The Routledge International Handbook on Hate Crime

This edited collection brings together many of the world's leading experts, both academic and practitioner, in a single volume Handbook that examines key international issues in the field of hate crime. Collectively it examines a range of pertinent areas with the ultimate aim of providing a detailed picture of the hate crime 'problem' in different parts of the world. The book is divided into four parts:

- An examination, covering theories and concepts, of issues relating to definitions of hate crime, the individual and community impacts of hate crime, the controversies of hate crime legislation and theoretical approaches to understanding offending.
- An exploration of the international geography of hate, in which each chapter examines a range of hate crime issues in different parts of the world, including the UK, wider Europe, North America, Australia and New Zealand.
- Reflections on a number of different perspectives across a range of key issues in hate crime, examining areas including particular issues affecting different victim groups, the increasingly important influence of the Internet and hate crimes in sport.
- A discussion of a range of international efforts being utilised to combat hate and hate crime.

Offering a strong international focus and comprehensive coverage of a wide range of hate crime issues, this book is an important contribution to hate crime studies and will be essential reading for academics, students and practitioners interested in this field.

Nathan Hall is a Principal Lecturer in Criminology and Policing at the Institute of Criminal Justice Studies at the University of Portsmouth.

Abbee Corb is a university professor, holds a PhD in Criminology, and bears the designation of CMAS (Certified Master Anti-Terrorism Specialist).

Paul Giannasi is a Police Superintendent, working within the Ministry of Justice in the United Kingdom.

John G. D. Grieve is a Senior Research Fellow at the University of Portsmouth and Professor Emeritus at London Metropolitan University.

'Hate crimes are a global problem and a serious human rights challenge that require a comprehensive response from governments and other stakeholders wherever they occur. This Handbook is an important new tool in the formulation of policies to combat hate crime, offering the latest thinking from top experts on the nature, incidence and impact of hate crime, as well as an honest account of the progress made and challenges that remain in law enforcement, criminal justice, and other policy responses to these crimes and the intolerance in which they are rooted.'

Paul LeGendre, Human Rights First, USA

'You do not have to agree with all the conclusions of the experts who contributed to this important book to recognize that it is an invaluable tool for officials who help set policy vis-à-vis hate crimes, as well as the frontline officers who have to deal with the impact of hate on diverse communities.'

Rabbi Abraham Cooper, Associate Dean of the Simon Wiesenthal Center, USA

The Routledge International Handbook on Hate Crime

*Edited by Nathan Hall, Abbee Corb,
Paul Giannasi and John G. D. Grieve*

Foreword by Neville Lawrence, OBE

Routledge
Taylor & Francis Group

LONDON AND NEW YORK

First published in paperback 2018
First published 2015
by Routledge
2 Park Square, Milton Park, Abingdon, Oxon, OX14 4RN

and by Routledge
711 Third Avenue, New York, NY 10017

Routledge is an imprint of the Taylor & Francis Group, an informa business

© 2015, 2018 selection and editorial material, Nathan Hall, Abbee Corb, Paul Giannasi and John G. D. Grieve; individual chapters, the contributors.

The right of Nathan Hall, Abbee Corb, Paul Giannasi and John G. D. Grieve to be identified as editors of this work has been asserted in accordance with sections 77 and 78 of the Copyright, Designs and Patents Act 1988.

All rights reserved. No part of this book may be reprinted or reproduced or utilised in any form or by any electronic, mechanical, or other means, now known or hereafter invented, including photocopying and recording, or in any information storage or retrieval system, without permission in writing from the publishers.

British Library Cataloguing in Publication Data
A catalogue record for this book is available from the British Library

Library of Congress Cataloging-in-Publication Data
The Routledge international handbook on hate crime/edited
by Nathan Hall, Abbee Corb, Paul Giannasi and
John G. D. Grieve. – First Edition.
     pages cm
     Includes bibliographical references and index.
     ISBN 978-0-415-81890-2 (hardback : alk. paper) – ISBN 978-0-203-57898-8 (ebook) 1. Hate crimes–Handbooks, manuals, etc.
     I. Hall, Nathan, editor of compilation. II. Title: International handbook on hate crime.
HV8079.H38R68 2014   2013047731
364.15–dc23

ISBN13: 978-0-415-81890-2 (hbk)
ISBN13: 978-1-138-30353-9 (pbk)
ISBN13: 978-0-203-57898-8 (ebk)

Typeset in Bembo
by Sunrise Setting Ltd, Paignton, UK

Contents

List of illustrations	ix
List of contributors	x
Foreword by Neville Lawrence, OBE	xviii
Introduction *Nathan Hall, Abbee Corb, Paul Giannasi and John G. D. Grieve*	1

PART ONE
Theories and concepts — 11

1	Framing the boundaries of hate crime *Neil Chakraborti*	13
2	Beyond the Silo: Rethinking hate crime and intersectionality *Hannah Mason-Bish*	24
3	The personal injuries of 'hate crime' *Paul Iganski and Spiridoula Lagou*	34
4	Exploring the community impacts of hate crime *Barbara Perry*	47
5	Legislating against hate *Gail Mason*	59
6	Understanding hate crimes: Sociological and criminological perspectives *Nathan Hall*	69
7	Understanding hate crimes: Perspectives from the wider social sciences *Nathan Hall*	81

Contents

PART TWO
The international geography of hate   93

  8 Hate crime in Europe   95
      Michael Whine

  9 Hate crime in the United Kingdom   105
      Paul Giannasi

 10 Sectarianism and hate crime in Northern Ireland   117
      Marian Duggan

 11 Global antisemitism   129
      Dave Rich

 12 The European extreme right: In search of respectability?   138
      Emmanuel Godin

 13 Hate crime in the United States   153
      Jordan Blair Woods

 14 Hate and hate crime in Canada   163
      Abbee Corb

 15 A governance of denial: Hate crime in Australia and New Zealand   174
      Nicole L. Asquith

PART THREE
Key issues in hate crime   191

 16 Hate crime against people with disabilities   193
      Chih Hoong Sin

 17 Disability hostility, harassment and violence in the UK:
      A 'motiveless' and 'senseless' crime?   207
      Paul Hamilton and Loretta Trickett

 18 Alternative subcultures and hate crime   226
      Jon Garland and Paul Hodkinson

 19 Hate crimes against Gypsies, Travellers and Roma in Europe   237
      Zoë James

20 Reflections on gendered masculine identities in targeted
    violence against ethnic minorities   249
    Loretta Trickett

21 LGBT hate crime   266
    Leslie J. Moran

22 Anti-transgender hate crime   278
    Jordan Blair Woods and Jody L. Herman

23 A personal reflection on good and evil on the Internet   289
    Sol Littman

24 Hate on the Internet   293
    Sarah Rohlfing

25 Online hate and cyber-bigotry: A glance at our radicalized online world   306
    Abbee Corb

26 Hate crime in sport   318
    Nick Hawkins

PART FOUR
Combating hate and hate crime   **329**

27 Policing and hate crime   331
    Paul Giannasi

28 Intelligence and hate crime   343
    John G. D. Grieve

29 Forensic science and hate crime   356
    Paul Smith

30 "You're a victim, don't become a perpetrator": A study
    of the 'moral career' of racist hate crime victims   367
    Corinne Funnell

31 Working with perpetrators   381
    Liz Dixon and David Court

32 Helping offenders to 'think again': A practitioner's perspective
    on developing an intervention for hate offenders   391
    Eila Davis

Contents

33	Repairing the harms of hate crime: A restorative justice approach *Mark Walters*	400
34	Challenging sectarianism *Graham Spencer*	411
35	Deradicalization *Daniel Köhler*	420
Index		430

Illustrations

Figures

3.1 Proportions of 'hate crimes' by identity motivation: household crime and personal crime — 36
3.2 How police came to know about incidents of crime: 'hate crime' and otherwise motivated crime — 38
3.3 Injuries sustained in violent crime: 'hate crime' and otherwise motivated crime compared — 39
3.4 Specific injuries sustained in violent crime and medical attention received: 'hate crime' and otherwise motivated crime compared — 40
3.5 General emotional reactions to crime victimisation: 'hate crime' and otherwise motivated crime compared — 41
3.6 Respondents reporting 'very much' of an emotional reaction to crime victimisation: 'hate crime' and otherwise motivated crime compared by crime type — 42
3.7 Specific emotional reactions to crime victimisation: 'hate crime' and otherwise motivated crime compared — 42
3.8 Specific behavioural reactions to crime victimisation: 'hate crime' and otherwise motivated crime compared — 43

Tables

3.1 Proportions of incidents of crime perceived by victims to be motivated by the offender's attitude towards their identity — 36
3.2 Proportions of incidents of crime perceived by victims to be motivated by the offender's attitude towards their identity in which the police came to know about the matter — 37
10.1 Number of incidents with a hate motivation, 2004/05 to 2011/12 — 122
10.2 Number of crimes with a hate motivation, 2004/05 to 2011/12 — 123
28.1 Summary: comparative table of usages of the word 'intelligence' — 345
28.2 Timeline Intelligence and Hate Crime Developments — 348

Contributors

Nicole L. Asquith is an Associate Professor at the School of Social Sciences and Psychology, University of Western Sydney, Research Associate with the Centre for Globalisation and Citizenship at Deakin University, and Associate Senior Research Fellow with the Tasmania Institute of Law Enforcement Studies. Her current research investigates motivated hate crime, intrafamilial hate crime, fear of heterosexism and the ripple-effect of hate crime victimisation. Her work in this field has been published in a range of edited collections and journal articles including Perry's five-volume collection, *Hate Crimes*. She is the author of *Text and Context of Malediction*, and co-author (with Rob White and Janine Haines) of *Crime and Criminology*, and co-editor (with Isabelle Bartkowiak-Théron) of *Policing Vulnerability*.

Neil Chakraborti is a Reader in Criminology at the University of Leicester and an Adjunct Professor at the University of Ontario Institute of Technology. He has published widely within the field of hate crime, and his books include *Responding to Hate Crime: The Case for Connecting Policy and Research* (The Policy Press, 2014 with Jon Garland); *Islamophobia, Victimisation and the Veil* (Palgrave Macmillan, 2014 with Irene Zempi); *Hate Crime: Concepts, Policy, Future Directions* (Routledge, 2010); *Hate Crime: Impact, Causes and Responses* (Sage, 2015 and 2009 with Jon Garland); and *Rural Racism* (Routledge, 2004 with Jon Garland).

Neil is currently the Principal Investigator of research funded by the Economic and Social Research Council exploring victims' experiences of hate crime, and Co-Investigator of an EU-funded study of populist political discourse. He has also been appointed as a Commissioner on the first-ever inquiry into sex in prisons within England and Wales, established by the Howard League for Penal Reform. He sits on the editorial board of the *The British Journal of Criminology*, is Chair of Research at the Board of Trustees for the Howard League for Penal Reform, and is Director of the Leicester Centre for Hate Studies.

Abbee Corb works as a consultant with the law enforcement and intelligence services within Canada and abroad. Abbee Corb provides educational instruction to law enforcement and government agencies around the world. She is a university professor. Corb has a PhD in Criminology and bears the designation of CMAS (Certified Master Anti-Terrorism Specialist). Corb has been working in the field of hate and extremism for over 20 years. She began her career dealing with Internet-based hatred and right wing extremists. Corb worked dealing with Nazi War criminals for almost 10 years. Abbee is a court-qualified expert on hate and extremism, specifically as it applies to the online environment. She has produced three award-winning films dealing with hate crime. Corb is a published author and is periodically called upon by the Canadian media and pro-active community based organizations as a consultant on right wing extremism. Corb is an expert on countering violent extremism and hate crime.

David Court is a Practice Development Officer and Probation Officer in the London Borough of Greenwich having previously specialised in working with Prolific and Priority Offenders, 2009 to 2012. Between 2001 and 2009 David was seconded to work in a targeted policing and crime reduction partnership initiative addressing initially race hate crime, then all forms of hate crime in the London Boroughs of Greenwich and Lewisham. David graduated in 1983 from London University with BA Hons in History and Physical Education, initially working for the West Midlands Probation Service in a Probation Hostel, then with adolescents in both open and secure unit conditions in east and south London. David is a Qualified Social Worker and Probation Officer (PostGraduate Diploma in Applied Social Studies, Certificate of Qualification in Social Work, South Bank University), and worked in Child Protection Teams in the London Boroughs of Haringey, Greenwich and Lewisham before rejoining the Probation Service in 1994. David is trained and specialised in supervising Sex Offenders with the Probation-Bracton Centre Partnership Challenge Project (1997 to 2001). David remains the lead officer for Hate Crime in Greenwich along with Restorative Justice.

Eila Davis' professional background is within the Probation Service. She has been interested in the characteristics of hate crime perpetrators since being awarded a Home Office scholarship (2004) to adapt the Priestley One to One programme to suit racially motivated offenders. In 2010 Eila completed a thesis 'What Works with Hate Crime?' at the Institute of Criminology, University of Cambridge, after which she developed an intervention now delivered in several Probation Trusts. The name of the intervention, 'Think Again', is not just a clarion call to perpetrators but an invitation to academics and practitioners to re-visit earlier conceptions of what works with hate crime. Eila contributes this chapter in a personal capacity as a practitioner and a manager.

Liz Dixon is the Restorative Justice Co-ordinator in London Probation. She has developed RJ for cases of acquisitive crime, violence and hate crime. She produced the Diversity and Prejudice Pack, a toolkit for working with racist and hate offending and has developed hate crime training for criminal justice staff. She has also produced a toolkit for interventions for those charged with terrorist-related offences She worked for many years as a Senior Lecturer in Criminal Justice Studies and has published a number of articles.

Marian Duggan is a Senior Lecturer in Criminology at Sheffield Hallam University. Her research interests focus on gender, sexuality and hate crime victimisation, including homophobia in Northern Ireland, gendered experiences of hate crime and male engagement in 'violence against women' prevention strategies. Marian is the author of *Queering Conflict: Examining Lesbian and Gay Experiences of Homophobia in Northern Ireland* (Ashgate, 2012) and co-editor (with M. Cowburn, P. Senior and A. Robinson) of *Values in Criminology and Community Justice* (Policy Press, 2013).

Corinne Funnell is a Senior Lecturer in criminology at the University of the West of England. Corinne has researched hate crime and also illegal drug markets and worked as a government policy and practice advisor in these fields. Her ESRC-funded PhD, undertaken at Cardiff University, explored victims' perceptions of racist hate crime and the impact of

Contributors

these experiences on their lives. Corinne is particularly interested in ethnographic research methods and the potential social, emotional and physical harms to qualitative researchers generated by fieldwork.

Jon Garland is a Reader in Criminology in the Department of Sociology, University of Surrey. His research interests are in the fields of hate crime, rural racism, community and identity, the far-right, policing and victimisation. He has published five books: *Racism and Anti-racism in Football* (with Mike Rowe); *The Future of Football* (with Mike Rowe and Dominic Malcolm), and *Rural Racism*, *Hate Crime: Impact, Causes, and Consequences* and *Responding to Hate Crime: the Case for Connecting Policy and Research* (all with Neil Chakraborti). He has also had numerous journal articles and reports published on issues of racism, the far-right, hate crime, policing, cultural criminology, and identity.

Paul Giannasi is a Police Superintendent, working within the Ministry of Justice in the United Kingdom. He leads a cross-governmental hate crime programme which brings all sectors of government together to coordinate efforts in order to improve the response to hate crime from across the criminal justice system. Paul is the UK 'National Point of Contact' to the Organisation for Security and Co-operation in Europe (OSCE) on hate crime and has worked to share good practice within the OSCE region and within Africa. Paul is also a member of the Association of Chief Police Officers (ACPO) Hate Crime Group and is one of the authors of the Police Hate Crime Manual, which provides guidance to UK police officers and their partners.

Emmanuel Godin is a Principal Lecturer in European studies (politics) at the University of Portsmouth, UK. His research interests cluster around the political dynamics of the French right within its European context, including the mainstreaming of the extreme right. With Andrea Mammone and Brian Jenkins, he edited *Mapping the Extreme Right in Contemporary Europe From Local to Transnational* (2012) and *Varieties of Right-Wing Extremism in Europe* (2013) as part of Routledge's Extremism and Democracy series. He is currently working on the impact of Marine Le Pen's leadership on French mainstream parties and their responses to it.

John G. D. Grieve joined the Metropolitan Police in 1966 at Clapham and served as a police officer and detective throughout London, in every role from undercover officer to policy chair for over 37 years. His duties involved the Drugs, Flying, Robbery and Murder Squads senior investigator. He was also the borough commander at Bethnal Green and head of training at Hendon Police College and was the first Director of Intelligence for the Metropolitan Police. He led the Anti-Terrorist Squad as National Co-ordinator during the 1996–1998 bombing campaigns and created the Race and Violent Crime Task Force. In the latter role he was responsible with others for the creation and development of the Cultural Change, Critical Incident and Community Impact models for strategic crisis management. He retired in May 2002. He was appointed as one of four Commissioners of the International Independent Monitoring Commission for some aspects of the peace process in Northern Ireland in 2003 by the UK Government until 2011. He is a Senior Research Fellow at the University of Portsmouth and Professor Emeritus at London Metropolitan University and has taught in Europe, USA, Russia, China, Japan, Africa, Caribbean and Australia. He currently chairs the MoJ/HO Independent Advisory Group on Hate Crime and advises a number of policing bodies/individuals.

Nathan Hall is a Principal Lecturer in Criminology and Policing at the Institute of Criminal Justice Studies at the University of Portsmouth. He is a member of the Cross-Government Hate Crime Independent Advisory Group (IAG) and the Association of Chief Police Officers Hate Crime Working Group. Nathan has also acted as an independent member of the UK government hate crime delegation to the Organization for Security and Co-operation in Europe, and is a member of the Crown Prosecution Service (Wessex) Independent Strategic Scrutiny and Involvement Panel, Hampshire Constabulary's Strategic IAG, and the Metropolitan Police Service's Hate Crime Diamond Group.

Paul Hamilton is a course leader (BA) and lecturer in Criminology at Nottingham Trent University (NTU). Paul's main research interests are in the fields of 'crime and prejudice', offender motivation(s), desistance from crime and the role of human and social capital in facilitating behavioural change. Paul is an active member of Nottinghamshire's 'Hate Crime Steering Group', which provides an opportunity to engage with and influence key policymakers and practitioners delivering hate crime interventions in the Nottinghamshire area. Paul has also recently been involved in research projects evaluating a number of resettlement initiatives within HMPS. Underpinning this is a commitment to improving the societal 're-entry' experiences of ex-offenders (and ultimately to reduce the incidence of reoffending). Prior to academia, Dr Hamilton spent eight years in the commercial sector, including IT consultancy and privately-funded social research.

Nick Hawkins has been a Chief Crown Prosecutor in England for 15 years and is the National Lead on sports matters. He has prosecuted a variety of hate crimes including sports-related offences. He deployed as legal adviser to the UK police team for the football World Cups in Germany in 2006 and South Africa in 2010 and has advised Brazilian authorities in the run up to the World Cup in 2014. He has also worked with the English Cricket Board/ICC on two international tournaments in England and Wales, and has links with a number of other sports. He is also a keen, but ageing, amateur sportsman.

Jody L. Herman is the Peter J. Cooper Public Policy Fellow and Manager of Transgender Research at the Williams Institute, UCLA School of Law. She holds a PhD in Public Policy and Public Administration from The George Washington University. She has published studies and co-authored reports on the topic of gender identity and transgender discrimination.

Paul Hodkinson is Reader in Sociology at the University of Surrey. He is author of *Goth. Identity, Style and Subculture* (Berg, 2002), *Media, Culture and Society* (Sage, 2010) and a range of journal articles and book chapters focused on matters connected to youth cultures, the role of online media in subcultural identities and ageing subcultural participants. He is also co-editor, with Wolfgang Deicke, of *Youth Cultures: Scenes, Subcultures and Tribes* (Routledge, 2007) and co-editor, with Andy Bennett, of *Ageing and Youth Cultures* (Berg, 2012). He is co-editor of the journal *Sociological Research Online*. His most recent research project, conducted with Jon Garland, provides the first detailed qualitative examination of experiences of targeted harassment and victimisation among participants of the goth scene.

Paul Iganski is Professor of Criminology and Criminal Justice in the Lancaster University Law School, UK. For well over a decade he has specialised in research, writing, teaching, public engagement and impact activity on 'hate crime'. He mostly conducts his research in

Contributors

collaboration with, or commissioned by, NGOs and the equalities sector. His books include *Hate Crime and the City* (2008), *Hate Crimes Against London's Jews* (2005 with Vicky Kielinger and Susan Paterson) and the edited volumes *Hate Crime: The Consequences of Hate Crime* (2009), and *The Hate Debate* (2002).

Zoë James is an Associate Professor (Senior Lecturer) in Criminology at Plymouth University. Her key research interests lie in policing and diversity issues. Zoë worked for the Home Office Research and Statistics Directorate in the 1990s and subsequently completed her PhD at the University of Surrey on the policing on New Travellers. Since joining Plymouth University in 1999, Zoë has gone on to research further issues relating to policing, particularly focusing on Gypsies, Travellers and Roma. Zoë leads Teaching and Learning in Criminology at Plymouth and lectures undergraduates and postgraduates on criminology, policing and organised deviance. Zoë's current research explores Gypsies, Travellers and Roma experiences of hate crime and policing responses to them.

Daniel Köhler studied Religious Studies, Political Science and Economics at Princeton University and Free University, Berlin and completed his postgraduate studies in peace and conflict research at the University of Hamburg. He is specialized on political and religious extremism and terrorism, radicalization and deradicalization processes. He is currently the Director of Research at the Institute for the Study of Radical Movements (ISRM www.istramo.com) and the founder as well as editor-in-chief of the world's first peer-reviewed journal on deradicalization (www.journal-exit.de). He also works for EXIT-Germany, one of the leading deradicalization programmes for right-wing extremists worldwide and Hayat, a German family counselling programme working with relatives of foreign fighters.

Spiridoula Lagou is a research analyst with *H8hurts* (www.H8hurts.com) which provides commissioned evaluation research, consultancy, training and public engagement activities concerned with tackling the problem of hate crime, supporting victims and working with offenders. She contributed data analysis for the Equality and Human Rights Commission's (EHRC) (Scotland) project on the *Rehabilitation of Hate Crime Offenders* (2011), and on projects recently commissioned by the EHRC to analyse data from the British Crime Survey and the Scottish Crime and Justice Survey on equality groups' perceptions and experience of harassment and crime.

Sol Littman is a sociologist turned journalist and community activist. Some 30 years ago he wrote an article predicting that the Internet, in spite of its great promise, would become an instrument of hate and confusion owing to its obliquity, anonymity and lack of editorship. Littman spent 14 years in the employ of the Anti-Defamation League where his focus was the exposure of native racist hate groups. He subsequently spent 15 years as Canadian Director of the Simon Wiesenthal Centre during which he searched international archives for evidence against the several hundred Nazi war criminals who had taken shelter in Canada and the United States. His career as a journalist included editorship of the Canadian Jewish News, editorial and feature writing for the *Toronto Star* and the production of news documentaries for the Canadian Broadcasting Corporation on subjects ranging from the evils of confinement in Canadian prisons to comic book conferences.

Gail Mason is Professor of Criminology in the Sydney Law School, University of Sydney, Australia. Her research centres on crime, social justice and exclusion, particularly: racist and homophobic violence; hate crime law and punishment; and resilience amongst former refugee communities. Gail is co-ordinator of the Australian Hate Crime Network. She is currently undertaking an international comparison of hate crime laws. She has recently edited *Restorative Justice and Adult Offending: Emerging Practice* (2012: Sydney Institute of Criminology).

Hannah Mason-Bish is a lecturer in Criminology and Sociology at the University of Sussex. Her main areas of research are on hate crime policy and victimisation with a particular focus on gender and disability. She co-edited a text with Prof Alan Roulstone which provides a comprehensive and interdisciplinary examination of Disability, Hate Crime and Violence, exploring its emergence on the policy agenda. Hannah is currently working on research which looks at intersectionality and hate crime policy and a monograph looking at the emergence of hate crime policy.

Leslie J. Moran is Professor in the School of Law, Birkbeck College, University of London. In 2004 he published *Sexuality and the politics of violence and safety* (Routledge) with B. Skeggs, P. Tyrer and K. Corteen, a theory informed empirical study of safety in response to homophobic violence. He has worked with stakeholder organisations including London's Metropolitan Police as a LGBT Advisory Group member and as Chair of GALOP, a London LGBT anti-violence community organisation. He is currently International consultant working with Gail Mason on an Australian Research Council grant on hate crime. Current projects include hate crime in the news, sexual violence in prisons and sexual diversity in the judiciary.

Barbara Perry is Professor and Associate Dean of Social Science and Humanities at the University of Ontario Institute of Technology, and Visiting Fellow at Leicester University in the UK. She has written extensively in the area of hate crime, including several books on the topic, among them, *In the Name of Hate: Understanding Hate Crime*; and *Hate and Bias Crime: A Reader*. She has also published in the area of Native American victimisation and social control, including one book entitled *The Silent Victims: Native American Victims of Hate Crime*, based on interviews with Native Americans (University of Arizona Press). She has also written a related book on policing Native American communities – *Policing Race and Place: Under- and Over-enforcement in Indian Country* (Lexington Press). She was the General Editor of a five-volume set on hate crime (Praeger), and editor of *Volume 3: Victims of Hate Crime* of that set. Dr. Perry continues to work in the area of hate crime, and has begun to make contributions to the limited scholarship on hate crime in Canada. Most recently, she has contributed to a scholarly understanding of the community impacts of hate crime, anti-Muslim violence, and hate crime against LGBTQ communities.

Dave Rich is Deputy Director of Communications at the Community Security Trust (CST), which provides security advice and assistance to the UK Jewish community and represents British Jewry to police, government and media on antisemitism and Jewish security. Dave is CST's lead analyst of antisemitic hate crimes and the author of CST's annual *Antisemitic Incidents Report*. Dave is also a Research Student Associate at the Pears Institute for the Study of Antisemitism, Birkbeck College, University of London, where he is studying for his PhD.

Sarah Rohlfing is a PhD candidate within the Department of Psychology at the University of Portsmouth. She has previously studied Forensic Psychology and has worked for the Department of Psychology in various research assistant and research support roles. This work contributed towards her decision to continue to pursue postgraduate studies, and she started her PhD in October 2011 under the supervision of Aldert Vrij, Stefanie Sonnenberg and Samantha Mann. Her PhD research investigates the relationship between the Internet, the development of prejudice, and hate offending.

Chih Hoong Sin is Director at OPM; a not-for-profit public interest organisation based in London, UK. He directed the major study into hate crime against disabled people in Great Britain on behalf of the Equality and Human Rights Commission, and the study into hate crime experienced by people with learning disabilities for the learning disability charity, Mencap, amongst others. Chih Hoong also supports local communities and police services in formulating and delivering hate crime strategies and action plans. He is also engaged in efforts exploring similarities and differences across the different types of hate crimes, having edited a special issue of the journal *Safer Communities* and convened a national conference *No Place for Hate*, to this effect.

Paul Smith worked as a crime scene investigator (CSI) with Leicestershire Constabulary. During this time he investigated a range of major and volume crimes and trained as a crime scene manager and coordinator, advancing to an assistant senior CSI in the summer of 2004. He continued in this role and studied for a Masters in forensic archaeology which led to a PhD in embedded technologies for scene investigations. He graduated in 2008 and soon after moved into his current role as a senior lecturer with the University of Portsmouth.

Graham Spencer is a Reader in Politics, Conflict and the Media, University of Portsmouth, Distinguished Senior Research Fellow, Edward M. Kennedy Institute for Conflict Intervention, NUI, Maynooth, Ireland, Honorary Senior Research Fellow, Department of Politics, University of Liverpool and a Fellow of the Royal Society of Arts. He has published widely on the Northern Ireland peace process and is involved in a number of cross-community conflict resolution initiatives there. His two books *The British and Peace in Northern Ireland* (Cambridge University Press) and *From Armed Struggle to Political Struggle: Republican Tradition and Transformation in Northern Ireland* (Bloomsbury) are both due in 2015.

Loretta Trickett is a Senior Lecturer in the Nottingham Law School, NTU and is Module Leader for Criminal Law (BA Criminology), Criminology (LLB) and for the LLM in International Criminal Law and Human Rights and Criminal Justice. Loretta's research interests are on masculinities, crime and victimisation and she has published articles on male fear of crime, boys and bullying and men's violence within gangs.

Loretta is an Assistant Editor for the Internet Journal of Criminology and for the past two years she has been a member of the Nottingham Hate Crime Steering Group along with Dr Paul Hamilton. The Steering Group is made up of several criminal justice organisations and Nottinghamshire Community Safety Partnership who work together to develop and implement Hate Crime Policy in the Nottinghamshire Area. Loretta is currently undertaking research on police questioning and data collection on disability hate crime in Nottinghamshire.

Mark Walters is a lecturer in law at the University of Sussex where he teaches criminal law and criminology. Mark completed his DPhil in law (criminology) at the Centre for Criminology, University of Oxford in 2011. Mark has published widely in the field of hate crime, focusing in particular on the criminalisation of hate-motivated offences, the use of restorative justice in hate crime cases, and criminological theories of causation. Some of his most recent publications include: Walters, M. A. and Hoyle, C. (2012) 'Exploring the Everyday World of Hate Victimization through Community Mediation', *International Review of Victimology*, 18(1): 7–24; Walters, M. A. (2011) 'A general *theories* of hate crime? Strain, doing difference and self control', *Critical Criminology*, 19(4): 313–330. Mark's monograph *Hate Crime and Restorative Justice, Exploring Causes and Repairing Harms* will be published by OUP in April 2014.

Michael Whine is the Government and International Affairs Director at the Community Security Trust, and a member of the Hate Crime Independent Advisors Group at the UK Ministry of Justice. Between 2010 and 2012 he acted as Lay Advisor to the Counter Terrorism Division of the Crown Prosecution Service. In 2013, he was both appointed to the Hate Crime Scrutiny and Involvement Panel of the London CPS, which assesses and evaluates hate crime prosecution cases, and the UK member of the European Commission Against Racism and Intolerance (ECRI), the monitoring agency of the Council of Europe.

Jordan Blair Woods is the Richard Taylor Law Teaching Fellow at the Williams Institute at UCLA School of Law. He is also a Gates Cambridge Scholar and PhD candidate at the Institute of Criminology at the University of Cambridge, UK. He received his M.Phil. in Criminological Research from the University of Cambridge, J.D. from UCLA School of Law, and A.B. in Social Studies from Harvard University.

Foreword

The challenge faced by my family and me when my son Stephen was so brutally murdered in 1993 has been recorded and captured by organisations, agencies and institutions around the world. This challenge is epitomised by the range of things that have happened since my son's murder. Legislation has been passed, Law Enforcement agencies have tried to improve services to Black and other minority communities, and Governments across all political persuasions have tried to help ensure that my family and I secure some justice.

I feel though that the greatest changes have taken place in education. Young students have embarked on research and taken up academic studies to understand why hate crime caused the killers of my son to murder him. They have become more sensitive to, and active in, challenging issues that previously were left solely to activists. I have travelled around the UK communicating with students and I have noticed a renewed passion for justice which was lacking from sections of the community before.

This international record of the evils of hate crime and its pervasive nature is further evidence of how educators and academic institutions are working hard to highlight how hate crime damages communities, and helps to explain the reasons why we should never relent in our fight against those who want to destroy our communities through hate.

It is a privilege and an honour to support the hard work put into writing this book and it is further evidence of how education institutions, academics, practitioners, and students are making every effort to raise the awareness of people across the world.

Neville Lawrence, OBE
13th April 2014

Introduction

Nathan Hall, Abbee Corb, Paul Giannasi and John G. D. Grieve

Welcome to *The Routledge International Handbook on Hate Crime*. For us as editors, the construction of this book has been a challenging but rewarding experience. The idea for a Handbook of this nature was conceived in the preparations for an academic seminar hosted by the UK Ministry of Justice on the 11th of May, 2011. At that time it was clear to us that a significant amount of very good work was being undertaken by academics and practitioners around the UK, but that it was largely disparate and, curiously, in many cases was not widely known about by others similarly working in the field of hate crime. In an effort to remedy this the academic seminar, hosted in London, brought together many leading hate crime scholars to share their work, their ideas and their visions for the future direction of hate crime research, policy and practice. It seemed to us that capturing this vast array of expertise in the form of a book was an appropriate and useful activity to undertake.

The original intention was to concentrate on the issues that informed that seminar – a move that would have probably seen this book entitled the 'Routledge UK Handbook on Hate Crime'. We quickly decided, however, that such a narrow focus on the UK, as valuable as that would be, was limited, not least because of the global nature of many of the issues in hand. The idea of an international approach to the issues relating to hate and hate crime was universally welcomed by everyone that we consulted, and thus this Handbook was born.

Designing and constructing a book such as this is not easy. Deciding which topics to include, which experts to approach (or chase – delete as appropriate!), the nature of the chapter contents to request, and so on, coupled with the sheer size of the volume, have meant that patience has become a virtue for all of us, and not least for Tom Sutton and Heidi Lee (especially Heidi) at our publishers, Routledge. All the patience and the effort was, we believe, worth it. We are hugely grateful to all our contributors, who have taken time to share their thoughts, and have produced chapters of great interest and worth, and we hope that this book will prove to be a valuable addition to the international literature base on hate and hate crime.

We do however believe that it is important to be aware of the limitations of the book. We make no claim to have included every issue or debate, every discussion or subject area. This is the Routledge Handbook *on* Hate Crime, *not* the Routledge Handbook *of* Hate Crime. As we explain a little later in this introduction, the expansive nature of the subject area means that to have included every issue relating to hate crime would have proved impossible, but the scope of the chapters are such that as many issues that we could have reasonably included *are* included somewhere, even if not in a chapter that specifically names them in the title. Perhaps the most obvious example is that relating to issues of Islamophobia and anti-Muslim hate crime, which is not the subject of a standalone chapter, but is discussed in one way or another in fourteen of the thirty-five chapters. We have also aimed for as broad a scope as possible, from the so-called 'low-level' to the extreme, and as such we hope that this volume will be of value to a similarly broad range of scholarly and practitioner interests. With all this in mind, what follows is a brief overview of the chapters within this Handbook.

Part One: *Theories and Concepts*

Part One of this Handbook discusses issues relating to theories and concepts. The subject of hate crime is inextricably bound up with a range of complex theoretical and conceptual issues that have come to define scholarly, and indeed wider, debates within the field. The chapters within this section of the book therefore seek to explore many of these complexities, and in so doing, provide the broader context within which to situate the more specific issues discussed in *Parts Two*, *Three* and *Four*.

Everything that we subsequently associate with hate crime is determined, to one degree or another, by the way in which the problem is defined and conceptualised. The question '*what is hate crime?*' is therefore of central importance to our understanding of the subject area. The significance of this issue is made starkly apparent in the opening chapter by *Neil Chakraborti*, who explores the ways in which hate crime has been 'framed' through a range of existing definitions, and discusses the considerable implications, both conceptual and practical, associated with establishing, maintaining and widening the 'boundaries' of the subject area.

One of the particular issues identified in *Chapter One* concerns the use of discrete characteristics in the construction of both hate crime definitions and existing policy around the world. That is to say that there is a historical and contemporary tendency to talk about hate crime issues in relation to this identifiable characteristic, or that identifiable characteristic. This 'silo' approach to the hate crime, and the issues and limitations associated with it, is explored in depth by *Hannah Mason-Bish* in *Chapter Two*. In considering the concept of 'intersectionality', she argues the case for rethinking the rather simplistic silo approach, and examines the need for hate crime policy to circumvent traditional notions of primary identity characteristics and to understand the fluidity of identity and the multiple ways in which prejudice and violence might be experienced.

The different ways in which hate crime is experienced are the subjects of *Chapters Three and Four*. It has long been suggested, and indeed assumed, that hate crimes 'hurt more' than comparable, non-hate motivated, events, and have additional wider impacts that extend beyond the immediate victim or victims of an attack. These claims have been, and indeed remain, the subject of considerable scholarly debate between those who *support* and those who *oppose* viewing hate crime as a distinct, even unique, form of crime.

In *Chapter Three*, and in support of the former position, *Paul Iganski* and *Spiridoula Lagou* extend the evidence base further by examining some new data on the physical, emotional, and behavioural injuries of hate crime. In doing so, they suggest that understanding the particular impacts of hate crime can, and should, serve to inform appropriate and effective support for victims and inform the training of those working with victims.

Beyond these 'personal' impacts of hate crime on the individual victim or victims, such victimisation is generally considered distinctive because of its distal effects – that is, the victim of hate crime is not restricted to the individual. Rather, the harm and the 'message' contained within the perpetrator's actions also extend to the victim's community. This particular aspect of victimisation is the subject of *Chapter Four*, in which *Barbara Perry* explores three layers of these wider effects, namely the impacts on targeted communities; impacts on shared values of inclusion; and, unusually, the mobilising effects of targeted violence.

These seemingly disproportionate impacts of hate crime on both the victim and wider communities have been central tenets of often-controversial attempts in many countries around the world to challenge hate crime through the use of criminal law. Although discussions around specific attempts to combat hate crime are reserved for *Part Four*, here in *Chapter Five*, *Gail Mason* considers a number of theoretical and conceptual issues in relation to legislating against hate. In particular, she examines the ways in which the concept of hate crime is translated into, and regulated by, law, and posits a tripartite model for understanding hate crime legislation across national borders and, in turn, for understanding the common elements that distinguish a hate crime from an ordinary crime under the law. As such, the chapter offers a transnational snapshot of hate crime laws and some of the key debates and dilemmas that currently surround them.

Notwithstanding the debates and dilemmas surrounding the use of criminal law in attempting to control hate, the very existence of hate crime laws points to the existence of a particular, and indeed distinct, form of offending behaviour. Writing in 1999, Ben Bowling lamented, in relation to race-hate offenders, that *"there has been almost no research on perpetrators. Whilst the most basic of descriptions have been formulated, they remain something of an effigy in the criminological literature"*. Similarly, a decade later, Barbara Perry noted that *"it is curious that hate crime has not been an object of extensive theoretical inquiry"*. In light of these concerns, in *Chapters Six* and *Seven*, *Nathan Hall* first presents an *overview* of sociological and criminological knowledge in relation to the perpetrators of hate crime, followed by a consideration of explanations of hate offending offered by the wider social sciences. Combined, these two chapters seek to shed some light on both what is known about the perpetrators of hate crime, and what might cause this type of offending.

Part Two: *The International Geography of Hate*

Having examined some of the key theoretical and conceptual issues underpinning the various debates within the field of hate crime, the chapters contained within *Part Two* of this Handbook both illustrate and examine a range of specific hate-related, and broader hate crime, issues from around the world.

In *Chapter Eight*, *Mike Whine* examines a range of issues relating to hate crime across Europe, and in particular considers the efforts of international bodies to recognise, measure, and address the problem in different countries across the continent. The chapter also provides a useful historical account of the emergence and evolution of political concerns relating to hate and hate crime in Europe. Moreover, as a consequence of these concerns, the chapter further discusses the broad range of commitments made by the resulting international governmental organisations (IGOs), including those which focus their efforts on (and commit their member states to) confronting the problem, including legislative reviews, collection of data, criminal justice agency training programmes, assistance to civil society organisations (CSOs) and vitally, regularly reviewing states' progress in combating the problem.

Whilst the reasons for the emergence of hate crime as a contemporary social and political concern differ by country, in England and Wales (and indeed the UK more generally) most policy and legislation has direct links to the 1999 Public Inquiry report into the racist murder

3

of Stephen Lawrence. As such, the UK's evolving engagement with hate crime has often been described as a 'journey'. In *Chapter Nine*, then, *Paul Giannasi* explores this 'journey' and argues that, whilst in comparative terms at least, this path is relatively advanced, much remains to be done in order to address the range of contemporary hate crime issues currently facing the UK.

Such is the diversity of the UK-related issues that Northern Ireland, and its particular association with sectarianism, commands its own chapter. In *Chapter Ten, Marian Duggan* analyses the factors informing and sustaining sectarian hostility, victimisation and segregation, with a view to understanding the changing nature of this deeply embedded form of prejudice. In doing so, she outlines the specific characteristics of sectarianism in Northern Ireland, from the establishment of the province and the ensuing 'Troubles' period, through to the legacy of this conflict in the form of paramilitary groups, identity symbolisers and 'peace' measures which serve to further segregate opposing communities. Her evaluation of sectarian hate crime questions how such acts are distinguished from the on-going, everyday processes of partition which promote safety and security through separation and segregation. The chapter concludes by considering the feasibility of political drives for greater cohesion and integration from parallel, but somewhat more peaceful, communities.

Chapter Eleven returns us to the broader international arena, where *Dave Rich* examines issues relating to anti-Semitic hate crime in a number of different countries. As the editors of a collection such as this, one of the inevitable dilemmas is to determine where to place each respective chapter. As an illustration of this, this particular chapter has found itself moved regularly between *Parts Two* and *Three*. Ultimately, as editors, we decided that whilst anti-Semitism is undoubtedly a key issue in hate crime (and therefore suited to a place in *Part Three*), such is Dave Rich's contribution to understanding international geographical variations in anti-Semitic hate crime that his chapter is equally at home in *Part Two*. As such, the chapter explores existing data, both official and unofficial, to form tentative snapshots of the different social and political dynamics that influence anti-Semitic hate crime in different countries, with a particular (but not exclusive) focus on the United Kingdom, France, Hungary, and Canada.

A similar editorial dilemma was presented by *Chapter Twelve*, in which *Emmanuel Godin* examines the European Far Right. Whilst similarly a key issue in hate crime (and therefore also suitable for inclusion in *Part Three*), the international flavour of the chapter persuaded us to include it in *Part Two* instead. In his chapter, Godin seeks to demonstrate that if extreme-right parties in Europe have moved from the margins to the mainstream of the political spectrum, they have not necessarily become more moderate for it. Furthermore, the chapter also identifies some of the non-party channels (think-tanks, social movements and new social media, transnational organisations) through which extreme-right values and ideas permeate the different strata of European societies, and thus influence and shape 'hateful' views amongst sections of the populace.

The next three chapters concentrate on hate-related issues in territories outside of Europe. In *Chapter Thirteen, Jordan Blair Woods* discusses hate crime in the United States, where he considers the evolution of various legislative efforts to address the problem. In addition, he examines the available data on hate crime, highlighting that existing empirical studies on hate crime in the United States focus primarily on hate crime victimisation, resulting in limited information about hate crime offending, policing and prosecution. A similar approach is taken in *Chapter Fourteen* where *Abbee Corb* considers issues relating to hate crime in Canada. Here she discusses the domestic hate crime problem, and in particular examines the challenges faced by Canadian law enforcement and the wider legal communities when dealing with hate crimes.

Finally for *Part Two*, *Chapter Fifteen* presents a discussion of hate crime issues in Australia and New Zealand, where *Nicole Asquith* examines the variety of legislative, policy and practice responses to 'hate speech' and prejudice-related violence in existence across the ten jurisdictions of those two countries. The chapter also outlines the institutional and cultural contexts in which these responses have emerged as a criminal justice issue, before proceeding to a critical discussion of antipodean hate crime governance.

Part Three: *Key Issues in Hate Crime*

Part Three of this Handbook has presented us with our biggest editorial challenges. As one of us (Hall, 2013) has noted elsewhere, somewhat ironically, the process of identifying which 'key issues' to include here is somewhat reflective of one of the often-cited criticisms of hate crime itself, noted in *Chapter One*, namely that selective decisions necessarily have to be made about which issues to include and which to omit. In many respects we find ourselves in a 'no-win' situation at the outset of this section – by selecting some issues over others we suspect that we will inevitably cause consternation amongst some readers for whom we will have left out issues close to their heart. But (and not withstanding the practical issues of constructing a book such as this) the inevitably expansive nature of this subject area means that including all of the seemingly infinite number of issues that might possibly and reasonably be considered 'key' becomes an impossible task. So with this in mind, the chapters within this section are the product of our selective decision-making (open to disagreement, obviously), but are chosen to reflect what we believe to be some, but not all, of the most prominent contemporary concerns at the time of writing. That said, however, even where a particular issue is not the subject of its own chapter, such is the breadth of discussion within the chapters of this Handbook that it is likely addressed in a number of different places within the pages of this book.

With this in mind, *Part Three* begins with two chapters that address issues relating to disability hate crime. In *Chapter Sixteen*, *Chih Hoong Sin* identifies a number of consistent features of hate crime against disabled people reported in the available international literature. The chapter explores, specifically, certain features of hate crime against disabled people that appear to be distinct from other types of hate crime, or at least where it exhibits important nuances. While discussing such distinctiveness, the chapter nonetheless asserts the importance of the need to understand hate crime through the lens of multiple identities (note the link with the discussion in *Chapter Two*) without reifying disability as the sole or primary identity that explains or helps us understand the incidence and experiences of hate crime against disabled people.

Whilst the previous chapter concentrates largely upon issues of victimisation, *Chapter Seventeen* draws attention to the perpetrators of disability hate crime. Here, *Paul Hamilton* and *Loretta Trickett* argue that whilst it would be wrong to suggest that nothing is known about the motivations of those committing such insidious expressions of hostility, harassment and violence, what is patently missing is a cohesive, nuanced body of research with offenders themselves. As such, their chapter examines what is known about these offenders, whilst simultaneously suggesting ways forward to better understand the perpetrators of disability hate crime.

Chapter Eighteen, by *Jon Garland* and *Paul Hodkinson*, provides a critical outline of some of the core arguments relating to an emerging area of policy, practice and academic study within the UK – the targeted victimisation of those within alternative subcultures. Despite falling outside of national hate crime policy for protected characteristics, it is suggested here that various aspects of this victimisation are comparable with that which recognised hate crime victim groups suffer, including the frequency and nature of 'low-' and 'high-level' incidents, and their potential psychological impact upon the victim and those in their community. The chapter also discusses some of the difficulties and dilemmas involved with including alternative subcultures under the hate crime 'umbrella'.

Having then considered a hitherto largely unrecognised form of hate crime, *Chapter Nineteen*, by *Zoë James*, addresses issues relating to Gypsies, Travellers and Roma, who, it is often argued, experience more bias-motivated crime and discrimination in Europe than any other minority communities. In examining this issue, her chapter explores how and why hate crimes have manifested against Gypsies, Travellers and Roma in Europe in the twenty-first century. In order to do this, she considers the context within which hate crime has arisen, and in doing so addresses some of the histories of Gypsies, Travellers and Roma in Europe. The chapter then examines the extent of contemporary hate crimes against Gypsies, Travellers and Roma, and identifies the range of hate crime experiences inflicted upon them. Importantly, the chapter also considers how hate incidents have been conflated with the experiences of discrimination and prejudice that Gypsies, Travellers and Roma experience as hate crime. The chapter also examines how the existence, or notion, of 'Europe' as a political and legal entity, has attempted to resolve this problem.

Arguably more traditional notions of racism are explored by *Loretta Trickett* in *Chapter Twenty*. In this chapter, though, she notes that contemporary debates about hate crime have had surprisingly little to say about gender, particularly when considering perpetrators. To address this shortcoming, the chapter provides an exploration of data from interviews with a group of white males who regularly targeted Asian shopkeepers for physical and verbal abuse, and the data demonstrates how the respondent's motivations for attacks were often informed by their reflections upon their own masculine identities. The chapter concludes that a greater focus on perceived threats to masculine identities could produce a more nuanced appreciation about why and how certain hate crimes manifest themselves.

Issues of gender extend into *Chapter Twenty-one*, where *Leslie Moran* examines key issues relating to Lesbian, Gay, Bisexual and Transgender (LGBT) hate crime, and argues that violence associated with sexual orientation and gender discrimination is at the heart of LGBT hate crime. The focus of the chapter is the challenges that LGBT experiences and perceptions of these forms of violence raise for the hate crime agenda, campaigning and activism, law and institutional reform, and the realisation of safety and security. In drawing attention to the potential for change, and some of the associated problems, the chapter aims to raise awareness, promote critical engagement, and thereby promote the more effective realisation of the ultimate goal of respect and recognition for all citizens.

In *Chapter Twenty-two*, the topic of crimes motivated by bias against a victim's actual or perceived gender identity or expression is explored by *Jordan Blair Woods* and *Jody L. Herman*. They argue that hate crime is part of a wider pattern of discrimination and marginalisation that many transgender and gender non-conforming people experience in vital spheres of daily life. More specifically, the chapter discusses some definitional issues involving this category of hate crime, summarises existing statistics and empirical research on hate crime motivated by anti-transgender bias, and discusses arguments for and against hate crime laws that include gender identity or expression.

Having examined a range of issues largely specific to certain group characteristics, *Part Three* of this Handbook then moves on to examine a number of increasingly important issues associated with hate, hate crime and the Internet. *Sol Littman* sets the scene in *Chapter Twenty-three* with a short but thoughtful and personal reflective piece that considers the emergence of the Internet and its role as a medium for both good and evil.

Chapter Twenty-four examines and synthesises existing research relating to online hatred. In a wide-ranging piece, *Sarah Rohlfing* discusses the Internet as a tool for hate groups to spread and incite hatred, and considers the challenges the Internet delivers for those whose responsibility it is to combat online hatred, including the problems associated with legislative responses. She also considers some of the current research limitations, including the challenges that the complexity of online hatred delivers, the 'end-product-approach' taken by many researchers, and the lack of knowledge regarding the impact of online hatred on its victims. Finally, some concluding thoughts about the future of research into online hatred and related policy making are discussed.

In a related piece, *Abbee Corb* discusses issues relating to the Internet as an unrestrained setting for extremist activity in *Chapter Twenty-five*. Here she argues that hate-motivated offences perpetrated by extremist groups and their "lone wolf" soldiers have increased over the past decade. This rise in worldwide hate crimes, coupled with the changes in social and political environments, and the flourishing of various global groups, have been propagated and advanced through the use of technology by means of the Internet. As she discusses, these changes have lead to an increase in contentious websites, questionable material and, to say the least, dubious uses of available technology that reach out to impressionable people using popularised social networking venues in a venture to indoctrinate them with their fundamental, and at times fervidly racist and odious messages.

Finally for *Part Three*, in *Chapter Twenty-six*, *Nick Hawkins* bridges a key contemporary issue that has links to social media and implications for responses to the hate crime problem, namely hate crimes in sport. In this chapter, he argues that sport by its very nature produces an environment which can be a force for good and which actively promotes equality and diversity amongst participants, officials and spectators. However, and conversely, the nature of sport also sets people against each other and this can (and has) cause(d) an environment in which incidents of hate crime can occur. This chapter therefore examines all aspects of hate crime in sport, in the UK and worldwide, and considers ways of tackling hate crime by looking at the role of sports authorities and police and prosecutors. Throughout the chapter, examples are given covering a range of sports from around the world.

Part Four: *Combating Hate and Hate Crime*

Part Four of this Handbook is devoted to specific efforts to combat hate and hate crime, and begins with three chapters that examine different aspects of the policing of hate crime. In *Chapter Twenty-seven*, *Paul Giannasi* outlines some of the significant operational challenges that the police face in their efforts to prevent hate crime, bring offenders to justice, and build positive relationships with the affected communities. In particular, he uses examples from the UK to demonstrate these challenges with specific reference to the under-reporting of hate crime, the relationship between hostility and public disorder, the challenges of policing hate crime on the Internet, and hate crime targeting disabled victims.

Chapter Twenty-eight, by *John Grieve*, specifically discusses the role of intelligence-led policing in dealing with hate crime. Here, an argument is developed that suggests that what is needed in general are 'community friendly' police intelligence systems, but that there are tensions, practical and logical, between this aspiration and the proximate social and cultural, professional and political context, and distal wider and international environment in which any intelligence developments are taking place. This chapter expressly addresses the application of intelligence, with all the current context of concerns that have arisen, to the policing of hate crime.

Continuing the policing theme, *Paul Smith* provides an overview of forensic science with reflections on its use in hate crime cases, in *Chapter Twenty-nine*. The discussion assumes little or no knowledge of forensic science by the reader and its purpose is to provide an overview of the key aspects in the application of science to hate crime. The context within which forensic science operates is discussed, and the contemporary issues and constraints affecting its use in practice are presented along with the fundamentals of forensic science. To facilitate this the 1999 London nail bombings are used as a case study as they exemplify the use of forensic science processes in a large complex investigation, which utilised a multi-disciplinary and multi-agency response along with the proactive use of intelligence resources, used to inform the strategic deployment of forensic science to the investigation.

We start to move away from policing per se in *Chapter Thirty*, in which *Corinne Funnell* presents findings from an ethnographic study that aimed to explore victims' perceptions and experiences of racist hate crime. The research took place at an agency located in England that was run by victims of racist incidents for such victims and which provided a casework-based service. The experience of victimisation is analysed here with reference to a principal aspect of the caseworkers' role, which was to "empower" clients. The focus is victims' perceptions of acts of provocation by the perpetrator and 'under-protection' by the police service and the potential for "retaliation" by the victim. Running through the analysis is a consideration of the operation in practice of the victim-centred Stephen Lawrence definition of hate crime in terms of how those who perceived that they were victims maintained or lost victims status vis-à-vis recording agencies such as the police service, but also how victims could be constituted as perpetrators.

From working with victims, the following two chapters discuss differing aspects of working with offenders. In *Chapter Thirty-one*, *Liz Dixon* and *David Court* rightly note that the publication of the Stephen Lawrence Public Inquiry report heralded revolutionary changes in the prosecution of race hate crime in the UK as police services and other criminal and community justice agencies began to address the phenomenon of racist crime. They argue that the focus on this form of criminal activity has had the effect of extending the criminal gaze to other strands of hate crime, and to the appreciation that there are moving targets when thinking about potential victims. Their chapter therefore seeks to reflect on this ongoing work with convicted perpetrators of hate crime, drawing on practitioner experience in London specifically. In doing so, they reflect on the emerging landscape to establish the extent to which the lessons learned with race hate perpetrators can apply to other forms of hate.

In *Chapter Thirty-two*, *Eila Davis* builds upon the previous chapter's discussion by examining the theories and processes behind the development of an intervention programme for hate offenders. In doing so, she reflects upon her experience of adapting an existing rehabilitative programme for *generalist* offenders into one specifically suited to *hate* offenders. In considering the delivery of such a programme, she argues that an intervention that is rounded, problem solving in content, and motivational in style, is likely to be more effective than one that attends directly to discriminatory attitudes and their origins.

Much has been written in this Handbook about the causes and consequences of hate crime, and about the use of legislation (and therefore increased punishments) to try to tackle the problem. But as *Mark Walters* notes in *Chapter Thirty-three*, whilst there are sound reasons why legislatures should pursue such an approach to tackling hate-motivated offences, critics have noted that penalty enhancements do little to actively repair the emotional, social and cultural damage caused by hate-motivated incidents. In this chapter, then, he examines whether restorative justice can help to repair the harms caused by hate crime. He begins by briefly summarising several commonly used restorative practices that have been empirically examined in the context of hate crime offending. He then explores the key process variables within restorative practice that have been identified as aiding the recovery of hate victims, before examining the potential limitations of restorative justice, including the secondary harms that "community" participants may expose hate victims to. It is here that he outlines the measures that restorative practitioners must undertake in order to guard against the risks posed to victims of hate crime by restorative justice.

The theme of reparation between parties continues into *Chapter Thirty-four*, where *Graham Spencer* reflects upon the ways in which sectarianism, with particular reference to Northern Ireland, might be challenged. In considering what might be done to address this incredibly complex issue, he argues that boundaries, walls and fears indicate the more fixed aspects of identity and the desire to preserve and protect what one is, and essential for this are rigid depictions of the 'other' who has little to offer 'us'. He suggests that though it would be ridiculous to claim that the sectarian mind inhabits all in conflict societies, it is nevertheless apparent that a sectarian minority can create fears and tensions which can hold that society back and in turn incite further violence and hatred. In this instance, it is movement or process that the sectarian fears most, at one level viewing this as contributing to the dissolution of identity and at the other presenting the 'other' as a distorted construct, who is revealed as such through engagement and dialogue. He therefore argues that a new future-oriented context which moves beyond 'us' and 'them' and which facilitates expectations of compromise, precisely because identity is conceived in terms of a wider social context rather than a communal one, has the ability to dissolve the sectarian tendency.

In our final contribution, *Daniel Köhler* examines issues of deradicalisation in *Chapter Thirty-five*. Here he argues that deradicalisation as a field of research and as a practical counter terrorism and anti-extremism tool is still in its infancy, but is one of the most promising future areas for academics and policy makers in that regard. Nevertheless, he suggests, a strong need for more comprehensive and substantial research in individual deradicalisation processes, as well as comparative interdisciplinary works, is among the factors impeding the development of deradicalisation programmes. In addition, he argues that policy makers still need to recognise the strategic value of deradicalisation tools for domestic security and to combat other forms of asymmetric threats. What nevertheless is clear from the existing research and practical experience, he notes, is that Deradicalisation and Disengagement Programmes are a valuable contribution to a comprehensive democratic culture, to the security and safety of every citizen, and an essential tool to combat terrorist and extremist threats.

Concluding comments

As we hope will have become clear by now, this Handbook examines a range of hate and hate crime related issues. The subjects discussed cover a host of contemporary problems, but with a strong emphasis on how these might be addressed, and it is within this spirit that we chose the cover of this book. It might seem a little odd to be discussing the choice of a book's cover within its introduction, but the story here is, we think, worth a moment or two of the reader's time.

There comes a point in the process of writing a book where an email will arrive from the publisher, usually with the subject of 'Cover Concepts', or something similar. For some, this is neither here nor there, and the process of choosing from the half-dozen or so mocked-up covers sent by the publisher ranges from being a minor inconvenience to quite good fun. For others it can become something of a headache as one wrestles with the 'meaning' behind the images to be permanently and forever on the front of their work. For this project, vast as it is in its scope and the range of issues covered, we couldn't decide on an appropriate cover. Some implied more North American issues, others British or European. Some suggested extremism, others one form of hate or another. Nothing seemed to capture the totality of the issues.

It was at this point that we decided upon something a little more abstract (itself a significant advancement in the process). It was here that images of lightning started to appear in the email inbox, and so another dilemma began: *which one looked the prettiest?* On this wholly superficial basis Nathan, Abbee and Paul had agreed to disagree, and so it was left to John (despite his protests, considered by the rest of us to be by far the most cerebral of our editorial team) to provide the answer. And he did. Sort of. Whilst the three of us were thinking about the visual attractiveness of the cover, John sent us an email, some of the content of which we shall share with you here:

> Have just read article on how little we know about the science behind lightning (although we know a lot about the science of storms) . . . The lightning is dramatic but I think it is about the totality of the storm . . . Reinforces my view that the 'lightning in the distance' are the better ones for the cover. So there could be a symbolism about what we know and what we still need to find out.

So this insightful input narrowed us down to a choice of two, at which point we asked Heidi Lee at Routledge to referee and make the final choice, which she duly did. The important point here though relates to John's comments about the 'totality of the storm', and what we know and what we still need to find out, and the road symbolises our (in the widest sense) collective journey in this regard. It is our hope then that this Handbook contributes to our understanding of the totality of this particular 'storm', but also that, in areas where it can't, it will nevertheless help to identify the things that we still need to find out. And in the event that it does neither, we hope that you still like the cover.

NH, AC, PG & JG, 2014

Reference

Hall, N. (2013). *Hate Crime* (2nd edition), Abingdon: Routledge.

1
Theories and concepts

1
Framing the boundaries of hate crime

Neil Chakraborti[1]

Hate crime has become an increasingly familiar term in recent years as the harms associated with acts of bigotry and prejudice continue to pose complex challenges for societies across the world. It is rightly seen as a human rights issue that has wider social and political ramifications beyond simply identifying criminal justice 'solutions' and the culpability of individual offenders. However, whilst hate crimes are now afforded greater recognition throughout all levels of society – from law-makers, law-enforcers, academics, students, activists and from 'ordinary' members of the public – some significant challenges remain. These continue to create uncertainty within the domains of hate crime scholarship and policy, particularly when it comes to making sense of the concept in a way that allows us to maximise its 'real-life' value to victims of hate crime.

On the one hand, questioning the value of our hate crime scholarship and policy-making may feel counter-intuitive to many of us who continue to praise the underlying principles of the hate crime movement and to marvel at its strengths: both as an umbrella construct to connect various forms of bigotry and as a bureaucratic term that lends itself to policy- and not just theory-building. Hate crime is a politically and socially significant term that cuts across disciplines, across communities and across borders. It is a concept which has inspired legal and social change designed to protect people from being persecuted simply because of who they are, or who they are perceived to be. It is an area of policy that has been prioritised regionally, nationally and internationally and which has been central to the governance of community cohesion.

At the same time, most of us would agree that there remains much about hate crime which we do not know, and this has implications for the 'real-life' value of our theorising and policy-making. This has a great deal to do with how we frame the parameters of hate crime. A vivid illustration of this can be seen in the official hate crime figures that are presented by different countries in an attempt to understand the scale of the problem within the Organization for Security and Co-Operation in Europe (OSCE) region. Figures collated by the Office for Democratic Institutions and Human Rights show considerable variations between OSCE member states: for instance, the number of hate crimes recorded by police in England, Wales and Northern Ireland in 2011 – 44,519 – contrasts quite dramatically with the corresponding numbers for countries such as Germany (4,040), Poland (444), Spain (115) and Italy (68) (ODIHR, 2012: 23–25). In reality, these figures are not an accurate measure through which to gauge international comparisons of hate crime: they are more a reflection of the way in which hate crimes are defined, publicised, recorded, reported and statistically collated by different countries, than of any genuine disparity in levels of hate crime.[2] Moreover, whilst this set of police-recorded figures from England and Wales paints a much more realistic picture than that offered by most other states, it does not begin to paint anything like a full picture. Recent sweeps of the Crime Survey for England and Wales – which accounts for experiences of victimisation not necessarily reported to the police – indicate that approximately 278,000 hate crimes are committed each year (Home Office, 2013), a total which is far higher than corresponding 'official' figures. Moreover, I would argue that the 'real' figure of hate crimes taking place is likely to be higher still but remains elusively unquantifiable, as many cases of hate crime are simply not recognised as hate crimes by criminal justice agencies, non-governmental organisations or by victims themselves.

This point is important because it shows that our understanding of hate crime is contingent upon the way in which we choose to frame the boundaries of hate crime. Within the discussion that follows, I call for a re-think in how we frame these boundaries, and I challenge the way in which narrow constructions of identity and community have led us to overlook a range of significant issues. As long as such issues remain peripheral to the 'hate debate' we risk marginalising the experiences of many victims, and thereby reducing the 'real-life' impact of hate crime theorising and policy-formation. Before outlining those issues, let us first consider the key features that have shaped our common understanding of hate crime.

Conventional boundaries

Hate crime is a social construct which has multiple meanings to different actors and which is subject to a myriad of interpretations. There is therefore no single universal framework that defines the way in which we conceive of the problem, although some notable efforts have been made by policy-makers and scholars to develop a common understanding that can generate workable responses to hate crime. One such attempt has come from The Office for Democratic Institutions and Human Rights (ODIHR), whose guidance for OSCE member states describes hate crimes as 'criminal acts committed with a bias motive' (2009: 16). For ODIHR, this bias does not have to manifest itself as hate for the offence to be thought of as a hate crime, nor does hate have to be the primary motive. Rather, it refers to acts where the victim is targeted deliberately because of a particular 'protected characteristic . . . shared by a group, such as "race", language, religion, ethnicity, nationality, or any other similar common factor' (2009: 16). Importantly, ODIHR's guidance does not seek to specify which protected characteristics should form the basis of a member state's hate crime policy, aside from making reference to aspects of identity that are 'fundamental to a person's sense of self' and to the relevance of 'current social problems as well as potential historical oppression and discrimination' (2009: 38).

This broad, pan-national framework for understanding hate crime was developed in recognition of the significance of hate crime across Europe and the pressing need for states, statutory and non-governmental organisations to acknowledge and respond to the problem. However – and as illustrated by the divergence in hate crime figures collated by different countries referred to above – there is little evidence of a shared understanding of the concept across nations. As such, inconsistencies abound when it comes to defining what a hate crime is, who the potential victims are and what type of legislative response is most appropriate (for further discussion, see Garland and Chakraborti, 2012). To some extent, this is an inevitable and understandable result of the way in which different countries' histories have shaped their prioritisation of different forms of hate crime. In countries such as Germany, Austria and Italy, for example, the connection of hate crime to right-wing extremism and anti-Semitism is clearly a legacy of tragic events from the twentieth century, while an emphasis on challenging racism in the UK is perhaps attributable to the mass migrations from the Caribbean and south Asia to the UK from the late 1940s onwards. Although a universal consensus on the implementation and prioritisation of hate crime policy may be unfeasible, the significance of ODIHR's guidance in the context of the discussion that follows lies in its broad interpretation of hate and the targets of hate.

A similarly broad interpretation is evident too within the hate crime policy framework of the UK. A key source of guidance comes from the Association of Chief Police Officers (ACPO), whose operational definition is enshrined within their guidelines for police forces in England, Wales and Northern Ireland (ACPO, 2000; 2005; 2014). As with ODIHR's hate crime guidance ACPO's policy framework makes specific reference to prejudice as well as hate, and it requires police forces to record not just hate *crimes* but all hate *incidents*, even if they lack the requisite elements to be classified as a notifiable offence later in the criminal justice process. In this context ACPO takes its lead from the landmark Macpherson Inquiry, whose attempts to address the deep-rooted institutional racism identified as being embedded within police culture by that Inquiry resulted in the adoption of a more flexible interpretation of a racist incident.[3] Accordingly, the hate crime guidance issued by ACPO stipulates that any hate incident, whether a *prima facie* 'crime' or not, should be recorded if it meets the threshold originally laid down by the Macpherson definition of a racist incident – namely, if it is perceived by the victim or any other person present as being motivated by prejudice or hate.

As for the protected characteristics that give rise to a hate crime, ACPO's guidance refers to five strands of monitored prejudice or hatred: race, religion, sexual orientation, gender identity and disability. This has facilitated a level of consistency in the way in which hate crimes are recorded and monitored by police forces, and successive governments have now passed a series of laws offering protection against expressions of hate crime falling under each of these strands. However, this does not preclude other forms of prejudice or hatred from being treated as hate crimes by local areas, as acknowledged within a recent government action plan (HM Government, 2012), and illustrated in April 2013 when Greater Manchester Police became the first police force within the UK to record attacks against members of alternative subcultures as hate crime.

In an academic sense Barbara Perry's (2001) conceptual framework is arguably the most influential. Whilst it is not the only one to have influenced the development of hate crime scholarship (see for example, Lawrence, 1999; Jacobs, 2002), it has left an indelible imprint upon contemporary hate crime discourse throughout the world (see, *inter alia*, Hall, 2005; Iganski, 2008; Chakraborti, 2010; Garland, 2012). It also offers much-needed theoretical substance to the more operationally-oriented frameworks described above. For Perry, hate crimes are acts of violence and intimidation directed towards marginalised communities, and are therefore synonymous with the power dynamics present within modern societies that reinforce the 'othering' of those who are seen as different. Indeed, the process of 'doing difference' is a central theme of Perry's framework which sees hate as rooted in the ideological structures of societal oppression that govern normative conceptions of identity. Within such a process, hate crime emerges as a response to the threats posed by 'others' when they attempt to step out of their 'proper' subordinate position within the structural order. It is, in other words, a mechanism through which violence is used to sustain both the hegemonic identity of the perpetrator and to reinforce the boundaries between dominant and subordinate groups, reminding the victim that they are 'different' and that they 'don't belong'.

Perry's framework has been of considerable value, not least because it helps us to think about hate crime within the broader psychological and socio-political contexts that condition hostile reactions to the 'other', and to recognise that hate crimes are part of a process of repeated or systematic victimisation shaped by context, structure and agency (Kelly, 1987; Bowling, 1993). But notwithstanding the significant advances made as a result of this framework – and through the operational guidance described above – I would argue that there is scope to develop our thinking even further to maximise the 'real-life' value of our theorising and policy-making. There remains much about hate crime that remains un- or under-explored, and this is a result of the way in which conventional constructions have been used to shape the parameters of what is categorised as hate crime without giving due regard to whether this satisfactorily accounts for the experiences and motivations that are connected to various manifestations of hate. As a result, certain realities of hate crime victimisation and perpetration have remained peripheral to the 'hate debate'. In the section that follows I outline a series of significant, yet 'peripheral' issues that could, and should, be considered alongside the more familiar aspects of hate crime discourse.

The case for extending boundaries

It is often said that hate crime policy creates and reinforces hierarchies of identity: some victims are deemed worthy of inclusion within hate crime frameworks whereas others invariably miss out. This is a now-familiar criticism of conventional hate crime policy (see, *inter alia*, Mason-Bish, 2010; Jacobs and Potter, 1998) but one that has not been adequately resolved. To some extent, this is an unavoidable outcome of having policy that makes a qualitative distinction between 'hate'-fuelled victimisation and 'ordinary' victimisation, where the needs and experiences of certain groups are prioritised over those of others. However, even if we accept that as a necessary, if uncomfortable, reality of hate crime policy, the process of deciding upon this 'hierarchy' is perhaps less palatable. As Mason-Bish (2010: 62) notes:

> ... hate crime policy has been formed through the work of lobbying and advisory groups who have had quite narrow remits, often focusing exclusively on one area of victimisation. This has contributed to a hierarchy within hate crime policy itself, whereby some identity groups seem to receive preferential treatment in criminal justice responses to hate crime.

Activists and campaigners have undoubtedly played a key role in pushing hate crime to the forefront of political and social agendas. Whether through generating debate about the nature of prejudice and intolerance of 'difference' or through evidencing the problem of targeted violence in its various guises, activists and campaigners can generate the momentum necessary to influence law making and policy enforcement (Lancaster, 2014; Perry, 2014). This is a process which has been crucial to the maturation of hate crime as an issue of international significance, yet there is a downside to this process too: namely, that the parameters of what we cover under the hate crime 'umbrella' can be contingent upon the capacity or willingness of campaign groups to lobby for recognition under this umbrella. Whether because of greater resources, a more powerful voice, public support for their cause or a more established history of stigma and discrimination, campaigners working to support certain strands of hate crime victim will invariably be able to lobby policy-makers harder than other potential claim-makers. It is that capacity to 'shout louder' that can sometimes influence who receives protection from hate crime laws and who does not, meaning that some victims of hate crime may not receive the recognition they expect or deserve.

Moreover, some groups may be denied altogether the privilege of having any campaign or advocacy groups lobbying on their behalf. This is especially true for certain 'others' who can find themselves marginal to or excluded from hate crime policy and scholarship despite being targeted because of characteristics fundamental to perceptions of who they are or their sense of self. Wachholz (2009), for instance, questions the failure to recognise the acts of violence and intimidation directed towards the homeless within the US as hate crime, whilst in the UK similar points could be made in relation to the targeted victimisation suffered by elderly and isolated victims (Meikle, 2011); by those with mental health issues or drug and alcohol dependency (Doward, 2010); by sex workers (Campbell, 2014); or by foreign nationals, refugees, asylum seekers, migrant workers and overseas students (Athwal et al., 2010; Fekete and Webber, 2010). These groups have much in common with the more established victim groups within hate crime discourse, in that they too are often singled out as targets of hate, hostility or prejudice specifically because of their 'difference'. However, lacking either the support of lobby groups or political representation, and typically seen as 'undesirables', *criminogenic* or less worthy than other more 'legitimate' or historically oppressed victim groups, they are commonly excluded from conventional frameworks.

Understanding the interplay between 'difference', vulnerability and hate crime is important if the concept is to have 'real-life' value beyond its existing confines. Of course, being 'different' does not automatically mean that someone will be singled out for harassment or abuse. Nor is it the case that *all* crimes against people who are 'different' will invariably be hate crimes: as we know, legal frameworks tend to require evidence of bias motivation against the victim, whether this takes the form of hostility, prejudice, bigotry or hate, in conjunction with the crime itself (ODIHR, 2009). However, we know both from contemporary research, and from simply opening our eyes to the world around us, that there are some 'others' in especially vulnerable situations who are at heightened risk of being victimised because of who they are – and this victimisation is likely to 'hurt' every bit as much as that suffered by the more established hate crime victim groups, and in some senses much more so (Chakraborti and Garland, 2012). And yet, by continuing to 'marginalise the marginalised' within our studies of hate crime we have little understanding of the victimisation directed towards less visible targets who lack the power of class or language, the privilege of advocacy groups and support networks, or the bargaining clout of political, economic or social mobility to draw from.

Currently these experiences of victimisation tend to fall between the cracks of existing scholarship and policy frameworks. So too does another dynamic pivotal to our understanding of hate crime: the intersectionality of identity characteristics that can be targeted by perpetrators of hate crime. Conceiving of hate crimes simply as offences directed towards individual strands of a person's identity fails to give adequate recognition to the interplay of identities with one another and with other personal, social and situational characteristics. Broadening our lines of enquiry beyond conventional singular constructions of identity has two key advantages. First, it acknowledges the intersections between a range of identity characteristics – including sexual orientation, ethnicity, disability, age, class, mental health, or body shape and appearance (to name but some) – thereby exposing what Moran and Sharpe (2004: 400) describe as 'the differences, the heterogeneity, within what are assumed to be homogeneous identity categories and groups'. In reality, these are not homogeneous categories and groups consisting of people with uniform characteristics and perceptions (see also Garland, 2012). Just as none of us should be defined exclusively by any one single identity characteristic (by being an ethnic minority, by having a disability, by being gay, for instance) nor should hate crime scholars and policy-makers automatically assume that perpetrators target their victims exclusively because of a single identity characteristic.

Second, recognising that hate crime can be the outcome of prejudice based upon multiple distinct yet connected lines is important not just for recognising the reality behind both the experience of victimisation and the commission of the offence, but for recognising the interplay between hate crime victimisation and socio-economic status. Many especially harrowing cases of hate crime take place in areas on the economic margins – in areas that many of us can conveniently avoid, ignore or write off – and yet the relevance of class and economic marginalisation to the commission of hate crime has rarely been a central line of enquiry to scholars and policy-makers. To use one well-known UK-based example, the years of disablist harassment directed towards Fiona Pilkington and her family – which tragically led to her taking her own life and that of her daughter Francecca[4] – has since been referred to as a watershed for the prioritisation of disablist victimisation. However, whilst the case serves as a powerful reminder of the nature and impact of prejudice directed towards disabled people, the relevance of related factors such as the family's social isolation and their economically deprived locality should not be discounted. Hate crimes can often be triggered and exacerbated by socio-economic conditions, and some potential targets of hate crime will invariably be better placed than others to avoid persecution by virtue of living at a greater distance from prejudiced neighbours or in less overtly hostile environments (Walters and Hoyle, 2012). Again, the probing of these factors should feature more prominently within contemporary hate crime studies.

A related shortcoming of our conventional approaches to understanding hate crime has been a failure to recognise the 'ordinariness' of much hate crime: ordinary not in relation to its impact upon the victim but in the sense of how the offence is conceived of by the perpetrator, and sometimes by the victim too, as discussed shortly. A consistent theme running through much of the hate crime literature is the association of hate with the prevailing power dynamics that reinforce the dominant position of the powerful and the marginal position of the 'other'; the idea that hate crimes prop up the perceived superiority of the perpetrators whilst simultaneously keeping victims in their 'proper' subordinate place. But while this stance accounts for many expressions of hate crime, it obscures those more spontaneous actions which occur in the context of a highly individualised 'trigger' situation rather than being a result of entrenched prejudice (Iganski, 2008; McGhee, 2007). While hate crimes are undeniably linked to the underlying structural and cultural processes that leave minorities susceptible to systemic violence, conceiving of these offences exclusively as a mechanism of subordination overplays what for some perpetrators will be an act arising from more banal motivations, be it boredom, jealousy or unfamiliarity with 'difference'.

This is another uncomfortable, and often-overlooked reality of hate crime. Political, public and scholarly responses can still be governed by a tendency to conflate hate crimes with the ideology of organised hate groups, supremacists or far-right extremists. And yet the evidence would suggest that many hate crimes tend to be committed by relatively 'ordinary' people in the context of their 'ordinary' day-to-day lives (Iganski, 2008; Mason, 2005; Ray et al., 2004). These offences are not always inspired by a sense of entrenched prejudice or hate on the part of the perpetrator but may instead arise as a departure from standard norms of behaviour; or through an inability to control language or behaviour in moments of stress, anger or inebriation; or from a sense of weakness or inadequacy that can stem from a range of subconscious emotional and psychological processes (Dixon and Gadd, 2006; Gadd, 2009).

Equally, our reliance on the labels 'victim' and 'offender' assumes dichotomous roles in hate crime offences, but research has shown that this reinforces a de-contextualised picture of some cases, particularly neighbourhood conflicts, where both parties can share culpability for the anti-social acts which form the basis for the broader conflict and hate offence (Walters and Hoyle, 2012).

This has a number of practical implications for the way in which we frame the boundaries of hate crime. First, it tells us that hate crimes are not committed exclusively by obvious 'haters'; by those whom one might immediately associate with 'hate'-fuelled beliefs. Instead, we must look beyond the realms of convention and recognise the 'everyday' acts of prejudice that blight victims' lives. The narrower our framework, the lower the chances of capturing these experiences. Second, it reminds us of the capacity for members of minority groups to be perpetrators as well as victims of hate crime. The kinds of biases, prejudices and stereotypes that form the basis of hate crimes are not the exclusive domain of any particular group, and yet the foundations of much hate crime policy and scholarship have been built on the assumption that these are exclusively 'majority versus minority' crimes. However well-intentioned, such an assumption fails to account for the acts of hate, prejudice and bigotry committed by minorities against fellow minorities, or indeed against those who might be described as majority group members. Again, this is too significant an issue to remain peripheral to the domains of scholarship and policy.

And finally – but perhaps even more significantly – the 'ordinariness' of hate crime has important implications for what victims themselves see as hate crime. For many victims of hate crime, harassment, bullying and violence form an entrenched, routine part of their day-to-day lives to the extent that this victimisation becomes a normalised feature of being 'different', and not something that they would recognise or report as 'hate crime'. Indeed, as noted earlier, there will invariably be high numbers of victims who are unfamiliar with the term 'hate crime' and who may be reluctant to share (or incapable of sharing) their experiences with a third party. Unless we recognise the many and varied forms that hate crime can take, more experiences of hate crime victimisation will continue to go unnoticed and unchallenged.

Using research to examine hidden truths

The preceding discussion identifies a series of issues which would be better placed at the forefront, rather than the periphery, of our thinking if we – as scholars, as activists, as policy-informers and as citizens – are to develop effective responses to the problems posed by hate crime. As noted earlier, interpretations of hate crime vary considerably and some of these issues may be beyond the scope of policy, law enforcement and scholarship in certain countries. Moreover, calls to think more broadly about a notion already as conceptually ambiguous and diffuse as hate crime are unlikely to be welcomed by all. Nonetheless, I would contend that thinking more broadly is an essential part of the process in understanding what hate crimes are, whom they affect and in what ways they create damage. Perhaps even more importantly, this line of thinking is key to maximising the real-life value of scholarship and policy to those countless numbers of victims whose experiences of hate crime go unnoticed.

By way of illustration, let me refer briefly to The Leicester Hate Crime Project,[5] a two-year study of hate crime victimisation funded by the Economic and Social Research Council.[6] This study has adopted a deliberately broad interpretation of hate crime – acts of hate, prejudice or bigotry directed towards the victim because of their identity or perceived 'difference' – in order to learn more about the profile of people affected, the nature of their experiences of victimisation and their expectations of agency responses. Although the research is ongoing as I write, a number of notable themes have started to emerge. First, as a research team we have already heard numerous accounts detailing harrowing experiences of prejudice – including physical attacks, harassment, criminal damage and online bullying – from victims who have often found themselves on the margins of conventional hate crime frameworks. This includes people targeted because of their body shape, their 'unusual' appearance or manner of dress, their mental health issues, or because of their perceived deviancy or 'bottom-of-the-ladder' status as asylum seekers, refugees, Gypsies or Travellers, to name just some examples. These are groups of people who each have very different sets of identity characteristics and yet who share a form of 'difference' that gives rise to repeated acts of targeted violence and intimidation.

Second, many of the victims whom we have engaged with so far are people who have little or no familiarity with the concept of hate crime, despite having suffered what most scholars and practitioners would automatically class as hate crime on repeated occasions. For these victims, experiences of hate crime are normalised as an everyday, unwanted but routine part of being 'different' rather than being seen as an act of victimisation that should be reported. Moreover, such victims will often find themselves based outside the perimeters of the 'knowledge' society: in environments where awareness of hate crime policy and associated publicity campaigns and reporting structures is invariably lower; where people are likely to feel less comfortable about sharing their experiences through official channels; and where the sense of bitterness, alienation and resentment that often triggers the scapegoating of 'others' is likely to be all the more pervasive as a result of prevailing economic conditions (see also Chakraborti and Garland, 2012; Gadd, 2009).

Third, the research has revealed that it is not just someone's identity *per se* (their ethnicity, their sexuality, their disability and so on) that makes them vulnerable to hate crimes, but rather the way that identity intersects with other aspects of self and with other situational factors and context. In this sense, the likelihood of being targeted is increased by the presence of factors that are distinct from an individual's 'main' or visible identity characteristic. Certainly, within the context of our ongoing research, the process of victim selection appears to have been influenced by factors such as the victim's manner of dress, their command of English, their isolation, their routine activities, their lack of physical presence or the type of area they live in – in association with what one might class as their main identity characteristic. Equally, some victims have found it difficult to limit the reasons for their selection by the perpetrator to one specific identity feature, and instead have referred to the relevance of multiple identity characteristics: being Asian *and* gay, elderly *and* disabled, or a veiled Muslim woman, for instance.

Finally, judging from the cases we have come across so far in our research it would seem that the notion of hate crimes being 'majority versus minority' crimes is much too simplistic. For instance, within our study some victims of racist and religiously motivated hate crimes described the perpetrators as being fellow ethnic minorities from different ethnic or faith backgrounds, while some victims of homophobic and transphobic hate encountered prejudice from within minority ethnic and faith communities and from within the lesbian, gay, bisexual and transgender (LGBT) community itself. Clearly, both victims and perpetrators of hate crime can belong to minority communities, and sometimes – if we are to group people under the broad homogenous banners of minority ethnic, LGBT, and so on – even to what might be described as the same minority community. Everyone has the capacity to express hate towards others, irrespective of their own background or identity.

Conclusion

The themes outlined in the preceding section offer support for the central message of this chapter: namely, that thinking more broadly about hate crime enables us to acknowledge important truths that would otherwise remain peripheral, at best, to the way in which we theorise, develop and enforce policy, support victims and punish offenders. As we have seen, international and domestic policy guidance gives us scope to think broadly about which prejudices, which groups of victims and which types of experiences we might choose to classify as hate crime. The faultlines associated with responses to hate crime, therefore, lie not so much with official policy and legislative frameworks but with the way in which we collectively – as scholars, practitioners, campaigners and citizens – limit the parameters of what we categorise as hate crime without accounting for the experiences and motivations that are connected to various expressions of hate.

As we all know, hate crime is an elastic concept that has multiple meanings for multiple audiences. Whilst this can be a source of frustration, it is also an inevitable consequence of using an umbrella term to cover a diverse and complex range of emotions and behaviours, whose meanings are contingent upon contextual factors relevant to individual cases and open to the interpretation of law enforcers. The search for a universally accepted, all-encompassing definition of hate crime may therefore be futile, but the search for greater conceptual and operational clarity is not. Rather, the onus is on us to extend the boundaries of our own cognitive frameworks in order to capture the realities of hate crime victimisation and perpetration. In so doing we can promote a common language of hate crime discourse – a language which is open to differences in interpretation across time, place and space, and one which can shape more effective responses to any expressions of prejudice that reinforce the persecution of 'others'.

Notes

1. This chapter has been adapted from the following article: Chakraborti, N. (2015) 'Re-Thinking Hate Crime: Fresh Challenges for Theory and Practice', *Journal of Interpersonal Violence*, 30 (1).
2. In England and Wales, a hate crime is recorded if the victim or any other person feel a criminal offence is 'motivated by prejudice or hate' (ACPO, 2005: 9). This 'victim-oriented' approach results in higher numbers of hate crimes being recorded than in most other states. The post-Macpherson priority given by the police, Ministry of Justice and other bodies in England and Wales to tackling hate crimes has also been a significant factor in encouraging more victims to report them.
3. Recommendation 12 of the Macpherson report defines a racist incident as 'any incident which is perceived to be racist by the victim or any other person' (Macpherson, 1999: para. 45.17).
4. Fiona, a 38-year-old mother of Francecca, an 18-year-old girl with learning difficulties, was driven to kill herself and her daughter in October 2007 by setting light to her car, with them both inside, near their home in Leicestershire, England, following years of disablist abuse from local youths directed at her family.
5. The Leicester Hate Crime Project is a two-year study which is due to be completed in October 2014. Further information about the research and its findings can be found at www2.le.ac.uk/departments/criminology/research/current-projects/hate-crime.
6. The Economic and Social Research Council (ESRC) is the UK's largest organisation for funding research on economic and social issues. It supports independent, high quality research which has an impact on business, the public sector and the third sector. More information can be found at www.esrc.ac.uk.

Bibliography

Association of Chief Police Officers (ACPO) (2005) *Hate Crime: Delivering A Quality Service – Good Practice and Tactical Guidance*. London: Home Office Police Standards Unit.

Association of Chief Police Officers (ACPO) (2000) *Guide to Identifying and Combating Hate Crime*. London: Home Office Police Standards Unit.

Athwal, H., Bourne, J. and Wood, R. (2010) *Racial Violence: The Buried Issue*. London: The Institute of Race Relations.

Bowling, B. (1993) 'Racial Harassment and the Process of Victimisation'. *British Journal of Criminology* 33 (2): 231–250.

Campbell, R. (2014) 'Linking Sex Work and Hate Crime in Merseyside', in N. Chakraborti and J. Garland (eds) *Responding to Hate Crime: The Case for Connecting Policy and Research*. Bristol: The Policy Press.

Chakraborti, N. (2010) 'Crimes against the 'Other': Conceptual, Operational and Empirical Challenges for Hate Studies'. *Journal of Hate Studies* 8 (1): 9–28.

Chakraborti, N. and Garland, J. (2012) 'Reconceptualising Hate Crime Victimization through the Lens of Vulnerability and "Difference"'. *Theoretical Criminology* 16 (4): 499–514.

Dixon, B. and Gadd, D. (2006) 'Getting the Message? 'New' Labour and the Criminalisation of "Hate"'. *Criminology and Criminal Justice* 6 (3): 309–328.

Doward, J. (2010) 'Vulnerable Tenants Targeted by Drug Gang "Cuckoos"'. *The Observer*, 3 October, p. 16.

Fekete, L. and Webber, F. (2010) 'Foreign Nationals, Enemy Penology and the Criminal Justice System'. *Race and Class* 51 (4): 1–25.

Gadd, D. (2009) 'Aggravating Racism and Elusive Motivation'. *British Journal of Criminology* 49 (6): 755–771.

Garland, J. (2012) 'Dilemmas in Defining Hate Crime Victimisation'. *International Review of Victimology* 18 (1): 25–37.

Garland, J. (2010) '"It's a Mosher just been Banged for No Reason": Assessing the Victimisation of Goths and the Boundaries of Hate Crime'. *International Review of Victimology* 17 (2): 159–177.

Garland, J. and Chakraborti, N. (2012) 'Divided by a Common Concept? Assessing the Implications of Different Conceptualizations of Hate Crime in the European Union'. *European Journal of Criminology*, 9 (1): 38–51.

Hall, N. (2005) *Hate Crime*. Cullompton: Willan.

Home Office (2013) with Ministry of Justice and Office for National Statistics, *An Overview of Hate Crime in England and Wales*, London: Home Office.

HM Government (2012) *Challenge It, Report It, Stop It: The Government's Plan to Tackle Hate Crime*. London: HM Government.

Iganski, P. (2008) *'Hate Crime' and the City*. Bristol: The Policy Press.

Iganski, P. (2001) 'Hate Crimes Hurt More'. *American Behavioral Scientist* 45: 697–713.

Jacobs, J. (2002) 'Hate Crime: Criminal Law and Identity Politics'. *Theoretical Criminology* 6 (4): 481–484.

Jacobs, J. and Potter, K. (1998) *Hate Crimes: Criminal Law and Identity Politics*. Oxford: Oxford University Press.

Kelly, L. (1987) 'The Continuum of Sexual Violence', in J. Hanmer and M. Maynard (eds) *Women, Violence and Social Control*. London: Macmillan, 46–60.

Lancaster, S. (2014) 'Reshaping Hate Crime Policy and Practice: Lessons from a Grassroots Campaign', in N. Chakraborti and J. Garland (eds) *Responding to Hate Crime: The Case for Connecting Policy and Research*. Bristol: The Policy Press.

Lawrence, F. (1999) *Punishing Hate: Bias Crimes under American Law*. Cambridge, MA: Harvard University Press.

Macpherson, Sir W. (1999) *The Stephen Lawrence Inquiry: Report of an Inquiry by Sir William Macpherson of Cluny*, CM 4262-1, London: Home Office.

Mason, G. (2005) 'Hate Crime and the Image of the Stranger'. *British Journal of Criminology*, 45 (6): 837–859.

Mason-Bish, H. (2010) 'Future Challenges for Hate Crime Policy: Lessons from the Past', in N. Chakraborti (ed.) *Hate Crime: Concepts, Policy, Future Directions*. Cullompton: Willan, 58–77.

McGhee, D. (2007) 'The Challenge of Working with Racially Motivated Offenders: An Exercise in Ambivalence?' *Probation Journal* 54 (3): 213–226.

Meikle, J. (2011) '"Night Stalker" Jailed for Life'. *The Guardian*, 25 March.

Moran, L. and Sharpe, A. (2004) 'Violence, Identity and Policing: The Case of Violence against Transgender People'. *Criminal Justice* 4 (4): 395–417.

ODIHR (Office for Democratic Institutions and Human Rights) (2012) *Hate Crimes in the OSCE Region: Incidents and Responses. Annual Report for 2011*. Warsaw: OSCE Office for Democratic Institutions and Human Rights.

ODIHR (Office for Democratic Institutions and Human Rights) (2009) *Hate Crime Laws: A Practical Guide.* Warsaw: OSCE Office for Democratic Institutions and Human Rights.

Perry, B. (2001) *In the Name of Hate: Understanding Hate Crimes.* London: Routledge.

Perry, J. (2014) 'Evidencing the Case for "Hate Crime"', in N. Chakraborti and J. Garland (eds) *Responding to Hate Crime: The Case for Connecting Policy and Research.* Bristol: The Policy Press.

Ray, L., Smith, D. and Wastell, L. (2004) 'Shame, Rage and Racist Violence'. *British Journal of Criminology* 44 (3), 350–368.

Wachholz, S. (2009) 'Pathways through Hate: Exploring the Victimisation of the Homeless', in B. Perry (ed.) *Hate Crimes Volume Three: The Victims of Hate Crime.* Westport, CT: Praeger, 199–222.

Walters, M.A. (2011) 'A General *Theories* of Hate Crime? Strain, Doing Difference and Self Control'. *Critical Criminology* 19 (4): 313–330.

Walters, M.A. and Hoyle, C. (2012) 'Exploring the Everyday World of Hate Victimisation through Community Mediation'. *International Review of Victimology* 18 (1): 7–24.

2
Beyond the Silo
Rethinking hate crime and intersectionality

Hannah Mason-Bish

During my doctoral research on the emergence of hate crime legislation I interviewed a number of campaign group activists who were working on improving the criminal justice response to hate crime victimisation. Many of these worked on one specific hate crime "strand" and were members of monitoring groups looking at racist, religious, homophobic, disablist or gendered crimes. However, one respondent worked independently and had been victimised herself in a violent attack in the street. She observed "I am disabled, gay and a woman. If I am targeted am I supposed to say which aspect was the most hurtful and damaging?" She was frustrated at a criminal justice response which would only allow her to tick one aspect of her identity as the potential cause of the attack and also at campaigners who were wedded to one aspect of identity in their lobbying efforts. This was not an uncommon opinion, with many also highlighting the competition between different charities and lobbying groups over resources, police attention and media coverage. What was clear was that hate crime policy had emerged through an identity politics which tended to oversimplify victim groups and did not necessarily take into account the diverse experiences of victims and the nuances of the harms that they might suffer.

The development of hate crime legislation has been characterised by this "silo" approach to identity, where groups are added to policy as time goes on. The Crime and Disorder Act 1998 set out specific offences for some racially aggravated crimes and that was expanded in 2001 to include crimes with a religious aggravation. In 2003 the Criminal Justice Act detailed sentence enhancements for crimes which were motivated by prejudice towards disability and sexual orientation. Transphobic hate crimes were added in 2012 under the Legal Aid, Sentencing and Punishment of Offenders Act. In June 2013 the Law Commission published its consultation looking into the further extension of hate crime provisions, suggesting that the group-based approach would continue for the foreseeable future. While this strategy does allow for the monitoring of criminal justice performance under each strand, this chapter suggests that the continuing focus on the group dimension of victimisation could be problematic. Scholars have noted that it creates a "competition to be counted" whereby some victim groups are included and others are left out (Morgan, 2002). The impact of excluding some categories of identity means that they are not only overlooked by policy, but they are also ignored as aspects of identity in other victim groups. Seeing that the original aim of hate crime legislation was to send a positive message to communities, then this exclusion or misrepresentation of identity groups warrants attention.

The aim of this chapter is to challenge the victim group approach to policy and to consider what can be gained from an intersectional understanding of hate crime. This will be achieved by first outlining the problems of policy which is wedded to identity politics, touching upon assumptions made about what it is to experience hate crime. The chapter then moves to examine the importance of considering intersectionality by looking at an emergent body of research that assesses the impact of multiple systems of oppression on the hate crime victim experience. Fundamentally it will be suggested that hate crime policy needs to circumvent traditional notions of primary identity characteristics and to understand the fluidity of identity and the multiple ways in which prejudice and violence might be experienced. In research this means studying the lived experience of the victim and to tease out the unique harms and risks that people might face in order to gain a more comprehensive understanding. For policy, this would require increased awareness about the risks faced by people who inhabit more "complex" identities, greater community engagement and the ability to record data to take account of this.

Hate crime policy

Internationally, policy definitions of hate crime differ broadly but most statutes are accompanied by a list of victims or identity groups who can seek redress and potentially a harsher punishment for their perpetrator. Typically, the groups included tend to be categories with a long history of oppression and in particular, a challenging relationship with the police and criminal justice system. What also appears to be the case is that once hate crimes are enshrined in law, campaign groups mobilise in an attempt to expand the list of victims and to gain recognition for the harms that they suffer (Jenness and Grattet, 2001). In the UK, the hate crime policy domain emerged after the racist murder of Stephen Lawrence in 1993 and the subsequent Macpherson Inquiry, which identified key failings in the Metropolitan Police Service. Calls for a specific offence of racial violence were made and garnered the support of New Labour, who made a manifesto commitment to do so once in power. The calls for enhanced punishment chimed with their political objective to appear "tough on crime". In 1998 the Crime and Disorder Act did just that, with the aim of sending a positive message but also providing a practical impetus for change within the justice system (Iganski, 1999). Already there was discord amongst some politicians and campaigners who queried the message sent to excluded groups. Lord Mackay of Drumadoon for example, wondered what message would be sent about other motivations and was concerned that they would be downgraded (Hansard (HL), 16 Dec. 1997). The exclusion of religion was a particular concern and MPs made specific reference to Islamophobia. The legislation was expanded to include religion in 2001, following revenge attacks against Muslims in the wake of the US terrorist attacks on the Twin Towers. Although Muslim organisations had been documenting Islamophobic attacks for a number of years, the 9/11 attacks also garnered media coverage about their victimisation and enabled a more concerted campaign to extend hate crime provisions (Law Commission, 2013a: 10). Importantly, campaigners wanted their victimisation correctly recognised as being linked to religious, rather than racial identity.

Hate crime provisions in Britain were further extended in 2003 to include sexual orientation and disability. Although not a specific offence, the Criminal Justice Act allowed for judicial discretion in adding a sentence enhancement. This too followed a high profile hate crime in which neo-Nazi David Copeland targeted the black, Bangladeshi, and gay communities, which demonstrated a broad spectrum of hate crime and similarities in the impact on victims. The debates in the House of Lords surrounding the amendment show that politicians drew upon victimisation surveys to show the scale of the problem of homophobic and disablist hate crimes when discussing these categories (Hansard (HL), 5 Nov. 2003). Transgender identity was added to this list in 2012, again with policymakers having viewed convincing evidence that these communities faced increasing violence that needed to be deterred. However, the work of lobbyists does not finish at the enshrinement of statute and research has shown that once included in hate crime law, victim groups have continued to work hard to ensure that provisions are implemented. For example, the Crown Prosecution Service did not produce a policy on prosecuting disability hate crime until 2007, which only came about after a series of murders of disabled people added impetus to the claims being made by the disability movement (Mason-Bish, 2012b). The involvement of myriad activists, monitoring organisations and advisory groups has been central to maintaining pressure on the criminal justice system to work on hate crime policy.

Identity politics and intersectionality

The character of hate crime legislation in Britain has been defined by an identity politics approach to which recognition is the main aim. According to Nancy Fraser, such objectives tend to be merely affirmative in recognising a simplistic aspect of identity and do little to really transform underlying structures (Fraser, 2003). Hate crime legislation shares this characteristic with other "recognition struggles" which have been critiqued for their tendency to create competition between victim groups. As Barbara Hobson notes:

> Recognition politics are dynamic: social actors seize political opportunities, reclaim and refashion public discourse and reconfigure the politics surrounding recognition and redistribution. But claims and claims-makers exist in political cultures. Socio-political context can be seen as a field of constraints and opportunities both in terms of a) who and what gets recognised; and b) where and how cultural identities are embedded.
>
> *(Hobson, 2003: 8)*

This demonstrates the way that activists have to grab opportunities as they arise in order to have an impact. This comes with a compromise in that some groups will not achieve the same level of recognition. Hate crime policy in Britain demonstrates this quite clearly because only five types of identity characteristic have been enshrined in law. Jon Garland's work on the exclusion of subcultural identity is a case in point. In 2007 Sophie Lancaster was brutally murdered for her appearance as a Goth and despite the judge labelling it as a "hate crime" there was no legal mechanism to prosecute it as such (Garland, 2010: 41; see also this volume). However, the case shared many characteristics associated with traditional forms of hate crime such as a history of marginalisation and being attacked because of perceived difference.

Chakraborti and Garland also draw attention to "undesirable" groups including the homeless, those with drug and alcohol dependency and refugees for not being included because they lack lobby group support and political experience (Chakraborti and Garland, 2012: 504). Therefore, hate crime is both a moral and legal construct that requires groups to engender "emotional thinking that encourage[s] others to see them as the undeserving victims of prejudice" (Mason, 2007: 249). Academic Jo Morgan takes this point further, arguing that hate crime laws are particularly damaging because:

> Competition to be "counted" and the political clout required to be counted has not only frozen out disorganised groups and individuals that experience hate crime, it has also led to in-fighting between social movements in the US.
>
> *(Morgan, 2002: 32)*

Morgan's work looks particularly at attacks on people who work in abortion clinics, sex workers and paedophiles and shows the similarities in their experiences when compared with more established hate crime groups. She observes that excluding groups because they lack political impetus is distinctly damaging in that it further fails to recognise their victimisation and renders them powerless. Furthermore, it creates a competition between groups who are seeking to show that their particular experience is worse and therefore needs recognition in law. This message is something that policymakers have clearly been acutely aware of. When the provisions for racially aggravated offences were being discussed in 1998, concerns were raised about the signal sent to other groups. Now in 2013, the Law Commission are considering amending hate crime provisions and their impact assessment warns against the "potential for harm to the reputation of the CJS as other groups . . . do not get the same protection" (Law Commission, 2013b: 3). For hate crime policy, you are either in or out.

An important by-product of the identity strand approach to hate crime policy has been to oversimplify the victim experience and to fail to acknowledge the lived reality for victims. This simplification of identity is described by Moran and Sharpe as the "either/or logic" (Moran and Sharpe, 2004: 410). Essentially, hate crime legislation has functioned by adding categories as seemingly separate entities – race or sexual orientation, disability or religion – and has not encouraged an understanding of identities that intersect. This sends the potentially harmful message that one aspect is irrelevant. Moran and Sharpe illustrate that it is impossible to find policy that makes reference to the transgender experience of racial violence, thus rendering it insignificant, difficult or invisible. Writing about the experiences of lesbian, gay, bisexual and transgender (LGBT) people, Doug Meyer found that approaches which only consider one aspect of oppression tend to provide "homogenized and distorted views of marginalized groups, advancing the interests of more privileged individuals" (Meyer, 2012: 850). Such criticisms have certainly been levelled at organisations such as Stonewall for failing to adequately campaign on behalf of black and minority ethnic (BME) people and for the large disability charities which have been criticised for speaking for and not with disabled people. Similarly, as is often a characteristic of identity politics, deeper structural and economic issues affecting victims of hate crime are often subsumed under the broader and simpler title of an identity characteristic (Fraser, 2003: 133). How might a wealthy gay man experience hate crime differently to a gay man living in poverty? Obviously such nuances are not just for policy to consider, but also relate to the importance of hate crime scholarship, which will be examined shortly.

The nuances of victimisation are also lost when totalising assumptions are made about group characteristics. For example, the Crown Prosecution Service (CPS) disability hate crime policy was criticised for failing to account for the diverse ways that disabled people experience hate crime. The CPS had to revise its policy to reflect the fact that disabled people might face very particular forms of hatred which had not necessarily been considered before – such as being attacked by pseudo-friends (Mason-Bish, 2012b). Of further importance has been the assumption that disabled people are inherently vulnerable and "easy targets" of hate crime, rather than victims of intentional hatred. Roulstone et al. observe that there has been a long history of labelling disabled people in this way and assuming that their identity is rooted in weakness and requires a paternalistic response (Roulstone et al., 2009: 8). It has been suggested that this has been at the root of difficulties in getting disabled people to report hate crime. Furthermore, the role of social exclusion, class and 'space' in the impact of hate crime on disabled victims warrants further attention. Chakraborti and Garland note that it is important to recognise that "hate crime can be the outcome of prejudice based on multiple, distinct yet connected, lines is important for recognizing the reality behind both the experience of victimization and the commission of the offence" (Chakraborti and Garland, 2012: 504). As was evidenced by the monitoring efforts of disability campaigners, adding a category to a list of hate crime victims then requires great efforts to understand the diversity of experiences within that simple grouping.

As hate crime policy is defined by the list of victim groups included, it draws attention to those left out of the list. The limits of a group-based approach to hate crime have also been evidenced by the absence of gender from provisions. It has been suggested that gender-based violence is different from hate crime for a number of reasons. First, some have suggested that women are not a 'minority' group and so do not require the protection that legislation affords. Second, gender-based violence might be more likely in the context of a personal relationship and women already have significant protection under other legislation (Mason-Bish, 2012a). These reasons, amongst others, demonstrate again that the silo approach to hate crime policy has meant that victim groups are evaluated in rather simplistic ways to see if they 'fit' or not. The limited debate that there has been draws on assumptions about the nature of violence that women experience and seeks to categorise it as either hate crime or something else. In reality, there might be instances of violence which are and which are not. But gender is seen as a complicated identity category that is best left out of the hate crime canon. A further impact of this has been that campaigners also evaluate the limits of hate crime policy as a tool to combat violence against women. In recent research by Gill and Mason-Bish it was discovered that campaigners on violence against women and gender-based violence were often cautious about hate crime policy, feeling that it lacked the sophistication to handle intersectionality and diversity (Gill and Mason-Bish, 2013). The London Feminist Network conference in 2010 raised concerns that such an approach would essentialise gender and ignore the intersection of race, class, religion and sexual orientation (Anthias, 2011). Furthermore, campaigners consider the effect of simply adding categories, meaning that a new identity group would be at the bottom of a long list. Academic Phyllis Gerstenfeld notes the victims of gender-based hate would be "subsumed under the larger rubric of bias crime, and thus will be largely forgotten" (Gerstenfeld, 2004: 9). This results in making women invisible from hate crime policy.

Squaring the circle

So far this chapter has critically assessed the strand-based approach to hate crime policy and thought about its limits in terms of simplifying or totalising the victim experience. However, there are some studies which have begun to look at the complexities of identity in relation to hate crime and these utilise an intersectional approach. Arguing that identity politics "conflates or ignores intragroup difference", intersectional theorists argued that it also tended to "expound identity as a woman or person of colour as an either/or proposition, they relegate the identity of women of colour to a location that resists telling" (Crenshaw, 1991: 1242). Instead of being members of separate groupings, the reality is that identity can be fluid, with aspects of oppression and inequality overlapping each other. The concept of intersectionality has been used to expose the flaws in a criminal justice response that assumes uniformity within categories (Marchetti, 2008; Crenshaw, 1991). Furthermore, an increasing number of researchers are using it to highlight the impact of multiple systems of oppression on a person's life. As such, intersectionality is an appealing concept for better understanding hate crime and victimisation. It is used in this chapter as a concept that "aims to make visible the multiple positioning that constitutes everyday life and the power relations that are central to it" (Phoenix and Pattynama, 2006: 187).

In his study on LGBT experiences of homophobic violence, Doug Meyer used the concept of intersectionality to understand how social position might impact on how victims evaluate harm. He was critical of the way that previous studies had assumed that the victim experience of violence and hate could be hierarchically ranked (Meyer, 2010: 982). For example, victimisation studies would require those surveyed to rank their most serious experience and to assume that people within a victim category did this in the same way. After conducting in-depth interviews, Meyer found that LGBT people with a white middle class background would frequently view the violence experienced as severe, whereas those from a working class background did not. The latter often had non-LGBT friends who had experienced worse violence and so posited that "it could be worse" (Meyer, 2010: 986). Part of this was down to support networks and friendship groups. For example, Meyer suggests that the white middle class respondents were often encouraged to report their victimisation because violence was an exceptional event in the circles that they mixed. The lower income LGBT groups had their violence minimised – usually by a family member. Quoting a respondent named Jayvyn, a 33-year-old black gay man who was assaulted in the street, he says:

> For the longest time, I didn't see it as a big deal. Everyone kept telling me, "well, you weren't hurt, you weren't killed, like so and so." But I was hurt. I mean, I had the scars to support it.
>
> *(Meyer, 2010: 985)*

As such the social networks of victims affect their perceptions of the severity of their victimisation. Furthermore, Meyer found that class and race also had an impact on their expectations about whether they would be victimised in the first place. Poor LGBT black people anticipated violence because their "race, class, gender and sexual identities had been attacked in the past" (Meyer, 2010, 987). This tended to lead to them minimising the brutality of their experiences as something normal that they would probably not report.

Adopting an intersectional approach to hate crime can be particularly illuminating where gender is concerned. In their examination of Muslim women who encounter Islamophobia, Chakraborti and Zempi argue that the Muslim veil itself is an intersectional issue (Chakraborti and Zempi, 2012: 274). The veil carries with it connotations of gender dominance and is viewed as a symbol of the oppression of Muslim women. Therefore, it is not sufficient merely to understand hate crimes against them as Islamophobic attacks because women will experience this differently from men. For Muslim women, the veil is part of their female identity but also means that they are targets and will avoid certain situations if they feel they might be at risk. Behaviour which might come under the title of "Islamophobia" cannot really be understood without examining how gender compounds or complicates it. Research has also demonstrated this in relation to lesbian experiences of hate violence. Corteen's study found that as lesbians were seen to transgress both gender and sexuality norms, they were at increased risk from violent attacks (Corteen, 2002: 266). Women were more likely to be attacked when they were not performing gender appropriately – such as when wearing trousers, no make-up or flat shoes (Corteen, 2002: 270). In Meyer's study he concluded that gay men decrease in status when identifying as feminine and were particularly attuned to verbal insults as an attack on their gender and sexuality. For lesbians, sexual violence was one of the most damaging forms of homophobic abuse because women are more likely to be subject to the threat of sexual assault in a way that men are not. As such, the experience of homophobia needs to be viewed through an intersectional lens. In these examples, Muslim women and lesbians are "doing gender inappropriately" and thus more at risk of attack and likely to be affected in different ways.

Some studies have looked at the difficulties of some victims of hate crime in seeking support and recognition within their own communities. In her study of violence against women in immigrant communities, Yasmin Jiwani found that the young women would "walk a tightrope" between violent racism that they would experience from the host or dominant society and the need to conform to different roles and norms in their own community (Jiwani, 2005: 846). They negotiate multiple identities on a daily basis and were acutely aware that it was necessary to assimilate into their new community in order to avoid racist violence committed against them (Jiwani, 2005: 868). This need to fit in meant that they had to privilege cultural norms of the new society over the ones associated with their home and family. Their immigrant status made them fearful of the police, so they would become more reliant on their family for support and even less likely to report violence experienced within their own community. Therefore:

> the othering resulting from gendered socialization combined with the othering resulting from racialisation heightens the complex and intersection forms of violence that girls and young women of colour experience.
>
> *(Jiwani, 2005: 851)*

Continuing this theme, Meyer found that black LGBT people experienced this jarring between communities where hate crime was concerned. He found that they would often interpret their violent experiences as an attempt to punish them for not representing their racial community appropriately (Meyer, 2012: 858). Black lesbians often felt that homophobic violence directed towards them was a statement that they had caused harm to the community by converting other women into lesbianism. Black gay men were often keen to highlight that they were still good role models for the black community, due to their physical and emotional strengths (Meyer, 2012: 861). This difficulty in managing roles also feeds into the ability of victims to overcome traumatic hate crimes. In their study of transgender people of colour, Singh and McKleroy observed that victims who had a strong sense of pride in both their racial and gender identity were more resilient after victimisation. This type of acceptance took time because their gender identity was not necessarily accepted within their family (Singh and McKleroy, 2011). Their minority status as being both black and transgender also made it hard to connect with activists and support networks. So their identity as people who were marginalised on many fronts meant that they could not always access support and validation of their lives.

Conclusion

This chapter has sought to re-examine the identity-based approach to hate crime policy by looking at its historical development. Hate crime legislation has been characterised by an approach which lists victim groups in a rather simplistic way. In keeping with other policy defined by identity politics, such groupings do not always acknowledge diversity and leave out victim groups who do not fit neatly within the hate crime framework. Taking a more intersectional approach highlights that this totalising logic inhibits our understanding of the victim experience. Policy is often reduced to one axis of oppression, meaning that intersections and diversity are rendered invisible. The impact of this is to "miscategorise" people who might then suffer from a lack of support and face difficulty in negotiating different social and cultural spaces. Some might also be at heightened risk of attack due to this and to the fact that they might be more visibly "different" and performing their identity inappropriately – as in the case of Muslim women for example. As Nancy Fraser would argue, this type of misrecognition means that policy is merely symbolic and does not have the power to really transform the experiences of victims.

The concept of intersectionality is a useful tool to break away from the strand-based approach to hate crime but it has its limitations. One might question how many aspects of identity need to be considered. While it is important to note how race and gender might intersect, these too are simplistic characteristics that offer limited appeal. What about sexuality, disability, class, age, weight or appearance? Can we ever have policy that truly takes account of each individual's experiences of oppression? The group-based approach to hate crime certainly possesses some intuitive appeal. It allows for the monitoring of recorded hate crimes by the police and criminal justice agencies – giving them a focus. Commentators have noted the importance of legislation for not only having a deterrent effect to perpetrators, but in forcing the criminal justice system to produce policy and be seen to take real action (Iganski, 1999). To take away the victim categories would be to make it difficult to monitor success in particular areas. As Chakraborti observes, placing limits on the groups attached to hate crime "is critical to its operational viability" (Chakraborti, 2010: 17). Criminal justice agencies including the CPS have been able to produce guidance for each strand after consulting with victim groups and campaigners. A generic hate crime policy might be unwieldy.

This chapter has shown that although not perfect, a consideration of intersectionality assists in better understanding the victim experience and points towards potential policy improvements. The role of policing is key in improving community engagement and an understanding about the diversity of its members. These individuals, who might be termed "hard to reach", need additional support due to the increased risk that they face (Moran and Sharpe, 2004: 409). So instead of adding new groups to hate crime policy, it is necessary to think about how identity categories interlock with multiple aspects of identity working simultaneously. Demographic factors such as class, social isolation, socio-economic status also need to be considered. As Chakraborti and Garland note:

> Vulnerability to hate crime stems from a broader range of factors than singular conceptions of identity allow and this should be factored into contemporary conceptual framework as should a further, often overlooked, dynamic of hate crime: namely, the capacity for members of minority groups to be perpetrators as well as victims of hate crime.
> *(Chakraborti and Garland, 2012: 504)*

The research findings which point towards the normalisation of violence for some groups also means that greater targeting of resources is needed to engage with them and provide support. It is also important for activists to work together to draw out their connections and share good practices, rather than seeing other strands as different or a competition for resources. Hate crime research needs to better understand how identity impacts on victimisation and how this notion shifts across time and space. Identity is messy. It is time for hate crime policy to better acknowledge this.

Bibliography

Anthias, S. (2011) Legislating gender inequalities: The nature and patterns of domestic violence experienced by South Asian women with insecure immigration status in the UK. *Violence Against Women*, 17 (10), 1260–1285.
Chakraborti, N. (2010) Crimes Against the 'Other': Conceptual, Operational and Empirical Challenges for Hate Studies. *Journal of Hate Studies*, 8 (9), 9–28.
Chakraborti, N. and Garland, J. (2012) Reconceptualizing hate crime victimization through the lens of vulnerability and 'difference'. *Theoretical Criminology*, 16, 499–514.
Chakraborti, N. and Zempi, I. (2012) The Veil under Attack: Gendered Dimensions of Islamophobic Victimisation. *International Review of Victimology*, 18 (3), 269–284.
Corteen, K. (2002) Lesbian Safety Talk: Problematizing Definitions and Experiences of Violence, Sexuality and Space. *Sexualities*, 5, 259–280.
Crenshaw, K. (1991) Intersectionality, Identity Politics and Violence Against Women of Color. *Stanford Law Review*, 43 (6), 1241–1299.
Fraser, N. (2003) Rethinking Recognition: overcoming displacement and reification in cultural politics, in Hobson, B. (Ed.) (2003) *Recognition Struggles and Social Movements: Contested Identities, Agency and Power*, Cambridge: Cambridge University Press.
Garland, J. (2010) The Victimisation of Goths and the Boundaries of Hate Crime. In Chakraborti, N. (Ed.) *Hate Crime: Concepts, Policy, Future Directions*, 40–57. Cullompton: Willan.
Garland, J. and Chakraborti, N. (2012) Divided by a common concept? Assessing the implications of different conceptualizations of hate crime in the European Union. *European Journal of Criminology*, 9, 38–51.
Gerstenfeld, P. (2004) *Hate Crimes: Causes, Controls, and Controversies*. USA: Sage.
Gill, A. and Mason-Bish, H. (2013) Addressing Violence against Women as a Form of Hate Crime: Limitations and Possibilities. *Feminist Review*, Issue 105.
Hansard (HL), 16 Dec. 1997, vol. 584, col. 584.
Hansard (HL), 5 Nov. 2003, vol. 654, cols 800 to 864.
Hobson, B. (Ed.) (2003) *Recognition Struggles and Social Movements: Contested Identities, Agency and Power*. Cambridge: Cambridge University Press.
Iganski, P. (1999) Why make "hate" a crime? *Critical Social Policy*, 19 (3), 386–395.
Jacobs, J. and Potter, K. (1998) *Hate Crimes – Criminal Law and Identity Politics*. New York: Aldine De Gruyter.
Jenness, V. and Grattet, R. (2001) *Making Hate a Crime – from Social Movement to Law Enforcement*. New York: Russell Sage.
Jiwani, Y. (2005) Walking a Tightrope: The Many Faces of Violence in the Lives of Racialized Immigrant Girls and Young Women. *Violence Against Women*, 11 (7), 846–887.
Law Commission. (2013a) *Consultation Paper 213 – Hate Crime: The case for extending the existing offences*. Appendix B: History of hate crime legislation, Crown: London.
Law Commission. (2013b) *Consultation Paper 213 – Hate Crime: The case for extending the existing offences*. Appendix C: Impact Assessment, Crown: London.
Marchetti, E. (2008) Intersectional Race and Gender Analyses: Why Legal Processes Just Don't Get It. *Social and Legal Studies*, 17 (2), 155–174.
Mason, G. (2007) Hate Crime as a Moral Category: Lessons from the Snowton Case. *Australian and New Zealand Journal of Criminology*, 40, 249–271.
Mason-Bish, H. (2010) Future Directions for Hate Crime Policy, in Chakraborti, N. (Ed.), *Hate Crime: Concepts, Policy, Future Directions*, 58–77. Cullompton: Willan.
Mason-Bish, H. (2012a) Examining the Boundaries of Hate Crime Policy: Considering Age and Gender. *Criminal Justice Policy Review*, 24 (3), 297–316.
Mason-Bish, H (2012b) Conceptual Issues in the Construction of Disability Hate Crime, in Roulstone, A. and Mason-Bish, H. (Eds.) (2012) *Disability, Hate Crime and Violence, an Edited Collection*, London: Routledge.
Meyer, D. (2012) An Intersectional Analysis of Lesbian, Gay, Bisexual and Transgender People's Evaluations of Anti-Queer Violence. *Gender and Society*, 26 (6), 849–873.
Meyer, D. (2010) Evaluating the Severity of Hate-Motivated Violence: Intersectional Differences among LGBT Hate Crime Victims, *Sociology*, 44 (5), 980–995.
Monro, S. (2010) Sexuality, Space and Intersectionality: The Case of Lesbian, Gay and Bisexual Equalities Initiatives in the UK Local Government. *Sociology*, 44 (5), 996–1010.

Moran, L. and Sharpe, A. (2004) Violence, Identity and Policing: The Case of Violence Against Transgender People. *Criminal Justice*, 4 (4), 395–417.

Morgan, J. (2002) US hate crime legislation: a legal model to avoid in Australia. *Journal of Sociology*, 38 (1), 25–48.

Park, H. (2012) Interracial Violence, Western Racialized Masculinities and the Geopolitics of Violence Against Women. *Social and Legal Studies*, 21 (4), 491–509.

Phoenix, A. and Pattynama, P. (2006) Intersectionality. *European Journal of Women's Studies*, 13 (3), 187–192.

Roulstone, A., Thomas, P. and Balderston, S. (2009) Hate is a Strong Word: A Critical Policy Analysis of Disability Hate Crime in the British Criminal Justice System. Paper Presented at the Social Policy Association Annual Conference, Edinburgh, July.

Singh, A. and McKleroy, V. (2011) Just Getting Out of Bed is a Revolutionary Act: The Resilience of Transgender People of Color Who Have Survived Traumatic Life Events. *Traumatology*, 17 (2), 34–44.

Tester, G. (2008) An Intersectional Analysis of Sexual Harassment in Housing. *Gender and Society*, 22, 349–366.

3
The personal injuries of 'hate crime'[1]

Paul Iganski and Spiridoula Lagou

'Hate crimes' hurt more than similar, but otherwise motivated crimes. This has increasingly been acknowledged and understood by criminal justice agencies in a number of countries, by supra-national policy bodies and civil society organisations concerned with fundamental human rights, and by those in the civil and public sectors working to support victims of 'hate crime'. A substantial body of evidence about the personal injuries of 'hate crime' has now accumulated to support the notion that 'hate crimes hurt more'. Initially, the evidence base developed across a number of studies carried out in the United States was constrained by the use of small samples of victims of 'hate crimes' and comparison crimes (cf. Garofalo, 1997) and non-random samples of respondents (cf. Herek et al., 1997; McDevitt et al., 2001). More recently, though, the evidence base has been strengthened by the use of large random samples in the secondary analysis of crime victimisation survey data. In the United Kingdom, research using crime victimisation data from the British Crime Survey (BCS) has considerably extended the depth of understanding and the reliability of the evidence about the personal injuries inflicted by 'hate crime' (cf. Botcherby et al., 2011; Coleman et al., 2013; Iganski, 2008; Iganski and Lagou, 2009; Nocon et al., 2011; Smith et al., 2012). This chapter extends the evidence base further by unfolding some new data on the physical, emotional, and behavioural injuries of 'hate crime'. It also suggests that understanding the particular impacts of 'hate crime' can serve to inform appropriate and effective support for victims and inform the training of those working with victims.

Research design and sample

The research for this chapter involved a secondary analysis of data from the Crime Survey for England and Wales (CSEW) (formerly known as the British Crime Survey, but renamed from April 2012 to better reflect its geographic coverage) obtained from the UK Data Archive.[2] A representative sample of approximately 46,000 respondents aged 16 and over living in households in England and Wales are interviewed in the survey every year, selected by a stratified and partially clustered design using the small users' Post Code Address file.[3] The survey does not cover those living in group residences or other institutions. Given the well-known limitations of police records, particularly because not all victims report crimes to the police for a variety of reasons, the Crime Survey for England and Wales is generally regarded as providing a more complete measure of crime compared with police records. The aim of the analysis reported here was to explore the post-victimisation impacts upon individual 'hate crime' victims as a group compared with victims of otherwise motivated crime.

In the reporting of the survey findings by the UK Home Office which initiated and reports on the survey, it is their preferred practice for two years of survey data to be combined to give a sufficient sample size for fine-grained analysis without a too prolonged reference period. However, given that the analysis reported here will be concerned with differences within the survey between samples of victims of 'hate crime' compared with victims of otherwise motivated crime, rather than with generalising beyond the samples to a wider population, consideration of the reference period is not as significant. Hence the analysis reported here combines three sweeps of the survey – from the 2009–10, 2010–11 and 2011–12 surveys (the three most recently available data sets at the time of writing) – to enable sufficient sample sizes for comparisons of sub-groups of respondents within the samples.

All respondents in the survey are asked whether they experienced certain types of crimes in the previous twelve months. For each crime reported respondents are asked a battery of questions. One of the questions is: "Do you think the incident was racially motivated?" They are also asked: "Do you think the incident was motivated by the offender's attitude towards . . . Your religion or religious beliefs . . . Your sexuality or sexual orientation . . . Your age . . . Your sex . . . Any disability you have . . . Your gender identity (transgender)." The analysis reported here focused on incidents perceived to be racially motivated and those which victims perceived were motivated by offenders' attitudes towards their religion or religious beliefs, sexuality or sexual orientation, and any disability they might have, as these are the 'strands' of 'hate crime' in the shared Criminal Justice System (CJS) definition of monitored 'hate crime' in England and Wales (and also Northern Ireland).[4]

Out of all the incidents of crime reported across the three sweeps of the survey – 34,440 incidents of crime – only a small proportion (2.8 per cent or approximately 1 in every 36 incidents) was perceived by individual victims to have been 'hate' motivated (Table 3.1). Racially motivated crimes were the most likely to be reported in the survey, although the difference compared with the proportions of other groups of perceived identity crime is very small. Incidents of personal crime were twice as likely to be perceived by victims as being 'hate motivated' than incidents of household crime, although the differential varies among the different 'strands' of identity crime, and the differences for crimes perceived to be motivated by the offender's attitude towards the victim's religion or religious beliefs, or sexuality or sexual orientation, are not statistically significant.[5]

Given that the numbers of reported household crimes are greater than the numbers of reported personal crimes (about three-and-a-half times greater), the number of incidents of household crime perceived to be because of the victim's disability exceed the number of incidents of personal crime which the victims perceived were similarly motivated (Figure 3.1). The same is the case for crimes where attitudes towards the victim's religion or religious beliefs were the perceived motivation. The reverse is the case for incidents of crime where attitudes towards the victim's race or sexual orientation were perceived to be the motivation behind the crime.

Relying on the victim's perception about motivation behind the crime is susceptible to over-reporting because some crimes perceived by the victim to have been motivated by the offender's attitudes towards some aspect of their identity could have been motivated by other reasons. But by the same token, it is also susceptible to under-reporting because in some crimes victims might not be aware that they were targeted because of their identity.

Paul Iganski and Spiridoula Lagou

Table 3.1 Proportions of incidents of crime perceived by victims to be motivated by the offender's attitude towards their identity

Column percentages	**England and Wales, adults aged 16 and over**		
	% of incidents Household crime	Personal crime	All crime
Perceived to be motivated by the offender's attitude towards the victim's			
'Race'	1.0	2.6*	1.6
Religion or religious beliefs	0.5	0.7	0.5
Sexuality or sexual orientation	0.3	0.7*	0.4
Disability	0.6	0.8	0.7
Any of the above identity characteristics	**2.0**	**4.2***	**2.8**[a]
Total number of incidents (n, unweighted bases)	26668	7772	34440

Source: Crime Survey of England and Wales, 2009–10, 2010–11, 2011–12.
*Statistically significant at least at 0.05 level of significance.
[a] This figure is less than the above combined as some incidents were perceived by victims to be motivated by the offender's attitude towards more than one of the listed identity characteristics. Because of small overlaps between the 'strands' in the table, comparison of the 'strands' must be treated with caution.

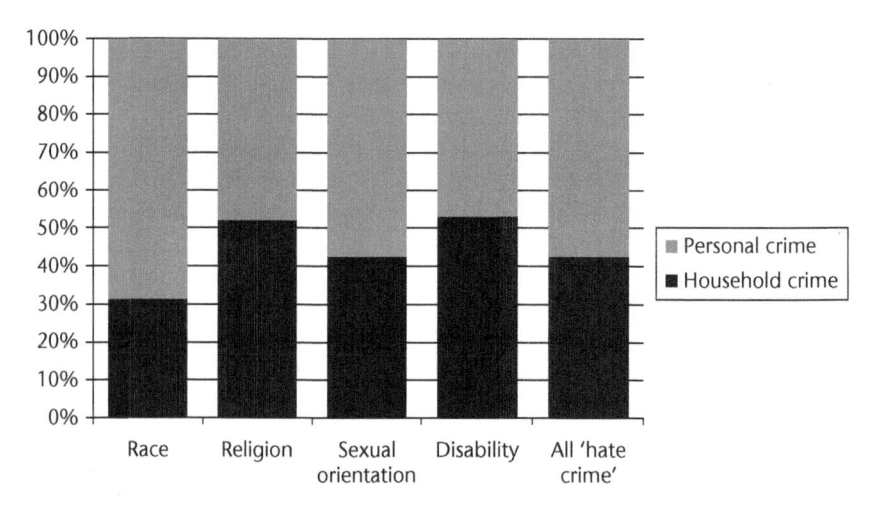

Figure 3.1 Proportions of 'hate crimes' by identity motivation: household crime and personal crime

However, consistency in the reports about crime victimisation across the years of the survey does indicate the reliability of this measure.

In incidents perceived to be racially motivated, racist language used by the offender was one of the most common reported indicators of racial motivation for victims. Unfortunately, a similar question has not been asked of respondents who perceived that the crime they experienced was motivated by the offender's attitude towards their religion or religious beliefs, sexuality or sexual orientation (or gender identity), or any disability they might have and so comparisons with these groups of crimes are not possible.

The personal injuries of 'hate crime'

Table 3.2 Proportions of incidents of crime perceived by victims to be motivated by the offender's attitude towards their identity in which the police came to know about the matter

Row percentages	England and Wales, adults aged 16 and over			
	Household crime		**Personal crime**	
	% of incidents	Number of incidents (n, unweighted bases)	% of incidents	Number of incidents (n, unweighted bases)
Incidents perceived to be motivated by the offender's attitude towards the victim's				
'Race'	62.8	174	39.1*	139
Religion or religious beliefs	51.1	82	19.3*	33
Sexuality or sexual orientation	45.3	61	39.9	50
Disability	63.8	119	51.6	85
Any of the above identity characteristics	**59.1**	**375**	**41.6***	**287**
All otherwise motivated crime	**38.8**	**26188**	**38.5**	**7465**

Source: Crime Survey for England and Wales, 2009–10, 2010–11, 2011–12.
*Statistically significant at least at 0.05 level of significance.

All respondents in the survey who report experiencing crime are asked for each incident they experienced whether the police came to know about the matter. It is well known that substantial numbers of crimes are not reported to the police for a variety of reasons.[6] According to the victims, police came to know about only approximately half (49.1 per cent) of all 'hate crimes' reported in the survey, although that is higher than the proportion (38.7 per cent) of otherwise motivated crimes that the police came to know about.

It has been long known that there are different reporting rates to the police for different types of crime (cf. Flatley et al., 2010, Figure 2.11, page 26). When household and personal crimes are considered separately as groups of crime, it is clear that for all strands of 'hate crime', the police were more likely to come to know about household crime than personal crime (Table 3.2). The long-recognised reporting differentials for some categories of otherwise motivated crimes (whereby theft of vehicles and burglaries with loss, for instance, have much higher rates of reporting than assaults with minor or no injury and theft from the person) are masked by the aggregation of incidents into these two broad categories as the police came to know about similar proportions of otherwise motivated household and personal crime overall.

In a majority of incidents in which the police came to know about the matter, it was from a report made to them by the victim, somebody else in the victim's household, or another person. In very few incidents were the police actually present at the time or found out about it by some other means (Figure 3.2). The pattern of reporting 'hate crime' to the police is very similar to the pattern for otherwise motivated crime as the only statistically significant difference concerned police being present at the scene or finding out about the crime by some other means.

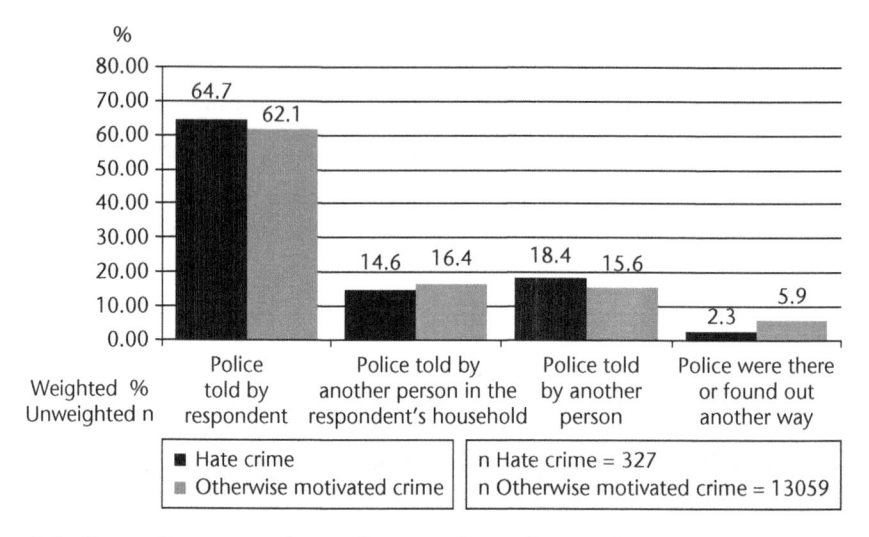

Figure 3.2 How police came to know about incidents of crime: 'hate crime' and otherwise motivated crime

The core of the analysis reported in this chapter was applied to the 664 incidents of crime believed by victims to have been 'hate' motivated and reported by 572 victims across the three sweeps of the survey used for the analysis.[7]

Physical injuries

Are victims of 'hate crime' more likely to suffer physical injury than victims of otherwise motivated crime? Two decades ago, in the foundational book for the field of 'hate crime' studies, *Hate Crimes: The Rising Tide of Bigotry and Bloodshed*, Levin and McDevitt concluded from their analysis of 452 'hate crimes' recorded by the Boston Police Department that 'hate crimes' "tend to be excessively brutal" (1993: 11). They noted that half of the recorded 'hate crimes' they analysed involved assaults and other personal attacks. This far exceeded the proportion for otherwise motivated crimes. Three quarters of the attacks resulted in some physical injury to the victim. The proportion of 'hate crime' victims who required hospital treatment for their injuries also exceeded the proportion of victims of otherwise motivated crime who wound up in hospital. These findings have left an influential footprint on understanding about the impacts of 'hate crime' upon victims. Frederick Lawrence, for instance, in his 1999 book *Punishing Hate*, informed by Levin and McDevitt's research, proposed that 'hate crimes', or 'bias crimes' to use Lawrence's preferred term, are "dramatically more likely to involve physical assaults than do crimes in general" (1999: 39). However, given that it is well-known that police recorded crime provides only a partial picture of crime victimisation, it is instructive to examine the BCS/CSEW data – which is a more reliable sample than police records – to determine whether indeed 'hate crimes' are particularly violent when compared with otherwise motivated crimes. Since Levin and McDevitt's findings, the investigation of the physical injuries inflicted in 'hate crimes' has not featured prominently to date in the growing body of evidence on the personal consequences of 'hate crime' – as the literature has mostly focused the emotional injuries inflicted. Therefore the findings offered here provide an added dimension to the extant body of evidence.

The personal injuries of 'hate crime'

Violent crimes as so-classified in the BCS/CSEW include wounding, assault with minor injury, assault without injury, and robbery. As it is a victim survey, homicides are not counted. Just over half of all 'hate crimes' (52.3 per cent) reported in the survey sample used for the analysis for this chapter were violent crimes: two-and-a-half times more than violent crimes as a proportion (21.3 per cent) of otherwise motivated crime. At first sight these findings do indeed seem to suggest that as a category of crime, 'hate crime' is particularly more violent than otherwise motivated crime. However, the findings might also indicate that the repertoire of offending by the perpetrators of 'hate crime' is much more limited than the offences which occur for other reasons than attitudes towards the victim's identity. For instance, property crimes such as burglary and theft of and from vehicles account for over half of otherwise motivated crimes reported in the BCS/CSEW. But it is clear that few offenders express their attitudes through 'hate motivated' car theft or house breaking, judging by the perceptions of victims. This might reflect a preference by 'hate crime' offenders for personal attacks. On the other hand it might also indicate a greater propensity for opportunistic and aggravated crimes, rather than premeditated offending, in the case of 'hate crime' triggered by personal encounters, compared with otherwise motivated crime.

A more reliable measure of the relative intensity of physical violence in 'hate crimes' compared with otherwise motivated crimes can be provided by victims' accounts of the injuries they suffer. The BCS/CSEW evidence on the matter runs counter to the accepted wisdom. In incidents of violent crime perceived to be 'hate motivated', victims were less likely to report being injured than to report suffering no injury. Fewer than half of victims in incidents of violent 'hate crime' reported being injured in any way (40.6 per cent). Whereas in incidents of otherwise motivated violent crime, victims were more likely to report injury than no injury (Figure 3.3) (each of these differences are statistically significant). This suggests that when all incidents of violent crime are considered as a group, the violence in hate motivated incidents is possibly less injurious on average than otherwise motivated incidents. Examination of the sub categories of violence supports this observation. There were higher

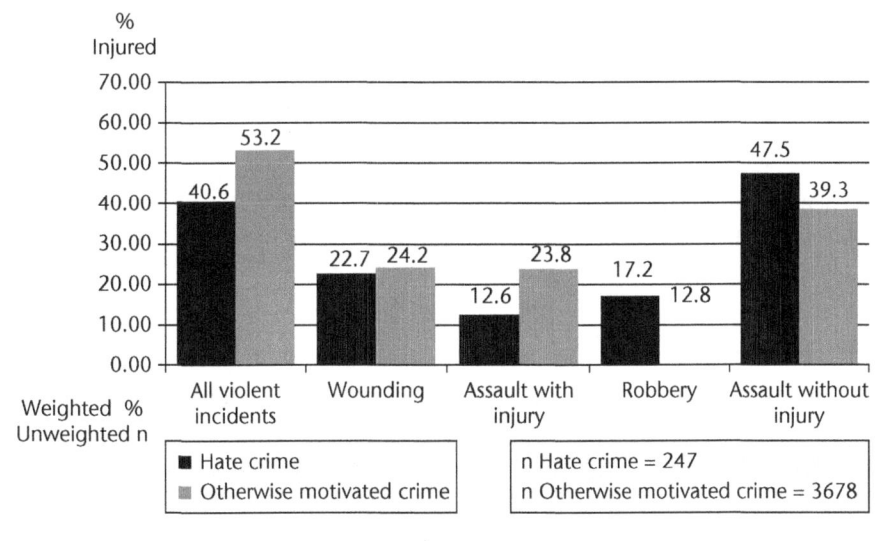

Figure 3.3 Injuries sustained in violent crime: 'hate crime' and otherwise motivated crime compared

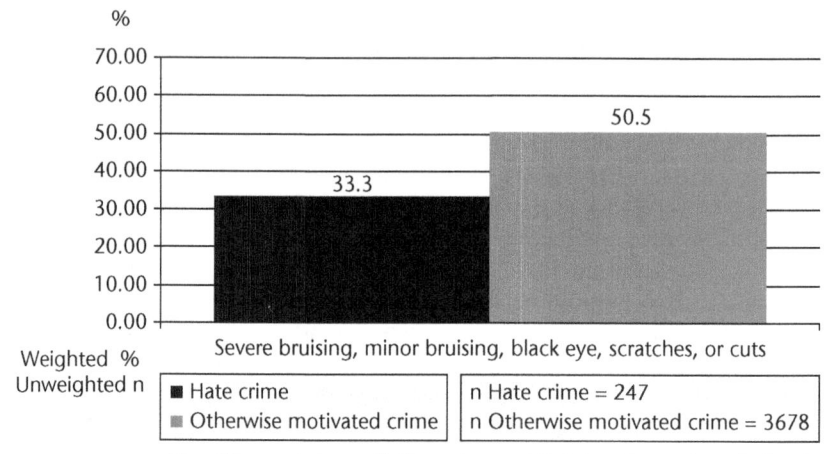

Paul Iganski and Spiridoula Lagou

```
%
70.00
60.00
50.00                          50.5
40.00
        33.3
30.00
20.00
10.00
 0.00
Weighted %    Severe bruising, minor bruising, black eye, scratches, or cuts
Unweighted n  ■ Hate crime                  n Hate crime = 247
              ■ Otherwise motivated crime   n Otherwise motivated crime = 3678
```

The difference between % Hate crime and % Otherwise motivated crime is statistically significant at least at .05 level of significance

Figure 3.4 Specific injuries sustained in violent crime and medical attention received: 'hate crime' and otherwise motivated crime compared

proportions of victims in incidents of wounding and assault with injury for otherwise motivated crimes compared with 'hate crimes', and lower proportions for robbery and assault without injury (Figure 3.3), although the differences for wounding and robbery are not statistically significant.

While the difference between the proportions of 'hate crime' victims and victims in violent incidents of otherwise motivated crime who suffered broken bones, a broken nose, broken, lost or chipped teeth was not statistically significant, over half of victims in incidents of otherwise motivated crime reported that they suffered severe bruising, minor bruising, a black eye, scratches, or cuts, compared with only two out of five victims in incidents perceived to be hate motivated (Figure 3.4). This observed difference between 'hate crime' victims and victims of otherwise motivated crime is statistically significant.

The difference in the proportions of victims in incidents of hate motivated violent crime and victims in incidents of otherwise motivated violent crime who received some form of medical attention was not statistically significant. Taken together then, these findings from the BCS/CSEW suggest that while victims of 'hate crime' as a group are possibly more likely to experience violent crime than victims of otherwise motivated crime, the injuries sustained by 'hate crime' victims as a group are less severe than victims of otherwise motivated crime as a group.

Emotional injuries

A growing body of research evidence indicates that victims of 'hate crime', as a grouped category of offence, are more likely to suffer post-victimisation emotional distress compared with victims of otherwise motivated crime as a group. While there is some variation within both groups and overlaps between the two groups in terms of the psycho-emotional injuries suffered, it is clear from the research evidence that 'hate crimes hurt more' on average. The research that has been carried out in the UK has underpinned policy by providing "definitive evidence" that 'hate crimes' can have a greater psychological impact upon victims (Giannasi, 2014).

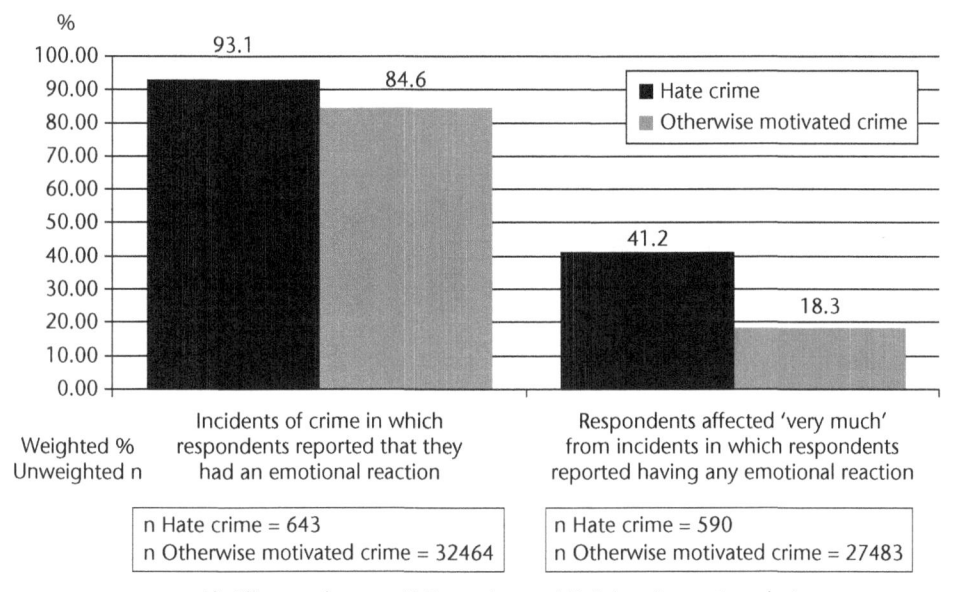

The personal injuries of 'hate crime'

Figure 3.5 General emotional reactions to crime victimisation: 'hate crime' and otherwise motivated crime compared

Most of the research studies have provided the evidence for single 'strands' of 'hate crime', although recently some have presented the evidence for all 'hate crime' victims combined into one group (cf. Smith et al., 2012). In continuing that approach in the analysis reported here, it is evident that victims in incidents which they believed were motivated because of the offender's attitude toward their identity were more likely to report having an emotional reaction to the incident and with a greater intensity, compared with otherwise motivated crimes. Respondents in the BCS/CSEW interview who report a crime are asked whether they had an emotional reaction. The great majority of victims of all crimes say that they did, although victims in incidents of 'hate crime' as a group are more likely to report having an emotional reaction than victims of otherwise motivated crime as a group (Figure 3.5). The difference between the two groups widens when the extent of the reported emotional reaction is considered. Victims in incidents of 'hate crime' were over twice as likely as victims in incidents of otherwise motivated crimes to state that they had been affected "very much".

The differences in reported post-victimisation distress between 'hate crime' victims as a group and victims of otherwise motivated crime cannot be accounted for by differences in the particular type of crime experienced. Across each major category of crime 'hate crime' victims as a group are more likely to report being affected "very much" (Figure 3.6).

For every crime they report in the survey, those victims who said they had an emotional reaction following the incident are asked: "Which of these reactions did you personally have ... anger, annoyance, anxiety/panic attacks, crying/tears, depression, difficulty sleeping, fear, loss of confidence/feeling vulnerable, shock, and other?" The respondents can choose as many as apply.

For each type of emotional reaction higher proportions of victims in crimes they believed to be motivated by the offender's attitude towards their identity reported the symptoms

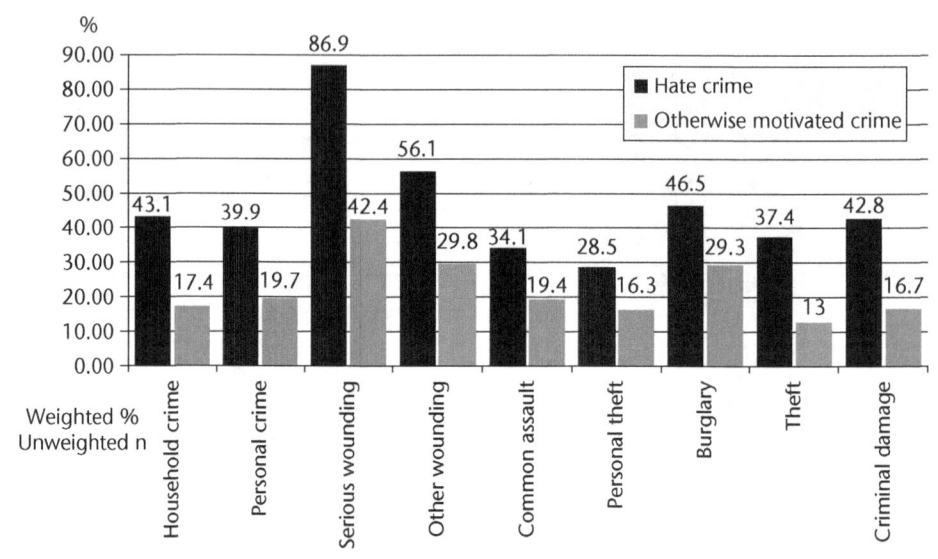

%

	Household crime	Personal crime	Serious wounding	Other wounding	Common assault	Personal theft	Burglary	Theft	Criminal damage
Hate crime	43.1	39.9	86.9	56.1	34.1	28.5	46.5	37.4	42.8
Otherwise motivated crime	17.4	19.7	42.4	29.8	19.4	16.3	29.3	13	16.7

All differences between % Hate crime and % Otherwise motivated crime are statistically significant at least at .05 level of significance

Hate crime n	327	263	14	46	120	83	87	57	183
Otherwise motivated crime n	21212	6271	211	576	1835	3649	3920	9594	7698

Figure 3.6 Respondents reporting 'very much' of an emotional reaction to crime victimisation: 'hate crime' and otherwise motivated crime compared by crime type

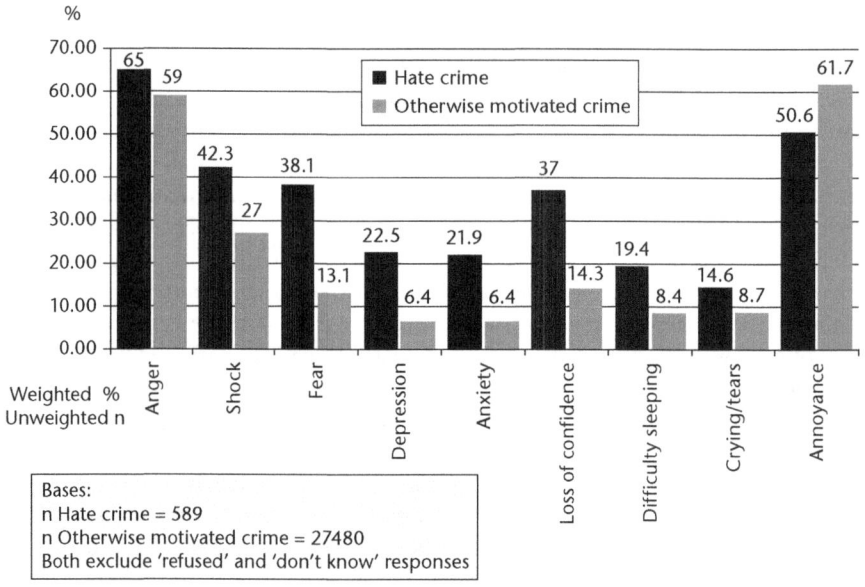

%

	Anger	Shock	Fear	Depression	Anxiety	Loss of confidence	Difficulty sleeping	Crying/tears	Annoyance
Hate crime	65	42.3	38.1	22.5	21.9	37	19.4	14.6	50.6
Otherwise motivated crime	59	27	13.1	6.4	6.4	14.3	8.4	8.7	61.7

Bases:
n Hate crime = 589
n Otherwise motivated crime = 27480
Both exclude 'refused' and 'don't know' responses

All differences between % Hate crime and % Otherwise motivated crime are statistically significant at least at .05 level of significance
Percentages add to more than 100% as multiple categories of response are possible

Figure 3.7 Specific emotional reactions to crime victimisation: 'hate crime' and otherwise motivated crime compared

The personal injuries of 'hate crime'

compared with victims in incidents of otherwise motivated crime, apart from the reaction of "annoyance" (Figure 3.7).

Behavioural injuries

Over two decades ago Rai and Hesse suggested, in drawing from their research on racist violence in the London borough of Waltham Forest, that members of communities targeted by 'racist attacks' carry "mental maps" in their heads of "no go areas" and other areas of relative safety (Rai and Hesse, 1992: 177). The impact of 'hate crime' victimisation upon the future behaviour of victims can be usefully assessed from the BSC/CSEW data as victims in incidents of reported crime asked whether they took a variety of protective and avoidance measures (Figure 3.8).

The numbers of victims reporting such behavioural responses is small. However, the data do suggest the possibility of a different pattern of response between 'hate crime' victims and victims of otherwise motivated crime. To take victims of household crime, 'hate crime' victims were more likely to report avoidance measures – moving home, and trying to be more alert and not so trusting of people – than victims of otherwise motivated crime who were more likely to increase the security of their vehicles and valuables. In the case of personal crime, 'hate crime' victims were more likely than victims of otherwise motivated crime to

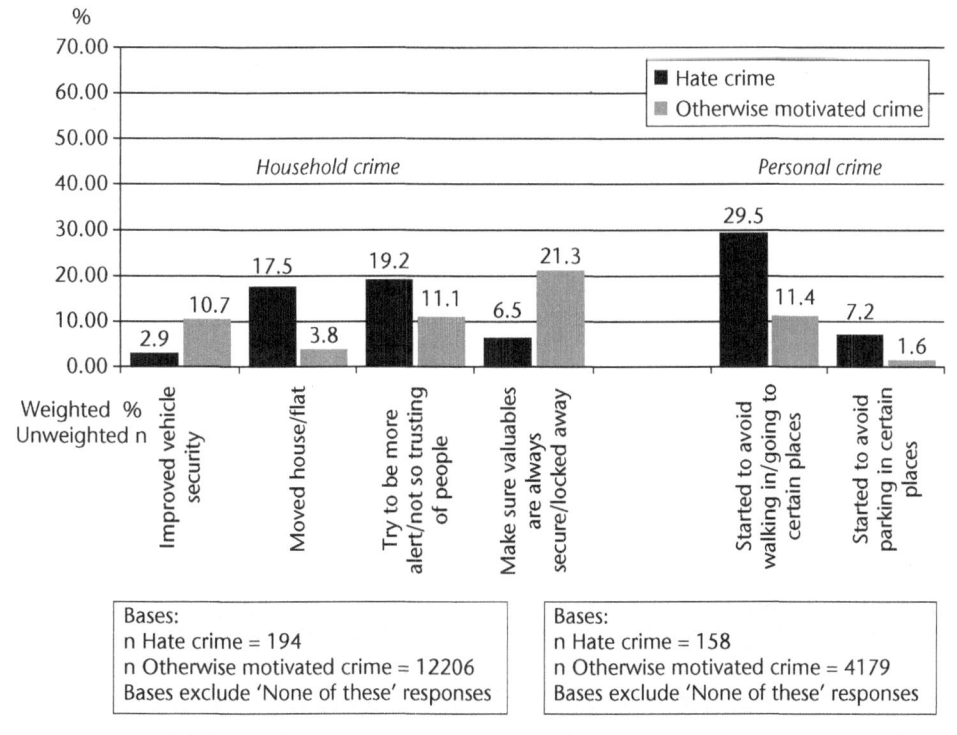

All differences between % Hate crime and % Otherwise motivated crime are statistically significant at least at .05 level of significance

Figure 3.8 Specific behavioural reactions to crime victimisation: 'hate crime' and otherwise motivated crime compared

avoid walking in certain places, while victims of otherwise motivated crime were more likely to avoid leaving their cars in certain places.

Understanding for supporting victims of 'hate crime'

While all crimes have some impact for the victims, the evidence presented in this chapter, which builds on an accumulating body of research evidence, shows that when crimes occur because of, or are aggravated by, the victim's 'race', ethnicity, or some other aspect of their identity – such as their religion, sexual orientation, disability, or gender identity – then the impacts and consequences of the crime are greater compared with the same types of crimes which occur for other reasons. Understanding the particular impacts of 'hate crime' can serve to inform appropriate and effective support for victims and inform the training of those working with victims (FRA, 2012: 20). The predominant type of impact demonstrated by the evidence in this chapter concerns post-victimisation emotional distress experienced by 'hate crime' victims. Given this understanding it is critical that victims of 'hate crime' are responded to appropriately and effectively as a matter of their fundamental human rights, but also to avoid secondary victimisation. Understanding the potential particular impacts of 'hate crimes', over and above the same types of crime which occur for other reasons, is critical for appropriate support. In light of the evidence presented in this chapter, and informed by practitioner experience of supporting victims of 'hate crime' (Iganski, 2012), some key suggestions are offered here to conclude the chapter.

- The emotional wounds inflicted by 'hate crime' are naturally very difficult for victims to talk about. It is important therefore that victims are responded to with sensitivity and offered empathic support.
- Putting the victim's wishes at the centre of managing a complaint, or empowering victims, is also fundamental.
- It is perhaps stating the obvious that those involved in supporting victims of 'hate crime' need to be fully aware of and appreciate the emotional and psychological impacts of such crimes to be sensitive and to be able to most effectively support victims.
- Such understanding offered by some of those supporting victims of 'hate crime', sadly – but unfortunately very valuably – comes from their own experience of being a victim. As many individuals engaged with non-governmental organisations (NGOs) and civil society organisations working against 'hate crime' have themselves been victims of 'hate crime', they potentially offer a significant experiential expertise which cannot be offered to the same extent by other agencies such as the police and other public authorities because many in such agencies tasked with responding to and managing 'hate crime' would not have experienced it themselves.
- While the experiential dimension is valuable for the understanding necessary to support victims of 'hate crime' such understanding is inevitably limited to the caseworker's own experience; it will be further enhanced by the understanding that comes from specialist work in supporting victims with a variety of experiences. Specialism enables the concentration of skills that are more diluted for organisations such as the police and victim support who work with a variety of victims – not only victims of 'hate crime'.
- Specialist skills in supporting 'hate crime' victims can be enhanced further still by engaging in professional development, training, and regular peer or supervisory casework reviews so that case workers can systematically reflect upon their interventions with victims to constantly develop their understanding and enhance their skills.

- Given that the criminal justice process is inevitably segmented with a division of labour between different agencies each playing their specialist part – the police, Crown Prosecution Service, courts, Victim Support, and local authorities – NGO and civil society organisations are uniquely positioned to support victims and engage in partnership with different agencies at all stages in the criminal justice process. This might include liaising with the police, chasing-up witness statements, encouraging the use of victim impact statements in court, and also attending the court with victims to provide support.
- Victims will expect something to be done, and keeping them informed of progress provides reassurance that action is being taken. Because of the multiple demands they face some agencies in the criminal justice process are less able to regularly keep victims in the picture. Again, NGO and civil society organisations can be uniquely positioned to provide consistent communication.
- While the caseworkers will have a very good appreciation of the impacts of their work, regular evaluation of the tangible outcomes for victims will enable them to systematically reflect upon the efficacy of their interventions.
- There is a need to identify and document good practice by NGOs and civil society organisations with regard to the provision of support to victims of 'hate crime', and a need to disseminate and share examples of good practice to potentially inform others (Iganski, 2011: 33).

Notes

1 The authors of this chapter prefer to surround the term 'hate crime' with single quotation marks to signify that, as critics of the term point out, 'hate' as a sentiment does not often figure in so-called 'hate crimes'. However, use of the term 'hate crime' is retained in this way as it is not entirely devoid of conceptual utility.
2 Material from Crown copyright records made available through the Home Office and the UK Data Archive has been used by permission of the Controller of Her Majesty's Stationery Office and the Queen's Printer for Scotland.
3 Since 2009 the survey has included a separate survey about the experiences of young people aged 10–15. We confine our analysis in this chapter, however, to the adult sample.
4 See: UK Association of Chief Police Officers *True Vision* website, 'Shared CJS Definition of Monitored Hate Crime', http://report-it.org.uk/files/hate_crime_definitions_-_v3_0.pdf
5 Household crimes include all vehicle and property-related crimes experienced by anyone residing in the respondent's household. Personal crimes include all crimes experienced by the individual respondent and do not include crimes experienced by others residing in the respondent's household.
6 This observation provides a staple discussion in undergraduate criminology textbooks.
7 A number of respondents reported more than one discrete separate 'hate crime' and therefore completed more than one victim form, hence the difference between the number of incidents of crime and the number of victims. Victims of a series of 'hate crimes', the same crime under the same circumstances probably committed by the same people, are asked to complete only one victimisation module for the most recent incident in the series.

References

Botcherby, S., Glen, F., Iganski, P., Jochelson, K. and Lagou, S. (2011). *Equality groups' perceptions and experience of crime: Analysis of the British Crime Survey 2007–08, 2008–09 and 2009–10*. Briefing Paper 4, Manchester: Equality and Human Rights Commission.
Coleman, N., Sykes, W. and Walker, A. (2013). *Crime and Disabled People: Baseline statistical analysis of measures for the formal legal inquiry into disability-related harassment*. Research Report 90, Manchester: Equality and Human Rights Commission.

Flatley, J., Kershaw, C., Smith, K., Chaplin, R. and Moon, D. (2010). *Crime in England & Wales 2009/10.* Home Office Statistical Bulletin, London: Home Office.

FRA-European Union Agency for Fundamental Rights (2012). *Making Hate Crime Visible in the European Union: Acknowledging Victims' Rights*, Vienna: FRA.

Garofalo, J. (1997). Hate crime victimization in the United States. In R.C. Davis, A.J. Lurigio, and W.G. Skogan (eds.) *Victims of Crime* (2nd ed., pp. 134–145). Thousand Oaks, CA: Sage.

Giannasi, P. (2014). 'Academia from a Practitioner's Perspective: A Reflection on the Changes in the Relationship between Academia, Policing and Government in a Hate Crime Context', in Neil Chakraborti and Jon Garland (eds.) *Responding to Hate Crime: The Case for Connecting Policy and Research.* Bristol: Policy Press.

Herek, G.M., Gillis, J.R., Cogan, J.C. and Glunt, E.K. (1997). Psychological sequelae of hate crime victimization among lesbian, gay, and bisexual adults: Prevalence, psychological correlates, and methodological issues. *Journal of Interpersonal Violence*, 12(2), 195–215.

Iganski, P. (2008). *Hate Crime and the City.* Bristol: Policy Press.

Iganski, P. (2011). *Racist Violence in Europe.* Brussels: European Network Against Racism.

Iganski, P. (2012). *This Should Be in Every Town.* Preston: Preston and Western Lancashire Racial Equality Council, www.report-it.org.uk/files/rhap_report_-_web_-_email_-_98_pdf.pdf

Iganski, P. and Lagou, S. (2009). 'How hate crimes hurt more: Evidence from the British Crime Survey', in P. Iganski (ed.) *The Consequences of Hate Crime*, Westport, CT: Praeger, pp. 1–13.

Lawrence, F. (1999). *Punishing Hate: Bias Crimes under American Law.* Cambridge, MA: Harvard University Press.

Levin, J. and McDevitt, J. (1993). *Hate Crimes: The Rising Tide of Bigotry and Bloodshed.* New York: Plenum.

McDevitt, J., Balboni, J., Garcia, L. and Gu, J. (2001). Consequences for victims: a comparison of bias and non-bias motivated assaults. *American Behavioral Scientist*, 45(4), 697–713.

Nocon, A., Iganski, P. and Lagou, S. (2011). *Disabled people's experiences and concerns about crime.* Briefing Paper 3, Manchester: Equality and Human Rights Commission.

Rai, D. K. and Hesse, B. (1992). 'Racial victimization: An experiential analysis', in B. Hesse, D. K. Rai, C. Bennett and P. McGilchrist (1992) *Beneath the surface: racial harassment*, Aldershot: Avebury (pp. 158–195).

Smith, K., Lader, D., Hoare, J. and Lau, I. (2012). *Hate crime, cyber security and the experience of crime among children: Findings from the 2010/11 British Crime Survey. Supplementary Volume 3 to Crime in England and Wales 2010/11.* London: Home Office.

4
Exploring the community impacts of hate crime

Barbara Perry

The fact that hate crime is often referred to as a message crime speaks to the importance of the audiences of the act. The intent of bias-motivated violence is to speak to not just the immediate victims of the act. Rather, the aim is much broader than that. Hate crime speaks to multiple communities not least of which are those from which both the perpetrator and the victim are drawn, as well as to all members of the civic culture in question. Based on research with multiple and diverse groups, this chapter outlines the consequences of hate crime for this array of audiences.

The phenomenon that has come to be known as hate crime is generally considered distinctive because of its distal effects. That is, the victim of hate crime is not restricted to the individual who might have been assaulted. Rather, the harm and the message extend to the victim's community. So, for example, vandalizing the home of one Jewish family is intended to send the message to all Jewish people that they are not welcome in the neighbourhood. Clearly, the broader social effects of hate crime must be examined both theoretically and empirically. How can we measure the impact of hate crime on the broader public? How does it affect perceptions of the liberties held dear in democratic states? To what extent is hate crime a reflection of broader hatreds, and to what extent does it exacerbate or alleviate these? Any combination of these questions provides a valuable starting point in our efforts to test widely held assumptions about the societal impact of ethno-violence. Here, I explore three layers of effects: impacts on targeted communities; impacts on shared values of inclusion; and, unusually, the mobilizing effects of targeted violence.

What's the harm?

Typically, legal definitions of hate crime have followed the lead of the model legislation as set out by the Anti-Defamation League, which states that "A person commits a Bias-Motivated Crime if, by reason of the actual or perceived race, color, religion, national origin, sexual orientation or gender of another individual or group of individuals, he violates Section _____ of the Penal code (insert code provisions for criminal trespass, criminal mischief, harassment, menacing, intimidation, assault, battery and or other appropriate statutorily proscribed criminal conduct)." This is very much like the language used in the Canadian sentencing enhancement provision (S718.2a): "a sentence should be increased or reduced to account for any relevant aggravating or mitigating circumstances relating to the offence or the offender, and, without limiting the generality of the foregoing, (i) evidence that the offence was motivated by bias, prejudice or hate based on race, national or ethnic origin, language, colour, religion, sex, age, mental or physical disability, sexual orientation, or any other similar factor."

However, such legalistic definitions say nothing about the power relations endemic to the act. Consequently, I have developed the following definition of hate crime, which has come to be widely cited in the sociological literature:

> It involves acts of violence and intimidation, usually directed toward already stigmatized and marginalized groups. As such, it is a mechanism of power, intended to reaffirm the precarious hierarchies that characterize a given social order. It attempts to recreate simultaneously the threatened (real or imagined) hegemony of the perpetrator's group and the "appropriate" subordinate identity of the victim's group.
>
> *(Perry, 2001: 10)*

What is especially useful about this definition is that it recognizes that hate crime is a structural rather than an individual response to difference. Moreover, it also speaks to the group impact of targeted violence. This is at least implicit in much of the literature, and even in court decisions on hate crime. These offences are qualitatively different in their effects, as compared to their non-bias-motivated counterparts. Specifically, Iganski (2001: 629) contends that there are five distinct types of harm associated with hate crime: harm to the initial victim; harm to the victim's group; harm to the victim's group (outside the neighbourhood); harm to other targeted communities; and harm to societal norms and values. The first of these has been the subject of considerable scholarly attention. Research suggests that first and foremost among the impacts on the individual is the physical harm: bias-motivated crimes are often characterized by extreme brutality (Levin and McDevitt, 1993). Violent personal crimes motivated by bias are more likely to involve extraordinary levels of violence. Additionally, the empirical findings in studies of the emotional, psychological, and behavioural impact of hate crime are beginning to establish a solid pattern of more severe impact on bias crime victims, as compared to non-bias victims (see, e.g., Herek et al., 2002; McDevitt et al., 2001).

When we move beyond the experiences of the immediate victim, we enter the realm of speculation. Many scholars point to the "fact" that hate crimes are "message crimes" that emit a distinct warning to all members of the victim's community: step out of line, cross invisible boundaries, and you too could be lying on the ground, beaten and bloodied (Iganski, 2001). Consequently, the individual fear noted above is thought to be accompanied by the collective fear of the victim's cultural group, possibly even of other minority groups likely to be victims. Weinstein (1992) refers to this as an *in terrorem* effect: intimidation of the group by the victimization of one or a few members of that group.

Another key concern is the possibility that hate crime has deleterious effects on the relationships between communities. Cultural groups that are already distant by virtue of language differences, or differences in values or beliefs are rendered even more distant by virtue of the fear and distrust engendered by bias-motivated violence. Intergroup violence and harassment further inhibit positive intergroup interaction. Again, explorations of changing intergroup dynamics in the face of bias-motivated violence will confirm – or deny – that such a relationship exists.

Hate crime throws into question not only the victim's and the community's identity, but also our national commitments to tolerance and inclusion. Speaking specifically of Native Americans, over fifty years ago, legal scholar Felix Cohen (1953) noted that mistreatment – legal or extralegal – of minorities "reflects the rise and fall of our democratic faith." In other words, the persistence of hate crime is a challenge to democratic ideals. It reveals the fissures that characterize its host societies, laying bare the bigotry that is endemic within each. As such, it may very well be the case that bias-motivated violence is not just a precursor to greater intergroup tension, but is an indicator of underlying social and cultural tensions. In this interpretation, hate crime is but one indicator that enshrined ideals of freedom and equality are illusory.

Alternatively, one possibility is that hate crime acts as a catalyst to positive change. That is, patterns of persistent violence, or highly publicized cases – like the 1998 Matthew Shepard or James Byrd cases – often have the unintended effect of mobilizing victim communities and their allies. Again, anecdotally, there is some evidence that this occurs. The racially motivated murders of Michael Griffith in Howard Beach in 1986 and Yusuf Hawkins in Bensonhurst in 1989 both resulted in flurries of organizing and demonstrating. An organization created after the first murder – New York City Civil Rights Coalition – was still available to lend its support to those involved in prosecuting the Hawkins case. Both incidents inspired widespread demonstrations condemning the racism of the perpetrators' communities, as well as the racist culture of New York City generally.

Before proceeding to explore the vicarious effects of hate crime, I would like to provide some contrasting background. In a campus hate crime study (N=807) I conducted with a colleague, we uncovered evidence of widespread denial of the realities of oppression and violence among marginalized communities. In an intriguing paradox, in spite of relatively high levels of observed acts of racism, sexism and so on, there were relatively low levels of agreement that the campus climate was in fact problematic for women and minorities (Perry, 2010). This indicates not a lack of awareness of the problem, but a lack of understanding of the cumulative impact of such incidents on underrepresented groups. It reflects Ditomaso et al.'s (2003: 197) claim that colour blindness "allows whites to ignore, deny, or disregard any notion that race matters in people's lives."

One indication that students did not take seriously the patterns of oppression on their campus were the responses to open-ended questions that challenged the utility of such a survey. For some, participating in the survey was thought to be a waste of time, which suggests that they did not think that the possibility of an inhospitable campus climate was worth exploring. The following is perhaps the most telling example of this:

> I can honestly say that this crap does little good; it also perpetuates the fear that stems throughout modern society. Stop doing these things, finish your business degree and go to the investors so you can run off to Cuba with lot of millions to buy your happy (*sic*), and leave me alone.

This student implies that there is little value in exploring racism, sexism, or homophobia on campus, and that such "undue attention" is itself to blame for creating a false sense of the disparities that might exist. Other students were even more direct in indicating their belief that systemic patterns of oppression were not apparent on campus: "No, from what I've experienced from (this university) is that this is a very friendly place, but I am one opinion and I have only my view;" similarly, "I think this is a great atmosphere to be in." Neither of these students is apparently cognizant of the likely impacts of extensive harassment, violence and discrimination faced by their minority peers. They are oblivious to the fact that the campus is not as comfortable for others as it may be for themselves.

Together the patterns of denial and apathy that were observed conspire to minimize the importance of bias incidents on campus. While members of the campus community may physically observe racist, or homophobic, or anti-Semitic behaviour, for example, they do not "see" it,

> ... partially because of its ubiquity. We simply do not see most racist conduct because we experience a world in which whites are supreme or simply "the world." Much racist conduct is considered unrelated to race or regarded as neutral because racist conduct maintains the status quo, the status quo of the world as we have known it.
>
> *(Lawrence, 1993: 63)*

The apparent disregard for the implications of the acts of bias and discrimination that students have witnessed on campus amounts to the failure to confer recognition, that is, a "response from the other which makes meaningful the feelings, intentions and actions of the self" (Feagin et al., 1996: 15). By denying the "fact" of an unwelcoming environment for minorities, students on campus are thereby denying the legitimacy of the pain and alienation associated with such experiences.

This chapter is a corrective to the broader tendencies to neutralize the reality and impacts of targeted violence by sharing the experiences and sentiments of people from diverse communities. The themes discussed here come from three projects I have conducted in the past five years: one specifically on community impacts experienced by seven diverse communities in Ontario (Perry and Alvi, 2011); one on violence against lesbian, gay, bisexual, transgender or queer (LGBTQ) communities in Canada (Perry and Dyck, 2013); and one on anti-Muslim violence in Ontario and Quebec (Perry, forthcoming). The qualitative data derived from surveys within all of the projects and from interviews and focus groups in the latter two are rich in themes that could inform this chapter. In the interests of brevity, however, I have chosen to focus on three broad areas of impact: effects on targeted communities; effects on shared national values; and positive effects on community engagement of targeted communities.

Message Crimes: Impacts on Targeted Communities

Because of its ripple effects (Noelle, 2002), hate crime is commonly referred to as a message crime. By this, we mean that it extends a warning to all members of a targeted community. Importantly, then, hate crime is also intended to manage not just the behaviour of particular individuals, but all members of their community. Without question, awareness of the potential for hate crime enhances the sense of vulnerability and fearfulness of affected communities. This, after all, is the intent of hate crime – to intimidate and instill fear in the whole of the targeted community, not just the immediate victim. Interestingly, when asked to define hate crime, many participants explicitly acknowledged the nature of these "message crimes":

> Hate crimes occur because people have learned to dislike difference. They occur because people want to feel superior to and have power over others. They are probably more likely to be committed by groups of young people who are looking to act out. They are meant to scare everyone, not just the victim.
>
> *(Asian female)*

For many, the message is received loud and clear; they do feel themselves to be equally vulnerable to victimization, and thus, fearful. Upon reading a scenario describing a hypothetical hate crime, an Asian male observed, "I feel for Jim – his safety and well-being. I also think that could've been anyone else leaving that meeting and that we all are vulnerable." Individuals do not have to be victims themselves to fear for their safety. Rather, "it only has to happen once or twice and that really affects, you know, and I think it has affected the overall community, right?" (Trans woman). Again, this speaks to the ripple effects of hate crime (Noelle, 2002, 2009; Perry and Alvi, 2011). It has the capacity to render all members of the community wary of their surroundings.

Clearly, from the responses of our participants, hate crime does have this broader effect of leaving communities, and not just individual victims, feeling vulnerable to further victimization. It renders communities fearful, and questioning with respect to their level of safety/unsafety. This was especially evident among trans communities. There is, to their mind, no safe space. It comes as no surprise, then, that so many trans women, in particular, spoke of the multiple and complex layers by which they defined "safety" and lack thereof. One Toronto trans woman spoke at length about her perceptions of safety and what that entailed for her:

> I think one of the real problems with safety, I don't know where it is safe in Toronto, when I started my transition people could easily identify that I was trans all the time and I faced constant harassment and people staring at me, giving me dirty looks, talking to each other ridiculing and mocking me. I had to adapt to the experiences of nearly being physically assaulted and my feeling was that I was never safe anywhere and that lead to being very reclusive, isolating, which then tied in with severe depression and suicide attempts. So there's the practical issue of safety, but then there's the subjective experience of safety that is radically altered by those experiences you have and without the involved balance, even just harassment, bullying, ridiculing and mocking takes a tremendous toll on us.

This is an inevitable outcome of a vulnerability that is experienced as normative and ubiquitous. Regardless of context, there is a constant fear of assault.

Without question, awareness of the potential for hate crime enhances the sense of vulnerability and fearfulness of most affected communities. Moreover, while hate crime is embedded in broader patterns of subjugation and oppression, it is also in and of itself an oppressive practice. It, too, is systematic (Young, 1990). It, too, has the effect of rendering targeted groups inferior and subjugated. A Muslim male captures this twin effect:

> So, the first thing I'd like to say is, what is really violence? Can other forms of threatening behaviour, can they have more effect than violence itself? So, I think that on a daily basis all of these accumulative looks, and the media, and the hurt, these things can have a deeper and much more harsher impact. For example, Muslims' confidence may go down because what they see in society, what happens to people they know.

One consequence of such normative threats and violence is that affected communities become distrustful. The connection is explicit in this Muslim woman's assessment: "Less trust between Muslims and non-Muslims. Muslims are made to feel inferior and like they don't belong, are unwelcomed. Non-Muslims see Muslims as aliens and a community of people to blame and their frustrations out on." Trans women also made frequent reference to their lack of trust. According to one trans woman, "I will say 'I,' but I mean, I think I can safely say, *we* don't trust anyone. We trust each other, as trans women trust each other, we don't trust anyone and that includes members of the queer community." Excluded as they are by a heteronormative culture that insists on gender conformity, these women have learned that there is risk in revealing themselves – literally and figuratively – to others. They know from experience that their "transgression" can be used against them at any moment.

One of the most dramatic effects of the threat of violence is that it can lead to self-destructive activities. It is enough to make people challenge the worth of their community and themselves. Too often, vulnerable communities internalize the hatred and the violence. Paolo Freire (1970: 31) refers to this as internalized oppression by which he means, "the oppressed having internalized the image of the oppressors and adopted his guidelines." What emerges for those who have adopted this stance is antagonism and hostility directed toward oneself and one's community:

> The effects of knowing that I and my community are reviled and hated by the majority of society, the majority of societal institutions and just the majority of people, it's very difficult not to internalize that and once it's internalized it's very difficult for me not to hate myself and to take things out on myself, to cut myself, to attempt suicide, abuse myself in other ways, so I don't actually have the experience of trusting myself, I'm the person I'm the very I'm most afraid of in a continuous basis.
>
> *(Trans woman)*

So pervasive are the violent reminders of their stigmatization that participants come to see themselves through that same lens. Again, the trans community is especially at risk in this context. They come to deflect the pain inward in ways that are self-destructive. In some cases, this meant coping through diverse risk-taking behaviours:

> I got to a point however that I started to fight back and in an attempt to fix myself I joined a gang and, you know, I started fighting back because well, that's what I wanted understood. I also found, as others have, that drugs and alcohol were a coping mechanism and it was only many, many years later that I found recovery. You know, they helped me get through an awful lot, but you know, as a, as a, I think that's not uncommon.

It is especially disturbing that so many talked about suicidal thoughts or even about having attempted suicide:

> First of all I almost tried suicide before I came out and now I'm wishing to God it would've worked because this life is hell. Outside of these friends here, I ain't got any friends, and like I said, I, I was loved by thousands. And it's really, really, really tough and that's ignorance.

The rate of suicide ideation and attempts is staggering for communities that are also frequent targets of hate crime: trans women, gay men and lesbians, and Aboriginal youth especially.

Collateral Damage: Impacts on Shared Values

In light of these cumulative effects on targeted communities, it is perhaps no surprise that ongoing patterns of violence and harassment also have collateral impacts on broader community relations. Hate crime challenges long and deeply held values of inclusion, equity, and justice. It is, in fact an exclusionary practice, a form of "intercultural exchange," which purposely increases the distance between communities rather than bridging that distance. It is divisive, in that "Incidents like these are likely to lead to deterioration of relationships between community and inter-group relations if not handled and controlled effectively" (Muslim female). A Muslim male frames similar sentiment, stating "I think it creates more tension and a reason to more clearly distinguish between dangerous thoughts such as 'us' vs. 'them'."

Targeted violence reinforces barriers between groups in multiple ways. On the one hand, it can lead to segregation and isolation of vulnerable communities. For some, this involves a process by which they seek to protect themselves by self-segregating. The known risk of violence limits people's movements and their perceived options, resulting in withdrawal:

> I would have been most likely very severely hurt and that's one of several anecdotes where it's just so close and those things really left me afraid, even remembering them now still leaves me afraid, I still isolate at times and it's been over two and half years since I last had an experience like that. These experiences don't just disappear.
>
> *(Trans woman)*

These violent reminders contribute to ongoing withdrawal and isolation. The hostility, and in this case violence, experienced "out there" produces what Wachtel (1999: 221) characterizes as "voluntary segregation," wherein those subject to the discriminatory and hateful patterns of behaviour may choose to return or simply remain in the relative safety of their community or, even more narrowly, their home.

The very motive and intent of targeted violence is to protect carefully crafted boundaries, in the physical and social sense. It is a purposive process of policing the line between white/not white, male/female, straight/gay, between dominant and subordinate. It stands, then, as both punishment for those who dare to transgress, and warning to those who are considering it. When considering First Nation reserves, or inner-city racialized "ghettoes" the lines of demarcation have a very real physical presence. Equally important are the infinitely less predictable, less tangible "social borders" that "are moving markers, boundaries that shift according to the positionings we negotiate and build in discursive interaction, in the conversations and actions of social exchange" (Valaskakis, 2005: 250).

Efforts to shift those markers can be met with controlling forms of violence that can also have the effect of creating hostility among target groups, as some participants in my research have argued. They have expressed not just fear of, typically, white people, but also retaliatory hatred and hostility. A young Muslim woman said, "I kind of tried not to be friends with white people, no offense. I mean I like them, it's just I'm very, very kind of self-conscious and scared of them." Two other Muslim males expressed more extreme possibilities:

> I believe this creates separation, hatred and rivalry as many might want to seek revenge and vice versa, then it will never stop.

> People were harassed against, they were making their own sort of a gang to retaliate with other people who were – who are – kind of harassing them. So, for example, this youth who started in grade seven or eight in my school, right. He was harassed a lot because of his views and where he comes from and all that. So for him to be protected he would be part of a gang, right, so that he can feel that he's welcomed, he's part of something, right?

Especially in a country like Canada, which so loudly espouses the mantra of multiculturalism, the reality of exclusionary violence has serious implications for Others' capacity to feel they are "part of something." Indeed, it challenges communities' sense of belonging in a social environment, and their faith in Canadian tenets of equity and multiculturalism. Their sense of being a valued part of Canadian society is dramatically curtailed. Rather than seeing themselves as embedded in the polity and culture of the nation, many of those who are actual or potential targets of violence come to see themselves and their communities as outside the boundaries of citizenship and its attendant rights. In short, "the hurt is strong as in Canada we are supposed to live in society without fear of attack" (south Asian female). Similarly, "I think that when you come to Canada, you have expectations – that you are coming to a civilized, democratic country. And therefore, if you are mistreated here, you get a much bigger shock than if you are mistreated elsewhere" (Muslim male).

Hate crime is a reminder that there are limits to inclusivity. It reinforces the outsider status of those who do not correspond to the mythical norm of what it is to be Canadian, or American, or English as the case may be. Generally, of course, this means anyone who is not white, Christian, straight, and able bodied. Consequently,

> It's just that we feel like we still feel cannot fit in society. And I think that's a main issue for a lot of Muslims because we want to be accepted; we want to be respected, but because of certain practices or beliefs that people do not understand, we feel like, okay, we have to hide that or conceal that in order to just have like a harmonious relationship maybe in the workplace, or in the school, or any realm in life for that matter. Just to be respected.
> *(Muslim female)*

In sum, "persons who do not feel valued in society cannot contribute or participate to their full potential" (OHRC, 2003: 34). Oppressive violence represents a will to power by which the very threat of otherwise unprovoked violence "deprives the oppressed of freedom and dignity" (Young, 1995: 83). In other words, it deprives them of their human rights, which is an egregious violation in nations that pride themselves on their commitment to inclusion.

The Other Side of Hate Crime: Community Cohesion and Mobilization

I noted earlier that hate crime can have the effect of isolating individuals and communities as a defensive mechanism. On the one hand, this is a limiting impulse, to the extent that it distances communities. Yet there is a positive effect, internally, in that it also serves to increase community cohesion among those affected, as in the following example:

> So, like, when you – and naturally, it's a human response. Naturally, when, you know, when you have a lot of pressure, you know, from outside the group, you know, the group interactions seem to increase more; you have more that's unifying. You have more talk, you have more of, like, oh, you got – you, oh, my God, you have been in the same position? Oh, I was, like, driving a car and I got, you know, a guy stuck the middle finger out too. Or really, when was that? It was in Ramadan, too, really, so that kind of thing. So, like, it unifies and just makes us – it's that moment that you can laugh about something, like, two people laugh about some things. It's just so ridiculous and so bizarre, really, you know, it brings people together, so you can laugh at it.
> *(Muslim male)*

The resultant solidarity can enhance group strength, and correspondingly increase the potential for community mobilization. In contrast to the debilitating effects of hate crime, which are characterized by fear, confusion, anger, even questioning Canadian values, it can also act as a catalyst to positive change. Frequently, those most affected by the patterns of harassment and violence resist their individual and cultural histories, and find strength rather than adversity in their identities. While anger and resentment are understandable, the converse is also possible. That is, the objects of hate violence can and do develop constructive alternatives to the prejudice and violence that confronts them. One respondent indicated that hate can be unlearned. "I think it is learned. It is learned partly in our educational system, it is learned in the home and is learned through the media culture. I would suggest that the only good news is that hate can be unlearned then" (Aboriginal male).

Whether individually or collectively, there is value in challenging hate crime and the biases that inform it. There were participants who were relatively optimistic about the potential for change, and who suggested progressive strategies for harnessing the energy of vibrant communities to counteract both the potential for and the impact of hate crime. One constructive shift noted by many was that they felt inspired to react at an individual and/or collective level. For example,

> In an attempt to promote gay rights and tolerance I donate money to EGALE, join protests, have written in local newspapers, questioned charitable/social agencies with regards to their policies and resources for dealing with LGBT community clients. In the scenario above I would help to ensure factual media coverage of the event to shed light on the issue of homophobia/gay bashing – perhaps work with a neighbourhood community group to deal with the issue.
>
> *(Lesbian)*

Some young Muslim women were particularly committed to challenging efforts to render them invisible and silent. While the threat of Islamophobic violence, specifically, led some women to cease covering, it actually took others in just the opposite direction. Indeed, many Muslims with whom I spoke insisted on embracing visibility:

> I had never really worn the hijab before, but for a short period of time, right after 9/11 I started wearing it as a sign of defiance, you know? And I also knew that it wasn't my style and I wasn't going to keep it on for too long but it was definitely a time when I felt like being more visibly Muslim was necessary for me to deal with all the anti-Muslim sentiments and hate that was going around in my school and but I remember . . . and it wasn't ever directed at me and I wasn't really challenged after that. I just wanted to feel defiance.
>
> *(Muslim female)*

This is a powerful reminder that persistent targeting can be directly challenged through equally persistent expressions of Muslim identities. Visibility becomes a show of strength that reflects the wielding of power by its very subjects. It reimagines "the performance of visible differences as the locus of political agency because of its potential to deconstruct foundational categories of identity" (Walker, 1993: 868). It is, in essence, a demand for recognition and acknowledgement of their identities as valued rather than subjugated.

Implications for change

It is apparent from our findings that hate crime has the effects intended by perpetrators: it instills fear and a sense of vulnerability among those communities that are targeted. It reminds all audiences of where the boundaries lie with respect to inclusion. Consequently, it also has dramatic consequences for communities' sense of belonging and their illusions of Canada's reputation for tolerance and inclusivity.

In contrast, however, participants across projects also reveal their willingness to respond in ways that were not intended by the perpetrator. For example, one would not think that perpetrators are much interested in stimulating their targets to resist, yet this was a common reaction. Rather than allowing their victimization to silence them, many individuals and communities react by mobilizing themselves and their communities to counteract hate and bias crime. It is this set of findings that provides the most promising avenues for interventions that challenge hate crime. Solutions to the problem of hate crime lie not only in the dominant culture. Targeted communities also recognize the role they must play, both in confronting hostility, but also in empowering themselves. Indeed, as the above discussion makes evident, the communities bearing the brunt of hate-motivated crime have not been passive victims of the varied forms of violence they experience. On the contrary, in recent years many have become very active in asserting the legitimacy of their identities, challenging heterosexism, patriarchy, racism and bigotry, and resisting the cultural and individual forms of violence to which they are subjected.

For some, this begins with an awareness of the rights to which they are entitled – legal, political, and social – but then extends to an exercise of those rights. In short, all communities must be educated on the nature and use of the rights to which they have access, and to become more self-aware:

> I guess something that I think is really important is, ah, getting the community to be more confident in itself. Because, I think people, I think we should see ourselves as any other minority that has rights, ah, and that should advocate for them. The francophone community, for example, in Ontario doesn't shy away from that at all. I mean they make themselves heard, which is good. It's great. Um, but I feel like Muslims are, like, sometimes apologetic, sometimes we're, I mean we see, a lot of, a lot of the time, I mean, we see, the opportunities that are given to us are like our rights as something like, something like, charity . . . But I think that will come with also, you know, with time because I feel that second or third generation Muslims, ah, are more confident about that.
>
> *(Muslim female)*

Interestingly, some community members have identified internal barriers to their ability to realize similar solidarity, and thus respond to discrimination and hate crime. It is, of course, insufficient to talk about *the* Jewish community, or *the* LGBT community, or *the* black community. Rather, there is dramatic variation within groups. However, we too often homogenize communities and assume a sameness of experience. Yet each of these groups is in fact constituted by multiple communities, which may or may not share experiences, perspectives, or place. Not surprisingly, then, conflicts within communities may also present challenges. A trans woman complains that there is "a lot of transphobia within the gay and lesbian community as well – that needs to be addressed." She went on to say that:

> (post-Stonewall) however almost immediately the people got involved to sanitize what being gay, lesbian, queer meant. And so that meant that gay men had to be straight acting and gay women had to be straight acting and the trans women had to be invisible, because they don't exist and so in terms of our rights today, we do not have the same queer rights as other queer people.
>
> *(Trans woman)*

Similarly, a Muslim woman challenges her community to:

> ... see who is not in the room? If you're in a room and it's completely made of the Muslim community and there's no one there who is Shi'a and you know there's a sizable Shi'a population in your city ... But they are not there. And there's also no one from the Somali community and we have a large Somali community here. You should be like: where's the Somali community because that's a huge voice that you don't understand that you need to have at the table. But we really don't do that. That's a serious challenge.

Ultimately, community members who noted these contradictory positions emphasized the need to build solidarity and strength within the community. In the words of one lesbian, "What I would like to see is a real showing of solidarity. It's becoming so cliquey, you know, but a lot of that is because our community became incestuous; 'cause it was so small." A Muslim male speaks of his involvement in a Muslim coordinating council meant to bring together Muslims with non-Muslims, but also Muslims with Muslims:

> This is the first time that we've tried to get all the Muslims together to uplift the most vulnerable in the community who now have to depend on the government or they cease to help like the, battered wives, or youth in detention, or people with disabilities or mentally ill, or refugees and so on. And our second objective is to reach out to fellow Canadians of other faiths to try to promote human rights, and dignity and equality for all Canadians, including aboriginal people in particular. And this is the first time that we've brought Shi'as and Sunnis together in Ottawa.

Initiatives like these suggest that there is potential in communities developing supports organically, within or across ethnic, racial, religious, or gender lines. In short, they recognize the value of community building through coalitions. Hate crime is a multiethnic and multicultural problem. It is, indeed, more than a black/white issue. Moreover, differences are themselves overlapping and intersecting. Each of us occupies multiple identities, as a woman, and a Latina, and a Catholic, for example. So it is with communities, whether locally or globally. Only by acknowledging and overcoming the "fragmentation" of community can collective action be an effective brake against hate crime.

References

Cohen, F. 1953. The Erosion of Indian Rights, 1950-1953: A Case Study in Bureaucracy. *Yale Law Journal*, (62) 348–390.

Ditomaso, N., Parks-Yancy, R., and Post, C. 2003. White views of civil rights: Color blindness and equal opportunity. In A. Doane and E. Bonilla-Silva (eds.), *White Out: The Continuing Significance of Racism* (pp. 199–214). New York: Routledge.

Feagin, J., Vera, H., and Imani, N. 1996. *The Agony of Education*. New York: Routledge.

Freire, P. 1970. *Pedagogy of the Oppressed*. New York: Continuum Publishing Company.

Herek, G., Cogan, J. and Gillis, J. R. 2002. Victim experiences in hate crimes based on sexual orientation. *Journal of Social Issues*, 58 (2): 319–339.

Iganski, P. 2001. Hate crimes hurt more. *American Behavior Scientist*, 45 (4): 627–638.

Lawrence, C. 1993. If he hollers let him go: Regulating racist speech on campus. In M. Matsuda, C. Lawrence, R. Delgado, and K. Crenshaw (eds.), *Words that wound: Critical race theory, assaultive speech, and the first amendment* (pp. 53–88). San Francisco: Westview.

Levin, J. and McDevitt, J. 1993. *Hate crimes: The rising tide of bigotry and bloodshed*. New York: Plenum.

McDevitt, J., Balboni, J., Garcia, L. and Gu, J. 2001. Consequences for victims: A comparison of bias- and non-bias motivated assaults. *American Behavioral Scientist*, 45 (4): 697–711.

Noelle, M. 2002. The ripple of effect of the Matthew Shepard murder: Impact on the assumptive worlds of members of the targeted group. *American Behavioral Scientist*, 46 (1): 27–50.
Noelle, M. 2009. The psychological and social effects of anti-bisexual, anti-gay, and anti-lesbian violence and harassment. In P. Iganski (ed.), *Hate Crimes: The Consequences of Hate Crime* (pp. 73–106). Westport, CT: Praeger.
Ontario Human Rights Commission (OHRC). 2003. *Paying the price: The human cost of racial profiling.* Toronto: Ontario Human Rights Commission.
Perry, B. (forthcoming). "All of a Sudden, There Are Muslims": Identities, Visibilities, and Islamophobic Violence in Canada. *Ethnic and Racial Studies.*
Perry, B. 2010. "No biggie": The denial of oppression on campus. *Education, Citizenship, and Social Justice*, 5 (3): 265–279.
Perry, B. 2001. *In the name of hate.* New York: Routledge.
Perry, B. and Alvi, S. 2011. "We are all vulnerable:" The *in terrorem* effects of hate crime. *International Review of Victimology*, 18 (1): 57–72.
Perry, B. and Dyck, R. 2013. "I Don't Know Where It Is Safe": Trans Women's Experience of Violence. *Critical Criminology*, August.
Valaskakis, G. 2005. *Indian Country: Essays on Contemporary Native Culture.* Waterloo, ON: Wilfrid Laurier University Press.
Wachtel, P. 1999. *Race in the Mind of America.* New York: Routledge.
Walker, L. 1993. How to Recognize a Lesbian: The Cultural Politics of Looking Like What You Are. *Signs*, 18 (4): 866–890.
Weinstein, J. 1992. First amendment challenges to hate crime legislation: Where's the speech? *Criminal Justice Ethics*, 11 (2): 6–20.
Young, I. 1995. Five faces of oppression. In D. Harris (ed.), *Multiculturalism from the margins* (pp. 65–86). Westport, CT: Bergin and Garvey.
Young, I. 1990. *Justice and the politics of difference.* Princeton, NJ: Princeton University Press.

5
Legislating against hate

Gail Mason

The criminalisation of behaviour that manifests prejudice or group hatred is not a new legal phenomenon. There is a long history in parts of Europe and the US of criminalising racial and ethno-religious propaganda, intimidation and incitement to violence. Since the 1980s, however, western nations have witnessed a proliferation of criminal laws specifically designed to address what has come to be called the problem of 'hate crime'.

Many global and local factors have come together to produce this current wave of hate crime laws. Initially, the emergence of the concept of hate crime in the US in the 1980s provided an umbrella term under which a range of new social movements – such as the civil rights movement and the gay and lesbian movement – could agitate not just for human rights or equal opportunities but also for legal protection against the violent manifestations of prejudice (Jenness and Grattet, 2001). These calls for law to specifically address racial, religious or homophobic violence found support from a wider movement advocating for the rights of victims within the criminal justice system. Throughout the 1990s, legislatures thus became increasingly receptive to the idea that purpose-built laws were necessary to punish, deter and denounce prejudice-motivated crime; and increasingly cognisant of the political benefits of demonstrating state support for minority groups in this way (Iganski, 2008; Jacobs and Potter, 1998; Jenness and Broad, 1997; Mason, 2009a).

This approach to regulating prejudice-related crime gradually spread from the US to other common law countries, including Canada, the United Kingdom, Australia and New Zealand, as well as to many civil law countries in Europe. Had these laws been introduced in an earlier welfare-oriented period of penal policy, they may well have taken a more rehabilitative approach to the problem. However, emerging as they did in a global period of increasing retributivism, advocates for hate crime laws were able to achieve considerable traction by framing their calls for law reform within popular 'tough on crime' discourses of crime control. Within the context of these broad global influences, eruptions of high profile and extreme cases of prejudice-motivated crime at the local level also strengthened calls for reform and shaped the kinds of prejudice deemed to warrant legislative intervention in particular countries (especially when read against the background of national histories of, for example, colonisation, slavery or extremism). Together, these social and political forces have generated a well-intentioned but problematic legal response to the social problem of crime that is related, in various ways, to prejudice, hostility or intolerance of 'the other'.

Gail Mason

This chapter will examine the ways in which the concept of hate crime is translated into, and regulated by, law. It will posit a tripartite model for understanding hate crime legislation across national borders and, in turn, the common elements that distinguish a hate crime from an ordinary crime under the law. As a means of considering arguments for and against hate crime laws, it will highlight three contemporary challenges for the way in which such laws are constructed and interpreted: the kind of test used to prove the element of hatred or bias; the victim attributes protected by the law; and the justifications that are advanced for the punitiveness of these laws. The chapter aims to offer a transnational snapshot of hate crime laws and some of the key debates and dilemmas that currently surround them.

Models of intervention: purpose and justifications

Despite the popularity of the phrase 'hate crime', most statutes that are characterised as such avoid the abstract concept of hatred itself in favour of less extreme or more flexible terminology such as 'prejudice' or 'hostility'. It is for this reason that hate crime is sometimes, more accurately, referred to as 'prejudice crime' (Jacobs and Potter, 1998). Thus Lawrence (1999) defines hate crime as a criminal manifestation of prejudice, while the Organization for Security and Co-operation in Europe states that '[c]rimes motivated by intolerance towards certain groups in society are described as hate crimes' (ODIHR, 2009a: 7). Legislative definitions of the crime itself will often differ from operational definitions of hate crime used by police or in policy documents (Jenness and Grattet, 2005; Goodey and Aromaa, 2008; Hall, 2005): for example, in the interests of developing community trust and confidence, the Association of Chief Police Officers in England and Wales defines a hate crime to include all 'hate incidents' whether they amount to a criminal offence or not (ACPO, 2005: 9). Under the law, however, it is necessary that a criminal act is committed that constitutes an offence, although as will be explained, in many instances, the actual offence that constitutes the hate crime will be one that already existed under the criminal law before the introduction of reforms in this area.

There is great variation between legislation that is commonly grouped under the umbrella of 'hate crime law' (and also great diversity in how these statutes are interpreted by the courts). A number of models have been proposed to help categorise the way in which hate crime reforms have been inserted into the criminal law (Lawrence, 1999; ODIHR, 2009a; Jenness and Grattet, 2001). Mapping these laws across international borders risks over-simplifying their elements and the variation between them but, reworking existing classifications, Mason (2009) has proposed three very broad models that are useful for capturing the key features of hate crime laws across jurisdictions: i) the penalty enhancement model; ii) the sentence aggravation model; and iii) the substantive offence model. Some jurisdictions have more than one model of hate crime legislation in force and in some countries, such as the US, hate crime laws have been enacted, amidst controversy, at both the federal and state levels (there are also laws that mandate the collection of statistics and associated matters).

The penalty enhancement model is probably the most common form of hate crime legislation in Europe and the US (ODIHR, 2009a). It specifies an additional maximum, sometimes minimum, penalty on (some or all) pre-existing offences if the conduct is motivated or aggravated by racial, religious or other forms of prejudice or group hostility. For example, the maximum term of imprisonment for a conviction of assault occasioning actual bodily harm in England and Wales is five years, while the maximum penalty for the same offence committed in circumstances of racial or religious aggravation is seven years imprisonment (*Crime and Disorder Act 1998* (UK), s 29(2)(b)).

Under the sentence aggravation model, the element of prejudice or aggravation is taken into account at sentencing thus allowing more judicial discretion than the penalty enhancement model. For example, in Canada, it will be an aggravating factor at sentencing if there is evidence that the offence was motivated by bias, prejudice or hate based on race, national or ethnic origin, language, colour, religion, sex, age, mental or physical disability, sexual orientation, or any other similar factor (Criminal Code, s 718.2(a)(i)). Sentence aggravation provisions also operate in Great Britain, New Zealand, Australia and some European countries.

The substantive offence model captures a diverse body of stand-alone offences that include prejudice or bias as an 'integral element of the legal definition of the offence' (ODIHR, 2009a: 32). Although these offences do more than enhance the criminality of a pre-existing offence, most still operate to impose harsher penalties than those available for 'parallel' offences, that is, for comparable offences which do not involve an element of prejudice (it has been suggested that without heightened penalties law enforcement officers would simply choose to charge and prosecute under the conventional criminal law). It is not unusual for substantive hate crime offences to centre on criminal words, images or conduct that are deemed threatening or that incite certain forms of hatred, including criminal civil rights laws. For example, in California it is a crime to injure, intimidate, interfere with, oppress or threaten another person, by force or threat of force, in the free exercise or enjoyment of Constitutional rights or privileges 'because of' specified characteristics of that person (California Penal Code, ss 422.6(a)). Many jurisdictions in the US have substantive hate crime offences (in addition to penalty enhancement provisions) as does Canada, Great Britain and some jurisdictions in Australia. According to the ODIHR (2009a), this model is not common in Europe but there are, nonetheless, a range of provisions that criminalise hate speech and the like, introduced in the wake of World War II and the Holocaust.

Despite these differences, there are several common denominators between these statutory models that enable us to talk about hate crime law with some degree of generality. First, hate crime laws all explicitly target crime where group hostility, bias, prejudice or hatred is an integral or associated element of the offender's behaviour (ie: crime + prejudice); as we will see, it is not always necessary that this prejudice amounts to motive. Second, this prejudice, bias or hostility is directed towards a group attribute or characteristic of the victim that is usually spelt out in the legislation. Third, in most jurisdictions express hate crime laws are not necessary to police, prosecute or sentence prejudice-related crime as most of the conduct they target is already criminalised. As a consequence, hate crime laws 'top up' the traditional criminal law by imposing, in most instances, a heavier penalty than that which is applicable to parallel crimes. The imposition of an extra penalty for the element of prejudice is thus a core feature of hate crime law. In a very broad sense, then, hate crime laws are designed to address multiple and diverse criminal manifestations of prejudice towards specified group characteristics, which they conceptualise as a very particular kind of social problem, one that seemingly demands its own label of criminality and punishment.

Where does the hate threshold lie?

It is often said that hate crimes are criminal acts that are *motivated* by prejudice or bias towards the victim because of his/her membership of a particular social group (ODIHR, 2009a; Lawrence, 1999). Under the criminal law, this is not always true and gives the impression that a very high degree of animosity on the part of the perpetrator is necessary to enliven the provisions. Attempting to bring a semblance of order to the multiple tests that are used to establish the prejudicial element in hate crime law is fraught with difficulty and over-simplification.

Nonetheless, it is helpful to identify some broad and important points of distinction in the tests that are used to satisfy the 'prejudice' element in hate crime offences and, thus, the degree or kind of prejudice that is required under the law.

The most commonly accepted distinction is between the 'motive' or 'discriminatory selection' tests, also referred to as the 'animus' or 'group selection' tests. In general, the motive test requires evidence that the offender was motivated to commit the offence by prejudice, hatred or hostility towards a group to which the victim is presumed to belong. The inclusion of motive as an element of a hate crime offence has attracted considerable criticism. Motive is not normally an element in the determination of guilt and, arguably, it is contrary to principles of criminal liability to require the prosecution to prove it (Hurd, 2001; Quill, 2010). The motive test has attracted strong opposition in the US where it is said to criminalise an offender for his/her bad thoughts or feelings and thus breach the Constitutional right to freedom of expression (Gellman, 1992). In contrast, judicial consideration of an offender's motive is accepted as a relevant factor at sentencing in many jurisdictions (Mason and Dyer, 2013) and thus, perhaps not surprisingly, hate crime sentencing aggravation provisions do often require proof that the offender was actually motivated by prejudice/hate/hostility (eg: in Canada and New Zealand).

In the US in particular, constitutional challenges to hate crime legislation have, according to some, necessitated the construction of different kinds of tests, particularly the 'discriminatory selection' test (Lawrence, 1999; but see Goodall, 2013). Under this test it is only necessary to prove that the offender intentionally selected the victim on the basis of his/her membership of a group protected under the legislation, for example if the offender selected the victim 'because of' or 'by reason of' his or her religion (Lawrence, 1999; Wang, 1999). While the discriminatory selection test provides a way of constructing motive without requiring actual proof of *why* the offender selected the victim, in the sense that selecting a victim because of their group membership is assumed to be tantamount to a motive of bias or prejudice, in practice it tends to set a lower threshold for liability as it is not always necessary to prove the reason the offender discriminated in choosing the victim but only that he/she did so (Mason, 2010). The discriminatory selection test thus has the potential to apply to a wider range of circumstances than the motive test. For example, if A commits a robbery against B because he/she believes that B is Jewish and that all Jewish people are wealthy this crime may well be caught by a discriminatory selection test but not necessarily by a motive test (although this will depend on other factors, such as how the discriminatory selection test is interpreted by the courts and whether we are comparing it to a motive test that requires prejudice to be the sole motive or merely a partial motive). Questions about how much bias is necessary to satisfy the causal link under this test are largely unresolved, with some courts settling for a 'but for' threshold and/or a 'substantial' causal connection rather than a causal link that demonstrates a 'preponderance of evidence' (Quill, 2010). Concerns about the discriminatory selection test thus include the fact that it is likely to be met in circumstances where the crime is opportunistic or motivated only by mild bias or stereotypes rather than by strong hatred or prejudice (Mason, 2010; Goodall, 2013; Jenness and Grattet, 2001).

Some jurisdictions have taken an even more expansive approach by criminalising speech and other forms of expression that incite hatred or demonstrate prejudice in the context of a criminal offence (Glet, 2009; Mason, 2009). The penalty enhancement provisions in the UK are of particular interest (these provisions are also replicated in Western Australia). As noted above, the *Crime and Disorder Act 1998* (UK) aggravates an offence where there is evidence of racial or religious 'hostility' on the part of the offender. There are two ways for hostility to be proven. While one is through motive, the other is through evidence that the offender 'demonstrated' racial or religious hostility immediately before, during or after the commission of the offence (see *R v Rogers* [2007] 2 AC 62). The vast majority of prosecutions rely upon proof that the offender demonstrated such hostility rather than proof that the offender was actually motivated by hostility to commit the offence (Burney and Rose, 2002). Spoken or written insults will be sufficient. For example, in *R v Londesbrough* ([2005] EWCA Crim 151) it was held that statements including 'fucking Paki . . . fuck off out of our country . . . I will fucking shoot you, paki bastard, go home' made by the offender during an assault arising out of a dispute over a parking space were sufficient to elevate the offender's offence. This test gives the UK's penalty enhancement provisions far reaching application and may partly account for the significantly larger number of hate crimes recorded, prosecuted and sentenced in the UK compared to other nations in Europe and the US (ODIHR, 2009b; Hall, 2005; Goodey and Aromaa, 2008). Although the 'demonstration' test seeks to recognise the harm to the victim that flows from the use of prejudiced insults during an offence, it has been criticised for criminalising hate speech and for setting a low threshold that captures offenders who are not driven by strong prejudice but, instead, express prejudicial values or stereotypes in the heat of the moment (Chakraborti and Garland, 2012; Dixon and Gadd, 2006).

The degree of prejudice required to enliven hate crime statutes thus presents an on-going challenge not only for legislatures but also for the courts. While many statutes are interpreted to apply in circumstances where the offender was driven by mixed motives (eg: financial gain and racism), considerable difficulty lies in determining how 'substantial' the element of prejudice or bias need be to warrant the imposition of a harsher penalty upon the offender (Lawrence, 1999; Goodall, 2013; Quill, 2010). In jurisdictions where proof of the offender's motive is required, prejudice or bias that is determined to be peripheral to the commission of the offence itself is unlikely to be sufficient (Phillips, 2009). For example, under hate crime sentencing laws in Australia, racial insults by the offender have been held to be insufficient in circumstances where the offender and the victim are already engaged in a conflict that has nothing to do with race (Mason and Dyer, 2013). Hence, the tests that are used to establish the element of prejudice, bias or group hostility raise important questions about where the 'hate threshold' should lie; questions that are answered in very different ways under different legislative and judicial frameworks.

Which forms of difference should be protected?

Like equal opportunity and anti-discrimination laws before them, hate crime statutes usually only cover prejudice towards specified victim characteristics or categories of identity (eg: race, religion, sexual orientation or disability). Although the initial impetus for reform in this area came from minority groups who successfully demonstrated to legislatures that their group identity or 'difference' from the majority made them vulnerable to prejudice-related violence and intimidation, the principle of equality before the law has meant that the vast majority of hate crime legislation has had to adopt a symmetrical approach to the protection of victim attributes or categories of identity (eg: race is the protected attribute not 'blackness'). This generic construction of hate crime has also enabled the law to recognise crimes of prejudice that are committed by minority group members upon majority group members and minority-upon-minority offences. This has produced a tension between the original impetus for hate crime laws to protect marginalised and stigmatised minorities and their increasing application to disadvantaged groups and minority offenders (Gadd and Dixon, 2011; Franklin, 2004).

The question of which victim characteristics, and thus which forms of prejudice, should be protected under hate crime laws has been contested from the very beginning. Protected attributes tend to reflect identity categories that are already well recognised under human rights legislation and have the backing of influential social movements and organised modes of identity politics. Thus race is the attribute most widely protected globally. In many jurisdictions, governments have gradually responded to increasing political pressure to include more group categories. For example, advocates for the inclusion of sexuality and disability have struggled, with varying levels of success, for their recognition under hate crime statutes (Sherry, 2010). A surge in genuine public concern or media-generated alarm about particular forms of prejudice-related violence, both locally and globally, has also prompted some legislatures to expand hate crime laws to attributes previously not protected; such as including religion in response to a perceived rise in anti-Muslim violence in the wake of September 11 and other terrorism attacks. Gender continues to divide advocates of hate crime laws, with some recognising the misogynist nature of much sexual and domestic violence against women but others expressing concern that gender will swamp other hate crime offences and is better addressed under criminal laws already developed for this purpose (Gelber, 2002; Lunny, 2011). Some rarely protected categories include marital status, birth, wealth, class and political affiliation (ODIHR, 2009a).

This piecemeal, inconsistent and politically charged approach to coverage of victim attributes generates concern about groups that are also vulnerable to targeted crime, such as the homeless, sex workers and asylum seekers, but who are rarely included as 'legitimate' hate crime victims under the law. By singling out selected victim attributes, and forms of prejudice, legislatures are 'sending a clear message' both that some attributes are 'deserving of more protection than others' (Schweppe, 2012: 178) and that offenders who act on some forms of prejudice are deserving of more punishment than others (Mason, 2013). Thus it has been argued that, despite their generic application, hate crime laws continue to jeopardise the principle of equality before the law by privileging particular victim attributes for protection and failing to treat all victims the same; for example, by protecting victims on the basis of their race but not their gender (Morgan, 2002). This has led to the characterisation of hate crime laws as a quick-fix political solution, fuelled by a sense of resentment on the part of minority groups, that run the risk of further balkanising destructive divisions between identity groups instead of tackling the problem at its source (Jacobs and Potter, 1998; Goodall, 2007).

These concerns are undoubtedly valid but the difficulty with continuing to add more and more victim attributes to hate crime legislation is that it risks, first, watering down the provisions to the point that they are meaningless and difficult to enforce in practice (Hall, 2005; ODIHR, 2009a) and second, obfuscating the initial purpose of the provisions, which was to address the violent and criminal manifestations of prejudice towards stigmatised and oppressed minorities. While previous responses to this challenge have been to advance the claims of individual groups to protection, a preferable approach, and one that appears to be gaining increasing traction, is to reconsider the criteria that scholars, policy-makers, non-governmental organisations (NGOs) and legislatures use to determine statutory protection. Some time ago, Stanko (2001) proposed that the concept of 'targeted crime' more helpfully encapsulated the vulnerability of multiple groups to prejudice-related violence and hostility. Building on this insight, some scholars have argued against the presumption that the only worthy victim attributes are those that have long histories of oppression and/or well articulated forms of group identity. Thus criteria of 'targeted vulnerability' (Roulstone et al., 2009) or 'vulnerability and difference' (Chakraborti and Garland, 2012) have been proposed as a way of breaking open the narrow, singular and fixed configurations of victim protection criteria. A parallel line of argumentation has proposed that the principles of social equality and respect for diversity that guide discrimination and human rights law provide an important potential touchstone for determining human attributes deserving of protection (Schweppe, 2012). Together, a combination of these approaches may ultimately assist criminal law to rise to the challenge of greater inclusiveness by recognising vulnerability to victimisation based, not necessarily all forms of difference but, rather, on forms of difference that have a claim to equal rights and freedom from unfair or unjustifiable prejudice (Mason, 2013).

Punitive justice in the name of social justice: Are hate crimes worse?

Despite the many differences between hate crime laws that have proliferated throughout western nations during the last few decades, the vast majority of statutory provisions are punitive in nature, that is, they impose a heavier penalty upon offenders than that which is applicable to comparable crimes where there is no evidence of prejudice or bias on the part of the offender (Al-Hakim and Dimock, 2012; Schweppe, 2012; Mason, 2009; Lawrence, 1999). While it is true that hate crime laws have not emerged in response to populist pressure from mainstream society (Iganski, 2008), the raw fact remains that, by and large, they do provide the opportunity, sometimes the mandate, for heavier penalties to be imposed. In light of their purported purpose, which is to protect the human right to be different, safe from the threat of violence and the means by which they seek to do this, which is to explicitly criminalise and punish violent manifestations of prejudice towards this difference, it is difficult to avoid the conclusion that hate crime laws rely upon the mechanisms of punitive justice to achieve, not just the instrumental goals of retributivist justice, but also the wider symbolic goals of social justice (Mason, 2009a).

Advocates for hate crime laws argue that the heightened punishment they impose is justified because crimes that manifest prejudice are more serious than parallel crimes. Two main arguments are advanced to support this claim: i) hate crime is said to inflict greater harm upon the individual victim, the targeted community and/or society as a whole; and ii) the offender's moral culpability is said to be greater than that of similar offenders whose conduct lacks the element of prejudice or hostility (Lawrence, 1999; ODIHR, 2009a; Levin and McDevitt, 2002; Sherry, 2010; Iganski, 2008). To this way of thinking, the harsher sentence imposed upon the offender is proportionate to the seriousness of the crime and thus consistent with traditional aims of punishment (Wellman, 2006). The underlying logic of these 'just deserts' rationales – and the feature that purportedly sets hate crime apart from other crime – is that such crimes are said to 'violate the ideal of equality between members of society' and that this 'equality norm is a fundamental value that seeks to achieve full human dignity and to give an opportunity to all people to realize their full potential' (ODIHR, 2009a: 19). In other words, the criminal law constructs hate crime as more serious than parallel crimes because it negates the 'values of tolerance, respect and equality' for diversity, difference, multiculturalism and the like (Mason and Dyer, 2013: 882).

The need for hate crime laws is also frequently justified on symbolic or denunciative grounds (Gerstenfeld, 2004; Chakraborti, 2010). Advocates argue that the state has a responsibility to make a declaration of support for the safety and security of groups who are targeted because of their difference (Iganski, 2008; Wellman, 2006) and to affirm 'prosocial values of tolerance and respect' (Jenness and Grattet, 2001: 179). This requires hate crime to be explicitly recognised and punished *as* hate crime (Lawrence, 1999; ODIHR, 2009a) and, as Kahan (1999: 69) puts it, '[s]evere punishment is the idiom' that these laws use to 'get the message across'. The enactment of hate crime laws is thus a 'statement that these actions will no longer be tolerated and that severe penalties will be applied if such offences are committed' (Hall, 2005: 132). In effect, the symbolic or expressive justifications for hate crime laws, and the harsher penalties they impose, also comes to rest on the 'strong interest liberal democracies have in promoting diversity and demonstrating equal concern and respect for all citizens' (Al-Hakim and Dimock, 2012: 572).

Opponents of hate crime laws, and principally of the punitive quality of these laws, make a number of counter-arguments. Many point out that empirical evidence that hate crimes inflict greater harm upon individual victims is weak (Al-Hakim and Dimock, 2012; Hurd, 2001; Mason and Dyer, 2013). Although there is research to suggest that hate crimes do inflict damage upon the targeted group and other minorities by reinforcing a sense of marginalisation and vulnerability (Mason, 2002), as well as damaging wider social values of tolerance and respect (Al-Hakim, 2010), critics contend that this harm is no greater than that which is inflicted by some other crimes, such as sexual assault (Morgan, 2002). To this way of thinking, the enhanced penalties imposed by these laws violate the principle of proportionate punishment (Al-Hakim and Dimock, 2012), unfairly penalise an offender for his/her bad character and undermine the commitment of liberal democracies to neutrality and freedom of thought/expression (Gellman, 1992; Hurd, 2001). Moreover, given the weakness of evidence to support imprisonment as a form of deterrence in other areas of criminal justice (Wan et al., 2012), it is questionable that the heightened penalties imposed by hate crime laws are actually capable of deterrence (Dixon and Gadd, 2006). In light of the extensive prosecutorial options available under modern criminal law, it has also been suggested that hate crime laws are superfluous (Jacobs and Potter, 1998). Finally, critics argue that in seeking to exploit the expressive function of the criminal law to the extent that they do, such laws effectively operate as a form of 'affirmative action' (McLaughlin, 2002: 495) that attempts to 'extend the civil rights paradigm into the world of crime and criminal law' (Jacobs and Potter, 1998: 27).

Even if we were to accept that the harsher punishment imposed by hate crime laws can be justified under principles of proportionality, the issue of punishment raises questions of ethics and policy that run deeper than principles of criminal liability alone. The problem of mass imprisonment and a culture of control across many, albeit not all, western nations should prompt us to query whether legal responses to hate crime need be punitive. For example, recent work points to the potential of restorative justice as a means of addressing hate crime (Walters and Hoyle, 2010). While we need to recognise that hate crime laws are an important symbol of state support for those who are victimised because of prejudice towards their 'otherness', it is time that we pushed harder to imagine a path to legislating against hate, and promoting social justice, that is not paved with penal punitiveness.

Conclusion

Criminal law has always been at the heart of the anti-hate crime movement. It has provided parameters for the construction of hate crime as a social problem, the definition of its elements, the scope of its application and, arguably, it has been promoted as the key remedy to the problem. While the concept of hate crime has taken root in some places in the absence of statutory reform, this has always been slower and less pronounced. The enactment of specific hate crime offences lends the authority of the law to the issue that spreads to other domains, including policy, education and media. For better or worse, it is fair to say that hate crime *becomes* the elements that are bestowed upon it by the criminal law: a particular kind of problem with a particular kind of solution.

While law thus provides a tangible avenue for addressing the harm and the hurt of targeted victimisation, as the above discussion suggests, the multiple, contradictory and shifting ways in which law articulates hate crime reveal the contingent nature of the concept itself and the social reality it seeks to capture. Internationally, it is possible to discern patterns in legislative intervention that reflect broad models of reform but debates over how far to set the threshold for the element of prejudice, which groups to protect and whether punitiveness can be justified all point to on-going challenges. On the one hand, we could see these challenges as indicative of the incoherent state of hate crime law and policy or, on the other hand, as a sign of the dynamic and passionate investment that continues to characterise and strengthen hate crime discourse. This is a discourse that, despite the seeming centrality of criminal law to the meaning of hate crime, develops and moves in directions that are much bigger than law itself: directions that prompt us to remember that criminal law is only one small, often problematic, part of the solution to the problem.

References

Al-Hakim, M. (2010). Making room for hate crime legislation in liberal societies. *Criminal Law and Philosophy*, 4, 341–358.

Al-Hakim, M. and Dimock, S. (2012). Hate as an aggravating factor in sentencing. *Criminal Law Review*, 15, 572–611.

Association of Chief Police Officers (2005). *Hate Crime: Delivering a Quality Service – Good Practice and Tactical Guidance*, London: ACPO.

Burney, E. and Rose, G. (2002). Racist Offences: How is the law responding? Research Study no. 244, Home Office, July 2002.

Chakraborti, N. (2010). Crimes against the 'other': Conceptual, operational, and empirical challenges for hate studies. *Journal of Hate Studies*, 8(9), 9–28.

Chakraborti, N. and Garland, J. (2012). Reconceptualising hate crime through the lens of vulnerability and 'difference', *Theoretical Criminology*, 16, 499–514.

Dixon, B. and Gadd, D. (2006). Getting the message? 'New' labour and the criminalisation of 'hate', *Criminology and Criminal Justice*, 6(3), 309–328.

Franklin, K. (2004). Good intentions: The enforcement of hate crime penalty-enhancement statutes. In P. Gerstenfeld and D. Grant (eds), *Crimes of hate: Selected readings*. Thousand Oaks: Sage.

Gadd, D. and Dixon, B. (2011). *Losing the race*. London: Karnac.

Gelber, K. (2002). *Speaking back: The free speech versus hate speech debate*. Amsterdam: John Benjamins Ltd.

Gellman, S. (1992). Brother, you can't go to jail for what you're thinking. *Criminal Justice Ethics*, 11(2), 24–29.

Gerstenfeld, P. (2004). *Hate Crimes: Causes, controls and controversies*. Thousand Oaks: Sage Publications.

Glet, A. (2009). The German hate crime concept: An account of the classification and registration of bias-motivated offences and the implementation of the hate crime model into German's law enforcement system. *Internet Journal of Criminology*, www.internetjournalofcriminology.com, pp. 1–20.

Goodall, K. (2007). Incitement to religious hatred: All talk and no substance? *Modern Law Review*. 70(1), 89–113.

Goodall, K. (2013). Conceptualising 'racism' in criminal law. *Legal Studies*, 33(2), 215–238.

Goodey, J. and Aromaa, K. (eds) (2008). Hate crime: Papers from the 2006 and 2007 Stockholm Criminology Symposiums, European Institute for Crime Prevention and Control, affiliated with the United Nations (HEUNI), Helsinki, Finland, Publication Series No. 57.

Hall, N. (2005). *Hate Crime: Crime and Society Series*. Cullompton: Willan Publishing.

Hurd, H. (2001). Why liberals should hate 'hate crime' legislation. *Law and Philosophy*, 20(2), 215–232.

Iganski, P. (2008). *Hate crime and the city*. Bristol: The Policy Press.

Jacobs, J. and Potter, K. (1998). *Hate crimes: Criminal law and identity politics*. Oxford University Press.

Jenness, V. and Broad, K. (1997). *Hate crimes: New social movements and the politics of violence*. New York: Gruyter.

Jenness, V. and Grattet, R. (2005). The law-in-between: The effects of organizational perviousness on the policing of hate crime. *Social Problems*, 52, 337–359.

Jenness, V. and Grattet, R. (2001). *Making hate a crime*. New York: Russell Sage Foundation.

Kahan, D. (1999). The progressive appropriation of disgust. In S. Bandes (ed.), *The passions of law*. New York: New York University Press, pp. 63–79.

Lawrence, L. (1999). *Punishing hate: Bias crime under American law*. Harvard University Press.

Levin, J. and McDevitt, J. (2002). *Hate Crimes Revisited: America's War on Those Who Are Different*. Westview Press.

Lunny, A. (2011). *Victimhood and Socio-Legal Narratives of Hate Crime Against Queer Communities in Canada, 1985–2003*. Doctoral dissertation, University of Toronto.

Mason, G. (2002). *The Spectacle of Violence: Homophobia, Gender and Knowledge*. Routledge.

Mason, G. (2009). Hate crime laws in Australia: Are they achieving their goals? *Criminal Law Journal*, 33(6), 326–340.

Mason, G. (2009a). 2009 JV Barry Memorial Lecture: The penal politics of hatred. *Australian and New Zealand Journal of Criminology*, 42(3), 275–286.

Mason, G. (2010). R v Gouros: Interpreting motivation under Victoria's new hate crime laws. *Criminal Law Journal*, 34(5), 323–327.

Mason, G. (2013). Paedophiles and hate crime laws: Legitimate victims? Pursuit of Justice Conference, Gonzaga Law School, Washington, USA.

Mason, G. and Dyer, A. (2013). 'A negation of Australia's fundamental values': Sentencing prejudice-motivated crime. *Melbourne University Law Review*, 36(3), 872–917.

McLaughlin, E. (2002). Rocks and hard places: The politics of hate crime. *Theoretical Criminology*, 6(4), 493–498.

Morgan, J. (2002). US hate crime legislation: a legal model to avoid in Australia. *Journal of Sociology*, 38(1): 25–48.

ODIHR (2009a). Hate crime laws: A practical guide. Office for Democratic Institutions and Human Rights, Organization for Security and Co-operation in Europe.

ODIHR (2009b). Hate crimes in the OSCE Region – incidents and responses: Annual report for 2009, Office for Democratic Institutions and Human Rights, Organization for Security and Co-operation in Europe.

Phillips, N. (2009). The prosecution of hate crime: The limitations of hate crime typology. *Journal of Interpersonal Violence*, 24, 883.

Quill, G. (2010). Motivation, causation, and hate crime sentence enhancement: A cautious approach to mind reading and incarceration. *Drake Law Review*, 59, 181–216.

Roulstone, A., Thomas, P., Balderston, S. and Harris, J. (2009). Hate is a strong word: A critical policy analysis of disability hate crime in the British criminal justice system. Paper presented at the Social Policy Association Annual Conference, Edinburgh, July.

Schweppe, J. (2012). Defining characteristics and politicising victims: A legal perspective. *Journal of Hate Studies*, 10(1), 173–198.

Sherry, M. (2010). *Disability hate crimes: Does anyone really hate disabled people?* Ashgate.

Stanko, E. (2001). Re-conceptualising the policing of hatred: Confessions and worrying dilemmas of a consultant. *Law and Critique*, 12, 309–329.

Walters, M. and Hoyle, C. (2010). Healing harms and engendering tolerance: The promise of restorative justice for hate crime. In N. Chakraborti, (ed.), *Hate Crime: Concepts, policy, future directions*. Cullompton: Willan Publishing.

Wan, W.Y., Moffatt, S., Jones, C. and Weatherburn, D. (2012). The effect of arrest and imprisonment on crime. Crime and Justice Bulletin, NSW Bureau of Crime Statistics and Research: Contemporary Issues in Crime and Justice, 158.

Wang, L. (1999). The complexities of 'hate'. *Ohio State Law Journal*, 60, 799.

Wellman, C. (2006). A defense of stiffer penalties for hate crimes. *Hypatia*, 21(2), 62–80.

6

Understanding hate crimes

Sociological and criminological perspectives

Nathan Hall[1]

Bowling (1999) suggests that academic and professional interest in issues of race and racism in relation to crime (and therefore, by analogy, interest in hate crime) can be traced back to the early 1980s in the UK through two key events. The first was the urban riots of 1981, most notably in Brixton, south London, which saw the emergence of race, prejudice and discrimination as significant social issues. The second was the re-emergence of victimology in the late 1970s and early 1980s as a significant social science in its own right, and the subsequent development of social surveys that for the first time began to provide a wealth of data relating to the plight of the victim, and in particular the disproportionate victimisation of certain minority groups.

Together, these two events served to ensure that the victim was placed at the centre of the criminal justice, criminological and political focus – a situation that largely remains to date. Whilst this is of course absolutely right and the victim of any crime should be of central concern to all parties in the criminal justice system, this focus on the victim has meant that the perpetrator as an actor in the equation has hitherto been largely ignored. This is particularly true for perpetrators of hate crime and poses something of a problem for our understanding of this form of offending behaviour. The following two quotes from Ben Bowling, which as we shall see still resonate today, adequately outline the consequent challenges facing those seeking to explain hate-motivated offending as a result of the predominantly victim-oriented focus. First:

> There has been almost no research on perpetrators. Whilst the most basic of descriptions have been formulated, they remain something of an effigy in the criminological literature ... The perpetrator is unknown and, consequently, the possibility for any understanding or interpretation of his or her behaviour becomes impossible.
>
> *(1999: 163)*

And second:

> What is needed for the purposes of explaining [hate crime] is for attention to be turned away from an analysis of the characteristics of victims to focus on the characteristics of offenders: their relationship with those they victimise; the social milieux in which anger,

aggression, hostility, and violence are fostered; and the social processes by which violence becomes directed against minority groups ... Criminologists operate with scant evidence about what is going on in the lives of these people. Instead, we have only a devilish effigy for symbolic sacrifice.

(1999: 305)

Writing of this situation from North America, Barbara Perry (2003) has argued similarly. In addition to the impact of the victim-oriented focus of which Bowling speaks, Perry has suggested that theorising about perpetrators has been scant partially because hate crime is still relatively 'new' to the criminological horizon, and also because of the general lack of consensus about how exactly 'hate crime' should be defined (see Chakraborti, this volume), and of course, the implications that necessarily follow for the production of reliable data upon which to base research and to construct conceptual frameworks (Perry, 2009). In addition, Perry has pointed to the fact that, historically, when criminology has taken an interest in minority groups *per se*, the focus has tended to be on their criminality, rather than on crimes committed against them.

Despite Bowling and Perry's concerns being a decade or more old, it is perhaps something of an indictment on the social sciences that Perry was able to reiterate these sentiments as recently as 2009, lamenting that:

> It is curious that hate crime has not been an object of extensive theoretical inquiry. Conceptually, it lies at the intersection of several themes that are currently to the fore, for example, violence, victimisation, race/ethnicity, gender, sexuality, and difference. In spite of the centrality of violence as a means of policing the relative boundaries of identity, few attempts have been made to understand theoretically the place of hate crime in the contemporary arsenal of oppression. It is not an area that has been seriously examined through a theoretical lens ... The goal of hate crime theory, then, is to conceptualise this particular form of violence within the psychological, cultural, or political contexts that condition hostile perceptions of, and reactions to, the Other.

(2009: 56)

In light of the various concerns expressed above, this chapter will present an *overview* of current sociological and criminological knowledge in relation to the perpetrators of hate crime. It will attempt, as far as possible given the available literature and the space available to discuss it, to shed some light on both what is known about the perpetrators of hate crime and what causes this type of offending, and in so doing present something (hopefully) a little more useful than the 'devilish effigy' we have thus far largely been confined to.

Anomie

Many sociological accounts of hate crime have their roots in anomie, and more specifically, strain theory. Hopkins-Burke and Pollock (2004), for example, suggest that hate crime should be considered a normal, rational and fully understandable activity within our society and, as a result, sociologically informed criminological theory, in particular that founded on the European and US anomie traditions, can be adapted to explain and understand the existence and persistence of hate motivation at all levels of the social world.

In particular, they suggest, insights can be derived from the early work of Durkheim (1933) in relation to social solidarity and the nature of social change, which they suggest, help us to make sense of the notion that hate crime motivation has its foundations in the origins and later development of societal structure. More recent, mid-twentieth century US anomie theorising, such as that concerning adaptations (Merton, 1938 – see next section), differential association (Sutherland, 1939, 1947), deviant subcultures (Cohen, 1955), and delinquency, drift and techniques of neutralisation (Matza, 1964 – see later), they further suggest, demonstrate how hate crime motivation has not just strongly founded macro-societal origins, but can occur as the outcome of rationally developed strategies developed, or encountered, by socio-economically disaffected people, with disparate commitment levels, at a local or micro societal level (Hopkins-Burke and Pollock, 2004: 7). They further argue that more recent radical European traditions with nonetheless firm identifiable foundations in both earlier anomie traditions help to explain the complexities and variations of hate crime motivation in contemporary fragmented communities. Here they point in particular to the radical, neo-Marxist sub-cultural theories of the Birmingham Centre for Contemporary Cultural Studies formulated in the 1970s. There is not the space here to adequately consider all of these issues (but see Hopkins-Burke and Pollock, 2004, for an in-depth and interesting consideration of each of these aspects), so we shall satisfy ourselves with an overview of some of the more commonly utilised sociological and criminological theories in this field.

Strain

Accounts of Mertonian strain theory are widely available, so we will satisfy ourselves with a simple overview here. Merton (1949) argued that crime was a product of the mismatch between the goals by which Western society judges 'success' (wealth and material possessions) and the means available to individuals to achieve those goals. Whilst society by its very nature pressures everyone to achieve those valued goals, not everyone has the opportunity or ability to do so legitimately (for example through hard work, education, and so on). Those who are unlikely to legitimately achieve the goals valued by society, Merton argued, would be placed under a 'strain' to achieve them through alternative means. In other words, it is achieving the goals that is important, and not necessarily how you achieve them.

Given these pressures, Merton argued that people would adapt to their situation in different ways. Some would *conform* and 'play by the rules', and others would deviate from those rules. Of the four categories of deviants (ritualists, retreatists, rebels and innovators) we shall concern ourselves with *innovators* and *rebels* (although it should be noted that Hopkins-Burke and Pollock, 2004, suggest that latent hate may often be present but not actualised in the other categories too). Innovators, according to Merton, accept society's goals but reject the legitimate means of achieving them. Instead, because they are unable to legitimately achieve 'success' (for example, because of unemployment, poor education, poor skills, and so on), these people will innovate and use illegitimate means that may prove more efficient for them to achieve the very same goals. In essence, then, the frustration, or strain, caused by the desire for 'success' and the inability to achieve it legitimately gives rise to criminal behaviour. Moreover, Agnew (1992) suggests that this strain often gives rise to negative emotions including disappointment, depression, fear and, crucially, anger because of the situation they find themselves in.

If we relate this theory to hate crime then it is tempting to conclude that such offences are committed by people in response to a perceived instability (or strain) in their lives, for example through increased competition for jobs and other scarce resources caused by 'foreigners', exploitation and marginalisation, and people's economic security being threatened by 'outsiders' (Perry, 2001). According to strain theory, then, hate crime is a way of *responding* to *threats* to the legitimate means of achieving society's proscribed goals. Minority groups therefore serve to increase the perception of strain that the majority population feel, and hate crime is a product of, and a response to, that strain.

This is illustrated, for example, in a small sample of studies cited by Sibbitt (1997). In outlining the role of social factors in shaping racist attitudes, the Association of London Authorities (1993) identified the key issues as unemployment, competition for housing, a lack of facilities for young people, and the need for people to find scapegoats to blame for their situation and therefore for the *strain* in their lives. In addition Sibbitt also draws upon a study conducted in Germany by Heitmeyer in 1993 that claimed hostility towards foreigners to be a product of social and political disintegration, the search for identity, experiences of powerlessness and isolation, and anxiety relating to social conditions, most notably in relation to jobs and housing. Likewise, the results of a Scandinavian study conducted by Bjorgo (1993). Such arguments are also frequently presented and fuelled by, for example, the British tabloid press in their recent coverage of immigration and asylum.

With regard to *rebellion*, which Merton labelled as those people who both reject society's systems and goals *and* seek to change them, some useful theoretical insights into more extreme and contemporary aspects of hate might be derived. Hopkins-Burke and Pollock (2004) suggest, for example, that Merton's concept of anomic rebellion is particularly useful in explaining the growth of Islamic fundamentalism against the dominant capitalist world order and its culture.

However, whilst strain theory may be suitable for explaining some hate crimes, or perhaps more suitably as a part-explanation, as a comprehensive theory Mertonian strain (as a specific part of the broader anomic tradition to which Hopkins-Burke and Pollock refer) falls down at a number of critical points. Perry (2001: 37) argues that

> ... there is no doubt that hate crime occurring in the historical (recession) and sociogeographical (inner city) context of economic instability may be in part a response to perceived strain. Those facing downward mobility may indeed lash out against scapegoats whom they hold to be responsible for their displacement ... However, not least of the inconsistencies here is that if strain accounted for hate crimes, then those most prevalent among the victims would instead be the perpetrators! Who is more disadvantaged – economically, socially and politically – than women and racial minorities? Yet these groups are much more likely to be victims than offenders.

In other words, if those experiencing the greatest strain should be those most likely to commit hate crimes, then minority groups should logically also be the largest perpetrator groups, but in reality this is not the case. Whilst the intention of hate crime policy is sometimes subverted and minorities may in some instances be disproportionately represented in the official statistics as perpetrators, it is minority groups who are predominantly the victims of hate crime. Perry also points to the fact that hate crime is not just committed at times when strain and cultural tension may be present, and nor is it always committed by those who are powerless in society and who are therefore most likely to perceive strain.

Indeed, Perry highlights the fact that hate crime crosses all class boundaries. She argues that the perpetrators of hate crime regularly include those who hold positions of relative power within society and not just those who are alienated or deprived. Indeed, those in the highest positions of power have perpetrated some of the worst examples of hate crimes throughout history. Perry also highlights the professional backgrounds of the leaders of certain organised hate groups and, perhaps more closer to home, the historical evidence relating to the secondary victimisation of minority groups by the criminal justice system, most notably by the police who hold a clear position of power within society. Furthermore, even where offenders are relatively powerless, through hate crime they are in fact exercising a degree of power over what they perceive to be 'subordinate' groups and in doing so are maintaining their 'rightful' place in a perceived hierarchy of power within society.

Differential association, subcultures, and drift

Despite Perry's criticisms of strain as an explanation of hate crime, Hopkins-Burke and Pollock (2004) imply that a more holistic take on the anomic tradition provides stronger theoretical foundations upon which to build our understanding. For example, by adding Sutherland's 'differential association' (which holds that a person is more likely to offend via a process of social learning if they have associations with individuals engaging in similar activities) into the mix, then the link between social structural conditions and individual behaviours might be better explained, as might the transmission of 'hate' from one individual to another.

Similarly, they suggest, *subcultural theories*, rooted in Cohen's (1955) work on delinquent youths, help to further illustrate how individuals come together as groups with shared views and cultural values. Whilst Cohen and others concentrated their theorising on the subcultural responses emerging from the disjoint between disadvantaged youths and mainstream middle-class society, Hopkins-Burke and Pollock (2004) suggest that, coupled with differential association, this can usefully be adapted to explain group 'hate' (and not just that found in disadvantaged communities) by providing insights into the ways in which people become socialised into a particular world view. This of course has links to aspects of social identity and culture in shaping prejudice, and has implications for our understanding of the Far Right and other organised hate groups.

One of the criticisms of subcultural theories, however, relates to their seemingly overly deterministic nature. Matza (1964) was acutely aware of these theoretical vulnerabilities, observing as he did the tendency of *most* young offenders to *drift* in and out of delinquency, to find excuses for their criminal behaviour and, ultimately, to 'grow out of' crime. This theoretical take on offending is perhaps best illustrated by research from McDevitt et al. (2002); Sibbitt (1997); and from Byers et al. (1999).

For example, of the 169 cases they analysed, McDevitt et al. concluded that 66 per cent (or 111 of the total) of the offences, mostly committed by youths, were motivated by the *thrill* or for the excitement of the act. This finding supports Sibbitt's (1997) contention that many younger racist offenders commit offences out of a sense of boredom and a need for excitement in their lives. The former report that in 91 per cent of these 'thrill' cases the perpetrators left their neighbourhood to search for a victim, and deliberately selected their target because they were 'different' to themselves, and the attacks were underpinned by an immature desire to display power and to enhance the offender's own feeling of self-importance at the expense of others.

Similarly, the perspectives of anomie presented here also support Sibbitt's broader view that it is the interplay of *contextual factors* and the *psychology* of certain individuals that produces perpetrators. Offenders, she suggests, are likely to be involved in other forms of criminal or antisocial behaviour, of which hate offending is a part, and will operate with the passive support (or at least without the condemnation) of some sections of the wider community who share similar views but who are not necessarily inclined towards, or engaged in, criminal behaviour themselves.

Furthermore, research conducted in the US by Byers et al. (1999) has also revealed some interesting insights into hate crime offending by drawing on Sykes and Matza's (1957) techniques of neutralisation, which sought to identify how perpetrators of crime justify their offending behaviour. Sykes and Matza found that offenders in general often attempted to justify their actions in a number of ways that mitigated their involvement, and that these justification techniques provided useful information about the motivation of criminals.

In their study of hate crimes committed against the Amish, Byers et al. found that whilst some offenders showed little or no remorse for their actions, others attempted to justify or rationalise their behaviour by using a number of 'neutralisation techniques'. The first technique described by Byers et al. is that of *denial of injury*. Here offenders attempted to neutralise their behaviour by suggesting that no real harm was done to the victim, that the offence was in effect 'harmless fun', and that the victim should in any case be used to being subject to certain forms of abuse, all of which combined to make the offender's behaviour somehow acceptable.

The second identified technique was that of the *denial of the victim*. According to Byers et al., this makes the assumption that the victim either deserved what they got, or that the victim is effectively worthless and offences against them are inconsequential either socially or legally. Essentially, then, victims are somewhat dehumanised and seen as deserving of their victimisation.

The third identified technique is the *appeal to higher loyalties*. Here, offences may be committed through allegiance to a group. Offenders therefore may see their behaviour, and subsequently not revealing that behaviour or the behaviour of their peers, as a form of group bonding and security within their 'in-group'.

Fourth, Byers et al. suggest that some offenders will engage *condemnation of the condemners*. Here offenders attempt to neutralise their behaviour by questioning the right of their condemners to sit in judgement of them. This may be done by suggesting that those that condemn them are in reality no better, share similar views to the offender, and given the chance in similar circumstances would act, or may have previously acted, in a similar way to the perpetrator.

The final technique relates to a *denial of responsibility*. Here, Byers et al. explain, offenders attempt to neutralise their responsibility for their actions by claiming other factors to be the cause of their behaviour, such as, the researchers suggest, the offender's socialisation and the way they were brought up. In other words, the blame for their behaviour lies somewhere other than with them.

Furthermore, Byers et al. found that many offenders broadly fitted the 'thrill' category described by Levin et al., earlier, and also pointed to the importance of peer support, which has links to Sibbitt's work on the 'perpetrator community', by highlighting the significance of shared views, and the reinforcement of those views. Offenders' attempts at justifying their actions also lend support to the view that victims are frequently dehumanised by their attackers, are perceived as subordinate to the offender, and are somehow deserving of their victimisation. This in turn reflects Perry's notion of power, the expression of power, and the use of hate crime as a method for maintaining perceived social hierarchies and for 'punishing' those who attempt to disturb the social order, to which we shall now turn our attention.

Structural accounts

Barbara Perry (2001: 46) argues that the United States (and therefore by analogy the UK)

> ... is a nation grounded in deeply embedded notions of difference that have been used to justify and construct intersecting hierarchies along lines of sexuality, race, gender, and class, to name but a few. In other words, difference has been socially constructed, but in ever-changing ways across time and space. Nonetheless, these constructions have reinforced similarly changing practices of exclusion and marginalisation.

In other words, there is essentially a form of classification in society with different categories of 'belonging'. For example, as Perry explains, one is either male or female, black or white, or Asian, Christian, Jew or Muslim, and so on. Here, the boundaries are held to be fixed and impermeable, and membership is usually given and not chosen. With these divisions, according to Perry, come assumptions about the members of each of the other categories. In creating an identity for itself, a group necessarily creates its antithesis. Similarly to Allport's (1954) theorising concerning 'in-groups' and 'out-groups', whilst one group perceives itself as dominant and privileged, so it also sees other groups as subordinate, disadvantaged and 'different'. Significantly, Perry (2001: 47) states that

> ... difference has been constructed in negative relational terms. A dominant norm ... has been established, against which all others are (unfavourably) judged. This is the case whether we speak in terms of race, class, gender, sexuality, beauty, or any other element of identity. So it is those who are not white or male or Christian or moneyed who are marked or stigmatised as different.

So those who do not fit the 'mythical norm' of dominance and power in Western society (that is, those who are not white, male, young, financially secure, heterosexual, Christian, physically attractive, and so on) are categorised as 'different'. With the notion of 'difference', Perry argues, comes the assumption of inferiority and the assignment of a subordinate place in society. Thus we are left with a hierarchical structure of power in society based upon notions of 'difference', with the 'mythical norm' at the top and those who are 'different' assigned subordinate positions. According to Perry these hierarchies are reinforced through labour and employment, politics, sexuality, and culture, the facets of which serve to continually construct, reinforce and maintain the dominant order.

Therefore, Perry (2001: 55) explains that:

> ... when we do difference, when we engage in the process of identity formation, we do so within the confines of structural and institutional norms. In so doing – to the extent that we conform to normative conceptions of identity – we reinforce the structural order. However, not everyone always performs 'appropriately'. Frequently, we construct our gender or race or sexuality in ways that in fact challenge or threaten sociocultural arrangements. We step out of line, cross sacred boundaries, or forget our 'place'. It is in such a context that hate crime often emerges as a means of responding to the threats. The tensions between hegemonic and counterhegemonic actors may culminate in violent efforts to reassert the dominance of the former and realign the position of the latter.

As such, through Perry's theory hate crime can be viewed as a 'tool' by which perpetrators attempt to reaffirm their perceived dominance when 'subordinate' groups attempt, for example, to 'better their lot' and threaten the 'natural' relations of superiority and inferiority within society. Such theorising, Perry contends, allows hate crime to be placed within the wider context of oppression that is found in a complex structure of power relations firmly and historically grounded in various notions of 'difference':

> In other words, hate motivated violence is used to sustain the privilege of the dominant group, and to police the boundaries between groups by reminding the Other of his/her 'place'. Perpetrators thus re-create their own masculinity, or whiteness, for example, while punishing the victims for their deviant identity performance.
>
> *(Perry, 2001: 55)*

However, whilst Perry's work represents a (or, arguably *the*) significant contribution to theorising hate crime, critical, structural theories such as Perry's are not without their critics. The suggestion that hate crimes are expressions of power aimed at reaffirming the offender's perceived hierarchy of appropriate social positions, some argue, masks a number of complexities associated with individual offences and offenders and indeed victims. There are effectively two problems. First, if hate crime is indeed used to sustain the privilege of the dominant group, then the implication appears to be that members of a dominant group can only ever be offenders, and conversely that members of minority groups can only ever be victims. Yet, victims of hate crimes are often members of the dominant social group, and members of minority groups are often the perpetrators of hate crime. Such a reality clearly does not sit easily with structural theories.

Second, to suggest that every hate crime is always about maintaining power is arguably a little too simplistic. This notion of power can be expressed in a variety of ways, and to differing degrees to the extent that no two motivations for hate offences can ever be said to be truly identical. Andrew Sullivan (1999) suggests that structural accounts are far better at alleging structures of power than at delineating the workings and complexities of the individual heart and mind. Structural theories necessarily tell us very little about how the victims or the offenders feel, nor indeed who the offenders might be. Power may be the underpinning factor in many cases, but prejudice and hate are expressed in many different ways, and no two 'hates' are ever qualitatively the same. The varieties of human emotion and human behaviour encapsulated by the word 'hate' are considered by some to be too varied to be explained as they are in structural accounts.

Merging theories

In considering theories of causation in relation to hate crime, Walters (2011: 314) neatly summarises many of the issues to emerge from the content of this chapter:

> while the extant literature on causation is of great epistemological value, several shortcomings can be identified. Firstly, there has been little which attempts to examine the intersections between the various theories espoused within criminology and other disciplines. The tendency to focus on disparate disciplinary analyses of hate crime has meant that the aetiology of 'hate' and more specifically hate motivated behaviour has been shaped within this or that field of study. Even within individual fields of study, researchers have failed to get to grips with linking macro level theory to individual

agency. For example, within the criminological body neither strain theory nor 'doing difference' have been used to adequately explain why only some individuals commit hate crimes while others, equally affected by socio-economic strains and social constructions of 'difference', do not.

To close this theoretical gap, at least partially, Walters suggests that theories of strain and theories of structure are better understood when they are synthesised through the interconnecting emotion of *fear*. He proposes that it is the fear that Others will encroach upon dominant group identity *and* socio-economic security that fuels the climate of prejudice against them, and as this fear spreads throughout a community it can affect everyone, regardless of their socio-economic status (thereby arguably bypassing some of the shortcomings of both sets of theories). That said, however, Walters also acknowledges that even with fear as the interconnecting element, neither theory explains why only certain individuals commit hate crimes while others, equally open to the same strains and hegemonic constructions of identity, choose not to. Indeed, he notes that there is little within the hate crime literature that addresses this.

In seeking to undertake this task, Walters taps into a hitherto unused source of criminological theory, namely Gottfredson and Hirschi's (1990) theory of self-control, in which they argue that it is a lack of self-control on the part of individuals that causes them to succumb to criminal opportunity (or, conversely, the presence of self-control on the part of most that stops them succumbing to such opportunities). In so doing, Walters (2011: 328) attempts to fill the gap between macro level causational mechanisms and micro level offending patterns, concluding that:

> an individual's propensity to commit hate crime may ultimately turn on his or her levels of self-control. By viewing hate offending in terms of self-control we begin to understand why many disgruntled racists or homophobes remain simply that and why others' prejudiced sentiments trigger a criminal response. Indeed, the current research body on hate perpetrator typology provides a persuasive account of offending suggesting that most perpetrators will display one or more of the following characteristics: thrill seeking, a tendency towards taking physical risks, defensive of territory, low tolerance levels of difference, a disposition towards violence and other anti-social behaviours, a lack of academic qualifications and/or low-skilled employment. The profile of hate offenders therefore creates a picture of offending which fits into almost all aspects of *Gottfredson and Hirschi's theory of self control*.

Although he accepts that this approach does not explain all forms of hate crime, Walters' contribution to the theoretical literature does begin to move us towards a more holistic approach to explaining hate crime and, given the rather disparate nature of the accounts offered by the different disciplines highlighted in this chapter, represents a move towards a more sophisticated way of analysing the problem of hate-motivated offending.

The 'normality' of hate offending

Iganski (2008) also notes the shortcomings of abstract and deterministic theorising, and has attempted to illuminate the connections between background structures of bigotry and the foreground of offenders' actions by combining theory with empirical fieldwork. By drawing upon what Garland (2001) has labelled 'the new criminologies of everyday life', which encompasses criminological perspectives including *routine activities theory* (see, for example, Felson, 2002), *rational choice theory*, and *situational crime prevention*, Iganski's own research makes for some uncomfortable reading.

Iganski concludes that hate crimes are predominantly 'low-level' offences, but are overwhelmingly committed by 'ordinary' people rather than by 'extremists', as media headlines might suggest. Thus, there is a 'normality' to everyday hate crime that, for Iganski, carries with it the rather uncomfortable reality that the majority of hate offenders are not hate-fuelled bigots who actively seek out their victims in a calculated and premeditated manner, but rather are 'people like us' (2008: 42) who offend in the context of their everyday lives. The value here lies in Iganski's focus on, and discussion of, the situational dynamics and social circumstances of hate crime offending that is derived from empirical evidence drawn from the lived experience of victims, resulting in the conclusion that hate crimes predominantly result from 'the normal frictions of day-to-day life'. Whilst this focus on lived experience predominantly relates to victims of racist and religiously motivated offences, Iganski also usefully explores the experiences of victims of disability and homophobic hate crimes and in so doing begins to fill something of a void in the existing literature. His analysis of the data therefore reveals a myriad of distinctive features of city life that provide potential opportunities for 'everyday' hate victimisation.

Conclusion

This chapter has sought to shed some light on the contribution made by sociological and criminological theorising in seeking to explain hate-motivated offending. What is clear is that this remains a complex issue to comprehensively (or indeed adequately) explain. It seems then that the views expressed by Kellina Craig more than a decade ago still ring true today. In her review of the socio-psychological literature, Craig (2002: 120) identified specific areas that relate to the characteristics of hate crime perpetrators, and in doing so noted the difficulties and limitations of theorising hate crime:

> Although several explanations may be applicable to hate crime occurrence, no existing one can fully account for all types of hate crime. This is because the factors that contribute to hate crime (i.e. perpetrators' motives, victims' characteristics, and cultural ideologies about the victim's social groups) differ markedly for each incident . . . Thus, in order to explain hate crimes, a consideration of all potentially relevant explanations is necessary.

Simply then, it seems that hate crime perpetrators can effectively be motivated by one or more of a wide range of social, psychological, political, cultural and other factors. On the basis of Craig's statement, the search for a single, universal causal factor for hate crime is likely to be fruitless. Rather, it is the interplay of a number of different factors that produces perpetrators. As such, the investigation and analysis of hate-motivated offending, and the search for causal explanations, within discreet disciplines of the social sciences has clearly yielded many avenues for us to explore. Indeed, the social sciences have much to offer, but despite this explanatory frameworks remain rather disparate and, consequently, we cannot say with any certainty why it is hate crime occurs.

Indeed, as Allport (1954) wryly noted:

> It required years of labor and billions of dollars to gain the secret of the atom. It will take a still greater investment to gain the secrets of man's irrational nature.

In line with Allport's suggestion, whilst we may now be able to say a *little* more about *who* offenders are in terms of identifying some of their basic characteristics, the search for a satisfactory answer to the *why?* question remains elusive. The theories discussed in this chapter offer numerous possible explanations, but none that provide us with concrete and holistic answers as to why hate crime occurs.

We should not forget though that hate crime is still a relatively new area of scholarly interest, and although there is *relatively* little by way of *applied* research on, or *theorising* about, hate crime offenders and the factors that cause such offending to occur, the evidence presented here, and indeed throughout this volume, suggests a degree of progress in both of these endeavours.

Note

1 Extracts of this chapter have previously been published in Hall, N. (2013) *Hate Crime* (2nd edn), Abingdon: Routledge.

Bibliography

Agnew, R. (1992) Foundation for a general strain theory of crime and delinquency. *Criminology*, 30: 47.

Allport, G. W. (1954) *The Nature of Prejudice*. Massachusetts: Addison-Wesley.

Association of London Authorities (1993) Racial Abuse: An Everyday Experience for Some Londoners. Submission by the Association of London Authorities to the House of Commons Home Affairs Committee Inquiry into Racially-Motivated Attacks and Harassment.

Bjorgo, T. (1993) Terrorist Violence against Immigrants and Refugees in Scandinavia: Patterns and Motives. In T. Bjorgo and R. Witte (eds) *Racist Violence in Europe*. London: Macmillan.

Bowling, B. (1999) *Violent Racism: Victimisation, policing and social context*. New York: Oxford University Press.

Byers, B., Crider, B. W. and Biggers, G. K. (1999) Bias crime motivation: a study of hate crime and offender neutralisation techniques used against the Amish. *Journal of Contemporary Criminal Justice*, 15(1): 78–96.

Chakraborti, N. (2010) (ed.) *Hate Crime: Concepts, Policy, Future Directions*. Collumpton: Willan Publishing.

Cohen, A. K. (1955) *Delinquent Boys: The Culture of the Gang*. New York: Free Press.

Craig, K. M. (2002) Examining Hate-Motivated Aggression: A Review of the Social Psychological Literature on Hate Crimes as a Distinct Form of Aggression. *Aggression and Violent Behaviour*. 7, 85–101.

Durkheim, E. (1933, originally 1893) *The Division of Labour in Society*. Glencoe: Free Press.

Felson, M. (2002) *Crime and Everyday Life* (3rd edition). Thousand Oaks, CA: Sage.

Garland, D. (2001) *The Culture of Control: Crime and Social Order in Late Modernity*. Oxford: Clarendon Press.

Gottfredson, M. and Hirschi, T. (1990) *A General Theory of Crime*. Stanford, CA: Stanford University Press.

Heitmeyer, W. (1993) Hostility and Violence Towards Foreigners in Germany. In T. Bjorgo and R. Witte (eds) *Racist Violence in Europe*. London: Macmillan.

Hopkins-Burke, R. and Pollock, E. (2004) A Tale of Two Anomies: some observations on the contribution of (sociological) criminological theory to explaining hate crime motivation. *Internet Journal of Criminology*. 1–54.

Iganski, P. (2008) *Hate Crime and the City*. Bristol: Policy Press.

McDevitt, J., Levin, J. and Bennett, S. (2002) Hate crime offenders: an expanded typology. *Journal of Social Issues*, 58(2): 303–17.

Matza, D. (1964) *Delinquency and Drift*. New York: John Wiley.

Merton, R. K. (1938) Social structure and anomie. *American Sociological Review*, 3 (October): 672–82.

Merton, R. K. (1949) *Social Theory and Social Structure*. New York: Free Press.

Perry, B. (2001) *In the Name of Hate: Understanding Hate Crimes*. New York: Routledge.
Perry, B. (2003) Anti-Muslim retaliatory violence following the 9/11 terrorist attacks. In B. Perry (ed.) *Hate and Bias Crime: A Reader*. London: Routledge, pp. 183–202.
Perry, B. (2009) The Sociology of Hate: Theoretical Approaches. In B. Perry (ed.) *Hate Crimes* (vol. 1). Westport: Praeger.
Perry, B. (2010) The More Things Change . . . post 9/11 Trends in Hate Crime Scholarship. In N. Chakraborti (ed.) *Hate Crime: Concepts, Policy, Future Directions*. Abingdon: Routledge.
Sibbitt, R. (1997) The Perpetrators of Racial Harassment and Racial Violence. Home Office Research Study No. 176. London: Home Office.
Sullivan, A. (1999) What's so bad about hate? The illogic and illiberalism behind hate crime laws. *New York Times Magazine*, 26 September.
Sutherland, E. H. (1939) *Principles of Criminology* (3rd edition). Philadelphia: J. P. Lippincott.
Sutherland, E. H. (1947) *Principles of Criminology* (4th edition). Philadelphia: J. P. Lippincott.
Sykes, G. and Matza, D. (1957) Techniques of neutralisation. *American Sociological Review*, 22: 664–70.
Walters, M. A. (2011) A general theories of hate crime? Strain, doing difference and self control. *Critical Criminology*, (19): 313–30.

7

Understanding hate crimes
Perspectives from the wider social sciences

Nathan Hall[1]

In the previous chapter I reflected on the contribution made by sociology and criminology to our understanding of hate crime. The various theories explored there provided some useful insights into why hate crimes might occur, but failed to provide any holistic answers. But of course it is not just these two academic disciplines that have contributions to make to our understanding of hate crime. Considerable understanding can also be derived from other branches of the social sciences. Perhaps unsurprisingly, though, given the often secular nature of the social sciences, explanations of hate and hate crime offending have been proffered in a rather disparate and often isolated manner, leaving us with a somewhat disjointed framework of analysis. In this chapter, then, we shall briefly consider what some of the social sciences, and their associated elements, have to say about our area of study, and assess the extent to which they further our understanding of 'hate' and 'hate crime'.

Psychology

The various definitions of hate crime considered in the chapters of this volume clearly illustrate that this form of offending isn't always about *hate*, but rather it is predominantly about *prejudice*, of which hate is just a small part. It follows then that if we want to understand hate crime then we must understand the nature of prejudice. Fortunately, as Stangor (2000) points out, there are few if any topics that have engaged the interests of social psychologists as much as those of *prejudice*, *stereotypes* and *discrimination*. This, he suggests, is a consequence of the immense practical importance that such studies hold for understanding the effects of these issues on both individuals and societies, particularly given the increasing diversity of the world we live in. And as Perry (2003) suggests, these concepts mark the starting point for theorising about the perpetrators of hate crime. Indeed, she notes that the literature has been dominated by psychological and social-psychological accounts that necessarily emphasise individual-level analyses (2009: 56), including significant contributions from Allport on the nature of prejudice (1954); Tajfel and Turner on social identity (1979); Sherif and Sherif on realistic conflict (1953); and Bandura on social learning (1977), to name but a few (see Hall, 2013, for a broader discussion of psychological theorising in relation to hate crime).

However, for all our theorising about these concepts, the existing literature tells us remarkably little about *how* prejudice transforms into actions that would constitute hate crimes. Indeed, there is little consensus for theories that seek to explain this phenomenon. It is also clear that there are many kinds of prejudice that vary greatly and have different psychological dynamics underpinning them, and this can have important implications for responding to hate crimes (as many of the chapters in Part Four of this volume make clear). Furthermore, because prejudices are independent psychological responses they can be expressed, as Allport illustrates, in a bewildering number of ways, ranging from a mild dislike or general aversion to others to extreme acts of violence. But (and this is crucial for our understanding of hate-motivated offending) as Green et al. (2003: 27) suggest in a position that still holds true today;

> It might take the better part of a lifetime to read the prodigious research literature on prejudice . . . yet scarcely any of this research examines directly and systematically the question of why prejudice erupts into violence.

So, when we talk about hate in the context of hate crime, we are really referring to prejudice, but despite the wide research that has been conducted into prejudice as a psychological phenomenon, we still cannot say with any degree of certainty why it is that prejudice leads to violent behaviour. But, as Gaylin (2003) argues, to suggest that *hatred* (but not in its contemporary politically constructed sense) is normal to the human condition is too simplistic an argument to sustain. After all, he suggests, even given the opportunity and freedom to hate or express hatred without obstruction or sanction, most of us would still not choose to do so. Yet when this does occur, we do not know enough about prejudice to say how or why.

Stern (2005) reiterates this point. Whilst *psychology* informs us that most people are capable of hatred and gives us some insights into the relationship between identity and hate, its rather narrow focus on the individual as an explanation is necessarily limited and needs, if it is to provide more comprehensive answers, to be integrated into a larger framework. The broader approach taken by *social psychology*, which considers the individual in social situations where certain attributes may come to the fore, offers arguably greater insight into intergroup conflict and, as Stern points out, this 'treasure trove' of research also suggests some possibilities for responding to the problem. Nevertheless, whilst collectively psychology has some important contributions to make to our understanding of hate, these individual-level analyses do not provide the complete explanation of hate-motivated offending that we might hope for. As such, we need to concern ourselves with exploring alternative explanatory frameworks that might help us to fill the gaps left by the psychological literature.

History

As Stern (2005: 5) rightly points out:

> History is the study of the past and, as such, provides a framework for understanding hatred and how it has manifested itself at different times and places. It focuses our attention on the societal origins of intergroup hate, on the rise and lifespan of various ideologies and theologies, on the role of dehumanization, on how institutions are used, and how old battles are recycled symbolically to energize new ones. It also helps us understand the 'triggers', the events that combine the ingredients of hate into a combustible brew.

He also makes the important point that, in addition to recognising historical triggers (for example, events in the Middle East that may impact upon levels of anti-Semitism and Islamophobia; the collapse of the Soviet Union in relation to the plight of the Roma and Sinti in Eastern Europe; and 9/11 in relation to the demonisation of Muslims), history is also a discipline often abused to promote hatred. In particular Stern (2005) points to the issue of Holocaust denial, which is no longer just the preserve of neo-Nazis, and to the content of white supremacist, Afrocentric, and fundamentalist Islamist teachings, which respectively subvert the meaning and interpretation of historical events for nefarious purposes.

Similarly, for example, Frost (2008) argues that the hostility towards, and demonisation of, Islam today is part of a longer legacy of anti-Muslim sentiment that stretches back to Renaissance Europe during the Middle Ages. This historical legacy, she suggests, has been contemporarily shaped by a host of 'trigger' events (and the manner of the reporting of these) including the Salman Rushdie/*Satanic Verses* affair in 1988, the invasion and occupation of Iraq, the situation in the Middle East and the use of suicide bombers, 9/11 and the stereotyping of 'Islam' and 'terrorism', the Danish anti-Muslim cartoons where the responses of radical Islamists dominated the media and were held to be 'representative' of the response of all Muslims, and so on.

But history more generally also provides some useful insights into hate offending. For example, in her examination of hate crimes in the United States, Carolyn Petrosino (1999) provides an interesting comparative analysis of past and present hate crimes and, by comparing historical events with contemporary hate crimes, she finds a number of striking similarities. To summarise, Petrosino's work illustrates a number of important themes, many of which are just as applicable to the UK as they are to the US. First, that the hate crime 'problem' is not a distinctly modern phenomenon and dates back to at least the seventeenth century (and much further in the UK and elsewhere in the world). Second, that hate crime has deep historical roots. Third, that hate crime was at least as prevalent in the past as it is today. Fourth, that most hate crimes relate to racial prejudice. Fifth, that diversity is not generally well tolerated. Sixth, that offence, victim and perpetrator characteristics have remained broadly similar over the past 400 or more years. Seventh, perpetrators are predominantly white males. Eighth, that minority groups are used as scapegoats for perceived social problems suggesting a 'culture of hate' (see following section). And finally, in something of a historical contrast, that hate crimes are characteristically less violent today than in the past. History tells us, then, that there are many distinct parallels that can be drawn between past and present-day hate crimes over a range of indicators.

Cultural studies

Closely aligned to the role of history in understanding hate crimes are issues relating to culture. The limitations of individual-level analyses of hate as a motivation for criminal behaviour, coupled with the 'normality' of prejudice suggested by psychology means that, as Levin and Rabrenovic (2009: 42) have put it, hate hardly depends for its existence on individual pathology or abnormal psychology. This latter point is neatly illustrated by one of the most widely cited studies of hate offenders conducted by McDevitt et al. (2002) who concluded that the rarest type of hate offender (less than 1 per cent of their sample) was that which they labelled as 'mission'. Here the offender is totally committed to his or her hate and bigotry, and views the objects of their hate as an evil that must be removed from the world.

So, for Levin and Rabrenovic, and in line with McDevitt et al.'s findings (and indeed those of Iganski discussed in the previous chapter), hate is rarely about abnormal or 'extreme' psychology, and neither is it necessarily a form of deviance from the point of view of mainstream society. Rather, hate is, they suggest, a part of the culture of the society in which it exists and when conceived as such, it is part of the totality of an individual's learned and accumulated experiences, including beliefs, values, attitudes, roles, and material possessions, which intensifies as it incorporates widely shared myths and stereotypes. Indeed research by Chandler and Tsai (2001) suggests that public views of immigration, for example, are shaped more by perceived cultural threats than by economic concerns, political ideologies, or fear of crime (cited by Stacey et al., 2011).

Levin and Rabrenovic (2009) argue that cultural hate has, and does, play an important role in justifying hate crimes against those who differ from the offender in socially significant ways. This cultural element of hate, they argue, can be identified in a number of different ways, including the ability of a hatred towards a certain group to be broadly shared across a range of other groups, the spanning of hatred across generations, and the acquisition of common culturally-based hatreds from an early age. Indeed, Sibbitt's (1997) research examining racist offending in London suggested that the perpetrators of racist offences spanned all age ranges, from young children to old age pensioners, and involved both sexes who often acted in groups. Sibbitt suggests that the experiences of older people are therefore crucial in providing a framework that shapes the hate-based attitudes and behaviours of others within a family or a community, and that the attitudes of younger offenders are often derived from those of their elders.

For Levin and Rabrenovic (2009), then, cultural hate identifies appropriate targets, increases the impact of victimisation, and, crucially, maintains intergroup conflict in the face of efforts to reduce the incidence of hate crime. The study of culture and its component parts therefore seems to have much to offer in aiding our understanding of hate and hate offending.

Geography

Beyond looking at what is occurring across international borders (as is the case in the chapters contained within Part Two of this volume), geography as a discipline has much to contribute to our understanding of hate crime. As Stacey et al. (2011) point out, over the past decade or so hate crime research has focused increasingly on the social and ecological context in which hate crime occurs, often focusing on issues of demographic change within and between geographical locations to explain variations in rates of offending and victimisation from place to place (see for example, Green et al., 1998b; Grattet's 2009 research on 'defended neighbourhoods'; and Chakraborti and Garland's 2004 work on rural racism).

The influence of 'territory' in the commission of hate crimes has also been illustrated by McDevitt et al. (2002). In 25 per cent of the cases analysed, they categorised the motivation as being 'defensive' in its nature. In these cases, the offender committed hate offences against what he or she perceived to be outsiders or intruders in an attempt to defend or protect his or her 'territory'. Echoing the view discussed by Perry (in this volume) that hate crimes are 'message crimes', the researchers found that many 'defensive' offenders believed that minority groups had undeservedly moved into their neighbourhood and that their hate crimes served to send a message to the victim and other members of the victim's group that they are unwelcome and should relocate. McDevitt et al. suggest that defensive attacks are often associated with demographic shifts at a local level, particularly where neighbourhoods or communities begin to experience a transition from being dominated by one ethnic group towards a more diverse population. This mirrors the findings of Sibbitt (1997) who highlighted rapid demographic changes in the UK in the 1960s as a key factor in the development of community prejudice and resentment towards ethnic minority groups – a factor held by Sibbitt to underpin racist offences against these groups.

More recently, Poirier (2010: 1) has further highlighted the depth of the importance of geography to understanding hate:

> A key concept is that bias crimes have ubiety – that is, that they occur in specific physical places. Moreover, they are legible – that is, they express (or are understood to express) facts about the safety and security in particular places of people and things (buildings, graves, ritual objects, etc.) that are identified with specific social categories. In contrast to hate speech, which is solely discursive, bias crimes engage both physical place and discursive space. In so doing they constitute a claim to territory.

In addition to pointing out the need for a physical location for hate crimes to occur (which one might suggest seems rather obvious), Poirier (2010: 2) also makes reference to an issue that is of increasing importance in the digital age:

> In contrast to physical place, discursive space can be considered nullibietous – that is, having no physical dimension . . . In an age of media scrutiny, the dialogues that bias crimes engender can occur anywhere. They are potentially worldwide. But they are often at the same time local. Much depends on what various media notice.

Although he acknowledges that in reality there is always a physical substrate to discourse and communication, Poirier's interpretation of geography serves to emphasise that the 'geography of hate crimes' in the twenty-first century includes both public and private spaces, but also other 'spaces' that go beyond traditional interpretations of 'geographical location', but which can have implications for a variety of ideological, political and economic perspectives, each of which we shall touch upon in due course.

Economics

Inextricably linked to the general concern about the apparent increase in hate crimes and other targeted violence in some countries where the impact of the current world financial crisis has hit particularly hard, it seems, is the issue of *economics*. This is hardly surprising given the general importance attached by criminologists to the strength of a given economy as a predictor of crime levels.

Whilst we considered the theoretical issues of economic and social strain in the previous chapter when we discussed the contribution of sociology and criminology to our understanding of hate-motivated offending, for now an illustrative example that links the past to the contemporary will serve to demonstrate the potential significance of economics to the problem of hate crime. We noted an historical link between economic hardship and membership of far right groups, such as the Ku Klux Klan in the US in the early part of the twentieth century. Similarly, the popularity of the Nazi Party in Germany in the 1930s was fuelled in large part by high rates of unemployment and the resulting feelings of relative deprivation and loss of status amongst swathes of the German population (Falk and Zweimuller, 2005) that helped to make the political rhetoric of the Nazis attractive and palatable.

In this country, Sibbitt (1997) has presented historical evidence to suggest that in particular, the rapid demographic changes in the UK during the 1960s, coupled with the inability of some communities to cope with this change has played a part in the development of community prejudice. The situation is somewhat amplified, Sibbitt suggests, by factors such as unemployment, economic hardship and/or deprivation, competition for scarce resources (for example, housing), and a lack of community facilities (particularly in relation to youth and leisure facilities). Thus, economic strain, although not always the sole cause of hate crime, may instead provide a platform from which it can emerge. In this sense people will require a scapegoat upon which to blame the situation in which they find themselves. Here the problems experienced by certain communities are inevitably perceived as being not of their own making or a product of circumstance, but as the fault of certain groups who are seen as responsible for causing or intensifying these social problems.

In short, then, there is a prominent hypothesis that links economic hardship, often in the shape of unemployment, to far right extremism and associated offending behaviour, and to hate crime more generally. In empirically testing this hypothesis using data from Germany, Falk and Zweimuller (2005) concluded that there is indeed a significant positive relationship between unemployment and right-wing criminal activities. They also found that unemployment was closely related to both violent and non-violent crimes, although the association with non-violent crimes was much stronger. In this sense, then, unemployment, or the fear of unemployment, helps to explain negative attitudes towards foreigners who are perceived to take jobs from the majority population and who therefore fulfil the need for a scapegoat – a position that 'foreigners' have long occupied.

Notwithstanding the findings provided by Falk and Zweimuller, as an *holistic* account of hate crime occurrence, the value of economics as an explanatory framework remains a little hazy. For example, in their analysis of the impact of immigration on anti-Hispanic hate crime in the US, Stacey et al. (2011) note that research on the relationship between economic conditions and racially motivated hate crime has provided mixed results. In justifying this, Stacey et al. present findings from research by Lyons (2007), which found that racially motivated hate crime was more prevalent in the more affluent neighbourhoods in Chicago, and conversely from Green et al. (1998a), who found that changes in economic conditions in New York, specifically the unemployment rate, were not significantly related to monthly counts of hate crime incidents in the city. In their own research, Stacey et al. found little evidence to suggest that anti-Hispanic hate crimes were triggered by economic threat. Rather, their results appear to align more closely with the views of Levin and Rabrenovic (2009), above, by implying that the primary threat posed by immigration may be *cultural* rather than economic.

Theology and religious studies

Given the position and influence of religion in both historical and contemporary hate crime issues, the field of religious studies is of considerable importance in terms of both understanding and responding to the problem. Stern (2005) argues that religion encompasses the best and the worst of human interaction with hatred. On the one hand, he suggests, religion has set the norms for universal human dignity, whilst on the other it has served as a justification for some of the most barbaric carnage in human history, becoming most dangerous when theology and ideology are combined. Indeed, one doesn't have to look very far into the history books to find examples of the kind of events to which Stern alludes, but these concerns are not simply confined to those history books. They are of course reflected in contemporary anxieties over extremism, fundamentalism, radicalisation, and so-called 'radical Muslim clerics' and other 'preachers of hate'.

For Stern, though, the issue of religion goes beyond just theology and belief to include the role of religious institutions and the impact they can have on individuals, groups, their politics, and so on, as we shall see later. This is particularly important in terms of understanding not just how religion is used to promote hatred, but also how it can be empowered to help combat it, which Stern acknowledges involves institutional concerns as well as theological ones. Similarly, he highlights the role of government in relation to religion, noting that the way in which governments understand and deal with religious issues will be of increasing importance, particularly in Europe, where concerns over government responses to these challenges persist.

Two contemporary examples will suffice in illustrating such concerns. The first is the post 9/11 counter-terrorism strategy in the UK, which McGhee (2010) suggests has developed in the main at the expense of an appreciation of the wider contexts of radicalisation and extremism, and has arguably had the unintended consequence of further tingeing the general public's view of Muslim communities with fear and suspicion. The second is the French government's decision to outlaw the public wearing of Muslim headscarves and veils with the aim of achieving secularism – a move that seems to me to be likely to risk precisely the opposite effect to the one intended by further alienating Muslim communities.

Appleby (2012) has similar concerns both about the role of the media and a relative lack of sophistication in policy circles in conflating religion with fundamentalism, and fundamentalism with terrorism. In particular he expresses his concern at the lazy commonplace pairing of the words 'religious' and 'violence', which he argues gives the unfortunate impression of a natural connection between the two. In reviewing the extensive available literature on 'religion' and 'violence', Appleby (2012: 2–3) suggests that there are *three* lines of analysis that help us to understand when it is that religion becomes the motivation for violence, which he terms *strong religion, weak religion,* and *pathological religion*:

> the term Strong Religion [is used to] cluster works that see religion itself as the source of, or justification for, deadly violence, or that emphasize distinctive religious practices, beliefs, and ideologies as the decisive ingredients in violent movements that may also draw on nationalist, ethnic, or other motivations . . . Weak Religion, refers to works that present religion as a dependent variable in deadly violence, the primary source of which is secular in origin (e.g., enacted by the state or by nationalist or ethnic extremists). Finally, a network of scholars explores what might be termed Pathological Religion, namely, religious actors whose embrace of fundamentalist or extremist religious modes of behavior reflect symptoms of psycho-social deviance.

But despite this impressive attempt to simplify and categorise what Appleby refers to as an 'incoherent avalanche' of publications in this field, a general comprehensive theory of religious violence remains elusive.

Politics and political science

Of course, the two examples of government responses to religion, above, also bring us inside the discipline of *politics and political science*, which itself may contain all sorts of insights into the causes of hate crime. We have already considered in previous chapters the role of politics, and in particular identity politics, in bringing hate crime to the fore as a specific area of concern (see Mason-Bish, this volume). Here of course the goal of making hate a political issue was so that something might be done to challenge it and, ultimately, to 'make things better'. But what about where the opposite occurs? Once again history is littered with examples where hate, and hateful rhetoric and discourse, has been used for nefarious political purposes.

The various genocides that have taken place around the world offer some prime examples, but more recently (and perhaps a little more subtly) so do the issues raised in relation to the political stances taken in some European countries in relation to the Roma and Sinti, and 'new migrant' communities respectively (see Hall, 2013).

Another contemporary example might include Iran's anti-Israeli foreign policy (although there is some debate about whether or not Iran's former President Ahmadinejad has explicitly called for 'Israel to be wiped off the map' – see Hasan, 2012, for an interesting discussion of the political discourse in this regard). Nevertheless, Stern (2005) states that of all the anti-Semitic discourses, political anti-Zionism (the belief that Jews do not have the right to self-determination in a land of their own) is the least understood and the most resurgent in recent years. Stern is also critical of, for example, Israel's support for Hamas from the late 1970s to counter the Palestine Liberation Organization (PLO), and the US government's support for Islamist groups in Afghanistan to fight the old Soviet Union towards the end of the Cold War – moves that may have served short-term political goals, but have had less than desirable longer-term implications.

Closer to home, and linked to domestic rather than international politics, apparent recent increases in the occurrence of disability hate crime are, in part, being attributed to what is perceived to be irresponsible political rhetoric from the British government in relation to statements concerning the numbers of people claiming incapacity benefit who are 'faking' disabilities (Riley-Smith, 2012). Research by ComRes (2012) on behalf of the disability charity Scope, for example, found that disabled people identified the small number of people falsely claiming disability benefits *and* the way the actions of this minority of claimants are reported as primary causes of public hostility. Scope concluded that it was impossible to ignore that the results came at the same time as the Government continued to focus the welfare debate on a few benefit 'scroungers' as part of efforts to make the case for more radical reform to the welfare system.

Similarly, a poll on behalf of the Trades Union Congress in the UK in 2013 suggested that 'prejudice and ignorance' was being fuelled by 'myths' spread by politicians in relation to the welfare system. The poll of 1,800 people found that four out of ten people believed that the benefits system is too generous whilst three in five believed that the system has created a culture of dependency. The poll also found that those who know *least* about the realities of the system were the *most* hostile towards benefits claimants, with more than half of such respondents declaring it too generous. Conversely, only one in three of those 'in possession of the facts' thought similarly (Grice, 2013). In other words, it seems that in this instance people's perceptions of the welfare system, and levels of hostility towards those that claim benefits, differ markedly depending upon whether they are in possession of none, some, or all of the facts. Clearly, then, the disciplines of politics and political science have a contribution to make to our understanding of hate crime, both on the international and the domestic stage.

Ideology

Many of the disparate issues we have discussed are often brought together in the form of ideological beliefs that are then used as justifications for hate and hate offending, most notably by what we might call 'hate groups'. As such, it is worth briefly drawing together a number of the points considered so far in this chapter to illustrate the significance of ideology to our field of study.

In considering contemporary hate groups in the United States, Barbara Perry (2001), Phyllis Gerstenfeld (2004) and others have identified a number of common core ideological claims to superiority that are used by hate groups to 'justify' their beliefs and actions. In many cases these are just as applicable to hate groups here in the UK and elsewhere in the world. Whilst a detailed examination of these is beyond the scope of this chapter (readers are advised to see Perry, 2001; Gerstenfeld, 2004) it is nevertheless important to briefly consider these ideologies because they allow us to gain an insight into the motivations and belief systems that serve to justify and legitimise the behaviour and actions of the members of such groups.

Gerstenfeld suggests that arguably the most important of these ideologies relates to *power*. Historically, hate groups have tended to form and grow in popularity at times where the dominant group feel somehow threatened. Indeed the history of the Ku Klux Klan is characterised by such peaks and troughs in popularity when faced with perceived threats to white dominance. The notion of power, then, is particularly central to White Supremacist discourse and the belief that power is rightfully theirs is based largely on the misguided premise that the white race is biologically superior to all other races. Specifically, Gerstenfeld suggests that such groups believe that the power of the white race is being stolen, for example, by blacks through their criminal behaviour; by mass immigration and the taking of jobs and the 'swamping' of the white population; by a Jewish conspiracy to control government and the media; and by non-whites race-mixing and thereby 'polluting' and 'weakening' the 'pure' Aryan gene pool.

The second ideology that Gerstenfeld outlines is *racial separatism*. She suggests that most hate groups advocate either complete or at least partial racial separatism, with many members believing that their perceived superiority gives them the right to define what constitutes a natural citizen of their country and that entry into that country can only happen on their terms. Indeed this focus on racial separatism is not restricted to white supremacists, as non-white organisations are known to advocate similarly.

The third ideology relates to *religion*. Gerstenfeld suggests that whilst not all hate groups have a religious basis, for many it is the key to their belief system. For white supremacists the most important (but not always exclusive) religious sect is that of *Christian Identity*. Gerstenfeld points out that the teachings of Christian Identity are attractive to white supremacists because they provide these groups with a 'theological seal of approval'. The sect teaches that Aryans are God's chosen people and that non-whites are sub-human, and that white people are descendents of Adam, whilst Jews are descendents of Satan. These 'facts' provide a rationale for racist views, particularly given that Christian Identity teaches that Adam's descendents are engaged in an apocalyptic struggle against the descendents of Satan. Gerstenfeld suggests that in this sense white supremacists believe that they are literally doing 'God's work'.

Two other key ideologies that Gerstenfeld and others have identified first concern a common antipathy for certain groups, particularly Jews who are frequently perceived to be descendants of the devil and who are also involved in a conspiracy to take over the world, and non-whites who are perceived to be a wholly inferior race, and second, a common antipathy for certain beliefs and actions, in particular abortion, communism, feminism and political liberalism (Gerstenfeld, 2004).

Conclusion

This chapter has briefly considered some of the explanations of 'hate' and 'hate crime' proffered by some of the branches of the wider social sciences. As was the case in the previous chapter, there are no complete, holistic explanations of hate crime occurrence to be found within this chapter either. This should come as little surprise. The lack of conceptual consensus, and the seemingly expansive nature of hate crime can, as Chakraborti (2010; this volume) rightly points out, overshadow the efforts of scholarship to be constructive in providing comprehensive and purposeful answers to a whole raft of questions about the subject. As such, our understanding of many aspects of hate crime, including explanations of causation, necessarily remains underdeveloped, and in some cases, substantially incomplete.

That said, however, the apparent increasing engagement of the social sciences with the problem of hate crime, both in those branches that you would perhaps expect to have an interest (such as psychology, sociology and criminology) and encouragingly those that are arguably less obviously related (such as geography, cultural studies and political science) have produced what Iganski (2008) and Chakraborti (2010) have both described as a 'welcome surge' in scholarly interest in our subject area. This 'welcome surge' is producing a 'welcome flurry' of research and other scholarly activity, bringing with it 'an astounding diversity of methodologies ... to more fully document and comprehend the problem' (Perry, 2010: 19). As such, in my view there are reasons to be optimistic about slowly edging closer to finding the answers to the *why?* question.

Note

1 Extracts of this chapter have previously been published in Hall, N. (2013) *Hate Crime* (Second Edition). Abingdon: Routledge.

References

Allport, G. W. (1954) *The Nature of Prejudice*. Massachusetts: Addison-Wesley Publishing Co.
Appleby, R. S. (2012) Religious violence: the strong, the weak, and the pathological. *Practical Matters*, 5: 1–25.
Bandura, A. (1977) *Social Learning Theory*. Englewood Cliffs, NJ: Prentice Hall.
Chakraborti, N. (2010) (ed.) *Hate Crime: Concepts, Policy, Future Directions*. Cullompton: Willan Publishing.
Chakraborti, N. and Garland, J. (eds) (2004) *Rural Racism*. Cullompton: Willan Publishing.
Chandler, C. R. and Tsai, Y.-M. (2001) Social factors influencing immigration attitudes: an analysis of data from the General Social Survey. *Social Science Journal*, 38: 177–88.
ComRes (2012) Scope Disability Survey. Accessed 31 October 2012 from www.comres.co.uk/poll/712/scope-disability-survey.htm.
Falk, A. and Zweimuller, J. (2005) Unemployment and Right-Wing Extremist Crime. IZA Discussion Paper, series no. 1540. Bonn: IZA.
Frost, D. (2008) Islamophobia: examining causal links between the media and 'race hate' from 'below'. *International Journal of Sociology and Social Policy*, 28 (11): 564–78.
Gaylin, W. (2003) *Hatred: the psychological descent into violence*. New York: Public Affairs.
Gerstenfeld, P. B. (2004) *Hate Crimes: Causes, Controls and Controversies*. Thousand Oaks, CA: Sage.
Grattet, R. (2009) The urban ecology of bias crime: a study of disorganized and defended neighborhoods. *Social Problems*, 5: 132–50.
Green, D. P., Glaser, J. and Rich, A. (1998a) From lynching to gay bashing: The elusive connection between economic conditions and hate crime. *Journal of Personality and Social Psychology*, 74: 82–92.
Green, D. P., Strolovitch, D. Z. and Wong, J. S. (1998b) Defended neighborhoods, integration, and racially motivated crime. *American Journal of Sociology* 104 (2): 372–403.
Green, D. P., McFalls, L. H. and Smith, J. K. (2003) Hate Crime: An Emergent Research Agenda. In B. Perry, (ed) *Hate and Bias Crime: A Reader*. New York: Routledge.
Grice, A. (2013) Voters 'brainwashed by Tory welfare myths', shows new poll. *The Independent*, 4 January.
Hall, N. (2013) *Hate Crime* (Second Edition). Abingdon: Routledge.
Hasan, M. (2012) Does Ahmadinejad really want to 'wipe Israel off the map'? *New Statesman*. 8 March.
Iganski, P. (2008) *Hate Crime and the City*. Bristol: Policy Press.

Levin, J. and Rabrenovic, G. (2009) Hate as Cultural Justification for Violence. In B. Perry (ed.) *Hate Crimes* (vol. 1). Westport: Praeger.

Lyons, C. J. (2007) Community (dis)organization and racially motivated crime. *American Journal of Sociology*, 113: 815–63.

McDevitt, J., Levin, J. and Bennett, S. (2002) Hate crime offenders: an expanded typology. *Journal of Social Issues*, 58 (2): 303–17.

McGhee, D. (2010) From hate to 'prevent': community safety and counter-terrorism. In N. Chakraborti (ed.) *Hate Crime: Concepts, Policy, Future Directions*. Abingdon: Routledge.

Perry, B. (2001) *In the Name of Hate: Understanding Hate Crimes*. New York: Routledge.

Perry, B. (ed.) (2003) *Hate and Bias Crime: A Reader*. Abingdon: Routledge.

Perry, B. (2009) The Sociology of Hate: Theoretical Approaches. In B. Perry (ed.) *Hate Crimes* (Vol. 1). Westport: Praeger.

Perry, B. (2010) The More Things Change ... post 9/11 Trends in Hate Crime Scholarship. In N. Chakraborti (ed.) *Hate Crime: Concepts, Policy, Future Directions*. Abingdon: Routledge.

Petrosino, C. (1999) Connecting the past to the future: hate crime in America. *Journal of Contemporary Criminal Justice*, 5 (1): 22–47.

Poirier, M. R. (2010) The Multiscalar Geography of Hate Crimes. Seton Hall Public Law Research Paper No. 1654350.

Riley-Smith, B. (2012) Disability hate crime: is 'benefit scrounger' abuse to blame? *The Guardian*, 14 August.

Sherif, M. and Sherif, C. W. (1953) *Groups in Harmony and Tension: An Integration of Studies on Inter-group Relations*. New York: Harper.

Sibbitt, R. (1997) The Perpetrators of Racial Harassment and Racial Violence. Home Office Research Study No. 176. London: Home Office.

Stacey, M., Carbone-Lopez, K. and Rosenfeld, R. (2011) Demographic change and ethnically motivated crime: the impact of immigration on anti-Hispanic hate crime in the United States. *Journal of Contemporary Criminal Justice*, 27 (3): 278–98. doi: 10.1177/1043986211412560.

Stangor, C. (ed.) (2000) *Stereotypes and Prejudice*. Philadelphia: Psychology Press.

Stern, K. (2005) *Hate Matters: The Need for an Interdisciplinary Field of Hate Studies*. New York: American Jewish Committee.

Tajfel, H. and Turner, J. C. (1979) An Integrative Theory of Intergroup Conflict. In W. G. Austin and S. Worchel (eds) *The Social Psychology of Intergroup Relations*. Monterey: CA: Brooks/Cole, pp. 33–47.

2
The international geography of hate

8

Hate crime in Europe

Michael Whine

The term 'hate crime' is a relatively recent addition to the international lexicon, originating in the USA but coming into general use comparatively recently. However, recognition of the harm caused by hate crime had already begun to preoccupy governments in the 1990s.

In 1990, the 35 participating states of the Conference on Security and Cooperation in Europe (CSCE) had pledged to take:

> effective measures to provide protection against any acts that constitute incitement to violence against people or groups based on national, racial and ethnic hatred, anti-Semitism, xenophobia and discrimination against anyone as well as persecution on religious and ideological grounds. In this context, they recognise the particular problems of Roma (gypsies). They declare their firm intention to intensify the efforts to combat these phenomena in all their forms and therefore will take effective measures ... to provide protection against any acts that constitute incitement to violence against persons or groups based on national, racial, ethnic or religious discrimination, hostility or hatred, including anti-semitism.[1]

In 1991, the Organisation for Security and Co-operation in Europe (OSCE), which succeeded the CSCE, expressed participating states' concerns over crimes based on prejudice, discrimination, hostility or hatred, and pledged to take action against them.[2] Their decision to take action was reaffirmed at the OSCE 2003 Ministerial Council Meeting, when the term 'hate crime' was first used. The participating states made a commitment "to consider enacting or strengthening, where appropriate, legislation that prohibits discrimination based on, or incitement to hate crimes".[3]

In 2006, the OSCE Ministerial Council decided inter alia to promote capacity-building among law enforcement authorities through training and the development of guidelines on effective ways to respond to bias-motivated crime, encouragement of reporting by hate crime victims, and by tasking its Office for Democratic Institutions and Human Rights (ODIHR) to serve as a collection point for information and statistics on hate crimes and relevant information, to make this information publicly available, and to strengthen its early warning function to identify, report and raise awareness of hate crime.[4] Subsequently, the OSCE

Ministerial Council adopted a decision in 2009 exclusively devoted to combating hate crime.[5]

It should be noted that the European Court of Human Rights (ECHR) had ruled some years earlier that states are obliged to 'unmask' the motivation behind racist crimes or crimes committed because of the religious belief of the victim, where relevant. It further observed that a criminal justice system that overlooks the bias motivation behind a crime violates Article 14 of the European Convention on Human Rights.[6]

As a consequence of governments' concerns, the international governmental organisations (IGOs) have agreed a broad range of commitments which focus their efforts, and commit their member states to confronting the problem, including legislative reviews, collection of data, criminal justice agency training programmes, assistance to civil society organisations (CSOs) and vitally, reviewing states' progress in combating the problem on a regular basis.

IGO efforts reviewed in this chapter include those undertaken by the Council of Europe and its monitoring agency, the European Commission against Racism and Intolerance (ECRI), the European Union Agency for Fundamental Rights (FRA), and the ODIHR.

The work of the Committee on the Elimination of Racial Discrimination, which monitors the United Nations International Convention on the Elimination of All Forms of Racial Discrimination, is not discussed as its focus is not hate crime but racial discrimination, and because it has no institutionalised mechanisms for combating hate crime.[7]

International commitments and oversight mechanisms

Three substantive agreements aimed at combating hate crime have been initiated by the European Union (EU). The first, contained within Article 21 of the Charter of Fundamental Rights of the EU, recognises the right to be free from discrimination, including on the basis of race, ethnic or social origin, religion or belief, political or any other opinion.[8] Article 19 of the Treaty on the Functioning of the European Union grants the EU powers to combat discrimination, and the Racial Equality Directive provides comprehensive protection against direct and indirect discrimination, as well as harassment, on the grounds of race or ethnicity in several areas including employment and training, education and social protection.[9]

The 2005 Warsaw Declaration binds EU Member States to "greater complementarity between European Union and Council of Europe legal texts", but in reality policy responses to hate crime can differ widely.[10] For this reason, Member States sought to agree a common approach and minimum standards, and it was with the 2008 Council Framework Decision on combating certain forms and expressions of racism and xenophobia by means of criminal law that the EU finally enacted legislation against hate crime. The Framework Decision requires member states to criminalise public incitement to violence or hatred against religious, racial ethnic and other groups, and publicly condoning, denying or grossly trivialising genocide, crimes against humanity and war crimes. The purpose was designed to approximate Member States' domestic criminal laws, and to more effectively promote full and effective judicial cooperation. Member States were given two years to comply, and during 2013 a review of their domestic legislation was carried out by FRA on behalf of the Council, the Commission and the European Parliament.[11]

A requirement for any concerted effort to combat hate crime was a regional overview, and the first Europe-wide survey of hate crime was undertaken in April 2005 by the European Union Monitoring Centre on Racism and Xenophobia (EUMC), the predecessor to FRA. Their report presented the information gathered from 2001 up to part of 2004 by the EUMC RAXEN network of national focal points.[12]

The first part of the report sought to define 'race', 'ethnicity' and 'racism', present an overview of legal definitions, and offered critical commentary on attempts to measure the extent and nature of racist violence, particularly as a comparative cross-national undertaking, as well as the effectiveness of official and alternative data collection mechanisms.[13] In the second part, the EUMC explored the available data from each of the (then) 15 Member States. The third part presented a comparative review, noting the limitations of trying to compare the sparse and different data sets, an examination of the cultural and criminological context in which racist violence occurs, and finally an assessment of states' responses.[14]

In summary, the EUMC found that no two states had data that was strictly comparable; that three states had no public official data at all; one state released only limited figures; three states concentrated their data collection on 'discriminatory offences' alone; two states focused their attention on the activities of (right wing) extremists only; and that only four, Finland, France, Ireland and the UK, had comprehensive data collection mechanisms.[15]

The discrepancies in the hate crime data that was collected were therefore apparent. Official data under-recorded hate crime to a substantial degree, either because official recording systems did not exist, or because they were not thorough or comprehensive enough. Since then data collection systems have improved. The FRA annual report in 2011 acknowledged that "some EU Members States are taking steps to improve data collection on racist crime", but that they still have a long way to go as "many Member States still do not have systematic mechanisms of data collection in place to record the incidence of racist crime at the national level". Consequently, "it therefore remains difficult to quantify the prevalence of racist crime in the EU or to compare trends over time among Member States".[16] Some improvements were noted in the 2012 report, and that a number of states had changed and enhanced their data collection systems.[17] The report further noted that one state had no data available (Croatia, the latest accession state); 12 states had limited data collection systems; 11 states had good systems and only four, Finland, Netherlands, Sweden and the UK, had comprehensive systems.[18]

FRA noted in another report published in 2012 that the situation was not improving, despite EU Member States' best efforts and commitments to counter discrimination and intolerance, including hate crime. It called for legislation at the EU and national level that would oblige Member States to collect and publish data, that states should encourage confidence among victims to report hate crime, and that law enforcement agencies should be attentive to bias motivation when investigating and prosecuting crime. It further recommended enhanced penalties for hate crime in order to underline their seriousness, and that courts should address these bias motivations publicly.[19]

In order to circumvent under-recording by states, and to fill in the gaps, FRA instituted a series of Europe-wide surveys on experiences of criminal victimisation. The first, the European Union Minorities and Discrimination Survey (EU-MIDIS), reported its findings in 2009. Among the questions asked were a series about respondents' experiences of being a victim of crime in five areas (theft of or from a vehicle, burglary or attempted burglary, theft of personal property not involving force or threat, assault, and threat and harassment of a serious nature). The focus of the survey was on easily identifiable minorities such as Roma and African migrants.[20]

In 2008, FRA commissioned a further survey, the results of which were published in 2012. Unlike the first, which examined experiences in the five years preceding the survey, the second examined experiences in the twelve months preceding the poll, and requested detailed information including whether racially or religiously offensive language was used, whether the matter was reported to the police, and the reasons why no report was made to the police in cases of negative responses.[21]

At the time of writing, there are three other FRA surveys at different stages of implementation, which cover less identifiable minorities. They are on experiences and perceptions of antisemitism among Jewish communities in nine selected European states, discrimination against and victimisation of lesbian, gay, bisexual and transgender (LGBT) persons, and violence against women. Taken together, it is expected that the surveys will provide a more complete picture of hate crime and criminal victimisation among the most populous minority groups.[22]

The Organisation for Security and Cooperation in Europe

ODIHR hate crime reports differ from those of FRA as they also include larger quantities of data submitted by partner organisations, IGOs and non-governmental organisations (NGOs). OSCE commitments to combating hate crime were laid down by the 2006 Ministerial Council meeting, and focused on the organisation's role in combating hate crime. These tasked ODIHR to serve as a collection point for information and statistics on hate crimes and relevant legislation, to make this information publicly available through its Tolerance and Non Discrimination Information System (TANDIS), strengthen its early warning function to identify, report and raise awareness of hate-motivated incidents and trends, provide recommendations and assistance to participating states and to report annually on challenges and responses to hate-motivated incidents in the OSCE region.[23]

This mandate was subsequently developed and strengthened by the Ministerial Council in 2009, where participating states committed to:

- Enact, where appropriate, specific tailored legislation to combat hate crimes, providing for effective penalties that take into account the gravity of such crimes;
- Take appropriate measures to encourage victims to report hate crime, recognising that under-reporting of hate crimes prevents states from devising effective policies. In this regard, explore, as complementary measures, methods for facilitating, the contribution of civil society to combat hate crimes;
- In co-operation with relevant actors, explore ways to provide victims of hate crimes with access to counselling, legal and consular assistance as well as effective access to justice;
- Introduce or further develop professional training and capacity building activities for law enforcement, prosecution and judicial officials dealing with hate crimes;
- Consider drawing on resources developed by the ODIHR in the area of education, training and awareness-raising to ensure a comprehensive approach to the tackling of hate crimes.[24]

Additionally, the ODIHR recognised specific types of hate crime including those against Jews, Muslims, Roma and Sinti and the LGBT communities. These categories have been recognised in Ministerial Council decisions, and latterly by the appointment of Special Representatives of the Chairman in Office whose tasks are to focus participating states' attention on the threats encountered by these communities.[25]

ODIHR too complains at the paucity of data. In 2011, it stated that the data submitted by participating states were of higher quality and more relevant than in previous years, but that there continued to be disparities which presented an obstacle to making sound comparative analyses. They added that even where statistics existed they were not always disaggregated according to bias motivation, type of crime or outcome of prosecution, and that if submissions were more uniform it would be possible to undertake a more meaningful comparative analysis. In fact at the time the report was finalised only 30 out of 56 states (now 57 with the accession of Macedonia) had completed their questionnaires.[26]

The approach taken by ODIHR is more multi-faceted than that of FRA, and includes strengthening the role of law enforcement, providing tolerance education, protection of and outreach to communities affected by hate crime, prevention of discrimination and improving access to justice and social services for victims.

ODIHR gathers data for its annual hate crime report through a questionnaire sent to states' national point of contacts on hate crime (NPCs – usually a designated official within a state's criminal justice agencies or interior ministry), which contains questions about data collection methods, legislation, reported hate crime and policies and initiatives. NPCs in turn respond by completing a questionnaire on a restricted access section on the TANDIS website, where information provided in previous submissions can also be accessed.[27] NGOs are also invited to submit reports on hate crime according to ODIHR requirements, to fill the gaps left by NPC reports and to add context. Other IGOs including the United Nations, EU agencies, and others are also consulted.

The European Commission Against Racism and Intolerance (ECRI)

ECRI adopts yet another approach to those of FRA and ODIHR, relying on five-yearly country reports. These examine progress in countering racism, racial discrimination, xenophobia, antisemitism and intolerance, and are compiled by ECRI staff and independent expert monitors who visit states to question officials and representatives of relevant NGOs. In addition, thematic reports provide general policy recommendations for Member States that are intended to serve as guidelines for policy makers dealing with racism and intolerance, and advice on assisting civil society with information and communication requirements. ECRI does not therefore directly focus on hate crime, but rather on the political and legal environment that gives rise to hate crime, and on states' adoption and use of legislation to counter racism.[28]

The latest ECRI annual report notes that the deteriorating economic crisis has contributed to a rise in racism and intolerance and that the resulting tension sometimes leads to racist violence.[29] It adds that advocacy of national, racial and religious hatred constitute incitement to discrimination, hostility and violence, and that these have become "a major problem in Europe today". It especially notes the role of the internet in "attracting likeminded people who encourage/reinforce each other's prejudices".[30]

ECRI country reports particularly highlight "instances of small-scale but persistent attacks targeting historical minorities, such as the desecration of cemeteries and widespread racist graffiti", and ECRI advises states' authorities "not to neglect these phenomena but to react promptly, in order, inter alia, to avoid escalation".[31]

The obstacles to combating hate crime

The obstacles to combating hate crime effectively are therefore apparent. The first of these is that the lack of data provided by states hinders any meaningful analysis. This in turn frustrates the search for solutions. The most recent ODIHR report therefore notes that:

> The full extent of hate crimes in the OSCE region continues to be obscured by a lack of adequate or reliable data. Although data collection by governments improved in 2011, it

is clear from the information provided to ODIHR that significant gaps in data collection remain a major obstacle to understanding the prevalence and nature of hate crimes within most participating States and across the OSCE as a region.[32]

Analysis of victim and perpetrator groups is also frustrated by the failure of many states to disaggregate their data. Only the four states noted above do so according to the ODIHR requirements. Consequently the three IGOs who focus on hate crime increasingly encourage CSOs to supplement the information provided by governments. However, data supplied by them may sometimes be derived from media reporting and will consequently fall below criminal justice standards. It may also be based on differing definitions or imprecise bias indicators. Although the quality of information supplied by civil society and victims groups adds vital context to government data it is often not possible to compare official and non-official information in any accurate manner.

The IGOs have therefore sought to encourage civil society to improve the quality of the data that it can provide. Among the recent projects to educate and empower CSOs was the EC-funded *Facing Facts* programme, initiated and managed by four CSOs (three Jewish and one representing the LGBT community) to train others over two years to collect data on hate crime against minority communities.[33]

The *Facing Facts* project began with a survey of CSO efforts to gather hate crime, and proceeded by building and publishing two manuals: the first on methods of data collection, categorisation, verification and reporting on hate crime; the second, a manual to enable trainers to train others. The first manual also listed states' obligations and demonstrated how the data collected can be used for advocacy purposes and to empower minority communities. At all stages during the process, ODIHR, EC and FRA officials were consulted and involved in the drafting process in order to ensure that the final publications met the needs of both the IGOs and civil society.

A second ODIHR project has brought together OSCE participating states' NPCs with representatives of victims groups and other civil society bodies in order to exchange best practices. Regular meetings have also taken place between the Personal Representatives of the OSCE Chairman in Office and CSOs, in order to exchange information.[34]

Two recently published FRA reports, *Making hate crime visible in the European Union: acknowledging victims' rights* and *EU-MIDIS Data in Focus: minorities as victims of crime* address these linked issues. The first highlights the substantial gaps in national data collection methods, leading to a distorted picture of the scale of hate crime; the second reveals the extent to which minority groups perceive themselves to be victims of racially motivated crime.[35]

One important consideration, which has emerged after several years of publishing data, is that high levels of recorded hate crime do not necessarily reflect the accurate measurement of hate crime in a country. As the ODIHR guide to hate crime laws notes, "countries with effective data collection mechanisms usually show higher levels of hate crimes than countries that do not have effective data collection systems".[36]

A second obstacle to combating hate crime is the lack of comparability between different data sets compiled by states parties. Statistics may be collected by the police, prosecutors, justice or interior ministries, statistical offices or other agencies, and may contain recorded hate crimes, criminal prosecutions and convictions. They may also contain reports of hate incidents that fall below the criminal threshold. Thus, while the quality and quantity of information collected by states parties is improving, clear comparisons are obscured because they publish different data sets, and like for like comparisons are therefore not easily made.

This leads directly to consideration of a third obstacle, which is that unless states adopt a holistic approach to prosecuting hate crime they will fail to combat the problem effectively. Not only must police officers be trained to recognise hate crime, in order to investigate properly, but prosecutors, and the judiciary, must also be trained to use the laws their governments have passed. Only in this fashion will states' criminal justice agencies send out the message that hate crime damages social cohesion.

ODIHR has addressed this obstacle by publishing two guidebooks for use by government officials and civil society. *Preventing and responding to hate crime* was prepared by ODIHR staff with help from a small number of expert NGOs, and provides a guide to essential concepts, strategies, and a list of useful resources.[37] *Hate Crime Laws – A Practical Guide* provides benchmarks for drafting hate crime legislation, highlighting good practices and risks without being prescriptive, in recognition of the fact that hate crime is specific to its social context. The *Guide* sets out the major questions to be addressed by legislators, provides examples of drafting choices made by Member States, comments on the implications of different approaches and provides details of additional resources.[38]

A third guide, for hate crime prosecutors, has been prepared with the assistance of the Hague-based International Association of Prosecutors but has not yet been published at the time of writing. This guide provides elements of the background and characteristics of hate crime that prosecutors need to consider as well as the jurisprudential framework. It also provides some practical considerations for lawyers engaged in prosecuting a hate crime.[39]

A fourth set of obstacles to effective efforts is that some states lack the capacity to implement the international agreements they have entered into. The 57 participating states of the OSCE, and the overlapping member states within the EU have agreed (and in the case of the EU are legally required) to gather data on hate crime, and publish the data in disaggregated form in order that the different strands of hate crime can be identified. However, as the records show, few states do so, or do so to the agreed standards. Their failures may be due to capacity, or they may not yet have provided the required legal mandate, or they may be precluded by pre-existing laws from doing so. The collection of data does require an efficient, centralised and systematic approach. It may also require the computerisation of records, and a working interface between different sets of records (for example, police, prosecution and the courts).

It was, in part, to address this need that the ODIHR Law Enforcement Officers Programme (LEOP) training for police officers was amended to take greater account of the legislative background, and a requirement for effective interaction with other criminal justice agencies in the Training Against Hate Crimes for Law Enforcement (TAHCLE) programme. Its programme description notes that:

> This manual describes the programme and provides information for governments interested in participating. This manual sets out how the TAHCLE programme works and explains how it can assist participating States in meeting their commitments. TAHCLE is the substantially revised and updated successor to the Law Enforcement Officer Programme, developed by ODIHR in 2004.[40]

It must be noted that states' capacities to upgrade and modernise their systems are inevitably compromised by the current economic climate, even assuming that they have the political will to do so. Combating hate crime is therefore often accorded a low priority, especially when it is in competition with other pressing issues.

The fifth obstacle is that victims are reluctant to report hate crime. Victims' surveys note the wide scale and prevalence of hate crimes, yet official data fails to illustrate this adequately:

> Victims and witnesses of hate crimes are reluctant to report them, whether to law enforcement agencies, the criminal justice system, non-governmental organisations or victim support groups. As a result, victims of crime are often unable or unwilling to seek redress against perpetrators, with many crimes remaining unreported, unprosecuted and, therefore invisible. In such cases, the rights of victims of crime may not be fully respected or protected and EU Member States may not be upholding the obligations they have towards victims of crime.[41]

The danger posed to communal cohesion is therefore clearly recognised by the IGOs and their member states, but states' efforts to deal with the threat is often characterised by an inconsistent approach, lack of capacity and the political will to combat a problem that can easily develop into broader unrest, and escalate into wider social conflict. The Council of Europe Commissioner for Human Rights put it succinctly:

> Political rhetoric on human rights in Europe is different from daily reality. Almost every politician is on record as favouring the protection of freedom and justice. Standards on human rights have been agreed at European and international level; many have been integrated into national law; but they are not consistently enforced. There is an implementation gap.[42]

Notes

1 Document of the Copenhagen Meeting of the Conference on the Human Dimension of the CSCE, paras. 40–1, Copenhagen, 29 June 1990, www.osce.org/odihr/elections/14304, downloaded 17 May 2013.
2 Document of the Moscow Meeting of the Conference on the Human Dimension of the CSCE, p. 29, Moscow, 3 October 1991, www.osce.org/odihr/elections/1432, downloaded 17 May 2013.
3 Decision No.4/03, Tolerance and Non-Discrimination, Eleventh Meeting of the Ministerial Council, Maastricht, 1–2 December 2003, www.osce.org/mc/40533, downloaded 17 May 2013.
4 Decision No.13/06, Combating Intolerance and Discrimination and Promoting Mutual Respect and Understanding, 5 December 2006, www.osce.org/mc/23114, downloaded 24 June 2013.
5 Decision No.9/09, Combating Hate Crimes, Ministerial Council, OSCE Athens, 2 December 2009, www.osce.org/cio/40695, downloaded January 2010.
6 Making hate crime visible in the European Union: acknowledging victims' rights, p. 7, European Union Agency for Fundamental Rights, Publications Office of the European Union, Luxembourg, 2012.
7 Committee on the Elimination of Racial Discrimination, Office of the United Nations High Commissioner for Human Rights, Geneva, www2.ohchr.org/english/bodies/cerd, downloaded 27 December 2012.
  See also Annual Report on ECRI's Activities, 2011, Council of Europe, Strasbourg, May 2012.
8 Charter of Fundamental Rights of the European Union, Official Journal of the European Communities, 18 December 2000, http://eur-lex.europe.eu/LexUriServ/LexUriServ.do?uri=OJ:2010, downloaded 24 June 2013.
9 Consolidated Version of the Treaty on the Functioning of the European Union, C83/47, 30 February 2010, http://eur-lex.europa.eu/LexUriServ/LexUriServ.do?uri=OJ:C:2010, downloaded 24 June 2013.
  Council Directive 2000/43/EC of 29 June 2000 implementing the principle of equal treatment between persons irrespective of racial or ethnic origin, Official Journal L 80, 19/07/2000 P.0022-0026,

http://eur-lex.europa.eu/LexUriServ/LexUriServ.do?uri=CELEX:32000L00:en:HT downloaded 24 June 2013.
10. Warsaw Declaration, Council of Europe, para 10, www.coe.int/t/dcr/summit/20050517_decl_varsovie_en.asp, downloaded 24 June 2013.
11. Council Framework Decision on combating certain forms and expressions of racism and xenophobia by means of criminal law, Official Journal of the European Union, 2008/913/JHA, 28 November 2008.
12. Racist Violence in 15 EU Member States: A Comparative Overview from the RAXEN National Focal Points Reports 2001–2004, Summary Report, European Monitoring Centre on Racism and Xenophobia (EUMC), Vienna, April 2005.
13. ibid., p. 8.
14. ibid., p. 9.
15. ibid., pp. 9–10.
16. Fundamental Rights: challenges and achievements in 2011, p. 155, EUMC, Vienna, 2012.
17. Fundamental Rights: challenges and achievements in 2012, p. 179, FRA, Vienna, 2013.
18. ibid., p. 188.
19. Making hate crime visible in the European Union: acknowledging victims' rights, p. 11, FRA, Vienna, 2012.
20. EU-MIDIS at a glance, Introduction to the FRA's EU-wide discrimination survey, European Union Agency for Fundamental Rights, Vienna, 2009.
21. Data in Focus Report – Minorities as Victims of Crime, 06, European Union Minorities and Discrimination Survey, European Union Agency for Fundamental Rights, Vienna, 2012.
22. FRA survey on gender-based violence against women, http://fra.europa.eu/en/project/2012/fra-survey-gender-based-violence-against-women, downloaded 25 June 2013.
European Union lesbian, gay, bisexual and transgender survey, FRA, Vienna, 2012.
FRA survey of Jewish people's experiences and perceptions of antisemitism, http://fra.europa.eu/sites/default/files/fra-uploads/2029-FRA-2012-factsheet-jewish-population-survey_eEN.pdf
23. Decision No.13/06, Combating Intolerance and Discrimination and Promoting Mutual Respect and Understanding, Ministerial Council, MC.DEC/13/06, OSCE, 5 December 2006.
24. Decision No.9/09, Combating Hate Crimes, Ministerial Council, MC.DEC/9/09, OSCE, 2 December 2009.
25. Decision No.12/04, Tolerance and Non-Discrimination, Ministerial Council, MC.DEC/12/04, 7 December 2004, www.osce.org/mc/41813, downloaded 25 June 2013.
The appointment of the Special Representatives of the Chairman in Office is renewed by each incoming Chairmanship. For the latest appointments see: CiO Representatives to promote tolerance, www/osce.org/cio/44357, downloaded 25 June 2013.
26. Hate Crimes in the OSCE Region: Incidents and Responses, Annual Report for 2011, OSCE ODIHR, Warsaw, November 2011.
27. Tolerance and Non-Discrimination Information System, http://tandis.odihr.pl/, downloaded 25 June 2013.
28. ECRI's mandate, www.coe.int/t/dghl/monitoring/ecri/activities/mandate_en.asp, European Commission against Racism and Intolerance (ECRI), downloaded 5 April 2013.
Country Monitoring Work, ECRI, www.coe.int/t/dghl/monitoring/ecri/activities/counytrybycountry_en.asp downloaded 5 April 2013.
Work on General Themes, ECRI, www.coe.int/t/dghl/monitoring/ecri/activities/GeneralThemes_en.asp downloaded 5 April 2013.
29. Annual Report on ECRI's Activities covering the period from 1 January to 31 December 2011, para. 11, ECRI, CRI(2012)23, Strasbourg, May 2012.
30. ibid., para. 10.
31. ibid., para. 11.
32. Hate Crimes in the OSCE region: Incidents and Responses, Annual Report for 2011, p. 7, OSCE ODIHR, Warsaw, November 2012.
33. Facing Facts, www.ceji.org/facingfacts/, downloaded 27 June 2013.
34. For initial appointments and mandates see: OSCE Chair extends appointments of Personal Representatives to promote tolerance, www.osce.org/cio/57117, downloaded 27 June 2013.
For Personal Representatives' reports see: OSCE Personal representatives, http://tandis.odihr.pl/imdex.php?p=qu-pr, downloaded 27 June 2013.

For latest appointments see: CiO Representatives to promote tolerance, www.osce.org/cio/44357, downloaded 27 June 2013.

35 Making hate crime visible in the European Union: acknowledging victims' rights, European Union Agency for Fundamental Rights, Vienna, 2012.
EU-MIDIS, data in Focus 6, Minorities as Victims of Crime, European Union Agency for Fundamental Rights, Vienna, 2012.
36 Hate Crime Laws – A Practical Guide, p. 11, OSCE ODIHR, Warsaw, 2009.
37 Preventing and responding to hate crimes – A resource guide for NGOs in the OSCE region, OSCE ODIHR, Warsaw, 2009.
38 ibid., Hate Crime Laws.
39 Effective prosecution of hate crimes focus of ODIHR event for prosecutors, www.osce.org/odihr/91990, downloaded 28 June 2013.
The author was invited to peer review the draft *Prosecuting Hate Crimes: A Practical Guide*, which was discussed at the pilot training session for prosecutors in Warsaw on 5 and 6 July 2012.
40 Training Against Hate Crimes for Law Enforcement, p. 4, OSCE ODIHR, Warsaw, 2012.
41 ibid., Making hate crime visible, p. 7.
42 Human rights in Europe: no grounds for complacency, p. 9, Thomas Hammarberg, Commissioner for Human Rights, Council of Europe, Strasbourg, April 2011.

9
Hate crime in the United Kingdom

Paul Giannasi

This chapter will outline the policy and legislative responses to hate crime in the United Kingdom. It will concentrate on England and Wales, as Scotland and Northern Ireland have independent legislative and judicial procedures, however it should be stated that the devolved legislatures have broadly similar natures and some functions such as foreign policy responses are shared.

Whilst there was recognition of hate crime, and particularly racist hate crime, in the UK beforehand, the catalyst for current policy and legislation was the murder of Stephen Lawrence in London in April 1993. Whilst Stephen's murder is now recognised to be one of the most significant events in the history of the criminal justice system in the United Kingdom, his murder was not immediately recognised as having such historical importance. Hall et al. (2009) demonstrate that the legacy of Stephen Lawrence was a paradigm shift in the criminal justice system, and particularly in its relationship with minority communities. Whilst we will concentrate here on those changes that relate to hate crime, the actual impact was much broader, bringing around change in many functions of the criminal justice system including critical incident management, community intelligence and victim and family support.

The tragic circumstances of Stephen's death were sadly not exceptional; such racist crimes were not uncommon, either before or after Stephen's death. What gave Stephen's murder such historical gravitas was the failings of the criminal justice system (and particularly the police), the tireless lobbying for change from activists led by Stephen's parents, Doreen and Neville Lawrence, and the Public Inquiry led by Sir William Macpherson, which reported in 1999.

The examination of hate crime data by international observers such as the Office for Democratic Institutions and Human Rights (ODIHR), who measure hate crime responses from the 57 participating states of the Organisation for Security and Co-operation in Europe (OSCE), would indicate that the UK is amongst the most advanced states when responding to hate crime. In their report summarising the situation in 2011, they published data submitted from participating states. Police in the UK (including Scotland and Northern Ireland) recorded 50,688 hate crimes. Many states were not able to submit data at all and some reported single figures.

By way of comparison, this data equates to 1 crime per 1,243 of the population in the UK, compared to 1 per 42,735 in the USA and 1 per 882,353 in Italy. If recording were equitable, that would suggest that the UK has 34 times the risk of victimisation compared to the USA, and 710 times the risk faced in Italy.[1] I do not believe it is possible to make actual comparisons of risk from these figures however, because recording practices vary from state to state. However, unless you subscribe to the view that the UK is significantly more hostile than other states – which I do not – this is clear evidence that reporting practices are more advanced in the UK than they are in many states with similar demographics.

Despite the comparatively strong reporting practices and transparency of data in the UK, there is no mainstream political party or criminal justice leader who has claimed that the response is complete, with all mainstream parties and criminal justice leaders accepting the distance we still have to go in encouraging fuller reporting and reducing the harm such targeted crime can cause.

Whilst most policy and legislation has direct links back to the 1999 Inquiry report, its development has been more often described as 'a journey', with no single turning point. Whilst the UK has a clearer guide than most states about where it wants to get to and the possible routes to get there, it knows that there is still a long way to go. In this chapter I will give my views about where we are on that journey and describe the route we have taken since Stephen Lawrence was murdered.

Hate crime policy development – 'the journey'

By the time Sir William Macpherson reported the findings of the Inquiry in February 1999, the impending impact on the criminal justice system was obvious. The daily media coverage of the evidence given to the Inquiry raised consciousness and the failings of the police in particular were obvious to all. The Metropolitan Police had appointed Deputy Assistant Commissioner John Grieve to head up its response, leading the Racial and Violent Crimes Task Force to re-investigate Stephen's murder, and to begin to build back the confidence in the Police's ability to deliver untainted services, free from the 'Institutional Racism' that the Inquiry found had contributed to the failure, at that time, to bring any of Stephen's murderers to justice.

The formal UK Government response to the Inquiry came in the Home Secretary's Action Plan published in April 1999, and was updated in an Annual Report published in February 2000. The Home Secretary accepted the vast majority of the 70 recommendations made by Sir William Macpherson, including the following important principles that have underpinned the subsequent policy response to hate crime:

- **Perception based recording** – The Inquiry believed professionals were making decisions influenced by their own discrimination and that if the victim perceived a crime to be racist then the police should record it as such. This has underpinned policy since 1999. It is not without its opponents as some have claimed that it is an entry route to a two-tier service, but it is important to note that the perception relates to 'motivation'. For anyone to receive any form of enhanced sentence, the prosecutor would need to provide admissible evidence that this was the case. However, this recording principle is important for purposes of police recording as it allows scrutiny of supervisors and encourages the consideration of the broader harms caused by hate crime.
- **Responding to incidents as well as crimes** – The Inquiry recognised the importance of early responses to hostility and presumed that offenders motivated by racism who go on to commit serious crime would have demonstrated that hostility at an earlier stage. Government and police leaders accepted the recommendation

that they should respond to racist incidents as well as crimes and although enforcement powers may not be available, there should still be cognizance of the harm caused and potential for escalation. This has also proved to be controversial and some opponents claim that the police have become the 'Thought Police' rather than 'crime-fighters'. Police leaders have consistently rejected this argument for the reasons identified above and this remains an important part of police response in the 2014 police guidance. The guidance does, however, stress the importance of proportionate responses, which consider the needs of the victim as well as encouraging 'problem-solving' response to reduce future hostility.

- **Improving the recording of, and addressing the under-reporting of hate crime** – This challenge has been a major thrust of policy since 1999 with successive Governments recognising that most crimes are unrecorded and wishing to see increased levels of recorded hate crime, so long as the actual incidence of hate crime does not increase. This issue is explored below when discussing hate crime data.
- **That information should be shared between different agencies** – Government and agencies have recognised that shared work is likely to achieve better results and many areas have some form of oversight group to deliver multi-agency work to reduce the harm caused by hate crime.
- **That the Association of Chief Police Officers (ACPO) should issue a Manual of Guidance** – This guidance is described in Chapter 27 of this volume.
- **That the racist element should not be subject to 'plea bargaining'** – This was accepted by the Crown Prosecution Service and the guidance of successive Directors of Public Prosecution has made it clear that such practices are not acceptable.

The period between 1999 and 2005 saw a flurry of activity in response to the Inquiry; it saw the enforcement of most of the legislation outlined below and the publication of three iterations of the ACPO hate crime manual. The commitment of agencies was, however, tested on numerous occasions, including the attacks on the black, Asian and gay communities in London from the bombings of David Copeland in 1999; the disorder that broke out in many English northern towns in 2001; and continued racist violence including the tragic murder of Anthony Walker in Liverpool in 2005. These incidents are explored in more detail in Chapter 27 of this volume.

In 2003, Professor Gus John was asked to examine the Crown Prosecution Service's decision-making to identify possible racial bias within the prosecution process. His report, Race for Justice (2003) included the following recommendation:

> CPS through the good offices of the Attorney General should take the lead in establishing a holistic approach, across the Criminal Justice System, to the issues highlighted by this research, not least in respect of the handling of race crimes by the police, the CPS and the Courts.

In response to the above recommendation, the then Attorney General Lord Goldsmith, established a task force under the chairmanship of The Honourable Mr. Justice Fulford. The Task Force reported in June 2006, in their report also called Race for Justice. They stated that:

> Our work revealed that there are varying levels of performance monitoring by Criminal Justice System agencies in respect of handling these crimes. The problems include

a significant failure to record these crimes accurately and different ethnicity classification systems being used by the various agencies, which in turn speak a different statistical language. We consider it necessary that all the agencies track cases from the receipt of an allegation until the end of the court process using some core, common terminology.

The Task Force made a series of recommendations, covering all criminal justice agencies and including issues such as common definitions, training, monitoring and service delivery.

In response to the Task Force report, the Government established a work programme, initially called Race for Justice, but latterly known as the Cross-Government Hate Crime Programme. The programme brought together relevant government departments, criminal justice agencies and the judiciary on a board which had oversight of the programme, hosted within the Office for Criminal Justice Reform, and latterly the Ministry of Justice. In addition to the board, the programme was established with a dedicated Independent Advisory Group to ensure that victims, advocates and academics have the opportunity to influence future policy and legislation.

Soon after the programme was established in April 2007, it began work to agree a common definition of hate crime which would provide clarity and also allow system changes to provide more accurate data on the extent of hate crime. Until this time, hate crime evaluation had largely concentrated on race, and there was no consistency as to which other 'strands' of hate crime were included. At this time the Crown Prosecution Service had included domestic violence within their hate crime policy, but the police did not, which made comparative data almost impossible.

The Race for Justice Board agreed that there was a need to have a shared definition of hate crime to allow for improved data recording and clarity of policy but that it should include the core principles of the Stephen Lawrence Inquiry. The Inquiry report had said that the definition should be that:

'A racist incident is any incident which is perceived to be racist by the victim or any other person', and:

'That it must be understood to include crimes and non-crimes in policing terms. Both must be reported, recorded and investigated with equal commitment.'

The board accepted these core principles, but noted two areas of divergence in local implementation. The first was that some agencies had conflated incidents and crimes to make performance measurement more difficult, and the second was the variation of monitored strands covered by the hate crime policy. Whilst the board recognised the importance of non-crime incidents as well as crimes, it felt that there needed to be clarity to allow transparent data collection.

During the consultation, there were many individuals who argued against the expansion of the hate crime categories beyond race. A common argument was that we should not lose the focus on our efforts to eradicate racism and until we have done so, we should not consider other motivations. This view was, however, rejected by Government and criminal justice agencies. In November 2007, the then Attorney General, Baroness Scotland, who was the Superintending Minister for the programme, made a speech to the European Hate Crime Conference, which was held in London. She said:

I have heard arguments that say that by broadening our attention, we dilute the effort to eradicate racism – I can not accept that argument. The same bigotry that fuels racism fuels other types of hate . . . We must seek to provide the same high degree of service to all hate crime victims. This must mean that all areas achieve the same high standard; I can assure you that I would never allow this to mean that our efforts to combat racism should be diluted in any way.

The programme took Baroness Scotland's direction and established that there were four victim groups who were considered to be susceptible, but where reporting of such crimes was less likely. These were asylum and refugee communities, Gypsy and Traveller communities, disabled and transgender victims.

It considered the inclusion of 21 different 'strands', which had been suggested should be included. These ranged from racism, which was universally included, to attacks on people who work in animal experimentation laboratories, which some claimed bore the same hostilities and impact on the victim. The Board accepted the need to set parameters but felt it would be wrong to deny the existence of other forms of hostility. As such it agreed that the shared definition should be of 'Monitored Hate Crime'.

The following definition was agreed by ACPO Cabinet in November 2007 and subsequently accepted by all other criminal justice agencies.

Monitored hate crime definition

Hate Motivation

Hate crimes and incidents are taken to mean any crime or incident where the perpetrator's hostility or prejudice against an identifiable group of people is a factor in determining who is victimised.

Monitored Hate Crime

A hate crime is any criminal offence which is perceived, by the victim or any other person, to be motivated by a hostility or prejudice based on a person's race or perceived race
or;
A person's religion or perceived religion
or;
a person's sexual orientation or perceived sexual orientation
or;
a person's disability or perceived disability
or;
against a person who is transgender or perceived to be transgender

Monitored Hate Incident

Any non-crime incident which is perceived by the victim or any other person, to be motivated by a hostility or prejudice based on a person's race or perceived race,
or;
a person's religion or perceived religion
or;
a person's sexual orientation or perceived sexual orientation
or;
a person's disability or perceived disability
or;
against a person who is transgender or perceived to be transgender

Paul Giannasi

Hate Crime Prosecution

A hate crime prosecution is any hate crime, which has been charged in the aggravated form or where the prosecutor has assessed that there is sufficient evidence of the hostility element to be put before the court when the offender is sentenced.

The definition takes a broad view on these strands – they include majority as well as minority groups, and in explanation the definition offers the following:

Included Subjects;
- *Any racial group or ethnic background including countries within the United Kingdom and 'Gypsy and Traveller groups'*
- *Any religious group including those who have no faith*
- *Any person's sexual orientation*
- *Any disability including physical disability, learning disability and mental health*
- *People who are transsexual, transgender, transvestite and those who hold a Gender Recognition Certificate under the Gender Recognition Act 2004.*

For recording purposes, the perception of the victim, or any other person, is the defining factor in determining whether an incident is a hate incident or in recognising the 'hostility' element of a hate crime. The victim does not have to justify or evidence their belief and it is important that police officers or staff do not directly challenge this perception. Evidence of the hostility is not required for an incident or crime to be recorded as a 'hate' crime or 'hate' incident.

If the alleged actions of the perpetrator amount to a crime under normal crime recording rules, then the perception of the victim, or any other person, will decide whether the crime is recorded as a hate crime. If the facts do not identify any recordable crime but the victim perceived it to be a hate crime, then the circumstances would be recorded as a non-crime hate incident and not a hate crime. For a conviction to receive enhanced sentencing in court, it is necessary to provide sufficient evidence for the prosecution to prove hostility to the court.

Understanding hostility is important to understanding the extent of hate crime in England and Wales. The term 'hate' implies a high degree of animosity, whereas the definition, and the legislation outlined below, require that the crime must be motivated (wholly or partially) by hostility or prejudice, or the offender must demonstrate such hostility.

The Crown Prosecution Service gives the following guidance to prosecutors:

In the absence of a precise legal definition of hostility, consideration should be given to ordinary dictionary definitions, which include ill-will, ill-feeling, spite, contempt, prejudice, unfriendliness, antagonism, resentment, and dislike.

Whilst the board found there was a need to set parameters to hate crime policy, it acknowledged that there were other crimes based on hostility to a person's characteristics, and that it would be unjust to deny the victim's right to be recognised as having suffered a hate crime. In Chapter 27, I discuss the challenges relating to some of these crimes.

Data developments

The agreement of a common definition of Monitored Hate Crime allowed for consistent data collection to be implemented. Building on this work, all police areas in the UK record and publish hate crime data broken down into the five monitored strands. Since April 2008 the data was published by ACPO but from April 2011 this has been included in the National Crime Statistics published by the Home Office. In 2011/12 this data showed that the police in England and Wales recorded 43,748 crimes. Of these;

35,816 (82 per cent) were race hate crimes
1,621 (4 per cent) were religion hate crimes
4,252 (10 per cent) were sexual orientation hate crimes
1,744 (4 per cent) were disability hate crimes
315 (1 per cent) were transgender hate crimes

England and Wales has an annual household survey which questions over 40,000 households about their experiences of crime, the impact this had on them, and the perception of the response of criminal justice agencies. In parallel to the recorded crime data collection, The British Crime Survey (BCS) (2010/11) (now called The Crime Survey of England and Wales) suggests that there are around 260,000 hate crimes each year in England and Wales, and it further indicates that around 127,000 of these 'came to the attention of the police'.

Hate crime prosecution data

The Crown Prosecution Service publishes its own data on hate crime and in its report covering the period 2011/12 it recorded that:

- The number of hate crime cases referred to the CPS by the police for decision was 14,781;
- The number of cases charged was 10,845;
- The number of successful prosecutions across all types of hate crime was 11,843 ('cases' can have more than one offender or offence hence the greater number);
- The volume of cases prosecuted was 14,196;
- The proportion of successful outcomes due to guilty pleas was 10,658;
- The most commonly prosecuted crimes were offences against the person at 49.5 per cent and public order offences at 31.5 per cent;
- 82.9 per cent of defendants were male;
- 73.9 per cent of defendants were identified as belonging to the White British category;
- 54.2 per cent of defendants were aged between 25–59, and 28.9 per cent between 18–24;
- 10–17-year-olds' involvement as defendants was 14.1 per cent.

The comparison of the three strands of data mentioned above provide the best indicators to the extent of hostility that exists in the UK, the willingness of victims to report to the police, and the success of the criminal justice system in bringing perpetrators to court. It identifies the key challenges identified by Government in its 2012 action plan – to prevent hate crime, to encourage reporting, and to improve the response of the criminal justice system.

Given my assumption that there is no society that does not experience hostility, perhaps the most pressing of these challenges is to increase the reporting and recording when crimes do occur. It is counter-intuitive to aspire to record higher crime levels but it is a positive sign that successive governments and criminal justice leaders have recognised the importance of this, and it is indicative that the one commitment in the current Coalition Government's Manifesto was to increase the recording of hate crime because it believed that such crimes often do not get reported or recorded.

Paul Giannasi

Hate crime legislation in England and Wales

Legislation in England and Wales has provided three specific options to assist in combating hate crime. These are:

- Racially or religiously aggravated offences.
- Specific offences that will always be classified as a hate crime.
- Enhanced sentencing legislation for any offence.

Racially and religiously aggravated offences

These offences had the effect of 'mirroring' some of the more prevalent hate crime offences, but they are limited in that they only relate to four offence groups (nine offences in total) namely; minor assaults, criminal damage, minor public order, and harassment offences.

The Crime and Disorder Act 1998 introduced the racially aggravated offences and the Anti-Terrorism, Crime and Security Act 2001, added religiously aggravated equivalents. Sections 29–32 of the 1998 Act states that the offences are made out if the core offence is motivated by hostility or where the offender demonstrates hostility.

Despite the limited scope of these offences, they have some advantages over the enhanced sentencing option as they carry a higher maximum sentence and they are more transparent, which makes them easier to trace through the criminal justice system. The Equality and Human Rights Commission raised this point in their 2011 'Hidden in Plain Sight' report into the harassment of disabled people. The report recommends that the Government should consider duplicating these offences for other types of hate crimes, including disability. In response to this recommendation, the Justice Secretary has asked the independent Law Commission to review this legislation and advise whether there is a case to extend these offences to cover the five strands of Monitored Hate Crime. The Law Commission is due to report back to the Justice Secretary in 2014.

Specific offences that will always be classified as a hate crime

The best known, and contentious, of the specific offences is the legislation to make illegal the stirring up of hatred on the grounds of race, religion and sexual orientation. Section 18 of the Public Order Act 1986 makes it an offence for a person to use threatening, abusive or insulting words or behaviour, or to display any written material which is threatening, abusive or insulting, intending to stir up racial hatred, or where having regard to all the circumstances racial hatred is likely to be stirred up. Section 29B of the same Act makes it an offence for a person to use threatening words or behaviour, or display any written material which is threatening, with the intention to stir up religious hatred or hatred based on sexual orientation. These offences also cover the distribution, broadcasting, performance, public display and possession of inflammatory material.

The three separate offences were created by Parliament at different times and inserted into the Public Order Act. They are not the same, and the race offence has a much lower burden of proof. It can include threatening, insulting or abusive activity and can be intended to stir up hatred or likely to do so. The religion and sexual orientation offence can only be threatening, and the prosecution must also prove that the perpetrator intended to stir up that hatred. The passage through Parliament for the latter two offences was not straightforward and there was much overt opposition from a minority of Parliamentarians who opposed the legislation.

Recognising the need to protect freedom of speech as well as to protect citizens from harm, the legislation includes safeguards to protect human rights and each prosecution needs the permission of The Attorney General to proceed to court. Prosecutions are relatively rare under these offences. In 2011/12 the Crown Prosecution Service prosecuted nine cases resulting in a total of 17 charges with 13 guilty verdicts and four not guilty. They included:

- 10 charges relating to distributing written material intended to stir up hatred on the grounds of sexual orientation;
- six of publishing racially inflammatory material or possession of racially inflammatory material with the intention of distributing it; and
- one of publishing written material with the intention of stirring up religious hatred.

In addition to the above there is a specific offence of Racist Chanting where the Football (Offences) Act 1991 makes it an offence to engage or take part in chanting of an indecent or racialist nature at a designated football match (see also Hawkins, this volume).

Enhanced sentencing legislation

The cornerstone of the legislative provision for hate crime is the enhanced sentencing provision provided by Sections 145 and 146 of the Criminal Justice Act 2003. Section 145 requires the courts to consider racial or religious hostility as an aggravating factor when deciding on the sentence for any offence (which has not been identified as a racially or religiously aggravated offence as outlined above). Section 146 has the same effect for sexual orientation, disability or transgender.

In cases where the prosecution are able to prove that the offender:

> was motivated (wholly or partly) by hostility towards a person's (actual or perceived) race, religion, sexual orientation, disability or who is transgender.
>
> or;
>
> at the time of committing the offence, or immediately before or after doing so, the offender demonstrated such hostility towards the victim of the offence, the court—
>
> > must treat that fact as an aggravating factor, and;
> >
> > must state in open court that the offence was so aggravated.

Equality Act 2010

In addition to the legislation to control criminal behaviour, the Equality Act 2010 creates a positive duty on public bodies, including the police and other criminal justice agencies. Essentially this compels agencies to consider issues such as hate crime.

Section 149 of the Equality Act 2010 requires that;

> A public authority must, in the exercise of its functions, have due regard to the need to (amongst other duties);
>
> > eliminate discrimination, harassment, victimisation and any other conduct that is prohibited by or under this Act;
> >
> > foster good relations between persons who share a relevant protected characteristic and persons who do not share it.

The act covers a number of 'protected characteristics', including the five monitored hate crime strands. It is perhaps too soon to clearly understand how the courts would interpret these provisions as the case law has yet to demonstrate what they would consider to be a breach of the duties.

Conclusion

I believe that the above described legislation and policy framework places the UK at the international forefront of state responses to hate crime, but there remain significant hurdles to clear before the race is run.

The relatively high recording rates and the growing percentage of actual crimes that are reported to the police, particularly for racist crime, is a testament to the work fuelled by the determination to see justice from the Lawrence family, but also to the commitment of all mainstream political parties and the leadership demonstrated by criminal justice heads, and key political figures such as Jack Straw MP, the Home Secretary who commissioned the Stephen Lawrence Inquiry.

The transparency of data to highlight the actual incidence of hate crime as well as the recorded crime and prosecution data provides the foundation to build for the future, but there remains a number of significant challenges including;

The under-recording of hate crime

This is explored in greater detail in Chapter 27, but the comparison between the BCS and recorded crime details the extent of this challenge, particularly for some victim groups where there is less likelihood of equitable access to justice. We can never expect full reporting of hate crime as we know that many people suffer crime in general without reporting it to the police, but the data shows us that there is an unacceptable gap.

The recorded crime and BCS figures can not be directly related as the survey is limited to people in a household who are over 16 years of age and the crime data includes child victims, but even with this caveat the gap is stark. It tells us that the figure of 43,748 recorded crimes in England and Wales is less than 1 in 5 of the crimes suffered by victims, although some are likely to have been recorded as crimes, without the hostility being recognised. This picture is even starker for disability and transgender and is likely to be so in the more isolated ethnic groups such as Gypsy and Traveller and asylum and refugee communities. The data shows us that less than 1 in 30 disability hate crimes are recorded as such.

Improving data

The shared definition of Monitored Hate Crime has allowed for consistent data to be published but this is relatively new and has some limitations. Whilst the data of the incidence of crime, the recorded crime and the prosecution data is now established, the courts and sentencing data is not complete. The Government Action Plan includes a commitment to improve this situation, however the challenges of diverse recording mechanisms mean that this data will not be easy to complete.

Another restriction of the data is that it is not nationally disaggregated within the five strands to identify which group was targeted by the hostility. There are many community groups and advisors who have called for this data to show, for example, the religion subject to hostility. However, whilst this data has traditionally been recorded by the police and partnerships locally, it has been recorded for intelligence purposes to inform management decisions and to measure community tensions. The many and variable groups has not made it easy to provide consistent national data.

Improving victim confidence

Despite the efforts described above and recognising the advances made since 1999, the BCS shows that victims of hate crime are less likely to be satisfied with the service they receive when they report. Only 53 per cent of respondents were satisfied with the response they got from the police, compared to 69 per cent of victims in general.

Hate on the Internet

The emergence of the Internet as a major part of everyday communications creates significant new challenges for authorities. This concept is explored further in this volume (see chapters by Littman, Rohlfing, and Corb) and I explore the operational challenges in Chapter 27. Authorities have seen a significant rise in complaints about Internet material, particularly since the emergence of Web 2.0 and the opportunities it provided to publish harmful media without the need to personally 'host' the material.

These challenges are exacerbated by the global nature of the media, the lack of capacity in the criminal justice system, the disparity of legislative approaches globally, and the difficulty in establishing jurisdiction for any offences that are reported.

In general, though, the UK has advanced significantly in the two decades since Stephen Lawrence was murdered but, as his father, Neville Lawrence OBE put it in August 2012:

> This problem is not solved: we've only just scratched the surface.

Note

1 Based on, UK – 50,688 crimes and 63m population, USA – 7,254 crimes and 310m population, Italy – 68 crimes and 60m population.

Bibliography

Attorney General's Office (2006) Race for Justice Task Force Report.
Crown Prosecution Service (2012) Hate crime and crimes against older people report for 2011–2012. London, CPS.
EHRC (2012) Out in the Open: tacking disability-related harassment – a manifesto for change. www.equalityhumanrights.com/uploaded_files/disabilityfi/out_in_the_open_dhi_manifesto.pdf.
EHRC (2011). Hidden in Plain Sight: Inquiry into Disability Related Harassment. Retrieved from EHRC website: www.equalityhumanrights.com/uploaded_files/disabilityfi/ehrc_hidden_in_plain_sight_3.pdf
Federal Bureau of Investigation (USA), Hate Crime Statistics for 2011 (Accessed October 2013 at www.fbi.gov/about-us/cjis/ucr/hate-crime/2011/narratives/incidents-and-offenses)
Hall, N., Grieve, J. and Savage, S.P. (eds) (2009) *Policing and the Legacy of Lawrence*. Abingdon: Routledge.
Hall, N. (2013) *Hate Crime* (2nd edition). Abingdon: Routledge.
HM Government (2012) Challenge it, Report it, Stop it: The Government's plan to tackle hate crime. Retrieved from: www.homeoffice.gov.uk/publications/crime/hate-crime-action-plan/
HM Government (2010) The Coalition: Our Plan for Government. Retrieved from www.direct.gov.uk/prod_consum_dg/groups/dg_digitalassets/@dg/@en/documents/digitalasset/dg_187876.pdf

Home Office (2002) Community Cohesion: A Report of the Independent Review Team Chaired by Ted Cantle.

John, G. (2003) Race for Justice www.cps.gov.uk/publications/docs/racejustice.pdf

OSCE (2012) Hate Crimes in the OSCE Region – Incidents and Responses. Annual Report for 2011. Warsaw: OSCE.

Smith, K., Lader, K., Hoare, J. and Lau, I. (2012) Hate Crime, Cyber Security and the Experience of Crime Among Children: Findings from the 2010/11 British Crime Survey. Retrieved from: www.homeoffice.gov.uk/publications/science-research-statistics/research-statistics/crime-research/hosb0612/hosb0612?view=Binary

10

Sectarianism and hate crime in Northern Ireland

Marian Duggan

Northern Ireland has dominated much academic research and scholarship, yet is less than a century old. British colonisation from the sixteenth century resulted in the creation of this semi-autonomous province from what was once part of a united Ireland.[1] Centuries of ethno-political tension between Catholics and Protestants (both Christian denominations) have quelled significantly since the 1998 Belfast (Good Friday) Agreement. However, deep-rooted cultural differences continue to demarcate and dictate interactions between the 'two communities' to a point whereby 'sectarianism' is almost synonymous with Northern Ireland.[2]

Northern Ireland's population is at its most balanced: 48 per cent Protestant and 45 per cent Catholic (Census, 2011). Although identities, and communities, are divided along religious markers, Cairns (2000) advises against perceiving prejudicial action towards the 'other side' as religious. Denoting which 'side' a person is on is about the height of it: no one side is looking to convert the other. Therefore, sectarianism in Northern Ireland encompasses more than two opposing faith groups, as McVeigh (1995: 643) observes:

> Sectarianism in Ireland is that changing set of ideas and practices, including, crucially, acts of violence, which serves to construct and reproduce the difference between, and unequal status of, Irish Protestants and Catholics.

Significant legal, social and political changes have enabled a more peaceful Northern Ireland. Overt forms of sectarian violence, such as the bombings, shootings, kneecapping and punishment beatings that characterised the worst years of the 'Troubles' – the three decades of violent conflict culminating in the 1998 Agreement – have been diminishing annually (PSNI, 2012). However, 'everyday' forms of sectarianism, situated in the ordinary discursive practices which function to denigrate the sectarian 'other' and collectively bond within the sectarian discourse continue to prevail (Cairns, 2000; Jarman, 2005).

This chapter analyses the factors informing and sustaining sectarian hostility, victimisation and segregation with a view to understanding the changing nature of this deeply embedded form of prejudice. Sectarianism became a 'hate crime' in Northern Ireland in 2005/06. Unlike other 'minority' communities who may require state-sanctioned protection from persecution, neither 'side' constitutes a minority, setting this particular form of hate crime apart. Bearing such differences in mind, the chapter outlines the specific characteristics of sectarianism in Northern Ireland, from the establishment of the province and the ensuing 'Troubles' period, through to the legacy of this conflict in the form of paramilitary groups, identity symbolisers and 'peace' measures which serve to further segregate opposing communities. The evaluation of sectarian hate crime questions how such acts are distinguished from the on-going, everyday processes of partition which promote safety and security through separation and segregation. The discussion concludes by considering the feasibility of political drives for greater cohesion and integration from parallel, but somewhat more peaceful, communities.

A history of violence

Literature on Northern Ireland focuses heavily on identity binaries: Republican/Loyalist, Nationalist/Unionist, Catholic/Protestant, Irish/British (Whyte and FitzGerald, 1991; Ruane and Todd, 1996). In reality, these are rarely neat divides: Unionists may align with a Northern Irish identity, a myriad of Protestant denominations exist, Nationalists may range from favouring a somewhat limited amount of British intervention to none whatsoever (Whyte and FitzGerald, 1991). Issues pertaining to identity and discrimination are important to understand divisions and ethno-political conflict in Northern Ireland. Drawing on key historical factors, McVeigh and Rolston (2007) reconceptualise sectarianism as a culturally specific form of racism, rooted in the wider processes of British imperialism in Ireland. The economic, social, political and legal inequalities that followed were founded upon an ideological justification that conceptualised the imperialist rulers as more civilised than the colonised indigenous population.

Prior to the Plantation period (sixteenth–seventeenth century), the island of Ireland was an autonomous, largely agricultural, Catholic country, where religious adherence bound otherwise rural, isolated communities (Ruane and Todd, 1996). British Protestant settlers, many of whom were Scottish, inhabited the north-east area of the country, forcing the native Irish to rent back land which previously belonged to the wider Catholic community. As well as wealth, the settlers brought the Presbyterian religion: a more puritan form of Protestantism that was more regimented than Catholicism. By 1641, as a result of this forced dispossession, Protestants controlled 41 per cent of the land in Ulster (Ruane and Todd, 1996: 20). One of the key historic moments in Protestant history is the Battle of the Boyne in 1690, when the Protestant King William of Orange defeated the Catholic King James II, deposing him of the British crown and effectively establishing Protestant supremacy in Ireland (Amstutz, 2004).

The Industrial Revolution brought wealth through linen, shipbuilding and engineering production to the largely Protestant-inhabited north-east (Hayes and McAllister, 2001). In 1800, a quarter of Ireland's four million population were descendants of the Protestant settlers, thus the Act of Union created what became the United Kingdom of Great Britain and Ireland. Hostility towards British rule increased following the 1845–1849 famine years during which the failure of the staple potato crops meant that thousands of poorer Catholic Irish people starved or migrated. Irish Catholics put forth a series of motions for what became a succession of Home Rule Bills advocating the removal of the British from Dublin Castle (where they were governing the Irish administration). The Bills were opposed by the Protestant minority who feared religious and political oppression (Amstutz, 2004). Years of violence resulted in the Government of Ireland Act 1920, which established partition between the predominantly Catholic-inhabited geographical south, and the predominantly Protestant-inhabited six north-eastern counties in 1921.

The legacy of the 'Troubles'

The extensive academic and journalistic coverage of 'the Troubles' is discernibly disproportionate to the actual size and scale of the issue (see Bell, 1991; Whyte and FitzGerald, 1991; Ruane and Todd, 1996; Fay et al., 1999; McKittrick and McVea, 2001; McEvoy, 2001). Violence between the British State and the various paramilitary organisations, namely the Irish Republican Army (IRA), Ulster Defence Force (UDF), Ulster Defence Association (UDA), and Ulster Freedom Fighters (UFF), account for most of the scholarly focus.

Bias and discrimination against Catholics in policing and criminal justice resulted in growing support for Republican paramilitaries during the latter half of the twentieth century in Northern Ireland. In 1969, the Royal Ulster Constabulary (RUC) – a predominantly Protestant police force – attacked Catholic citizens taking part in a civil rights protest against a political system which they claimed favoured Protestants. Ensuing counter-demonstrations resulted in an escalation of violence between members of Loyalist and Republican paramilitary groups. The British Government responded with internment: arrest and detention without trial. Interning almost 2,000 people in a short period of time to protect the British Army from further attacks hugely increased public support for the IRA. During another civil rights march three years later, this time against internment, British soldiers opened fire on unarmed demonstrators, killing 13 people and injuring 14 others (one of them fatally) in what has come to be known as 'Bloody Sunday'.

With no confidence remaining in the criminal justice system, Republicans turned to the IRA, who battled the British Army, Loyalist Paramilitaries and the RUC (predicated on a 'two-thirds Protestant, one-third Catholic' quotient) (McVeigh and Rolston, 2007).[3] Violence along the lines of murders, shootings, pipe bomb attacks, intimidation, hoax bombs, criminal damage, arson, punishment beatings, petrol bomb attacks, kneecappings, robberies and extortion rackets prevailed with 1,601 conflict-related deaths since 1969 (Shirlow, 2008: 338). The majority of these victims were Catholics, and many of these were killed by members of their *own* side, illustrating divisions *within* as well as *between* groups at the height of the conflict. The perceived illegitimacy of the criminal justice system meant that within communities, violent methods of 'moral policing' by self-selected leaders was evident. In addition, a clear demarcation was established between 'political' and 'criminal' violence; the former reinforced by political protests such as the Dirty Protest and the Blanket Protest (see Hillyard, 1985; Sluka, 1989; Silke, 1998).

With a heightening of violence came changes in responses to it. A 'blurring' of the purpose and severity of violent acts created a situation whereby in comparison to 'political' or 'serious' violence 'a communal blind eye [was] often turned to other forms of violence' (Steenkamp, 2005: 262). The condemnation of violence depended upon who was doing what to whom, and why. Steenkamp suggests that the failure of the State to effectively address and challenge this behaviour in turn served to reinforce a 'climate of permissiveness' in relation to some forms of violent expression (2005: 262). In his consideration of the nature and extent of paramilitary violence, Knox suggests that certain concessions may have arisen as a result of the peace process, which has shifted conceptualisations of, and responses to, violence. Of note is the precarious position of traditionally marginalised, yet increasingly visible minority groups in light of the tenuous nature of the 'peace process' in Northern Ireland:

> This raises the wider question as to whether paramilitary violence, the by-product of a negotiated political settlement in Northern Ireland, would be tolerated as a 'price worth paying' in other areas of domestic, homophobic or racist violence.
>
> *(Knox, 2002: 181)*

The regulation of historically 'deviant' minority groups by paramilitaries (see Kitchin and Lysaght, 2004; Duggan, 2012) does not command as much political interest as inter- and intra-group conflict. Knox's (2002) analysis of paramilitary policing *within* communities suggests that the 'blind eye' turned by the State to particular forms of unofficial policing is strategic: hierarchies of violence may ensure the continuance of an 'imperfect peace'. An increasing trend in Loyalist or Republican attacks on members of their own communities has been towards *non-fatal* shootings and assaults (PSNI, 2012). In 1994, the IRA was the first of the paramilitary organisations to call a ceasefire, leading to the gradual diminishment of 'political' violence. In the following decade however, 2,500 'paramilitary-style attacks' were reported and 167 people died as a result of violence attributed to dissident groups, internal feuds, informal community policing, or localized 'interface' conflict (where opposing communities share a territorial border) (McGrellis, 2005).

Things are improving: during 2011/12 the murder of a police officer accounted for the single security related death recorded; 14 fewer than in 2002/03 (PSNI, 2012). In 2011/12, the police recorded 67 shooting and 56 bombing incidents, somewhat lower than 2010/11 (72 and 99 respectively) but significantly down from a decade ago (348 shooting and 178 bombing incidents in 2002/03) (PSNI, 2012). In 2011/12, the 33 recorded 'paramilitary style' shootings represented a fifth of the number recorded a decade ago (165 in 2002/03). Divides exist in punishment styles too: since 2007/08 the majority of all paramilitary style shootings, including *all* 33 incidents recorded in 2011/12, were attributed to Republicans. By contrast, the majority (approximately two thirds) of paramilitary style assaults carried out in the same period have been attributed to Loyalists (PSNI, 2012).

Paramilitary membership continues to thrive in post-conflict Northern Ireland for several reasons. Organisations provide income opportunities for those with low employment prospects, educational achievements or social mobility; there may be generational aspirations passed down through families; criminal activity has evolved to more organised forms such as smuggling and drug rackets; and the shaping of post-conflict masculinities may also be a factor (Getty, 2003). Paramilitaries were linked to the flag riots of December 2012, when disorder broke out in response to Belfast city council's decision to only fly the union flag on designated days, rather than all year round. Many of the Loyalist working class youth involved are disconnected from politics and society, unrepresented by Unionist parties and have few employment opportunities. Paradoxically, the media attention devoted to these disturbances discourages economic investment, growth, and expansion thus exacerbating structural inequalities, poverty and general unemployment. Previous fluctuations in foreign investment linked to political and social stability are evident in Northern Ireland's history with a marked decrease in such capital being visible during the worst years of the Troubles and remaining that way until the 1994 ceasefires (Birnie and Hitchens, 1999).

Symbolism, security and segregation

In Northern Ireland, symbolism is of utmost importance. The open display of pictures of royalty, Union Jack flags and bunting (all year round, but particularly around significant events), community murals and painted kerbstones in Loyalist heartlands all indicate space, place, identity and belonging (Cairns, 2000: 444). Shirlow (2006: 103) demonstrates how murals function as a 'recognisable form of territorial marking and an illustration of territorialized power'. Therefore, as part of the on-going peace process and movement away from the terrors of the past, the reimaging of murals and walls, particularly those in close proximity to schools, has been a vital part of the efforts to move towards a more integrated and peaceful future (Shirlow, 2012: 244).

Several other methods of advancing peace appear at first counter-intuitive. Enduring processes of geographical, social and political segregation enable a significant proportion of people to go about their daily business with little or no interaction with members of the 'other' community. Despite experiments with shared housing and shared education, over 92 per cent of enrolments are in single-community schools and 90 per cent of social housing is allocated for single-community groups. This segregation proves functional in that it serves to reduce fears and possibilities of sectarian victimisation or intimidation (Jarman, 2005; Shirlow, 2008). For example, in order to try and quell cross-community tensions, 14 'peace lines' were built in and around the most incendiary interface areas of Northern Ireland between 1969 and 1999, most usually within the Belfast area (Shirlow, 2001). These barriers range from a few hundred yards to over three miles (5km) long, are up to 25 feet (7.6m) high, are made of iron, brick and steel and may or may not have gates in them which are open during the day but locked at night. Despite being imposing structures, the barriers are considered necessary by those in close proximity to them, creating a sense of personal safety and property security. Rather than being dismantled following the 1998 Agreement, the number of peace lines gradually increased to the current total of 48, with 18 of the 27 barriers in Belfast being enhanced in order to curb perceived tensions (Jarman, 2005). During the decade following paramilitary ceasefires (1994–2004) nearly 14,000 people required rehousing as a result of experiencing intimidation (Jarman, 2005: 24).

The underlying problem that the permeation of post-conflict sectarianism may be so ubiquitous that rather than being challenged, it is instead accommodated or overlooked in a manner which enhances its hegemonic state and allows an 'imperfect peace' to ensue (Jarman, 2005). A state of 'everyday sectarianism' may be so woven into the fabric of Northern Ireland that it is regarded as a fact of life and thus only problematic when of a particular violent or impactful nature (Cairns, 2000). Hamilton et al. (2008) demonstrate how 'everyday sectarianism' is dependent upon both geographical location and how affected an area was at the height of the Troubles. Economic prosperity has played a significant role in enhancing the number of neutral spaces (such as city centre pubs and bars or shopping centres) and facilitating cross-community integration. However, this was offset by the continued existence of heavily segregated areas and the fears around identification as a result of markers such as school uniforms (Hamilton et al., 2008). Segregation may be more or less visible according to a specific community's events too: whereas on a day-by-day basis a parallel but non-confrontational existence may be evident, this is subject to change in light of marches, parades or other notable events celebrating one side's history.

Workplace intimidation due to religious affiliation may affect people's choices when seeking employment (Dickson et al., 2002). Trademark's (2012) investigation into sectarianism in the workplace indicated how levels of segregation in employment are improving but remain a source of concern for many. The report cited the existence of several 'chill factors' whereby the mere threat of sectarian victimisation ensured that people kept a protective distance from perceived threatening environment. This could be through limiting their use of social space, interactions with others or disclosing personal information which might be received in a manner which caused them to fear retaliation. Trademark (2012) also indicated how contextually significant, low-level incidents like wearing poppies or displaying Help for Heroes stickers (both affiliated to British security forces) in and around the workplace proved a subtle yet effective means of reinforcing affiliation to a particular 'side'. Fears that flagging up or complaining about such paraphernalia may exacerbate tensions or single a person out for future victimisation dissuaded many from speaking out. Perhaps more importantly, changes made in the public sector as a result of the good relations legislation are not applicable to the private sector where similar problems may exist. These seemingly small issues take on greater significance when contextualised in relation to the importance placed upon historical events in Northern Ireland. As well as annual commemorations such as St Patrick's Day (Catholics) and the 12th July (Protestants) several centenary celebrations are soon forthcoming, including the Plantation of Ulster (2013), the First World War (2014), the Battle of the Somme and Easter Rising (2016) and the Partition and Government of Ireland Act (2021).

Sectarianism and 'hate crime'

Steenkamp (2005) claims that the legacy of political conflict in Northern Ireland has rendered it a place where pre-existing 'cultures of violence' may prevail. Despite having progressed to a comparably peaceful situation, the nature of conflict may have left a legacy on some members of society that may affect perceptions of violence and victims: perhaps violence does not abate, but rather shifts targets. However, the attitudes informing such violence are not restricted to the violent actors, but may permeate through wider communities. Therefore, she argues, the impact of violent norms and values in society are seen to create communities where there exists 'a greater social tolerance of individuals' violent behaviour' as this behaviour is on some conscious level juxtaposed to the violence which preceded it (2005: 253–254). In a thematic review into hate crime in Northern Ireland, the Criminal Justice Inspectorate appeared to echo such sentiments: 'There are worrying signs that groups such as ethnic minorities, homosexuals and the disabled are becoming the new scapegoats on whom those so inclined are now exercising their aggression' (CJINI, 2007: vii).

Identity and spatial struggles between the two communities have overshadowed other minority identities, rendering them politically invisible (Kitchin and Lysaght, 2003, 2004; Duggan, 2012). As a result, the sectarian issue has dominated (identity) politics to the point whereby identification within this sectarian currency was required before individuals and groups claimed access to a politically-recognised 'self' (Conrad, 1998: 55).[4] However, Northern Ireland could not ignore the fact that violence not linked to the conflict was still

Table 10.1 Number of incidents with a hate motivation, 2004/05 to 2011/12

Type of motivation	2004/05	2005/06	2006/07	2007/08	2008/09	2009/10	2010/11	2011/12
Racist incidents	813	936	1,047	976	990	1,038	842	696
Homophobic incidents	196	220	155	160	179	175	211	200
Sectarian incidents	n/a	1,701	1,695	1,584	1,595	1,840	1,437	1,344
Faith/religion incidents	n/a	70	136	68	46	23	21	8
Disability incidents	n/a	70	48	49	44	58	38	33
Transphobic incidents	n/a	n/a	32	7	10	14	22	4

Table 10.2 Number of crimes with a hate motivation, 2004/05 to 2011/12

Type of motivation	2004/05	2005/06	2006/07	2007/08	2008/09	2009/10	2010/11	2011/12
Racist crime	634	746	861	757	771	712	531	458
Homophobic crime	151	148	117	114	134	112	137	120
Sectarian crime	n/a	1,470	1,217	1,056	1,017	1,264	995	885
Faith/religion crime	n/a	78	120	62	35	15	17	6
Disability crime	n/a	38	6	42	28	41	31	15
Transphobic crime	n/a	n/a	14	4	2	4	8	3

Source: PSNI Annual Bulletin, 2012: 9[5]

an issue, particularly in light of the growing diversity of its citizens. In line with England and Wales, the Police Service of Northern Ireland (PSNI) have recorded race and sexual orientation hate incidents and crimes since 2004/05. This was soon followed by sectarian, faith/religion and disability motivated incidents and crimes in 2005/06 and transphobic motivations in 2006/07. As can be seen from Tables 10.1 and 10.2, sectarian incidents and crimes far outweigh other forms of targeted victimisation, but in 2011/12, the 1,344 incidents and 885 crimes recorded indicated the lowest level for both types since recording began (PSNI, 2012).

In keeping with other forms of hate crime (Hall, 2005), sectarian incidents/crimes are defined as being perceived as such by the victim or any other person and attributable to a Catholic/Protestant, Nationalist/Unionist, or Loyalist/Republican identity. Hate crime can take the form of assault (verbal or physical) or criminal damage. In addition, the targeting of a premises attributed to a particular 'side' in Northern Ireland may enhance the message being imparted or inferred by virtue of the symbolism affiliated to the building (Perry, 2001, 2003). Such targets have included churches/chapels, Gaelic Athletic Association (GAA) or Ancient Order of Hibernians Halls, Orange Halls or Apprentice Boys Halls, and schools. PSNI data for 2011/12 indicates that of this group, Orange or Apprentice Boys Halls are most likely to be targeted, followed by churches/chapels, then GAA or Ancient Order of Hibernians Halls and finally schools (PSNI, 2012).

The Institute for Conflict Research has demonstrated that of the 13,655 hate-motivated incidents reported to the police between 2008 and 2012, only 12 cases were successfully prosecuted using the hate crime legislation (NICEM, 2013). In the majority of cases, the hate element was lost in the criminal justice process, so crimes were being recorded without the hate motivation factor. Not only does this affect the tariff (hate crimes incur additional penalties in the form of enhanced sentences) but it also indicates a high level of attrition in hate crime cases. The Public Prosecution Service (PPS) attribute this in part to the high burden of proof required to show beyond reasonable doubt that a crime was motivated by hatred. However, the Criminal Justice Inspectorate for Northern Ireland (CJINI) has challenged the way in which hate crime cases are processed, with particular criticisms levied at the recording stage and the ability of some police officers to understand the subjective perception element of hate crimes and the different evidential requirements (CJINI, 2007: 14). These are crucial factors setting hate crimes apart from other types of criminal offences and having a significant impact on highlighting the victimisation of 'hidden' populations with already contested 'victim' status in Northern Ireland, such as sexual minorities (Duggan, 2010).

Taking a culturally specific focus, it can be difficult to discern the rationale for a particular act as being a 'hate crime' or being part of the wider differences characterising community relations in Northern Ireland. Family influences in promoting or facilitating sectarian divisions, hatred and activities may reduce outside influences aimed at addressing 'hate crime'. Smyth et al. (2004) found that parents often told stories and introduced young people to certain aspects of the Troubles in a way that was strongly influenced by their own interpretations of events. Two-thirds of the young people surveyed had been exposed to negative images or stereotypes of people from the opposite religious background by members of their family. More worryingly, Kelly (2002) found that parents had encouraged young people in his study to take part in riots or to assist in making petrol bombs. While such influences may diminish with adulthood and socialisation in a wider context, exposure to such negativity in these formative years can have significant outcomes on young people's hostile behaviour to those they deem 'other'.

The impact of such social learning environments was demonstrated by Connolly et al. (2002) whose research into the cultural and political awareness of children aged between three and six years old in Northern Ireland demonstrated some important findings. Generally, the older the children in the sample were, the greater affiliation, knowledge or understanding they illustrated about different 'sides' and where they fit in relation to these. Some key findings included half (51 per cent) of the three year olds and most (90 per cent) of the six year olds had some awareness of the cultural/political significance of at least one event or symbol (i.e. parades, flags and Irish dancing). In terms of identifying with Protestant or Catholic communities, on average 6 per cent of three- to four-year-olds achieved this, rising to 13 per cent of all five-year-olds and 34 per cent of the six-year-old children. When addressing whether this identification came with a tendency for hostility to the 'other side', engaging in sectarian or prejudiced comments was rare among the three- to four-year-olds, but 7 per cent of the five-year-olds and 15 per cent of all six-year-olds demonstrated a tendency to make comments that could be inferred as sectarian in nature. Current research being conducted by the Northern Ireland Association for the Care and Resettlement of Offenders (NIACRO) seeks to address this imperviousness to prejudice, highlighting the impact of exposure to bias at a young age as having significant implications on the perceived 'wrongness' of acts at a later stage. 'Hate crime' to the young people they are currently working with, means little in light of the culturally specific context of their upbringing.[6]

Ewart and Schubotz's (2004) study into young people's views of sectarianism since the onset of the peace process demonstrated a desire for six key changes ranging from practical implementations through to altering perspectives and outlooks. These were: more formally integrated schools; more informal mixing between schools; more cross-community contact schemes (both through schools and across neighbourhoods, so that they can get to know the 'other' community); better facilities and activities for them to mix in a non-sectarian atmosphere (particularly pertinent given the embedded nature of sectarianism in sport); the banning of territorial markers (such as murals, flags and kerb-painting); and more acknowledgement of compromises, commonalities and commitments to a peaceful future. Recognising the intense work undertaken to realise many of these requests, Shirlow (2012: 242) indicates that in terms of political, social and media recognition, concerted efforts by Loyalists and Republicans to reduce interface area violence have been successful yet largely unacknowledged in the grander scheme of things.

Conclusion: working towards shared futures?

It would appear that sectarianism in Northern Ireland is changing rather than diminishing. Whether politicians in the province have any real impetus to bring about a truly post-conflict, integrated society is questionable. Following the reinstatement of Stormont in 2007, members of the Northern Ireland Assembly[7] began discussing a strategic vision for community cohesion developed by Northern Ireland politicians to replace the 2003 policy, 'A Shared Future: Improving Relations in Northern Ireland', which had been implemented by the British Government during the short period of direct rule (when the Assembly is suspended in light of conflict and political decisions are transferred back to Westminster) (OFMDFM, 2003). The focus was to be the same: promoting the integration and sharing of communities; eliminating sectarianism and racism; encouraging communication, tolerance and respect between segregated communities; and promoting the celebration of diverse cultures and heritages. However, in the 2003 'Shared Futures' document, it was *explicitly* stated that separate but equal (parallel) living was *not* a viable option.

Following a protracted political process, a 'Cohesion, Sharing and Integration' (CSI) document was produced and disseminated for public consultation (OFMDFM, 2010). As of 2013 a final decision on the CSI strategy had still not been reached: negotiations which began with representatives from all five main political parties (as part of a working group established to seek consensus on the issues raised by the public consultation) slowly eroded during 2012, with the Alliance Party withdrawing involvement first, followed by the Ulster Unionist Party shortly after. Evidently there is still 'trouble at the top' when it comes to the political parties' abilities to engage in 'cohesion, sharing and integration' with one another.

Taking a broader (and more positive) perspective, Devine et al. (2011) examined general changes in attitudes towards community relations in Northern Ireland since 1989, drawing on available data from two key annual attitudinal surveys: the Northern Ireland Social Attitudes (NISA) Survey (which ran between 1989 and 1996) and the Northern Ireland Life and Times (NILT) Survey (operational since 1998). A significant growth in optimism regarding relations between Protestants and Catholics was evident, despite aforementioned 'political stalemates'. In 2009, nearly two-thirds (60 per cent) of those surveyed stated that relations were better than five years previously whereas prior to the 1994 ceasefires only a quarter (24 per cent) felt that relations were improving. With the onset of the peace agreements, Devine et al. (2011) suggested that two perspectives were evident in relation to outlooks on Northern Ireland's future: either the two communities would eventually integrate generationally (harmonising as part of the continuing peace process) or segregation would flourish, albeit with reduced levels of violence in an otherwise 'separate but equal' parallel lives situation (as opposed by the British Government).

As Northern Ireland moves towards its centenary, sectarianism is still evident, albeit in a far less violent, fearsome and debilitating guise for most. Clearly, an issue which has been woven into the fabric of society through decades of turbulence, troubles and tension is not going to be resolved overnight. However, for a province born out of, underpinned by and divided along sectarian lines, merely envisaging – never mind enacting – a sectarian-free future may be beyond the capabilities of those currently tasked with such a mission.

Notes

1 Northern Ireland retains significant political, economic and cultural links with Great Britain and to a lesser degree the Republic of Ireland.

2 Sectarianism is also recognised as underpinning much football violence in Scotland, thus was recognised as such in changes to Scottish hate crime laws in 2012.
3 Now rebranded as the Police Service of Northern Ireland (PSNI), quotas have sought to balance representation across all identity strands.
4 This is even so in the devolved Northern Ireland Assembly, where Members must assign themselves to one of three options: 'Nationalist', 'Unionist' or 'Other'.
5 As there may be more than one crime recorded within an individual incident, it is possible for the number of crimes with a particular hate motivation to be higher than the number of incidents with that motivation.
6 The NIACRO *Challenge Hate Crime* three-year project was launched in 2010 and seeks to reduce hate crime through intensive support for people who have committed this sort of offence. The project also aims to improve the level of debate and understanding around hate crime (especially when motivated by sectarianism), develop a definition of sectarian hate crime, extend the debate beyond the criminal justice system, design and pilot a workable, effective model of helping offenders – in custody and in the community – tackle their offending, increase the skills of those working with offenders, and share the learning through seminars and publications. See www.niacro.co.uk/challenge-hate-crime/ for further details.
7 Within this, the power-sharing Executive comprises ten ministers and two junior ministers: five Democratic Unionist, four Sinn Fein, two Ulster Unionists, and one Social Democratic and Labour Party. The Executive is headed by First Minister Peter Robinson and Deputy First Minister Martin McGuinness.

Bibliography

Amstutz, M. (2004) *The Healing of Nations: The Promise and Limitations of Political Forgiveness*. Oxford: Rowman and Littlefield Publishers.
Bell, J.B. (1991) *The Gun in Politics: An Analysis of Irish Political Conflict. 1916–1986*. New Jersey: Transaction Publishers.
Birnie, E. and Hitchens, D. (1999) *Northern Ireland economy: Performance, prospects, policy*. Aldershot: Ashgate.
Cairns, D. (2000) 'The Object of Sectarianism: The Material Reality of Sectarianism in Ulster Loyalism', *The Journal of the Royal Anthropological Institute*, 6(3): 437–452.
Census (2011) Northern Ireland Statistics and Research Agency. Accessed 01.03.2013. Available at www.ninis2.nisra.gov.uk/public/Theme.aspx?themeNumber=136&themeName=Census%202011
CJINI (2007) *Hate Crime in Northern Ireland: A Thematic Inspection of the Management of Hate Crime by the Criminal Justice System in Northern Ireland*. January 2007.
CJINI (2010) *Hate Crime: A Follow-Up Inspection of the Management of Hate Crime by the Criminal Justice System in Northern Ireland*. July 2010.
Connolly, P., Smith, A. and Kelly, B. (2002) *Too Young to Notice? The Cultural And Political Awareness Of 3–6 Year Olds In Northern Ireland*. Belfast: Community Relations Council.
Conrad, K. (1998) 'Women troubles, queer troubles: Gender, sexuality, and the politics of selfhood in the construction of the Northern Irish State', in M. Cohen and N. Curtin (eds) *Reclaiming Gender: Transgressive Identities in Modern Ireland*. New York: St. Martin's Press.
Cramphorn, C. (2002) 'Faith and prejudice: Sectarianism as hate crime', *Criminal Justice Matters*, 48(1): 12–13.
Devine, P., Kelly, G. and Robinson, G. (2011) *An Age of Change? Community Relations in Northern Ireland*. ARK Research Update Number 72, January 2011.
Dickson, D., Hargie, O. and Nelson, S. (2002) *Relational Communication Between Catholics and Protestants in the Workplace: A Study of Policies, Practices and Procedures*. Office of First Minister and Deputy First Minister, Equality Unit – Research Branch. University of Ulster, Jordanstown.
Duggan, M. (2010) 'Homophobic hate crime in Northern Ireland', in N. Chakraborti (ed.) *Hate Crime: Concepts, Policy, Future Directions*. Collumpton: Willan.
Duggan, M. (2012) *Queering Conflict: Examining Lesbian and Gay Experiences of Homophobia in Northern Ireland*. Farnham: Ashgate.
Ewart, S. and Schubotz, D. (2004) *Voices behind the Statistics: Young People's Views of Sectarianism in Northern Ireland*. London: National Children's Bureau.

Fay, M., Morrissey, M. and Smyth, M. (1999) *Northern Ireland's Troubles: The Human Costs*. London: Pluto Press.

Getty, E. (2003) 'Building peace in Northern Ireland: Christian reconcilers in an economy of hate', *Journal of Hate Studies*, 2: 47–62.

Hall, N. (2005) *Hate Crime*. Collumpton: Willan Publishing.

Hamilton, J., Hansson, U., Bell, J. and Toucas, S. (2008) *Segregated Lives: Social Division, Sectarianism and Everyday Life in Northern Ireland*. Belfast: Institute for Conflict Research.

Hayes, B. and McAllister, I. 2001. 'Sowing dragon's teeth: public support for political violence and paramilitarism in Northern Ireland', *Political Studies*, 49, 901–922.

Hillyard, P. (1985) 'Popular justice in Northern Ireland: continuities and change', in S. Spitzer and A.T. Scull (eds) *Research in Law Deviance and Social Control*. London: Jai Press.

Jarman, N. (2005) *No Longer A Problem? Sectarian Violence in Northern Ireland*. Belfast: Institute for Conflict Research.

Kelly, B. (2002) 'Young people's views on communities and sectarianism in Northern Ireland', *Child Care in Practice*, 8(1): 65–72.

Kitchin, R. and Lysaght, K. (2003) 'Heterosexism and the geographies of everyday life in Belfast, Northern Ireland', *Environment and Planning A*, 35(3): 489–510.

Kitchin, R. and Lysaght, K. (2004) 'Sexual citizenship in Belfast, Northern Ireland', *Gender, Place & Culture*, 11(1): 83–103.

Knox, C. (2002) '"See no evil, hear no evil": Insidious paramilitary violence in Northern Ireland', *British Journal of Criminology*, 42(1): 164–185.

Knox, C. (2011) 'Peace Building in Northern Ireland: A Role for Civil Society', *Social Policy and Society*, 10(1): 13–28.

Lambert, R. (2008) 'Ignoring the lessons of the past', *Criminal Justice Matters*, 73(1): 22–23.

Lloyd, K. and Robinson, G. (2008) *Intimate Mixing – Bridging the Gap? Catholic–Protestant Relationships in Northern Ireland*. ARK Research Update Number 54, April.

McEvoy, K. (2001) *Paramilitary Imprisonment in Northern Ireland: Resistance, Management and Release*. Oxford: Oxford University Press.

McEvoy, L., McEvoy, K. and McConnachie, K. (2006) 'Reconciliation as a dirty word: Conflict, community relations and education in Northern Ireland', *Journal of International Affairs*, Fall/Winter, vol. 60(1): 81–106.

McGrellis, S. (2005) 'Pushing the boundaries in Northern Ireland: Young people, violence and sectarianism', *Contemporary Politics*, 11(1): 53–71.

McKittrick, D. and McVea, D. (2001) *Making Sense of the Troubles*. Belfast: Blackstaff Press.

McVeigh, R. (1995) 'Cherishing the Children of the Nation Unequally: Sectarianism in Ireland', in P. Clancy, S. Drudy, K. Lynch and L. O'Dowd (eds) *Irish Society: Sociological Perspectives*. Ireland: Institute of Public Administration.

McVeigh, R. and Rolston, B. (2007) 'From Good Friday to Good Relations: Sectarianism, racism and the Northern Ireland state', *Race & Class*, 48 (4).

Northern Ireland Council for Ethnic Minorities (NICEM) (2013) *Race and Criminal Justice in Northern Ireland: Towards a Blueprint for the Eradication of Racism from the CJSNI*.

Office of the First Minister and Deputy First Minister (OFMDFM) (2003) *A Shared Future*. Accessed 01.03.13. Available at: www.northernireland.gov.uk

Office of the First Minister and Deputy First Minister (OFMDFM) (2010) *From A Shared Future to Cohesion, Sharing and Integration: Developments in Good Relations Policy*. Accessed 01.03.13. Available at: www.niassembly.gov.uk/researchandlibrary/2009/7109.pdf

Perry, B. (2001) *In The Name Of Hate: Understanding Hate Crime*. New York: Routledge.

Perry, B. (2003) 'Accounting for hate crime: Doing difference', in B. Perry (ed.) *Hate and Bias Crime: A Reader*. New York: Routledge.

Police Service of Northern Ireland (PSNI) (2012) *Trends in Hate Motivated Incidents and Crimes Recorded by the Police in Northern Ireland 2004/05 to 2011/12*. Annual Bulletin, July 2012.

Rolston, B. (2010) '"Unjustified and unjustifiable": Vindication for the victims of Bloody Sunday', *Criminal Justice Matters*, 82(1): 12–13.

Ruane, J. and Dunne, R. (2010) *From 'A Shared Future' to 'Cohesion, Sharing and Integration': An Analysis of Northern Ireland's Policy Framework Documents*. Joseph Rowntree Charitable Trust.

Ruane, J. and Todd, J. (1996) *The Dynamics of Conflict in Northern Ireland: Power, Conflict and Emancipation*. Cambridge: Cambridge University Press.

Shirlow, P. (2001) 'Fear and ethnic division', *Peace Review: A Journal of Social Justice*, 13(1): 67–74.
Shirlow, P. (2006) 'Belfast: The "post-conflict" city', *Space and Polity*, 10(2): 99–107.
Shirlow, P. (2008) 'Sympathies, apathies and antipathies: the Falls–Shankill Divide', *Irish Geography*, 41(3): 337–340.
Shirlow, P. (2012) 'A prosperity of thought in an age of austerity: The case of Ulster Loyalism', *The Political Quarterly*, April–June 83(2): 238–246.
Silke, A. (1998) 'Cheshire-cat logic: The recurring theme of terrorist abnormality in psychological research', *Psychology, Crime, and Law*, 4(1): 51–69.
Sluka, J. (1989) *Hearts and Minds, Water and Fish: Popular Support for the IRA and INLA in a Northern Irish Ghetto*. Greenwich, CT: JAI Press.
Smyth, M., Fay, M.T., Brough, E. and Hamilton, J. (2004) *The Impact of Political Conflict on Children in Northern Ireland*. Belfast: Institute for Conflict Research.
Steenkamp, C.K. (2005) 'The legacy of war: Conceptualizing a culture of violence to explain violence after peace accords', *The Round Table*, 94(379): 253–267.
Trademark (2012) *Sectarianism in the Workplace: Research on Sectarianism in the Private Sector Workplace Report prepared by Trademark ICTU Anti-sectarian Unit*. May 2012.
Whyte, J. and FitzGerald, G. (1991) *Interpreting Northern Ireland*. Oxford: Oxford University Press.

11
Global antisemitism

Dave Rich

The legacy of the Holocaust ensures that the question of antisemitism and hate crimes against Jews will always be of emblematic importance to wider efforts to combat racism and hate crime. In 45 years of debates in the British Parliament to pass laws against racism and discrimination, for example, "For both supporters and opponents of race relations legislation, Jews were deployed as paradigmatic victims of racism."[1] Serious antisemitic hate crimes, such as the murder of French Jew Ilan Halimi in 2006, or the desecration of Finsbury Park Synagogue in London in 2002, can attract significant media and political attention and debate. Yet as Michael Whine explains elsewhere in this volume, governmental efforts to monitor, measure and assess all hate crimes have been slow to develop and remain inconsistent. It was only in 2004 that Organisation for Security and Cooperation in Europe (OSCE) participating States committed themselves to collecting reliable data on antisemitic hate crimes, and this commitment is far from being fulfilled.[2] For the purposes of this chapter, this state of affairs has one significant consequence: anyone hoping to make a useful assessment of contemporary antisemitic hate crime across States will encounter a troubling lack of official data.

According to the OSCE Annual Report on hate crimes for 2011, 21 of the 57 OSCE participating States collect data on antisemitic crimes, but only five submitted hate crime statistics for inclusion in the Annual Report itself, while a sixth provided case examples.[3] A working paper on antisemitism published by the European Union Agency for Fundamental Rights (FRA) in 2012 similarly noted that "only a few EU Member States operate official data collection mechanisms that record the incidence of antisemitism in any great detail". What data exists are collected using different methodologies and definitions across Member States, making it difficult to conduct any useful cross-comparisons. This not only leads to "gross underreporting", the paper explained:

> The lack of data also limits the ability of policy makers and other relevant stakeholders at national and international levels to take measures and implement courses of action to combat antisemitism effectively and decisively. This blind spot in the policy field means that offenders are able to carry out attacks with relative impunity and Jewish populations continue to face antisemitic violence.[4]

As a result, "no clear-cut conclusions can be drawn on the situation of antisemitism in the EU on the basis of the data that are currently available from Member States".[5] It is not surprising that civil society organisations and non-governmental organisations (NGOs), principally Jewish community bodies, have stepped into this breach to produce their own, unofficial, data on antisemitic hate crimes. The 2011 OSCE Report included data on antisemitic hate crimes submitted by 20 NGOs from 20 participating States.[6] If collected and analysed properly, this community-based data can supplement official data on antisemitic hate crimes to provide a more rounded, community-focused picture. However, the FRA working paper noted that in many cases NGOs or civil society organisations do not collect data in a systematic way, relying instead on media reports, which undermines the reliability of their reports.[7]

Efforts to reach a common understanding of antisemitic hate crime are further obscured by politicised arguments over the scale of the phenomenon, the role (if any) of different types of political extremism in antisemitic hate crime and the identities of antisemitic hate crime offenders. One typical view is found in Stauber, for example, who argues that in the past decade "Jewish communities have faced probably the largest wave of antisemitic manifestations since World War II", and that this comes from three sources: Islamists; radicalised young Muslims; and left-wing intellectuals.[8] This is part of what is commonly known as the 'new antisemitism' theory. On the contrary, Kushner argues: Jews, Muslims and other minorities are all vulnerable to "the impact of exclusive nationalism manifesting itself violently", and Jews probably less so than other, more visible and recently-arrived, minorities.[9] Lerman goes further: Jews "are not visible targets for racists in the way that people of African, Caribbean or Asian origin are" and claims of rising antisemitic incidents are exaggerated.[10] This is not merely an academic argument. In 2003 efforts by the EU to address antisemitism suffered a minor scandal when FRA's predecessor, the European Union Monitoring Centre on Racism and Xenophobia (EUMC), attempted to bury a report that claimed to have identified a connection between events in the Middle East and antisemitic hate crime in Europe. This finding was seemingly unwelcome for some EUMC officials.[11] Peace argues that hostility to the 'new antisemitism' theory correlates with hostility to Israel.[12] One example of this is found in Bakan and Abu-Laban's dismissive treatment of a 2009 gathering in London of nearly 100 Parliamentarians from 35 countries, and a similar number of experts, for the inaugural conference of the Inter-Parliamentary Coalition Combating Antisemitism, which the authors claimed was not motivated by concern about antisemitism but was in fact "a tribute to the deepening influence" of the campaign for a boycott of Israel.[13] Fekete, also in *Race & Class*, stretched this hostility so far as to claim that the 'new antisemitism' is an Islamophobic conspiracy theory that helped to shape the thinking of Norwegian terrorist Anders Breivik.[14] Aspects of the 'new antisemitism' theory are worthy of criticism but there is a danger of throwing the baby out with the bath water. *Race & Class* is an influential British journal covering racism, including hate crime, from a radical left wing perspective but it publishes very little about antisemitism. A 2013 article on 'racial violence and the politics of hate' in Britain ignored antisemitism entirely.[15] This elimination of the study of antisemitism from the study of racism in general is unlikely to aid understanding of either phenomenon.

These obstacles have not deterred some political and academic bodies from making transnational analyses of the level and nature of antisemitic hate crime. The 2012 edition of an annual survey of global antisemitism published by the Kantor Center for the Study of Contemporary European Jewry at Tel Aviv University, assessed that there had been "A considerable escalation in the level of violent and vandalistic acts against Jewish individuals, sites and private property" worldwide in 2012.[16] A report published by the United States Department of State in 2008 revealed that over the previous decade, "U.S. embassies worldwide have noted an increase in anti-Semitic incidents, such as attacks on Jewish people, property, community institutions, and religious facilities." However, the State Department report cautioned that, because NGOs and academic bodies are more able to gather and publish information about antisemitism in open, democratic societies, "global statistics about anti-Semitic incidents are disproportionately skewed against Western democratic countries".[17]

As if to emphasise this last point, the countries with the highest numbers of violent antisemitic incidents in the Kantor Center's 2012 report are France, the United States, the United Kingdom, Canada and Australia.[18] If correct, this adds more weight to the idea previously outlined here that there is little value in quantitative comparisons of antisemitic hate crime data collected in different countries. In fact, Goodey has argued that quantitative comparisons are often a more useful guide to the effectiveness of hate crime recording mechanisms in those countries than to the actual number and distribution of hate crimes themselves.[19] However, it is possible to use the existing data, both official and unofficial, to form tentative snapshots of the different social and political dynamics that influence antisemitic hate crime in different countries, without making any judgements as to the relative scale and seriousness of the problem in each location, and that is what this chapter will attempt to do, taking four countries in turn: the United Kingdom; France; Hungary; and Canada.

In the United Kingdom, official data for antisemitic hate crime has only been published nationally since 2009. This is a consequence of the findings of the All-Party Parliamentary Inquiry into Antisemitism that was held in 2006. The 14 Members of Parliament who made up the Inquiry panel heard evidence from the Association of Chief Police Officers (ACPO) that all but eight of the 44 regional police forces across England, Wales and Northern Ireland that made up its membership subsumed antisemitic hate incident and hate crime data within their statistics for racist incidents and crimes. Nor did ACPO collate or publish national figures for antisemitic incidents and crimes. The Report of the Inquiry described this as "a matter of concern" and recommended that it be rectified, a recommendation that was welcomed by the government in their official Response to the Report.[20] The official data published since 2009 records 703 antisemitic crimes in 2009; 488 in 2010; and 440 in 2011.[21] These figures only included recordable crime and do not include non-crime incidents, the data for which is not collated at a national level. They also do not account for unreported crimes. There are no published figures showing the extent of unreported antisemitic hate crime in the United Kingdom, but the British Crime Survey found that from 2009–2011, only 49 per cent of all racist crime came to the attention of the police, either from a direct report by the victim or via some other route (this was still more than the 39 per cent of all crime that became known to the police).[22]

ACPO's data is broken down by police force area, but there is no further disaggregation of the data by, for example, crime type or victim or offender profile, or to relate the data to any external factors. The force area data shows, unsurprisingly, that the three forces with the highest number of antisemitic hate crimes are the three forces with the highest number of Jewish residents: the Metropolitan Police Service in London; Greater Manchester Police; and Hertfordshire Police. Yet there are other forces with small, but significant, Jewish communities, who according to the ACPO data recorded no antisemitic crimes at all: West Midlands, Nottinghamshire and Merseyside Police are three examples. This is where the unofficial data generated by community-based reporting can help fill gaps left by official data. In 2012 the Community Security Trust (CST), a Jewish charity that has recorded antisemitic incident data since 1984 (and for which I work), recorded 11 antisemitic incidents in the West Midlands Police area, four antisemitic incidents in Nottinghamshire and eight in

Merseyside. CST's Antisemitic Incidents Reports also provide a detailed breakdown of the data that is missing from the official statistics. These show that the most common type of antisemitic incident reported to CST involves spontaneous verbal abuse or minor assault, delivered in public areas to randomly-selected Jewish victims. Often, the victim will be visibly Jewish due to their religious or traditional clothing or a Jewish school uniform. The proportion of antisemitic incidents reported to CST that involve violence fluctuates between 10 per cent and 20 per cent of the overall total. Synagogues are particular targets for antisemitism, whether in the form of graffiti, hate mail or abusive and threatening phone calls, as are Jewish communal organisations.[23]

Antisemitic hate crime has proven to be particularly sensitive to trigger events that can cause temporary but significant spikes in the number of antisemitic incidents and crimes that are recorded. The highest annual total ever recorded by CST, for example, came in 2009, due to reactions to the fighting between Israel and Hamas in Gaza and Southern Israel in January 2009. CST recorded 929 antisemitic incidents that year, compared to the previous annual high of 598 incidents in 2006. That 2006 total was itself triggered by reactions to the war that was fought that summer between Israel and Hizbollah in Lebanon and northern Israel. Other incident spikes were triggered by reactions to the outbreak of the Second Palestinian Intifada in October 2000, or the 9/11 terrorist attacks in September 2001. These spikes in incidents also affect the types of offenders who carry out antisemitic incidents and crimes. In an average year, the proportion of antisemitic incident offenders who are described to CST as being of white appearance is normally over 50 per cent (of those incidents where an offender description is obtained), and can be over 60 per cent. However, in 2009 the proportion of offenders described to CST as being of white appearance was 48 per cent of those incidents where an offender description was obtained, while in January 2009 – the month when the fighting in Israel and Gaza occurred – fully 54 per cent of antisemitic incident offenders were described to CST as being of south Asian or Arab appearance, compared to 43 per cent for 2009 as a whole.[24] This suggests that not only do more antisemitic incidents take place during these temporary spikes in incidents, but also that the 'extra' antisemitic incidents are being carried out by people who would not offend in this way at other times.

CST reports also show that every year a minority of antisemitic incidents involve the use of political extremist discourse, usually either neo-Nazi or anti-Zionist in nature, alongside antisemitic language, motivation or targeting. In several cases the offender appears to be motivated by an extremist ideology or is, at some superficial level, a supporter of an extremist movement – for example, by daubing 'BNP' on a synagogue, or shouting 'Hamas' at visibly Jewish people walking to synagogue – although rarely is there evidence that they are actually a member of an extremist organisation. In other cases, offenders who use extremist discourse are merely selecting from a discursive reservoir for language that they know will offend or threaten their Jewish victim. Again, as with the ethnic appearance of offenders, this use of discourse changes to reflect external trigger events that may be in the news at any one time.[25]

This can give the impression that antisemitic hate crime in the UK is part of a global phenomenon, driven more by transnational identities and allegiances than by local factors. However, on its own this would be a misleading conclusion. The part of the UK which has seen the largest number of reported antisemitic hate crime relative to the size of its Jewish population in recent years is Greater Manchester, and in particular the boroughs of Bury and Salford to the north of the City Centre. Here, antisemitic hate crime is most definitely local. The number of antisemitic incidents reported to CST in Greater Manchester has risen steadily over the past decade with a relatively minor spike in 2009 and no other discernible correlation to overseas trigger events. Similarly, in Gateshead, a town in the north east of England that is a centre of Jewish learning for Strictly Orthodox, or *Haredi*, Jews, hate crime officers from Northumbria Police report that antisemitic hate crime offenders are mainly local youths; and they offend either for their own entertainment, or as a result of domestic friction between different communities living side-by-side.[26] Iganski and Kosmin have argued that most hate crime is not perpetrated by political extremists, but by offenders seeking a thrill or to gain the admiration of their peers.[27] Iganski, Keilinger and Paterson further claim that antisemitic hate crime, like all hate crime, is not driven by political extremism but mostly occurs as part of everyday life, "in cultural contexts where bigotry, and in some instances the use of violence as a social resource, are norms that serve as a social basis for offenders' actions by determining who is an appropriate target".[28] Thus, as well as overseas events acting as triggers for spikes in antisemitic incidents in the UK, the number of incidents recorded by CST also increases around the time of Jewish festivals, when there are more visibly Jewish people on the streets and more CST security volunteers and police officers available to receive reports of incidents.[29] The data collected by CST over several years suggest that this picture of quotidian hate crime as part of a more general pattern of criminal or anti-social behaviour explains most antisemitic hate crime in the UK, particularly at a local level; while extremist attitudes and reactions to overseas trigger events make up the remainder and influence annual fluctuations in the national total.

During the years of the Second Palestinian Intifada, French Jews were at the centre of the international debate that a 'new antisemitism', emanating from Muslim youth in Europe rather than from far right sources, was the driving force behind increased anti-Jewish hate crimes.[30] France, like Britain, saw an increase in reported antisemitic hate crime in October 2000. According to official data from the Commission Nationale Consultative des Droits de l'Homme (CNCDH), from 2000 onwards "Arab-Muslims" overtook far right sympathisers as perpetrators of antisemitic incidents. CNCDH also reported that the number of recorded antisemitic incidents in France spiked significantly in 2000, 2002, 2004, 2009 and 2012.[31] The first three of these years saw the beginning of, and significant moments in, the Second Palestinian Intifada; the fourth correlates to the fighting between Israel and Hamas in Gaza and southern Israel in January 2009; and the fifth has been attributed to reactions to a domestic trigger event with international implications: the jihadist murder of four French Jews, including three children, at a Jewish school in Toulouse. There were 90 antisemitic incidents recorded in France in the 10 days following that shooting in Toulouse in March 2012, and 28 incidents recorded in the eight days following the dismantling of another anti-Jewish terrorist cell in Sarcelles in October 2012.[32] The Toulouse shooting was itself an antisemitic hate crime of the most violent and murderous kind, as was the 2006 murder of Ilan Halimi, that at the time of writing has no recent parallel in the UK.

While superficially this picture bears similarities to the situation in the United Kingdom, France provides a significantly different domestic context. The Jewish and Muslim communities in France are both a little over double the size of the respective communities in the UK, and they have a shared history in colonial Algeria that is absent from the parallel relationship in the UK. Attitudes towards Jews and antisemitism have played central roles in some of the seminal moments in the creation of modern France, from the Revolution, to the Dreyfus Affair, to Vichy and the German occupation.[33] Consequently the question of antisemitism features in mainstream French political debates over immigration, crime and security to a much greater extent in France than in the UK. This may be one reason why "France has some of the most sophisticated methods for monitoring racist and antisemitic acts in the whole of the European Union."[34] In the French system, official and unofficial data for antisemitic hate crimes are effectively merged: the Service de Protection de la Communauté

Juive (SPCJ), a Jewish NGO, publishes official data that has been verified by the Ministry of the Interior. According to Silverstein, antisemitism is so entangled with French domestic and foreign policy that "contemporary antisemitism in France constitutes in practice a form of proxy violence" that merges with violent actions against the French state. Young Franco-Maghrebis who are angry at American and Israeli actions in the Middle East and frustrated with the discrimination and marginalisation they face at home, Silverstein argues, "reinterpret ... their battles with French forces of law and order as an *intifada* of their own, as a resistance to the forces of imperialism".[35] In this analysis, political extremism and day-to-day street antisemitism in France are so closely interwoven as to be barely distinguishable as separate phenomena.

Unlike the United Kingdom and France, Hungary does not collect any official data on antisemitic incidents or crimes. The OSCE Annual Report on hate crimes for 2011 includes just two antisemitic incidents reported to them by Athena Institute, a Hungarian NGO.[36] The FRA working paper on antisemitism noted nine antisemitic incidents in Hungary in 2009, eight in 2010 and 10 in 2010, all reported to them by Athena Institute.[37] Yet despite this lack of antisemitic hate crime data, a perception has grown in recent years of a serious problem of antisemitism in Hungary. The far right party Jobbik became the third-largest party in the Hungarian Parliament in 2010, polling 17 per cent of the vote, to add to its three seats in the European Parliament. Since that election Jobbik has expressed public antisemitism with increased confidence, both in the statements of its officials and in public marches and demonstrations by its paramilitary followers, creating fears that this would lead to an increase in antisemitic hate crime.[38] So significant was this perception of growing antisemitism in Hungary that the Nobel Laureate and Holocaust survivor Elie Wiesel returned the Grand Cross Order of Merit, a decoration he had received from the Hungarian President in 2004, in protest against the growth of fascist activity in the country,[39] while in 2013 the World Jewish Congress brought its assembly from Jerusalem to Budapest to highlight its concerns.

Largely because of this international interest, for the first time the Hungarian Jewish community published a report on antisemitism in the country during 2012. This used a broad definition of an antisemitic incident, to include violence, verbal abuse, vandalism, online activity, statements by politicians and in the media, and political demonstrations. These were gathered primarily from media reports and the report was written by volunteers. The report noted 102 antisemitic incidents during the year, overwhelmingly from far right extremist sources and several by Jobbik members and officials themselves. They included antisemitic activity directed at symbols of Israel, also carried out by far right activists. Although this was the first year in which data was published by the Jewish community, the report claimed that antisemitic incidents had increased in number in recent years and also become more violent. It ascribed this to the growing popularity of Jobbik amongst young Hungarians and "the proliferation of hate groups, speeches inciting violence and assault at neo-Nazi mass demonstrations and the military training of radical paramilitary skinhead groups".[40] Both the extent and the character of the political extremism in play here present a very different profile from the antisemitic hate crimes reported in the UK or France.

Canada collects official data on antisemitic hate crimes, but did not submit any to the OSCE for their 2011 report. The League for Human Rights of B'nai Brith Canada, a Jewish NGO, produced a report on antisemitic incidents in 2012 that showed 1,345 antisemitic incidents, a small rise compared to 2011. Just 13 of these involved violence, a tiny percentage compared to the UK or France. Over the previous decade the number of incidents recorded by the League had risen steadily from 569 in 2003, with no apparent spikes that correlate to international trigger events. The League note that due to Canada's national stability, "extremist ideologies have not established any firm foothold or attracted mainstream acceptance", meaning that the number of antisemitic incidents is not attached to "global trends". However, the connection to global events appears to be weak rather than entirely absent: the highest monthly total came in November 2012, when fighting between Israel and Hamas escalated briefly in Gaza and southern Israel.

In the absence of strong indigenous extremist organisations, the League noted the role of the Internet in spreading antisemitic ideas and cyber bullying. A large proportion of the recorded incidents, 521 or 39 per cent, took place online, about half of which involved social media applications. The League also noted anti-Jewish prejudice from other Canadian minority groups: 87 of the 147 incidents they recorded in 2012 where a description of the offender was obtained involved offenders "self identifying as Muslims supportive of Islamist anti-Jewish sentiments . . . No other ethnic or religious group came anywhere near this number in the line-up of perpetrators identified by religious or ethnic group." Separately, the report notes that there were 151 incidents linked to "white supremacist activity". 79 incidents took place at universities, 20 of which coincided with 'Israel Apartheid Week' programmes, suggesting a political context for those incidents. Reporting to the police is low: approximately 34 per cent of all hate incidents in Canada are reported to the police. Meanwhile 28 per cent of the incidents reported to the League were also reported to the police, of which 20 led to suspects being charged.

The four countries surveyed in this chapter provide different answers to the role of extremism and international trigger events in antisemitic hate crime. In the United Kingdom both play a role, but most antisemitic hate crime is a matter of banal interactions between Jews and others, set in the context of their daily lives. In France, social exclusion, political extremism and global politics are more entwined and together play a significant role in antisemitic hate crime. In Hungary, political extremism is a dominant factor in antisemitism, but it is of a domestic variety and has little to do with global events. Meanwhile Canada displays elements of all these factors, but none could be argued to be the defining influence in anti-Jewish hate crime. These brief overviews provide enough differences and contrasts to demonstrate that simplistic worldwide assessments of antisemitic hate crime risk flattening the significant differences between, and within, countries. Qualitative comparisons that draw out these distinctions are worthwhile; but the picture will not be complete until all countries provide official data on antisemitic hate crime that can be cross-referenced with antisemitic incident reports from community-based NGOs.

Notes

1 Didi Herman, '"The Wandering Jew has no Nation": Jewishness and Race Relations Law', *Jewish Culture and History*, 12:1–2 (Summer/Autumn 2010), 131–158 (p. 140)
2 'Hate Crimes in the OSCE Region: Incidents and Responses', *Annual Report for 2011* (OSCE: Warsaw, 2012), p. 60 http://tandis.odihr.pl/hcr2011/pdf/Hate_Crime_Report_full_version.pdf [accessed 20 May 2013].
3 'Hate Crimes in the OSCE Region: Incidents and Responses', *Annual Report for 2011* (OSCE: Warsaw, 2012), p. 61 http://tandis.odihr.pl/hcr2011/pdf/Hate_Crime_Report_full_version.pdf [accessed 20 May 2013].
4 'Antisemitism: Summary overview of the situation in the European Union 2001–2011', *FRA Working Paper* (June 2012), pp. 4–5.
5 'Antisemitism: Summary overview of the situation in the European Union 2001–2011', *FRA Working Paper* (June 2012), p. 51.
6 For full disclosure, my own organisation, CST, was one of the submitting NGOs.

7 'Antisemitism: Summary overview of the situation in the European Union 2001–2011', *FRA Working Paper* (June 2012), p. 5.
8 Roni Stauber, 'The Academic and Public Debate Over the Meaning of the "New Antisemitism"', Stephen Roth Institute for the Study of Contemporary Antisemitism and Racism, 24 April 2008 www.kantorcenter.tau.ac.il/sites/default/files/stauber-debate-fin%20.pdf [accessed 27 October 2012), pp. 8–9.
9 Tony Kushner, 'Anti-Semitism in Britain: Continuity and the Absence of a Resurgence?', *Ethnic and Racial Studies*, 36:3 (2013), 434–449 (p. 445).
10 Antony Lerman, 'Sense on Antisemitism', in *A New Antisemitism? Debating Judeophobia in 21st-Century Britain*, ed. by Paul Iganski and Barry Kosmin (London: Profile Books/Institute for Jewish Policy Research, 2003), 54–67 (p. 66).
11 Michael Whine, 'Two Steps Forward, One Step Back: Diplomatic Progress in Combating Antisemitism', *Israel Journal of Foreign Affairs*, 4:3 (2010), 91–102 (pp. 94–95).
12 Timothy Peace, 'Un Antisemitisme Nouveau? The Debate about a "New Antisemitism" in France', *Patterns of Prejudice*, 43:2 (2009), 103–121 (pp. 112–113).
13 Abigail B. Bakan and Yasmeen Abu-Laban, 'Palestinian Resistance and International Solidarity: the BDS Campaign', *Race & Class*, 51:1 (2009), 29–54 (p. 50 n. 12).
14 Liz Fekete, 'The Muslim conspiracy theory and the Oslo massacre', *Race & Class*, 53:3 (2012), 30–47 (pp. 42–43).
15 Jon Burnett, 'Britain: Racial Violence and the Politics of Hate', *Race & Class*, 54:4 (2013), 5–21.
16 *Antisemitism Worldwide 2012: General Analysis* (Tel Aviv: Kantor Center for the Study of Contemporary European Jewry, 2013), p. 1.
17 *Contemporary Global Anti-Semitism: A Report Provided to the United States Congress* (Washington, D.C.: United States Department of State, March 2008), p. 11.
18 *Antisemitism Worldwide 2012: General Analysis* (Tel Aviv: Kantor Center for the Study of Contemporary European Jewry, 2013), p. 39.
19 Jo Goodey, 'Racist violence in Europe: Challenges for official data collection', *Ethnic and Racial Studies*, 30:4 (July 2007), 570–589 (p. 579).
20 *Report of the All-Party Parliamentary Inquiry into Antisemitism* (London: All-Party Parliamentary Group Against Antisemitism, 2006), pp. 9–11; *Report of the All-Party Parliamentary Inquiry into Antisemitism: Government Response* (London; The Stationery Office, 2007), p. 4.
21 www.report-it.org.uk/hate_crime_data1 [accessed 22 May 2013]; Data for 2012 was not available at the time of writing.
22 Kevin Smith (ed.), Deborah Lader, Jacqueline Hoare and Ivy Lau, *Hate crime, cyber security and the experience of crime among children: Findings from the 2010/11 British Crime Survey* (London: Home Office, 2012), p. 20.
23 *Antisemitic Incidents Report 2012* (London: Community Security Trust, 2013).
24 *Antisemitic Incidents Report 2009* (London: Community Security Trust, 2010), pp. 21–22. All percentages are of those incidents where an offender description was obtained, not of the annual incident total as a whole. In 2009 CST obtained an offender description for 35 per cent of the antisemitic incidents recorded during the year.
25 *Antisemitic Incidents Report 2009* (London: Community Security Trust, 2010), pp. 23–25; *Antisemitic Incidents Report 2012* (London: Community Security Trust, 2013), p. 22.
26 Conversation with the author.
27 Paul Iganski and Barry Kosmin, 'Globalized Judeophobia and its Ramifications for British Society', in *A New Antisemitism? Debating Judeophobia in 21st-Century Britain*, ed. by Paul Iganski and Barry Kosmin (London: Profile Books/Institute for Jewish Policy Research, 2003), 275–297.
28 Paul Iganski, Vicky Keilinger and Susan Paterson, *Hate Crimes Against London's Jews* (London: Institute for Jewish Policy Research, 2005).
29 *Antisemitic Incidents Report 2012* (London: Community Security Trust, 2013), p. 11.
30 For example, Pierre-André Taguieff, *Rising from the Muck: The New Anti-Semitism in Europe* (Chicago: Ivan R. Dee, 2004).
31 Timothy Peace, 'Un Antisemitisme Nouveau? The Debate about a "New Antisemitism" in France', *Patterns of Prejudice*, 43:2 (2009), 103–121 (pp. 106–110); 'Antisemitism: Summary overview of the situation in the European Union 2001–2011', *FRA Working Paper* (June 2012), pp. 27–29; *2012 Report on Anti-Semitism in France, Statistics and Analyses* (Paris: Service de Protection de la Communauté Juive, 2013).

32 *Report on Anti-Semitism in France, Statistics and Analyses* (Paris: Service de Protection de la Communauté Juive, 2013), p. 13.
33 Robert Zaretsky, 'Mind Games', Tablet (27 July 2011), www.tabletmag.com/news-and-politics/73123/mind-games-2/print/ [accessed 23 May 2013].
34 Timothy Peace, 'Un Antisemitisme Nouveau? The Debate about a "New Antisemitism" in France', *Patterns of Prejudice*, 43:2 (2009), 103–121 (pp. 105–106).
35 Paul A. Silverstein, 'The Context of Antisemitism and Islamophobia in France', *Patterns of Prejudice*, 42:1 (2008), 1–26 (pp. 5, 19).
36 'Hate Crimes in the OSCE Region: Incidents and Responses', *Annual Report for 2011* (OSCE: Warsaw, 2012), pp. 61–62 http://tandis.odihr.pl/hcr2011/pdf/Hate_Crime_Report_full_version.pdf [accessed 20 May 2013].
37 'Antisemitism: Summary overview of the situation in the European Union 2001–2011', *FRA Working Paper* (June 2012), p. 34. The discrepancy between the OSCE and EU data for 2011, both sourced to Athena Institute, is not explained in either report.
38 *Antisemitism Worldwide 2012: General Analysis* (Tel Aviv: Kantor Center for the Study of Contemporary European Jewry, 2013), p. 11.
39 'Elie Wiesel rejects Hungarian award over Nazi memorial', Times of Israel (19 June 2012) www.timesofisrael.com/elie-wiesel-rejects-hungarian-award-over-nazi-memorial/ [accessed 23 May 2013].
40 *Anti-Semitic Incidents in Hungary 2012*, http://antisemitism.org.il/webfm_send/56 [accessed 23 May 2013].

12
The European extreme right
In search of respectability?

Emmanuel Godin

Over the past 20 years or so, throughout Europe, extreme-right parties have consolidated their electoral gains, and in some cases, entered government coalitions. In countries where their electoral success remains mediocre, their ideas have often been co-opted by mainstream parties. Their success has received widespread attention in the media and has been the subject of many academic debates. These debates have, for the most part, raised contentious questions about the political nature of such parties (Mudde, 2007), notably their degree of kinship with fascism (Wolfreys, 2013; Ignazi, 2003); the reasons for their relative electoral success (Carter, 2005); their actual impact on both party competition (on the right: Godin and Hanley, 2013; on the left: Rydgren, 2012) and policy making (Howard, 2010; Schain et al., 2002); and the strategies to combat their influence (Downs, 2012; Bertelsmann Stiftung, 2009). There is a general consensus that these parties form a heteroclite family, albeit with obvious ideological and organisational differences. This family draws on different national traditions to articulate concurring ideas about immigration, race and identity. Family members are able to learn fast from one another and regularly, formally or informally, engage in the transnational exchange of ideas, staff and resources (Rydgren, 2005). The search for a generic definition, encompassing both the family's diversity and the political principles that form its ideological core, has led to persistent arguments.

The use of labels such as 'populist right', 'radical right', 'extreme right', 'neo-nationalist right', 'neo-fascism', to name a few, is fraught with difficulties: it can say more about the researcher's own conceptual grounding than the object studied (Mudde, 1996). Labels, of course, are always problematic and their profusion can be confusing. First, they mask the fact that such parties are often rife with internal, ideological tensions: not all of them can ensure a level of political consistency and organisational cohesion that highly hierarchical – but often illusionary – representations of such parties habitually convey. As is the case with any other party, a level of ideological discrepancy between leaders, officials, activists and voters, is to be expected, as the defence of political orthodoxy – whatever this may be – is not always the single or most important objective to be achieved through political engagement. Doctrinal rigidity or coherence, readily conferred to extreme parties, must be critically assessed rather than reproduced, as should their ability to change and review their core ideological tenets. Whether such changes amount to an opportunistic electoral gloss or correspond to a profound ideological shift is, as we will see, an area of significant debate. Indeed, arguments about the ideological nature of parties situated on the right of the right of the political spectrum seem endless. New typologies aimed at providing a clear and cogent panorama of such parties are routinely presented, dismissed and soon reconfigured. Yet, their very imperfections reveal the complex nature of the phenomenon and raise some important questions about the renewed vitality of such parties and their dynamics, and whether, how and why they should or could be tamed. More than in other fields, research on extreme parties does not always clearly untangle empirical from normative and prescriptive arguments.

In this chapter, I seek to demonstrate that if in Europe extreme-right parties have moved from the margins to the mainstream, they have not necessarily become more moderate for it. To understand their nature, it is perhaps more important to evaluate the kinds of relations which they entertain with foes and allies than to analyse their shifting and ambiguous discourse. Much is to be gained by going beyond the realm of narrow electoral, party politics, and instead relocating the study of right-wing extremism within a wider, composite social movement (Rydgren, 2007). Extreme-right think-tanks (such as the high-brow GRECE), social movements (such as CasaPound in Italy), subcultures (such as skinheads, or football ultras) and virtual communities (on the Internet) have recently been the object of new research (Mammone et al., 2013): the extreme right in Europe is better understood as a polymorphous phenomenon, a galaxy whose ideological contortions are often difficult to explain, but whose synchronised development across borders and transnational exchange of ideas are evident enough to warrant it the title of a European political family.

Political parties

One of the prevalent, but disputed, arguments about the nature of the European extreme right can be summarised as follows: the European extreme right has been able to free itself from its fascist past and the stigma attached to an ideology promoting biological racism and outright authoritarian, anti-democratic solutions (Ignazi, 2003). It now operates within a new, modern master frame: it combines a 'populist', anti-establishment rhetoric (a naturally virtuous people is routinely opposed to a corrupt, ineffective and sometimes cosmopolitan elite) with an ethno-pluralist doctrine, a form of cultural racism which posits that different, ethnically-grounded cultures are equal but incompatible and best kept separated (Rydgren, 2005). The consequences of such a position are clear: on a given territory, groups which are considered as alien to the dominant culture must have their rights curtailed to reduce the impact of their presence and limit their ability to disseminate their values. Native cultures, it is argued, must be protected by the state against the dangers of hybridity, generated by mass migration, and uniformisation, derived from global consumerism and/or bureaucratic centralising tendencies of Brussels. Within this context, from the early 2000s onwards, the fear of Islamisation of Western societies has proved particularly potent: it has provided new and effective ammunition for established right-wing extremist parties and propelled new ones into the political limelight.[1] Islam is presented as culturally different and incompatible with what is defined as a homogeneous national or/and European identity (Rosenberger and Hadj-Abdou, 2013; Camus, 2013). For instance, the Dutch Party for Freedom (PVV, *Partijvoor de Vrijheid*), founded in 2005 by Geert Wilders, has built its political identity on Islamophobia, linking Islam to fascism and the Koran to *Mein Kampf* (Vossen, 2010). Whereas the logical consequence of such discourses is invariably the formulation of discriminatory and exclusionary policies, nativist discourses are now saturated with positive, but ultimately hazy references to 'liberal', mainstream values, such as freedom (from the 'system', the EU, global capitalism, alien cultures and religions), democracy (calls for referendum and demands for a re-energised local democracy are common currency) and even the preservation of diversity (that is, the defence of native culture against Europeanisation, globalisation, Islamisation or multiculturalism's alleged homogenising tendencies). This paints an image that is at odds with fascism and its core anti-democratic and anti-pluralist tenets. Yet, the nature, depth, authenticity and finality of this new discourse are often disputed. Indeed, if it is clear that the European extreme right has considerably repackaged its message, it is less certain that this amounts to a clear rupture with the past.

Initial research into extreme-right parties has tended to pay more attention to their public discourses, aimed at voters, than to the core principles prevailing among party cadres, activists and the rank and file. In this context, research has stressed quite clearly wide-ranging shifts in values, programmes and policy, reflecting attempts to 'modernise' established extreme-right parties through the rejection of their fascist heritage (Ignazi, 2003 and for a general discussion Mudde, 2007). The astonishing transformation of the Italian extreme right since the early 1990s under Gianfranco Fini's leadership provides undoubtedly the most striking – even caricatural – example of this 'modernisation' process. By the mid-1990s, a fringe party, the Italian Social Movement (Movimento Sociale Italiano, MSI), created after the Second World War by Mussolini's supporters, became a senior partner in successive Berlusconi's coalition governments. Throughout the 2000s, this self-styled 'post-fascist' party, renamed National Alliance (Alleanza Nazionale, AN) articulated a new programme whose ostensibly 'liberal' principles indicated a significant departure from traditional fascist rhetoric: a repudiation of all forms of dictatorships and totalitarianism, a commitment to democracy and liberty, a declared aversion to racism and anti-Semitism, and the recognition of the positive impact of immigration on the Italian economy (Fella, 2006). Fini directed his most acerbic criticisms against the Italian 'system', condemning both the corrupt elites and the ineffectiveness of the parliamentary system. The party's ideological frame of reference became decidedly less objectionable, focusing as it did on freedom (of choice), (presidential) democracy, accountability, and a stronger work ethic. This new stance created major tensions within the party, leading some of its cadres to find refuge in the plethora of smaller neo-fascist splinter parties which uneasily gravitated around and away from the AN.[2] But most of them stayed put: when looking at the internal working of the party machinery, the eradication of fascist tendencies is less clear.

Indeed, if one focuses on the ideas circulating within the AN, the depth and nature of this transformation are less obvious: nostalgia for Mussolini remains high among the rank and file and his dictatorship is still perceived in a very positive light (Ignazi, 2003). When a prominent cadre of the party, Gianni Alemanno, was elected Mayor of Rome in 2008, he was acclaimed to the cries of '*Duce, Duce!*' and the fascist salutes of dedicated activists. Fascism remains the core ideological frame of reference for the training of young activists, who have no qualms studying fascist canonical texts as a basis for understanding politics today or accepting fascist interpretations of Italian and European history. Contrary to the instinctive rejection of politics ('all corrupt!') and simplistic approach to policy issues ('why don't they just do this?'), both of which characterise a populist attitude, AN members tend to value political activism and leadership (politics is a noble activity and requires the sort of skills that the *vulgum pecus* does not often possess); they are knowledgeable about politics, situate themselves clearly on the right of the political spectrum (the nature of their values is clear and coherent); they are able to present their case in a rational rather than emotive way (Dechezelles, 2013).

The Italian extreme right is not unique in presenting this dual, Janus-like figure (Mammone, 2009): the same strategy has been pursued by other European parties, with varying degree of political and electoral success. Admittedly, Nick Griffin, the leader of the British National Party (BNP) since 1999 has been less successful than his European counterparts in lifting his party out of its electoral ghetto and providing it with a veneer of respectability. Nevertheless, the same strategy has been used: Griffin sought to avoid crude racial rhetoric in public, banned white supremacist references, dropped calls for the compulsory repatriation of immigrants from the BNP manifesto and became the defender of British culture against the homogenising tendencies of Europe, global markets and multiculturalism. To attract the growing number of voters dissatisfied with – rather than opposed to – British democracy, he sought to boost the party's credentials through a re-appropriation of the most potent symbols of British political culture: Churchill's 'V for victory' was to replace the foreign, Nazi-imported salute. The BNP's posters for the 2009 European elections intimated to voters that Churchill would have supported the BNP's nativist approach to immigration policy rather than tearing into the BNP's fascist roots. At the same time, Griffin constantly reassured the party base that such a significant ideological shift owed more to pragmatism than principles: for instance, grassroots were reminded that the 'underlying rationale from shifting the debate from race inequality to the preservation cultural diversity was that the latter "raises no alarming questions of superiority or inferiority"' (Goodwin, 2011: 68).

In France, Marine Le Pen's so-called 'de-demonization' strategy also necessitated a very public rupture with neo-fascist and neo-Nazi groups. In December 2011, she declared that 'radical, grotesque and anachronistic groups, such as ultra-Catholics, supporters of Pétain [the French leader of the collaborationist Vichy regime (1940–1944)], and Holocaust deniers had no role to play in the party [. . .]. The Front National (FN) [would] not be used as a platform for their obsessions' (*Le Figaro*, 1 December 2010). In marked contrast to her father, whose anti-Semitic comments peppered his political career, she publically repudiated his reading of the Second World War and the trivialisation of Nazi barbarism. She challenged whoever defined the FN as an extreme party, explaining that 'extreme' was a derogatory adjective conferred upon the FN by its enemies in order to stigmatise and isolate it. Yet, there is one ideological component that has not changed under her leadership: the defence of an ethno-pluralist vision of society. The FN's stance against immigrants, and particularly Muslims, is explained by the belief that they cannot be assimilated into the national community because of the radical incompatibility between their ethnic and cultural roots and that of the French nation.

Parties on the right of the right welcome the 'populist' label as a way of gaining a surplus of legitimacy, as they seek to shake off their extremist ideas for a more desirable image, that of the defender of the 'people' (Mammone, 2009). The label conveniently indicates what is rejected rather than what is defended and serves well their electoral interests precisely because their public discourses evade the ideological foundations of their manifesto. Their political identity and success cannot be solely imputed to the populist utterances that their leaders address to potential voters (Collovald, 2004). This populism is not so much about a virtuous people, with alleged homogeneous interests and opinions that must be consulted when formulating policy options, it is also about a people which must be successfully led by a charismatic leader and managed by an effective organisation. The leadership qualities of such parties, the effectiveness of their organisation and above all their ability to find new allies, must also be taken into account if one wants to understand their success.

Conversely, it would be erroneous to believe that explicit references to fascism necessarily confine a party to the margins of a given party system. Neo-fascist and neo-Nazi parties are usually seen as marginal parties. They have dismal records at the ballot-box, weakened by their nostalgia for past heroes, outmoded ideologies and their predilection for rhetorical and physical violence. Examples include the myriad of Francoist splinter parties in Spain with a decidedly ageing, if not demographically extinct, electoral base, the tiny Dutch People's Union (Nederlandse Volks-Unie), whose members often parade in SS uniform, or the German NPD (Nationaldemokratische Partei Deutschlands), whose electoral results remain very low, despite some passing local victories (as discussed later), and whose neo-Nazi rhetoric has to be constantly kept in check, or so it seems, if it wishes to avoid being banned by the German constitutional court (Backes, 2006; Rayder, 2012).

Yet, the automatic marginalisation of parties displaying overt neo-fascist and neo-Nazi doctrines is not obvious anymore. Association with a fascist ideology and routine perpetration of violent acts do not automatically hinder electoral success or warrant political isolation. In Greece, the recent electoral breakthrough of Golden Dawn (7 per cent of the vote, 2012 general elections, and 18 MPs out of 300) proves that voters can reward the use of physical violence and full-frontal attacks against democracy. Golden Dawn has indeed a taste for vicious vigilante operations against foreigners and hardly conceals its preferences for the sort of biological nationalism commonly found in Nazi ideology. It flaunts its anti-Semitism and extols Greek biological superiority in a way that sets it apart even from previous Greek extreme-right parties (Ellinas, 2013).[3] Of course, it is possible that Golden Dawn is a mere flash party, whose success is primarily related to the extraordinary Greek financial and economic crisis rather than the political expression of deep ideological preferences. Yet a poll released in October 2012 put public support for the party at 21 per cent, far higher than its 7 per cent showing at national elections four months earlier (FRA, 2013). Recent research into Golden Dawn suggests that if it is to ensure its continuing influence in Greek politics, the modernisation of its ideology may not be the most important issue: rather the quality of its organisation, leadership and its ability to find reliable or compliant allies, among other parties or within civil society, would be a more determining factor (Ellinas, 2013).

The Hungarian Movement for a Better Hungary (Jobbik Magyarországért Mozgalom) is a clear-cut example of how a party favouring neo-fascist ideas and tactics, with a strong organisation and a set of reliable allies, can become a significant political actor. In the 2010 general elections, Jobbik won 12 per cent of the vote and sent 47 MPs to the Hungarian parliament. Its rhetoric is clearly reminiscent of Nazi ideology: in November 2012 it called for a listing of all Jews in Government and Parliament, arguing that they posed a security risk to the country. Believing that Hungarians form a superior ethnic group, the party especially fears its 'contamination' by Jews, a view directly inherited from Ferenc Szálasi, the interwar Nazi leader of the Arrow Cross Party (Haynes and Rady, 2011). To support and propagate its ideology, suffused with anti-Semitism, historical revisionism, anti-Communism and anti-global capitalism, Jobbik has long relied on the support of a militia – the Magyar Gárda – which, until its dissolution in 2009, often verbally and physically intimidated Roma, Jewish and gay communities. Fully uniformed, occasionally illegally using dogs and makeshift weapons, the militia's cadres were meant to 'prepare youth spiritually and physically for extraordinary situations that might require the mobilization of the people' (OSCE, 2010).

The dissolved militia has now re-emerged as a civic and cultural foundation, one of the many 'non-political' associations orbiting around the party and facilitating the propagation of its ideas within Hungarian society. Jobbik can also count on its 'nearby' mainstream rival, Fidesz, the conservative party of Prime Minister Viktor Orbán. They share ethno-nationalist views, as demonstrated by their close collaboration in reforming Hungarian citizenship law in 2010 (Pytlas, 2013). Jobbik also benefits from the leniency of the police force, whose lack of zeal in pursuing perpetrators of hate crime is well documented (Amnesty International,

2013). Recent mayoral by-elections have shown that Jobbik can increase its electoral share and win elections, not despite but because of its violent rhetoric and violent 'punitive' actions. In 2011, the village of Gyöngyöspata elected a Jobbik mayor, whose manifesto's sole engagement was to 'invite' the residing Romas to leave, as militias patrolled its streets, intimidating the local Roma population (Pidd, 2012).[4] Clearly, Jobbik is neither electorally nor politically, nor ideologically marginalised, and as such, it points to the fact that today, in the very heart of Europe, violent parties with an agenda inspired by biological racism can also do well.

The search for respectability

An analysis of manifestoes and public discourse point to the huge diversity of the European extreme right. This is hardly surprising, as each party seeks to mobilise images, symbols and specific ideas which allow it to present itself as being part of a national tradition. Yet, other elements point towards some common trends too. All parties, populist, fascist or otherwise labelled, seek to be perceived as 'respectable'. In recent years, even the sulphurous German NPD has tried to alter its image and become more respectable, by putting forward social and environmental protection as one of its primary concerns. Yet its leadership is unable to impose a clear line on the troops, not least the party cadres who seem unable to conceal, even in public, their admiration for Nazism (Rayder, 2012).

This search for respectability has a series of important consequences on the way we should approach extreme-right parties. First, the way parties manage the tensions that exist between their members and their potential electoral base is crucial: what is happening within the party is as important as its discourse. Therefore, one must analyse what the party does, including the internal mechanisms that lead to the production of a programme or the definition of the party's political line (Dézé, 2007; Wolfreys, 2013).

Second, parties should not be analysed in isolation, but in their relations with other organisations. In that respect, the search for respectability is not solely geared to increase their electoral appeal, but crucially to expand the range of their political allies (Crépon, 2012). Whether this is achieved by adopting a more moderate stance (in order to form an electoral alliance or participate in local or national coalitions) or blackmailing rivals to respond to the agenda that extreme-right parties have set, depends on specific contexts. Potential allies are to be found among conservative parties or fringe parties, such as smaller 'moral order' or Eurosceptic parties.[5]

What is more interesting are new alliances forged with non-party actors. Here again, the French case is revealing. Marine Le Pen has effectively attracted talented, professional party cadres, who have had successful careers as senior civil servants, opinion leaders or professional experts. This new generation of cadres is not necessarily less extreme than their forerunners, but more interested in gaining and exercising power than waiting for the elusive crisis which would bring it within their reach. They have successfully marginalised within the party those holding neo-fascist and neo-Nazi ideals, but also – and this is the crucial point – their professional expertise has enabled them to cultivate contacts and build alliances with a variety of political stakeholders, both on the left and on the right of the political spectrum (Godin, 2013).

The message is less modernised than professionalised. For instance, the FN has sought to reach specific groups considered, so far, to be the least receptive to its discourse, such as school teachers who have traditionally formed the electoral bedrock of the French left.[6] During the 2012 presidential campaign, the FN promised to restore 'republican discipline' in the classroom and return to traditional methods of teaching. On this issue, Marine Le

Pen was careful to stress that she was ready to work with people from different political persuasions: her proposals, she argued, were largely consensual and echoed those made in other political milieux, from the authoritarian-left to the ultra-conservative right. As she admitted, she sought to become a 'normal and respected' contributor to debates pertaining to education, a subject less polarising than say, immigration, but ultimately related to the production of national values (Foessel, 2012).

Third, extreme-right parties rely on non-party organisations in order to disseminate their ideas within civil society and among the elites. Parties only form the most visible part of the extreme-right galaxy. Non-party organisations (think-tanks, militia, social movements, and so on . . .), which do not normally enter the electoral fray, offer a fresh perspective on the extreme-right galaxy where notions of moderation and respectability vary considerably.

Non-party organisations

The extreme-right family certainly is not simply made up of parties seeking to win public office or, at the very least, influence political and policy agenda. First, the family includes grass-root social movements (Caiani et al., 2012) seeking to influence and sometimes mobilise public opinion and specific social, religious or professional groups by offering 'interpretative frameworks for specific problems' (Minkenberg, 2009: 15). For instance, in France, this is the case of the Institut Civitas, composed of hardliner Catholics whose broad objective is to undertake a political and social crusade against the 'de-Christianisation' of the country. Civitas trains its members in how to effectively use new social media, offers workshops in public discursive techniques, edits its own review and, taking its cue from the trade union movement, has created 'professional sections' within private companies and local public administrations. In 2013, it played a crucial role in hardening public demonstrations against the Socialist-sponsored law to legalise gay marriage and was held partly responsible for encouraging violent homophobic actions.

Second, the extreme-right family also encompasses a network of think-tanks and publishing houses disseminating quite highbrow ideas in journals, reviews, seminars, radio stations and, of course, on the Internet. These intellectual networks often act as contact points with mainstream conservatives and non-conformist milieux, offering a much sought-after veneer of respectability and legitimacy. For instance, the Danish Association (Den Danske Forening), which acts as both a think-tank and pressure group, successfully recruited in academic circles in the 1980s and 1990s. It was then instrumental in moving immigration to the top of the political agenda in Denmark and served as a launch pad for the Danish People's Party (Dansk Folkeparti, DF) in 1995, providing it with both a set of effective discursive frames and competent personnel (Rydgren, 2004).

The most influential trans-European think-tank is undoubtedly the GRECE (Groupement de Recherche et d'Etudes pour la Civilisation Européenne), the standard bearer and the spearhead of the New Right and its school of thought. Created in France in the aftermath of May '68, and directed by Alain de Benoist, the GRECE's project is to restore the intellectual and cultural hegemony of the right over that of the left (Taguieff, 1994). This, of course, would be a 'New Right' freed from the 'nefarious' conservative, liberal and above all Christian-democratic heritage. It embraces the non-materialist, spiritual and war-like virtues of pre-Christian Europeans seen as the only viable solution against the onslaught of global mediocrity (American consumerism), multiculturalism and universalism (notably the liberal obsession with universal 'human rights'). For the GRECE, natural communities are and should remain ethnically homogeneous if they are to ensure their survival. In that context, recent non-European immigration is associated with a form of slow, subversive 'genocide', threatening the very essence of European civilisation.

In many respects, the GRECE's project replicates the European dreams of past fascist intellectuals and leaders (Bar-on, 2013; Mellon, 2013). Today, it attracts highly educated professionals who wish to wage a cultural war against the 'hegemonic' liberal and left-wing establishment. Through a wide range of activities (publication of books and journals, symposia and conferences, seminars and summer schools, and so on . . .), it seeks to challenge the perceptions of what is acceptable (notably in terms of race relations) and redefine the 'meta-political' language through which issues are constructed and solutions put forward for the whole European continent. For the most part, the GRECE ideology is now very much part of the political identity of European extreme-right parties.[7] Its fundamentally anti-egalitarian and elitist references are a far cry from the more amorphous populism which prevails on the extreme-right parties' electoral trail. Today, its homogenising, nativist definition of the nation, based on ethnic differentialism, serves to strengthen such parties' core doctrinal principles rather than dilute them.

Finally, the extreme right is made up of a plethora of smaller groups and networks operating relatively independently from parties. Their membership is fluid and their ideology radical. They are particularly active on the Internet, which enhances the capacity of disparate groups and different 'cells', often advocating violence, to work together and develop a common language and world view. Skinheads, pagan groups, as well as networks modelled on the German free camaraderies (*Freie Kameradschaften*) also offer alternative lifestyles: they convey extreme ideas to a younger public, less interested in conventional forms of political participation but finding in sport, music and new social media an original and appealing form of political socialisation (Whine, 2012; François, 2007). As fairly unregulated vehicles for extremist ideas, these groups are usually violent (online and offline), act as a facilitator for street mobilisation, form an important recruitment pool for parties despite the ambivalent relations they entertain with them, and above all propagate a common extreme language and common political identity across borders (Whine, 2012).

This is the case, for instance, of the German, Czech and Flemish Autonomous Nationalists (Autonome Nationalisten), a transnational grassroots 'leaderless resistance' movement, whose lack of central organisation makes it difficult to monitor (and to ban). Primarily involved in violent attacks against anti-fascist organisations and their members ('anti-antifa' campaigns) the movement promotes a white supremacist ideology (Mareš, 2010). In the state of Mecklenburg-Western Pomerania, Germany, some of its members have taken over economically devastated rural areas, and created their own 'national liberated zones'. Having rejected the skinhead image and supporting the de-subculturalisation of the neo-Nazi movement ('wearing ties, not boots'), they are now presenting a professional image, staffing 'the local fire departments, running leisure activities for young people and even providing citizens' advice for welfare claimants'. By vetoing new entrants, they are seeking to establish their own ethnically pure villages (Crossland, 2011). They have also radicalised the local NPD's cadres, making it impossible for this extreme-right party to pursue the strategy of 'moderation' and 'respectability' that it has intended to implement (Rayder, 2012).

The two following sections will look at in more detail two street-based social movements, the Italian CasaPound and the English Defence League. Both have different interests and strategies, and entertain complex relations with extreme-right parties; yet both cast some doubt on the de-radicalisation of right-wing extremism in Europe, which is so often associated with the study of electorally successful parties.

CasaPound

CasaPound is an Italian social movement created in 2003 when a group of neo-fascist activists squatted a state-owned building in Rome to provide decent accommodation to Italian families forced out of their home by high rents and real estate speculation.[8] It is estimated to have 5,000 members, but its net-like organisation points to a much wider reach. Indeed, CasaPound provides a range of welfare (mainly housing, but also support for single mothers, meals for isolated pensioners) and cultural services (bookshops, a publishing house, dance, drama and music classes), aimed at poorer Italian families and disfranchised youth. It often manages emergency services, rescuing victims of the earthquakes that frequently ravage the Italian peninsula. Politically, it has championed a variety of laws, from the promotion of social housing, to the re-nationalisation of public utilities. It can count on the support of a violence-prone students' organisation, Blocco Studentesco (BS), particularly strong in Rome and the Lazio region. Glorifying its members as courageous street warriors, the BS's website claims to represent the 'fascists of the third millennium'.[9] CasaPound can also rely on a dense network of sporting clubs, from football to boxing, climbing and scuba diving, a significant reservoir of activists and supporters, who can be easily mobilised. It has produced its own art manifesto – *Manifesto del Turbodinamismo* – largely inspired by the Italian futurist movement, which calls for radical and violent eradication of decadent practices through the multiplication of gratuitous, violent and reckless acts of destruction or provocation.

Gianluca Iannone, CasaPound leader, comes from a neo-fascist splinter party (Fiamma Tricolore), which has rejected Fini's search for respectability and moderation. Today, CasaPound's ideology explicitly espouses Mussolini's fascism, notably its social legislation, and aims to transcend divisions between left and right. The protection of ethnic Italians against poverty, unemployment, and above all poor housing has become its main preoccupation. It argues that an inefficient and corrupt Italian state, a market-obsessed EU and the economic burden of immigration on social services have left ethnic Italians to fend for themselves. Immigrants are mainly presented as victims of globalisation – a modern form of slavery, a global 'resource' exploited by global capitalism – who would be happier to live in a culture which is their own. CasaPound argues that natives – Italian or otherwise – ought to remain master of their own countries.

On the one hand, CasaPound extols the virtues of the state, successively defined as the 'spiritual and moral guide of the national community' and 'the provider of its vital energy'. Outside the state, it argues, individuals and groups remain 'unthinkable'. On the other hand, CasaPound encourages direct action (political stunts, squatting abandoned buildings, festive and violent occupations of public spaces), providing attractive forms of political mobilisation for those who are deeply dissatisfied with traditional politics. The stress put on the 'cult of the body' (it enjoins its members to undertake strenuous physical exercise and to 'dress well' (*vestirsi bene*)), and the requirement that members develop a degree of resistance to physical pain ('*cinghamattanza*', for instance, is a practice when young male activists whip each other with belts, until bleeding)[10] indicate a predilection for violence: Roma, Jewish, immigrant and gay communities, as well as left-wing and liberal activists, have been physically targeted, sometimes with fatal consequences.[11]

CasaPound steers clear of fascist nostalgia (no display of fascist salutes, uniforms and memorabilia), without rejecting fascism. It engages with contemporary issues without following the road of moderation. Here, fascism is modernised rather than diluted. It is not a marginal movement: it started in Rome and the Lazio region, but has now branched out throughout Italy. Admittedly, its recent attempt to enter the electoral fray as a political party has been met with abysmal failure.[12] It is not popular with voters but its social and cultural organisations reach sections of the Italian society that traditional parties or other movements (the Church and unions) find increasingly difficult to re-engage. Its social and cultural appeal means that there exists a strong anti-system and anti-democratic force at the heart of the Italian polity.

The English Defence League

Islamophobia is absent from CasaPound's sophisticated programme and does not register as a major preoccupation for its most active members (Bartlett et al., 2012). Conversely, the English Defence League (EDL) portrays Muslims in the West as a threat to European culture, natural allies to jihadist terrorists whose ambition is to establish a Caliphate in enslaved Europe. The EDL is a street movement, which was created in 2009 in Luton as a response to a demonstration organised by Islam4UK, an extremist Islamist group that provocatively insulted British soldiers parading in Wootton Basset on their return from service in Afghanistan. The EDL warns that Islamisation of Europe through the stealthy implementation of Islamic law (Sharia) will lead to war, an inevitable clash of civilisations. The inability of the British establishment – especially the police – to take the necessary measures to prevent such a scenario is a matter of anger, distress and incredulity among EDL members. It calls for compulsory assimilation of immigrants into a pre-defined national identity, while rejecting any values deemed 'alien' to the English traditions (Jackson, 2011). The EDL promotes exclusion, division and violence, and thrives on confrontation and community tensions.

The EDL's Islamophobia has made it a magnet for neo-fascist and neo-Nazi groups, from the BNP to Combat 18. It has been struggling to dissociate itself from overtly racist organisations that would dent its ability to attract people who merely wish to register their general discontent with British politics (UKIP is doing much better here). This is why the EDL is verbally forbidding BNP members to join the movement. The EDL insists that its demands are motivated by 'cultural', not racial, nationalism (Woodbridge, 2011). To respond to accusations of racism, it has created Jewish, Sikh and Hindu 'divisions' which 'appear to exist primarily as a Facebook page'. Similarly, to boost its 'liberal' credentials, it has set up a lesbian, gay, bisexual and transgender (LGBT) 'division' to counter the homophobia and anti-gay violence that is usually associated with extremist Islamists (Meleagrou and Brun, 2013). Yet its rhetorical defence of an English 'culture' remains mono-cultural. It hardly conceals the racial hatred displayed during EDL marches and the violence of its local campaigns (such as routinely displaying pig's heads in or around mosques) that have led to the arrest and prosecution of many of its members.

The EDL membership is difficult to estimate.[13] It would be an exaggeration to describe the EDL as a huge, mobile street army: its members are first of all 'keyboard warriors', who rarely travel any distance to partake in street demonstrations (Bartlett and Littler, 2011). The use of new media, from Facebook, to personal blogs and websites, is a vital tool for the EDL. Social media are used to launch and organise campaigns, mobilise and energise supporters and disseminate its messages further afield. The EDL has been less successful in using social media to assert its specific identity and strengthen its organisation as is the case with other social movement in Europe (Caiani and Parenti, 2013). It remains poorly organised: the EDL's central organisation is struggling to build a collective identity and 'regulate' effectively the messages that are displayed on social media. It relies heavily on loosely connected grass-roots networks to provide feeds, videos and comments for its own online site or the plethora of sites linked to it. The latter are often more violent, more inflammatory and more overtly racist than the EDL's own brand of cultural nationalism and have by association, a negative effect on its image (Jackson, 2011). It is the tone of such messages and the violence displayed during public marches that put the public off, much more than the EDL's core ideas (Extremis Project, 2012). Its failure to capitalise on the right-wing 'popular' themes (immigration, law and order) is one of strategy rather than one of principle.[14]

The Internet has also played a major role in providing links between the EDL and other European 'counter-jihad movements' (Meleagrou-Hitchen and Brun, 2013). Information, ideas, emotions and plans for the future have long been exchanged through Islamophobic websites such as the 'Europenews' or 'The Gates of Vienna'. The introduction of a stream-lined system for the translation of texts and the subtitling of videos (Rosetta Stone projects) is aimed at facilitating the dissemination of information across the continent. Through online activism, the EDL has initially played an active role in exporting the 'defence league' concept throughout Europe (we have now the Swedish Defence League, Danish Defence League etc. . . . .). In March 2012, it played a pivotal role in setting up a transnational 'counter-jihad movement': 'Stop the Islamisation of Nations' (SION) (Meleagrou-Hitchen and Brun, 2013). It received the backing of American counter-jihadist leaders (such as Pamela Geller, from 'Stop the Islamisation of America' (SIOA), which served as its model) and witnessed the strong participation of Scandinavian defence leagues. SION rejects the existence or possibility of an Islam which is not extreme and systematically contrasts the benefits of Western democracy with the oppression of 'Islamic supremacists': 'freedom of speech against Islamic prohibitions of blasphemy and slander; freedom of conscience against Islamic death penalty for apostasy; equality of rights for all people before the law – as opposed to Sharia's institutionalized discrimination against women and non-Muslims' (Meleagrou-Hitchen and Brun, 2013). Some prominent activists in the European counter-jihad movement, such as the Norwegian blogger Peder Nøstvold Jensen, have refused to condemn the ideas defended by Anders Breivik, who killed 77 people in Norway in 2011, whereas others, such as Philip Traulsen, once leader of the Danish Defence League, have clear links with neo-Nazi groups, such as Blood and Honour (Hope, not Hate, nd; Orange, 2012). In the end, not much is expected to come out of such transnational collaboration, primarily because national and transnational organisations are poorly led and poorly managed (the Dutch Defence League has now collapsed). Nevertheless, such international networks raise some doubt about the EDL's claims to be a non-violent, non-racist movement, untainted by extremist ideas.

Conclusion

This chapter has identified some of the non-party channels (think-tanks, social movements and new social media, transnational organisations) through which extreme-right values and ideas permeate the different strata of European societies. The ethno-pluralist vision of European societies promoted by the GRECE is now widely diffused not only within the political system but also within civil society. Likewise, there is a high frequency of low-level acts of violence associated with the extreme right movements. This is in marked contrast with the search for respectability that characterises extreme-right political parties today.

It is tempting to equate their 'modernisation' to a process of de-radicalisation, and their shift from the margins to the mainstream as a sign of democratic acculturation. A closer analysis of these parties' ideas, beyond the manifestos and public discourses addressed to potential voters, indicates that they continue to abide by a belief system which is at odds with the core value of the polity in which they operate (even when they enter coalitions: see Albertazzi, 2009). The historian Robert Paxton, however, suggests that we shift our attention from what such parties have to say to what they actually do and with whom they actually work. In *The Anatomy of Fascism* (2005), Paxton suggests that a degree of ideological pragmatism, a quest for respectability and the willingness to forge new alliances with mainstream parties, but also professional, civil and even religious associations have all historically characterised the way in which fascism has sought to root itself in a given political context. It is worth hypothesising whether this provides enough of a parallel to see in these parties a contemporary form of fascism.

The extreme right has different faces that it presents to different audiences. This chapter thus warns against the tendency to envisage what is happening on the right of the right through the sole prism of 'populism'. It is true that successful parties owe part of their appeal to a populist rhetoric, an empty but convenient signifier that can accommodate all grievances, all solutions. Yet once their public discourses are compared to their internal debates, their modes of organisation and the links they have established with a wide variety of groups are analysed, it appears that the 'people' which are at the heart of their discourse bear little resemblance to the plural 'people', with their contradictory interests, ideas and desires, who make up our societies. The 'people' of the extreme right is monolithic, and also needs to be strongly guided by enlightened elite. This populism is an anti pluralist and anti democratic one, with a strong authoritarian streak.

Notes

1 For some established parties, such as the Belgian VlaamsBelang, the Austrian FPO and the French FN, the shift between anti-Semitism and Islamophobia provoked serious internal tensions.
2 The rather unstable Italian party system, based on proportional representation and rife with factionalism, means that leaders of small factions or micro-parties can have a disproportionate leverage within parliament when governmental coalitions are formed. It also means that factions are more readily identified with their leader than a clear ideology. Fini has now evolved to a social-liberal position, leading a new small centrist party: Future and Freedom (Futuro e Libertà per l'Italia). The ex-AN's more orthodox cadres, such as Gianni Alemanno, have formed a major 'pressure group' (New Italy) within Berlusconi's mainstream right party.
3 Including the military junta (1967–1974) which found the justification for its oppressive, anti-democratic regime in anti-Communism and the defence of a strict moral order inspired by Christian orthodox values, rather than biological arguments.
4 In the end, they did, unable to bear more harassment and intimidation.
5 The increasing ideological porosity between the mainstream and extreme right is now well documented: established parties have reacted to the growing strength of the extreme right by adopting and legitimising some of its ideas, notably on immigration and identity (Godin and Hanley, 2013). In a number of states (such as Austria, Denmark, Italy, Netherlands, Norway, Poland, Romania, Slovakia, and Switzerland) extreme-right parties have been part of coalition governments or crucial supporters of minority conservative governments. This represents a major shift from earlier patterns in which established parties effectively ostracised extreme parties (Minkenberg, 2002).
6 Using Islamophobia, the FN has sought to attract Jewish and gay communities, with limited success (Camus, 2013).

7 Relations with parties are not always easy: for instance, the GRECE's relations with the FN are tempestuous. Within the FN, those who defend an ultra-nationalist position, or make references to the Christian roots of France, are viewed with suspicion.
8 CasaPound takes its name from the fascist American writer and poet, Ezra Pound, whose pro-fascist broadcast in Italy during World War II led to his internment in the US until 1958.
9 Blocco Studentesco gained some 11,000 votes in the 2011 students' elections in Lazio, the region around Rome. It has also made some inroads into secondary schools.
10 References to the film *Fight Club* (1999) are common in CasaPound's discourse.
11 For instance, a CasaPound sympathiser went on a shooting spree in Florence in 2011, killing two Senegalese workers and wounding others.
12 In 2012, it failed to gain any regional seat in the Lazio region, its natural stronghold. In the 2013 general elections, it obtained 47,317 votes (0.14 per cent).
13 There is no membership card and thus no fees to be paid. The EDL claims around 100,000 members, its Facebook page indicates that 153,000 people 'like this' (July 2013), but membership is likely to be around 35,000 members, including 500 committed activists (Bartlett and Littler, 2011).
14 British voters hold more negative views about immigration than in other West European countries. In 2010, British respondents were the most likely to regard immigration as a problem (Ford, 2011).

Bibliography

Albertazzi, D. (2009) Reconciling 'Voice' and 'Exit': Swiss and Italian Populists in Power, *Politics* 29(1), pp. 1–10.
Amnesty International (2013) Annual Report: Hungary 2013. Available at: www.amnestyusa.org/research/reports/annual-report-hungary-2013
Art, D. (2011) *Inside the Radical Right: The Development of Anti-Immigrant Parties in Western Europe*, Cambridge: Cambridge University Press.
Backes, U. (2006) The electoral victory of the NPD in Saxony and the prospects for future extreme-right success in German elections, *Patterns of Prejudice*, 40(2), pp. 129–144.
Bar-On, T. (2007) *Where Have All the Fascists Gone?* London: Ashgate.
Bar-On, T. (2013) Fascism and the Nouvelle Droite: The quest for a pan-European empire. In A. Mammone, E. Godin and B. Jenkins (eds), *Varieties of right-wing extremism in Europe*, pp. 69–84, London: Routledge.
Bartlett, J. and Littler, M. (2011) *Inside the EDL*, London: Demos.
Bartlett, J., Birdwell, J. and Froio, C. (2012) *Populism in Europe: Casapound*, London: Demos.
Bertelsmann Stiftung (2009) *Strategies for combating right-wing extremism in Europe*, Verlag Betelesmann Stiftung, Gütersloh.
Caiani, M. and Parenti, L. (2013) *European and American Extreme Right Groups and the Internet*, London: Ashgate.
Caiani, M., della Porta, D. and Wagemann, C. (2012) *Mobilizing on the Extreme Right: Germany, Italy, and the United States*, Oxford: Oxford University Press.
Camus, J.Y. (2013) The French extreme right, anti-Semitism and anti-Zionism (1945–2009). In A. Mammone, E. Godin and B. Jenkins (eds), *Varieties of right-wing extremism in Europe*, pp. 121–133, London: Routledge.
Carter, E. (2005) *The Extreme Right in Western Europe: Success Or Failure?* Manchester: Manchester University Press.
Collovald, A. (2004) *Le "populisme du FN", un dangereux contresens*, Bellecombe-en-Bauges, Ed. du Croquant.
Copsey, N. (2010) *The English Defence League: A Challenge to our Country and our Values of Social Inclusion, Fairness and Equality*, London: Faith Matters.
Crépon, S. (2012) *Enquête au cœur du nouveau Front National*, Paris: Nouveau Monde.
Crossland, D. (2011) Fighting the Far Right: One German State's Losing Battle Against Extremism, *Der Spiegel*, 6 September. Available at: www.spiegel.de/international/germany/fighting-the-far-right-one-german-state-s-losing-battle-against-extremism-a-784686.html
Dechezelles, S. (2013) Not so new? The Cultural Basis of Youth Involvement in Italian Extreme Right Organisations. In A. Mammone, E. Godin and B. Jenkins (eds), *Varieties of Right-Wing Extremism in Contemporary Europe*, pp. 182–196, London: Palgrave.

Dézé, A. (2007) Le Front national comme « entreprise doctrinale ». In F. Haegel (ed.), *Partis Politiques et Système Partisan en France*, pp. 255–284, Paris: Presses de Sciences Po.

Downs, William M. (2012) *Political extremism in democracies: combating intolerance*, London: Palgrave Macmillan.

Ellinas, A. (2013) The rise of Golden Dawn: The new face of the far right in Greece, *South European Society and Politics*, pp. 1–24.

Extremis Project (2012) Under the microscope: Public attitudes toward the English Defence League (EDL). Available at: http://extremisproject.org/2012/10/the-english-defence-league-edl-what-do-people-think/

Fella, S. (2006) From Fiuggi to the Farnesina: Gianfranco Fini's Remarkable Journey, *Journal of Contemporary European Studies*, 14(1), pp. 11–23.

Foessel, M. (2012) Marine Le Pen ou la captation des 'invisibles', *Esprit*, February (2), pp. 20–31.

Ford, R. (2011) Public opinion and immigration: policy briefing. All-Party Parliamentary group on migration. Available at: www.appgmigration.org.uk/sites/default/files/APPG_migration-Public_opinion-June_2011.pdf

FRA (European Agency for Fundamental Rights) (2013) *Fundamental rights: challenges and achievements in 2012*. Available at: http://fra.europa.eu/sites/default/files/annual-report-2012-chapter-6_en.pdf

François, S. (2007) The Euro-Pagan scene: Between paganism and radical right, *Journal for the study of radicalisation*, 1(2), 35–54.

Godin, E. (2013) The porosity between the mainstream right and extreme right in France: *les droites décomplexées* under Nicolas Sarkozy and Marine Le Pen's leadership, *Journal of Contemporary European Studies*, 21(1), pp. 53–67.

Godin, E. and Hanley, D. (2013) No Enemies on the Right? Competition and Collusion between Conservatives, Moderates and Extreme Right Parties in Europe [Special issue]. *Journal of Contemporary European Studies*, 21(1), pp. 2–4.

Goodwin, M. (2011) *New British Fascism: The rise of the British National Party*, London: Routledge.

Haynes, R. and Rady, M. (eds) (2011) 'Ferenc Szálasi, "Hungarism" and the Arrow Cross', *In the Shadow of Hitler: Personalities of the Right in Central and Eastern Europe*, London: Tauris, pp. 261–277.

Hope, not Hate (nd) Counter-Jihad, Available at: www.hopenothate.org.uk/counter-jihad/country/

Howard, M. (2010) The Impact of the Far Right on Citizenship Policy in Europe: Explaining Continuity and Change, *Journal of Ethnic and Migration Studies*, 36(5), pp. 735–751.

Ignazi, P. (1996) From Neo-Fascists to Post-Fascists? The Transformation of the MSI into the AN, *West European Politics*, 19(4), pp. 693–714.

Ignazi, P. (2003) *Extreme-right Parties in Western Europe*, Oxford: Oxford University Press.

Jackson, P. (2011) *The EDL: Britain's far right social movement*, University of Northampton, September. Available at: www.radicalism-new-media.org/wp-content/uploads/2011/09/The_EDL_Britains_New_Far_Right_Social_Movement.pdf

Le Figaro (4 December 2010) 2012: Marine Le Pen ira pour gagner.

Mammone, A. (2009) The Eternal Return? Faux Populism and Contemporarization of Neo-Fascism across Britain, France and Italy, *Journal of Contemporary European Studies*, 17(2), pp. 171–192.

Mammone, A., Godin, E. and Jenkins, B. (2013) *Varieties of right-wing extremism in Europe*, London: Routledge.

Manifesto del Turbodinamismo, CasaPound, Available at: www.ideodromocasapound.org/?p=677

Mareš, M. (2010) Transnational Activism of Extreme Right Youth in East Central Europe, Paper presented at the International Conference "Far right networks in Northern and Eastern Europe", 25–27 March, Uppsala University. Available at: www.anst.uu.se/matwe309/Mares.pdf

Meleagrou-Hitchen, A. and Brun, H. (2013) *A neo-nationalist network: The English Defence League and Europe's Counter-Jihad Movement*, The International Centre for the Study of Radicalisation and Political Violence (ICSR), King's College, London.

Mellon, J.-A. (2013) The idées-force of the European New Right. In A. Mammone, E. Godin and B. Jenkins (eds), *Varieties of Right-Wing Extremism in Contemporary Europe*, pp. 53–68, London: Palgrave.

Minkenberg, M. (2002) The New Radical Right in the Political Process: Interaction Effects in France and Germany. In M. Schain, A. Zolberg and P. Hossay (eds), *Shadows over Europe: The Development and Impact of the Extreme Right in Western Europe*, pp. 245–268, New York: Palgrave Macmillan.

Minkenberg, M. (2009) The radical right in Europe: challenges for contemporary Research, in Bertelsmann Stiftung (2009) *Strategies for combating right-wing extremism in Europe*, Verlag Bertelesmann Stifung, Gütersloh, pp. 13–28.

Mudde, C. (1996) The War of Words Defining the Extreme Right Party Family, *West European Politics*, 19(2), 225–48.

Mudde, C. (2007) *Populist Radical-right Parties in Europe*, Cambridge: Cambridge University Press.

Orange, R. (2012, 12 March) English Defence League sacks European demo head after brutal assault. *The Telegraph*, Available at: www.telegraph.co.uk/news/worldnews/europe/denmark/9138323/English-Defence-League-sacks-European-demo-head-after-brutal-assault.html

Organization for Security and Co-operation in Europe (OSCE). 15 June 2010. Office for Democratic Institutions and Human Rights (ODIHR). Addressing Violence, Promoting Integration: Field Assessment of Violent Incidents against Roma in Hungary. Key Developments, Findings and Recommendations June–July 2009. Available at: www.osce.org/odihr/68545

Paxton, R. (2005) *The Anatomy of Fascism*, London: Penguin.

Pidd, H. (2012) Poor, abused and second-class: the Roma living in fear in Hungarian village, *The Guardian*, 27 January. Available at: www.guardian.co.uk/world/2012/jan/27/hungary-roma-living-in-fear

Pytlas, B. (2013) Radical-right narratives in Slovakia and Hungary: Historical legacies, mythic overlaying and contemporary politics, *Patterns of Prejudice*, 47(2), pp. 162–183.

Rayder, B. (2012) The ideological development of the NPD from 1996 to 2011: A critical analysis of Germany's oldest existing right-wing party. Paper presented at the UACES conference, Passau, Germany, 3–5 September 2012. Available at: http://uaces.org/documents/papers/1201/rayder.pdf

Rosenberger, S. and Hadj-Abdou, L. (2013) Islam at issue: Anti-Islamic mobilization of the extreme right in Austria. In A. Mammone, E. Godin and B. Jenkins (eds), *Varieties of right-wing extremism in Europe*, pp. 149–163, London: Routledge.

Ruzza, C. and Fella, S. (2011) *Re-inventing the Italian Right: Territorial politics, populism and 'post-fascism'*, London: Routledge.

Rydgren, J. (2004) Explaining the Emergence of Radical Right-Wing Populist Parties: The Case of Denmark, *West European Politics* 27(3), 474–503.

Rydgren, J. (2005) Is extreme right-wing populism contagious? Explaining the emergence of a new party family, *European Journal of Political Research*, 44, 413–437.

Rydgren, J. (2007) The sociology of the radical right, *Annual Review of Sociology*, (33), pp. 241–262.

Rydgren, J. (2012) *Class Politics and the Radical Right*, London: Routledge.

Schain, M., Zolberg, A. and Hossay, P. (eds) (2002) *Shadows Over Europe: The Development and Impact of the Extreme Right in Western Europe*, Basingstoke: Palgrave Macmillan.

Taguieff, P.-A. (1994) *Sur la Nouvelle Droite. Jalons d'une analyse critique*, Paris: Galilée.

Vossen, K. (2010) Populism in the Netherlands after Fortuyn: Rita Verdonk and Geert Wilders compared, *Perspectives on European Politics and Society*, 11(1), pp. 22–38.

Whine, M. (2012) Trans-European trends in right-wing extremism. In A. Mammone, E. Godin and B. Jenkins (eds), *Mapping the extreme right in contemporary Europe*, pp. 317–333, London: Routledge.

Wolfreys, J. (2013) The European extreme right in comparative perspective. In A. Mammone, E. Godin and B. Jenkins (eds), *Varieties of right wing-extremism in Europe*, pp. 19–37, London: Routledge.

Woodbridge, S. (2011) 'Ambivalent admiration? The response of other extreme-right groups to the rise of the BNP'. In N. Copsey and G. Macklin (eds), *British National Party: Contemporary perspectives*, pp. 103–122, London: Routledge.

13

Hate crime in the United States

Jordan Blair Woods

This chapter provides an overview of hate crime in the United States. It focuses on two main topics: (1) hate crime legislation and (2) hate crime statistics. As the chapter discusses, dozens of hate crime laws have been enacted across the United States at the federal and state levels. Although hate crime statistics are more comprehensive in the United States than in many other countries, the data likely fail to capture the true extent of the problem because of methodological shortcomings. Moreover, existing empirical studies on hate crime in the United States focus primarily on hate crime victimisation, resulting in limited information about hate crime offending, policing, and prosecution.

Hate crime legislation in the United States

Federalism – the concept by which governing authority is distributed between the U.S. Federal government and the States – lies at the heart of how hate crime laws are created and enforced in the United States (Lawrence, 2009). As a consequence of the broad police powers that the United States Constitution vests in the states, most hate crime laws – and criminal laws generally – derive from state codes created by state legislatures. From early American history until the 1960s, Congress had very limited involvement in creating criminal legislation (Marion, 1994). The role of the U.S. Federal government to enact criminal laws has expanded since then, which is illustrated by the growth of federal hate crime protections.

Federal hate crime laws

Although there is a long history of hate-motivated violence in the United States, Congress did not enact hate crime legislation until 1968 (Woods, 2008a). *See* 18 U.S.C. § 245. This early hate crime law, passed as part of the Civil Rights Act of 1968, gave federal officers the authority to investigate and to prosecute crimes motivated by hatred against a victim's race, colour, religion, or national origin if the victim was engaging in specific federally-protected activities when the crimes occurred. These activities included: (1) applying or enrolling for admission to a public school or college; (2) participating in benefit or service programs and facilities administered by state and local governments; (3) applying for private or state employment; (4) serving in a jury; (5) traveling in or using a facility of interstate commerce or common carrier; and (6) using a public accommodation or place of exhibition or entertainment, including hotels, motels, restaurants, lunchrooms, bars, gas stations, theatres, concert halls, sports arenas or stadiums. *See* 18 U.S.C. § 245.

The need to address racial violence committed primarily against African Americans motivated Congress' decision to include hate crime provisions as part of the Civil Rights Act of 1968. This racial violence swept across the United States in three waves (Levin, 2002). An overview of this history of violence is necessary to understand the context in which hate crime laws in the United States came about.

The first wave of racial violence occurred during the Reconstruction Era (1865–1877). After the U.S. Civil War ended in 1865, Congress passed the Thirteenth, Fourteenth, and Fifteenth Amendments to the U.S. Constitution, which intended to protect the civil rights of newly freed slaves (Lively, 1999). These amendments fell far short of this goal, largely because states enacted various laws to circumvent the requirements of the amendments (Valelly, 2009). These new amendments also inspired violent backlash against newly freed slaves. The Ku Klux Klan (KKK) was the most notorious organisation that used violence as means to deter African Americans from exercising their civil rights, and gaining political, economic, and social power (Samito, 2009). Its membership included politicians, law enforcement officers, and the general public. Racial violence against African Americans often went unpunished because many local law enforcement officers refused to arrest white perpetrators of this violence (Foner, 1988). And, even if arrested, all-white juries commonly refused to indict white perpetrators. To address these issues, Congress enacted laws to punish government officials and private individuals who threatened to deprive, or actually deprived, citizens from exercising their constitutional and statutory rights. *See* 18 U.S.C. §§ 241, 242. In spite of these federal legislative reforms, pervasive racial violence against African Americans continued.

The second wave of racial violence occurred after an immigration surge immediately following World War I. During this period, the KKK reached its organisational peak (Fox, 2011). Many people, including an unprecedented number of women, joined the KKK and other white supremacist organisations in an attempt to maintain social and political dominance in post-war society (Blee, 1991). The KKK not only targeted African Americans, but also victimised Catholics, Jews, and other new immigrant groups.

African Americans were still disproportionately terrorised by white-supremacist violence – and by the practice of lynching in particular – after World War I. The return of African American veterans and labour shortages in essential industries prompted white mob violence (Gitlin, 2009). In the summer of 1919, what became known as the "Red Summer," white mobs murdered hundreds of African Americans during race riots that exploded in many U.S. cities; 73 African Americans were murdered by lynching in this summer alone (Gitlin, 2009; Davis, 2008). The National Association for the Advancement of Colored People (NAACP) led the initiative for a federal law addressing lynching, which was never enacted (Berg, 2011; Holden-Smith, 1996). To address the systemic practice of lynching, over a dozen U.S. states passed anti-lynching laws between the 1890s and the 1930s. These laws were among the first laws to outlaw a specific form of hate-motivated violence. Lax police enforcement and all-white juries that refused to convict white perpetrators, however, often prevented these laws from being enforced (Berg, 2011).

The third wave of hate-motivated violence occurred during the Civil Rights Movement in the 1960s. After the Great Depression of the 1930s, the U.S. Supreme Court decided several cases that intended to strengthen the civil rights of African Americans in different contexts, such as education (*Brown v. Board of Education*, 347 U.S. 483 [1954]; *Missouri ex rel. Gaines v. Canada*, 305 U.S. 337 [1938]), jury participation (*Patton v. Mississippi*, 332 U.S. 463 [1947]), public transportation (*Morgan v. Commonwealth of Virginia*, 328 U.S. 373 [1946]), and voting (*Smith v. Allwright*, 321 U.S. 649 [1944]). Lack of enforcement at the state and local levels again inhibited African Americans from fully exercising these expanded civil rights.

In the 1960s, demonstrators led by Martin Luther King Jr. and other renowned civil rights leaders protested unequal treatment and discrimination against African Americans through boycotts, rallies, black voter registrations, and marches. Many opponents of the Civil Rights Movement violently targeted African Americans to intimidate them from politically organising and exercising their civil rights (Chalmers, 2005). In response, Congress enacted the Civil Rights Act of 1968, which included a provision that gave federal officers the authority to investigate and to prosecute crimes of violence motivated by a victim's race, colour, religion, or national origin if the victim was engaging in certain federally-protected activities when the crimes occurred. *See* 18 U.S.C. § 245.

The Hate Crime Statistics Act of 1990 (HCSA) was the first piece of federal hate crime legislation enacted after 18 U.S.C. § 245 (Woods, 2008b). *See* 28 U.S.C. § 534. The HCSA mandated the Attorney General to gather data about hate crimes motivated by bias against a person's race, religion, disability, sexual orientation, or ethnicity. The bill also required the Attorney General to 'establish guidelines for the collection of such data including the necessary evidence and criteria ... for a finding of manifest prejudice'. Following this mandate, the Federal Bureau of Investigation (FBI) has gathered and published annual hate crime statistics since 1992.

In 1994, Congress enacted the Hate Crimes Sentencing Enhancement Act (HCSEA). *See* 28 U.S.C. § 994. The HCSEA required the U.S. Sentencing Commission to provide enhanced penalties for crimes motivated by animus towards a person's actual or perceived race, colour, religion, national origin, ethnicity, gender, disability or sexual orientation. As directed by Congress, the U.S. Sentencing Commission in 1995 implemented a three-level enhancement for hate crimes under the Sentencing Guidelines. The enhancement applied exclusively in cases where federal jurisdiction was proper. Because 18 U.S.C. § 245 granted federal jurisdiction with respect to crimes motivated by bias against a person's race, religion, colour, and national origin, the federal government could only prosecute crimes motivated by bias against a person's sexual orientation, gender identity, gender, or disability if it obtained jurisdiction in another way. This jurisdictional barrier made it very difficult to apply the enhancement in those latter categories of cases.

The Matthew Shepard and James Byrd, Jr. Hate Crimes Prevention Act of 2009 eased this jurisdictional obstacle. *See* 18 U.S.C. § 249. Congress enacted this law after several unsuccessful attempts to expand federal hate crime legislation during the late 1990s and early 2000s (Woods, 2008b). The Act bears the names of two victims – Matthew Shepard and James Byrd, Jr. – whose brutal murders received nationwide media coverage. In 1998, two homophobic assailants brutally attacked Matthew Shepard – a gay, 21-year-old university student – and left him to die in a remote area of Wyoming. That same year, three white men in Jasper, Texas picked up James Byrd, Jr. – a 49-year-old black man – on a country road in their truck, beat him, slit his throat, chained him to the back of the truck, and dragged his body for three miles. At the time, Wyoming and Texas did not have hate crime laws.

The Matthew Shepard and James Byrd, Jr. Hate Crimes Prevention Act expands federal hate crime law protection to include actual or perceived sexual orientation, gender, gender identity, or disability of the victim. It also provides financial and personnel assistance to state and local governments to investigate and to prosecute bias crimes. Further, the law expands the federal government's authority to prosecute hate crimes even when the victims are not engaging in the federally-protected activities specified in 18 U.S.C. § 245.

State hate crime laws

In 1978, California became the first state to enact hate crime legislation. During the 1980s and 1990s, state legislatures passed most existing hate crime laws in the United States. It is uncertain whether states experienced greater levels of hate-motivated violence against minorities during this period. Nevertheless, addressing this violence became a priority of various social movements and state legislatures (Jenness and Grattet, 2001).

Today, nearly every state has passed some form of hate crime legislation. The content of hate crime laws and their scope of prohibited conduct differ widely from state to state. These laws might include civil penalties, criminal penalties, resource allocation to collect statistics on hate crime, and/or resource allocation to train law enforcement officers to appropriately handle and investigate hate crime.

The characteristics that are protected under hate crime laws also vary from state to state and are continuously expanding. As of May 2013, 44 states and Washington D.C. have hate crime laws that include race/ethnicity/colour, religion, and national origin/ancestry.[1] The hate crime laws of 32 states and Washington D.C. include disability[2]; 31 states and Washington D.C. include sexual orientation[3]; 28 states and Washington D.C. include sex/gender[4]; 14 states and Washington D.C. include age[5]; 13 states and Washington D.C. include gender identity or expression[6]; five states and Washington D.C. include homelessness.[7]

Statutory definitions of hate: animus v. intentional selection

Hate crime laws across the United States also take different approaches to defining "hate" (Woods, 2008c). The prototypical hate crime is motivated by animus against a victim's actual or perceived difference (Wang, 1999). In the case of opportunistic bias crimes, however, perpetrators intentionally select victims for personal gain who they perceive to be more vulnerable to hate crime – the perpetrators are not necessarily motivated by animus (Woods, 2008c; Wang, 1999). For instance, consider a perpetrator who does not have personal views about homosexuality, but targets gay men as robbery victims because he believes that they are "easy targets" and will not report the crimes.

Whether a showing of actual animus is required to pursue hate crime charges varies among jurisdictions. Federal, state and local governments have adopted two models of hate crime law: the Group Animus Model and the Discriminatory Selection Model. Hate crime laws in some states (e.g., Florida, New Hampshire, and Pennsylvania) follow the Group Animus Model, which defines "hate" as motivated substantially or in part by animus against victims because of their actual or perceived group membership. *See* FLA. STAT. ANN. § 755.085 (2005); N.H. REV. STAT. ANN. § 651:6(1)(f) (2008); PA. CONS. STAT. ANN. §2710(a) (2008). Under the Discriminatory Selection Model, a crime qualifies as a hate crime whenever perpetrators intentionally select victims on the basis of their group membership, regardless of the reasons for the selection. Wisconsin is the only state with a hate crime law that unambiguously follows the Discriminatory Selection Model. *See* WIS. STAT. ANN. §939.645(2)(b) (2000).

Most U.S. states have adopted hate crime laws that do not refer explicitly to either the group animus or the intentional selection of victims (Lawrence, 2009; Woods, 2008c). These statutes define hate crimes as occurring "because of or by reason of" the victims' group membership, or, with "malicious intent" towards victims because of their group membership. In most states with hate crime laws that adopt this language, neither legislatures nor the courts have declared that animus is required to prosecute hate crimes. Given this lack of guidance, the scope of conduct that falls under the purview of these hate crime laws is not entirely clear.

The constitutionality of hate crime laws

The U.S. Supreme Court has addressed the constitutionality of hate crime laws in two decisions – *R.A.V. v. City of St. Paul* (505 U.S. 377 [1992]) and *Wisconsin v. Mitchell* (508 U.S. 476 [1993]).

In *R.A.V.*, the Supreme Court invalidated a local hate crime ordinance that prohibited specific modes of expression. Specifically, the ordinance prohibited the display of symbols or objects (e.g., a burning cross or Nazi swastika) by which 'one knows or has reasonable grounds to know arouses anger, alarm, or resentment in others on the basis of race, color, religion, or gender'. The Supreme Court held that hate crime ordinances that criminalise specific expressive acts violate free speech guarantees under the First Amendment to the U.S. Constitution (p. 391).

In *Mitchell*, the Supreme Court reached the opposite result and upheld the constitutionality of Wisconsin's hate crime law. That statute enhanced the penalty of an offence whenever the defendant '[i]ntentionally select[ed] the person against whom the crime . . . is committed . . . because of the race, religion, color, disability, sexual orientation, national origin, or ancestry of that person'. The Court concluded that unlike the ordinance at issue in *R.A.V.* that criminalised expressive acts, the Wisconsin statute targeted violent conduct, which is not afforded First Amendment protection (p. 484). The Court stressed the relationship between the purpose of the Wisconsin penalty-enhancement statute and the harms of hate crime, stating that the 'Wisconsin statute singles out for enhancement bias-inspired conduct because this conduct is thought to inflict greater individual and societal harm . . . [and is] more likely to provoke retaliatory crimes, inflict distinct emotional harms on their victims and incite community unrest' (pp. 487–488). The Court further reasoned, 'the State's desire to redress these perceived harms provides an adequate explanation for its penalty-enhancement provision over and above mere disagreement with the offenders' biases and beliefs' (p. 488).

After Congress passed the Matthew Shepard and James Byrd, Jr. Hate Crimes Prevention Act in 2009, commentators have debated whether Congress had the constitutional power to enact the law and whether the law impermissibly violates freedom of expression (Bessel, 2010; Walsh, 2009; DiPompeo, 2008; Lawrence, 2008; Woods, 2008b). Although the Supreme Court disposed of free speech arguments in *Mitchell*, the Court has not considered whether Congress had the constitutional authority to pass the Act. The Supreme Court's decisions in *R.A.V.* and *Mitchell* did not address this specific challenge because the cases involved a local ordinance and a state law.

Statistics on hate crime in the United States

The main source of official U.S. crime data is the FBI's Uniform Crime Report (UCR). In accordance with the HCSA, the FBI has released a separate annual publication on hate crime data in the United States, entitled *Hate Crime Statistics*. The report is based on voluntarily submitted data from over 18,000 law enforcement agencies across the United States. The report, however, likely underrepresents the true extent of hate crime in the United States due to lack of participation, lax recording, and different hate-crime classification practices of law enforcement agencies (Hall, 2005; Rubenstein, 2004; McDevitt et al., 2003; Perry, 2001). Nevertheless, the 2011 report reflects that 1,944 law enforcement agencies reported 6,222 hate crime incidents involving 7,254 offenses[8] (FBI, 2012). The report also provides further information on the different hate crimes committed against persons and property, hate crime perpetrators, victims, location type, and jurisdiction. Currently, the report only includes data on hate crime motivated by bias against a person's race, religion, sexual orientation, ethnicity/national origin, and disability. Beginning in 2013, it will include hate crimes motivated by bias against a person's gender and gender identity.

Many states also gather and release data on hate crime. California has one of the most comprehensive hate crime reporting schemes. Since 1995, the Office of Attorney General of California has released an annual report on hate crime in the state. According to the 2011 report, the total number of hate crimes has decreased 33 per cent since 2002, from 2,009 to 1,347 (California Attorney General, 2012). Hate-motivated violent offenses have decreased 45.6 per cent since 2002 (from 1,517 to 825), while hate-motivated property offenses have increased 4.5 per cent since 2002 (from 492 to 514). The report also reflects that in 2011 hate crimes motivated by bias against a person's race/ethnicity/national origin are most common in California (57.5 per cent), followed by sexual orientation (23 per cent) and religion (16.9 per cent). It is uncertain whether these statistics accurately reflect hate crime occurrences or whether they reflect changes in hate crime reporting.

The National Crime Victimization Survey (NCVS), conducted jointly by the U.S. Department of Justice and the U.S. Census Bureau, is the largest ongoing victim survey in the United States. The NCVS is based on a nationally representative sample of about 40,000 households (approximately 70,000 to 75,000 people). The households are included in the sample for three years, and the participants are interviewed twice a year about their victimisation experiences with violent and property crimes. One advantage of the NCVS is that it has the potential to capture both reported and unreported hate crimes. The NCVS questionnaire asks participants whether they 'have any reason to suspect' that an incident 'was a hate crime or crime of prejudice or bigotry'. If so, then it asks participants whether they suspected that the offender targeted them because of race, religion, ethnicity/national origin, disability, gender, or sexual orientation. It also asks about what evidence led the participant to believe that the incident was motivated by hatred and whether the participant reported the incident to the police.

In 2013, Bureau of Justice Statistics researchers released a report on hate crime victimisation rates based on NCVS data from 2003 to 2011 (Sandholtz et al., 2013). It reported that an estimated annual average of 259,700 non-fatal violent and property hate crime victimisations occurred against persons age twelve or older residing in U.S. households between 2007 and 2011. During this period, whites, Blacks, and Hispanics had similar rates of violent hate crime victimisation, and about one-third of all victimisations occurred at or near the victim's home. The report further noted that there was no change in the annual average number of total, violent, or property hate crime victimisation across the periods from 2003–06 and 2007–11. Moreover, the percentage of hate crimes motivated by religious bias more than doubled between 2003–06 and 2007–11 (from 10 per cent to 21 per cent), while the percentage motivated by racial bias dropped slightly (from 63 per cent to 54 per cent). Between 2003–06 and 2007–11, the percentage of hate crime victimisations reported to police declined from 46 per cent to 35 per cent.

In addition to official statistics and victimisation surveys, several researchers have studied hate crime in the United States. Most of this empirical research focuses on victimisation and touches on three themes (Woods, 2008a). First, U.S.-based researchers have reported that hate crimes cause greater physical injury to victims than parallel crimes (Lombardi et al., 2001; Herek et al., 2002; Lawrence, 1994). Second, they have reported that hate crimes cause greater psychological injury to victims than parallel crimes (Herek et al., 2002; McDevitt et al., 2001; D'Augelli and Grossman, 2001; Lombardi et al., 2001; Herek et al., 1999). Third, they have reported that the harms of hate crime extend beyond immediate victims to targeted communities in the United States (Herek and Berrill, 1992). Some scholars challenged the research in support of each of these themes (Hurd and Moore, 2004; Jacobs and Potter, 1998). In spite of these challenges, the Supreme Court's reliance on these themes to uphold the constitutionality of hate crime laws in *Wisconsin v. Mitchell* demonstrates their importance. *See* 508 U.S. at 477–78.

Some researchers have also focused on hate crime offenders (Dunbar et al., 2005; McDevitt et al., 2002; Levin and McDevitt, 1993). This area of research, however, is much more limited. Based on case files from the Boston Police Department, McDevitt et al. (2002) advanced the most popular typology of hate-crime offender motivations to date, which includes four categories: thrill-seeking, defensive, retaliatory, and mission. Offenders who commit *thrill-seeking* hate crimes – which they contend are the most frequent – are 'motivated by a desire for excitement or thrills' (p. 307). Offenders commit *defensive* hate crimes 'to protect his neighbourhood from those [they] considered to be outsiders or intruders' (p. 308). *Retaliatory* hate crimes intend to respond to a previously perceived hate crime with hate-motivated violence. Finally, during *mission* hate crimes, 'the perpetrator becomes totally committed to bigotry' and 'seeks to rid the world of evil rather than to respond to any specific event that threatens him' (p. 309). Several law enforcement agencies across the United States have used and continue to use this typology to assist in hate crime investigations (Levin and McDevitt, 2012).

Researchers have also focused on hate crime policing in the United States. Similar to research on hate crime offending, research in this area is also limited. The existing studies focus generally on two themes. The first theme is the factors that influence law enforcement agencies to participate in hate-crime reporting schemes (Grattet and Jenness, 2008; Cronin et al., 2007; Nolan and Akiyama, 2002, 1999; Balboni and McDevitt, 2001). Researchers have found that the existence of departmental policies and protocols on hate crime encourages police participation in hate crime reporting (Grattet and Jenness, 2008; Nolan and Akiyama, 2002, 1999; Balboni and McDevitt, 2001). The second theme is the factors associated with the police enforcement of hate crime laws and the creation of hate crime policies in law enforcement agencies (King, 2007; Jenness and Grattet, 2005; Bell, 2002; Franklin, 2002; Boyd et al., 1996; Martin, 1996).

Very few scholars have investigated the factors that influence hate crime prosecutions in the United States (Byers et al., 2012; Phillips, 2009; King, 2008; Levin et al., 2007; McPhail and Jenness, 2005). Phillips' (2009) study found that hate crime typology is useful for understanding prosecuted cases in which hatred is the sole motivation, but inadequate to explain prosecuted cases in which hatred is one of many or a peripheral motivation. King's study (2008) reported that racial demographics, religious views, and political ideology influence the number of hate crime prosecutions and the institution of hate crime policies. In McPhail and Jenness' (2005) study, prosecutors reported that the facts of the case, strategic advantage, the seriousness of the crime, and a desire to send a message motivated their decisions to prosecute hate crimes.

Conclusion

In summary, this overview has shown that several different hate crime laws exist across the United States at the federal and state levels. It has also demonstrated that there are numerous sources of hate crime statistics in the United States, but that the data from these sources likely underrepresents the extent of the problem due to methodological shortcomings. Finally, the overview has shown that there is a need for more developed empirical studies on hate crime in the United States, especially in terms of offending, policing, and prosecution.

Notes

1 States that include race/ethnicity/colour, religion, and national origin/ancestry in hate crime laws include: AL, AK, AZ, CA, CO, CT, DE, FL, HI, IA, ID, IL, KS, KY, LA, MA, MD, ME, MI, MN, MO, MS, MT, NC, ND, NE, NH, NJ, NM, NV, NY, OH, OK, OR, PA, RI, SD, TN, TX, VA, VT, WA, WI, WV and Washington D.C.
2 States that include disability in hate crime laws include: AL, AK, AZ, CA, CO, CT, DE, FL, HI, IA, IL, KS, LA, MA, MD, ME, MN, MO, NE, NH, NJ, NM, NV, NY, OK, OR, RI, TN, TX, VT, WA, WI and Washington D.C.
3 States that include sexual orientation in hate crime laws include: AZ, CA, CO, CT, DE, FL, HI, IA, IL, KS, KY, LA, MA, MD, ME, MI, MN, MO, NE, NH, NJ, NM, NV, NY, OR, RI, TN, TX, VT, WA, WI and Washington D.C.
4 States that include sex/gender in hate crime laws include: AK, AZ, CA, CT, HI, IA, IL, LA, MD, ME, MI, MN, MO, MS, NC, ND, NE, NH, NJ, NM, NY, OK, RI, TN, TX, VT, WA, WV and Washington D.C.
5 States that include age in hate crime laws include: CA, FL, HI, IA, KS, LA, ME, MN, NE, NH, NM, NY, TX, VT and Washington D.C.
6 States that include gender identity or expression in hate crime laws include: CA, CO, CT, HI, MA, MD, NJ, NM, NV, OR, RI, VT, WA and Washington D.C.
7 Homelessness: FL, MD, ME, RI, WA, and Washington D.C.
8 A perpetrator can commit multiple offenses during a single hate crime incident.

References

Balboni, J. and McDevitt, J. (2001). Hate crime reporting: Understanding police officer perceptions, departmental protocol, and the role of the victim: Is there such a thing as a hate crime? *Justice Research and Policy*, 3, 1–27.
Bell, J. (2002). *Policing hatred: Law enforcement, civil rights, and hate crime.* New York: New York University Press.
Berg, M. (2011). *Popular justice: A history of lynching in America.* Chicago: Ivan R. Dee.
Bessel, A. L. (2010). Preventing hate crimes without restricting constitutionally protected speech: Evaluating the impact of the Matthew Shepard and James Byrd, Jr. Hate Crimes Prevention Act on First Amendment free speech rights. *Hamline Journal of Public Law and Public Policy*, 31, 735–775.
Blee, K. M. (1991). Women in the 1920s' Ku Klux Klan movement. *Feminist Studies*, 17, 57–77.
Boyd, E. A., Berk, R. A. and Hamner, K. M. (1996). "Motivated by hatred or prejudice": Categorization of hate-motivated crimes in two police divisions. *Law & Society Review*, 30(4), 819–850.
Brown v. Board of Education, 347 U.S. 483 (1954).
Byers, B., Warren-Gordon, K. and Jones, J. A. (2012). Predictors of hate crime prosecutions: An analysis of data from the national prosecutors survey and state-level bias crime laws. *Race and Justice*, 2(3), 203–219.
California Attorney General (2012). *Hate crime in California 2011.* Available at https://oag.ca.gov/sites/all/files/agweb/pdfs/cjsc/publications/hatecrimes/hc11/preface11.pdf (last visited June 9, 2013).
Chalmers, D. M. (2005). *Backfire: How the Ku Klux Klan helped the civil rights movement.* Oxford, UK: Rowman & Littlefield Publishers, Inc.
Cronin, S. W., McDevitt, J., Farrell, A. and Nolan, J. J. (2007). Bias-crime reporting: Organizational responses to ambiguity, uncertainty, and infrequency in eight police departments. *American Behavioral Scientist*, 51(2), 213–231.
D'Augelli, A. R. and Grossman, A. H. (2001). Disclosure of sexual orientation, victimization, and mental health among lesbian, gay, bisexual older adults. *Journal of Interpersonal Violence*, 16, 1008–1027.

Davis, D. A. (2008). Not only war is hell: World War I and African American lynching narratives. *African American Review*, 42, 477–491.
DiPompeo, C. (2008). Federal hate crime laws and United States v. Lopez: On a collision course to clarify jurisdictional-element analysis. *University of Pennsylvania Law Review*, 157, 617–672.
Dunbar, E., Quinones, J. and Crevecoeur, D. A. (2005). Assessment of hate crime offenders: The role of bias intent in examining violence risk. *Journal of Forensic Psychology Practice*, 5(1), 1–19.
Federal Bureau of Investigation (FBI) (2012). *Hate crime statistics 2011*. Available at www.fbi.gov/about-us/cjis/ucr/hate-crime/2011 (last visited June 9, 2013).
Foner, E. (1988). *Reconstruction: America's unfinished revolution, 1863–1877*. New York: Harper and Row.
Fox, C. (2011). *Everyday klansfolk: White protestant life and the KKK in 1920s Michigan*. East Lansing, MI: Michigan State University Press.
Franklin, K. (2002). Good intentions: The enforcement of hate crime penalty-enhancements statutes. *American Behavioral Scientist*, 46(1), 154–172.
Gitlin, M. (2009). *The Ku Klux Klan: A guide to an American subculture*. Santa Barbara, CA: ABC-CLIO.
Grattet, R. and Jenness, V. (2008). Transforming symbolic law into organizational action: Hate crime policy and law enforcement practice. *Social Forces*, 87(1), 1–28.
Hall, N. (2005). *Hate crime*. Cullompton: Willan.
Herek, G. M. and Berrill, K. T. (eds) (1992). *Hate crimes: Confronting violence against lesbians and gay men*. Newbury Park, CA: Sage Publications.
Herek, G. M., Cogan, J. C. and Gillis, J. R. (2002). Victim experiences in hate crimes based on sexual orientation. *Journal of Social Issues*, 58(2), 319–339.
Herek, G. M., Gillis, J. R. and Cogan, J. C. (1999). Psychological sequelae of hate-crime victimization among lesbian, gay, and bisexual adults. *Journal of Consulting and Clinical Psychology*, 67, 945–951.
Holden-Smith, B. (1996). Lynching, federalism, and the intersection of race and gender in the progressive era. *Yale Journal of Law and Feminism*, 8, 31–78.
Hurd, H. M. and Moore, M. S. (2004). Punishing hatred and prejudice. *Stanford Law Review*, 56, 1081–1146.
Jacobs, J. B. and Potter, K. (1998). *Hate crimes: Criminal law and identity politics*. New York: Oxford University Press.
Jenness, V. and Grattet, R. (2005). The law-in-between: The effects of organizational perviousness on the policing of hate crime. *Social Problems*, 52(3), 337–359.
Jenness, V. and Grattet, R. (2001). *Making hate a crime: From social movement to law enforcement*. New York: Russell Sage Foundation.
King, R. D. (2008). Conservatism, institutionalism, and the social control of intergroup conflict. *American Journal of Sociology*, 113(5), 1351–1393.
King, R. D. (2007). The context of minority group threat: Race, institutions, and complying with hate crime law. *Law and Society Review*, 41(1), 189–224.
Lawrence, F. M. (2009). *Punishing hate: Bias crimes under American law*. Cambridge, MA: Harvard University Press.
Lawrence, F. M. (2008). The evolving federal role in bias crime law enforcement and the Hate Crimes Prevention Act of 2007. *Stanford Law and Policy Review*, 19, 251–282.
Lawrence, F. M. (1994). The punishment of hate: Toward a normative theory of bias-motivated crimes. *Michigan Law Review*, 93, 320–381.
Levin, B. (2002). The vindication of hate violence victims via criminal and civil adjudications. *Journal of Hate Studies*, 1, 133–165.
Levin, J. and McDevitt, J. (2012). Public sociology: Research, action, and change. In P. Nyden, L. Hossfeld, and G. Nyden (eds), *Public sociology: Research, action, and change*, pp. 265–270. New York: Sage.
Levin, J. and McDevitt, J. (1993). *Hate crimes: The rising tide of bigotry and bloodshed*. New York: Plenum.
Levin, J., Rabrenovic, G., Ferraro, V., Doran, T. and Methe, D. (2007). When a crime committed by a teenager becomes a hate crime. *American Behavioral Scientist*, 51(2), 246–257.
Lively, D. E. (1999). *Landmark Supreme Court cases: A reference guide*. Westport, CT: Greenwood Press.
Lombardi, E. L., Wilchins, R. A., Priesing, D. and Malouf, D. (2001). Gender violence: Transgender experiences with violence and discrimination. *Journal of Homosexuality*, 42(1), 89–101.
Marion, N. E. (1994). *A history of federal crime control initiatives, 1960–1993*. Westport, CT: Praeger Publishers.
Martin, S. E. (1996). Investigating hate crimes: Case characteristics and law enforcement responses. *Justice Quarterly*, 13(3), 455–480.

McDevitt, J., Balboni, J. M., Bennett, S., Weiss, J. C., Orchowsky, S. and Walbolt, L. (2003). Improving the Quality and Accuracy of Bias Crime Statistics Nationally: An Assessment of the First Ten Years of Bias Crime Data Collection. In B. Perry (ed.), *Hate and bias crime: A reader*, pp. 77–89. New York: Routledge.

McDevitt, J., Balboni, J., Garcia, L. and Gu, J. (2001). Consequences for victims: A comparison of bias and non-bias-motivated assaults. *American Behavioral Science*, 45(4), 697–713.

McDevitt, J., Levin, J. and Bennett, S. (2002). Hate crime offenders: An expanded typology. *Journal of Social Issues*, 58(2), 303–317.

McPhail, B. and Jenness, V. (2005). To charge or not to charge? That is the question: The pursuit of strategic advantage in prosecutorial decision-making surrounding hate crime. *Journal of Hate Studies*, 4(1), 89–119.

Missouri ex rel. Gaines v. Canada, 305 U.S. 337 (1938).

Morgan v. Commonwealth of Virginia, 328 U.S. 373 (1946).

Nolan, J. J. and Akiyama, Y. (2002). Assessing the climate for hate crime reporting in law enforcement organizations: A force-field analysis. *Justice Professional*, 15, 87–103.

Nolan, J. J. and Akiyama, Y. (1999). An analysis of factors that affect law enforcement participation in hate crime reporting. *Journal of Contemporary Criminal Justice*, 15, 111–127.

Patton v. Mississippi, 332 U.S. 463 (1947).

Perry, B. (2001). *In the name of hate: Understanding hate crimes.* New York: Routledge.

Phillips, N. D. (2009). The prosecution of hate crimes: The limitations of the hate crime typology. *Journal of Interpersonal Violence*, 24(5), 883–905.

R.A.V. v. City of St. Paul, 505 U.S. 377 (1992).

Rubenstein, W. B. (2004). The real story of U.S. hate crime statistics: An empirical analysis. *Tulane Law Review*, 78, 1213–1246.

Samito, C. G. (2009). (ed.). *Changes in law and society during the civil war and reconstruction.* Carbondale: Southern Illinois University Press.

Sandholtz, N., Langton, L. and Planty, M. (2013). *Hate crime victimization, 2003–2011.* Special report NCJ 241291: U.S. Department of Justice, Office of Justice Programs, Bureau of Justice Statistics. Available at www.bjs.gov/content/pub/pdf/hcv0311.pdf (last retrieved on June 16, 2013).

Smith v. Allwright, 321 U.S. 649 (1944).

Valelly, R. M. (2009). *The two reconstructions: The struggle for black enfranchisement.* Chicago, IL: University of Chicago Press.

Walsh, B. W. (2009). Federal hate crimes statute: An unconstitutional exercise of legislative power. Available at: www.heritage.org/research/reports/2009/04/federal-hate-crimes-statute-an-unconstitutional-exercise-of-legislative-power (last visited June 9, 2013).

Wang, L. (1999). The complexities of "hate." *Ohio State Law Journal*, 60, 799–900.

Wisconsin v. Mitchell, 508 U.S. 476 (1993).

Woods, J. B. (2008a). Reconceptualizing anti-LGBT hate crimes as burdening expression and association: A case for expanding federal hate crime legislation to include gender identity and sexual orientation. *Journal of Hate Studies*, 6, 81–115.

Woods, J. B. (2008b). Ensuring a right of access to the courts for bias crime victims: A section 5 defense of the Matthew Shepard Act. *Chapman Law Review*, 12, 389–431.

Woods, J. B. (2008c). Taking the "hate" out of hate crimes: Applying unfair advantage theory to justify the enhanced punishment of opportunistic bias crimes. *UCLA Law Review*, 56, 489–541.

14
Hate and hate crime in Canada

Abbee Corb

Hate crimes have been vilified in our everyday vernacular. The seemingly increasing occurrence of hate crimes, and related hate crime prosecutions, in Canada has been accompanied by numerous reports, governmental studies, think tanks and working groups relating to the topic. Despite the increase in hate crime research though, few quantitative studies exist. This chapter discusses the hate crime problem in Canada, and examines the challenges faced by law enforcement and the legal communities when dealing with hate crimes.

Freedom of expression is central to all healthy democracies. Accordingly, although racist and hateful comments are offensive to the vast majority of Canadians, they are not necessarily illegal. The first issue I see warranting critical reflection appears to be little more than a question of mere semantics. Specifically I am referring to the term "hate crime" itself. As Chakraborti (this volume) has already explained, the phrase is fraught with dilemmas and difficulties. Community and lay leaders, the general public, professionals and scholars often tend to interpret "hate crime" (a term, which tends to suffer from overuse) far too literally. They quite often insist that all crimes are hate crimes, or alternatively, they claim that perpetrators of the hateful acts don't necessarily hate their victims, nor do they feel any type of recognizable bias for the victims.

In the United States the term "hate crime" was first coined in the mid-1980s with reference to crimes and incidents directed at specific ethnic and other identifiable groups. The Federal statutes of the US define hate crime and bias crimes as criminal offences committed against a person, property or group motivated by a bias against race, religion, disability, sexual orientation, ethnicity or ethnic origin. According to the US Department of Justice, federal civil rights statutes which reference bias crimes apply to all states, however only 49 states have hate crime statutes. For example, in the US state of Wyoming, no hate crime laws exist whatsoever. States vary with regard to the groups protected under hate crime laws (e.g., religion, race or ethnicity, and sexual orientation), the range of crimes covered, and the penalty enhancements for offenders (USDOJ website).

In Canada, hate crime is dealt with in Sections 318, 319, and 320 of the Canadian Criminal Code. It has been suggested, however, that this legislation is cumbersome and, at times, impedes law enforcement officers. A police officer can arrest and charge individuals for homicide, for assault, and so on, but cannot proceed with charges against an individual accused of hate crimes without consent of a higher body. Canadian legislation requires the police officer to obtain written consent from the Attorney General in order to proceed with charges under the hate crime laws. Moreover, Canadian law is narrowly written and the Crown has to prove an accused was motivated by hate in order to secure a conviction.

The design of the legislation creates a backlog for law enforcement, and applications to the Attorney General for consent can languish in their offices waiting for responses. There have been cases that have been delayed for over two years as a consequence of this process. This system stagnates the investigative process and does not benefit the victim, serve society or benefit the policing community. The fact that only a handful of people in Canada have been prosecuted under hate crime legislation since the 1970s speaks volumes about the legal issues facing the Canadian judicial system.

Up until recently, the Canadian Human Rights Commission utilized a different mechanism (Section 13 of the Canadian Human Rights Act empowers the Canadian Human Rights Commission to deal with complaints regarding the use of the Internet as a tool for the transmission of hate) to deal with hate crime. It made use of a tribunal system where the burden of proof is lessened. The tribunal was able to make decisions that were binding and that would be enforced by the federal courts. These findings had the ability to impose the same penalties as the Federal Courts. Section 13 of the Canadian Human Rights Act was, however, repealed in June 2013.

The nature and scope of hate crime in Canada have been pondered and deliberated by researchers, government officials, community organizations, lobbyists and the legal community for decades. So, before engaging in an in-depth discussion surrounding the policing of hate crime in Canada, one needs to understand some of the pertinent issues at hand. What, for example, have legal, sociological and other experts said about this topic? When did the issue of hate and hate crimes in general enter the public debate forum? What is the discourse associated with this phenomenon? These are some of the key questions that can be best addressed by a review of the available literature.

While hate crime laws are a relatively new phenomenon within the criminal justice systems in both Canada and the United States, it is not new when applied to other contexts. The types of events and incidents associated with hate and hate crime are deeply rooted in global history. From the persecution of the Christians during the height of the Roman Empire, the Crusaders, the Nazis' "final solution" of the Jews and other persecuted groups during the Second World War, to the recent "ethnic cleansing" in the former Yugoslavia and genocide in Rwanda, hate (crime) has been an evident fact in the history of the world (Bureau of Justice Assistance, 1997).

In Canada, the conception of "hate" as a social/criminal policy concern emerged following the release of the 1965 Report to the Minister of Justice of the Special Committee on Hate Propaganda in Canada, known as the *Cohen Committee*. The mandate of the Cohen Committee was to ascertain the nature and scope of hate propaganda present in Canada. Some of its conclusions stressed that although the extent of the problem in Canada was limited to a relatively small number of people, such activity could create a climate of malice and destructiveness to the core values of Canadian society (Cohen Report, 1966: 24). As a result of the Committee's efforts, Parliament amended the Canadian Criminal Code in 1970, thus rendering hate propaganda as a punishable offence (Law Reform Commission of Canada, 1986: 7). These laws are found at sections 318–320 of the Canadian Criminal Code. Recently, as a result of the terrorist attacks committed on September 11th, 2001, the mischief section of the Criminal Code, found at Section 430 has been amended to include attacks on religious property and institutions as hate crimes.

Canadians enjoy certain rights and freedoms. Section 2 of the Canadian Charter of Rights and Freedoms guarantees freedom of thought, belief, opinion and expression to all Canadians. However, all Charter rights are subject to reasonable limits that can be demonstrably justified in a free and democratic society. In 1990, the Supreme Court of Canada considered whether or not section 319(2) of the Canadian Criminal Code (the crime of willfully promoting hatred) violates our constitutional right to freedom of expression, as seen in the case *R. v. Keegstra*. James Keegstra was a high school teacher in the Province of Alberta, who taught his students that the Holocaust did not occur and was part of a Jewish conspiracy. The Court decision held that, although section 319(2) does protect the right of free speech it was reasonable to limit such rights justifiably demonstrated in a democratic society, and is therefore constitutional. The *Keegstra* case was one of the landmark cases in the arena of hate crimes in Canada.

Chief Justice Dickson, in *Keegstra*, expressed his thoughts on the values promoted by the legislation in question:

> In my opinion, it would be impossible to deny that Parliament's objective in enacting s. 319(2) is of the utmost importance. Parliament has recognized the substantial harm that can flow from hate propaganda and in trying to prevent the pain suffered by target group members and to reduce racial, ethnic and religious tension in Canada has decided to suppress the willful promotion of hatred against identifiable groups. At the core of freedom of expression lies the need to ensure that truth and the common good are attained, whether in scientific and artistic endeavors or in the process of determining the best course to take in our political affairs. The message put forth by individuals who fall within the ambit of s. 319(2) represents a most extreme opposition to the idea that members of identifiable groups should enjoy this aspect of the s. 2(b) benefit. The scope to which the unhindered promotion of this message furthers free expression values must therefore be tempered insofar as it advocates with inordinate vitriol an intolerance and prejudice which view as execrable the process of individual self-development and human flourishing among all members of society.
>
> *([1990] 3 S.C.R. 697 [Keegstra])*

The Canadian Human Rights Commission administers the Canadian Human Rights Act. (Repealed) Section 13 of the Canadian Human Rights Act prohibited the communication by means of a telecommunication, including telephone, Internet or other means undertaking of messages that are likely to expose or subject people to hatred on the basis of the following factors: race, national or ethnic origin, colour, religion, age, sex, sexual orientation, marital status, family status, and disability. Although repealed in June 2013, it still remains important to be aware of this piece of legislation. Difficulties in the prosecution of accused hate monger, Ernst Zundel, arose due to the vagueness of the laws and to definitional issues. The case eventually moved from the mainstream judicial system to that of the Canadian Human Rights Commission and their tribunal system. In January 2002, the Canadian Human Rights Tribunal ordered Zundel to cease and desist from publishing hate messages on the Zundel site because his writings violate section 13. Ernst Zundel's legal battles are another example of the difficulty encountered in the policing and prosecution of hate crime in Canada. The 2002 Canadian Human Rights Tribunal was specific to the Internet. At the time, the Zundel site was located on a server situated in Carlsbad, California and continued to post hateful messages because it was located in the United States and was, therefore, outside the jurisdiction of the Canadian tribunal.

Although lobbying for hate propaganda laws came from select identifiable groups, primarily Jewish and Black pro-active organizations, the mid-1970s gave rise to a second phase of racist activity and hate propaganda directed at other groups (Janhevich, 1997). Associated with this second phase of hate and racist activity were high profile legal cases, which gave notoriety to a number of Holocaust deniers in Canada. What also appeared to emerge was the increased presence of violence. As a result, there was increased pressure for legislative changes. Emphasis was now placed on measuring the frequency of the problem in order to improve the criminal justice system response (Karmen, 1990: 262). At the time, these efforts were far more evident in the United States of America; however, similar pressures soon arose in Canadian society and culture.

Following this second phase, the issue of hate crime became a more prolific and, indeed, a public one. Hate crimes were, at that time, viewed as a global phenomenon. The 1990s in Canada marked a fundamental change in the activity of those perpetrating crimes motivated by a bias or hate factor. Skinhead groups were responsible for extreme violence against members of many minority groups in the City of Edmonton, in Alberta in 1990. Similar incidents also occurred in the City of Toronto in both 1990 and 1993; the murder of a Sikh caretaker occurred in British Columbia in 1998; and a series of murders and attacks on the gay community took place in Montreal in the 1990s. In addition, in 1989, 13 young female students at the École Polytechnic in Montreal, Quebec were killed by a gunman, Mark Lepine, whose misogynistic crime was committed because he held a personal bias against women.

The increasing concern about hate crime was reflected in the establishment of various police hate/bias crimes units, government funded studies, and the tabling of specific hate crime legislation in the sentencing reform section of Bill C-41 of 1996. Although the Hate Propaganda provisions in the Canadian Criminal Code have existed since 1970, the Criminal Code was amended in 1996 to include sentencing enhancement principles (CC section 718.2) where there is evidence that the offence was motivated by bias, prejudice or hate based on race, national or ethnic origin, language, colour, religion, sex, age, mental or physical disability, sexual orientation, or any other similar factor. It was again amended after the terrorist acts of September 11th, 2001, to include stronger laws against hate crime, propaganda and damage to religious property. Importantly, the establishments of police hate crime units provided the avenue for the criminal justice system in Canada to officially recognize this growing criminal and social problem as a specific category of crime.

In 1998, with reference to Section 718 of the Criminal Code of Canada, the Canadian Association of Chiefs of Police (CACP) agreed that the identified groups within this section be incorporated into a uniform definition of what constitutes a hate crime. As a reminder to the reader, the identified groups in this particular section are race, national or ethnic origin, language, colour, religion, sex, age, mental or physical disability, sexual orientation, or any other similar factor. Many law enforcement officials work with their respective Crown Attorneys to enhance sentencing via the route of Section 718. This is especially important if the legal professionals and law enforcement could not meet the burden of proof for hate crime charges.

Numerous studies exist that are specific to Canadian society, which classify hate crimes and crimes motivated by a bias differently. Various academic disciplines incorporate different paradigms to elucidate and identify hate crimes. For example, the hate crime label has been applied to describe a wide variety of behaviour, ranging from international violent acts such as ethnic cleansing (Hamm, 1993, 1994) and right-wing terrorism (Bjorgo, 1995) to severe criminal behaviour such as homicide and assault, to less serious incidents of vandalism and property crime. A series of interviews was conducted with citizens around the country; the majority of respondents defined the term "hate crime" differently (Corb, 2007). There didn't seem to be any consistency in the term, yet the vernacular was a familiar one. The main typical feature with hate crimes is that, overall, the offences include a specific motivating factor not found in other crimes, yet any crime can be a hate crime (Former Chief Murray Faulkner: London Police Service: June 2006).

In order for an offence to be processed and preceded with as a hate crime in Canada, the motivation must be proven. In the educational documentary "What is a Hate Crime?" (HCEIT, 2007) both lawyers and police officers state that proving the motivating factor of a hate crime is both imperative and difficult. As is typical with most criminal offences, a number of motivating factors may exist and underlie any one act or incident. Interpretation and perception on the part of the investigators and the victim is important to the entire case. An exclusive definition which classifies a hate crime as an act solely motivated by hate of the victim's status will likely result in fewer reported offences, while other definitions which only require that an act be motivated in whole or in part by hate will spawn a greater number of reported hate crimes (Roberts, 1995: 11; HCCWG, 2007).

In their report, *Addressing Hate Crime in Ontario*, the Hate Crime Community Working Group aptly stated that standardized definitions of hate crime and hate incidents need to be tailored in order for those dealing with the crimes to be able to understand and identify the activity:

> The Working Group's proposed definition of 'hate crime' broadens, in modest but important ways, definitions already in use by the Canadian Centre for Justice Statistics, the Ontario's Policing Standards Manual and the sentencing provisions of the Criminal Code. Adoption of the proposed definitions, together with the recommendations that urge mandatory, standardized statistical records of hate crimes and incidents, will create a trustworthy baseline against which to gauge trends in reported hate crimes and incidents across the province.
>
> *(HCCWG, 2007)*

Despite the clear importance of responding to hate crimes, very little has been written critiquing the overall process of dealing with the purported hate crime from inception to judicial and legal process in Canada. One such study was, however, conducted by this author (Corb, 2008, 2011), and surveyed 100 members of the law enforcement and legal communities from across Canada with a survey of questions pertaining to hate crime and hate crime prosecution in Canada. The results suggested that:

- An existing unit or officer to deal specifically with hate related crimes and incidents was common;
- Few police officers had investigated bona fide hate crimes, although about 30 percent had investigated crimes with hate overtones;
- The majority of the police had never laid a 318/319 charge;
- The majority of officers had never received a call that they felt fell under Sections 318/319 of the Criminal Code;
- The response time from the Attorney General's Office for consent to lay a charge ranged from two weeks to a year;
- Most police respondents considered the responses from the Attorney General's Office to be positive;
- The majority of the police participants had requested that section 718 be used to enhance sentencing;
- A number of respondents felt that hate crimes charges were difficult to lay in Canada;
- The majority of police respondents felt that hate offenders were likely to reoffend;

- The majority of respondents felt that the penalty did not always reflect the seriousness of the crime, and that the adjustments to the Criminal Code were necessary for this to occur;
- Around half of the respondents stated that their agency, organization, or institution offered counselling and support to victims;
- The majority of respondents stated that their group, organization, or institution did not share their information with other pro-active community groups (i.e. B'nai Brith, Canadian Arab Federation, and other similar organizations);
- The majority of respondents indicated that they were concerned with how hate crimes were dealt with;
- Members of the Legal Community, Crowns, or members of Attorney General's Office were asked to define the hate crimes sections of the Canadian Criminal Code. Responses were varied but included: racism, gender or particular religious affiliation, genocide and public incitement of hatred;
- Responses indicated that more hate crime training was necessary for members of the legal community;
- Legal community participants were asked whether they had ever been approached with respect to 318/319 applications for prosecution. The evidence indicated that most of the members of the Attorney General's Office had not been approached with respect to 318/319 applications for prosecution;
- Those participants who responded in the affirmative to being approached with 318/319 applications were consequently asked to define how they felt about the working process. As the Crown Attorney is responsible for pre-charge approval, members consider the file and then provide an opinion to the regional Crown counsel. In addition, they were asked whether it had been expedient or slow and what the process had been. Several felt that the process was lengthy and that too many hands per se were 'in the pot';
- Survey participants were asked whether they felt there was a need for 318/319 applications to be authorized by the Attorney General's Office. In addition, they were asked whether they felt that the local or regional Crown's office should have been able to make that decision. The responses support that either only the Attorney General's Office should handle this or it should be case specific;
- The participants were asked whether they had ever applied a 718 application. The evidence indicated that most of them had applied for 718 applications and that they were content with the result;
- Finally, police respondents were asked what changes if any they would make to the hate crimes sections of the Canadian Criminal Code and how hate crimes were dealt with. Several suggested that increasing penalties would prevent reoffending. Other respondents felt the system was fine. As for waiting for approval of the Attorney General, several respondents felt that it was necessary because of the balance that had to be struck between the Charter and one's freedom of expression. Some felt that definitional disparity existed in the Criminal Code; that existing legal definitions for hate crimes can be limiting in terms of prosecuting cases and supporting victims/survivors, particularly when it comes to dealing with systemic issues and bias activity. Some felt that the Criminal Code needed some tweaking, that the definition of religious property needed to be expanded upon, and that there needed to be a greater willingness of police and Crowns to lay appropriate charges.

Conclusions and recommendations

Hate crime is significantly underreported in Canada. This particular problem exists for various reasons, including fear of repercussions, fear of exclusion from the community at large, fear of being stigmatized, fear of police resulting from pre-existing perceptions of the law enforcement methods from home countries and the list goes on. Community members must be encouraged to report all crimes, hate associated or otherwise. Moreover, there is a need for definitive and understandable definitions of hate and hate crime. A comprehensive definition will ensure less disparity in the policing of hate crimes, and aid understanding and therefore (hopefully) increase reporting levels.

Law enforcement community members should have more latitude when dealing with hate related occurrences. Streamlining must occur with respect to the process in place for dealing with Sections 318/319 of the Criminal Code of Canada applications. Crown Attorneys and Attorney Generals need to develop a more comprehensive and effective method of managing applications submitted for prosecution under the current legislation. Furthermore, they must be able to deal with these applications in a more timely fashion. At present the waiting time is often far too long and the entire process needs to be streamlined. Time restrictions should perhaps be emplaced in regards to the response time of the Attorney General's Office when dealing with 318/319 applications.

Increased awareness of hate and hate related criminal offences must be increased to ensure and guarantee a more informed citizenry. Community group and community member education and involvement are essential to both reduce the crimes and increase reporting of hate related crimes.

Communities, and members of the judiciary, must speak out against intolerance, racism, and hate crime. Community members and the leaders and lay leaders of community based and religious groups must recognize that hate crimes, and bias-motivated behaviours that are not criminal, victimize not only the targeted individual or group, but also the entire community. Communities at large become injured and offended when hate crimes corrode mutual respect and civility, and undermines the individuals' sense of comfort and belonging.

In order to effectively respond to criminal occurrences, perceived to be hate related or motivated by a bias, a comprehensive definition of hate, and what is constitutionally defined as a hate crime, needs to be established. It is important to note that any incident can be deemed to be a hate crime if the motivation of the offence can be proven to be provoked by an existing bias. Prejudicial actions exist along a gamut including negative speech, discriminatory practices, property damage, physical assault, and murder. Legally, a hate crime is any crime enumerated in hate crime legislation in which the person responsible for the action is subject to an enhanced penalty if the crime was motivated by bias, as defined by the existing legislation. Community leaders, victim groups and justice agencies need a common language and definition for what constitutes a hate crime. This will facilitate and encourage the reporting of crimes to law enforcement. In doing so, the community will avoid misconceptions of the police if charges cannot be laid.

Definitional disparities similarly exist between the lawmakers and those enforcing the laws. This disparity can be eliminated by supporting new, and revising old, legislation, which encompass criminal offences committed against persons, property, or society, which are motivated by the perpetrators' bias against an individual, his community or a group's actual or perceived race, religion, ethnicity, national or ethnic origin, disability, sexual orientation, age or gender. Additionally, for the benefit of the community groups and community members, the differences between incidents of hate and hate crime should be clarified. For example, an incident in which a person is subjected to offensive speech is not a criminal offence, yet still affects the victim. Therefore, the definition of hate crime must be clear, concise and commonly understood and accepted. As well, the legislation pertaining to hate crime should be clearly defined for community stakeholders and members of the legal community.

With respect to the law enforcement officers themselves, members of the policing community must be better trained to recognize hate crimes and crimes motivated by a bias. These individuals must be familiar with the motivators and indicators of said crimes. They need to be familiar with the various specialized agencies and community groups/religious institutions that exist and to which they can in turn refer the victims. Police officers are generally the first people to respond to the scene of any crime, hate or otherwise. As such, their actions significantly affect the outcome of the criminal investigation as well as the community's response to the incident. Therefore enhanced knowledge and understanding of the various ethnic communities that exist within Canada, is of utmost importance.

With respect to representatives of the legal community, a more comprehensive knowledge of the existing legislation is a necessary imperative. Enhanced training on the legislation, the motivators of hate crimes, and indicators is necessary for more expedient handling of this type of crime. Training and education will result in more thorough and efficient examination and prosecutions of hate crime.

With respect to the perpetrators of hate related crimes, police officers and members of the legal community must hold hate crime offenders answerable and accountable for their actions. Wherever possible, they must provide opportunities for these perpetrators to expand their perspectives and change their overall value system. Offenders must be made to understand that hate crime will not be tolerated in our communities and those who commit them will be held liable and appropriately sanctioned. Enhancements therefore, need to be made to Canadian hate crime legislation and to the imposed penalties, especially for repeat and violent offenders.

After careful consideration and evaluation of the data and literature, further recommendations and ideas for future study have evolved. These include:

- Enhanced education/further education on all levels (victim groups, community and religious organizations, policing community and legal community) on all aspects of hate related crimes, and the legislation and legal remedies available to all is of fundamental importance. In addition, further education on cultural groups and localized hate groups and their operations are essential;
- A clear and comprehensive definition of hate and hate crime needs to be established;
- Ensure that all reported hate incidents and crimes are thoroughly documented and studied to assess existing correlations among the characteristics of the victims, the perpetrators, demographics and the actual situations in which the hate crimes occurred. Continuous intelligence gathering is necessary to enable the policing community to be pro-active and vigilant. Continuous intelligence gathering by the community groups should be made available to members of the policing community to enable them to be more involved and more pro-active;
- Further evaluation of existing legislation is necessary.

Unfortunately Canada's legal community's work in confronting hate and bias and the aggression that is engendered is not over. With populations changing as they are, and with the complex issue of immigration, the number of hate related crimes may well increase over time. Hate crimes present a challenge to the community at large. The law enforcement community and the legal community have been challenged by hate crime too. The legal community needs to effectively come to some accord and devise mechanisms and safeguards for responding to the discordant and disparaging impact of hate.

Bibliography

Beck, J. H., Reitz, J. G. and Weiner, N. (2002), 'Addressing Systemic Racial Discrimination in Employment: The Health Canada Case and Implications of Legislative Change', *Canadian Public Policy/Analyse de politiques* 28 (3): 373–394.

Bell, J. (2002), *Policing Hatred: Law Enforcement, Civil Rights and Hate Crime*. New York, NY: New York University Press.

Bensinger, G. (1992), 'Hate Crime: A New/Old Problem', *International Journal of Comparative and Applied Criminal Justice*, 16: 115–123.

Berk, R., Boyd, E. and Hamner, K. (1992), 'Thinking More Clearly About Hate-Motivated Crimes', in Herek, G. and Berrill, K. eds., *Hate Crimes: Confronting Violence Against Lesbians and Gay Men*. Newbury Park, CA: Sage: 123–143.

Bjorgo, T. (1995), 'Extreme Nationalism and Violent Discourses in Scandinavia: "The Resistance", "Traitors", and "Foreign Invaders"', *Terrorism And Political Violence*, 7 (1), 182–220.

Bureau of Justice Assistance www.bja.gov/Default.aspx/ (last accessed July 12, 2013).

Canada (1966), Report to the Minister of Justice of the Special Committee on Hate Propaganda in Canada. Ottawa: Queen's Printer.

Canadian Centre for Justice Statistics, (2001), *Hate Crimes in Canada: An Overview of Issues and Data Sources*.

Canadian Human Rights Act, Department of Justice: Canada laws-lois.justice.gc.ca/eng/ (last accessed August 17, 2013).

Canadian Sentencing Commission, *Sentencing Reform: A Canadian Approach* (Ottawa: Minister of Supply and Services, 1986).

Carswell's form and precedent collection: criminal law precedents, Toronto: Carswell, 2007. 2 v. ; : ill.

CBC News. 2007, Ernst Zundel sentenced to 5 years for Holocaust denial. CBC News Online, February 15, www.cbc.ca/world/story/2007/02/15/zundel-germany.html (last accessed August 14, 2013).

Claghorn, Kate H. (1917/18), 'Crime and Immigration', *Journal of the American Institute of Criminal Law and Criminology*, 8: 675–693.

Commission sur le racisme systémique dans le système de justice pénale en Ontario. (1995). Rapport de la Commission sur le racisme systémique dans le système de justice pénale en Ontario. Toronto.

Commission on Systemic Racism in the Ontario Criminal Justice System. (1995). Report of the Commission on Systemic Racism in the Ontario Criminal Justice System: A community survey. Toronto: Government of Ontario

Corb, Abbee (2008, 2011), An examination and remedy to the systemic failures in Canadian hate crime prosecution (position paper) Hate Crime Extremism Investigative Team: Toronto.

Corb, Abbee (2007), What is a Hate Crime? (DVD). HCEIT: Ontario.

Coutu, Jean Charles. (1995), *La Justice pour et par les autochtones*. Québec: Ministre de la Justice du Québec.

Craig, K. (2002), 'Examining hate-motivated aggression: A review of the social psychological literature on hate crimes as a distinct form of aggression', *Aggression and Violent Behavior*, 7: 85–101.

Currie, A. and Kiefl, G. (1994), *Ethnocultural Groups and the Justice System in Canada: A Review of the Issues*. Ottawa: Department of Justice Canada.

Delman, Howard (ed.) (1994), 'Canadian Immigration and Refugee Policy and Practice', *Migration*, Vol. 21/22.

Federal Bureau of Investigation. Hate Crime Statistics, (2011). Washington, DC: U.S. Department of Justice, Federal Bureau of Investigation.

Federal Bureau of Investigation (website) www.fbi.gov/about-us/cjis/ucr/crime-in-the-u.s/2011/crime-in-the-u.s.-2011/hate-crime-statistics (last accessed July 20, 2013).

Grattet, R. and Jenness, V. (2001a), 'The Birth and Maturation of Hate Crime Policy in the United States', *American Behavioral Scientist*, 45 (4): 668–696.

Grattet, R. and Jenness, V. (2001b), 'Examining the Boundaries of Hate Crime Law: Disabilities and the "Dilemma of Difference"', *Journal of Criminal Law and Criminology*, 91: 653–697.

Hamm, M. (1993), *American Skinheads: The Criminology and Control of Hate Crime*, Cincinnati, OH: Anderson.

Hamm, M. (1994), '*Conceptualizing Hate Crime in a Global Context*', Hate Crime: International Perspectives on Causes and Control. Cincinnati, OH: Anderson: 173–194.

Harlow, C.W. (2005), *Hate Crimes Reported by Victims and Police*. Special Report. Washington, DC: U.S. Department of Justice, Bureau of Justice Statistics, NCJ 209911.

Hate Crime Community Working Group Addressing Hate Crime in Ontario (2006), www.attorneygeneral.jus.gov.on.ca/english/about/pubs/hatecrimes/HCCWG_full.pdf (last accessed August 10, 2013).

Hate Crime: United States Department of Justice (website) January 2007 from www.ojp.gov/nij/topics/crime/hate-crime/welcome.htm (last accessed January 2008).

Hate Propaganda Working Paper: Law Reform Commission of Canada (1986).

HCEIT (2007) Corb, Where does Hate Begin?, Hate Crime Extremism Investigative Team video production. Toronto 2007.

IACP National Law Enforcement Policy Centre. Hate Crimes. Concepts and Issues Paper; Arlington, Virginia: IACP National Law Enforcement Policy Center (1991).

Illarraza, F., Angle, Becker, P. (2001), 'Hate Crime Data and its Sources: An assessment', *Journal of Social and Behavioural Sciences*, 38 (2): 128–138.

Interim Report of the Commission on Systemic Racism in the Ontario Criminal Justice System. (1994). Racism Behind Bars: The Treatment of Black and Other Racial Minority Prisoners in Ontario Prisons. Toronto: Queen's Printer for Ontario.

International Association of Chiefs of Police (1999), Hate Crime in America Summit: Recommendations. Washington, DC: IACP.

Jacobs, J. and Potter, K. (1998), *Hate Crimes: Criminal Law and Identity Politics*. New York: Oxford University Press.

Janhevich, D. (2001), Hate Crime in Canada: An overview of Issues and Data Sources; (Statistics Canada). Ottawa: Minister of Industry.

Jankowicz, A. (1995), *Business Research Projects*. London: International Thomson Business Press, pp. 16–35.

Karmen, Andrew (1990), *Crime Victims: An Introduction to Victimology*. Pacific Grove, CA: Brooks/Cole Publishing.

Lambert, John R. (1970), *Crime, Police, and Race Relations: A Study in Birmingham*. Oxford: Oxford University Press.

Law Reform Commission of Canada, Aboriginal Peoples and Criminal Justice (Ottawa: Law Reform Commission of Canada, 1991).

Leedy, P.D. (1989), *Practical research: planning and design*. New York: Macmillan, pp. 120–132.

Levin, B. and Levin, J. (1999), Annals of the American Academy of Political and Social Science, Vol. 566, The Social Diffusion of Ideas and Things (Nov., 1999), pp. 190–192.

London Police Service (June 2006) personal interview.

Mason, G. (2001), 'Not Our Kind of Hate Crime', *Law and Critique*, 12: 253–278.

McDevitt, J. et al. (2000), *Improving the Quality and Accuracy of Bias Crime Statistics Nationally: An Assessment of the First Ten Years of Bias Crime Data Collection*. Boston, MA: Center for Criminal Justice Policy Research.

Ontario Human Rights Commission (2003), Paying the Price: The Human Cost of Racial Profiling. Toronto.

Ontario Ministry of Citizenship (1988), Intercultural Communications Workshop.

Pocket Criminal Code 2007 (Print-Non-Fiction). Carswell Thomson Professional Publishing, 2006.

The Prejudice Institute www.prejudiceinstitute.org/(last accessed via archive.org July 2013).

National Institute against Prejudice and Violence/Prejudice Institute, 1993: 1–2.

Ray, L. and Smith, D. (2004), 'Racist Offending, Policing and Community Conflict', *Sociology*, 38: 681–699.

Remenyi, D., Williams, B., Money, A. and Swartz, E. (1998), *Doing research in business and management: an introduction to process and method*. London: Sage Publications, pp. 28–35.

Restorative Justice: fact sheet; Policy Centre for Victim Issues; Department of Justice Ottawa, Ontario www.justice.gc.ca/en/ps/voc/rest_just.html (last accessed January 2008).

Roberts, C.M. (2004), *The dissertation journey: a practical and comprehensive guide to planning, writing, and defending your dissertation*. Thousand Oaks, CA: Corwin Press.

Roberts, J. (1995), Disproportionate Harm: Hate Crime in Canada (Working paper), Department of Criminology: University of Ottawa.

Roberts, J.V. (1994), 'Hate Motivated Crimes Deserve Harsher Penalties', *Ottawa Citizen*, November 24, 1994.

Roberts, J.V. (1994), 'Statistics on Race and Crime: Towards a Canadian Solution', *Canadian Journal of Criminology*, 36: 175–186.

Satzewich, V. (ed.) (1998), *Racism & Social Inequality in Canada: Concepts, Controversies & Strategies of Resistance*. Toronto: Thompson Educational Publishing Inc.

R. v. Keegstra (1990) 3 C. S. R. (www.canlii.org/en/ca/scc/doc/1990/1990canlii24/1990canlii24.html).

Shaw, M. (2002), Preventing Hate Crimes: International Strategies and Practice. International Centre for the Prevention of Crime: April 2002.

Shively, M. 'Study of Literature and Legislation on Hate Crime in America'. Final report submitted to the National Institute of Justice, June 2005, NCJ 210300. www.ncjrs.gov/App/Publications/abstract.aspx?ID=210300 (last accessed August 12, 2013).

Standing Committee on Justice and the Solicitor General, Canada, First Principles: Recodifying the General Part of the Criminal Code of Canada. (Ottawa: Queen's Printer, 1993) [White Paper].

Statistics Canada: Hate Crime in Canada: An Overview of Issues and Data Sources. January 2001 Catalogue no. 85-551-XIE.

Trochim, William M. *The Research Methods Knowledge Base*, 2nd Edition. Internet page, at URL: www.socialresearchmethods.net/kb/ (version current as of August 2013).

Uniform Crime Reporting Survey; Statistics Canada 2003, 2005.

United States Department of Justice (website) USDOJ www.usdoj.gov (last accessed August 3, 2013).

Urban Alliance on Race Relations (1995), Race and the Canadian Justice System.

Wessler, Steve (2001), *Promising Practices Against Hate Crime: Five State and Local Demonstration Projects*. Portland, ME: Center for the Study and Prevention of Hate Crime.

15
A governance of denial
Hate crime in Australia and New Zealand

Nicole L. Asquith[1]

Notwithstanding over two decades of 'hate speech' legislation, hate crime regulation in Australia and New Zealand (ANZ[2]) is in its infancy, with limited criminal sanctions introduced in the last ten years. Across the ten jurisdictions,[3] there are a variety of legislative, policy and practice responses to 'hate speech' (vilification) and prejudice-related violence (hate crime). This chapter will outline the institutional and cultural contexts in which these responses emerge as a criminal justice issue before proceeding to a critical discussion of antipodean hate crime governance. In Australia and New Zealand, as occurs elsewhere, the strategies employed by governments to remedy prejudice, intolerance and hatred occur on a continuum; ranging from global mission statements about multiculturalism/biculturalism, through to the enactment of civil anti-discrimination and anti-vilification legislation. These civil remedies have also been extended in some cases to criminal codes and sentencing legislation, and the enshrinement of individual rights to freedom from violence in human rights charters. A complete survey of all these strategies is not possible within the limits of this chapter. Instead, case studies from throughout the region are presented here as exemplars of the strategies employed, and issues and critical barriers faced, in reducing prejudice-related violence.

The case studies presented in this chapter complement the model proposed by Mason (2009; see also Mason, this volume) for understanding the criminal law strategies adopted to regulate hate crime. As Mason's taxonomy begins and ends with the law, a wider variety of examples have been used in this chapter, so as non-legal strategies can also be considered. In this region, New South Wales (NSW) and Victoria are often presented as case studies in hate crime regulation due to the longer history and wider scope of government and community responses. This is especially the case with NSW, where the critical mass of population, combined with deeper cultural and ethnic diversity (primarily as a result of immigration), has necessitated a speedier response from government and led to more cases of hate crime reaching the stage of prosecution or mediation. Rather than re-state the legal and political analysis on the hate crime provisions in NSW,[4] alternative case studies are offered from the margins. Hate crime governance, in these examples, is at the margins of research and scholarship, geography and the criminal justice approaches enacted. These examples also offer important insights into some of the key issues in Australasia, including the relationship between colonisation and hate crime governance, the individual and social attributes recognised and protected under hate crime provisions and the inter-play between, and barriers created by, civil *and* criminal provisions. When hate crime regulation is considered across the continuum of strategies and within the political and cultural contexts of each nation – especially, the context of colonisation – it is questioned whether the symbolic and justice goals of these strategies are achieved or, indeed, are achievable.[5]

Institutional and cultural contexts of hate crime regulation

Understanding the regulation of hate crime in Australia and New Zealand requires being mindful of the structural impediments to effective crime control. While New Zealand has a unitary system of government similar to that of England and Wales, where a single parliament regulates criminal justice responses, Australia (as with the USA) has a federated system that has three levels of government; two of which (federal and state) have explicit constitutional powers to legislate on criminal matters. The Australian federal government has limited crime control powers, though it is responsible for ensuring that its obligations under international agreements – such as the *International Covenant on Civil and Political Rights* and *International Convention on the Elimination of Forms of Racial Discrimination* – are provided for in Australian law. In relation to hate crime regulation, the federal *Criminal Code Act 1995* empowers the Australian government to regulate criminal acts that exceed state jurisdictions in the incitement to violence (s. 11.4), seditious incitement to violence (by race, religion, nationality or political opinion) (s. 80.2(5)), and the use of the telecommunications and postal systems to disseminate threats, menace, harassment or offence (s. 471.11). None of these provisions were created or framed with hate crime regulation as a stated purpose. The structural limitations imposed on legislative development in Australia contrast with New Zealand, where a unicameral parliament sets the legislative and policy direction for the nation as a whole. While the initial six provinces were effectively expunged with the enactment of the British *New Zealand Constitution Act 1852*, the *Treaty of Waitangi* necessarily ensures that local and regional interests of Iwi (tribes) remain central to governance in New Zealand (Humpage and Fleras, 2001; Tauri and Webb, 2011).

These political and structural differences between Australia and New Zealand are shaped, however, by some similar historical and cultural processes associated with colonisation (White, 2002). Australia and New Zealand were both British colonies, founded in the late eighteenth century on the dispossession of lands from indigenous peoples. Since colonisation, both countries have adopted institutional strategies that have dispossessed and fundamentally disempowered each nation's first peoples, including, in the case of Australia, the genocide of the entire Palawa people in Tasmania (Madley, 2008; Reynolds, 2001; Tatz, 2003). However, unlike the declaration of *terra nullius*[6] in Australia, New Zealand's indigenous peoples asserted their sovereign independence in 1835 in the *Declaration of Independence of New Zealand (He Wakaputanga o te Rangatiratanga o Nu Tirene)* and were formally recognised as 'guardians' by the *Treaty of Waitangi (Te Tiriti o Waitangi)*. What the *Treaty* means, its interpretation (and translation) in each of its languages, and the interpretation of the powers divested by Māori chiefs on signing the *Treaty*, continue to be contested.[7] Whatever its status as a legal document, the *Treaty* is a foundational document of the nation and critical to the recognition of Māori sovereignty and self-determination (Humpage and Fleras, 2001; Mutu, 2011). It is noteworthy then, that this foundational agreement was not integrated into either the *Bill of Rights Act* in 1990 or the *Human Rights Act* in 1993. Despite the absence of the *Treaty* from the wider human rights instruments, unlike indigenous Australian, Māori are deeply, if unequally, entrenched in the cultural and political life, and the governmentality of the nation – including reserved seats for Māori parliamentary representatives[8] (Iorns, 2003).

The de facto assumption of *terra nullius* in Australia in 1788 expunged the sovereign rights of those peoples residing in the southern islands – including the islands of Aotearoa until the *Treaty of Waitangi* in 1840. With the signing of the *Treaty* in the early days of colonisation, Māori were acknowledged and recognised by the British government as the nation's first peoples. In contrast, indigenous Australians were refused recognition as citizens for 179 years, and their primary sovereign rights to land were not reluctantly acceded until the *Mabo* decision in the late twentieth century (*Mabo & ors v Queensland (No.2)* [1992]). Each nation's relationship with its indigenous peoples has influenced how race and ethnic relations are played out more generally. This is overt in the political rhetoric and legislative practices of Australian and New Zealand governments on issues to do with 'beaches, border, boats and bodies' (Perera, 2009), such as 'uninvited' refugees in the case of Australian governments (Cameron, 2013; Saul, 2013), and rights to seas, seabeds, shores and fisheries in New Zealand (Bess, 2011; van Meijl, 2010). While the legal declaration of *terra nullius* may have been overturned in *Mabo*, and rejected in New Zealand with the signing of *He Wakaputanga o te Rangatiratanga o Nu Tirene* in 1835 and the *Treaty of Waitangi* in 1840, a 'psychological *terra nullius*' (Behrendt, 1999) continues to shape how each nation responds to hatred and intolerance.

While not obvious at the level of case law, or even when considered through the lens of a single jurisdiction, the lack of 'figurehead' or 'ideal victim' (Mason, 2013) cases in Australia and New Zealand has been a significant barrier to greater 'mainstream' community awareness about hate crimes, and as such, government responses to community concerns. In contrast to the UK cases of Stephen Lawrence and Fiona Pilkington and Francecca Hardwick, and the conviction of David Copeland in the UK, or the James Byrd, Jr. and Matthew Shepard cases in the USA, no hate crime victim (or their family) has had sufficient capital to activate a social imagination about hate crime in this region. Horrific hate crimes in Australasia have failed to gain political traction or imprint on the social memory in ways achieved in the USA and UK. Nor have the calls for increased regulation of hate crime been taken up as a cause célèbre by politicians, the police or the judiciary. The limited adoption of hate crime provisions has been a product of ad hoc lobbying from marginalised communities, often working independently of each other. The actions of the Australian Nationalist Movement (ANM) in the 1980s provide a partial exception. The ANM were active throughout the 1980/90s in Western Australia (WA), using racist graffiti, posters and publications to advocate against the 'Asianisation' of Australia and promote Holocaust denial (Brown, V, 2004). Throughout this period, the issue of racist violence was a critical issue for WA governments and the community (including, impromptu community 'clean-up' squads who removed the ANM materials).[9] Yet, the impact of these racist attacks on the hate crime policy, practice and legislative development across the region was limited, with no other jurisdiction adopting either the 'substantive offence' and 'penalty enhancement' approaches enacted on the west coast.

The recent publicity to arise from the murders of gay men in New South Wales in the late 1980s (Tomsen, 2002) and the attacks on Indian students in Melbourne and Sydney (Dunn et al., 2011; Mason, 2012), while having an impact on local policy or practice, have also had a limited impact on wider community responses to hate crime. In the case of the latter, as Mason and Dunn et al. have documented, the official response to a perceived targeting of some victims due to their racial or ethnic identity was the rejection of hate as a motivating (or aggravating) factor, and the inversion of culpability. Victoria Police, at the time, recognised that some of these crimes were motivated by prejudice but asserted that most were crimes of opportunity, and suggested that, in addition to being simply more vulnerable to victimisation, Indian students put themselves at greater risk by carrying expensive electronic objects on public transport at night and 'being in the wrong place at the wrong time' (Flower and Evans, 2010). The public denial and minimisation of hate crime is also illustrated in the recent revelation of a 'shameful crime wave' in Sydney, NSW during the 1980/90s, which resulted in the deaths of up to 80 men, including Steve Johnson (Sheehan, 2013; Ozturk, 2013). While it has only now come to the attention of the popular press, these murders were well documented by the gay and lesbian press at the time and by Tomsen in his 2002 study of anti-homosexual homicides. Since his murder in 1988, Steve Johnson's family has lobbied the NSW government and NSW Police to consider his death as a possible hate crime. Resulting from their privately funded investigations, a second coronial inquest was held, and the initial verdict of suicide was overturned (Levy, 2013). This automatically activated a referral to the unsolved homicide team, which led to the creation of Strike Force Macnamir. Twenty years after these deaths, NSW Police have directed the Strike Force to re-investigate these cases as possibly related, and part of an organised campaign of hate crime against gay men (NSW Police Force, 2013; Tomsen, 2002). While these two cases – attacks against Indian students and deaths of gay men – received relatively significant media coverage at the time and were to lead to critical criminal justice interventions, the issues relating to criminal hatred have rarely moved beyond sensationalised accounts of violence (with the 'hatred' ignored, minimised or individualised) or localised protests at police inaction (Millar and Doherty, 2009).

The limited criminal law responses from ANZ governments are the result of several factors, not least of which is the lack of public awareness about hate crimes and the impact of these on individuals and communities. Yet, within the institutional and cultural context of ANZ, this lack of awareness is not as much about not knowing, as it is about not *wanting* to know. As suggested by Steyn (2012: 21), in relationships of colonisation, ignorance is a necessary tool for the ethnic-majority's well-being, as it shields them from the 'realities that undergird their privilege'. The denial to witness and acknowledge hate crimes, therefore, may be more a product of the political, institutional and social denial necessary for the creation of a colonial nation than any considered evaluation of the increased harms caused by hate crime. If, as is the case with Australia, the nation can ignore or minimise domestic genocide, it is no wonder that the government and its people are capable of ignoring or minimising the 'everyday exterminabilities' (Hage, 2006) of prejudice and hatred. In addition to the limited public knowledge of hate crime, the denial or minimisation of hatred and prejudice can be also illustrated through the legal strategies developed.

Civil responses

New Zealand and Australian governments have responded to an increasing awareness of prejudice through social policies, institutional practices, and civil and criminal laws. Across the ten jurisdictions, and in some victimised communities (particularly, indigenous communities), the preference has been in favour of education and social change rather than punitive criminal sanctions. As framed by the New Zealand Human Rights Commissioner, Judy McGregor (2005), 'legislation alone is limited in curbing the most harmful effects of hate . . . the promotion of positive relations between groups in society through education and public awareness are equally important'. Here the emphasis has been on the symbolic function of the law to bring about social change and provide a model from which to 'unearth and de-normalise subtle and ingrained attitudes towards traditionally underprivileged groups' (Brown, C, 2004: 595). Apart from the policy and practice rhetoric on multiculturalism and

Nicole L. Asquith

biculturalism, both countries have also adopted various civil provisions for the arbitration of discrimination, harassment and vilification. While civil procedures enable individual complainants to seek remedy from individual or organisational offenders, the enactment of these laws was as much about the stated goals of pluralism as they were about the individual needs of victims of prejudice.

Anti-vilification provisions have been in place in Australia since 1989 (*Anti-Discrimination Act 1977* [NSW]), and racial disharmony provisions have been enacted in various ways in New Zealand since 1977 (*Human Rights Act 1993*, and before it, *Human Rights Commission Act 1977*). Despite the problems faced by complainants in seeking remedies for vilification since that time, several important cases have been heard, which have begun to map the line between 'mere words' and (criminal) vilification.[10] Between the jurisdictions, however, there have been contradictory rulings on these 'mere words'. In *Burns v Dye* [2002], the NSW Administrative Appeals Tribunal found that sufficient hostility was contained in the homophobic name-calling directed at Burns (such as 'poofter' and 'faggot'), yet in *Police v A Child*, the magistrate stated that the laws were 'intended to deal with severe abuse, and not petty name-calling' (cited in Weber, 2006). Unlike the UK, where 'name-calling' is sufficient to meet the lower threshold of the 'demonstration of hostility' test (Mason, 2009), anti-vilification (and criminal incitement to hatred) cases heard in ANZ have rarely met the tests for public act, incitement or hostility (or animosity, ill-will, contempt, offence, insult, humiliation, intimidation or ridicule as used in *Racial Hatred Act 1995* (Australia); *Human Rights Act 1993* (NZ); *Criminal Code Compilation Act 1913* (WA)).

The lack of case law on vilification is in spite of multiple public statements made by high profile Australians and New Zealanders that clearly create the conditions for contempt and humiliation of some vulnerable groups. The most remarkable example of this was the 2005 vilification and incitement to violence broadcasted by shock-jock, Alan Jones on national radio in the days leading up to Cronulla riots (Asquith, 2008b; Asquith and Poynting, 2011). In his broadcasts, he promoted the text of a racist text message, which called for 'Aussies' to '. . . get down to North Cronulla to help support Leb and wog bashing day' (Goggin, 2006). He also demonised Lebanese and Arab-Australians, and advocated for Australia's biker gangs to defend the beach against the 'Lebanese thugs', and that 'it would be worth the price of admission to watch these [Lebanese] cowards scurry back onto the train for the return trip to their lairs' (Alan Jones, 7 December 2005, cited in Australian Communication and Media Authority (ACMA), 2006: 57). ACMA found that his programme during that week was 'likely to [and did] encourage violence and brutality' (ACMA, 2006: 2), and, thus, breached the *Broadcasting Services Act 1992*. He, and his broadcaster, 2GB were expected to face sanctions such as a fine, training or mediation for on-air staff or the imposition of licence conditions (ACMA, 2006).[11] If dealt with as a matter of criminal incitement to violence by the NSW Police (rather than a breach of the telecommunications code), Alan Jones could have received a penalty as high as six months imprisonment under the *NSW Anti-Discrimination Act 1977* (s. 20D provisions for serious racial vilification), or seven years imprisonment under the *Criminal Code Act 1995* (Commonwealth of Australia) (s. 11.4 provisions for incitement).[12]

The New Zealand *Human Rights Act 1993* prohibits discrimination on 11 grounds (or protected classes) including those 'enduring' characteristics captured by the sentence aggravation provisions (*Sentencing Act 2002* (NZ)), along with other non-'enduring' characteristics such as family status, political opinion, and marital status. While the discrimination provisions are written broadly to cover a range of attributes and discriminatory practices, the vilification provisions are severely restricted, with only race, or national or ethnic identity recognised in both the definition of the provisions (s. 61.1) and the sentencing structure for breaches of vilification provisions (s. 131.1). Across the various New Zealand instruments used to protect against prejudice-related violence (including discrimination and vilification), there is a privileging of the experiences of racism, and a consistent omission of disability and sexuality – particularly the latter. Ironically, given that Part 1A of the *Human Rights Act 1993* relates to discrimination by government, the Act itself discriminates in favour of some experiences of hatred, whilst ignoring others conventionally considered under these types of provisions.

Anti-discrimination and anti-vilification strategies have been subject to sustained critique since their creation in the late 1970s, including the issues raised by the private conciliation of public offences, the necessity for a committed, well-resourced individual complainant, the inadequacy of incitement provisions for many of the one-on-one encounters between victims and perpetrators, and the lack of enforcement powers of the tribunals (Asquith, 2007, 2008a; Gelber, 2002; McNamara, 2002; Meagher, 2006). Some jurisdictions allow for representative complaints, yet the processes for evaluating these cases are tortuous, highly individualised and rarely provide a symbolic statement about the unacceptability of tolerance and hatred (Gelber, 2002; McNamara, 2002). The division in ANZ law between the civil offence of vilification (hate speech) and the criminal offence of prejudice-related violence (hate crime) has complicated the reporting and adjudication processes, and as Meagher (2006: 213) suggests, sent a 'mixed and diluted message' about rights to freedom from violence and the denunciation of prejudice and intolerance.

Criminal responses

In addition to civil provisions, New Zealand and Australian jurisdictions have also introduced changes to criminal provisions, and the practices of policing and prosecuting hate crime. Reforms to policing practices preceded legislative changes in most ANZ jurisdictions. As early as the late 1980s, NSW Police Force had introduced a range of strategies to increase hate crime reporting, and increase the capacity of frontline police officers to recognise and name hate crime, respond to hate crime victims in a culturally competent manner, and to collect unique hate crime 'evidence' (such as the verbal-textual hostility used by the offenders) (Asquith, 2012). These 'service enhancements' are designed to address the specific victimisation processes identified as central to the additional harm generated from hate crimes (Asquith, 2009; Iganski, 2001). As with other serious interpersonal violence such as sexual assault and intimate partner violence, policing services in ANZ have adopted increased victim support mechanisms at the levels of initial reporting, investigation and prosecution. As documented by Bartkowiak-Théron (2011, 2012), policing services in this region have also integrated (or added) a range of community policing approaches to facilitate increased trust between victimised communities and the police. At a minimum, these community approaches to hate crime have included the integration of community participation in, and design of, police training, community liaison officers, third-party reporting mechanisms, and community outreach (such as the NSW Police Force participation in the annual Gay and Lesbian Mardi Gras parade).

All ANZ policing services have a network of specially trained liaison officers for recognised vulnerable communities (for example, Gay and Lesbian Liaison Officers in NSW, New & Emerging Community Liaison Officers in Victoria, and Iwi Liaison Officers in New Zealand). In addition to bridging the gap between vulnerable and, in some cases, estranged communities and their policing services (Campbell, 2007; Dwyer, 2012), some of these liaison roles also included direct service delivery to vulnerable victims (Asquith, 2012).

Nicole L. Asquith

Over the last 20 years, however, these liaison roles have been altered by budget cuts and changing relationships between communities and policing services, with fewer liaison officers undertaking the frontline policing duties initially integrated into these positions (Bartkowiak-Théron, 2011). Apart from the 'soft' approaches to victim 'service enhancements', policing services have also begun to integrate increasingly sophisticated data reporting mechanisms to capture the most critical information about hate crimes (Asquith, 2012). This has not extended to the level of reporting undertaken by UK and USA policing services; however, it has facilitated greater internal awareness about the problems of hate crime, and has enabled policing services and vulnerable communities to target their preventative efforts and resources.

Once a report of prejudice-related violence is accepted by the police, the options for investigating the crime and the charging of a suspect vary according to the provisions in the criminal code, and/or the related sentencing legislation and guidance.[13] Even in those jurisdictions with the capacity for police officers to record an incident as possibly prejudice-related, the current approach in most ANZ jurisdictions is to deal with the incident as with any comparable crime without a hate motivation (Walters, 2005). In four jurisdictions – New Zealand, New South Wales, Victoria and the Northern Territory – amendments to sentencing legislation have enabled the judiciary to consider hatred and prejudice as an aggravating factor. For example, the New Zealand *Sentencing Act 2002* offers the judiciary options for crimes committed partly or wholly because of hostility against a group with an 'enduring characteristic', such as race, colour, nationality, religion, gender identity, sexual orientation, age or disability. The New Zealand provisions also require that hostility is '. . . because of . . .' the characteristic, and that the offender believed the victim was a member of one of these protected groups. This approach is similar to the 'sentence aggravation' provisions offered in the other jurisdictions.

Apart from the limited and largely untested civil offences of serious vilification (commonly contained in anti-discrimination legislation), Western Australia is the only jurisdiction in ANZ to enact a limited version of the 'substantive offence' model by way of criminalising *racist* incitement, harassment and the possession of racist materials (*Criminal Code Compilation Act 1913*, ss. 77–80). The same jurisdiction is also the only one in this region to adopt the 'penalty enhancement' model; as with the substantive offence provisions in ss. 70–80, the s. 313 penalty enhancement provisions only relate to *racial* aggravation. The 'substantive offences' of racial hatred and 'penalty enhancement' provisions were integrated into the *Act* in 2004 in response to the re-emergence of the ANM (Weber, 2004). As early as 1990 – and ahead of many other states of ANZ – the WA government, in response to a report into racist violence (Law Reform Commission of WA, 1989), was one of the first to criminalise incitement to racial hatred. Yet, despite ongoing campaigns of racist violence and threats against Jews, Muslims, migrants and refugees during the intervening 14 years, it was not until 2004 (in the same year these provisions were replaced with new 'vilification' offences) that an offender was charged under this section of the criminal code. By 2006, when van Tongeren was brought before the courts for his (and the ANM's) 20-year campaign of racial hatred (*Van Tongeren v State of Western Australia* [2006] WASC 10), the 1990 provisions had been repealed, and the new 'vilification' provisions in WA's criminal code had been expanded beyond the 1990 ambit of 'incitement' to include harassment and possession of racist material. Mason (2009) argues that the substantive offences of racial hatred in the WA criminal code have been ineffective in their primary stated goal of deterrence. As with the serious vilification provisions provided in other jurisdictions, the criminal provisions provided by the WA government have been untested, and their purpose appears more symbolic than illustrative of a real commitment to the redistribution of justice.

For the majority of jurisdictions (ACT, Tasmania, Queensland, South Australia, and Commonwealth of Australia), however, there are no specific hate crime provisions in any of the criminal justice legislation, codes or guidance documents, and attempts at reading hate crime into the generalist aggravation provisions in sentencing legislation have been sketchy, especially when the offence is *partially* motivated by hatred or prejudice. For example, in 2010 the Tasmanian Court of Criminal Appeal in *DPP v Broadby & ors* [2010] was asked to consider race as an aggravating factor under its generalist sentencing provisions. The court found no evidence of aggravating circumstances despite prior reported offences targeting Southeast Asian victims. As with the political discourse of 'boys behaving badly', in these cases – and as with the attacks against Indian students in 2009 in NSW and Victoria (Dunn et al., 2011) – the courts and the police have framed hate crime victimisation as opportunistic rather than aggravated or motivated by prejudice or hatred.

Mason and Dyer (2012) suggest that in addition to the significant under-utilisation of the criminal provisions (hate crime and criminal/serious vilification), the case law in Australia to date has highlighted three important, and recurring problems with the criminalisation of hatred. First, while several jurisdictions have adopted similar terminology in their definitions of hate crime – including versions of the phrase '. . . wholly or partially [partly] motivated by . . .' – the courts have taken a conservative line on cases not *wholly* motivated by hatred or prejudice (Mason, 2009). Additionally, no clear rulings have emerged to assist the judiciary in evaluating to what extent prejudice or hatred must be a factor for the hate crime provisions to be 'enlivened' (Mason and Dyer, 2012: 913). Second, they identify that the reliance on group selection tests could be counter-productive to the symbolic and deterrence goals of hate crime provisions, as group selection does not capture the necessary component of either motivation or intent. The group selection test also falls prey to exactly the same discriminatory processes employed by perpetrators of hate crime, whereby assumptions are made based simply on perceived membership of a recognised group. Finally, the case law and policing practices of the hate crime provisions also highlight the burning issue common to all jurisdictions that attempt to regulate and criminalise hatred: who will be protected? (Mason and Dyer, 2012).

Protected classes of victims

At the level of legislation, those protected by Australian and New Zealand hate crime provisions vary, with race/ethnicity as the only common attribute shared by all jurisdictions. The service enhancements offered by policing services, however, are usually extended to a wider group of people than are protected by, or named in legislation. For example, Youth Liaison Officers operate across the region yet ageism and hatred based on age are only considered aggravating factors in criminal sentencing in two jurisdictions, Victoria and New Zealand. In New Zealand, criminal provisions only protect 'enduring characteristics' (*Sentencing Act 2002* (NZ)); in other jurisdictions, such as Victoria, the legislation covers a variety of individual and social attributes including some that are mutable (*Sentencing Act 1991* (Victoria)). Hate crime provisions are said to serve the justice needs of vulnerable victims, but also the symbolic needs of the wider society in promoting the elimination of prejudice and hatred. The decisions in *A Child v The Police* (unreported, cited in Weber, 2006), and *Dunn v The Queen* (see Mason and Dyer, 2012) highlight the difficulties that arise when a normative list of victims is eschewed; albeit, for good reasons. *Dunn* also highlights the problems that can emerge when a group selection test is applied out of vaguely worded legislation (such as the NSW provisions that include a conventional but selective list of vulnerable groups preceded by '. . . prejudice against a group of people, *such as . . .*' (*Crimes (Sentencing Procedure) Act 1999*, s. 21A(2)(h); emphasis added). These cases contribute to a pattern emerging internationally, which has seen these types of provisions used against minority and/or vulnerable groups by majority complainants or the provisions have been extended to other characteristics uncommonly considered within the traditional notion of hate crime (such as paedophilia in *Dunn*). Whether those protected by legislation are explicitly named or not, identifying increased vulnerability to victimisation simply from a perceived or actual membership of a recognised community fails the justice goals of assisting those victims most vulnerable to the increased harms of targeted violence. The process of naming and protecting marginalised communities within legislation is central to the symbolic goals of responding to hate crime; yet, these are empty gestures if they fail to acknowledge the biopower of intolerance and prejudice, and that hatred is unevenly distributed in the first place.

The institutional responses to hate crime in Australia and New Zealand have been focused on racist violence; this is despite various statements by political leaders denying that racism exists, and insisting that racism is 'un-Australian' or 'un-Kiwi', or that we are not racist (Coorey, 2009; Davies and Peating, 2005; Kay, 2010; O'Malley and Drape, 2009). The development of the hate crime field for other victims of targeted violence has been much slower and less widely dispersed, and more contested publicly and politically. While homophobic and antisemitic prejudice was recognised by NSW Police as early as 1990 by way of their crime reporting system and network of community liaison officers (Asquith, 2008a), sexuality and (ethno-)religious identification – along with disability – are not consistently recognised in this region. As with three other jurisdictions, Tasmania has no specific hate crime provisions, nor a substantive offence of criminal vilification; though, incitement to hatred, contempt or ridicule has been included in s. 19 of the *Anti-Discrimination Act 1998* (Tasmania). The vilification provisions specifically identifies four protected attributes in relation to the incitement of hatred – race, disability, sexual orientation and religious belief. The inclusion of disability in the s. 19 vilification provisions is a first for Australia.[14] Yet, despite documenting over 50 complaints of disability vilification, the Tasmanian Anti-Discrimination Commissioner, Robin Banks reported in 2011 that none of these cases has managed to meet the test and burden of proof to sustain a complaint of vilification; let alone criminal or serious vilification. The commissioner suggests that these cases fail to meet the test because the emphasis is on incitement rather than 'offensive conduct' (Banks, 2011: 6), and that most disability hate speech was conducted in private and thus did not meet the public test of incitement.[15]

New Zealand and Australian governments have promoted mixed messages on issues relating to heterosexist and homophobic violence. Although recently assenting amendments to the *Marriage Act 1955* to recognise same-sex marriages, the New Zealand government continues to oscillate between providing protection from discrimination (*Human Rights Act 1993*) and recognition of sexuality in the hate crime sentencing provisions (*Sentencing Act 2002*), and failing to either collect data on experiences of heterosexist hate (Mayhew and Reilly, 2007a, 2007b) or extend vilification provisions to cover heterosexism. Additionally, as McDonald (2006) highlights, the courts have made use of the mitigating provisions for 'homosexual panic defence' more often than the s. 9(1)(h) sentencing aggravation provisions for hate crimes against gay men. As with Australia, the distribution of legislative responses in New Zealand has led to a 'policy career' that places greater importance on issues of race and ethnicity than all other experiences of prejudice and hatred. In Australia, the position of sexual and gender diverse communities is equally fraught; on the one hand, the recognition of same-sex relationships was briefly on the last Labor government's agenda in 2013, whilst at the same time, as discussed above in relation to the murders of gay men in Sydney in the 1980s, heterosexist hate crime is only recognised 20 years after a 'shameful crime wave' (Sheehan, 2013). The recently assented *Sex Discrimination Amendment (Sexual Orientation, Gender Identity and Intersex Status) Act 2013* comes 20 years after the first Bill relating discrimination and harassment based on sexual or gender identity was referred to Senate committee for review. This amendment comes nearly 40 years after the *Racial Discrimination Act 1975*, 30 years after the substantive Act for which the above is an amendment, the *Sex Discrimination Act 1984*, and 20 years after the *Disability Discrimination Act 1992* and *Racial Hatred Act 1995*.

Given the colonial histories of Australia and New Zealand, it is ironic that indigenous peoples of neither land have had recourse to use the criminal sanctions available to them nor promoted the development of hate crime provisions as an effective mechanism for remedying prejudice and hatred (see, for example, Victoria Aboriginal Legal Service Co-operative (VALS), 2010). This wariness about aggravated sentencing and penalty enhancements must be read in the wider context of the criminalisation of indigeneity. In its submission to the Eames review of Victoria's identity motivated hate crime provisions, VALS (2010) argued that criminal provisions were new forms of punitive crime control. They suggested that '[s]eeing first hand the failings of the criminal justice system to achieve positive justice outcomes through punitive measures, VALS retains a healthy scepticism when considering potential for punitive changes to the law' (VALS, 2010), and that any response to prejudice-related violence must include mechanisms for the prevention of hate crimes through the recognition of first peoples and the promotion of cultural diversity and equality.

Symbolic law

The original dispossession of lands from indigenous peoples in Australia and New Zealand has marked how each nation addresses the issues raised by colonisation, including the perception of racism, and the strategies employed to remedy what is constructed as either anomalous, individualised outbursts of pathological hatred, or 'boys behaving badly'. The 'frontier' racism to emerge from colonisation is matched in equal measure by deeply sexualised divisions of labour, power and justice, and while both nations have been 'social laboratories' at different times over the last 100 years, divisions continue to exist along a range of social and individual attributes. In some respects, however, New Zealand has been better prepared for responding to hate crimes, and for developing strategies that by-pass the criminalisation of individual behaviour in favour of whole-of-government initiatives. The differences between Australia and New Zealand are overt in the divergence between the two nations' responses to three critical, symbolic issues, which in themselves can act as 'dog-whistles' (Poynting and Noble, 2003) for those looking for justifications to enact their hatred or as a call to arms against prejudice. These three critical issues – indigenous self-determination, the rights of sexual and gender diverse communities and 'uninvited' humanitarian asylum seekers – are litmus tests of the capacity of each nation to match their global human rights commitments with legislative and policy frameworks that fully and coherently address the relationship between structures of prejudice and discrimination, and individualised acts of hatred. On each of these critical issues, New Zealand has maximised its opportunities to promote diversity and minimise the impact of prejudice and hatred. In this sense, at a symbolic level at the very least, it has had more success transforming social attitudes about diversity and preventing the conditions under which hate crime becomes possible.

Nicole L. Asquith

The differences between the ten ANZ jurisdictions belies a common theme that frames the delay in developing political and legislative responses to hate crime, but also in the paucity of civil and criminal cases to reach the point at which they begin to establish an agreed set of norms and values about the abhorrence of prejudice and hatred.[16] At most turns – whether political or public rhetoric, or legislative and policy development – there is a 'frontier' denial, minimisation and negation of prejudice and hatred (Soutphommasane, 2013). While some victimised groups and politicians may emphasise the non-criminal strategies employed by the state to facilitate cultural harmony, the symbolic gestures towards multiculturalism are incapable of achieving justice for many hate crime victims. Symbolic gestures alone cannot ameliorate the damage of targeted violence. Additionally, while 'service enhancements' may assist individual victims to better negotiate the criminal justice system, treating hate crimes as if they are the same as comparable crimes without a prejudicial motivation minimises the additional individual and community damage created by these incidents, and the different meaning of these incidents when they are motivated by prejudice or hatred. As illustrated by Mason (2009), Brown, C (2004) and McDonald (2006), hate crime provisions as developed in New Zealand and Australia have been largely ineffective in meeting the symbolic or deterrence goals of these types of interventions. In fact, in the case of Australia, some of the cases to reach adjudication (such as *Dunn*) undermine many of the stated reasons for developing a criminal response to hatred. Whether the criminal law is inefficacious in relation to managing prejudice and hatred, or whether the law as drafted in ANZ is incapable of doing so, is still open to debate. In late August 2013, the United Nations' Human Rights Committee found the government of Australia guilty of 150 violations of international law in relation to the Labor government's policy of mandatory and indefinite detention of refugees (Gordon, 2013). If the government, itself, cannot protect those who have been victims of crimes against humanity, it is naïve to expect these 'dog-whistle' violations will be drowned out by the symbolic effects of hate crime, anti-vilification or anti-discrimination legislation.

Notes

1 Associate Professor Nicole Asquith would like to acknowledge the contributions of Professor Scott Poynting (University of Auckland) – who worked closely with her in the early development of this chapter – and Ms Alice Tregunna (University of Auckland) for her assistance in reviewing the existing literature on hate crime in New Zealand.
2 ANZ is a common abbreviation of the two nations, including key multilateral and bilateral agreements such as *ANZAC* (Australia and New Zealand Army Corp) and *ANZUS* (Australia, New Zealand, United States Security Treaty), and has been used throughout this chapter. On some occasions, the term Australasia has been used; though, the use of this term is in its limited ANZ meaning, rather than the geographical 'Australasia', which also includes New Guinea, and less commonly, Polynesia and Melanesia.
3 New Zealand, Commonwealth of Australia, Australian Capital Territory, Northern Territory, Western Australia, South Australia, Queensland, Tasmania, Victoria and New South Wales.
4 For more detailed discussions about the regulation of hate crime in New South Wales and Victoria see, for example, Asquith (2007, 2008a); Dunn (2003); Dunn et al. (2007, 2011); Mason (2009, 2010, 2012); Poynting (2000a, 2000b, 2002); Poynting et al. (2004); Tomsen (2002); Tomsen and Markwell (2009); Walters (2005), but also the various studies undertaken before and after the Cronulla riots, such as those offered in Noble's (2009) edited collection, *Lines in the Sand*, and Walters (2006), Asquith and Poynting (2011) and Asquith (2008b).
5 See Mason (2013) for an extended discussion of the symbolic function of hate crime law, and the emotional labour required to legitimise a criminal or legislative response to hate crime.
6 *terra nullius* is a Latin term from Roman law that translates to English as 'land belonging to no one'.

Through convention, and English common law, the term at the time of colonisation meant 'land belonging to no *civilised* people'. As a legal precedent for dispossession in 1788, *terra nullius* was in fact not tested until 1827, declared until 1835, endorsed by the Privy Council until 1889, and remained as a law and doctrine until *Mabo v Queensland (No 2)* in 1992.
7 See for example, Belgrave et al. (2005); Durie (1998); Humpage and Fleras (2001); Kawharu (1989); Mutu (2011); Smith and Ruckstuhl (2010); Tauri (1999); Tauri and Webb (2011).
8 Importantly, while these reserved seats for Māori representatives may appear progressive in the contemporary era, when created in 1867, Māori were in the ethnic majority, which meant, in effect, that their representation was tokenistic at best.
9 There is no documented evidence of this unpublicised community response; however, the author was a member of the North Perth clean-up team in the mid to late 1980s.
10 See, for example, *Jones v Toben* [2002] in the federal jurisdiction, *Catch the Fire Ministries Inc v Islamic Council of Victoria Inc.* [2006] in Victoria, *A Child v Police* (unreported, Magistrate Auty, 14 September 2006) in Western Australia (cited in Weber, 2006), *Burns v Dye* [2002] NSWADT 32 (12 March 2002) in NSW, and *King-Ansell v Police* [1979] in New Zealand.
11 As an illustration of the inefficacy of the anti-vilification provisions to even act as a symbolic of the government's intent to eliminate prejudice and hatred, the 'sanctions' imposed on Jones were never reported.
12 Similarly, McGuire (another high profile media personality), like Jones, was charged with racism when he suggested that an indigenous football player, Adam Goodes, would be an ideal person to launch the musical, *King Kong* (Le Grand, 2013). This comment came only days after Goodes was called an 'ape' by a football spectator. As with Jones, the most strident public response was not to condemn McGuire (though the young female football spectator and her family were denounced in the media); instead, his detractors were pilloried for being 'thin-skinned' and for the deep offence caused *to* McGuire by calling his behaviour racist (Soutphommasane, 2013).
13 For up-to-date details about each of the hate crime legislative frameworks in Australia, along with key case citations see the Law link on the Australian Hate Crime Network website, http://sydney.edu.au/law/criminology/ahcn/index.shtml.
14 In 2012, the Tasmanian *Anti-Discrimination Amendment Bill* also sought to include in their definition of protected groups those who are intersex, which reflects the amendments made to the *Sex Discrimination Act 1984* by the Federal government in 2013. The expansion of traditional definitions of 'sex' to include sexual, sexuality and gender identity is rare in ANZ.
15 In a further development with regard to this protected class, in September 2013, the Victorian Human Rights and Equal Opportunity Commission is expected to release its report on disability and victimisation, with particular focus on the barriers to successful disability hate crimes prosecutions.
16 In March 2014, the newly elected Coalition government tabled amendments to Australia's *Racial Hatred Act*, which eviscerates the intent and symbolic function of this Act.

Bibliography

A Child v Police (unreported, Magistrate Auty, 14 September 2006) (Western Australia)
Anti-Discrimination Act 1977 (New South Wales)
Anti-Discrimination Act 1998 (Tasmania)
Anti-Discrimination Amendment Bill 2012 (Tasmania)
Bill of Rights Act 1990 (New Zealand)
Broadcasting Services Act 1992 (Commonwealth of Australia)
Burns v Dye [2002] NSWADT 32
Catch the Fire Ministries Inc v Islamic Council of Victoria Inc. [2006] VSCA 284
Crimes (Sentencing Procedures) Act 1999 (New South Wales)
Criminal Code Act 1995 (Commonwealth of Australia)
Criminal Code Compilation Act 1913 (WA)
Declaration of Independence of New Zealand (He Wakaputanga o te Rangatiratanga o Nu Tirene) 1835 (Aotearoa)
Director of Public Prosecutions v Broadby, Cockshutt and Woolley [2010] TASCCA 13 (17 September 2010)
Disability Discrimination Act 1992 (Commonwealth of Australia)
Dunn v The Queen [2007] NSWCCA 312

Nicole L. Asquith

Human Rights Act 1993 (New Zealand)
Human Rights Commission Act 1977 (New Zealand)
Jones v Toben (No. 2) [2009] FCA 477
King-Ansell v Police [1979] 2 NZLR 531
Marriage Act 1955 (New Zealand)
Mabo and Others v Queensland (No. 2) [1992] HCA 23; (1992) 175 CLR 1
New Zealand Constitution Act 1852 (Britain)
Racial Discrimination Act 1975 (Commonwealth of Australia)
Racial Hatred Act 1995 (Commonwealth of Australia)
Sentencing Act 1991 (Victoria)
Sentencing Act 2002 (New Zealand)
Sex Discrimination Amendment (Sexual Orientation, Gender Identity and Intersex Status) Bill 2013 (Commonwealth of Australia)
Sex Discrimination Act 1984 (Commonwealth of Australia)
Treaty of Waitangi (Te Tiriti o Waitangi) 1840 (New Zealand)
van Tongeren v The State Of Western Australia [2006] WASC 10
Asquith, NL (2012). Vulnerability and the Art of Complaint Making, in I Bartkowiak-Théron and NL Asquith (eds), *Policing Vulnerability*. Sydney: Federation Press.
_____ (2009). The Harms of Verbal and Textual Hatred, in P Iganski, (ed), *Hate Crimes: The Consequences of Hate Crime [Vol. 2]*. Westport: Praeger.
_____ (2008a). *The Text and Context of Malediction: A Study of Antisemitic and Heterosexist Hate Violence*. Saarbrücken: VDM Verlag.
_____ (2008b). Race Riots on the Beach: A Case for Criminalising Hate Speech? in A Millie (ed) *BSC Online Journal – Criminological Futures: Controversies, Developments and Debates*, 8 (Dec), 50–64.
_____ (2007). Speech Act Theory, Maledictive Force and the Adjudication of Vilification in Australia, in J Ensor, I Polak and P van der Merwe (eds) *New Talents 21C: other contact zones*. Perth: Network Books, 179–188.
Asquith, NL and Bartkowiak-Théron, I (2012). Vulnerable People Policing: A Preparatory Framework for Operationalising Vulnerability, in I Bartkowiak-Théron and NL Asquith (eds), *Policing Vulnerability*. Sydney: Federation Press, 279–292.
Asquith, NL and Poynting, S (2011). Anti-Cosmopolitanism and 'Ethnic Cleansing' at Cronulla, in K Jacobs and J Malpas (eds) *Between the Outback and the Sea: Cosmopolitanism and Anti-Cosmopolitanism in Contemporary Australia*. Perth: UWA Press, 96–122.
Australian Communication and Media Authority (ACMA) (2006). *Investigation Report No. 1485 – Breakfast with Alan Jones*. Canberra: Australian Federal Government.
Australian Hate Crime Network (2013). Law. Retrieved August 2013, from http://sydney.edu.au/law/criminology/ahcn/legislation_nsw.shtml
Banks, R (2011). Outlawing Vilification: The Tasmanian Experience, *Hate Crimes against Persons with Disability – Time for Action*. Sydney: NSW Disability Discrimination Legal Centre.
Bartkowiak-Théron, I (2012). Reaching out to Vulnerable People: the work of Police Liaison Officers, in I Bartkowiak-Théron and NL Asquith (eds), *Policing Vulnerability*. Annandale: Federation Press.
_____ (2011). Community Engagement and Public Trust in the Police: a Pragmatic view on Police and Community Relationships and Liaison Schemes, *Australasian Policing*, 2(3), 31–32.
Behrendt, L (1999). White Picket Fences: Recognizing Aboriginal Property Rights in Australia's Psychological *terra nullius*, *Constitutional Forum*, 10(2), 50–58.
Belgrave, M, Kawharu, M and Williams, DV (2005). *Waitangi Revisited: Perspectives on the Treaty of Waitangi*. South Melbourne: Oxford University Press.
Bess, R (2011). New Zealand's Treaty of Waitangi and the Doctrine of Discovery: Implications for the foreshore and seabed, *Marine Policy*, 35(1), 85–94.
Brown, C (2004). Legislating against Hate Crime in New Zealand: The Need to Recognise Gender-Based Violence, *Victoria University of Wellington Law Review*, 35(3), 591–608.
Brown, V (2004, 28 July). Neo-Nazis launch weekend of racist vandalism, *Green Left Weekly*. Retrieved August 2013, from www.greenleft.org.au/node/31743
Cameron, M (2013). From 'Queue Jumpers' to 'Absolute Scum of the Earth': Refugee and Organised Criminal Deviance in Australian Asylum Policy, *Australian Journal of Politics and History*, 59(2), 241–259.

Campbell, D (2007). Regional Settlement of Refugees: Implications for Policing, Refugee Entrants and Host Communities, *TILES Briefing Paper* (No. 3). Tasmanian Institute of Law Enforcement Studies, University of Tasmania.

Coorey, P (2009, 2 June). Rudd reassures India after a year of alarm, *Sydney Morning Herald*. Retrieved June 2013, from www.smh.com.au/national/rudd-reassures-india-after-a-year-of-alarm-20090601-bszm.html

Davies, A and Peating, S (2005, 13 December). Australians racist? No way, says Howard, *Sydney Morning Herald*. Retrieved February 2006, from www.smh.com.au/news/national/australians-racist-no-way-says-howard/2005/12/12/1134236005950.html

Dunn, KM (2003). Using cultural geography to engage contested constructions of ethnicity and citizenship in Sydney, *Social and Cultural Geography*, 4(2), 153–165.

Dunn, KM, Klocker, N and Salabay, T (2007). Contemporary Racism and Islamaphobia in Australia: Racializing Religion, *Ethnicities*, 7(4), 564–589.

Dunn, KM, Pelleri, D and Maeder-Han, K (2011). Attacks on Indian students: The commerce of denial in Australia, *Race and Class*, 52(4), 71–88.

Durie, MH (1998). *Te Mana, Te Kāwanatanga: The Politics of Self Determination*. Auckland: Oxford University Press.

Dwyer, AE (2012). Policing visible sexual/gender diversity as a program of governance, *International Journal for Crime and Justice*, 1(1), 14–26.

Flower, W and Evans, T (2010). Acting Premier Rob Hulls urges calm as Deputy PM Julia Gillard condemns stabbing death of Indian student in West Footscray, *Herald Sun*. Retrieved August 2013, from www.heraldsun.com.au/news/thugs-beat-police-knife-crackdown/story-e6frf7jo-1225815769857

Gelber, K (2002). *Speaking Back: The Free Speech Versus Hate Speech Debate* (Vol. 1). Amsterdam and Philadelphia: John Benjamins Publishing Company.

Goggin, G (2006). SMS Riot: Transmitting Race on a Sydney Beach, December 2005, *M/C Journal*, 9(1). Retrieved August 2013, from http://journal.media-culture.org.au/0603/02-goggin.php.

Gordon, M (2013, 22 August). Australia violated refugees' human rights, UN says, *The Age*. Retrieved August 2013, from www.theage.com.au/federal-politics/federal-election-2013/australia-violated-refugees-human-rights-un-says-20130822-2sdxq.html

Hage, G (2006, September). Everyday Exterminability. Keynote paper to the *Everyday Multiculturalism* Conference. Macquarie University, Sydney.

Humpage, L and Fleras, A (2001). Intersecting Discourses: Closing the Gaps, Social Justice and the Treaty of Waitangi, *Social Policy Journal of New Zealand*, 16, 37–54.

Iganski, P (2001). Hate Crimes Hurt More, *American Behavioral Scientist*, 45(4), 626–638.

Iorns, CJ (2003). Dedicated Parliamentary Seats for Indigenous Peoples: Political Representation as an Element of Indigenous Self-Determination, *E-Law: Murdoch University Electronic Journal of Law*, 10(4).

Kawharu, IH (1989). *Waitangi: Māori & Pākehā Perspectives of the Treaty of Waitangi*. Oxford University Press, USA.

Kay, M (2010, 5 October). TVNZ feels heat over Henry's 'un-Kiwi' comment, *Stuff.co.nz*. Retrieved August 2013, from www.stuff.co.nz/entertainment/tv/4196680/TVNZ-feels-heat-over-Henrys-un-Kiwi-comment

Law Reform Commission of Western Australia (1989). *Incitement to Racial Hatred*. Perth, WA: Law Reform Commission of Western Australia.

Le Grand, C (2013, 31 May). Eddie McGuire's comment reflected a serious problem in Australia, says Mick Dodson, *The Australian*. Retrieved June 2013, from www.theaustralian.com.au/sport/afl/…

Levy, M (2013, 13 February). Gays hunted for sport, says dead man's family. *The Sydney Morning Herald*. Retrieved August 2013, from www.smh.com.au/nsw/gays-hunted-for-sport-says-dead-mans-family-20130212-2eb5j.html

Madley, B (2008). From Terror to Genocide: Britain's Tasmanian Penal Colony and Australia's History Wars, *Journal of British Studies*, 47(1), 77–106.

Mason, G (2013). The Symbolic Purpose of Hate Crime Law: Ideal Victims and Emotion, *Theoretical Criminology*, OnlineFirst, 11 September, 2013, DOI: 10.1177/1362480613499792.

____ (2012). 'I Am Tomorrow': Violence against Indian Students in Australia and Political Denial, *Australian and New Zealand Journal of Criminology*, 45(1), 4–25.

____ (2010). *R v Gouros*: Interpreting Motivation under Victoria's New Hate Crime Laws, *Criminal Law Journal*, 34(5), 323–327.

____ (2009). Hate Crime Laws in Australia: Are They Achieving Their Goals? *Criminal Law Journal,* *33*(6), 326–340.
Mason, G and Dyer, A (2012). 'A Negation of Australia's Fundamental Values': Sentencing Prejudice Motivated Crime, *Melbourne University Law Review, 36*(3), 1–45.
Mayhew, P and Reilly, J (2007a, April). *The New Zealand Crime & Safety Survey: 2006.* Wellington: Ministry of Justice.
____ (2007b, December). *Community Safety: Findings from the New Zealand Crime & Safety Survey 2006.* Wellington: Ministry of Justice.
McDonald, E (2006). No Straight Answer: Homophobia as both an Aggravating and Mitigating Factor in New Zealand Homicide Cases, *Victoria University of Wellington Law Review, 37*(2), 223–248.
McGregor, J (2005). *Submission to the Government Administration Committee into the Inquiry into Hate Speech.* Wellington: Human Rights Commission.
McNamara, L (2002). *Regulating Racism – Racial Vilification Laws in Australia.* Sydney: Sydney Institute of Criminology.
Meagher, D (2006). So far no good: The regulatory failure of criminal racial vilification laws in Australia, *Public Law Review, 17*(3), 209–232.
Millar, P and Doherty, B (2009, 1 June). Indian anger boils over, *The Age.* Retrieved May 2010, from www.theage.com.au/national/indian-anger-boils-over-20090531-brrm.html
Mutu, M (2011). *The State of Māori Rights.* Wellington: Huia Publishers.
New South Wales Police Force (2013). NSWPF Corporate Sponsor GLBTI. Facebook post, 6 August @ 1.52am. Retrieved August 2013, www.facebook.com/nswpoliceforce/posts/10151612120451185
Noble, G (ed) (2009). *Lines in the Sand: The Cronulla Riots, Multiculturalism and National Belonging.* Sydney: Federation Press.
O'Malley, S and Drape, J (2009). Australia isn't racist: Rudd tells India, *Sydney Morning Herald.* Retrieved July 2013, from http://news.smh.com.au/breaking-news-national/australia-isnt-racist-rudd-tells-india-20090601-bsm1.html
Ozturk, S (2013, 8 August). Sydney's killer: The gay-hate epidemic that claimed 80 men, *Sydney Star Observer.* Retrieved August 2013, from www.starobserver.com.au/news/local-news/new-south-wales-news/2013/08/08/sydneys-killer-the-gay-hate-epidemic-that-claimed-80-men/107657
Perera, S (2009). *Australia and the Insular Imagination: Beaches, borders, boats and bodies.* New York: Palgrave Macmillan.
Poynting, S (2000a). Criminalising Ethnicity and Ethnicising Crime, in J. Collins and S. Poynting (eds), *Communities, Identities and Inequalities in Western Sydney.* Sydney: Common Ground, 63–78.
____ (2000b). Accounting for Cultural Diversity? The Recent Record of the NSW Police Service, *Current Issues in Criminal Justice, 12*(2), 223–226.
Poynting, S (2002). "Bin Laden in the Suburbs": Attacks on Arab and Muslim Australians before and after 11 September, *Current Issues in Criminal Justice, 14*(1), 43–64.
Poynting, S and Noble, G (2003). Dog-whistle Journalism and Muslim Australians since 2001, *Media International Australia: Culture and Politics, 107,* 41–49.
Poynting, S, Noble, G, Tabar, P and Collins, J (2004). *Bin Laden in the Suburbs: Criminalising the Arab Other.* Sydney: Institute of Criminology.
Reynolds, H (2001). *An Indelible Stain? The Question of Genocide in Australia's History.* Melbourne: Viking.
Saul, B (2013). Dark Justice: Australia's Indefinite Detention of Refugees on Security Grounds under International Human Rights Law, *Sydney Law School Research Paper,* No. 13/02. Sydney: University of Sydney.
Sheehan, P (2013, 4 March). Gay hate: the shameful crime wave, *Sydney Morning Herald.* Retrieved August 2013, from www.smh.com.au/comment/gay-hate-the-shameful-crime-wave-20130303-2fe9w.html
Smith, J and Ruckstuhl, K (2010). The Case of 'Te Karaka': Ngai Tahu Print Media before and after settlement, *AlterNative: An International Journal of Indigenous Peoples, 6*(1), 25–37.
Soutphommasane, T (2013, 3 June). Racism, bigotry and debate, Australian-style, *The Sydney Morning Herald.* Retrieved July 2013, from www.smh.com.au/comment/racism-bigotry-and-debate-australianstyle-20130602-2nju5.html
Steyn, M (2012). The Ignorance Contract: Recollections of Apartheid Childhoods and the Construction of Epistemologies of Ignorance, *Identities: Global Studies in Culture and Power, 19*(1), 8–25.
Tatz, C (2003). *With Intent to Destroy: Reflections on Genocide.* London and New York: Verso Books.

Tauri, J (1999). Explaining Recent Innovations in New Zealand's Criminal Justice System: Empowering Māori or Biculturalising the State? *Australian & New Zealand Journal of Criminology, 32*(2), 153–167.

Tauri, J and Webb, RD (2011). The Waitangi Tribunal and the Regulation of Māori, *Journal of the Sociological Association of Aotearoa/New Zealand, 26*, 21–41.

Tomsen, S (2002). *Hatred, Murder and Male Honour: Anti-Homosexual Homicides in New South Wales, 1980–2000* (Research and Public Policy Series No. 43). Canberra: Australian Institute of Criminology.

Tomsen, S and Markwell, K (2009). *When the Glitter Settles: Safety and hostility at and around gay and lesbian public events* (Research and Public Policy Series No. 100). Canberra: Australian Institute of Criminology.

van Meijl, T (2010). Settling Maori Land Claims: Legal and Economic Implications of Political and Ideological Contests, in T van Meijl and F von Benda-Beckmann (eds), *Property Rights and Economic Development*. Abingdon and New York: Routledge, 259–290.

Victorian Aboriginal Legal Service Co-operative (2010). *Hate Crime Review: A Review of Identity Motivated Hate Crime (Responses to Consultation Issues Paper)*. Melbourne: VALS.

Walters, M (2006). The Cronulla Riots: Exposing the Problem with Australia's Anti-Vilification Laws, *Current Issues in Criminal Justice, 17*(3), 165–169.

———— (2005). Hate crimes in Australia: introducing punishment enhancers, *Journal of Criminal Law and Criminology, 29*, 201–216.

Weber, D (2006). WA court dismisses charges over racial insult, *AM Radio*. Retrieved August 2013, from www.abc.net.au/am/content/2006/s1741596.htm

———— (2004). Emerging race hate campaign in Perth, *PM Radio*. Retrieved August 2013, from www.abc.net.au/pm/content/2004/s1157360.htm

White, RD (2002). Hate Crime Politics, *Theoretical Criminology, 6*(4), 499–502.

3
Key issues in hate crime

16
Hate crime against people with disabilities

Chih Hoong Sin

Compared with racist and religiously-motivated hate crime, hate crime against disabled people has attracted significantly less attention in policy, practice and academic research internationally. There is still a severe paucity of robust evidence in this area, and significant gaps that limit the extent to which meaningful comparisons may be made internationally. Petersilia's observation in 2001 that much of the evidence "is not scientifically rigorous literature, consisting mostly of anecdotal evidence, data from convenience samples and non-random samples, and non-random programme evaluations" is still, unfortunately, valid (Petersilia, 2001: 658). Methods are not always reported in sufficient detail, or at all, to enable assessment of robustness and rigour. In addition, there is a paucity of material adopting comparative approaches (e.g. comparing different sub-groups of disabled people; comparing disabled and non-disabled people; comparing across different countries). This limits the extent to which we can assess the significance or generalisability of reported findings.

Nonetheless there has been progress in a few countries in recent years, including developments in policy and practice. Reflecting on the transformations in the United Kingdom (UK), for instance, the journalist and activist Katherine Quarmby noted that when she first embarked on documenting hate crime against disabled people in 2007, ignorance of such crime or disbelief that these things happen were prevalent, even amongst the police and prosecutors. Writing three years later, Quarmby (2010) found that the "disbelief and ignorance has fallen away". Not only are police and prosecutors keen to investigate and prosecute such hate crime (e.g. Crown Prosecution Service, 2010a; Home Office, 2012), disabled people and their organisations have also redoubled efforts to press for action (see Department for Work and Pensions, 2012; Disability Rights UK, 2012). The hate crime scholarship relating to disability has also exploded (e.g. Roulstone and Mason-Bish, 2012; Sheikh et al., 2011; Sin et al., 2009, etc.). Sherry (2010: xv) commented that "there have been probably more publications about disability hate crimes in the UK over the last five years than the rest of the world combined".

In the United States of America (USA), Grattet and Jenness (2001: 669) argued that hate crime against persons with disabilities is "at best, a second class citizen insofar as it is peripheral to the core of hate crime legislation in the United States". Writing at around the same time, Perry (2003: 173) noted that the "recognition of people with disabilities as potential victims of bias-motivated violence has come very late to the social sciences". In the ten years since these seminal publications, Levin (2012: 103) reported legislative progress and improvements in the evidence base. For example, while 18 states do not have hate crime statutes that protect people with disabilities, the passing of the Matthew Shepard and James Byrd, Jr. Hate Crimes Prevention Act (which covers disability, amongst other identities/characteristics) has brought a uniform federal approach to the protection of hate crime victims that was not formerly possible when matters were left only to the states. While not without flaws and delays, the FBI has been collecting data on hate crime based on 'physical' or 'mental' disability since 1997 (Sherry, 2003: 6) and is the longest-running and most comprehensive database on hate crime against disabled people in the world (Sherry, 2010: 1); while other useful data have been generated by the United States Bureau of Justice Statistics and the US Department of Justice (Harrell, 2011).

Aside from the few examples of country-specific developments, internationally hate crime against disabled people remains overlooked in research, policy and practice. The few efforts in making some progress in this area have all been very recent. For example, the first project of the European Union Agency for Fundamental Rights (FRA) in the area of disability, carried out in the spirit of the UN Convention on the Rights of Persons with Disabilities, was only undertaken in 2009 (reporting in 2010). This looked at the fundamental rights situation of those with intellectual disabilities and those with mental health problems (FRA, 2010). The Office for Democratic Institutions and Human Rights (ODIHR), part of the Organisation for Security and Co-operation in Europe (OSCE), on the other hand, convened a workshop on combating hate-motivated crimes against disabled people in Dublin on 24 May 2012 in partnership with the European Network of Independent Living. This was the first ODIHR event to specifically address hate crime against disabled people (see: www.osce.org/odihr/90807).

Given the potential breadth of the topic, this chapter adopts a focus that is necessarily selective. It identifies a number of consistent features of hate crime against disabled people reported in the available international literature, while drawing attention to gaps in the evidence base and challenges with consistent interpretation. The chapter explores, specifically, certain features of hate crime against disabled people that appear to be distinct from other types of hate crime, or at least where it exhibits important nuances. While discussing such distinctiveness, the chapter nonetheless asserts the importance of the need to understand hate crime through the lens of multiple identities without reifying disability as the sole or primary identity that explains or helps us understand the incidence and experiences of hate crime against disabled people.

Terminology

When writing about the international evidence base, we encounter different terminology reflecting different traditions and cultures, and have different implications for how we understand the associated evidence base and the relevant legislation, policy and practice. In the UK, the 'social model' of disability makes a clear distinction between 'impairment' and 'disability'. The 'social model' of disability is a way of thinking about disability developed by the Union of the Physically Impaired Against Segregation (UPIAS) in the 1970s that makes the crucial distinction between the biological and the social (UPIAS, 1976). It attempts to shift the emphasis away from individual impairments towards the ways in which physical, cultural and social environments exclude and disadvantage, thereby 'disabling', people (Oliver, 1983).

In the USA and elsewhere, the term 'people with disabilities' is commonly used. The penetration and currency of terminology, however, is not complete even within individual countries. For example, while the 'social model' is more deeply rooted in the UK, it is still not unusual to find references to 'people with disabilities' (see Vincent et al., 2009 for example). Similarly, the 'social model' has advocates in the USA, Canada and Australia (Sherry, 2010). Philosophical and political traditions are thus not easily read off the use of particular terminology. In addition, it is difficult to sustain consistent use of preferred terminology when discussing cross-country material due to the need to respect linguistic differences and to maintain fidelity in reporting original usage.

This brief overview of linguistic differences is not to serve pedantic purposes. They have concrete impacts on policy and practice, as well as on the thrust of research conducted in different social milieu. For example, Sherry (2012) argued that the 'social model' underpinning the use of the term 'disabled people' rather than 'people with disabilities' in the UK focuses attention on the collective experience of oppression and requires large-scale social change. Perhaps unsurprisingly, the UK disability movement has been noted as being particularly active in this area; seeing its role very much in terms of pressing for social change. The policy and practice response has also been on dismantling disabling barriers, while scholars and criminal justice agencies have increasingly been working to shift the emphasis away from uncritical assumptions around the inherent 'vulnerability' of disabled people, and using this assumed 'vulnerability' to explain why hate crimes happen to disabled people (Crown Prosecution Service, 2010b; Roulstone and Sadique, 2012; Sin, 2013).

In comparison, Sherry (2012) contends that the more individualistic culture in the USA has meant that disability has largely been framed as an issue relating to individual identity, and hence the tendency to talk about 'persons with disabilities'. This difference in perspective and approach influences, in some cases, the reference to 'disability hate crime' or 'disablist hate crime'. The latter, which is less commonly used than the former, is often used by those who embrace the social model of disability, as: "This term more clearly shows that the problem is with the perpetrator, and how disablist hate crime ... come from ... prejudice against groups" (Strengthening Disabled People's User-led Organisations Programme, 2012: 5).

These differences in how disability and disability hate crime are defined affect how disabled people, organisations and agencies, and wider society respond to hate crime; and how they approach the topic of intervention and redress. It is clear from the international evidence that different countries define 'disability' differently, leading to different inclusions and exclusions, and different responses to hate crime.

One definition of disability in Australia, used by the Australian Government's Australian Institute of Health and Welfare (AIHW), defines it as: "one or more of 17 limitations, restrictions or impairments which have lasted or are likely to last, for a period of six months or more, and which restrict a person's everyday activities" (AIHW, 2013). Instead of a prescribed list of limitations, restrictions or impairments, disability is defined in the UK as "a physical or mental impairment which has a substantial and long-term adverse effect on his [sic] ability to carry out normal day-to-day activities" (Office for Public Sector Information, 2005). In contrast to the definition used by the AIHW, the UK operationalises 'long-term' as lasting (or likely to last) at least 12 months. Diabetes and cancer, from the point of diagnosis, are also covered by the definition of disability in the UK (Office for Disability Issues, 2010). In Sweden, disability is understood as "enduring physical, mental or learning limitations of a person's functional capacities that have occurred at birth or later or can be expected to occur as a consequence of injury or disease" (European Commission, 2002). Unlike the UK, a person's functional limitations do not have to be 'substantial'.

A comparative analysis of definitions of disability published by the European Commission in 2002 found significant variations across national statutes, and even across different administrative boundaries within the same country. In general, definitions used in anti-discrimination policies are broader, and focus on the act of discrimination. Conversely, definitions used in social policy are more restrictive, as they are used in the context of allocating scarce resources to meet recognised needs. Disabled people may be regarded and treated differently by different organisations (and countries) because of different definitions. The specific implications for hate crime are, as yet, under-explored. For example, how do agencies working in health, social care, housing, and elsewhere perceive their role in identifying and tackling hate crime against disabled people when they may use different definitions of disability with associated differences in inclusions and exclusions? This issue has increasingly been rearing its head in the UK, where multi-agency response to hate crime against disabled people is being promoted in a context characterised by a lack of consistency in monitoring and recording practices (Sin et al., 2011).

Just as the definition of disability has to be understood in the context of the specific political and social milieu from which it originates, likewise Ray and Smith (2001: 211) argued that "the definition of hate crime is subject to a process of contestation and negotiation rather than being pre-given". Indeed the word 'hate' does not always appear in 'hate crime' statutes (Perry, 2009; Iganski et al., 2011). For example, Section 146 of the Criminal Justice Act 2003 in the UK recognises that 'hate crime' has occurred: "Where . . . at the time of committing the offence or immediately before or after doing so, the offender demonstrated towards the victim of the offence *hostility* based on . . . a disability (or presumed disability of the victim) . . ." (emphasis added).

The different definitions of (disability) hate crime introduce different inclusions and exclusions that, again, have concrete implications for how we assess reported findings internationally. Sherry (2012), for example, compared the definitions and operationalisation of 'hate crime' in the UK and USA, and explored the implications for resultant statistics. The UK considers "verbal abuse, insults or harassment" as examples of hate crime (see Crown Prosecution Service, n.d.), whereas the constitutional protection for freedom of speech in the USA means that these instances would not be regarded as hate crime in their own right (Cram, 2005). Sherry argued that the broader inclusion criteria in the UK may explain the higher reported figures in comparison with those for the USA. In Canada, Shaw and Barchechat (2002: 8) noted that hate propaganda was included in the Criminal Code in 1970, while amendments to the Criminal Code in 1996 (Article 718.2) made hate an 'aggravating circumstance' where there is: "evidence that the offence was motivated by bias, prejudice or hate based on race, national or ethnic origin, language, colour, religion, sex, age, mental or physical disability, sexual orientation, or any other similar factor".

Difference from other types of hate crimes

Regardless of the differences in terminology and definition, a number of common messages are reported in the literature pertaining to the differences between hate crime against disabled people and other forms of hate crime.

Levin (2012: 98) observed that "unlike racially and religiously motivated offences, attacks against people with disabilities tend to be committed less by strangers and more by family members, neighbours, employees, and friends who may also be caregivers". As Iganski et al. (2011) demonstrated, unfortunately, there is a real paucity of data on perpetrators of hate crime against disabled people internationally. This has been backed up by a more recent review of the international literature by Roberts et al. (2013) that went further by comparing the strength and depth of published literature on offenders of different types of hate crime. Nonetheless, the USA's Department of Justice statistics for 2010 show that 33 per cent of violent victimisations against persons with disabilities were committed by strangers to the victim (Harrell, 2011). Additionally, there is evidence from Australia (Sherry, 2000) and the UK (Sin et al., 2009) suggesting strongly that a significant proportion of hate crime against disabled people are perpetrated by people who are known to the victim, even if the level of familiarity may be quite tenuous. In proposing a typology of different hate crimes against disabled people and exploring how these are manifested in different 'hotspots', Sin et al. (2009) found that many cases take place near to where the victims live, often within the same neighbourhood or estate; in the victims' schools or workplaces; and in institutional settings such as day care centres or residential/in-patient care settings. Roberts et al. (2013), however, cited numerous examples of literature on other forms of hate crime that also challenged the predominant 'stranger danger' perspective, indicating that this may not be unique to hate crime against disabled people (see also Mason, 2005).

Nonetheless, there may be some differences in the composition of perpetrators who are 'known to' the victim. Clements et al. (2011), for example, argued that hate crime against disabled people are different from other forms of hate crime in that carers feature more prominently in the former. Human Rights First (2007: 27) similarly noted the preponderance of cases that occur in the 'private sphere' of disabled people's lives, and in institutions.

This characteristic of hate crime against disabled people has a number of implications that explain additional differences from other forms of hate crime. First, the fact that many perpetrators are known to the victim, including people with intimate relationships with the disabled person (e.g. family members, caregivers, friends, etc.), can often lead to cases being characterised as 'abuse' rather than 'hate crime'. This is especially so for cases that occur at home, and in care or custodial settings, almost regardless of the severity of the case (Human Rights First, 2007).

This tendency for cases to be labelled as 'abuse' has been widely reported in the published literature, leading to cases not being reported to the police. Literature on domestic violence against disabled women from the USA (Nosek and Howland, 1998), Canada (DAWN, 1994), Australia (Chenoweth, 1996; Salthouse and Frohmader, 2004), and the UK (Barclay and Mulligan, 2009; Thiara et al., 2012); and the burgeoning literature from the UK in relation to what has become known as 'mate crime' (i.e. crimes against disabled people carried out by people the disabled person considers to be their friends – Thomas, 2012) demonstrate the complications that arise when hate crimes are perpetrated by people close to, or intimate with, the disabled person.

Sin et al. (2011) observed that individual-, organisational- and systemic-level responses can often be orientated towards protection or the minimisation of risk rather than towards providing access to justice and effective redress via the criminal justice system. In fact, some have argued that hate crime against disabled people shares key commonalities with violence against women (Quarmby, 2011), although there are also significant differences.

Second, statutory agencies and those working with disabled people can feature prominently amongst those who perpetrate hate crime against disabled people. There are numerous examples reported in the literature of victimisation by someone associated with disability services or through services provided specifically for disabled people (e.g. Sobsey, 1994; Petersilia, 2001). This seems to be especially so for people with learning disabilities or 'developmental disabilities'. People with mental health conditions have also reported experiencing violence from the police and from staff in in-patient psychiatric wards (Burgess and Phillips, 2006; MIND, 2007). The experience or perception of the role played by these agencies and individuals in perpetrating hate crime can lead to under-reporting as well as unwillingness to engage with relevant agencies and staff to seek support.

Third, the role played by those known to disabled victims of hate crime is significant as it can mean that disabled people are subjected to persistent attacks. The wider literature suggests that incidents are often multiple, with a likelihood of escalation (Human Rights First, 2007). The UK Home Office, for example, published a report in 2007 that built on the findings from a Higgins survey of Scottish people with learning disabilities that reported that 20 per cent of respondents had experienced an attack 'at least once a week'. The Home Office report extrapolated this figure and noted that if such an incidence of attack occurred in England, this would result in 32,000 people experiencing a hate crime on a weekly basis (Home Office, 2007: 4). Hate crime can often be experienced on an ongoing basis perpetrated by the same person(s), or as frequent 'one off' incidents that become part of the victim's everyday life (McDonald and Hogue, 2007; Sin et al., 2009).

An important observation that arises from the recognition of the often persistent and escalating nature of experiences is that it can be vital for those working to combat hate crime against disabled people to monitor not only hate crimes but also hate incidents. This has been particularly noteworthy in the UK. Iganski (2008) conducted fresh analyses of data from the British Crime Survey and demonstrated compellingly that hate crimes caused more harm than the same offence without the bias motivation (see also Smith et al., 2012). This has also been demonstrated in the evidence from the USA (Herek et al., 1999). In relation to disabled victims, even so-called 'low level' non-criminal incidents have been shown to have high impact (Sin et al., 2009). They can also be important indicators of patterns of repeat victimisation (Sheikh et al., 2011; Sin, 2013), that may be a precursor to more severe hyperviolent and hypersexual crimes noted by commentators as being a significant feature of hate crime against disabled people in the international context (Levin, 2012; Sherry, 2012).

Prevalence

Issues with the quality and comprehensiveness of hate crime data relating to disability are widely acknowledged in the international evidence base. A review conducted by Hunter et al. (2007: 5) in the UK concluded that: "historically there has been very limited systematic recording of the amount of harassment or victimization experienced by disabled people", while Sherry (2003) offered clear analysis of why FBI statistics on hate crime against people with disabilities in the USA are woefully inadequate in giving a true sense of prevalence. Reports by ODIHR, and by others, similarly note the lack of such recording; with many countries demonstrating a complete absence of any recording mechanism. Even where there have been legislation or policy put in place requiring the recording of such data, there can be significant delays in implementation.

Recording practices can also be inconsistent, further weakening the reliability of reported data. In some cases, monitoring is hampered where hate crime against disabled people is not recognised legally across all parts of a country. For example, while race is covered under all hate crime laws across the various jurisdictions of Australia, disability and sexual orientation are not included in many statutes (Mason, 2010).

The literature recognises that the accuracy of estimates of prevalence continue to be hampered by under-reporting. The combination of under-reporting and under-recording (or inconsistent recording) means that prevalence statistics need to be interpreted with caution.

The OSCE, through the ODIHR, publishes annual hate crime reports since 2008. However, the comparability of data is compromised by different specific definitions of hate crime under domestic laws of participating States, by varying hate crime categories, and critically by varying emphases and commitment. Official monitoring of hate crime against disabled people is woefully limited. Thirteen participating States reported collecting this data in 2011: Belgium, Canada, Croatia, Cyprus, Finland, France, Georgia, Germany, Moldova, Netherlands, Serbia, the UK and the USA. Only Germany and the UK provided figures for the 2011 report. Data on the USA are publicly available, but were not submitted to ODIHR as part of the formal reporting process (Human Rights First and the Anti-Defamation League, 2012). Similarly, of the 27 EU Member States that reported hate crime data pertaining to 2010, only four indicated that they had data relating to hate crime against disabled people, three of which provided the relevant data (FRA, 2012).

Even these data are of doubtful utility. The ODIHR report showed that Germany's official law-enforcement figures documented 18 crimes motivated by a bias against disabled people for 2011. The corresponding figures for England, Wales and Northern Ireland were 2,095 (ODIHR, 2012). As Sin (2013) noted, while the UK is performing better in terms of monitoring hate crime against disabled people in comparison with most other OSCE participating States, the veracity of figures reported is still in doubt due to inconsistent recording practices across different police services and significant under-reporting by disabled people themselves. In a similar vein, the report by the FRA indicated that in 2010 Finland reported 20 cases of hate crime against disabled people; the Netherlands reported seven cases; while the UK reported 1,619 cases (FRA, 2012).

Likewise, data on crimes reported to and substantiated by police in Canada through the Incident-based Uniform Crime Reporting Survey indicated a total of eight cases of hate crime in Canada motivated by bias relating to 'mental or physical disability' in 2010 (Dowden and Brennan, 2012).

One of the consequences of poor or non-existent recording is that it can perpetuate the misperception of low levels of hate crime against disabled people. Certainly, there is confusion over whether there really is such a thing as 'hate crime' against disabled people and, if so, what it looks like (Adams-Spink, 2008; Sherry, 2010).

Two systematic reviews published in 2012, however, suggest that hate crime against disabled people is a real issue of significant magnitude. While highlighting the lack of data from low- and middle-income countries, and with a focus on violence, the reviews provided compelling evidence that disabled children and adults are at much higher risk of violence than their non-disabled peers. Overall disabled children are 3.7 times more likely to experience any sort of violence than non-disabled children, 3.6 times more likely to be victims of physical violence, and 2.9 times more likely to be victims of sexual violence. Children with 'mental or intellectual impairments' appear to be particularly at risk, with 4.6 times the risk of sexual violence than their non-disabled peers (Jones et al., 2012). A separate review on violence against disabled adults found that overall they are 1.5 times more likely to be a victim of violence than non-disabled adults. Those with mental health conditions are at nearly four times the risk of experiencing violence (Hughes et al., 2012).

Under-reporting

While hate crimes, in general, are widely acknowledged to be under-reported; there are specific features of the reporting of hate crime against disabled people that need to be highlighted. The fact that disabled people under-report to the police is well-documented in the international literature, although there is a paucity of statistical information with regards to reporting rates. Where these are produced or referenced, they tend to be somewhat out of date, or relate only to particular sub-groups (e.g. people with mental health conditions) in the context of specific experiences (e.g. in relation to sexual crimes).

While under-reporting is a feature across all forms of hate crime, the reasons underpinning this can be quite different. In the UK for example, the British Gay Crime Survey (Dick, 2008) found that the majority of victims of homophobic hate crime are aware that they have experienced something unacceptable and that they should (although they do not always) report to the police. In contrast, the literature on disabled victims of hate crime indicates that many are not even aware that what they have experienced is anything other than "part of their everyday lives" (Perry, 2004; Sin et al., 2009; Sherry, 2003).

At risk of over-simplification, the reasons why disabled people under-report to the police can be grouped under two broad categories. The first relates to experiences and perceptions of the police. These may involve specific experiences of reporting to the police, but can also involve impressions formed of the police as a result of other encounters. The second involves more general issues relating to the structural position of disabled people in society and the implications this has for relationships, attitudes and awareness.

Experiences and perceptions of the police

While the international evidence base contains numerous examples of disabled people's experiences of reporting to the police, these tend to be presented as individual case studies (Sharp, 2001). Nonetheless, a number of specific barriers are discernible.

First, there is some evidence that lack of access to police stations and inaccessible reporting systems can contribute to under-reporting (Cunningham and Drury, 2002). Poor wheelchair access, the lack of sign language interpreters, inaccessible information and reporting forms and systems, and a lack of disability awareness amongst frontline staff can create multiple layers of inaccessibility (Gilson et al., 2001).

Second, past experiences with the police can contribute towards unwillingness to report. The police may be dismissive and disabled people often indicate that they do not feel listened to or taken seriously (Levin, 2012; Carlson, 2013). Negative stereotypes around the capability and competence of disabled people can lead to them being seen as unreliable or 'lacking' (OSCE/ODIHR, 2009). There is also evidence that stereotypes about disabled people can lead to negative behaviours by the police. This seems to be particularly so for people with learning disabilities and/or mental health conditions, where reports of victimisation or low level harassment by the police exist. Levin (2012) noted that in the USA, ethnic background and immigration status can also introduce additional challenges to the willingness to engage with law enforcement personnel. More generally, disabled people have been found to have lower levels of confidence in the criminal justice system compared with non-disabled people (Quarmby, 2008; Home Office, 2012).

The relationship between the perpetrator and the victim

Disabled victims of hate crime can be prevented or discouraged from reporting due to complex sets of relationships within which they are enmeshed. As many perpetrators of hate crime against disabled people are 'known to' the victims, the disabled person may fear grave personal harm or retaliatory attacks on themselves, their family and their property if they make a report (Levin, 2012; McDonald and Hogue, 2007; Petersilia, 2001).

Due to the multiple exclusions experienced by many disabled people (Williams et al., 2008), some can find it difficult to form supportive and sustainable social networks. People with learning disabilities and/or mental health conditions, in particular, have been found to be susceptible to being 'befriended' by people who then exploit them. Disabled people may put up with acts of cruelty, humiliation, servitude, exploitation and theft from those whom they regard as 'friends' (Hunter et al., 2007; Thomas, 2012).

In other relationships involving family members (including spouse) as well as with others who may be providing care, the challenges become even more considerable due to complex issues around (inter)dependency (Elman, 2005; Faulkner, 2012; Levin, 2012; Saxton et al., 2001). Disabled people often have no idea what will happen to the information they provide to the police, and whether actions will be taken without their consent, as even well-intentioned actions may exacerbate their circumstances. These act as formidable barriers to reporting.

Wider structures and attitudes

Decisions around reporting are also influenced deeply by an individual's and society's attitudes towards disability and disabled people. Disabled people are often conditioned by their carers and family members, and by wider society, to accept and ignore negative behaviour targeted at them (Sherry, 2003; Sin et al., 2009). While some of this may be well-intentioned, the welfarist and protectionist assumptions underpinning such responses mean that the focus is on harm avoidance and risk minimisation through the disabled person changing his or her behaviours and routines (WHO, 2011).

Much of the response in relation to hate crime against disabled people has been underpinned by implicit or explicit assumptions around their 'vulnerability'. Hate crime can often be portrayed as something that happens to disabled people *because* of their vulnerability; that their vulnerability stems from them having impairments; and that their vulnerability is an inherent and fixed condition. This uncritical acceptance of the 'vulnerability' thesis can mean endemic low aspirations for disabled people as a group, leading to fatalistic acceptance that disabled people cannot expect anything different because they are inherently vulnerable. The best that may be done for them is to 'protect'. This does not recognise the structures that reproduce vulnerability and the contexts in which disabled people experience hate crime. This approach serves to locate disabled people in a way that enables them to be managed.

The recent move within the hate crime scholarship to critique the representation of vulnerability (e.g. Sin et al., 2009; Roulstone and Sadique, 2012; Sin, 2013) has been particularly strong in the UK. This is unsurprising given the almost hegemonic discourse around the 'social model' of disability. Sin (2014), for instance, proposed a 'layers of influence' model to help conceptualise hate crime against disabled people as the result of the interdependency of various levels of social aggregate within which any individual is positioned. Positionality is not fixed, and is always contingent and contextual.

Reporting behaviours

While disabled people under-report to the police, this does not mean that they do not report at all. Unfortunately, very little is known about who else they report to, and what happens with this information. The limited data in this area often relate to specific groups, and are often out of date. Coverage is, perhaps, most extensive in the UK literature. For example, data from Scotland suggest that 90 per cent of disabled victims of hate crime in Scotland have told someone about the incident, with friends and family being the most likely people to have been informed (Disability Rights Commission and Capability Scotland, 2004). Research with visually impaired people found that the majority of those who experienced hate crime tended to turn to their family and friends (Action for Blind People, 2008) while research with people with learning disabilities and/or mental health conditions who have experienced hate crime indicates that they have a tendency to tell social workers, support workers, advocates, health professionals, housing officers and others, rather than to the police (Mencap, 1999; MIND, 2007; Sin et al., 2009; Sheikh et al., 2011).

The policy and practice focus on the criminal justice system has meant that the critical role played by other individuals and organisations has been overlooked. Indeed, much of the international literature looking at the response to hate crime against disabled people has noted the lack of coordination across the various key agencies (McDonald and Hogue, 2007; National Council on Disability, 2008; Office for Victims of Crime, 2012a, 2012b; Sin et al., 2011). In fact, the term 'reporting' may not accurately represent the processes and dynamics involved, as the information may be divulged through informal conversations, and the topic of conversations may not be around hate crime (Sin et al., 2009). It can be through discussion of some other issue (e.g. health problem) that an experience of hate crime is mentioned, often incidentally.

Conclusion

The introduction to this chapter argued that research, policy and practice in relation to hate crime against disabled people suffer from serious gaps in the evidence base. This hampers severely efforts to combat such hate crime effectively. However, progress towards tackling hate crime against disabled people cannot simply be put down to the quality of the evidence base. The issue is still largely invisible in many countries, with little if not no recognition that it is a problem. While there is an urgent need to improve the quality and coverage of the evidence base, there must also be concomitant efforts to raise awareness and to shift attitudes towards disability and hate crime against disabled people.

While this chapter has approached the topic of hate crime through the lens of disability, it has to be acknowledged that a singular identity-based approach towards understanding hate crime has its limitations (Perry, 2009, 2012; Piggott, 2011). The discussion within this chapter has already highlighted international evidence pointing to the fact that disabled children and disabled women may experience disproportionate levels of victimisation even in comparison with disabled people in general. While the link between risk and resultant victimisation is highly complex, there is evidence suggesting that an accumulation of risk factors heightens significantly the likelihood of being a victim of hate crime. Sin et al. (2009) argued that this may be due to the combination of different identities that compound power imbalance, for example by having (or being perceived to have) more than one minoritised identity. The use of the word 'minoritised' (as opposed to minority) is important in this context. It points to unequal power dynamics played out in different socio-political milieu. After all, women are not a numerical 'minority', but nonetheless occupy a less privileged structural position in many societies. Real or perceived/ascribed identity labels (for example ethnicity, gender, religion, sexual orientation, etc.) as well as wider demographic characteristics (for example geographical distribution, socio-economic status, etc.) can interact in complex manners to bring about differential levels of risk in different contexts, and diverse experiences of victimisation. Unfortunately, there is little sustained exploration of 'intersectionality' in the wider evidence base.

Horvath and Kelly (2008) argued that 'simplistic' discrimination and equality formulations often fail to help us understand fully the 'lived experience' of victims of hate crime. They offer 'intersectionality' as a conceptual basis to understand the complexity and multi-layering of identities and experience. Hate crimes do not always fall neatly under one identity category and it is crucial that relevant agencies acknowledge the multiple identities and multiple needs of the victim, as well as the complex motivations behind the perpetrator's actions.

Disabled people are not a homogenous group, and experiences within the disabled population are extremely diverse. The evidence behoves us to develop more sophisticated ways of understanding the issue of hate crime against disabled people. The concept of intersectionality makes us realise that 'vulnerability' and 'risk', for example, are not simply by-products of some inherent and unchanging characteristics of disabled people. Instead, it encourages us to adopt structural as well as situational perspectives in understanding hate crime against disabled people.

References

Action for Blind People (2008) *Report on Verbal and Physical Abuse Towards Blind and Partially Sighted People Across the UK*, London, UK: Action for Blind People.
Adams-Spink, G. (2008) Does disability hate crime exist? 19 August 2008. Available at: http://news.bbc.co.uk/1/hi/magazine/7570305.stm. Accessed on 9 August 2013.
Australian Institute of Health and Welfare (AIHW) (2013) *Definition of Disability*. Available at: www.aihw.gov.au/definition-of-disability/. Accessed on 9 August 2013.
Barclay, H. and Mulligan, D. (2009) Tackling violence against women: lessons for efforts to tackle other forms of targeted violence, *Safer Communities*, 8(4), 43–50.
Burgess, A.W. and Phillips, S.L. (2006) Sexual abuse, trauma and dementia in the elderly: A retrospective, *Victims and Offenders*, 1(2), 193–204.
Carlson, T. (2013) People with Disabilities Open Up About Hate Crime, *The Huffington Post*, 20 July 2013. Available at: www.huffingtonpost.com/2013/06/20/people-with-disabilities-relay-hate-crimes_n_3473590.html. Accessed on 9 August 2013.
Chenoweth, L. (1996) Violence and women with disabilities: Silence and paradox, *Violence Against Women*, 2(4), 391–411.
Clements, S., Rohan, E., Sayce, L., Paul, J. and Thorneycroft, G. (2011) Disability hate crime and targeted violence and hostility: A mental health and discrimination perspective, *Journal of Mental Health*, 20(3), 219–225.
Cram, I. (2005) Hate speech and disabled people: Some comparative constitutional thoughts, in Lawson, A. and Gooding, C. (eds) *Disability Rights in Europe: From Theory to Practice*, pp. 65–86, Portland, OR, USA: Hart Publishing.
Crown Prosecution Service (CPS) (2010a) *Policy for Prosecuting Cases of Disability Hate Crime*, London, UK: CPS.
Crown Prosecution Service (CPS) (2010b) *Disability Hate Crime – Guidance on the Distinction between Vulnerability and Hostility in the Context of Crimes Committed Against Disabled People*, London, UK: CPS.
Crown Prosecution Service (CPS) (n.d.) Hate Crime, *CPS Fact Sheet*, London, UK: CPS. Available at: www.cps.gov.uk/news/fact_sheets/hate_crime/. Accessed on 6 August 2013.
Cunningham, S. and Drury, S. (2002) *Access All Areas. A Guide for Community Safety Partnerships on Working More Effectively with Disabled People*, London, UK: Nacro.
Department for Work and Pensions (2012) *Disabled People's Groups – Making a Difference to Disability Hate Crime*, London, UK: Department for Work and Pensions.
Dick, S. (2008) *Homophobic Hate Crime: The Gay British Crime Survey 2008*, London, UK: Stonewall.
Disability Rights UK (2012) *Let's Stop Disability Hate Crime: A Guide for Non-disabled People*, London, UK: Disability Rights UK in association with the Office for Disability Issues.
DisAbled Women's Network (DAWN) (1994) *Strengthening the Links, Stopping the Violence: A Guide to the Issue of Violence Against Women with Disabilities*, Toronto, Ontario, Canada: DAWN.
Disability Rights Commission (DRC) and Capability Scotland (2004) *Hate Crime against Disabled People in Scotland: A Survey Report*, Stratford upon Avon, UK: Disability Rights Commission.
Dowden, C. and Brennan, S. (2012) *Police-reported Hate Crime in Canada, 2010*, Component of Statistics Canada catalogue no. 85-002-X, *Juristat*, Statistics Canada.

Elman, A. (2005) *Confronting the Sexual Abuse of Women with Disabilities*, Harrisburg, PA, USA: VAWnet, a project of the National Resource Center on Domestic Violence/Pennsylvania Coalition Against Domestic Violence.

European Commission (2002) *Definitions of Disability in Europe. A Comparative Analysis*, Directorate-General for Employment and Social Affairs, Brussels, Belgium: European Commission.

European Union Agency for Fundamental Rights (FRA) (2010) *The Fundamental Rights of Persons with Intellectual Disabilities and Persons with Mental Health Problems*, Vienna, Austria: European Union Agency for Fundamental Rights. Available at: http://fra.europa.eu/en/publication/2010/fundamental-rights-persons-intellectual-disabilities-and-persons-mental-health. Accessed on 30 July 2013.

European Union Agency for Fundamental Rights (FRA) (2012) *Making Hate Crime Visible in the European Union: Acknowledging Victims' Rights*, Vienna, Austria: European Union Agency for Fundamental Rights.

Faulkner, A. (2012) *The Right to Take Risks: Service Users' Views of Risk in Adult Social Care*, York, UK: Joseph Rowntree Foundation.

Gilson, S.F., Cramer, E.P. and DePoy, E. (2001) Linking the assessment of self-reported functional capacity with abuse experiences of women with disabilities, *Violence Against Women*, 7(4), 418.

Grattet, R. and Jenness, V. (2001) Examining the Boundaries of Hate Crime Law: Disabilities and the 'Dilemma of Difference', *The Journal of Criminal Law and Criminology*, 91(3), 653–698.

Harrell, E. (2011) *Crimes Against Persons with Disabilities, 2008–2010 – Statistical Tables*, Department of Justice National Crime Victimization Survey (October), Washington, DC, USA: Bureau of Justice Statistics, U.S. Department of Justice.

Herek, G.M., Gillis, J.R. and Cogan, J.C. (1999) Psychological sequelae of hate-crime victimisation among lesbian, gay and bisexual adults, *Journal of Consulting and Clinical Psychology*, 67(6), 945–951.

Home Office (2007) *Learning Disability Hate Crime: Good Practice Guidance for Crime and Disorder Reduction*, London, UK: Home Office.

Home Office (2012) *Challenge It, Report It, Stop It: The Government's Plan to Tackle Hate Crime*, London, UK: HM Government.

Horvath, M. and Kelly, L. (2008) *From the Outset: Why Violence Should be a Priority for the Commission for Equality and Human Rights*, London, UK: End Violence Against Women Campaign and the Roddick Foundation.

Hughes, K., Bellis, M.A., Jones, L., Wood, S., Bates, G., Eckley, L., McCoy, E., Mikton, C., Shakespeare, T. and Officer, A. (2012) Prevalence and risk of violence against adults with disabilities: A systematic review and meta-analysis of observational studies, *The Lancet*, 2012; doi:10.1016/S0410-6736(11)61851-5. Available at: www.who.int/disabilities/publications/violence_children_lancet.pdf. Accessed on 6 August 2013.

Human Rights First (2007) *Hate Crimes: 2007 Survey*, New York, USA: Human Rights First.

Human Rights First and the Anti-defamation League (2012) *What the ODIHR's Hate Crime Annual Report for 2011 Reveals About States' Implementation of OSCE Commitments*, New York, USA: Human Rights First.

Hunter, C., Hodge, N., Nixon, J., Parr, S. and Willis, B. (2007) *Disabled People's Experiences of Anti-social Behaviour and Harassment in Social Housing: A Critical Review*, London, UK: Disability Rights Commission.

Iganski, P. (2008) *Hate Crime and the City*, Bristol, UK: Policy Press.

Iganski, P., Smith, D., Dixon, L., Kielinger, V., Mason, G., McDevitt, J., Perry, B., Stelman, A., Bargen, J., Lagou, S. and Pfeffer, R. (2011) *Rehabilitation of Hate Crime Offenders*, Equality and Human Rights Commission Research Report, Glasgow, UK: EHRC.

Jones, L., Bellis, M.A., Wood, S., Hughes, K., McCoy, E., Eckley, L., Bates, G., Mikton, C., Shakespeare, T., and Officer, A. (2012) Prevalence and risk of violence against children with disabilities: A systematic review and meta-analysis of observational studies, *The Lancet*, doi:10.1016/S0140-6736(12)60692-8. Available at: http://press.thelancet.com/childrendisabilities.pdf. Accessed on 6 August 2013.

Levin, J. (2012) Disablist violence in the US. Unacknowledged hate crime, in Roulstone, A. and Mason-Bish, H. (eds) *Disability, Hate Crime and Violence*, pp. 95–105, London, UK: Routledge.

Mason, G. (2005) Hate crime and the image of the stranger, *British Journal of Criminology*, 45(6), 837–859.

Mason, G. (2010) Hate crime laws in Australia: Are they achieving their goals? Paper presented at the Sentencing Conference, 6–7 February 2010, Canberra, Australia. Available at: http://njca.anu.edu.au/Professional%20Development/programs%20by%20year/2010/Sentencing%202010/Papers/Mason.pdf. Accessed on 30 July 2013.

McDonald, S. and Hogue, A. (2007) *An Exploration of the Needs of Victims of Hate Crime*, Ottawa, Ontario, Canada: Department of Justice Canada.

Mencap (1999) *Living in Fear: The Need to Combat Bullying of People with a Learning Disability*, London, UK: Mencap.

MIND (2007) *Another Assault*, London, UK: MIND.

National Council on Disability (2008) *Finding the Gaps: A Comparative Analysis of Disability Laws in the U.S. to the U.N. Convention on the Rights of Persons with Disabilities*, Washington, D.C., USA: National Council on Disability.

Nosek, M. and Howland, C. (1998) *Abuse and Women with Disabilities*, Harrisburg, PA, USA: VAWnet, a project of the National Resource Center on Domestic Violence/Pennsylvania Coalition Against Domestic Violence.

Organisation for Security and Co-operation in Europe (OSCE)/The Office for Democratic Institutions and Human Rights (ODIHR) (2009) *Preventing and Responding to Hate Crimes: A Resource Guide for NGOs in the OSCE Region*, Warsaw, Poland: OSCE/ODIHR.

OSCE/ODIHR (ODIHR) (2012) Hate Crimes in the OSCE Region – Incidents and Responses: Annual Report for 2011, Warsaw, Poland: OSCE/ODIHR.

Office for Disability Issues (ODI) (2010) *Equality Act 2010. Guidance. Guidance on Matters to be Taken Into Account in Determining Questions Relating to the Definition of Disability*, London, UK: ODI.

Office for Public Sector Information (2005) *Disability Discrimination Act*. Available at: http://webarchive.nationalarchives.gov.uk/20100407010852/http://opsi.gov.uk/acts/acts1995/ukpga_19950050_en_1. Accessed on 9 August 2013.

Office for Victims of Crime (2012a) *Multidisciplinary Response to Crime Victims with Disabilities: State-Level Replication Guide*, Washington, DC, USA: Office for Victims of Crime.

Office for Victims of Crime (2012b) *Multidisciplinary Response to Crime Victims with Disabilities: Community-Level Replication Guide*, Washington, D.C., USA: Office for Victims of Crime.

Oliver, M. (1983) *Social Work with Disabled People*, London, UK: Macmillan.

Perry, B. (ed.) (2003) *Hate and Bias Crime: A Reader*, New York, USA: Routledge.

Perry, J. (2004) Is justice taking a beating? *Community Care*, 1 April 2004, 44–45.

Perry, J. (2009) At the intersection: hate crime policy and practice in England and Wales, *Safer Communities*, 8(4), 9–18.

Perry, J. (2012) The wrong war? Critically examining the 'fight against disability hate crime', in Roulstone, A. and Mason-Bish, H. (eds) *Disability, Hate Crime and Violence*, pp. 40–51, London, UK: Routledge.

Petersilia, J.R. (2001) Crime victims with developmental disabilities: a review essay, *Criminal Justice and Behavior*, 28(6), 655–694.

Piggott, L. (2011) Prosecuting disability hate crime: A disabling solution? *People, Place and Policy*, 5(1), 25–34.

Quarmby, K. (2008) *Getting Away with Murder: Disabled People's Experiences of Hate Crime in the UK*, London, UK: Scope, Disability Now, UK Disabled People Council.

Quarmby, K. (2010) From Disbelief and Ignorance to Anger and Action, *The Huffington Post*, 8 February 2010. Available at: www.huffingtonpost.com/katharine-quarmby/from-disbelief-and-ignora_b_453088.html. Accessed on 30 July 2013.

Quarmby, K. (2011) *Scapegoat – How We Are Failing Disabled People*, London, UK: Portobello Books.

Ray, L. and Smith, D. (2001) Racist offenders and the politics of 'hate crime', *Law and Critique*, 12(3), 203–221.

Roberts, C., Innes, M., Williams, M., Tregidga, J. and Gadd, D. (2013) *Understanding Who Commits Hate Crime and Why They Do It*, Merthyr Tydfil, UK: Local Government and Communities, Welsh Government.

Roulstone, A. and Mason-Bish, H. (eds) (2012) *Disability, Hate Crime and Violence*, London, UK: Routledge.

Roulstone, A. and Sadique, K. (2012) Vulnerable to misinterpretation: disabled people, 'vulnerability', hate crime and the fight for legal recognition, in Roulstone, A. and Mason-Bish, H. (eds) *Disability, Hate Crime and Violence*, pp. 25–39, London, UK: Routledge.

Salthouse, S. and Frohmader, C. (2004) 'Double the odds' – domestic violence and women with disabilities, paper presented at the Home Truths Conference, Sheraton Towers, Southgate, Melbourne, Australia, 15–17 September 2004. Available at: www.wwda.org.au/odds.htm. Accessed on 30 July 2013.

Saxton, M., Curry, M.A., Powers, L.E., Maley, S., Eckels, K. and Gross, J. (2001) Bring my scooter so I can leave you: A study of disabled women handling abuse by personal assistance providers, *Violence Against Women*, 7(4), 393.

Sharp, H. (2001) Steps towards justice for people with learning disabilities as victims of crime; the important role of the police, *British Journal of Learning Disabilities*, 29(3), 88–92.

Shaw, M. and Barchechat, O. (2002) *Preventing Hate Crimes: International Strategies and Practice*, Montreal, Canada: International Centre for the Prevention of Crime.

Sheikh, S., Khanna, M., Pralat, R., Reed, C. and Sin, C.H. (2011) *Hate Crime Research for Stand By Me Campaign*, London, UK: OPM for Mencap.

Sherry, M. (2000) *Hate Crimes Against People With Disabilities*, Paper published by School of Social Work, University of Queensland, January 2000. Available at: www.wwda.org.au/hate.htm. Accessed on 30 July 2013.

Sherry, M. (2003) *Don't Ask, Tell or Respond: Silent Acceptance of Disability Hate Crimes*, Ontario, Canada: Disabled Women's Network Ontario.

Sherry, M. (2010) *Disability Hate Crimes: Does Anyone Really Hate Disabled People?* Surrey, UK: Ashgate.

Sherry, M. (2012) *International Perspectives on Disability Hate Crime*, in Roulstone, A. and Mason-Bish, H. (eds) *Disability, Hate Crime and Violence*, pp. 80–91, London, UK: Routledge.

Sin, C.H. (2013) Making disablist hate crime visible: addressing the challenges of improving reporting, in Roulstone, A. and Mason-Bish, H. (eds) *Disability, Hate Crime and Violence*, pp. 147–165, London, UK: Routledge.

Sin, C.H. (2014) Using a 'layers of influence' model to understand the interaction of research policy and practice in relation to disablist hate crime, in Chakraborti, N.A. and Garland, J. (eds) *Responding to Hate Crime: The Case for Connecting Policy and Research*, Bristol, UK: The Policy Press, forthcoming.

Sin, C.H., Hedges, A., Cook, C., Comber, N. and Mguni, N. (2009), *Disabled People's Experiences of Targeted Violence and Hostility*, Research Report 21, London, UK: OPM for the Equality and Human Rights Commission.

Sin, C.H., Hedges, A., Cook, C., Mguni, N. and Comber, N. (2011) Adult protection and effective action in tackling violence and hostility against disabled people: some tensions and challenges, *Journal of Adult Protection*, 13(2), 63–75.

Smith, K., Lader, D., Hoare, J. and Lau, I. (2012) *Hate Crime, Cyber Security and the Experience of Crime Among Children: Findings From the 2010/2011 British Crime Survey*, London, UK: Home Office.

Sobsey, D. (1994) *Violence and Abuse in the Lives of People with Disabilities: The End of Silent Acceptance?* Baltimore, USA: Paul H. Brookes Publishing Co.

Strengthening Disabled People's User-led Organisations Programme (2012) *Disabled People's User-led Organisations Making a Difference. Disability Hate Crime*, London, UK: Office for Disability Issues. Available at: http://odi.dwp.gov.uk/docs/dpulo/disability-hate-crime-rtf.rtf. Accessed on 30 July 2013.

Thiara, R.K., Hague, G., Bashall, R., Ellis, B. and Mullender, A. (2012) *Disabled Women and Domestic Violence: Responding to the Experiences of Survivors*, London, UK: Jessica Kingsley.

Thomas, P. (2012) Hate crime or mate crime? Disablist hostility, contempt and ridicule, in Roulstone, A. and Mason-Bish, H. (eds) *Disability, Hate Crime and Violence*, pp. 135–146, London, UK: Routledge.

Union of the Physically Impaired Against Segregation (UPIAS) (1976) *Fundamental Principles of Disability*, London, UK: UPIAS.

Vincent, F., Radford, K., Jarman, N., Martynowicz, A. and Rallings, M.-K. (2009) *Hate Crime Against People with Disabilities. A Baseline Study of Experiences in Northern Ireland*, Belfast, Northern Ireland: Institute for Conflict Research.

Williams, B., Copestake, P., Eversley, J. and Stafford, B. (2008) *Experiences and Expectations of Disabled People*, London, UK: The Office for Disability Issues.

World Health Organisation (WHO) (2011) *World Report on Disability*, Geneva, Switzerland: WHO.

17

Disability hostility, harassment and violence in the UK

A 'motiveless' and 'senseless' crime?

Paul Hamilton and Loretta Trickett

The 2012 London Paralympic Games were the subject of widespread media coverage and intense speculation about how sport might act as a catalyst for engendering positive perceptions of disability in the UK (and beyond). Polls undertaken since September 2012 indicate that, for disabled people, some of this initial optimism may have been misguided (Marsh, 2012; Mencap, 2012). Worse still, research suggests that hostile, and sometimes violent, behaviour towards disabled people in the UK remains depressingly commonplace. Whilst it would be wrong to suggest we know nothing about the motivations, attitudes and 'crime scripts' (Cornish, 1984) of those committing such insidious expressions of hostility, harassment and violence, what is patently missing is a cohesive, nuanced body of research with offenders themselves. This chapter seeks to revisit what we do know – and what we think we know – whilst simultaneously suggesting ways forward to better understand the perpetrators of so-called 'Disability Hate Crime' (DHC), including a discussion of a recently commissioned pilot study of research with DHC offenders designed by these authors.

Background

The 2012 London Paralympics were notable for a rarely seen positive portrayal of disability in the British media (Disability Horizons, 2012). The hope was that this would lead to positive progressive societal attitudes towards disability and an erosion of often endemic social exclusion. Regrettably, evidence from disability-support groups post-September 2012 (ITV (Mencap), 2012) indicate that this optimism has yet to translate into tangible attitudinal or 'quality of life' improvements on the ground. In explaining these findings, commentators suggest that the welfare debate instigated by politicians – but played out in the media – has visibly correlated disability with the concept of 'welfare cheats and scroungers'[1] (The Guardian, Feb 2012). Conceivably, everyday hate and prejudice will flourish in societies adopting normative anti-disabled sentiments.

Regrettably, negative attitudes towards disability have a long, entrenched history. Ancient Greek moral philosophers, for example, argued for the banishing of physical/mental 'defects' from the public realm and the notion of Eugenics were clearly influenced by Plato's assertion in *Republic* that 'only the fittest should survive' (Quarmby, 2011: 19). Understandably, overcoming entrenched and pervasive prejudice takes time and necessitates a combination of positive media representation(s), a review of existing policies, increased visibility in public life, greater contact between disabled and non-disabled people and not inconsiderable effort from lobbyists and activists (amongst other things). But what does disability prejudice look like in twenty-first century Britain? As Sherry (2010) has asked: does anyone really hate the disabled? At present, the answer would appear to be that we simply do not know.

Academic and criminal justice responses to DHC: A step in the right direction?

Before articulating what we (do not) know about DHC offenders, it is important to note that there has been a recent effort from academia and beyond to make sense of disabled victims' experiences. The case of Fiona Pilkington, who tragically killed herself and her disabled daughter Francecca Hardwick following years of intolerable, persistent abuse, visibly exposed the harassment that people with disabilities have to endure on a daily basis. Fortunately, since this case we find ourselves in a position where our understanding of DHC has improved considerably (e.g. EHRC, 2011a; Mencap, 2000; Quarmby, 2008, 2011; Sykes et al., 2011; Hoong Sin et al., 2009; Miller et al., 2004; Sherry, 2010; HM Government, 2012).

Consequently, the experiences of DHC victims and affiliated (poor) responses by the Criminal Justice System (CJS) are well documented. Given the remit of this chapter, the intention is not to replicate these findings here. Briefly, however, an abundance of evidence has emerged that disabled people in the UK are subjected to much higher rates of repeat victimisation than non-disabled citizens, including a wide spectrum of unreported harassment and abuse (see Miller et al., 2004; Sobsey, 1994; Clement et al., 2001; Mencap, 2000, 2012; EHRC, 2011a).

Research has also revealed that when incidents are reported, many disabled people feel let down by the police and the CJS, resulting in a reluctance to report future crimes (DWP, 2012). This lack of faith in the CJS is arguably exacerbated by the infrequent application of the uplift tariff available to the judiciary for DHC sentencing under s.146 of the Criminal Justice Act 2003[2] (HM Inspectorate, 2013; Scope, 2013). Further, given that there is no separate and specific offence for DHC, the seriousness of DHC as a 'signal crime' is not adequately conveyed (Law Commission, 2013).

That said, there have undoubtedly been some improvements in terms of how agencies of the CJS (including the police and the Crown Prosecution Service (CPS)) handle DHC. For example, whilst the ratio of recorded to prosecuted cases remains low (including a proliferation of 'no crimed' incidents), it is also noteworthy that between 2007/8–2010/11, there was been an increase of 311 per cent in the number of successful DHC prosecutions (CPS, 2011), although the number of DHC prosecutions actually fell by 17.5 per cent between 2010/11–2011/12 (CPS, 2013a).

Further, in the year prior to the publication of the Equality and Human Rights Commission's landmark inquiry into disability-related harassment (EHRC, 2011a), the police in England and Wales recorded 1,567 cases of DHC. In 2011 there were 1,788 recorded cases; an increase of more than 18 per cent on the previous year (Home Office, 2011). The suggestion is that this increase can be attributed to the willingness of victims to come forward and report incidents, rather than necessarily being representative of a proliferation of DHC (ACPO, 2012).

But can we say with certainty that CJS and third-sector agencies/organisations have uniformly learnt lessons from recent policies, research reports and Government strategies (e.g.

HM Government, 2012; EHRC, 2011a)? Examining Home Office data broken down by police force, the answer to this question appears to be that it probably depends on where you live. By way of illustration, Leicestershire, a force heavily criticised in the aftermath of the 'watershed' Pilkington case (IPCC, 2011), recorded twice as many DHC incidents in 2011 than the significantly more populous West Midlands force area. Anomalously, rural Suffolk recorded 152 DHC incidents (the most of any force for 2010/11), yet the urban, densely populated South Yorkshire conurbation only recorded seven incidents for the whole year.[3] This would suggest that either South Yorkshire is strangely devoid of disability-orientated prejudice, or – more likely – that there are significant discrepancies in the way different forces log and record DHC. In relation to this latter point, the breakdown of incidents by police force indicates that 16 police forces reported fewer than 15 cases for the whole of 2010/11. Moreover, there is clear evidence that certain forces are still failing to link incidents, instead treating them as isolated incidents of 'Anti-Social Behaviour' (CJJI, 2013).

Variation between forces can partly be explained by the findings of a recent Joint Inspectorate Review (CJJI, 2013), which revealed the failure to record incidents as DHC is largely attributable to poor definitional clarity. Further, there appears to be a lack of standardisation regarding police officers asking victims about the presence of a disability for fear of causing offence (ibid.). As well as the need for a clearer definition (The Guardian, 2013; CJJI, 2013), better training for the police, CPS and probation has been advocated. Amongst other things, the Joint Review noted that DHC should be afforded a higher profile in probation so that the rehabilitative needs of DHC offenders could be met.

The impact of DHC: Eroding happiness and 'friendship vacuums'?

Aside from these (inter)organisational challenges, research has also demonstrated a number of everyday considerations. Most notably, the types and frequency of crimes committed against disabled people in the UK are wide-ranging and that it is the cumulative effect of harassment, hostility and abuse that is particularly damaging certainly in terms of limiting what disabled people feel they can do and where they can go (e.g. Mencap, 2000; Nottinghamshire County Council, 2010).

Ominously, case studies have provided disturbing evidence of how such abuse can escalate into serious – and occasionally fatal – violence (EHRC, 2011a). In recent years, this has led to the creation of the – contested – term 'mate crime' to describe the befriending/'grooming' of people with learning difficulties by those who go on to exercise economic, verbal, and psychological violence.[4] Appallingly, this abuse often escalates into more serious physical violence, as demonstrated by the well-documented murders of Brent Martin and Steven Hoskin (EHRC, 2011a).

Despite claims from the judiciary that the violence associated with DHC is often 'motiveless' and 'senseless' (Quarmby, 2008: 26), there are striking similarities in the brutality of the violence and the derogatory language used. Consequently, one might reasonably conclude that such cases constitute examples of 'hatred' on the extreme end of a spectrum of prejudice. Controversially, 'mate crime' might – in part – be seen as a product of the unintended consequences of promoting 'independent living' for those with learning disabilities. Whilst the underlying ethos of living in the community is clearly grounded in constructs of equality and social inclusion, the reality is that rapid and under-resourced deinstitutionalisation has resulted in disabled people suffering from 'relationship vacuums' with non-disabled people (Bayley, 1997).

Allied to instances of ineffective multi-agency working amongst key support organisations, 'mate crimes' may represent an example of 'rational opportunism', whereby disabled people are targeted on the basis of their perceived vulnerability exacerbated by social and psychological isolation from the communities in which they reside. Significantly, case reviews of murders with an apparent 'mate crime' component consistently demonstrate that earlier, joined-up interventions may have saved the lives of these victims (see EHRC, 2011a; CJJI, 2013).[5]

Despite these institutional failings, there is a danger of 'blaming' DHC on the shortfalls of multi-agency working, or even worse, the behaviour/actions of victims themselves. The upshot is that the perpetrator often gets lost in this introspective evaluation. The rest of this chapter explores the folly of this introspection and summarises what (little) we know so far about those perpetrating DHC.

Understanding the perpetrators of DHC: Why bother?

Unquestionably, an appreciation of disabled people's experiences of hostility, harassment and violence is integral to helping future victims and encouraging better targeted early interventions. Arguably, however, this tells us only half the story. The aforementioned shortcomings of the CJS/third sector in identifying victims and pre-empting events before they escalate into something more serious, is in some capacity shaped by the lack of research data acquired from DHC offenders themselves. As it stands, most of what we know about offenders comes from secondary CJS data-sources and/or well-informed speculation from victims as to the offender's motivation(s). A common perception amongst victims is that they were an 'easy target' for crime because of their disability (DWP, 2012). But as Quarmby (2011: 193) points out:

> Vulnerability (in a child, a woman or a disabled person, for example) provides an opportunity for an underlying (perhaps even unconscious) hatred to manifest itself. [. . .].

In short, '. . . vulnerability only provides an opportunity for offenders to express their hatred' (Waxman, 1991 in Quarmby, 2011: 193).

Irrespective of the validity to the claim that hatred and vulnerability are correlated, the outcome is that victims may draw false – or partially accurate – inferences about why they were 'targeted'. Equally, of course, we need to exercise caution in assuming that offenders know themselves why they behaved in the way that they did (or that they will feel comfortable in explaining these motivations to academic researchers). Indeed, we need to recognise that offenders may reconstruct their crimes as a mechanism to neutralise their guilt. Nevertheless, there are a number of reasons why speaking directly with DHC offenders can be seen as the 'right thing to do'.

Research with DHC offenders may facilitate more effective policing and multi-agency strategies, particularly related to reporting and the early identification of, and intervention with, potential victims (and perpetrators). One of the mechanisms by which this may be achieved is through an understanding of what Cornish (1984) has identified as 'crime scripts'. Put simply, what are the crime contexts within which DHC manifests itself? For example, are DHC crimes always escalatory? Where a relationship previously existed between the victim and offender, what was the nature of this relationship, how did it materialise and what are/were the values that this relationship was built on? Where did offences take place? Who else was involved? Did anybody try to stop these crimes?

The reality is that qualitative research with offenders tells us a lot, particularly with regards to challenging the still-too-common tendency for events to be seen as single incidents, rather than joined-up, multi-dimensional processes.

Furthermore, research with offenders helps with the design of strategies for dealing with identified DHC perpetrators. Offender Behaviour Programmes are common for offenders within certain offence categories (for example, the Integrated Domestic Abuse Programme for domestic abuse offenders or CALM for violence offenders). But what interventions do we currently have in place for identified DHC offenders? Whilst there is much talk about strategies to reduce DHC (re)offending, in the UK, it appears that the only intervention relevant to DHC offenders currently is the Diversity Awareness and Prejudice Pack (DAPP), which amongst other things looks to develop an offender's 'motivation for change', challenge a perpetrator's underlying prejudice(s) and explore the impact of hate crime (HC) on victims (see, Dixon et al., 2010; EHRC, 2011b).

Whilst the DAPP is increasingly used in the CJS, it was originally designed for race hate offenders, with subsequent minor 'adaptations' for other hate crime (HC) strands, including DHC. Given the lack of realistic evaluation (Pawson and Tilley, 1997) for DHC-focused DAPP, the question remains as to what extent the DAPP has been informed by theoretical constructs of DHC. The answer it seems is very little, although the programme is clearly informed by desistance theory (McNeill, 2006). In considering these evaluative and programmatic shortfalls, it is not unreasonable to assume that research with DHC offenders might start to help us design more directed and theoretically-informed rehabilitative measures. It may also help us to decide what the future of DHC rehabilitation might look like (for example, an increased use of Restorative Justice (see Dixon et al., 2010; Gavrielides, 2011)).

Understanding perpetrators of DHC: Towards a conceptual framework?

Against this background, it is important to recognise that of all the hate crime strands, crimes against disabled people are perhaps the most difficult to comprehend. Conceivably this is representative of a somewhat paternalistic attitude towards disability. As Mike Smith points out in the 2011 EHRC inquiry into disability hostility:

> ... we are supposed to feel sorry for these people, so why would anyone be deliberately horrible to them? Maybe it just makes us too uncomfortable, thinking that might be the society in which we live.
>
> *(EHRC, 2011a: 7)*

Given the aforementioned need to better understand perpetrators of DHC, it is somewhat surprising that there remains a '... distinct lack of evidence on both the motivations and profile of perpetrators' (ibid: 87). Unfortunately, concerns about the paucity of published data on offender characteristics and motivations are nothing new; even at the turn of the last century, Bowling (1999 in Hall, 2005: 73) had noted how there was a need to better

> ... focus on the characteristics of offenders: their relationship with those they victimise, the social milieux in which anger, hostility and violence are fostered; and the social processes by which violence becomes directed against minority groups.

In the period since Bowling made these incisive observations, there has undoubtedly been some progress in our understanding of the socio-demographic profile, motivations and 'crime scripts' of hate crime offenders in the UK. Progress, however, has been sporadic and uneven across the five officially recognised hate crime strands. Most notably, we know considerably more about 'race hate' offenders – the very thing that Bowling was writing about back in 1999 – than we do about DHC perpetrators. That the knowledge-base is so under-developed in relation to DHC perpetrators, is perhaps unremarkable when considering that the key 'watershed' event associated with raising the public's awareness of DHC in the UK – the 'Pilkington Case' – came a full 14 years after the equivalent[6] 'watershed' event for race hate crime; that of the brutal murder of Stephen Lawrence in 1993. Arguably, race HC has tended to take centre-stage politically and academically.

The upshot of this 14-year hiatus is that, where hate crime offender data has been commissioned, this has tended to be undertaken with 'race/religious hate' perpetrators, often right-wing 'extremists' (e.g. Gadd et al., 2005; Byers et al., 1999; Bjørgo et al., 2009; Palmer and Smith, 2010; Sibbitt, 1997; Court, 2003). Research pertaining to DHC has been almost exclusively victim-centred. This, of course, should not undermine the immense value of such research, but as the previous section and McDevitt et al. (2010: 125) point out, there is only so much victims' service providers and law enforcement professionals can hope to achieve in the absence of data related directly to (D)HC offenders.

Without this empirical evidence-base, the temptation is to transpose research undertaken with race HC offenders to other forms of hate crime, including DHC. Take, for example, the work of Levin and McDevitt (1993; updated, McDevitt et al., 2002) which remains the most comprehensive attempt at providing a typology of hate crime offenders, encompassing 'hate-mongers, dabblers, sympathisers and spectators' (Levin and McDevitt, 2002). According to McDevitt et al.'s (2002) analysis of 169 hate crime cases investigated by the Boston (US) Police department, crimes being committed by 'bored youths' looking for the thrill of something to do are by far the most common type of offender. Although the data makes no claims to be exclusive to 'race hate', the authors acknowledge that HC cases in their analysis tended to be recorded on the basis of 'racial or ethnic slurs' (McDevitt et al., 2000 in McDevitt et al., 2010: 139). Significantly, DHC is not overtly mentioned anywhere in this research output.

Aside from: 1) the danger of over-simplifying a mono-causal model of motivational explanation (see Phillips, 2009); and 2) relying on secondary data analysis rather than speaking directly with offenders themselves, intuitively it is easy to see the appeal of applying the 'thrill seeker' classification to other hate crime strands, including DHC. Even a cursory glance of high-profile DHC cases in the UK indicate that the so-called 'thrill' is often not far from the surface. No doubt Anthony Anderson got some perverse 'thrill' from filming himself urinating on Christine Lakinski as she lay dying (Quarmby, 2008). The fact that none of the numerous onlookers intervened to stop Anderson, also adds credence to McDevitt et al.'s (2002 cited in McDevitt et al., 2010: 133) assertion that '. . . these young people [incorrectly] believe others in the community will support their actions'. Equally, one might speculate that William Hughes, Marcus Miller and Stephen Bonallie all got some inexplicable 'thrill' from the £5 bet they had to see who would be the first to knock Brent Martin unconscious (EHRC, 2011a).

This, of course, has parallels with structural concepts of crime, most notably sub-cultural theory (Cohen, 1955 in Hopkins-Burke, 2009), which stresses that economic reward is less important than one's reputation amongst the peer group. Accordingly, individuals come together in like-minded groups in order to demonstrate toughness and seek excitement. Allied to this, Franklin (2000 in EHRC, 2011b) talks of 'adolescent developmental needs' whereby 'thrill seekers commit assaults to alleviate boredom, to have fun and excitement, and to feel strong'. Put simply, peer groups commit assaults in order to '. . . prove their toughness and heterosexuality to friends' (ibid.). This has some theoretical appeal when considering other examples of intense and grotesque hate crime, particularly homophobic violence. Matza (1964 in Hopkins-Burke, 2009) and more recently Herek (2000) argue that, even in a climate of increased tolerance towards homosexuality, there remains pressure for adolescents to conform to a stereotypical male gender role. In these circumstances 'gay bashing' is seen as low-risk and high-status. Some psychologists also contend that intense, brutal homophobia may be 'reaction-formation' defence to admitting homosexual tendencies. Whether or not the same notions of 'the situation of company' (Matza, 1964 in Hopkins-Burke, 2009) and 'reaction-formation' defences are equally applicable to DHC perpetrators will – like many of the theoretical speculations in this chapter – require further research.

Inevitably, some of this may be the product of learned behaviour beginning in the home; the EHRC (2011b) note how children of hate crime perpetrators have the potential to perpetrate violence and harassment based on prejudice; as Adorno et al. (1950 in Craig, 2002) speculated, the origins of prejudice[7] may lie in the extent to which family life is characterised by the 'authoritarian personality'.

Equally, it is not unreasonable to venture that the 'social bonds' (Hirschi, 1969 in Hopkins-Burke, 2009) (or the presence of 'social capital' (Putnam, 1995; Bourdieu, 1986)) one has within society is likely to play a contributory and significant role here. However, rather than seeing this in terms of a 'lack of' bonding relationships, it may be perpetrators' exposure to damaging, anti-social relationships – rather than pro-social bridging capital – is of most significance. In short, relationships matter; social networks have both negative and positive value. In considering these factors together, it is perhaps unsurprising that both 'low-level' and extreme forms of DHC often take place in groups (either as perpetrators and/or as spectators); the majority of DHC tends not to be an isolated, individual activity.

Levin and McDevitt (2002) also draw our attention to the 'defensive' HC offender, who uses hate crime to send a message that 'your type is not welcome round these parts'. This has parallels with 'realistic conflict' theory (Sherif et al., 1961 cited in Gerstenfeld, 2011; Esses et al., 2001; Green, 1998; Green et al., 1998), which stresses that direct competition for limited economic resources plays a significant role in fostering prejudice. For 'critical' criminologists, it is the changing nature of economic competition within the working class, and the media representations of this conflict, that accounts for much of the prejudice against minority groups. In short, prejudice exists because somebody gains by it.

Further, as several social psychologists have pointed out (e.g. Brown, 1995; Nelson, 2002), all humans have an innate desire to 'feel good' about their self-identity and in circumstances where self-esteem may be low due to a feeling of inadequacy, under-achievement and/or, social-exclusion from mainstream society, human beings may resort to artificially manufacturing esteem through comparisons to – and undermining of – other social groups. This, of course, is one of the central tenets of 'social identity theory' (Tajfel and Turner, 1979).

One could see how this could apply to an antipathy towards the 'latest wave of immigrants/asylum seekers' 'flooding' Britain (BNP, 2013), but at first glance, it is less obviously applicable to DHC. Yet, as Cornish Councillor, Collin Brewer, so crudely demonstrated with his comments that 'disabled children cost too much money and should be put down' (BBC, 2013), the notion that those with disabilities are a 'drain on society' is potentially more prevalent than we would dare to think. Although the evidence-base does not exist to validate such claims, these views may have been compounded by the recent economic downturn and the reconfiguration of segments of the disabled 'community' as 'benefit scroungers' (Update Disability, 2013). A recent case in Northampton (Channel 4, 2012) highlights how DHC can be understood as a conflation of 'scapegoating' and the move towards encouraging those with (learning) disabilities to live independently. In this case, an 'able-bodied' neighbour expressed concern that her new disabled fellow citizen would negatively impact on the price of her flat.

Yet these socio-psychological and criminological theories tell us only part of the story. McDevitt et al.'s (2002) typology certainly tells us little directly of: 1) the activities that precede both maleficent, low-level hostility and more 'serious' violence towards disabled people; 2) the interplay between 'macro level causational mechanisms [and] micro level offending' (Walters, 2011: 328); or 3) the precise mechanisms by which perpetrators seek to neutralise their guilt through 'dehumanising' their victims. In other words, these generalist 'models' may be a necessary, but ultimately insufficient, explanatory framework to explain DHC. After all, there are plenty of young men (and women) in society willing to engage in delinquent and/or criminal activity to enhance their peer reputation, but who would no doubt recoil at the thought of verbally/physically abusing someone with a disability. Similarly, there may be those who view 'borderline' disabled benefit claimants with suspicion, but would not hesitate to denounce public hostility towards those with visible learning and/or physical disabilities (as is depressingly often the case with DHC). As Walters (2011) points out, we need to start seeing prejudice not just in terms of 'socio-cultural structures and socio-economic strains', but also in terms of why some individuals appear unable to exercise high levels of 'self-control'.

Moreover, we have no way of confirming if the homogenisation that accompanies Levin and McDevitt's American-based typologies has any value in helping understand DHC offenders in the UK (particularly without the appropriate evidence-base). In short, there is a real danger that in transplanting the findings from one jurisdiction (the USA) to another (the UK) the cultural canvas gets missed. This, of course, further assumes that we can espouse such typologies to DHC without actually speaking directly with offenders. It is not clear, for example, whereabouts in this model the phenomena of 'mate crime' would fit.

Levels of DHC palpably fluctuate over time and space and much of this may be reflective of technological advances – in particular the explosion of mobile communication and new 'social media' – and different modes of communicating 'ideas', prejudices and cultural identities. For example, Sherry's (2010) research into DHC reveals how some of the most prevalent and pernicious 'hate' takes place via the web. The extent to which this 'virtual' abuse manifests itself in 'real life' DHC, however, is unclear. Is it that some 'hate offenders' (or Internet 'trolls') are satisfied to reside in the virtual world, content in the misguided belief that such actions are immune to criminal justice sanctions? Would these Internet offenders identify with individuals such as Bonnalie et al., whose hate so hideously manifested itself physically against Brent Martin? As Allport (1954) points out in his seminal work on prejudice, antilocution is one thing, physical violence something entirely different. Equally, can the motivations that compelled Anthony Anderson to film himself on a mobile phone urinating on Christine Lakinski be understood in the current theoretical framework?

Compounding this theoretical guesswork, is the fact that we lack the complete socio-demographic and 'previous offending' picture of DHC perpetrators. Research in other spheres of HC research indicates that those committing crimes motivated by prejudice are often 'generalists' involved in a range of offending activity (EHRC, 2011a). Naturally, this may include offending behaviour across different HC strands. There is also some evidence that HC perpetrators tend to be young white men,[8] suffering from a range of socio-economic deprivations. Interestingly, and in line with Arendt's (1963) observations from the Holocaust, extreme acts of HC are characterised by the 'banality of evil'; thus, HC is rarely undertaken by fanatics or extremists, but frequently by so-called 'ordinary folk'. As Waller (2007) points out, genocidal perpetrators are arguably extraordinary for what they do, but ordinary for who they are. Similar principles might equally be applied to DHC perpetrators, but as it stands, we simply do not have the first-hand evidence-base to come to these conclusions.

Arguably, to get a complete picture of what motivates DHC offenders there needs to be a multi-disciplinary approach. Complementing socio-criminological explanations, social psychology offers much in helping our understanding of individual behaviour in the context of a group setting (e.g. Brown, 1995). However, the bad news from social neuro-science is that prejudice, it seems, is part of our genetic make-up, principally because it guides our daily activities and helps us to avoid danger and make sense of the world (Fiske, 2008). Yet, as Nelson Mandela points out, 'people [. . .] learn to hate, and if they can learn to hate, they can be taught to love' (Mandela, 1995). Ultimately, being genetically 'hardwired' does not 'equate to innate'; the 'social' can and does influence the biological. However, understanding the way in which these structural and socio-neurological factors interface for DHC offenders currently lacks clarity and should therefore necessitate a critical research agenda for those working in the field.

Finally, we know very little about how DHC offenders seek to make sense of their offending. How, for example, do DHC perpetrators attempt to neutralise their guilt (Sykes and Matza, 1957 in Newburn, 2013)? Again, we can speculate by examining evidence elsewhere in the HC literature. Building on the work of Sykes and Matza (1957), Levin and McDevitt (2002) observe that offenders may engage in a 'denial of injury' ('no-one got hurt, it's just a bit of harmless fun'), a 'denial of the victim' (through a process of dehumanisation and stating that 'they deserved what they got') or a 'denial of responsibility' (e.g., blaming their social situation). This is important, since looking at how DHC offenders justify their actions is likely to give us an insight into their motivations. Potentially it may indicate that DHC offenders' motivations are 'unique' and should not be conflated with other HC theoretical models. Speculating, the offending behaviours of some DHC perpetrators may be driven by a response to psychological discomfort towards disability; for others it may be that disability is a stark reminder of the mortality of all human beings. As Perry ventures in Quarmby (2011: 193), prejudice against the disabled may in large part be motivated by fear:

> . . . fear that the perpetrator could just easily become that person in the wheelchair, or that person with a brain injury, and thus it presents as preying on those perceived to be 'vulnerable' rather than threatening, as in racial prejudice.

Of course, until we find out more from perpetrators themselves, such theories remain in the realms of speculation. Without this core knowledge, it is certainly difficult to see how the CJS – and other agencies – can ever hope to respond in any capacity other than punitively and reactively.

Hostility, harassment and violence against disabled people: An offender's perspective

What is evident from the discussion above, is that our theoretical framework needs sharpening to make better sense of DHC; we have very few first-hand accounts from DHC offenders about their socio-demographic circumstances, offence motivations and/or 'crime scripts'.

In an attempt to 'kick start' the research dialogue with DHC offenders, the authors of this chapter secured a small amount of funding from Nottinghamshire Primary Care Trust (as was prior to recent NHS organisational changes) for a qualitative pilot project entitled: 'Disability

Harassment, Hostility and Violence in the East Midlands: An Offender's Perspective'. The key aims and objectives for this uncompleted research are based around the following five broad themes:

a) Offender's socio-demographic and social settings (especially housing and 'place'), together with evidence for: a) 'bridging' social capital (including the respondent's peer group); b) notions of 'realistic opportunism'; c) offender's 'routine activities'; d) dysfunctional social settings (especially social, economic and cultural deprivation); and e) attitudes towards, and experiences of, bullying.
b) 'Crime Scripts' (e.g. did the offender act alone, was it a 'one-off', had the offence been preceded by other incidents and how were these dealt with?), the presence of drugs/alcohol as crime facilitators and participant's relationship to, and perceptions of, their victim (especially any evidence of 'dehumanisation').
c) Offence Motivation and 'Techniques of Guilt Neutralisation'.
d) Attitudes towards disability and other areas of 'difference', together with a reflection of 'self'.
e) Post offence support/engagement with CJS/third sector agencies to address DHC offending behaviour.

Methodological reflections, process evaluation and preliminary findings

Despite having secured funding to speak with individuals prosecuted under s.146 of the 2003 Criminal Justice Act (and/or have a DHC element present alongside their 'principle offence'), the qualitative element of the fieldwork had yet to commence at the time of writing this chapter. Whilst this delay has been frustrating for the project team, it nevertheless flags a number of pertinent methodological insights correlated to the process of identifying perpetrators and recording and responding to DHC.

There are, of course, major challenges with undertaking research with hard-to-reach groups. Unfortunately when carrying out research amongst specific offender populations, the social researcher rarely has at his or her disposal access to organisations and/or databases from which a random sample can be generated. This is especially true of DHC offenders, where the numbers of offenders prosecuted for DHC remains low, especially when compared with race-hate offending (CPS, 2012). Consequently, tracing respondents that fit the research criteria requires a great deal of luck, persistence and outside assistance. Even then, this assumes that such individuals are willing to speak with 'outsider' University researchers. Because of this, social researchers have tended to employ techniques associated with convenience and non-random sampling when recruiting offender populations.

Initially, the approach taken to gain access to DHC offenders was to contact appropriate CJS and third-sector gatekeeper organisations. The most obvious starting point for this opportunistic sampling approach was to seek access to CPS files that had been arraigned and/or flagged as DHC[9] and to take this information to gatekeeper organisations to help expedite qualitative interviews. Unfortunately, CPS files are only in scope for 12 months and – perhaps unsurprisingly given the national picture – it transpired that there were very few cases flagged as DHC in the East Midlands[10] during this time period, despite the high levels of persistent, repeat DHC-motivated crimes identified in victim surveys. Even then, these cases were not prosecuted as such, although disappointingly there was little on the file to indicate why such decisions had been made. Pointedly, the identification of DHC on case files is a relatively recent development within the CPS (2012) and this may go some way to explaining why the CPS files were often cumbersome to follow and interpret.

There are several learning outcomes that arise from this process. First, missing or incomplete 'front sheets' meant it was sometimes impossible to establish whether the crime had been flagged as a DHC. Often the only information on the file that shed any light on the presence of DHC related to anecdotal comments from the police about the victim's disability.[11] In several cases the victim's disability lacked specificity about how this related to the logged incident. Further, there often appeared to be unsubstantiated assumptions that victims had been targeted on the basis of their 'vulnerability'. Unfortunately, this speculation was hindered by the difficulty in working out which charge had been pursued and/or what sentence had been employed.

Inevitably, the CPS is bound by legal pragmatism and will only pursue cases where there is a reasonable probability of securing a conviction. This may partially explain why the charge of DHC was so obviously lacking from the case files; implicitly there was a sense that the burden of proof was too onerous for the CPS to consider pursuing these crimes as DHC.[12] As previously discussed, this is understandable considering the inconsistency in how DHC gets recorded and the reluctance of the judiciary to interpret crimes as DHCs and to enforce the sentence uplift (Quarmby, 2008).

Further details supplied in six of the 15[13] CPS case files (see boxed text on pp. 218 and 219), clearly resonates with previous findings (ibid.) that the CJS often fails disabled people in terms of consistently applying the law and implementing early multi-agency strategies, together with presumptions that offenders are only motivated by perceptions of vulnerability and not prejudice. Disappointingly, in only one of the case files examined was the aforementioned sentence uplift used, despite evidence that disability played a role in all of the cases scrutinised. Of course, case files can tell us only so much, but the evidence below suggests that offender motivations may go beyond a simplistic notion of vulnerability; susceptibility may be a factor in understanding how the victim is targeted, but the language used is simultaneously suggestive of victims being dehumanised during the commissioning of criminal acts. Grooming/befriending and repeat victimisation is also present in many of the cases cited; very few of the cases involved strangers and many of the offences took place in or near the victim's home. In Case File 6 there is also evidence for 'realistic conflict' theory being operationalised as a mechanism for 'guilt neutralisation'. Regrettably, all of the cases resulted in long-term 'quality of life' implications for the victims, who for the most part were living independently in the community.[14] Some crimes were committed by individuals, but many involved more than one perpetrator. Whether or not, 'thrill', 'defence' or 'retaliation' motivations (Levin and McDevitt, 2002) were present is unclear from the case files. Although not cited below, there were several cases where it was clear that the police had not sought CPS advice, despite clear guidance emanating from the HC scrutiny panel and disabled people's organisations that '. . . every case involving a disabled victim must now be looked at for any evidence of hostility. In addition, the reasons as to why it is or is not to be considered are to be written on the file and at full file review' (CPS, 2012: 28). Incidentally, in an analysis of Nottinghamshire's Crime Reporting Management System (CRMS), 154 out of 172 reports of DHC in the previous 12 months were classified as undetected/non-crimed. In further analysis carried out by the police for the researchers, some of these non-crimes appear highly contentious. For example, in one instance a young victim was knocked to the ground and called a 'spastic'. No further action was taken.

Case File 1

Custody (YOI/STC) was used for a 15-year-old with previous convictions for theft, robbery and burglary. The perpetrator targeted the home of a disabled man for burglary and had been part of a 'gang' who had repeatedly harassed the victim at his home; the victim had visible physical and learning/communication difficulties. It was felt that the case needed a robust approach so that the victim did not become a repeat 'vulnerable' victim (like the former disabled neighbour of the accused; from a multi-agency, early intervention perspective, this raises a number of important questions). Since being targeted, the victim's quality of life had been severely affected; for example, he had taken to not going out and putting bin liners on his windows so the youths could not tell when he was home. No sentence uplift.

Case File 2

This case involved a vicious assault using weapons in which two co-accused planned an attack against a young disabled man with Asperger's Syndrome, Reactive Detachment Disorder and learning difficulties. The victim knew the offenders as they were friends of his associates who lived in the same building. The victim had previously been assaulted by one of the defendants and had been 'spoken' to by police about it, but had failed to mention a burglary committed at his home by the co-accused. The defendants broke into the victim's home and threatened two of his friends to leave. They then subjected the victim to a serious and sustained assault using a baseball bat and lamp, telling him that it was because he was a 'snitch'. The victim sustained several injuries after the attack and has since become very fearful in his home and when venturing out. Special measures were required at trial for him to give evidence. The co-defendants were charged with burglary, assault and intent to cause GBH under s.18 OAPA and each given 70 days custody. No sentence uplift.

Case File 3

A particularly pernicious example of 'mate crime', in which – prior to the incident – the accused spent lots of time at the victim's home, walked his dog and generally helped him out. The victim had physical disabilities, epilepsy and limited mobility. On the night in question, the victim briefly vacated his property where it was alleged the defendant had started a fire at the flat's front door, trapping the victim inside. The defendant rescued the victim's dog, but it was left to the police and fire brigade to put out the fire and rescue the victim. The victim was extremely distressed following the incident, his home was badly damaged and his health and confidence have since deteriorated rapidly. No sentence uplift.

Case File 4

A complicated case of 'mate crime' involving the burglary of a disabled victim by a young man he had befriended and allowed to stay at his home. The accused left a letter apologising for his crime and referring to the victim as a 'father figure'. Somewhat contradictorily however, when told the victim wanted to press charges the defendant accused him of being a paedophile (common 'dehumanising'/justificatory language used by DHC perpetrators, see also EHRC, 2011a: 24). The victim, who had learning difficulties and depression, had recently moved into his own bungalow with the help of a support worker and was said to be deeply traumatised by this series of events. No sentence uplift.

Case File 5

The only case applying the uplift tariff involved neighbours where the defendant was charged with threatening behaviour under s4(1) of the Public Order Act 1986. The defendant was already on an ASBO not to cause harassment, alarm or distress to any person or have anyone in her house after 10 p.m. The victim was outside the accused's flat asking her to turn the music down, to which the accused shouted: '. . . the police won't do anything, go on and grass, I'm going to burn your house down with you and your mongrel spaz daughter in it'. The victim's daughter suffers from cerebral palsy. A witness overheard these comments and the distress they caused the victim who stated she felt hurt, intimidated and scared. The uplift tariff was used, with an 18-month community order imposed.

Case File 6

A similar case to Case File 5 involved the repeated targeting of an elderly man by a neighbour. This case was also charged under s4 of the Public Order Act. The victim was repeatedly abused on the basis of his disability and 'fleecing the state' because of 'having a free car'. He was also accused of being a paedophile. On the day in question a neighbour with mental health issues told the defendant to calm down, at which point he was subjected to verbal abuse (referred to as a 'psycho') and threatened with violence. On the case files the penalty given for this offence was a restriction order. There was a note on file that the defendant was serially targeting and harassing these victims on the basis of their disability, but in this instance the uplift tariff was not used.

In summarising the limited data from the CPS files, one could reasonably conclude that many of the sentencing/recording decisions lacked an appreciation of theoretical constructs of DHC motivations, although it is recognised that case files can never replicate the workings of a Magistrates Court.

Whilst cognisant of these limitations, it was clear that we had insufficient caseloads to be able to secure the required number of offender interviews. Subsequent to accessing CPS case files, the researchers have spent considerable time with East Midlands probation trusts, police officers with a responsibility for (D)HC, the courts, members of the Hate Crime Steering Group (HCSG) and the prison service in an attempt to identify supplementary DHC offenders that fulfil the aims and objectives of the project. Unfortunately, opaque recording processes, a limited offender 'pool' to draw upon, offenders being out of scope and data protection issues have resulted in slow progress. As a result the qualitative fieldwork has yet to commence.

In an attempt to overcome these sampling barriers, the researchers are in the process of placing online advertisements in User Voice.[15] Using the media as a recruitment tool is favoured in circumstances where the research project is operating with short timescales, and/or alternative sampling techniques have been exhausted. Inevitably, this gain has to be balanced with the methodological challenges of such an approach, including the problems associated with a self-selected sample (Campbell, 1998: 158) and having to extend the project geographically beyond the East Midlands. In relying on the media (electronic or print), one arguably loses a degree of control over the sampling process, making it difficult to filter out respondents with ulterior motives, or to include those who are not exposed to the chosen media output. Although exposed to these methodological challenges, given the sampling barriers experienced, this is deemed to be the most realistic approach to overcome the lack of respondents recruited so far.

Summary and ways forward

Understanding perpetrators helps us to better understand potential victims. This raises a number of policy implications and it is envisaged that the findings from this project – when complete – will be of interest to local/national policy-makers and academics alike. For example, the mechanisms by which 'grooming' manifests itself from a victim's and offender's perspective could be translated into a package of interventions for those living independently (e.g. helping individuals recognise real and false friendship). It is also likely to help with the design and implementation of tailored offender management programmes for those convicted of perpetrating DHC. Of course, this alone is only part of the solution. As analysis of the CPS files suggests and as the EHRC (2011a: 5) point out:

> ... [the] police don't know how many victims of crime are disabled; the courts don't know how many disabled victims have access to special measures, what proportion of offences against disabled victims result in conviction or how many of these offences result in a sentence uplift; and the prisons don't know how many offenders are serving sentences for crimes motivated by hostility to disabled people.

These shortfalls further validate the importance of this research. Combined with appropriate 'crime mapping' and the potentially inter-dependent relationship with poverty and deprivation, understanding offender motivations, offending history and socio-demographic profile adds another important layer to consider when thinking about resourcing anti-DHC measures.

As it stands, however, motivational drivers are either interpreted through the lens of victim's experiences or through US-centric police records, which in our view is wholly unsatisfactory. Certainly, our own analysis of CPS records indicates this latter approach may be a risky strategy. Worse still, it is not inconceivable that money intended for intervention strategies may be poorly directed and we are possibly missing opportunities to minimise risk/harm more effectively. What our research has palpably demonstrated, however, is that DHC offenders are an extremely problematic group to access. Overcoming these obstacles, however, is imperative. As the EHRC (2011a: 163) elucidate '. . . understanding [the motivations of offenders] will be key to tackling the root causes of [DHC] hostility'. This research hopes to start the process of addressing this knowledge 'black hole' and – in the long run – to help design policies that reduce disabled citizens' exposure to persistent, life-affecting criminal acts.

Notes

1 The media correlates this notion of 'welfare cheats' with other social groups, including Asylum Seekers and the pejoratively-labelled White 'Underclass'.
2 S.146 of the Criminal Justice Act (2003) places a duty on the court to increase the sentence for any offence aggravated by hostility based on the victim's race, religion, disability or sexual orientation and more recently hostility motivated by the victim's transgendered identity.
3 In contrast it has recently been reported that Plymouth has witnessed a 900 per cent increase in disability hate crime; suffice to say that naturally some discretion is needed when interpreting statistics particularly when previous baseline figures are low.
4 Thomas (2011) has argued, for example, that 'mate crime' has more in common with domestic violence than it does 'hate crime'.
5 Although the term vulnerability has been criticised, if one considers the term as denoting 'vulnerability' in terms of the perception of the perpetrator, these may be avoided (see Chakraborti and Garland, 2012).
6 Although it should be noted that the impact of these watershed events lacks equivalence. Both cases were widely reported in the media, but it would be naive to claim that the IPCC report of the Pilkington case had the same organisational, structural and reflective impact as the Macpherson Report (1999).
7 The term prejudice can be difficult to pin down. The same definitional disputations certainly apply to the idea of 'hate crime'. Equally it could be argued that the broad term 'disability' fails to fully capture the nuances within this 'catch-all' categorisation. Whilst cognisant of these disputes, the intention is not to replicate – or add to – the discussion here; rather terms will be used in their broadest sense. For an overview of some of these debates see Hall, 2005.
8 Although, interestingly, compared with other crime types, women/girls appear to be over-represented (see: CPS, 2012).
9 The CPS is represented in Nottinghamshire's Hate Crime Steering Group, and the authors would like to thank the CPS for their help in negotiating the process/paperwork required to gain access to these files.
10 Consisting of Nottinghamshire, Leicestershire, Derbyshire, Lincolnshire and Northamptonshire.
11 Although how the police ascertained this information lacked clarity.
12 This may be partly as a result of the dichotomy recognised by the CPS themselves when prosecuting such cases on the basis of hostility/vulnerability. Where evidence of the former is lacking it is unlikely to be prosecuted as a hate crime (CPS, 2012).
13 Space precludes us from including an overview of all case files here. However, the examples cited are not aberrations, but rather representative of common themes.
14 Although as previously discussed, the extent to which these victims were 'existing' rather than 'living' in a non-institutional setting is a point of debate.
15 User Voice is an ex-offender-led organisation, with a central remit to reducing offending.

References

ACPO (2012). Disability Hate Crime. Simon Cole, Chief Constable of Leicestershire Police, ACPO Lead on Disability and Mental Health. 10th Sept. 2012. www.acpo.police.uk/ThePoliceChiefsBlog/201209SimonColeBlog.aspx [last accessed 28th June 2013].

Adorno, T.W. (1960). The Authoritarian Personality. New York: Norton.
Allport, G.W. (1954). The Nature of Prejudice. Cambridge, MA: Addison-Wesley.
Arendt, H. (1963). Eichmann in Jerusalem: A report on the banality of evil. London: Penguin Classics.
Bayley, M. (1997). What price friendship?: Encouraging the relationships of people with learning difficulties. Melbourne: Hexagon Publishing.
BBC (2012). After the Paralympics: Has anything changed for disabled people? 13th Dec. 2013, www.bbc.co.uk/news/magazine-20693647 [last accessed 15th June 2013].
BBC (2013). Councillor considers resignation over disabled comment [online]. Available at: www.bbc.co.uk/news/uk-england-cornwall-21594109 [last accessed 12th June 2013].
Bjørgo, T., van Donselaar, J. and Grunenberg, S. (2009). 'Exit from right-wing extremist groups: lessons from disengagement programmes in Norway, Sweden and Germany', in T. Bjørgo and J. Horgan, (eds.), Leaving Terrorism Behind, London: Routledge, pp. 135–151.
BNP (2013). 'Cuts, cuts, cuts for the British – but Lib/Lab/Cons allow foreigners to bleed our country dry' [online]. Available at: www.bnp.org.uk/news/national/cuts-cuts-cuts-british-liblabcons-allow-foreigners-bleed-our-country-dry [last accessed 12th June 2013].
Bourdieu, P. (1986). 'The forms of capital', in J.G. Richardson (ed.), Handbook of Theory and Research for the Sociology of Education. New York: Greenwood Press, pp. 241–258.
Bowling, B. (1999). Violent racism: Victimisation, Policing and Social Context. Harlow: Longman.
Brown, R. (1995). Prejudice: it's Social Psychology. Oxford: Blackwell.
Byers, B., Crider, B.W. and Biggers, G.K. (1999). 'Bias Crime Motivation: A Study of Hate Crime Offender Neutralization Techniques Used Against the Amish'. *Journal of Contemporary Criminal Justice*, 15(1): 78–96.
Campbell, R. (1998). 'Invisible men: making visible male clients of female prostitutes in Merseyside', in J.E. Elias, V.L. Bullough, V. Elias and G. Brewer, (eds), Prostitution: On Whores, Hustlers and Johns. New York: Prometheus.
Chakraborti, N. and Garland, J. (2012). Hate crime: impact, causes and responses. London: Sage.
Channel 4 News (2013). Disability Hate Crime: five years on from Fiona Pilkington [online]. Available at: www.channel4.com/news/disability-hate-crime-five-years-on-from-fiona-pilkington [last accessed 5th January 2013].
CJJI (2013). Living in a Different World: A joint review of Disability Hate Crime. London: CJJI.
Clement, S., Brohan, E., Sayce. L., Pool. J. and Thornicroft. G. (2001). 'Disability hate crime and targeted violence and hostility: A mental health and discrimination perspective', *Journal of Mental Health*, June 2011, 20(3): 219–225.
Cohen, A.K. (1955). Delinquent boys: the culture of the gang. New York: Free Press.
Cornish, D.B. (1994). 'The Procedural Analysis of Offending and its Relevance for Situational Prevention', in R.V. Clarke (ed.), Crime Prevention Studies, Vol. 3, pp. 151–196. Monsey, N.Y.: Criminal Justice Press.
Court, D. (2003). 'Direct work with racially-motivated offenders', *Probation Journal*, 50(1): 52–58.
CPS (2011). Hate Crime and Crimes Against Older People Report. Home Office. www.cps.gov.uk/publications/docs/cps_hate_crime_report_2011.pdf
CPS (2012). Hate Crime and Crimes against older people report 2010–2011. London: CPS (EQU).
CPS (2013a). Hate Crime and Crimes against older people report 2011–2012. London: CPS (EQU).
CPS (2013b). Disability Hate Crime – Guidance on the distinction between vulnerability and hostility in the context of crimes committed against disabled people [online]. Available at: www.cps.gov.uk/legal/d_to_g/disability_hate_crime_/#a06 [last accessed 12th June 2013].
Craig, K.M. (2002). 'Examining hate-motivated aggression: A review of the social psychological literature on hate crimes as a distinct form of aggression', *Aggression and Violent Behaviour*, 7, 85–101.
Disability Horizons (2012). Paralympic Games 2012: The Legacy and the Impact. 29th Oct. 2012 http://disabilityhorizons.com/2012/10/paralympics-games-2012-the-legacy-and-the-impact/ [last accessed 2nd June 2013].
Dixon, L., Noel, E. and Walters, M. (2010). Keeping communities safe: working with perpetrators of hate crime. In 2010 Hate Crimes Conference – Tackling Hatred Head On: Working with Hate Crime Offenders and Extremism, 21st September, Middlesex University.
DWP (2012). *Disabled People's user-led organisations making a difference: Disability Hate Crime.* (Dec 2012). Department for Work and Pensions. http://odi.dwp.gov.uk/docs/dpulo/disability-hate-crime-easy-read.pdf

Esses, V.M., Dovidio, J.F., Jackson, L.M. and Armstrong, T.L. (2001). 'The immigration dilemma: the role of perceived group competition, ethnic prejudice, and national identity', *Journal of Social Issues*, 57: 389–412.

EHRC (2011a). Hidden in Plain Sight: Inquiry into disability-related harassment. London: Equality and Human Rights Commission.

EHRC (2011b). Rehabilitation of hate crime offenders. London: Equality and Human Rights Commission.

Fiske, S.T. (2008). 'Are we born Racist', *Greater Good*, Summer 2008: 14–17.

Gadd, D., Dixon, B. and Jefferson, T. (2005). Why Do They Do It? Racial Harassment in North Staffordshire. Keele: Centre for Criminological Research, Keele University.

Gavrielides, T. (2011). 'Restorative Practices and hate crime: opening up the debate', *TEMIDA*, Dec 2011: 7–20.

Gerstenfeld, P. (2011). Hate Crimes Causes, Controls, and Controversies. London: Sage Publications.

Glasgow Media Group (2011). Bad News for Disabled People: How the media are reporting disability [online]. Available at: www.gla.ac.uk/media/media_214917_en.pdf [last accessed 3rd May 2013].

Green, D.P. (1998). 'From lynching to gay bashing: The elusive connection between economic conditions and hate crime', *Journal of Personality and Social Psychology*, 75: 82–92.

Green, D.P., Strolovitch, D.Z. and Wong, J.S. (1998). 'Defended neighbourhoods, integration, and racially motivated crime', *American Journal of Sociology*, 104(2): 372–403.

Hall, N. (2005). Hate crime. Cullompton: Willan Publishing.

Herek, G.M. (2000). 'The psychology of sexual prejudice', *Current Directions in Psychological Science*, 9, 19–22.

Hirschi, T. (1969). Causes of Delinquency. Berkeley: University of California Press.

HM Government. (2012). Challenge it, Report it, Stop it: The Government's Plan to Tackle Hate Crime. London: Stationery Office.

HM Inspectorate (2013). Living in a Different World: Joint Inspectorate Review of Disability Hate Crime, HMCPSI, HMIC, HMI Probation. www.hmic.gov.uk/publication/living-in-a-different-world-joint-review-of-disability-hate-crime/

Home Office (2011). Hate Crimes, England and Wales 2011–2012. [online] www.gov.uk/government/publications/hate-crimes-england-and-wales-2011-to-2012-2/hate-crimes-england-and-wales-2011-to-2012 [last accessed on 28th June 2013].

Hoong Sin, C., Hedges, A., Cook, C., Mguni, N. and Comber, N. (2009). Disabled people's experiences of targeted violence of hostility. EHRC, Manchester: OPU.

Hopkins-Burke, R., and Pollock, E. (2004). A tale of two anomies: some observations on the contribution of (sociological) criminological theory to explaining hate crime motivation [online] Available at: www.internetjournalofcriminology.com/ijcarticles.html

Hopkins-Burke, R.D. (2009). An Introduction to Criminological Theory, Cullompton: Willan Press.

IPCC. Report into the contact between Fiona Pilkington and Leicestershire Constabulary (24th May 2011) www.ipcc.gov.uk/news/Pages/pr_240511_pilkington.aspx [last accessed 23rd June 2013].

ITV News. Mencap: No difference in disability attitudes after games. Tuesday 18th Dec. 2012, 7.05 pm. www.itv.com/news/update/2012-12-18/mencap-no-difference-on-disability-attitudes-after-games/ [last accessed 5th July 2013].

Law Commission Consultation (27th June 2013). Hate Crime: The case for extending the existing offences. http://lawcommission.justice.gov.uk/consultations/hate_crime.htm [last accessed 5th July 2013].

Levin, J. and McDevitt, J. (1993) Hate Crimes: The Rising Tide of Bigotry and Bloodshed. New York: Plenum Press.

Levin, J. and McDevitt, J. (2002). Hate Crimes Revisited: America's War on Those Who are Different. Boulder, CO: Westview Press.

Marsh, S. (2012). For Britain's disabled people, the Paralympics couldn't make 2012 golden [online]. Available at: www.guardian.co.uk/commentisfree/2012/dec/31/britain-disabled-paralympics-cuts [last accessed 15th May 2013].

Macpherson, W. (1999). The Stephen Lawrence Inquiry, Report of an Inquiry by Sir William Macpherson of Cluny. London: Home Office.
Mandela, N. (1995). Long walk to freedom. New York: Back Bay Books.
McDevitt, J., Levin J., Nolan, J. and Bennett, S. (2002). 'Hate Crime Offenders: An Expanded Typology', *Journal of Social Issues*, 58(2): 303–317.
McDevitt, J., Levin J., Nolan, J. and Bennett, S. (2010). 'Hate Crime Offenders', in N. Chakraborti (ed.), Hate Crimes: Concepts, policy, future directions. Cullompton: Willan Publishing, pp. 124–145.
McNeill, F. (2006). 'A desistance paradigm for offender management', *Criminology and Criminal Justice*, 6(1): 39–62.
Mencap (2000). Living in Fear [online]. Available at: www.mencap.org.uk/download/fear.pdf [last accessed 12th October 2008].
Mencap (2010). Don't Stand By: Ending Disability Hate Crime Together. Hate Crime Research Report. Mencap: London.
Mencap (2011). Police Failings in Fiona Pilkington case, Tuesday 24th May 2011. See www.mencap.org.uk/news/article/police-failings-fiona-pilkington-case [last accessed 28th June 2013].
Miller, P., Parker, S. and Gillinson, S. (2004). Disablism: How to tackle the last prejudice. London: Demos.
Nelson, T.D. (2002). The Psychology of Prejudice. London: Allyn and Bacon.
Newburn, T. (2013). Criminology. Cullompton: Willan Publishing.
Nottinghamshire County Council (2010). Disability hate crime in Nottinghamshire: A summary of findings December 2010. NCC: unpublished.
Palmer, J. and Smith, D. (2010). 'Promoting Human Dignity: An evaluation of a programme for racially motivated offenders', *Probation Journal*, 57(4): 368–382.
Pawson, R. and Tilley, N. (1997). Realistic Evaluation. London: Sage.
Phillips, N. (2009). 'The Prosecution of Hate Crimes: The Limitations of the Hate Crime Typology', *Journal of Interpersonal Violence*, 24: 883–905.
Plymouth 'hate crime' against disabled people rises by over 900 per cent. www.thisisthewestcountry.co.uk/news/devon_news/10478544.Plymouth_hate_crime_against_disabled_people_rises_by_over_900_per_cent/ [last accessed 16 June 2013].
Putnam, R.D. (1995). 'Bowling alone: America's declining social capital', *Journal of Democracy*, Vol. 6 (1): 64–78.
Quarmby, K. (2008). Getting away with murder: disabled people's experiences of hate crime in the UK. London: Scope.
Quarmby, K. (2011). Scapegoat: Why we are failing disabled people. London: Portobello.
Scope (2013). www.scope.org.uk/news/scope-responds-new-report-on-disability-hate-crime
Sherry, M. (2010). Disability Hate Crimes: Does Anyone Really Hate Disabled People? Farnham: Ashgate.
Sherif, M., Harvey, O.J., White, B.J., Hood, W.R. and Sherif, C.W. (1961). Intergroup conflict and cooperation: The Robbers Cave experiment. Norman: University of Oklahoma Press.
Sibbitt, R. (1997). The perpetrators of racial harassment and racial violence, Home Office Research Study 176. London: Home Office.
Sobsey, D. (1994). Violence and abuse in the lives of people with disabilities: the end of silent acceptance? Baltimore: P. H. Brookes Publishing Company.
Sykes, G. and Matza, D. (1957). 'Techniques of Neutralisation', *American Sociological Review*, 22: 664–670.
Sykes, W., Groom, C. and Desai, P. (2011). Disability-related harassment: the role of public bodies. A qualitative research report. London: Equality and Human Rights Commission.
Tajfel, H., and Turner, J. C. (1979). 'The social identity theory of intergroup behaviour', in S. Worchel and W.G. Austin (eds), Psychology of Intergroup Relations (pp. 7–24). Chicago: Nelson.
The Guardian. Disability Hate Crime is at its highest level since records began (15th August 2012) www.guardian.co.uk/news/datablog/2012/aug/14/disability-hate-crime-increase-reported-incidents-data [last accessed 28th June 2013].
The Guardian. Benefit cuts are fuelling abuse of disabled people say charities. Sunday 5th Feb. 2012. www.guardian.co.uk/society/2012/feb/05/benefit-cuts-fuelling-abuse-disabled-people [last accessed 28th June 2013].
Thomas, P. (2011). '"Mate crime": Ridicule, hostility and targeted violence against disabled people', *Disability and Society*, 26(1): 107–111.

Update Disability (2013). Hate crime linked to newspaper stories of fraud and 'scroungers' [online]. Available at: www.update.org.uk/news-detail.php?page=193 [last accessed 24th June 2013].

Waller, J. (2007). Becoming Evil: How Ordinary People Commit Genocide and Mass Killing (2nd edition). Oxford: Oxford University Press.

Walters, M. A. (2011). 'A general theories of hate crime? Strain, doing difference and self control', *Critical Criminology*, 19(4): pp. 313–330.

18
Alternative subcultures and hate crime

Jon Garland and Paul Hodkinson

In April 2013 Greater Manchester Police (GMP) in the UK announced that it would henceforth be recording targeted attacks on members of what it termed 'alternative subcultures' as hate crimes. In a move covered prominently across national media, the force argued that 'adding this extra category of hate crime will help us better understand how some people are suffering from crimes because of their appearance, and better respond to the needs of victims of crime' (GMP, 2013). With implications for how such crime is measured and the kinds of support offered to victims, the move – at present – contrasts with current national hate crime policy in the UK, which covers race/ethnicity, religion/belief, disability, sexual orientation and gender identity.

The GMP's announcement represented a response to a concerted campaign on the part of the Sophie Lancaster Foundation, following the 2007 murder of Sophie Lancaster in Lancashire, UK. The case's trial judge had labelled the incident as a 'hate crime' on the basis that the victim and her boyfriend had been attacked solely because of their goth appearance. More recently, a UK government document on hate crime entitled 'Challenge it, Report it, Stop it', stated in relation to the Lancaster murder that 'although crimes such as this may fall outside of the nationally monitored strands, they are nonetheless hate crimes, and they should therefore be treated as such' (HM Government, 2012).

Yet while the GMP announcement was welcomed by some commentators – and by many alternative subcultural participants – others expressed scepticism, illustrating that the question of whether targeted attacks on members of alternative subcultures should indeed be treated as hate crimes is a contentious one. Against the background of these developments, this chapter explores the key arguments on either side of the debate on alternative subcultures and hate crime and, in so doing, raises broader questions about contrasting understandings of the concept of hate crime itself.

The case in favour

Patterns of harassment and prejudice

Although little concentrated research has been conducted on the subject to date, small-scale studies suggest that, while the Lancaster case was unusual in its violence, it was not a 'one-off'. As Smyth (2010: 58) reports, just a few weeks after Lancaster's murder there was another horrific attack of a group of three boys and a girl in Burnley, just eight miles from the site of Lancaster's assault. The group, all wearing 'mosher or goth-style clothing', were set upon by a gang of seven with such intent that two of the boys needed hospital treatment. The following year, a 26-year-old goth was punched, kicked and stamped upon by a group of males in a public park in Leeds. This assault resulted in him lapsing into a coma and losing an ear, while two other goths were hospitalised in the same incident (Gardner, 2009). Another goth spoke of being attacked every day while at school and then being hospitalised after receiving a severe beating from a group of 14 youths at a fairground (Taylor et al., 2013).

Although it is difficult to know precisely how often these assaults occur, some studies suggest that alternative subculture participants can be the frequent targets of verbal *and* physical abuse, so much so that some have 'lost count' of the number of times they have been victimised just because of their subcultural style and appearance (Goulding and Saren, 2009). In a fashion not dissimilar to that of racist harassment (Bowling, 1998), the violence suffered by such individuals represents the extreme end of a pattern of ongoing targeted victimisation which can occur on a regular basis, with so-called 'low-level' abuse a commonplace feature of many lives (Garland, 2010a, 2010b). As Taylor et al. (2013) note, some subcultural participants they interviewed reported being the recipients of verbal abuse on a 'day to day' basis, causing 'real damage' to victims' sense of wellbeing. Similarly, Price (2013) reports that 'low-level smalltown violence and aggression [towards alternative subculture participants] is common', while Jones (2013) suggests that such harassment is widespread.

The types of insult to which alternative subcultural participants are subjected can range from those aimed at their strikingly different appearance (such as 'corpse' or 'witch' in the case of goths) to those that imply that they are somehow unkempt or unclean (the attackers involved in the Leeds incident were heard yelling 'dirty moshers and goths' at their victims, a not uncommon slight (Gardner, 2009)). In the case of male goths, such general terms of abuse sometimes are mixed with homophobic slurs (Brill, 2008; Price, 2013) that target their often androgynous and effeminate appearance. Their difference in the eyes of perpetrators is therefore multi-layered; they are 'othered' due to their subcultural identity *and* their apparent performance of a gender and sexual identity deemed abnormal by the offender. As Walters (2011: 318) suggests, and in common with recognised forms of hate crime perpetration, such types of difference may be feared or despised as a result of the way they encroach upon the 'ingroup's' normative identity constructions:

> For some individuals this [encroachment] creates a feeling of helplessness and insecurity about their place in society. In response to these negative emotions, individuals frequently attempt to transpose their feelings of helplessness into animosity, an emotive reaction which is used to gain a sense of control over those who they see as causing their insecurity, thus temporarily relinquishing the original negative feeling of fear.

As is the case with racist or homophobic victimisation, for example, the target group – in this case, alternative subculture participants – apparently provokes negative and hostile feelings among those who may see their difference as a threat to dominant cultural and sexual norms. They are thus 'othered' and labelled as a deviant 'outgroup' to the extent that those in the 'ingroup' regard them as a legitimate target for abuse or assault. It also could be argued that, as with more recognised forms of hate crime, what is being targeted is less the individual identity of the victim and more their membership of a stigmatised 'outgroup' that the perpetrator despises. These incidents thus often seem to conform to the 'classic' stranger danger conception of hate crime where the victim could be interchangeable with another member of the same 'outgroup' (see Iganski, 2008; Perry, 2009).

This is not to say that the perpetrator necessarily *hates* their victim, but rather that they target them due to feelings of enmity that are provoked by prejudice that is in itself interwoven with fear of or animosity towards difference. As Chakraborti and Garland (2012) argue, often what we understand as 'hate crimes' are not actually motivated by hate, but instead by hostility that is the by-product of feelings of weakness, inadequacy or other, more complex emotional and psychological processes (see also Dixon and Gadd, 2006; Gadd, 2009). It only takes a 'trigger' incident, and perhaps one fuelled by intoxication, jealousy or the heat of an argument, to bring such negative subconscious feelings to the surface.

In other instances, acts of 'hate' may occur due to boredom and the perpetrator's need for excitement. As McDevitt et al. (2002) and Byers et al. (1999) found, often such incidents arise from groups of young males' desire for the 'thrill' and the 'rush' that they can attain by seeking out and targeting a local 'outgroup'. In Byers et al.'s study, this group was the local Amish community, whom young men would often chase, abuse and harass for the 'fun of it'. This does not mean that feelings of animosity were totally absent, but rather that they were only *part* of the motivation for such incidents.

And, while it is acknowledged that the motivations of those who target alternative subculture participants need more research, they, and the nature of many of the incidents of harassment they endure, do seem similar to those described in the work cited above. They often occur in public spaces late at night when perpetrators, either fuelled by alcohol or the need for excitement, target a stigmatised 'outgroup' for no other reason than they present an easily identifiable, and perhaps 'soft', target, possibly for latent anger and frustration (for an extended discussion of the intersection of strain theory and 'doing difference', see Walters, 2011). As Garland (2010a) posits, goths and members of at least some other alternative subcultures tend to be perceived as passive, 'bookish' and in the case of males, relatively weak and effeminate. As such, they may provide a particularly easy target when walking through a park or making their way home after a night out (Kidd and Witten, 2008). Their vulnerability, in this sense, provides a further parallel between the types of everyday, more 'banal' forms of hate crime experienced by recognised victim groups (Iganski, 2008) and those suffered by alternative subcultural participants.

Identity and community

Interestingly, the frequency of its occurrence means that being the subject of targeted harassment can become an integral part of being involved in visually distinctive subcultures (Barker, 2003: 43; Hodkinson, 2008: 32). It can even take the form of a 'rite of passage' for some participants, who may feel more embedded in the subculture as a result of the victimisation they experience (Hodkinson, 2002). However, for most of those who are targeted, any such 'badge of honour' is liable to be significantly outweighed by the alarm and distress they feel at being victimised. In addition to any immediate impacts, attacks are liable to affect their sense of self-worth, self-confidence, security and psychological wellbeing (Garland, 2010a; Taylor et al., 2013) in a manner comparable to the victimisation processes and experiences of recognised forms of hate crime (Garland, 2010b). Meanwhile, individuals often recognise that it is not only who they are that makes them vulnerable, but the intersection of their appearance and identity with place and time that can heighten their risk of victimisation. Thus, like victims of faith hate or transphobic hate, for example, alternative subcultural participants may develop avoidance strategies, such as steering clear of certain routes, spaces, venues or groups of people, to lessen this risk.

It also has become clear that alternative subcultures have a sense of community strong enough for them to feel the impact of the targeted victimisation of others within the group. In other words, just as the harassment or abuse of gay people (for example) can negatively impact upon gay communities both locally and nationally, it is plausible to suggest that the victimisation of goths and alternatives might affect the security and wellbeing of the subculture as a whole rather than the victim alone (Jones, 2013; Price, 2013). This was especially noticeable in the aftermath of the high-profile killing of Sophie Lancaster for her goth appearance in 2007, which sent out 'ripples' of alarm throughout the alternative community in the same way that another 'signal crime', the homophobic murder of Jody Dobrowski, did with gay communities two years earlier. Indeed, as Smyth (2010) and Garland (2014) note, the weeks and months following Lancaster's death saw a huge response from the goth and alternative communities, with thousands of messages of support and sympathy being sent to Sophie's mother, Sylvia, from within the UK and around the world. Tied in with this were the hundreds of examples of targeted victimisation of members of alternative communities that were posted on websites, message boards and in magazines. As Taylor et al. (2013) suggest, Sophie Lancaster's murder 'galvanised' these groups, engendering a feeling of communal horror at what had happened together with a sense of solidarity at their own shared experiences of being abused or assaulted. Indeed, it could be argued that these communities reacted just as recognised hate crime victim communities tend to do when a member is attacked.

The limited research available to date, then, suggests some striking similarities between alternative subcultures and 'traditional' hate crime groups with respect to the experiences of victims. For those commentators and campaigners who support the inclusion of the former as a hate crime victim group, one of the key aims of hate crime as a concept is to highlight the victimisation that all 'othered' groups suffer, whatever their background or historical context, as they are being victimised due to an identity characteristic in a manner that affects the victim, and their community, more than 'normal' crimes do (Chakraborti, 2010). According to this view, the point of the hate crime concept is to support the marginalised, the stigmatised and the 'othered', including those groups that have somehow 'slipped though the cracks' of policy and practice. As we have seen, there are a number of reasons why the targeting of alternative subcultures could fit within such a framework.

Difficulties and dilemmas

Yet, while some have welcomed Greater Manchester Police's decision on hate crime and alternative subcultures, others have raised concerns about the move. There are a number of complexities that might arise from extending the hate crime concept in such a way, some of which relate to details and practicalities and others to more fundamental concerns about 'watering down' or even trivialising the notion of hate crime itself. The next section of this chapter explores some of the most commonly raised objections and difficulties.

Subculture as 'choice'

One of the most frequently raised objections rests on the contention that, unlike traditional hate crime groups, subcultures represent a lifestyle choice rather than an ascribed aspect of identity. Members of ethnic minorities have no choice over the colour of their skin, so the argument goes, and neither do disabled people over the capacities of their bodies. Such characteristics constitute an essential and irremovable aspect of the very being of individuals and hate crime legislation constitutes a crucial protection against being targeted on the basis of them. Many would extend the argument to those whose sexual or gender orientation places them within a minority group and to those whose upbringing renders religious beliefs and identity a core element of self.

In contrast, alternative subcultures, as Hodkinson has noted elsewhere, often have been regarded as temporary affiliations attributable to the choices young people make as they go through the exploratory period of adolescence (Hodkinson, 2012). Not only does this suggest that alternative subcultural identities are ephemeral but also that, in the context of the possibility of harassment or attack, those involved have the option to choose a less distinctive appearance or community. As Colin Freeman, writing for the UK's *Daily Telegraph*, has put it,

> ... how will ethnic minorities and other 'vulnerable groups', for whom hate crime legislation was originally designed to protect, feel about goths and punks getting the same protection? ... I suspect there is one point they would feel tempted to make, which is that if things get really bad, goths and punks ... can always change the way they look.
> *(Freeman, 2013)*

Yet, such an argument veers uncomfortably close to suggesting that goths, punks and others are partially responsible for the abuse or violence they receive. More fundamentally, its inference is that difference is to be valued and protected only in those cases where individuals are not in any way responsible for their distinctiveness – hardly a ringing endorsement of the principle of diversity. Might we not wish to value the possibility for individuals to *elect* to express themselves in a way that differs from what is considered normal?

There are also ambiguities as to what it means to suggest an identity is 'chosen'. Research tends to illustrate that few experience their gravitation towards a subcultural identity as a simple choice. Participants typically recount the process of their becoming involved as a complex series of influences, coincidences and reinforcements over a period of time without a clear decision ever having been taken. For many the process partially connects to the resolution of prior difficulties such as social isolation or lack of status – something well-established in classic and recent subcultural theories (see Cohen, 1955; Hodkinson, 2002). Here subcultural involvement becomes an essential source of belonging, status and friendships in the context of insecurity and isolation elsewhere. And whether specific 'problems' are resolved or not, such groups often become pivotal to the identity, friendships and everyday life of those involved, to the extent that their abandonment would entail substantial personal and social costs. The following comment, from one of Hodkinson's goth respondents, was not untypical:

> W1 (male): It is the most important thing in my life, there's no doubt about it – it is the most important thing in my life – I couldn't fathom existing without it at all.
> *(cited in Hodkinson, 2002)*

Recent research, meanwhile, raises questions about traditional understandings of subcultures as short-lived forms of identity tied to adolescence. Certainly, most participants become interested during their teens, but the extent of the belonging and commitment generated is prompting increasing numbers to remain involved into and beyond their thirties, with subcultural identity acting as a consistent and central thread within developing adult lives (Bennett, 2006; Hodkinson, 2011; Bennett and Hodkinson, 2012).

Dominant or subordinate?

A potentially more compelling objection to categorising alternative subcultures as a hate crime victim group is that such a move may dilute understandings of hate crime as rooted in broader patterns of domination and subordination. In so doing, it may draw attention away from the specific importance – integral to early hate crime interventions – of preventing targeted attacks on already subordinated minority groups that reflect and reinforce systematic patterns of disadvantage that are deeply ingrained in society. For scholars such as Barbara Perry, the reinforcement of hegemony and the subordination of non-powerful groups are at the heart of what hate crime is:

> . . . hate crime provides a context in which the perpetrator can reassert his or her hegemonic identity and, at the same time, punish the victim for the individual or collective performance of his or her identity. In other words, hate motivated violence is used to sustain the privilege of the dominant group and to police the boundaries between groups by reminding the Other of his or her place.
>
> *(Perry, 2009: 71)*

According to this perspective, hate crime legislation is not about reducing targeted violence *per se* but is a means to address the broader inequalities of power in which such violence is deemed to be rooted.

To include alternative subcultures as hate crime victim groups would signal a shift away from the understanding of hate crime as perpetrated by the powerful against the powerless. There may, of course, be circumstances in which the victimisation of individual punks, goths or metallers relate to the intersection of subcultural identity with ingrained lines of division such as gender or sexuality, but few would argue that, in a general sense, the targeting of such groups reflects or reinforces their broader collective socio-economic subordination. Studies, for example, indicate that many participants are white, middle-class, heterosexual and relatively well educated (Brill, 2008) and that elements of the internal ideology and rhetoric of some groups implicitly privilege middle-class values (Thornton, 1995; Hodkinson, 2012). In contrast, those commonly cited by subcultural participants as perpetrators of violence against them tend to be from disadvantaged sections of society, something illustrated in the frequent description of such would-be attackers (in the UK context) as 'chavs', a term some regard as an acronym for Council-Housed And Violent (see Tyler, 2008; Jones, 2012).

Of course, not all alternative subculture participants are white, middle class and heterosexual. And neither does being well-educated or espousing broadly middle-class values exclude an individual from the possibility of finding themselves on the wrong end of discrimination or subordination, whether on the basis of race, religion, sexuality, disability, gender, age or other characteristics. Such complexities of identity raise broader questions as to how easy it is to establish who is 'dominant' and who is 'subordinate'. Nevertheless, in the case of alternative subcultures, it is hard to argue that the 'target' group is, in a general sense, a systematically subordinated one. As a consequence their inclusion as a victim group would imply a broadening – or 'watering down', depending on your perspective – of the notion of hate crime. And the fear of some is that the inclusion of alternative subcultures may become the thin end of the wedge, opening the floodgates for a plethora of other groups. As Freeman

(2013) puts it, 'if we extend the "hate crime" definition to things like youth subcultures, where exactly do we stop?'

Blurry boundaries and selectivity

A further problem is that the term 'alternative subcultures' is far from easy to define and it is unclear which groups or individuals would in practice be included, which would not, and why. Greater Manchester Police accompanied their announcement with the following definition:

> Greater Manchester Police, in consultation with the Sophie Lancaster Foundation, recognises alternative sub-culture as a broad term to define a strong sense of collective identity and a set of group-specific values and tastes. This typically centres on distinctive style, clothing, make up, body art and music preference. Those involved usually stand out to both fellow participants and to those outside the group. Groups typically under the 'alternative' umbrella include Goths, Emos, Punks and Metallers however this list is not exhaustive.
>
> *(Press release, Greater Manchester Police, 2013)*

Contributed to, at the request of the Sophie Lancaster Foundation, by the authors of this chapter, the definition sets out some useful parameters that many would recognise but is inevitably broad and flexible, leaving various questions unanswered.

First, while research demonstrates that 'core' participants often are highly committed to alternative subcultures, there are significant numbers of individuals who have more partial connections, sometimes with a range of different groups (Bennett, 1999; Muggleton, 2000). Under what circumstances would those whose appearance or identity places them on the margins of one alternative subculture or indeed several, be included or excluded? Meanwhile, even among those whose identities fall more squarely within groups such as goth, punk and metal, levels and types of involvement can vary – from those exhibiting the most spectacular forms of appearance to those whose visual distinctiveness may be limited to a band T-shirt and a pair of jeans, for instance.

There are also important questions about which groups count as 'alternative'. For example, would members of student-oriented indie rock scenes – which are less overtly distinctive in terms of dress than goths and punks but often associated with the notion of 'alternative music culture' (see Kruse, 1993) – be included? What about the various strands of dance or clubbing scenes, some of which have historical connections with elements of hippy culture and resistant forms of politics (Thornton, 1995; Malbon, 2000)? Or could 'alternative subcultures' be operationalised in a more literal sense, with the implication that any distinctive identity group related to style and music could be protected, from goths, to clubbers to hip hop fanatics?

Given such complexities, it is likely that, as Garland has pointed out elsewhere (Sedgewick, 2013), reliance on self-identification on the part of victims may be the only viable way to proceed, but it remains unclear what happens if an individual claims to have been targeted on the basis of their alternative subcultural identity if their outward appearance is at odds with the authorities' own understandings of the term. Such difficulties should not be overstated in the case of Greater Manchester Police's localised initiative and it should be noted that similar problems of categorisation exist in the case of existing hate crime categories, not least religion and belief. But if alternative subcultures were to be recognised in hate crime legislation, with implications for the sentencing of offenders, the complexities described would require a more satisfactory resolution.

More fundamentally, though, it would need to be clear why alternative subcultures *should* be singled out as opposed to various other victim groups, including other music-related cultures, distinctive consumer groupings and more structurally disadvantaged groups, such as the elderly and the homeless. Do such inclusions and exclusions reflect a careful, wholesale weighing up of the situation of different groups, or rather the amount of pressure such groups have been able to generate? Such pressure may reflect the newsworthiness of high profile incidents and the ways they are framed by media as well as the existence and effectiveness of campaign groups (Mason-Bish, 2014, forthcoming). The murder of Sophie Lancaster attracted extensive media attention – the striking image of a small, pretty and innocent-looking young girl being kicked to death by violent male youths providing a compelling narrative that engendered extensive public sympathy. Subsequently, the political awareness and commitment of Lancaster's mother, Sylvia, alongside the participants of predominantly well-educated subcultural groups, enabled the development of a highly effective campaign with a clear set of goals. Such circumstances prompt the following concern from Nelson Jones, writing in the *New Statesman*:

> There must be a suspicion, though, that without the efforts of the Sophie Lancaster Foundation in pushing for the recognition of anti-goth crime, and without the galvanising effect of the 2007 murder, today's announcement [from Greater Manchester Police] would not have happened. And this creates its own dangers. Simply adding another tickbox to an already substantial list won't solve the problem of a legal and bureaucratic scheme that continues to privilege some types of hate-crime as special while ignoring others.
>
> *(Jones, 2013)*

Rather than objecting specifically to the inclusion of alternative subcultures, Jones' comment points to a broader problem, as he sees it, with the formulation of hate crime legislation as something centred upon a selected list of recognised victim groups.

Conclusion: A challenge to traditional understandings of hate crime?

This chapter has provided a critical outline of some of the core arguments relating to an emerging area of policy, practice and academic study within the UK: the targeted victimisation of those within alternative subcultures. We have suggested that various aspects of this victimisation are comparable with that which recognised hate crime victim groups suffer, including the frequency and nature of 'low-' and 'high-level' incidents, and their potential psychological impact upon the victim and those in their community. We have also indicated that in many instances the victim could be interchangeable with someone else from their identity group as, like the acknowledged hate crime groups, these are often 'stranger danger' forms of crime where it is the victim's identity group that is targeted, rather than the individual themselves.

Yet the chapter has also discussed some of the difficulties and dilemmas involved with including alternative subculture participants under the hate crime 'umbrella'. Doubts were raised, here, about the helpfulness of arguments that alternative subculture identities are – unlike those of traditional victim groups – elective, ephemeral and easy to discard. Such claims are questionable, we suggested, and their use as an argument in this debate displays a position of some ambivalence about the societal value of difference and diversity. Of greater concern, we suggested, is the danger, as some see it, of 'watering down' the concept of hate crime by including groups that have not been systematically and historically marginalised or excluded in the same way that already recognised hate crime victim groups have. We also identified significant difficulties with respect to defining exactly who can be categorised as 'alternative' and with why such groups, however defined, should be included as hate crime victim groups when a range of other vulnerable groups are not.

Ultimately, it is difficult to separate the alternative subcultures case study discussed in this chapter from broader debates about what hate crime as a concept means and what hate crime legislation and interventions are for. Whichever position one ultimately takes on the subject, it seems clear that, were it to become more widespread, the inclusion of alternative subcultures as a hate crime victim group would comprise a departure from traditional understandings of hate crime as something centred upon the protection of structurally and/or historically marginalised groups. It also seems likely that, if accepted, the inclusion of alternative subcultures would open the way for equally compelling claims from other targeted groups that do not currently fall under the hate crime umbrella. Under such circumstances, the approach of adding more and more groups in a piecemeal fashion may become unsustainable, prompting more fundamental re-evaluations of hate crime that move away from a framework that specifies particular protected groups and towards a more general focus on identity-motivated attacks on the members of vulnerable, marginalised and/or distinctive cultures (see Chakraborti and Garland, 2012 for one possible approach). Debate will and should ensue, of course, over the feasibility and desirability of such a trajectory. Whichever way the debate goes, Greater Manchester Police's announcement about alternative subcultures represents a significant challenge to traditional understandings of hate crime.

References

Barker, M. (2003) 'Satanic Subcultures? A Discourse Analysis of the Self-Perceptions of Young Goths and Pagans', in T. Waddell (ed.), *Cultural Expressions of Evil and Wickedness: Wrath, Sex, Crime*, Amsterdam: Editions Rodopi BV, pp. 37–57.
Bennett, A. (1999) 'Subcultures or Neo-Tribes? Rethinking the Relationship Between Youth, Style and Musical Taste', *Sociology* 33 (3): 599–617.
Bennett, A. (2006) 'Punk's Not Dead: The Continuing Significance of Punk Rock for an Older Generation of Fans', *Sociology* 40 (2): 219–235.
Bennett, A. and Hodkinson, P. (2012) *Ageing and Youth Cultures: Music, Style and Identity*, Oxford: Berg.
Bowling, B. (1998) *Violent Racism: Victimisation, Policing and Social Context*, Oxford: Clarendon Press.
Brill, D. (2008) *Goth Culture: Gender, Sexuality and Style*, Oxford: Berg.
Byers, B., Crider, B.W. and Biggers, G.K. (1999) 'Bias Crime Motivation: A Study of Hate Crime Offender Neutralization Techniques Used against the Amish', *Journal of Contemporary Criminal Justice*, 15 (1): 78–96.
Chakraborti, N. (2010) 'Future Developments for Hate Crime Thinking: Who, What and Why?', in N. Chakraborti (ed.), *Hate Crime: Concepts, Policy, Future Directions*, Cullompton: Willan, pp. 1–14.
Chakraborti, N. and Garland, J. (2012) 'Reconceptualising Hate Crime Victimisation Through the Lens of Vulnerability and "Difference"', *Theoretical Criminology*, 16 (4): 499–514.
Cohen, A. (1955) *Delinquent Boys: The Culture of the Gang*, London: Collier-MacMillan.
Dixon, B. and Gadd, D. (2006) 'Getting the Message? "New" Labour and the Criminalization of "Hate"', *Criminology and Criminal Justice*, 6 (3): 309–328.
Freeman, F. (2013) 'Isn't "Hate Crime" Against Goths and Punks Just Old Fashioned Yobbery', *Daily Telegraph*, 4 April, http://blogs.telegraph.co.uk/news/colinfreeman/100210429/isnt-hate-crime-against-goths-and-punks-just-old-fashioned-yobbery/, accessed June 2013.

Gadd, D. (2009) 'Aggravating Racism and Elusive Motivation', *British Journal of Criminology*, 49 (6): 755–771.
Gardner, T. (2009) 'Rothwell: Man's Ear Sliced Off in Thugs' Rampage', *Rothwell Today*, 8 June, www.rothwelltoday.eo.uk/news/Rothwell-Man39s-ear-sliced-off.-5344242.jp, accessed 9 June 2013.
Garland, J. (2010a) '"It's a Mosher Just Been Banged for No Reason": Assessing the Victimisation of Goths and the Boundaries of Hate Crime', *International Review of Victimology*, 17 (2): 159–177.
Garland, J. (2010b) 'The Victimisation of Goths and the Boundaries of Hate Crime', in N. Chakraborti (ed.), *Hate Crime: Concepts, Policy, Future Directions*, Cullompton: Willan, pp. 40–57.
Garland, J. (2014) 'Reshaping Hate Crime Policy and Practice: Lessons from a Grassroots Campaign – An Interview with Sylvia Lancaster, Founder of the Sophie Lancaster Foundation', in N. Chakraborti and J. Garland (eds), *Responding to Hate Crime: The Case For Connecting Policy And Research*, Bristol: Policy Press, pp. 39–53.
Goulding, C. and Saren, M. (2009) 'Performing Identity: an Analysis of Gender Expressions at the Whitby Goth Festival', *Consumption Markets & Culture*, 12 (1): 27–46.
Greater Manchester Police (GMP) (2013) 'Hate Crime' at www.gmp.police.uk/content/section.html?readform&s=C4D5E39C4F3817F680257961004019B9, accessed 15 June 2013.
H.M. Government (2012) 'Challenge it, Report it, Stop it: the Government's Plan to Tackle Hate Crime', at www.gov.uk/government/uploads/system/uploads/attachment_data/file/97849/action-plan.pdf, accessed June 2013.
Hodkinson, M. (2008) 'On 11 August 2007 a Young Goth Died at the Hands of a Brutal Teenage Gang: One Year On, Thousands of Her Supporters the World Over Have United in the Name of Tolerance – and the Girl Who Dared to be Different'. *Observer Magazine*, 3 August, pp. 29–34.
Hodkinson, P. (2002) *Goth: Identity, Style and Subculture*. Oxford: Berg.
Hodkinson, P. (2011) 'Ageing in a Spectacular 'Youth' Culture: Continuity, Change and Community Amongst Older Goths', *British Journal of Sociology*, 62 (2): 262–282.
Hodkinson, P. (2012) 'Family and Parenting in an Ageing "Youth Culture": A Collective Embrace of Dominant Adulthood?', *Sociology*, online before print, at http://soc.sagepub.com/content/early/2012/12/10/0038038512454351.abstract
Iganski, P. (2008) *Hate Crime and the City*, Bristol: The Policy Press.
Jones, N. (2013) 'Are Attacks on Goths, Heavy Metal Fans and Other "Subcultures" Hate Crimes?' *New Statesman* at www.newstatesman.com/nelson-jones/2013/04/are-attacks-goths-heavy-metal-fans-and-other-subcultures-hate-crimes, 4 April, accessed June 2013.
Jones, O. (2012) *Chavs: The Demonisation of the Working Class*, London: Verso.
Kidd, J. and Witten, T. (2008) 'Transgender and Transsexual Identities: The Next Strange Fruit – Hate Crimes, Violence and Genocide against the Global Trans-communities', *Journal of Hate Studies*, 6 (1): 31–63.
Kruse, H. (1993) 'Subcultural Identity in Alternative Music Culture', *Popular Music*, 12 (1): 31–43.
Malbon, B. (2000) *Clubbing: Dancing, Ecstasy and Vitality*, London: Routledge.
Mason-Bish, H. (2014) 'We Need to Talk about Women: Examining the Role of Gender in Hate Crime Policy', in N. Chakraborti and J. Garland (eds), *Responding to Hate Crime: The Case For Connecting Policy And Research*, Bristol: Policy Press, forthcoming.
McDevitt, J., Levin, J. and Bennett, S. (2002) 'Hate Crime Offenders: An Expanded Typology', *Journal of Social Studies*, 58 (2): 303–317.
Muggleton, D. (2000), *Inside Subculture: The Postmodern Meaning of Style*, Oxford: Berg.
Perry, B. (2009) 'The Sociology of Hate: Theoretical Approaches', in B. Levin (ed.), *Hate Crimes: Understanding and Defining Hate Crime*, Westport, CT: Praeger, pp. 55–76.
Price, S. (2013) 'Violence against Goths is a Hate Crime', *Guardian*, at www.guardian.co.uk/commentisfree/2013/apr/04/violence-against-goths-hate-crime?CMP=twt_gu, accessed June 2013.
Sedgewick, M. (2013) 'How Are Goths and Emos Defined?', *BBC News Magazine* at www.bbc.co.uk/news/magazine-22026044, 14 April, accessed 13 June 2013.
Smyth, C. (2010) *Weirdo. Mosher. Freak: The Murder of Sophie Lancaster*, Reading: Pomona Books.
Taylor, J. (2013) 'Sophie Lancaster: The Murder that Caused a Subculture to Fight Back', *Independent* at www.independent.co.uk/news/uk/crime/sophie-lancaster-the-murder-that-caused-a-subculture-to-fight-back-8560733.html, 4 April, accessed 6 June 2013.

Taylor, J., Jaffer, N. and Renaud-Komiya, N. (2013) '"The Abuse Has Become a Daily Thing": Punks and Goths Hail Overdue Recognition', *Independent* at www.independent.co.uk/news/uk/crime/the-abuse-has-become-a-daily-thing-punks-and-goths-hail-overdue-recognition-8559181.html

Thornton, S. (1995) *Club Cultures: Music, Media and Subcultural Capital*, Cambridge: Polity.

Tyler, I. (2008) '"Chav Mum, Chav Scum": Class Disgust in Contemporary Britain', *Feminist Media Studies*, 8 (1). pp. 17–34.

Walters, M.A. (2011) 'A General *Theories* of Hate Crime? Strain, Doing Difference and Self Control', *Critical Criminology*, 19 (4): 313–330.

19
Hate crimes against Gypsies, Travellers and Roma in Europe

Zoë James

Gypsies, Travellers and Roma experience more bias-motivated crime and discrimination in Europe than any other minority communities (Council of Europe, 2011). This chapter will explore how and why hate crimes have manifested against Gypsies, Travellers and Roma in Europe in the twenty-first century. In order to do this, the chapter will initially consider the context within which hate crime has arisen and in doing so will address some of the histories of Gypsies, Travellers and Roma in Europe. It will then go on to examine the extent of contemporary hate crimes against Gypsies, Travellers and Roma. The chapter will therefore identify the range of hate crime experiences of Gypsies, Travellers and Roma in Europe that range from extreme violence and murder, through serious harassment to hate speech and minor hate incidents inflicted upon them. Importantly, the chapter will consider how hate incidents have been conflated with the experiences of discrimination and prejudice that Gypsies, Travellers and Roma experience as 'hate crime'.

Having established the circumstances within which Gypsies, Travellers and Roma have become the object of hate in Europe and how that hatred has manifested, the chapter will go on to examine how the existence, or notion, of 'Europe' as a political and legal entity, has attempted to resolve this problem. Gypsies, Travellers and Roma have been set out as the ultimate 'Europeans', who are 'stateless' nomads (Hepworth, 2012; Goldston, 2010). In reality though, Gypsies, Travellers and Roma are citizens of states and their lifestyle does not and should not preclude them from the rights that citizenship entails. The chapter therefore considers the impact of the identities of Gypsies, Travellers and Roma as mobile communities in order to unpack their experiences of hate crime and discrimination. In conclusion, the chapter argues that Gypsies, Travellers and Roma experience hate crime and discrimination as a consequence of a set of othering processes that function to provide settled communities with an acceptable scapegoat for their fears and insecurities. These fears and insecurities have been born of a changing European environment that has been through rapid political change in the East and fiscal instability in the West.

Gypsies, Travellers and Roma in Europe: A brief history

In this chapter, I refer purposively to 'Gypsies, Travellers and Roma' in an attempt to encapsulate a diverse range of peoples living in Europe who have some commonality of identity based on their ethnic origins, their culture or their way of living that is often associated with nomadism. European academics and policy makers tend to refer solely to 'Roma' in reports and writing as per agreement at the first World Romani Congress in 1971 (Council of Europe, 2011). My English European origins however, require me here to represent Gypsies and Travellers in the United Kingdom (UK) who do not identify with the moniker 'Roma'. In the UK, a clear distinction is made between Gypsies, Travellers and Roma and pride is associated with each of those titles. This differs greatly to the European mainland, where the use of the word 'Gypsy' is often considered offensive or degrading in some way. The complexity over titling the peoples discussed here is typical of issues faced by Gypsy, Traveller and Roma communities across Europe.

The identities of Gypsies, Travellers and Roma in Europe are extremely diverse, including the Sinti, Kale, Manus, Kalderas, Lovari and Romanichals that Liegeois refers to as 'a rich mosaic of ethnic fragments' (1994: 12; Kostadinova, 2011). However, as in the UK, many European countries are occupied by Travellers that are not ethnically defined, but rather, are identified as such due to their nomadic or cultural lifestyles (James, 2013; Council of Europe, 2011). It may be safe to say that despite their contemporary differences, some Gypsies, Travellers and Roma do share a common ancestry. Historiographies have identified their origin as from the Indian subcontinent, from where they appear to have travelled to Europe in the fourteenth century. On arrival in Europe, Gypsies, Travellers and Roma dispersed throughout the region, often mobilising for commercial purposes (Brearley, 2001).

Acton (2010) argues that Gypsies, Travellers and Roma responded to the economic conditions they met on arrival in Europe that led those in the East to settle to pursue their economic goals, while those that arrived in the West became commercial nomads. Despite the settlement of Roma in the East (and increasing settlement of Gypsies, Travellers and Roma in the West), nomadism remained an important aspect of Gypsies, Travellers and Roma identity. As noted by Shubin and Swanson (2010) the mobility of Gypsies, Travellers and Roma does not require them to constantly travel, but can refer to their emotional mobility. Indeed, the lifestyle associated with nomadism, living in close groups with strong bonds of familial attachment and strict moral codes, is what signifies Gypsy, Traveller and Roma cultures most and what the different communities have most in common. It is also the aspect of Gypsies, Travellers and Roma lives that is least understood by other communities and which creates the boundary between those communities that are Gypsies, Travellers and Roma and those that are not. Ultimately, Gypsy, Traveller and Roma identity therefore goes beyond their 'ethnicity' (Csepeli and Simon, 2007) or their movement and rests with their lifestyle that is born of their nomadism.

The nomadic tradition of Gypsies, Travellers and Roma has meant that they have always stood out as different to other communities, as their lifestyle and culture has set them apart (Acton, 2010). This cultural divide has resulted in Gypsy, Traveller and Roma communities having experienced harassment and persecution since their arrival in Europe (Fraser, 1992). For example they experienced enslavement in fifteenth-century Romania, were banned from entering England, on pain of death, in the sixteenth century and were hunted as animals in seventeenth-century Holland (Kenrick and Puxon, 1972). They were subject to numerous anti-'vagabond' legislations in the eighteenth century and were considered outlaws that were imprisoned, forcibly settled and had their children taken from them into the nineteenth century (Brearley, 2001). Gypsies, Travellers and Roma were therefore criminalised and subjected to fear and terror throughout Europe.

Despite the enlightenment of the nineteenth century which saw some recognition of the language, music and culture of Gypsies, Travellers and Roma, the twentieth century saw no

Hate crimes against Gypsies, Travellers and Roma in Europe

abatement to their persecution. Over time Gypsies, Travellers and Roma identities have been characterised as pathologically criminal and developments in science that explored the nature of human beings had profoundly negative consequences for them. The 'founding father' of criminology, Cesare Lombroso, described Gypsies as 'atavistic'; physiological 'throwbacks' that were born criminal. Such pathologising of Gypsies, Travellers and Roma fed directly into the development of criminal biology that was taken up by Robert Ritter in the National Socialist Party of Germany in the 1930s and ultimately led to their genocide as part of the Nazi 'final solution' in the 1940s (Widmann, 2007).

The genocide of Gypsies, Travellers and Roma in the Second World War has often been ignored or marginalised, but is essential to conceptualising their societal position today and particularly their continued experiences of hate. Gypsies, Travellers and Roma refer to the Holocaust as the 'Porrajmos', which means the 'devouring' in Romani language. It is estimated that between 250,000 and 1,500,000 Gypsies, Travellers and Roma were killed, though records are extremely poor (Hancock, 2004). As part of the Nazi regime's policy of ethnic cleansing, Ritter's research on criminal biology was utilised by Himmler to justify a racialised definition of 'Gypsies', despite their apparent Aryan appearance, and they were sent to concentration camps, particularly Auschwitz.

Tragically, Himmler's project was highly effective and Hancock (2004) suggests that the genocide of Gypsies was so comprehensive that it left Gypsy, Traveller and Roma communities decimated and in disarray. They had lost so many people and their traditions and stories in the concentration camps that they subsequently dealt with those losses by not speaking about their time there (Kenrick, 1999). In the post-war period they were not recognised by authorities as having suffered, not even by the Nuremberg Trials in 1947 (Kostadinova, 2011).

The oral tradition of Gypsies, Travellers and Roma, as opposed to the literary tradition of Jews, meant that few records of the Porrajmos were made by Gypsy, Traveller and Roma communities. In fact, the development of knowledge and understanding of the experiences of Gypsies, Travellers and Roma in the Holocaust were largely written by Jewish scholars (Hancock, 2004). Further, the propensity of Gypsies, Travellers and Roma to not speak about negative experiences meant that their story was withheld, in part, by their own inability to discuss their losses (Kenrick, 1999).

In the post-war period then, Gypsies, Travellers and Roma in Europe were disparate communities, ravaged by war and lacking recognition. It was at this point that the difference between Gypsies, Travellers and Roma in Eastern and Western areas of Europe again became distinct, as Eastern Europe was taken over by communist regimes and capitalism flourished in the West. Within each of these environments Gypsies, Travellers and Roma continued to experience discrimination, prejudice and hate as stereotyped notions of their lifestyles and culture developed that were not challenged by authorities within or beyond states, or by the Gypsies, Travellers and Roma themselves.

In Eastern Europe, Gypsies, Travellers and Roma gained some respite under communism as they were incorporated into regimes that enforced policies of work and welfare for all, providing them with a sense of security (Brearley, 2001). However, the cultural expression of Gypsies, Travellers and Roma was suppressed within these regimes as their language, nomadism, self-employment and way of living was repressed by assimilationist policies and as a consequence their identity was vilified by the state and increasingly by the public. When Eastern European communism broke down in the 1990s, Gypsies, Travellers and Roma were among the first to lose their jobs and subsequently their homes. Factories set up under communism closed in the competitive markets of capitalism and the old stigmas attached to

Gypsies, Travellers and Roma emerged amongst the new leaders of post-communist states, a developing free-press and the public alike (Cahn and Vermeersch, 2007; Raihman, 2007).

In the West of Europe, the failure to challenge stereotypical, negative perceptions of Gypsies, Travellers and Roma by any authorities meant that the burgeoning populist media grasped them as a scapegoat for the ills of capitalist excess. As land and property had become more valuable in Western Europe and wealth was gained from its sale or use, Gypsies, Travellers and Roma were removed from it (Morris and Clements, 2002). Increasingly then, Gypsies, Travellers and Roma had no places to stop or stay on and they faced a crisis of accommodation (Pusca, 2010; James, 2011). Media accounts of the lives of Gypsies, Travellers and Roma stigmatised their communities, informing a negative public discourse (Richardson, 2006). Gypsies, Travellers and Roma were drawn by the media as lazy and work-shy, and over-archingly as unclean in some way, or 'dirty'.

Sibley (1988) utilises the work of Douglas (1966) on 'purity and danger' in order to unpack societal responses to Gypsies, Travellers and Roma. In doing so he notes the need of people to make sense of the world through processes of classification, and that those who cannot be classified are identified as pollutants, 'as a threat to the integrity of the collective' (Sibley, 1988: 410). Discussion amongst scholars of Gypsy, Traveller and Roma issues focus on the genesis of the threat posed by these communities, which is largely placed in their propensity to nomadism or their mobility. The nomadic nature of Gypsies, Travellers and Roma lifestyles, as noted above, places them apart from the rest of society and subsequently is used as a tool to exclude them. Gypsies, Travellers and Roma have therefore become a 'problem' in the perception of non-Gypsy society, fed by a malignant media.

Hating Gypsies, Travellers and Roma

In the late twentieth century then, Gypsies, Travellers and Roma faced a commonality of issues, despite their diverse communities and breadth of experiences throughout Europe. Their nomadic lifestyle was limited by a deficiency of space and place, they suffered from a lack of employment and opportunity, and they were demonised by the rest of society as 'pollutants'. They were beginning to be recognised by European agencies as the poorest people in Europe, with the worst accommodation, health and welfare of any minority communities (Brearley, 2001).

Despite the fact that Gypsies, Travellers and Roma make up the largest minority in Europe (Council of Europe, 2011) their plight has only recently been addressed by research, writing and political movements. This can be explained in part by the very nature of their distance from the rest of society. The lack of public empathy towards Gypsies, Travellers and Roma is augmented by a lack of knowledge or understanding of their communities. Little light is shone on how Gypsy, Traveller and Roma communities really live due to the fact that such communities are loath to open their doors to outsiders; they keep to themselves, guarding their privacy after so many years of vilification.

An excellent example of the irony of the stigma attached to Gypsies, Travellers and Roma, is the key tool used to attack them: the notion of them as 'dirty'. Gypsies, Travellers and Roma actually commonly follow strict rules of hygiene, based on their historic nomadism. These rules dictate how they live, work and socialise and they inform moral codes of behaviour. Despite some recent attempts to bring the real lives of Gypsies, Travellers and Roma into the public gaze through television programmes particularly, they remain stereotyping, rather than informative and focus on aspects of their lives that are the most challenging to outsiders' perceptions (Munk, 2007; Hutchings, 2013; Jensen and Ringrose, 2013).

Gypsies, Travellers and Roma therefore remain the most disliked communities in Europe, as the twenty-first century advances. Numerous studies and surveys have identified negative public attitudes towards Gypsies, Travellers and Roma (for example, Frazer and Marlier, 2011; Csepeli and Simon, 2007; Gounev and Bezlov, 2006) and Goldston (2002: 157) suggests that prejudice against them is 'casual' and 'insidious' throughout Europe, resulting in it becoming normalised. It is unsurprising then that politicians and officials have been able to voice negative views against Gypsies, Travellers and Roma without recourse (Parker, 2012) and subsequently, governmental policies and legislations have been created that directly discriminate against and criminalise Gypsies, Travellers and Roma.

For example, in the UK legislation has prevented Gypsies, Travellers and Roma from staying on publicly owned land (James, 2007); in Italy Gypsies, Travellers and Roma were subject to fingerprinting and expulsion (Clough Marinaro, 2009); in Turkey they were removed forcibly from areas to allow for the gentrification of cities (Somersan and Kirca-Schroeder, 2007); and in Slovakia they were not allowed to live in certain areas (Goldston, 2006), to name but a few. These policies have acted to place Gypsies, Travellers and Roma within a 'discourse of punishment' (Bancroft, 2000), rather than provision and as such their identity has been framed as offenders, rather than as victims (James, 2013). Such populist punitive approaches to Gypsies, Travellers and Roma have resulted in increased victimisation of them.

Gypsies, Travellers and Roma are victimised in two distinct ways that are conflated by the fact that each is motivated by bias or 'hate' against their communities. First, they are discriminated against by both state and non-state agencies and they therefore experience prejudice in their daily lives. Second, they experience crimes committed against them that are motivated by hate. The conflation of discrimination and traditionally understood 'hate crimes' against Gypsies, Travellers and Roma in Europe has occurred for a number of reasons: Gypsies, Travellers and Roma tend to place their experiences of hate on a continuum that ranges from crimes committed against them, to their poor treatment by state and non-state agencies; the continued failure of states and agencies to challenge discrimination heightens their victimisation; and scholars of Gypsy, Traveller and Roma issues have incorporated analysis of *all* prejudicial actions and sentiments against them as 'anti-Gypsyism' (James, 2014).

In terms of discrimination, Gypsies, Travellers and Roma do not receive the same levels of care and welfare that other communities access. They suffer high levels of deprivation and live in poor accommodation, have high infant mortality rates, poor general health and low life expectancy, and are discriminated against in education systems throughout Europe, resulting in some countries placing high proportions of their Gypsy, Traveller and Roma children in schools for children with learning difficulties (for an excellent European-wide summary of the welfare outcomes for Gypsies, Travellers and Roma, see Frazer and Marlier, 2011). Gypsies, Travellers and Roma are commonly refused services, including entrance to amenities such as libraries, launderettes, sports facilities and local community spaces (Cemlyn et al., 2009). Further, they are often refused entrance to shops, bars and restaurants (Goldston, 2006).

Perhaps the most serious discrimination experienced by Gypsies, Travellers and Roma though, is that where state agencies are complicit in the bullying or exclusion they receive. Additional to the populist punitive policies and legislation applied to Gypsies, Travellers and Roma from the top of states down, as outlined above, research papers detail horrific acts meted out on Gypsies, Travellers and Roma by local policing agencies and local authorities. For example, in Hungary police physically abused suspects in their custody and took part in local violence against a Romani man (Szikinger, 2010). In Serbia police used torture against members of the Roma community, and were often violent and abusive towards them

(Kesetovic, 2009). In Romania, Roma communities were ghettoised by local authorities that constructed large walls to exclude and hide them from other Romanians (Bumbu, 2012) and in Slovakia police used cruelty and brutality against Roma and coercion and segregation was practised by local authorities (Buckova, 2012). In Italy Gypsies, Travellers and Roma were forced to live in 'camps' that equated to ghettos (Clough Marinaro, 2009) or they were expelled from the country (Costi, 2010). Similarly, in France, police brutality was used in forced evictions (James, 2007) and Gypsies, Travellers and Roma were expelled from the country (Pusca, 2010).

This discrimination experienced by Gypsies, Travellers and Roma from multiple agencies and actors across Europe (I have only provided a brief snapshot here), has fed into the vicious cycle of stereotyping. This stereotyping is fed by the media and has increased public dislike of their communities. Further, particularly in post-communist Eastern Europe, Gypsies, Travellers and Roma have suffered exclusion to the degree that they have turned to petty crime to survive. This criminality has been perceived as evidence of their inbred delinquency and has further augmented other communities' hatred of Gypsies, Travellers and Roma (Brearley, 2001). They have subsequently been met by mob violence that amounts to pogroms in many countries, including in Poland, Hungary, Slovakia, Romania and the Czech Republic (Brearley, 2001). Such shocking violence has rarely been held to account by either state or European authorities.

In both the East and West of Europe, Gypsies, Travellers and Roma are hated within their own countries due to public belief in stereotypes of their criminality and their lifestyles as previously discussed. They are also hated for their mobility. In the East they are hated because they are believed to have brought disrepute to Eastern European countries when they have moved into Western Europe. In the West, they are hated because they are perceived as invaders (Kabachnik, 2010) from the East, despite the fact that most Western European Gypsies, Travellers and Roma have resided there for generations, even centuries. Within this environment of hate and frustration, far-right political movements have latched on to the 'Roma-problem' as a tool to gain recognition, membership and electoral success.

Varying analyses of the role of far-right organisations in hate-motivated crimes against Gypsies, Travellers and Roma in Europe exist, with some placing their involvement at the root of all hate crimes (Brearley, 2001) and others seeing them as riding the populist wave of anti-Gypsyism (European Union Minorities and Discrimination Survey, 2012). It is quite likely that both of these analyses are true, as different states' histories determine the activity and prominence of far-right groups (Savelsberg and King, 2005). In real terms, knowledge of hate crimes committed against Gypsies, Travellers and Roma is limited, as countries lack effective recording practices. Furthermore, throughout Europe, Gypsies, Travellers and Roma rarely report hate crimes committed against them to the authorities, due to their lack of faith in criminal justice systems. For example, the European Union Minorities and Discrimination Survey (2012) found that despite very high levels of violence and harassment experienced by Roma, 75 per cent of victims were unwilling to report such offences to the police due to a lack of confidence in them. Also, Gypsies, Travellers and Roma do not report hate crimes for similar reasons to other hate crime victims: they lack faith in the police as above, they perceive that there is little that could be done to resolve the problem, the problem is normalised within their communities or they perceive the problem as too minor to involve authorities (Hall, 2005).

The lack of consistent recording of hate crimes across Europe raises particular issues in tackling it. In the UK recording tools have been set up by both state and non-state organisations to capture hate crime levels. Though these can be problematic in themselves (Christman and

Wong, 2010), they are comprehensive relative to other European countries. This means, however, that the UK hate crime statistics are high in comparison to the rest of Europe, which implies that the UK has a greater hate crime problem than other European states (Donnelly, 2002). Indeed, some states in Europe have denied any issues with hate crime, utilising a lack of records as evidence of this (Frazer and Marlier, 2011).

High levels of discrimination and hate crime against Gypsies, Travellers and Roma across Europe since the 1990s have been recorded by research however (Stewart, 2012; European Union Minorities and Discrimination Survey, 2012; OSCE, 2012, 2011) and public resentment of Gypsy, Traveller and Roma communities has even led to protests and riots (Ivanov, 2012). Even a brief review of literature provides comprehensive information on the serious crimes committed against Gypsies, Travellers and Roma that are not reflected in any official statistics. For example, in Hungary between 2008 and 2009 six Roma people were killed in incidents when 'Molotov cocktails' were thrown at their homes and they were shot as they attempted to flee (Daroczi, 2012). In the UK in 2003, a young boy was beaten to death as perpetrators said, 'he was only a Gypsy' (James, 2013) and similarly, in the Czech Republic a Roma man was stabbed to death following racial abuse in a bar (Goldston, 2010). In Italy in 2008, a Roma camp was set fire to following a conflict between the Roma community and their settled neighbours the previous day (Costi, 2010). OSCE reports on hate crimes in Europe (for example, 2012, 2011) detail numerous other examples of such serious hate crimes. Further, reports of other hate offences such as damage to homes, vehicles and sites, as well as other physical abuse against Gypsies, Travellers and Roma in Europe litter the pages of research papers (for example, James, 2014; Kyuchokov, 2012; Kabachnik and Ryder, 2010).

The role of 'hate speech' in the perpetuation of hate crimes in Europe evidences the other end of the spectrum of hate committed against Gypsies, Travellers and Roma. Hate speech is far less likely to be perceived as crime per se, but its impact on communities can be overwhelming as both individuals and whole communities can become beleaguered by it (Bowling, 1999). Again, the use of hate speech is identified in multiple research studies across Europe (Stewart, 2012; Vidra and Fox, 2012; Mirga, 2009). Goldston (2002) cites the hate speech of powerful elites in dictating negative public attitudes towards Gypsies, Travellers and Roma. So, he refers to a Hungarian Mayor in 2000, who he reports as saying, 'The Roma . . . have no place among human beings. Just as in the animal world, parasites must be expelled' (Goldston, 2002: 156). The media amplifies such negative attitudes and behaviour with similarly problematic hate speech. For example, in the UK in 2005, a popular national daily newspaper ran a campaign against Gypsies and Travellers entitled, 'Stamp on the Camps' (Dear, 2005). The use of hate speech then frames the stigma attached to Gypsies, Travellers and Roma in Europe, exacerbating their experiences of discrimination and hate crimes committed against them.

European responses to hate against Gypsies, Travellers and Roma

Hate speech against Gypsies, Travellers and Roma has been used for political gains by far-right groups in Eastern Europe (Mirga, 2009), which Csepeli and Simon (2007) suggest has interrupted the development of positive relations with Gypsy, Traveller and Roma communities. At the same time some Eastern European countries have courted membership of the EU and have tried to minimise the extent of their problematic issues with Gypsy, Traveller and Roma communities to that end (Sobotka and Vermeersch, 2012). As part of the process of accession to the EU, Eastern European states have been required to address their human rights record, and so the gaze of the EU and its related agencies, such as the Council of Europe and the Organisation for Security and Cooperation in Europe (OSCE), that have specific human rights agendas, have enhanced their consideration of the lives of Gypsies, Travellers and Roma.

This process has led to an interrogation of data and evidence on discrimination towards Gypsies, Travellers and Roma that has resulted in the 2011 EU Framework for National Roma Integration Strategies up to 2020 (Luggin, 2012) and increased monitoring of 'anti-Gypsyism' across Europe by the Office for Democratic Institutions and Human Rights under the remit of the OSCE. Reporting to these organisations remains poor, however, as countries aspiring to EU entry, or newly entered continue to hide hate and discrimination towards Gypsies, Travellers and Roma within their state boundaries (OSCE, 2012, 2011).

Individual state policies on prejudice and discrimination differ widely across Europe, dependent on their origins. As Savelsberg and King (2005: 579) note, 'collective memory' and 'cultural trauma' activate different national responses to hate victimisation for 'political, legal and moral purposes'. So, the resounding memory of the Holocaust in Western Europe has resulted in particular concerns regarding the development of far-right political activism, whereas this has been overtaken in the East by the more recent memory of communist control and repression, potentially leaving space for far-right political voices to be heard. The EU developed from the perspective of the West, with its onus on ensuring human rights and therefore its policies reflect this perspective. In the rest of Europe, organisations such as the OSCE attempt to drive the human rights agenda forward, but it is often non-governmental organisations that have pushed for change most effectively, partly due to their local knowledge of the realities of hate crimes and discrimination against Gypsies, Travellers and Roma.

Ignatoiu-Sora (2011) argues that the development of rights organisations, such as the European Roma Rights Centre in Hungary, has resulted in better recognition of discrimination and offending against Gypsies, Travellers and Roma. Despite EU programmes to improve knowledge of discrimination and hate towards Gypsies, Travellers and Roma and policies designed to tackle such problems, their implementation is met by bottlenecks at national, regional and local levels due to institutionalised prejudice, as outlined above (Sobotka and Vermeersch, 2012).

Therefore, minority rights law is being increasingly utilised by non-governmental organisations to ensure that Gypsies, Travellers and Roma in Europe are recognised as equal citizens of states and that resources are redistributed to them (Kostadinova, 2011). Such initiatives, from the bottom of states up, challenge local, regional and national approaches to Gypsies, Travellers and Roma in order to prevent discrimination against them and to lift them out of poverty more effectively (Goldston, 2010). Following successful use of minority rights law within states that have such laws enshrined, and use of EU law when they have not, resources have begun to make a positive impact on Gypsy, Traveller and Roma communities in Europe. Goldston (2002) suggests that there have been improvements in media representations of Gypsies, Travellers and Roma and EU grants have been utilised to improve educational opportunities. Some policing approaches have also subsequently improved, so training of police in Slovenia for example has resulted in improved relations between police and Gypsies, Travellers and Roma, which has also resulted in better overall community relations (Strobl et al., 2013). Also, in Poland, development of human rights legislation has improved public perceptions of Gypsies, Travellers and Roma (Celinska and Gutkowska, 2013).

Conclusion: Recognising hate against Gypsies, Travellers and Roma

In this chapter I have attempted to provide an overview of hate crimes committed against Gypsies, Travellers and Roma in Europe and some responses to them. In doing so, I have not prescribed boundaries of what 'Europe' constitutes, but have intentionally distinguished between the East and the West. I have done this in order that any commonality of problems can be drawn out, while their genesis can be distinguished. As such, the chapter refrains, I hope, from ethnicising the experiences of Roma in the East and nomadising Gypsies and Travellers in the West (Simhandl, 2006). Academic discourse surrounding Gypsies, Travellers and Roma is fraught with difficulty, as any attempt to homogenise such heterogeneous communities should. I have therefore tried here to be all-encompassing, to include all those people who may perceive themselves as Gypsy, Traveller or Roma, akin to the UK definition of hate crime that allows for the perception of prejudice by any person (James, 2014).

In presenting the hate experiences of Gypsies, Travellers and Roma here, the chapter initially identified their placing as 'others' in communities. This process of othering has occurred in Europe through historic ignorance of the cultural differences of Gypsies, Travellers and Roma, through pathological determination of their identity and their exclusion from society. The chapter has therefore provided an outline of the contemporary position of Gypsies, Travellers and Roma as framed by a stigma that has been perpetuated by the media and utilised by populist punitive political agendas throughout Europe. In such conditions Gypsies, Travellers and Roma have experienced high levels of hate crime and discrimination against them, some of which I have detailed here. A paucity of official records of hate crime is available however, and therefore state responses to hate crimes have been relatively limited. Nor have states seen the utility of addressing hate against Gypsies, Travellers and Roma, given the extent of public dislike of such communities. Nevertheless, an increasing gaze of European-wide agencies and pressure from local non-governmental organisations has slowly brought to light the extent of discrimination and hatred against Gypsies, Travellers and Roma which is making change possible. As such 'anti-Gypsyism', or 'Romaphobia' (Ljujic et al., 2012) is being tackled more.

Despite positive strides made, the extensive nature of hate crime against Gypsies, Travellers and Roma in Europe, and their exacerbation since the 1990s, as detailed in this chapter, need greater recognition. As post-communist countries in the East of Europe struggle to manage the vagaries of market economies, so community insecurities continue to rise and othering processes function to provide a scapegoat for these fears in the figures of Gypsies, Travellers and Roma. Similarly, in the West of Europe, state recession as a consequence of fiscal crises, has led to greater competition for resources and subsequent community tensions that place Gypsies, Travellers and Roma as scapegoats for the losses communities have experienced. Therefore throughout Europe, Gypsies, Travellers and Roma continue to struggle for a voice, a place and space to exist free of acrimony, hostility and hate.

References

Acton, T. (2010) 'Theorising Mobility: Migration, nomadism, and the social reconstruction of ethnicity'. In: *Romani Mobilities in Europe Conference*. University of Oxford.
Bancroft, A. (2000) '"No Interest in Land": Legal and Spatial Enclosure of Gypsy-Travellers in Britain'. *Space and Polity*, 4(1): 41–56.
Bowling, B. (1999) *Violent Racism: Victimisation, Policing and Social Context*. Oxford: Oxford University Press.
Brearley, M. (2001) 'The Persecution of Gypsies in Europe'. *American Behavioural Scientist*, 45(4): 588–599.
Bumbu, G. (2012) 'Antigypsyism in Romania'. In: Kyuchokov, H. (ed.), *New Faces of Antigypsyism in Modern Europe*. Prague: Decade Trust Fund.
Cahn, C. and Vermeersch, P. (2007) 'The group expulsion of Slovak Roma by the Belgian government: A case study of the treatment of Romani refugees in western countries'. *Cambridge Review of International Affairs*, 13(2): 71–82.

Celinska, K. and Gutkowska, A. (2013) 'The Polish Roma: From a persecuted to a protected minority'. *International Journal of Comparative and Applied Criminal Justice*. DOI: 10.1080/01924036.2013.813398. Published online: 05/07/2013.

Cemlyn, S., Greenfields, M., Burnett, S., Matthews, Z. and Whitwell, C. (2009) *Inequalities experienced by Gypsy and Traveller Communities: A review*. London: EHRC.

Christman, K. and Wong, K. (2010) 'Hate crime victims and hate crime reporting: some impertinent questions'. In: Chakraborti, N. (ed.), *Hate Crime: Concepts, policy and future directions*. Cullompton: Willan.

Clough Marinaro, I. (2009) 'Between Surveillance and Exile: Biopolitics and the Roma in Italy'. *Bulletin of Italian Politics*, 1(2): 265–287.

Costi, N. (2010) 'The spectre that haunts Italy: The systematic criminalisation of the Roma and the fears of the *Heartland*'. *Romani Studies*, 20(2): 105–136.

Council of Europe (2011) *The Council of Europe: Protecting the rights of Roma*. Strasbourg: Council of Europe.

Csepeli, G. and Simon, D. (2007) 'Construction of Roma Identity in Eastern and Central Europe: Perception and Self-identification'. *Journal of Ethnic and Migration Studies*, 30(1): 129–150.

Daroczi, A. (2012) 'Antigypsyism in Hungary'. In: Kyuchokov, H. (ed.), *New Faces of Antigypsyism in Modern Europe*. Prague: Decade Trust Fund.

Dear, P. (2005) 'Gypsy campaign raises ethics issue'. *BBC News*. 11/03/2005.

Donnelly, E. (2002) 'Hate Crimes Against Travellers'. *Criminal Justice Matters*, 48(1): 24–25.

Douglas, M. (1966) *Purity and Danger: An Analysis of Concepts of Purity and Taboo*. London: Routledge Kegan Paul.

European Union Minorities and Discrimination Survey (2012) *Data in Focus Report: Minorities as Victims of Crime*. EU: European Union Agency for Fundamental Rights.

Fraser, A. (1992) *The Gypsies*, Oxford: Blackwell.

Frazer, H. and Marlier, E. (2011) *Promoting the social inclusion of Roma*. EU: Employment, Social Affairs and Equal Opportunities.

Goldston, J. (2002) 'Roma Rights, Roma Wrongs'. *Foreign Affairs*, 81(2): 146–162.

Goldston, J. (2006) 'Public Interest Litigation in Central and Eastern Europe: Roots, Prospects, and Challenges'. *Human Rights Quarterly*, 28(2): 492–527.

Goldston, J. (2010) 'The Struggle for Roma Rights: Arguments that Have Worked'. *Human Rights Quarterly*, 32(2): 311–325.

Gounev, P. and Bezlov, T. (2006) 'The Roma in Bulgaria's Criminal Justice System: From Ethnic Profiling to Imprisonment'. *Critical Criminology*, 14(3): 313–338.

Hall, N. (2005) *Hate Crime*. Cullompton: Willan.

Hancock, I. (2004) 'Romanies and the Holocaust: A Reevaluation and an Overview'. In: Stone, D. (ed.), *The Historiography of the Holocaust*. New York: Palgrave Macmillan.

Hepworth, K. (2012) 'Abject citizens: Italian "Nomad Emergencies" and the deportability of Romanian Roma'. *Citizenship Studies*, 16(3–4): 431–449.

Hutchings, S. (2013) 'The gypsy as vanishing mediator in Russian television coverage of interethnic tension'. *Nationalities Papers: The Journal of Nationalism and Ethnicity*, DOI: 10.1080/00905992.2013.801417. Published online: 22/05/2013.

Ignatoiu-Sora, E. (2011) 'The discrimination discourse in relation to the Roma: its limits and benefits'. *Ethnic and Racial Studies*, 34(10): 1697–1714.

Ivanov, A. (2012) 'Antigypsyism in Bulgaria'. In: Kyuchokov, H. (ed.), *New Faces of Antigypsyism in Modern Europe*. Prague: Decade Trust Fund.

James, Z. (2007) 'Policing Marginal Spaces: Controlling Gypsies and Travellers'. *Criminology and Criminal Justice: An International Journal*, 7(4): 367–389.

James, Z. (2011) 'Gypsies and Travellers in the Countryside: managing a risky population'. In: Yarwood, R. and Mawby, R.I. (eds), *Constable Countryside? Policing, Governance and Rurality*. Aldershot: Ashgate.

James, Z. (2013) 'Offenders or Victims?: An exploration of Gypsies and Travellers as a policing paradox'. In: Phillips, C. and Webster, C. (eds), *New Directions in Race, Ethnicity and Crime*. Abingdon: Routledge.

James, Z. (2014) 'Policing Hate against Gypsies and Travellers: Dealing with the Dark Side'. In: Chakraborti, N. and Garland, J. (eds), *Responding to Hate Crime: The Case for Connecting Policy and Research*. Bristol: Policy Press.

Jensen, T. and Ringrose, J. (2013) 'Sluts that Choose vs Doormat Gypsies'. *Feminist Media Studies*, DOI: 10.1080/14680777.2012.756820. Published online: 25/01/2013.
Kabachnik, P. (2010) 'Place Invaders: Constructing the nomadic threat in England'. *The Geographical Review*, 100(1): 90–108.
Kabachnik, P. and Ryder, A. (2010) 'Nomadism and New Labour: Constraining Gypsy and Traveller mobilities in Britain'. In: *Romani Mobilities in Europe Conference*. University of Oxford.
Kenrick, D. (1999) *The Gypsies during the Second World War: In the shadow of the swastika*. Hatfield: University of Hertfordshire Press.
Kenrick, D. and Puxon, G. (1972) *The Destiny of Europe's Gypsies*. New York: Basic Books, Inc.
Kesetovic, Z. (2009) 'Understanding diversity in policing: Serbian perspectives'. *Policing: An International Journal of Police Strategies and Management*, 32(3): 431–445.
Kostadinova, G. (2011) 'Minority Rights as a Normative Framework for Addressing the Situation of Roma in Europe'. *Oxford Development Studies*, 39(2): 163–183.
Kyuchokov, H. (ed.) (2012) *New Faces of Antigypsyism in Modern Europe*. Prague: Decade Trust Fund.
Liegeois, J.-P. (1994) *Roma, Gypsies, Travellers*. Strasbourg: Council of Europe.
Ljujic, V., Vedder, P., Dekker, H. and van Geel, M. (2012) 'Serbian adolecents' Romaphobia and their acculturation orientations towards to Roma minority'. *International Journal of Intercultural Relations*, 36(1): 53–61.
Luggin, B. (2012) 'EU Anti-discrimination and Social Inclusion Politics'. In: Kyuchokov, H. (ed.), *New Faces of Antigypsyism in Modern Europe*. Prague: Decade Trust Fund.
Mirga, A. (2009) 'The Extreme Right and Roma and Sinti in Europe: A New Phase in the Use of Hate Speech and Violence?' *Roma Rights Quarterly*, 1/2009: 5–9.
Morris, R. and Clements, L. (2002) *At What Cost? The Economics of Gypsy and Traveller Encampments*. Bristol: The Policy Press.
Munk, V. (2007) '"Play to Me Gypsy!" How Roma Stars' Image Change in Hungarian Media'. In: Kallioniemi, K., Karki, K., Makela, J. and Salmi, H. (eds), *History of Stardom Reconsidered*. Turku: International Institute for Popular Culture.
OSCE (2011) *Hate Crimes in the OSCE Region: Incidents and Responses. Annual Report for 2010*. Warsaw: OSCE ODIHR.
OSCE (2012) *Hate Crimes in the OSCE Region: Incidents and Responses. Annual Report for 2011*. Warsaw: OSCE ODIHR.
Parker, O. (2012) 'Roma and the Politics of EU Citizenship in France: Everyday Security and Resistance'. *Journal of Common Market Studies*, 50(3): 475–491.
Pusca, A. (2010) 'The "Roma Problem" in the EU'. *Borderlands*, 9(2): 1–17.
Raihman, L. (2007) 'Between Litigation and Freedom of Speech'. *Roma Rights Quarterly*, 3/2007: 105–108.
Richardson, J. (2006) 'Talking about Gypsies: The Notion of Discourse as Control', *Housing Studies*, 21(1): 77–96.
Savelsberg, J. and King, R. (2005) 'Institutionalizing Collective Memories of Hate: Law and Law Enforcement in Germany and the United States'. *American Journal of Sociology*, 111(2): 579–616.
Shubin, S. and Swanson, K. (2010) '"I'm an imaginary figure": Unravelling the mobility and marginalisation of Scottish Gypsy Travellers'. *Geoforum*, 41: 919–929.
Sibley, D. (1988) 'Purification of space'. *Environment and Planning D: Society and Space*, 6(4): 409–421.
Simhandl, K. (2006) '"Western Gypsies and Travellers" – "Eastern Roma": the creation of political objects by the institutions of the European Union'. *Nations and Nationalism*, 12(1): 97–115.
Sobotka, E. and Vermeersch, P. (2012) 'Governing Human Rights and Roma Inclusion: Can the EU be a Catalyst for Local Social Change?'. *Human Rights Quarterly*, 34(3): 800–822.
Somersan, S. and Kirca-Schroeder, S. (2007) 'Resisting Eviction: Sulukule Roma in Search of Right to Space and Place'. *The Anthropology of East Europe Review*, 25(2): 96–107.
Stewart, M. S. (2012) 'New Forms of Anti-Gypsy Politics: A problem for Europe'. In: Stewart, M.S. (ed.), *The Gypsy Menace*. London: Hurst and Co.
Strobl, S., Banutai, E., Duque, S. and Haberfeld, M. (2013) 'Nothing to be done about them without them: The Slovenian National Police and Roma joint-training program'. *International Journal of Comparative and Applied Criminal Justice*. DOI: 10.1080/01924036.2013.813397. Published online: 15/07/2013.

Szikinger, I. (2010) 'The Roma in Hungary'. *Policing and Society*, 10(1): 91–106.
Vidra, Z. and Fox, J. (2012) 'The rise of the extreme right in Hungary and the Roma question'. *Accept Pluralism*, Issue 9/2012.
Widmann, P. (2007) 'The Campaign against the Restless: Criminal Biology and the Stigmatization of the Gypsies: 1890–1960'. In: Stauber, R. and Vago, R. (eds), *The Roma: A Minority in Europe: Historical, Political and Social Perspectives*. Budapest: Central European University Press.

20
Reflections on gendered masculine identities in targeted violence against ethnic minorities

Loretta Trickett

Contemporary debates about hate crime have had surprisingly little to say about gender, particularly when considering perpetrators. Based on a small empirical study in the UK, this chapter provides an exploration of data from interviews with a group of white males who regularly targeted Asian shopkeepers for physical and verbal abuse. The data demonstrates how the respondent's motivations for attacks were often informed by their reflections upon their own masculine identities. The chapter concludes that a greater focus on perceived threats to masculine identities could produce a more nuanced appreciation about why and how certain hate crimes manifest themselves.

Recent years have born witness to a considerable volume of research on victims of hate crime (see Chakraborti and Garland, 2012a); yet our knowledge on offenders is more limited (see Hamilton and Trickett, this volume). We assume that such crimes are based upon prejudice but remain unsure about exactly which socio-psychological factors are implicated. Further it is not always clear whether there are differences in the motivations of those who offend against disabled, lesbian, gay, bisexual and transgender (LGBT), ethnic and religious minority populations.

This chapter suggests that future research on hate crime offending needs to include an increased focus on gender. The consideration of gender has been somewhat limited in the hate crime field to date, albeit with some regard paid to it in research around hate crimes against the LGBT community. For example, Perry (2001: 107) has suggested that 'anti-gay' violence is an exercise in the construction of gender wherein victims of homophobic and transphobic violence are 'gender outsiders' within a 'heteronormative' society.[1] Gender has also been considered as a motivational factor in violence against women[2] and there have correspondingly been calls for the victimisation of women to qualify for inclusion as a separate category of hate crime (see McPhail, 2002; Drew, 2008).[3] Notwithstanding this, there has been scant academic attention paid to gender as a motivational factor in hate crime against ethnic minority groups.[4] Therefore, this chapter seeks to provide some insights into this area by examining extracts from interviews with white men living within a predominantly white area who regularly targeted Asian shopkeepers for physical and verbal abuse and their premises for acts of theft, criminal damage and vandalism.

Loretta Trickett

Theoretical background: Conceptualising hate crimes

Whilst there is disagreement about what the term 'hate crime' means (see Jacobs and Potter, 1998), a particularly useful conceptualisation has been that offered by Perry (2001) who envisages hate crime as involving a process of intimidation directed at particular communities to convey the message that they are 'different' and 'don't belong'. In this way hate crime involves attempts to assert authority and protect the hegemony (real or imagined) of the perpetrator's own group (Sheffield, 1995: 438).[5]

As noted by other scholars (see Hall, 2005) this definition is helpful in the way that it addresses both the political and social context through which hate crime develops, in particular, the 'relational disadvantages' (Stanko, 2001: 318) and the subsequent entrenched hierarchies of identity and power that underpin hate crimes.

In considering this, there is some value in using the lens of 'vulnerability' not only because it enables a wider range of victims to be examined but because it also takes account of the multi-layered context of hate crime incidents. This can help us to understand that the heightened risk posed to certain groups of individuals can arise through a complex interplay of different factors, including hate, prejudice, hostility, unfamiliarity, discomfort or simply opportunism or convenience (see Chakraborti and Garland, 2012b). Chakraborti and Garland (2012b) have suggested that these advantages outweigh any negative connotations associated with labelling hate crime victims as vulnerable because rather than victims actually being weak or powerless with limited capacity to resist, in fact the vulnerability concept can be used to encapsulate that this is the way that they are often viewed by many hate crime perpetrators.

A considerable advantage of the vulnerability approach is that it allows a more thorough examination of the context of victimisation including intersectionality (see also Mason-Bish, this volume). A person becomes a victim not due to a specific aspect of their identity per se, but rather because of how one particular aspect of their identity intersects with other facets of selfhood alongside situational factors to make them vulnerable in the eyes of perpetrators (see Chakraborti and Garland, 2012b). This enables us to move beyond singular constructions of identity to recognise the complex interplay of identities with other personal, social and situational characteristics that can be significant to hate crime incidents.

Of utmost importance to this chapter is that this complex interplay of personal, social and situational characteristics may affect the offender's perception of their own gendered identity and this may then manifest in perpetrating hate crimes. Arguably, hate crimes are not simply to do with the perceived vulnerability of the victim but they can also arise from a sense of weakness or inadequacy felt by the perpetrator involving a range of subconscious 'emotional and psychological processes' (Gadd and Dixon, 2009; Walters, 2011).

The remainder of the chapter will now turn to the importance of understanding how offenders may view victims through the lens of their own gendered identities. The question posed therefore is: what impact does the gendered self-identity of the perpetrator have on the targeting of ethnic minority victims for 'hate crimes'?

The research – methods

The dataset used in this chapter formed part of a larger study into the fear of crime and experiences of crime and victimisation with men and boys. The research was conducted in Birmingham, the second largest city in England, in an area that consisted largely of council housing. There were 45 respondents in total, broken down into 15 respondents from three age groups, 16–21, 21–45 and 60 plus.[6] All of the respondents were asked to provide demographic information on age, ethnicity, length of residence, schooling and work experience. They were questioned about their experiences of crime including their own offending behaviour, the area and communities in which they lived, their daily routines, and about earlier experiences including childhood and schooling. The interview schedule was based on open-ended questions and interviews lasted approximately one hour. Each interview was transcribed and the data coded using qualitative coding techniques extracting patterns across respondent's answers (Miles and Huberman, 2002; Mason, 2002).

This chapter is based on interview extracts from the youngest age group, ten of whom were part of a peer group regularly involved in crime and violence. Although, given the size of the sample, it is difficult to make large-scale generalisations from the data, it is nevertheless possible to identify issues which are important to a consideration of offending by young white men against men of ethnic minority status.

In terms of sampling the researcher used the method of non-probability quota sampling (see Miles and Huberman, 2002). The respondents discussed here were interviewed at or around the research site of a youth drop-in centre in the area. The researcher was introduced to the respondents by youth workers who were employed to work at the site and to walk the streets of the local area and a considerable amount of time was spent by the researcher 'hanging out' at the centre and sometimes on the streets with youth workers. Therefore over time the researcher became a familiar figure at the centre. Flyers and posters detailing the research were on view at the centre and young men were given plenty of information about the research and the ethics procedure; when consent was obtained a research protocol guaranteeing confidentiality was also provided. The researcher was a different sex to the research respondents and this must be taken into account when interpreting the data.

A researcher must always remain objective and professional when interviewing respondents even when faced with racist and sexist views and not allow their own feelings and opinions to affect the data-collection process. When faced with sexist and racist attitudes the researcher had to remain neutral in the situation but would ask respondents to explain why they felt as they did.

Intersectionality theory

Intersectionality theory explores the ways in which systems of oppression such as race, class, gender and sexuality simultaneously structure social relations (Collins, 1998; Crenshaw, 1991). Intersectional approaches posit that relations of domination should be understood as a mesh of mutually reinforcing power structures, operating in different yet overlapping ways being dependent on each other (Collins, 1998; Crenshaw, 1991; Bowleg, 2008; 2013; Shields, 2008). An intersectional approach encourages a fluid conceptualisation of gender,[7] which highlights its relationship with structure and personal agency. It is the practices of individuals over time that produce institutionalised structures seen as gender, race and class that in turn, inform individual practices.

One such institutionalised structure informing individual practices around gender is that of hegemonic masculinity; a term coined by Connell (1987, 1995) to describe a form of 'normative heterosexuality', which defines masculinity through difference from, and desire for, women. Hegemonic masculinity is normative in that it embodies the currently most honoured way of being a man and this involves the structuring of differing forms of masculinity within Westernised society wherein it is distinguished from other subordinated masculinities which are subsumed under it. As hegemonic masculinity is formed in relation to femininity and competing accounts, its position is constantly negotiated and sometimes altered following the resistance and challenge of such accounts. In this way hegemonic masculinity is understood as the pattern of practice that allows men's dominance over women to continue. Connell (1987, 1995) suggests that whilst only a minority of men might exemplify this Alpha male image; enough men are complicit with the hegemonic pattern to maintain its hierarchical position.

By drawing upon Connell's work, Messerschmidt (1993) makes the connection between agency and structure and emphasises the intersectional aspects of gender. He does so by conceptualising gender as a situational accomplishment of individuals wherein they simultaneously accomplish their race and class. During such situational accomplishments of identity individuals draw on existing and shared knowledge to configure the behaviour of themselves and others with reference to existing knowledge patterns and discourses; therefore hegemonic masculinity provides a resource to be used in such situational accomplishments of identity.

Over the life course building on a masculine identity involves a continual process (Jackson, 1990), which includes psychological and social factors such as sexual orientation, race and class together with one's historical experiences. It follows that the masculine identity of each man will be unique because each will select from the resources available to him and build these into his identity in a different way. The ability to draw upon potential identity resources will sometimes be limited by structural restraints (Messerschmidt, 1993), albeit how people draw upon resources will always involve a degree of personal choice. Whilst Hegemonic Masculinity has been extremely influential in research on gendered relations and masculinities – it has also been heavily criticised (see Beasley, 2008a, 2008b). One line of criticism has been the failure to develop any understanding of subjectivity and how men come to make discursive choices around masculinities (see Edley and Wetherall, 1995; Jefferson, 2002; Walklate, 1998; Whitehead, 2002) and the author has explained how these respondents make these choices in an earlier article (see Trickett, 2011).[8]

Intersectional aspects of respondent's identities

The respondents here were asked to describe what sort of man they saw themselves as and the masculine identities they discussed, which drew on discourses around hegemonic masculinity, put an over-riding emphasis on toughness, exhibiting power and control. This was similar to Hallsworth and Silverstone's (2009) 'on-roaders'; a term used to describe the chaotic 'gang' lifestyles of their respondents. What life 'on-road' tends to encourage is a daily existence characterised by a hyper-aggressive form of masculinity (see Campbell, 1993). This is a vision of purified masculinity informed by homophobia and misogyny (and in the case of the current respondents, racism) where being 'hard' assumes master status, there is no backing down to threats or provocation and violence is imperative when faced with disrespect both real and imagined (see Hallsworth and Silverstone, 2009).

The men in this chapter also engaged with this hyper-aggressive version of masculine identity largely because it was familiar and expected by their peers (it was more accessible than other versions of successful masculine identities albeit it also prevented them engaging with less damaging and violent versions – see Trickett 2011); in this way, the respondent's identities were largely defined by their membership of a gang which they self-defined as being based on friendship ties, shared social and geographical histories. The concept of a gang has been notoriously difficult to define (see Hallsworth and Young, 2008; Trickett, 2011)[9] but although the young men defined their gang as based on friendship within a geographical space, their descriptions of their gang also matched Hallsworth and Young's (2004) definition:

> A relatively durable, predominantly street-based group of young people who see themselves (and are seen by others) as a discernible group for whom crime and violence is integral to the group's identity.[10]

The respondents were also asked to explain how they saw themselves in terms of social class and were provided with selective categories and some explanation of these. They were also asked to describe their educational attainment and occupational history in detail. Whilst the respondents identified their lack of educational attainment and criminal records as being factors in their failure to obtain employment in discussions around their reflections on their daily lives, they still self-identified as working class albeit none of them was currently employed. Indeed, all were in receipt of benefits and all living with their mother or their mother and a step-father in council housing.

In terms of race these respondents identified as White English or British.[11] In contrast to their own claims of being British, the respondents referred to the shopkeepers concerned as Pakis and used this racist term to refer to anyone of Asian appearance. They did not consider Black or Asian people to be 'British'.

Gendered strain, difference and self-control

There were several themes which served as justifications when interviewees were discussing their actions against ethnic minority groups including both socio-economic strain and resentment towards difference. The interview extracts demonstrated hostility and racism towards minority people of colour (see also Bowling and Phillips, 2003) but these young men particularly disliked Asian shopkeepers for their ownership of businesses within the area.

In the interview discussions there were many examples of the practice of 'othering', which resonated with Kundnani's (2001) notion of popular racism (see also McGhee, 2005). Kundnani has referred to popular racism as 'kith and kin' racism that denotes a social process of exclusion based on colour, or latterly, cultural difference.

Larger cultural and political discourses informed the racism of the young men interviewed and it appeared that the racist opinions were largely influenced by family, friends and also the tabloid media. As argued by other researchers a general culture of racisms exist (see also Glaser et al., 2002) that can be contextualised with a context of socio-economic strain. Such cultures of prejudice are nurtured within families, friendship circles and by neighbours but have also been normalised by media and political discourses on race and immigration (Sibbitt, 1997; Ray and Smith, 2002; Ray et al., 2004; Gadd et al., 2005).

Within the discussions there were common ideas about both England and the local area being swamped with immigrants:

Sean (Aged 18)

They're taking over aren't they? They have so many kids and that, they'll be more pakis than white people soon.

The respondents drew on exaggerated claims that Asians were taking over 'their' area and used this to justify their hostility, in doing so they constructed Asians as non-white and unwanted inhabitants. These findings therefore echo those of other researchers who have found that as minority identity groups move into new areas they are often perceived as invaders of indigenous (or dominant) group territory (Green et al., 2001; Green et al., 1998; Perry, 2009b: 67; Sveinsson, 2009; Garner, 2011; Walters, 2011).

Lee (Aged 20)

They're trying to take over, they don't belong here, this is a white area, they should stay out of it.

Gary (Aged 21)

This is a white area and that's where I want to live, they should live with other pakis.

There were echoes of discourses around entitlement here based on whiteness which were linked to a familiar appeal to a nostalgic past of a White united Britain:

Mickey (Aged 16)

It was probably better when my dad was growing up, cos there was no pakis, I don't like 'em', Asian people, there was none in this country then, now there's loads.

Similar accounts have been provided by other studies on hate crime including those by Ray and Smith (2002) and Gadd et al. (2005) which also found that white inhabitants provided accounts of 'foreigners' as outsiders/outgroup and themselves as White British, belonging both to Britain and the immediate area (Gadd et al., 2005: 5).

In addition to arguments about the threat to a so-called 'white community' within the area and the 'British' way of life, these young men expressed 'socio-economic' resentment about Asian people being 'better off than them'. Indeed, whilst the respondents disliked Asians in general they particularly disliked Asian shopkeepers, who were arguably the most 'visible' Asians in the area and perceived to be 'wealthy'. In constructing Asians as 'outsiders' their business activities in the area were easily deemed to be illegitimate:

Kris (Aged 21)

I hate Pakis, they're money grabbing bastards.

Mickey (Aged 16)

This is England but you've got white men on the dole and pakis running shops, it's not on is it?

Sean (Aged 18)

We're on the dole and they are earning lots of money, it makes me sick.

The respondents claimed to be particularly aggrieved that Asian men in the area were 'making money' from the 'less well off' white people who were their customers:

Craig (Aged 17)

Why should pakis be better off than the white people who live here? Taking what little money they have.

Troy (Aged 18)

A lot of white people round here are on the dole or they've got crap jobs, and they are spending their money in the Paki shops, making them rich.

There was a suggestion that the white people who used Asian shops had no choice as white shops were miles away; in this way respondents deflected the fact that the Asian shops were providing a local service in the area:

Lee (Aged 20)

If you want to shop at a white shop now, you have to go miles away, to Tesco or something, most people can't be bothered to go there, so they are getting rich because white people have to shop there.

The contradiction in this quote is evident as it highlights the real reason that white people used the shops was because they were convenient which is alluded to in the statement 'most people can't be bothered to go to Tesco'.

Therefore many of the discursive attempts within the interview to construct ethnic minority shopkeepers as illegitimate inhabitants of the area were largely based on the rhetoric of White British 'entitlement' and attempts to reaffirm white ownership of geographical spaces; these themes were then used in order to justify actions as legitimate. Whilst justifying their hostility, respondents also used techniques of neutralisation (Sykes and Matza, 1957; Byers et al., 1999) to underplay their own agency and culpability in 'hate crime' incidents:

Brad (Aged 16)

I had a fight with one of them in there, they had banned me and I went in and they tried to get me out and I punched one, he asked for it.

Craig (Aged 17)

... me and my mates had a scuffle with them in there, we had nicked some cans of lager, they're loaded anyway, so why make them richer, they were telling us to get out and one of them kept pushing my mate, so he whacked him and then we all started fighting with them.

What these quotations illustrate are feelings of resentment towards foreigners for obtaining what are primarily perceived to be British businesses, housing and benefits (see also Esses et al., 2001; Bowling and Phillips, 2003; Ray and Smith, 2002; Gadd et al., 2005; Sveinsson, 2009; Garner, 2011). They are suggestive that these majority residents became fearful that incoming groups would impact on their social and economic security jeopardising positively valued goals (see also Green et al., 1998; Levin and McDevitt, 2002: 57; Ray and Smith 2002). Consequently minority identity groups conveniently became the scapegoat for the 'troubles' of the white majority living in the area (Agnew, 1992; Sibbitt, 1997; Young, 1999) whilst at the same time they were labelled as being 'inferior' and less respectable citizens (Levin and McDevitt, 2002; Levin and Rabrenovic, 2009; Craig, 2002).

Such research therefore demonstrates the pervasiveness of animosity held against certain ethnic minority groups that may be exacerbated by perceptions of socio-economic disadvantage. As Ray and Smith have argued this can frustrate individuals who see their general lack of social status, framed by their lack of obtaining material goods and property, as a personal failing. Whilst frustration is internalised as 'negative feelings' about the self it quickly re-surfaces as feelings of anger that are then directed towards 'outsiders'; who are seen as the source of the offender's own problems (see Sibbitt, 1997; Green, 1998; Gadd et al., 2005; Gadd and Dixon, 2009; Ray and Smith, 2002; Ray et al., 2004). In this way, some types of hate violence, particularly racist or anti-immigrant have been characterised as the culmination of unacknowledged shame rooted to a perpetrator's own social and economic disadvantage which is inevitably projected onto those perceived to be restricting the attainment of socially constructed goals (Ray and Smith, 2002).

However, although both older and younger respondents discussed such sentiments the difference was that the latter acted out their prejudice and the chapter now turns to further the explanation of why this was so. It is at this point that we can draw a connection with gendered feelings of inadequacy and shame, in that feelings around one's own social and economic disadvantage may lead to the questioning of one's masculinity and worth as a man.

A hard man or a failure? Contradictions in masculine identities, humiliation and resentment

Perry (2001) has argued that hate crime involves fears that Others will encroach upon the 'in-group's' identity and cultural norms and that this often leads to feelings of insecurity and negative emotions which individuals then transpose into animosity, an emotive reaction, which is used to gain a sense of control over those who they see as causing their insecurity, thus temporarily relinquishing the original negative feeling of fear (Perry, 2001). In this way individuals are doing 'difference' but as argued in the following examples, they are simultaneously 'doing masculinity'.

The respondents' resentment about socio-economic strain and their enactment of hate crimes as 'doing difference' were both partly as a result of prejudice but also linked to the respondents' reflections on their own masculine identities which involved grappling with contradictions around markers of manhood and indicators of success. In a previous article the author has discussed the precarious nature of the masculine identities of these respondents which were predominantly rooted in notions of being able to physically defend themselves and others. The fear of violence which may cause them to 'lose face' and consequently respect for their masculinity was a constant presence in the lives of these young men and the associated fear of humiliation was a driving factor behind the violence regularly used. Indeed, the driving force behind much of the violence used against other young men (often White men like themselves) was a fear of humiliation and losing face and control of the form of masculinity based on toughness, reputation and retaliation which was available to them (see Trickett, 2011).

This fear of humiliation over the questioning of one's masculine identity as not being 'a real man' also manifested itself in discussions about Asian inhabitants using their own language. The suspiciousness about this was linked to the fear of having one's masculinity questioned, such as someone suggesting that you were gay and not a real man whilst you did not realise that you were being insulted because you could not understand the language, as the following quotes illustrates:

Lee (Aged 20)

They could be saying anything about you couldn't they? Calling you a queer, a poof, and you wouldn't know about it.

Brad (Aged 16)

I hate how they talk in Paki language . . . you wonder if they are taking the piss, calling you a faggot or something.

Interestingly, the connection with 'gayness' is suggestive of the fear of the questioning of one's masculinity and sexuality. This is unsurprising given that these young men were extremely homophobic and the prevailing worry over being perceived 'as gay' and 'not truly male' lay at the heart of much of their anxiety about masculinity. The desire to know what was being said (to avoid being foolish and humiliated about one's masculinity) in order to challenge it with violence and re-establish oneself as truly male is illustrated by the next quote:

Troy (Aged 18)

He stands there and talks in his language, they should speak in English man, he could say anything about you, you ain't got a clue what he's saying, he could be really slagging you off, I don't wanna do French, that's no good to me. . . .I'd like to learn Paki language though, cos I'd want to know what they're saying about you, cos I could walk in the shop and he could say something about me but then I'd know and I could say 'what are you saying you fucking prick?'.

In addition to the fear of not being seen as a real man in terms of being tough and able to physically and verbally defend oneself, there was also a prevalent anxiety in discussions of reflections on daily lives and future prospects which were related to socio-economic strain, criminal records and limited ability to engage with alternative forms of successful masculinity. In a previous article the author has demonstrated how many of these young men wished to exit a gang lifestyle and expressed desires to have an easier and 'ordinary' life; some of them also expressed regrets about earlier lifestyle choices which had limited their options and when asked to reflect on their daily lives and whether there was anything that they would like to change several respondents expressed a desire to find employment:

Lee (Aged 20)

I'd like to have some money. I feel stuck. I don't get on with my step-dad and it causes arguments with my mum. It would be good to get out.

Ricky (Aged 18)

I've hardly had any work really since I left school . . . I mean had a job for a bit in a warehouse. It wasn't well paid, just casual, then I lost it. I was acting up and that and I got the push . . . I haven't been able to find anything since, that was over a year ago. I regret losing it now to be honest.

Some of them also expressed wishes to 'pay their way' and were aware of being dependent on others – 'embarrassingly' this was usually their mothers:

Sean (Aged 18)

I'd like to get a job, to give my mum some money, she's struggling, you know, so I'd like to help her out.

Ricky (Aged 18)

Since my dad died, I'm the man of the house like, but it's my mum and my sister that keep the house and everything going.

The contradictions in these interview accounts are informative, for in reality these 'so-called' hard men were still living as 'boys' and being kept by their 'mums'. None of them had a place of their own to live or their own transport and they travelled around the area on foot, by bus or often, on small child-like mountain bikes. This fuelled resentment of Asian shopkeepers and their younger sons. In the following quote jealousy about 'flash cars' – a long-known association with masculinity and lack of access to them is seen:

Gary (Aged 21)

I hate all of em . . . Pakis . . . some of the younger ones act all flash, driving round in BMWs and that and we are on mountain bikes. What a joke!

Moreover, these young men knew that far from being able to provide for themselves they were even less capable of providing for others:

Danny (Aged 20)

Once you've got a criminal record, you ain't gonna get a job. They just don't wanna know.

At the same time that some of these young men expressed desires to break away from a gang lifestyle and obtain a job and possibly have a family, they were aware that the likelihood of doing this was very limited i) through the difficulties in leaving a gang and a history of violence, and ii) through their lack of education and criminal convictions which made gaining employment, independence and associated benefits extremely difficult. Indeed, future opportunities were limited for these young men, as were their opportunities for engaging with alternative versions of masculinities that were not premised on violence and abuse. One of the respondents, Kris, had made an effort to limit his criminal and gang involvement due to having a young son, but had found that people he had offended in the past kept coming back to challenge him (see Trickett, 2011).

Therefore, whilst the acts of assault and vandalism against the Asian men and their premises were informed in large part by prejudicial attitudes around ethnicity, these were acutely linked to reflections upon masculine identities which included the questioning of what it meant to be a real man, in particular the claims to be a working class man whilst having no job and being dependent on others, often females, and the associated feelings of inadequacy and jealousy. In contrast, the Asian shopkeeper presented a 'visibly' alternative view of masculinity based on hard work, independence and provision for others, concepts that were unfamiliar to the young men in this study.

Whilst dislike of the Asian shopkeeper was partly fuelled by racism it was also premised on the ontological challenge that he presented to the precarious senses of selfhood of these young men. In short, he represented a challenge to their claims to define masculinity based on whiteness, territory, class and hardness and they resented him.

In order to constrain the threat posed by the figure of the Asian shopkeeper, as a possibly more successful man who was also ethnically 'different', these young men sought to disparage his version of masculinity by presenting him as a 'deluded' fool for providing for others and working hard and a 'weak' man who was unable to protect himself through violence. In this way they manage to deny him any kudos around independence and breadwinner roles, which they currently lacked, whilst using their own norms of masculinity based on toughness, defence and retaliation to find his masculinity wanting.

Containing the 'threat' to gendered identities

The respondents attempted to undermine the Asian shopkeeper's entrepreneurial spirit and work ethic by ridiculing his long working hours and provision for his family which was in stark contrast to their reflections and ruminations on their own current and future lives and being unable to provide for themselves and others:

Lee (Aged 20)

They think they're great don't they? Businessmen and all that, working all day and night in a poncey little shop, who would want to do that?

Gary (Aged 21)

. . . they've got a big car and a wife and loads of kids and that, I wouldn't want to be tied down like that and working all the time anyway, what a crap life.

Ricky (Aged 18)

They're mugs I reckon.

An alternative strategy was to ridicule the attempts of Asian men to defend themselves and their business interests in order to depict the Asian Man as weak in contrast to themselves as tough men who could look after themselves:

Kris (Aged 21)

They're pathetic . . . all mouth and no action.

This strategy involved accounts of Asian men as 'grassers' (when they had called the police). Once again this was deemed to be non-masculine according to gang norms around masculinity for grassing and was a despised practice within the gang (see also Heale, 2009; Hallsworth and Silverstone, 2009):

Troy (Aged 18)

The shop owners, I don't get on with none of them, I've had fights in there like, arguments with the owners and then they call the police, they got me arrested, they're sad, they can't deal with it on their own, so they just grass.

Sean (Aged 18)

He's grassed on me ain't he [shopkeeper] he got me took to court. It's just not right, he could have got me an extra twelve months on my sentence, they arrested me for affray and assault in the shop, he just couldn't deal with it himself, cos he's a wimp.

Even when Asian men attempted to fight back (a strategy always advocated by the gang), the legitimacy of their doing so was questioned. Although the respondents often resorted to group violence when dealing with threats from others and in self-defence and retaliation, efforts by Asian shopkeepers to defend themselves and their premises by using the same tactics were undermined:

> **Mickey (Aged 16)**
>
> ... I don't like any of them shopkeepers, they're all just nobs, just twats, they think they're hard and that, they try and mouth off at you, they tell me to get out of the shop, they get together and say 'Get out of the shop'. . .but they're not hard really, they just get loads of 'em together and mouth off, they don't do anything else . . . if they were really hard then one of them would take me on wouldn't they?
>
> **Lee (Aged 20)**
>
> ... they've tried to throw me out of the shop before, they got a load of them to do it, about ten or something, because they can't fight.

These accounts demonstrate how the respondents were doing masculinity and 'racial' difference in terms of their actions but also during their discursive practices in the interviews where they projected their own anxieties about being unable to provide for themselves and others onto the targets of their actions in order to call the masculinity of others in question rather than their own.

In doing so they attempted to depict themselves as successful, 'real white tough men' as compared to the weak Asian, non-white man, whose outer appearance of having a business, earning a wage and providing for others arguably established him as a more successful male. Feelings of fear here, as advocated by Perry, were based on the assumption that Others would encroach upon the 'in-group's' identity and cultural norms. But the cultural norms here concerned the respondent's masculinity as tough, White British working class men who exercised some power in the area. In this sense the Asian man presented a threat to all of these components of masculinity.

The resistance to these perceived threats to masculine self-identity took the form of violence and crime which had negative and serious implications both for others and the perpetrators themselves; the irony was that the more the men invested in these tough resistant masculine identities the more powerless they became and the more they blamed 'others' for their own powerlessness by diverting responsibility for their own situation.

The final piece of the jigsaw: gendered masculinities and self-control

In order to bridge the gap between the macro explanations of hate crime offending (social-economic strain and structured action, doing difference) with the micro level of individuals offending, Walters (2011) draws on Gottfredson and Hirschi's (1990) control theory. These authors suggested that most individuals do not commit crime because they have developed adequate self-control through socialisation processes within which the family is the primary influence; in contrast, most criminals will exhibit low-levels of self-control usually through inadequate parenting. Using Levin and McDevitt's typology of hate crime offenders, Walters (2011) suggests that some hate crime offenders including homophobic ones may commit hate crime partly for the thrill and the 'fun' presented by such offending. Certainly there were elements of that here.

These young men repeatedly targeted Asian shops even when they knew they had been banned and when the police had been called to earlier incidents. There was also the suggestion within the interview extracts that the respondents were 'defenders' of 'territory' (Levin and McDevitt, 1993) against invaders who have no rights to be living or working in the area. Both elements were present in the data discussed but importantly these individuals acted as they did because they had low levels of self-control in general and they were frequent users of violence to resolve inter-personal conflict (see Gadd et al., 2005; Ray and Smith, 2002).[12]

All of this, however, was linked to how they defined their masculinities. Indeed, being a frequent user of violence was the raison d'être of their masculinities. Therefore when offending against other young white men like themselves in the area they were asserting their physical dominance to offset threats to their reputations as tough men. Whereas when offending against ethnic minorities within the Asian shops, they were again attempting to assert that core toughness of masculine identity in response to the threat posed to their lack of ability to provide for themselves and others and claims to be working class. In contrast, other residents in the area may have harboured prejudicial opinions but their masculinity identities were not constructed in the same way; violence was not the central component and consequently they had more to lose by use of violence. Unfortunately, the respondents discussed here had very little to lose by their actions, the police were not always called to incidents, the men had criminal records and no jobs and they were asserting their masculinity and having 'a laugh' within their peer group. Therefore an emphasis on gendered strain, doing difference whilst doing masculinity and a lack of self-control linked to masculinity can do much to enhance our understanding of the encounters discussed.

Conclusion

This chapter has suggested that within hate crime encounters involving men attacking other men the factor of gendered masculinity may be extremely important.[13] In the examples discussed herein the incidents were partly motivated by hostility for difference (see Allport, 1954; Green, 1998) and also by socio-economic strain but importantly both were linked to the perceived threatened masculinity of the offender. This may mean that where hate crime offenders also commit crimes against their own ethnic group, many of the causes of hate crime overlap with their commission of ordinary crimes. The difference may lie in how the threat posed to masculinity by both indigenous and ethnically different groups manifests itself.

Notes

1. On the role of gender in anti-gay attitudes see Herek, 1984, 1988, 1993; Cotten-Huston and Waite, 1999; Dick, 2008; Witten and Taylor, 1999.
2. The inclusion of gender as a hate crime category varies globally, for a discussion of the issues see Choundas, 1995; Copeland and Wolfe, 1991; Kersten, 1996; Angelari, 1994; Pendo, 1994; Bunch, 1990; Weisburd and Levin, 1994.
3. For a discussion of policy implications around gender see Mason-Bish, 2013 and McPhail and DiNitto, 2005.
4. For an exception see Treadwell and Garland (2011) on masculinity and the EDL.
5. Sheffield, in particular, links blame for hate crimes with wider societal factors.
6. These were considered important life stages that informed fears around crime.
7. For an intersectional approach to hate crime to the study of LGBT victims see Meyer (2010).
8. For a defence of the concept of hegemonic masculinity see Connell and Messerschmidt, 2005.
9. For differences in definitions of 'gang' see Cohen, 1955; Miller, 1958; Jankowski, 1991; Klein, 1995; Klein et al., 2000; Katz and Jackson-Jacobs, 2003; Gunter, 2008; Pitts, 2008; Ralphs et al., 2009; Dying to Belong, 2009.
10. See Dying to Belong (2009) for a discussion of the competing definitions of 'gang'.

11 Racial categories as imperfect and as Garland et al. (2006) have argued ethnic categories fail to emphasise the complexities of identity positions within both victim and offender populations.
12 It should be noted that these respondents were prolific offenders who had a range of criminal convictions against other white residents in the area (both younger and older) as well as people from ethnic minority groups. Whilst claiming to speak for 'whites' in terms of belonging to the area and being British – they were actively disliked by other white residents from all age groups even those with similar demographic profiles to themselves. Indeed, other white respondents viewed them as being the most problematic group in the area because of the crime and violence they committed and this anxiety far exceeded any expressed by white residents about ethnic minorities living in the area and associated perceptions about resources/cultural implications.
13 Albeit this study is on gendered masculinity as a motivational factor in attacks against other men research on how gendered masculinity or femininity impacts upon attacks against women is to be welcomed.

Bibliography

Agnew, R. (1992). Foundation for a general strain theory of crime and delinquency. *Criminology*, 30, 47–87.
Allport, G. W. (1954). *The Nature of Prejudice*. Cambridge, MA: Addison-Wesley.
Angelari, M. (1994). *Hate Crime Statute: A Promising Tool for Fighting Violence Against Women*. Heinonline, Gender and Law, 2 A. M. U.J.
Beasley, C. (2008a). Rethinking hegemonic masculinity in a globalizing world. *Men and Masculinities*, 11 (1), pp. 86–103.
Beasley, C. (2008b). Reply to Messerschmidt and to Howson. *Men and Masculinities*, 11 (1), pp. 111–115.
Bowleg, L. (2008). When Black + Lesbian + Woman ≠ Black Lesbian Woman: The Methodological Challenges of Qualitative and Quantitative Intersectionality Research. *Sex Roles*, 59, pp. 312–325.
Bowleg, L. (2013). Once you've blended the cake, you can't take the parts back to the main ingredients: Black, Gay and Bisexual Men's Descriptions of Intersectionality. *Sex Roles*, 68 (11–12), pp. 754–767.
Bowling, B. and Phillips, C. (2003). Racist Victimization in England and Wales. In D. Hawkins (ed.), *Violent Crime, Assessing Race & Ethnic Difference*. Cambridge: Cambridge University Press.
Bunch, C. (1990). Women's Rights as Human Rights: Towards a Re-Vision of Human Rights. *Human Rights Quarterly*, 12 (4), pp. 468–498.
Byers, B., Crider, B. W. and Biggers, G. K. (1999). Bias Crime Motivation: A Study of Hate Crime Offender Neutralization Techniques Used Against the Amish. *Journal of Contemporary Criminal Justice*, 15 (1): 78–96.
Campbell, B. (1993). *Goliath: Britain's Dangerous Places*. London: Virago.
Chakraborti, N. and Garland, J. (2012a). *Hate crime: impact, causes and responses*. London: Sage.
Chakraborti, N. and Garland, J. (2012b). Reconceptualising Hate Crime Victimisation through the Lens of Vulnerability and 'Difference'. *Theoretical Criminology*, 16 (4), pp. 499–514.
Choundas, G. (1995). Neither equal nor protected: The invisible law of equal protection, the legal invisibility of its gender based victims. *Emory Law Journal*, 44, 1069–1185.
Cohen, A. K. (1955). *Delinquent boys: the culture of the gang*. New York: Free Press.
Collins, P. H. (1998). It's All in the Family: Intersections of Gender, Race and Nation. *Hypation: A Journal of Feminist Philosophy*, 13 (3), pp. 62–82.
Connell, R. W. (1987). *Gender and Power: Society, the Person and Sexual Politics*. Polity, Cambridge.
Connell, R. W. (1995). *Masculinities*. London: Polity Press.
Connell, R. W. and Messerschmidt, J. (2005). Hegemonic masculinity: rethinking the concept. *Gender and Society*, 19 (6), pp. 829–859.
Copeland, L. and Wolfe, L. R. (1991). *Violence Against Women as Bias Motivated Hate Crime: Defining the Issues*. Washington: Centre for Women's Policy Studies.
Cotten-Huston, A. L. and Waite, B. M. (1999). Anti-Homosexual Attitude in College Students: Predictors and Classroom Interventions. *Journal of Homosexuality*, 38 (3), pp. 117–133.
Craig, K. M. (2002). Examining hate-motivated aggression: A review of the social psychological literature on hate crimes as a distinct form of aggression. *Aggression and Violent Behaviour*, 7, pp. 85–101.

Crenshaw, K. (1991). Mapping the Margins: Intersectionality, Identity Politics and Violence Against Women of Color. *Stanford Law Review*, 43 (6), pp. 1241–1299.

Dick, S. (2008). *Homophobic hate crime: The Gay British Crime Survey 2008*. London, UK: Stonewall. Retrieved from www.stonewall.org.uk/documents/homophobic_hate_crime_final_report.pdf

Drew, J. (2008). *The epidemic of male violence against women*. Retrieved from www.thefword.org.uk/features/2008/04/the_epidemic_of

Dying to Belong: An In-Depth Review of Street Gangs in Britain. (2009). A Policy Report by the Gangs Working Group. The Centre for Social Justice.

Edley, N. and Wetherall, M. (1995). *Men in Perspective, Practice, Power and Identity*. Hertfordshire: Prentice Hall.

Esses, V. M., Dovidio, J. F., Jackson, L. M. and Armstrong, T. L. (2001). The immigration dilemma: the role of perceived group competition, ethnic prejudice, and national identity. *Journal of Social Issues*, 57, pp. 389–412.

Gadd, D. and Dixon, B. (2009). Posing the 'Why' Question: Understanding the Perpetration of Racially Motivated Violence and Harassment. In B. Perry (ed.), *Hate Crimes*, Volume One. London: Praeger.

Gadd, D., Dixon, B. and Jefferson, T. (2005). *Why Do They Do It? Racial Harassment in North Staffordshire*. Centre for Criminological Research: Keele University.

Garland, J., Spalek, B. and Chakraborti, N. (2006). Hearing Lost Voices: Issues in Researching 'Hidden' Minority Ethnic Communities. *British Journal of Criminology*, 46 (3), pp. 423–437.

Garner, S. (2011). *White Working Class Neighbourhoods: Common Themes and Policy Suggestions*. UK: Joseph Roundtree Foundation.

Glaser, J., Dixit, J. and Green, D. P. (2002). Studying Hate Crime with the Internet: What makes Racists Advocate Racist Violence? *Journal of Social Issues*, 58 (1), pp. 177–193.

Gottfredson, M. and Hirschi, T. (1990). *A General Theory of Crime*. Stanford, CA: Stanford University Press.

Green, D. P. (1998). From lynching to gay bashing: The elusive connection between economic conditions and hate crime. *Journal of Personality and Social Psychology*, 75, pp. 82–92.

Green, D. P., McFalls, L. H. and Smith, J. K. (2001). Hate Crime: An Emergent Research Agenda. *Annual Review of Sociology*, 27, pp. 479–504.

Green, D. P. and Seher, R. L. (2003). What Role Does Prejudice Play in Ethnic Conflict? *Annual Review of Political Science*, 6, pp. 509–531.

Green, D. P., Strolovitch, D. Z. and Wong, J. S. (1998). Defended neighbourhoods, integration, and racially motivated crime. *American Journal of Sociology*, 104 (2), pp. 372–403.

Gunter, A. (2008). Growing up bad: black youth, 'road' culture and badness in an East London neighbourhood. *Crime, Media Culture*, 4, pp. 349–366.

Hall, N. (2005). *Hate crime*. Cullompton: Willan Publishing.

Hallsworth, S. and Silverstone, D. (2009). 'That's life innit': a British perspective on guns, crime and social order. *Criminology and Criminal Justice*, 9, pp. 359–377.

Hallsworth, S. and Young, T. (2008). Gang talk and Gang talkers: a critique. *Crime Media Culture*, 4, pp. 175–195.

Hallsworth, S. and Young, T. (2004). Getting Real About Gangs. *Criminal Justice Matters*, 55 (1), pp. 12–13.

Heale, J. (2009). *One Blood: Inside Britain's New Street Gangs*. UK: Simon & Schuster.

Herek, G. M. (1984). Beyond 'Homophobia': A Social Psychological Perspective on Attitudes Towards Lesbian and Gay Men. *Journal of Homosexuality*, 10: 1–2 pp. 1–21.

Herek, G. M. (1988). Heterosexual's Attitude towards Lesbian and Gay Men: Correlates and Gender Differences. *Journal of Sex Research*, 25: 4, pp. 451–477.

Herek, G. M. (1993). Documenting Prejudice Against Lesbians and Gay Men on Campus: The Yale Sexual Orientation Survey, *Journal of Homosexuality*, 25 (4), pp. 15–30.

Jackson, D. (1990). *Unmasking Masculinity: A Critical Autobiography*. London: Unwin Hyman Ltd.

Jacobs, J. B. and Potter, K. (1998). *Hate Crimes*. New York: Oxford University Press.

Jankowski, M. (1991). *Gangs and American Urban Society*. Berkeley: University of California Press.

Jefferson, T. (2002). Subordinating Hegemonic Masculinity. *Theoretical Criminology*, 6(1), 63–88.

Katz, J. and Jackson-Jacobs, C. (2003). The criminologists' gang. In: C. Sumner (ed.), *The Blackwell Companion to Criminology*. Oxford: Blackwell, pp. 91–124.

Kersten, J. (1996). Culture, Masculinities and Violence against Women. *British Journal of Criminology*, 36 (3), pp. 381–395.

Klein, M. W. (1995). *The American Street Gang: Its Nature, Prevalence and Control*. Oxford: Oxford University Press.
Klein, M. W., Kerner, H. J., Maxson, C. L. and Weitekamp, E. (eds) (2000). *The Eurogang Paradox: Street Gangs and Youth Groups in the U.S. and Europe*. The Netherlands: Kluwer Academic Publisher.
Kundnani, A. (2001). In a Foreign Land: The New Popular Racism. *Race and Class*, 43, pp. 41–60.
Levin, J. and McDevitt, J. (1993). *Hate Crimes: The rising tide of bigotry & bloodshed*. New York: Plenum.
Levin, J. and McDevitt, J. (2002). *Hate Crimes Revisited: America's War on Those Who Are Different*. New York: Basic Books.
Levin, J. and Rabrenovic, G. (2009). Hate as Cultural Justification for Violence. In: B. Perry (ed.), *Hate Crimes*, Volume One. London: Praeger.
Mason, J. (2002). *Qualitative Researching*. London: Sage.
Mason-Bish, H. (2013). Examining the Boundaries of Hate Crime Policy: Considering Age and Gender. *Criminal Justice Policy Review*, 12 (3), pp. 309–329.
McDevitt, J., Levin, J. and Bennett, S. (2002). Hate Crime Offenders: An Expanded Typology. *Journal of Social Studies*, 58 (2), pp. 303–317.
McDevitt, J., Levin, J., Nolan, J. and Bennett, S. (2010). Hate Crime Offenders. In: N. Chakraborti (ed.), *Hate Crimes: Concepts, policy, future directions*. Cullompton: Willan Publishing, pp. 124–145.
McGhee, D. (2005). *Intolerant Britain?: Hate, citizenship and difference*. Berkshire: Open University Press.
McPhail, B. A. (2002). Gender-Bias Hate Crime: A Review. *Trauma, Violence, Abuse*. 3 (2), pp. 125–143.
McPhail, B. A. and DiNitto, D. M. (2005). Prosecutorial Perspectives on Gender-Bias Hate Crimes. *Violence Against Women*, 11 (9), pp. 1162–1185.
Messerschmidt, J. W. (1993). *Masculinities and Crime: Critique and Reconceptualisation of Theory*. Maryland: USA, Rowman & Littlefield Publishers, Inc.
Messerschmidt, J. W. (1997). *Crime as Structured Action: Gender, Race, Class, and Crime in the Making*. London: Sage.
Meyer, D. (2010). Evaluating the Severity of Hate Motivated Violence: Intersectional Differences Among LGBT Hate Crime Victims. *Sociology*, 44 (5), pp. 980–995.
Miles, M. B. and Huberman, M. A. (2002). *The Qualitative Researchers Companion*. London: Sage.
Miller, W. (1958). Lower class culture as generating mileau of gang delinquency. *Journal of Social Issues*, 14, 5–20.
Pendo, E. (1994). Recognising Violence Against Women: Gender and the Hate Crime Statistics Act. *Harvard Women's Law Journal*, 17, p. 157.
Perry, B. (2001). *In the Name of Hate: Understanding Hate Crimes*. New York: Routledge.
Perry, B. (ed.) (2009a). *Hate Crimes*. Volume One. London: Praeger.
Perry, B. (2009b). The Sociology of Hate: Theoretical Approaches. In: B. Perry (ed.), *Hate Crimes*, Volume One. London: Praeger.
Pitts, J. (2008). *Reluctant Gangsters: The Changing Face of Youth Crime*. Cullompton: Willan Publishing.
Ralphs, R., Medina, J. and Aldridge, J. (2009). Who Needs Enemies with Friends Like These? The Importance of Place for Young People Living in Known Gang Areas. *Journal of Youth Studies*, 12 (5), pp. 483–500.
Ray, L. and Smith, D. (2002). Hate crime, violence and cultures of racism. In P. Iganski (ed.), *The Hate Debate*. London: Profile Books.
Ray, L., Smith, D. and Wastell, L. (2004). Shame, Rage and Racist Violence. *British Journal of Criminology*, 44, 350–368.
Sheffield, C. (1995). Hate violence. In P. Rothenburg (ed.), *Race, class and gender in the United States* (pp. 432–441), New York, NY: St Martins.
Shields, S. A. (2008). Gender: An Intersectionality Perspective. *Sex Roles*, 59, pp. 301–311.
Sibbitt, R. (1997). *The perpetrators of racial harassment and racial violence*, Home Office Research Study 176. London: Home Office.
Stanko, E. A. (2001). Re-Conceptualising The Policy of Hatred: Confessions And Worrying Dilemmas of a Consultant. *Law and Critique*, 12 (3), pp. 309–329.
Sveinsson, K. P. (ed.) (2009). *Who Cares About the White Working Class?* UK: Runneymede Trust.
Sykes, G. and Matza, D. (1957). Techniques of Neutralisation, *American Sociological Review*, 22, 664–670.
Thraser, F. (1927). *The Gang: A Study of 1,313 Gangs in Chicago*. Chicago: University of Chicago Press.

Treadwell, J. and Garland, J. (2011). Masculinity, Marginalisation and Violence: A Case Study of the English Defence League, *British Journal of Criminology*, 51, pp. 621–634.

Trickett, L. F. (2011). Fears of the Fearless. *International Journal of Law, Crime and Justice*, 39, pp. 280–302.

Walklate, S. (1998). *Understanding Criminology: Current Theoretical Debates*. Buckinghamshire: Open University Press.

Walters, M. A. (2011). A general theories of hate crime? Strain, doing difference and self control. *Critical Criminology*, 19 (4), pp. 313–330.

Weisburd, S. and Levin, B. (1994). On the basis of sex. *Stanford Law and Policy Review*, 2, 21–47.

Whitehead, S. M. (1998). Hegemonic Masculinity Revisited. *Gender, Work and Organizations*, 6 (1), pp. 58–62.

Whitehead, S. M. (2002). *Men and Masculinities: Key Themes and New Directions*. Cambridge: Policy Press in Association with Blackwell Publishers.

Witten, T. M. and Taylor, A. E. (1999). Hate Crimes and Violence Against the Transgendered. *Peace Review: A Journal of Social Justice*. 11 (3), pp. 461–468.

Women's Aid. (2007). *Statistics: How common is domestic violence?* Retrieved from www.womensaid.org.uk/domestic-violence-articles.asp?section=00010001002200410001

Young, J. (1999). *The exclusive society: social exclusion, crime and difference in late modernity*. London: Sage.

21
LGBT hate crime

Leslie J. Moran

Violence associated with sexual orientation and gender discrimination is at the heart of lesbian, gay, bisexual and transgender (LGBT) hate crime. The focus of this chapter is the challenges that LGBT experiences and perceptions of these forms of violence raise for the hate crime agenda, campaigning and activism, law and institutional reform, and the realisation of safety and security. Throughout I use 'violence' to refer to the full spectrum of acts ranging from the most extreme and exceptional, bringing life itself to an end, to the pettiest and most frequent, so-called 'low level' acts such as harassment, intimidation, or fear-inducing name calling.

I begin with two preliminary related points. The first is illustrated by comments made in a video produced by the United Nations in 2011 to mark *International Day against Homophobia and Transphobia*. UN High Commissioner for Human Rights, Navi Pillay, contrasts the now widely accepted condemnation of some forms of discrimination such as racial and ethnic bias-related violence with the ongoing tolerance towards and sometimes advocacy of violence associated with sexual orientation and gender discrimination (Pillay, 2011). All forms of discriminatory violence are not treated equally and more specifically equally condemned. While Pillay calls for this state of affairs to end, it is and will remain an ongoing problem.

Jenness and Grattet's study of the emergence of the social, political and legal category 'hate crime' in the US, *Making Hate a Crime*, provides an illustration of the second related point. The authors note that the incorporation of sexual orientation and gender bias-related violence into the hate crime agenda was not a part of the first wave of initiatives and reforms (2001: 97). They describe sexual orientation as a 'second tier' rather than 'core' hate crime status category – the 'core' being race and ethnicity.[1] The specific recognition of transgender comes even later. The struggle to bring sexual orientation and gender-related discrimination under the banner of 'hate crime' is potentially different from that of other 'status categories'. Establishing the legitimacy of complaints about sexual orientation and gender-related violence has been more challenging and more problematic.

These two opening snapshots are indicative of hierarchies of acceptable and unacceptable violence and hierarchies of recognition operating within societies in general, and within hate crime agendas specifically and criminal justice agendas more generally. They both suggest some lives, some citizens, continue to be more worthy of respect than others (Tatchell, 2002). Some will be able to access safety and security provided by the State more easily and readily than others. These fundamental inequalities shape the hate crime landscape. For example, the European Union Agency for Fundamental Rights (FRA) reported that in 2010 only eight of 27 EU member states included information about sexual orientation hate crime and four of the 27 collected data on gender identity hate crime in official data (European Union Agency for Fundamental Rights, 2012).

In England and Wales, a jurisdiction in which much progress has been made to take seriously sexual orientation and gender bias-related violence, a review of the existing 'hate crime' laws was undertaken in 2013 by the Law Commission for England and Wales. The Commission noted the full range of legal protections designed to target hate crime are not available where the violence is connected to sexual orientation or transgender discrimination (Law Commission, 2013). In this respect LGBT people appear to be second-class citizens.

The objective of this chapter is therefore to identify and explore some of the key conceptual, social, political and practical factors that shape the LGBT-related aspects of the hate crime agenda. Inevitably it is a big task. In the limited space available the aim will be to map some of the fundamental issues and to examine some strategies developed in response, and also to identify some of their limitations.

Being critical of sexuality, taking gender seriously

Before going further it is important to pause a moment to focus on the now widely used acronym 'LGBT'. It is both a useful shorthand and deeply problematic (Moran, 2007a). Connecting the 'L', 'G', 'B' and 'T' together may be indicative of ways in which the experiences of different discriminations put into play though acts of sexual and gender-related violence are linked in and through these identity categories. 'LGBT' can also symbolise the practice and importance of alliances and common initiatives to help raise issues, facilitate tactical gains, and support new initiatives. At the same time 'LGBT' can have the opposite effect, conflating very different experiences of violence and insecurity, sustaining hidden hierarchies where gay male issues tend to dominate. Another common effect is that the 'T' tends to get subsumed under the 'LGB'. 'LGBT' can also have the effect of producing or sustaining new exclusions. What about those who don't fit or identify with the 'LGBT'; intersex 'I', those questioning sexuality 'Q', or those who experience discrimination because of their asexuality 'A' (DeLuzio Chasin, 2011; Emens, 2013)? The extension of 'LGBT' to 'LGBT-QIA' is certainly one response but does it adequately respond to all the problems or paper over them anew? Does it generate new problems?

This brings me to a related set of issues. I want to touch on two. The first is the use of the phrase 'sexual orientation' and the use of sexual identity categories such as 'lesbian' and 'gay' and 'sexuality' more generally. The second is concerned with the significance of gender in making sense of 'L', 'G', 'B' and 'T' experiences and perceptions of prejudice-related violence.

'Sexuality' as a concept, as a way of making sense of human relations, has a history and has its roots in particular social, political and institutional locations (Foucault, 1981; Moran, 1996). To acknowledge this is not to deny the widespread uses of 'sexuality' in very different and diverse settings, or to deny its value as a local as well as a global resource by which lives may be affirmed and discrimination and oppression resisted. But it does demand that we acknowledge the fact that 'sexuality' is neither a necessary nor inevitable way of making sense of human relations. It is highly contested and a site of intense political struggle. It also calls for recognition that 'sexuality' is both important and potentially deeply problematic. At the end of the day, problematising 'sexuality' as a way of making sense of the world, helps to understand its social, political and cultural nature (Tomsen, 2009). Papering over the political nature of 'sexuality' potentially limits opportunities and undermines potential for change.

A connected set of problems relates to the use of identity categories, such as 'lesbian', 'gay', and 'heterosexual' that connote the essence or truth of subjects. Again this is not to suggest that these terms have no political value for those who are the object of bias-related violence. Nor does a more critical approach lead to conclusions that 'lesbian' or 'gay' are categories of same-sex erotic relations that are novel, strange or exotic practices or ways of being imported from alien western cultures through the corrupting forces of colonialism, capitalism, globalisation or the dangerous forces of modernity shattering long-standing traditions. But the position I advocate does call for consideration to be given to the way in which sexual identity categories organise, emerge, frame and limit political engagement and social change. One particular concern is the way they have a tendency to separate out a complicated and messy reality into neat, box-like distinctions that give rise to a silo mentality (see also Mason-Bish, this volume).

Debates about 'intersectionality' have been one context in which scholars have attempted to expose problems associated with this silo mentality. 'Intersectionality' seeks to demonstrate how other forms of social exclusion such as that of social class, ethnicity, faith, work simultaneously to shape sexuality and gender identities, perceptions and experiences (Crenshaw, 1995; Lamble, 2008; Mason, 2002; Moran and Sharpe, 2004).

Sexual identity categories have the potential to police and manage social relations and claims for recognition, generating new frameworks of respectability, new social inclusions and new exclusions (Duggan, 2003). If you are gay or lesbian but don't fit the new, emerging, ideal of being 'openly gay', 'married with two kids', owning a 'nice home' in a 'nice neighbourhood', in short being the picture of respectability, then you may still struggle to have your injuries recognised. You may still struggle to access state provided and supported safety and security.

Last but by no means least I want to briefly refer to 'Queer theory'. 'Queer theory' offers some important insights to help think through the potential and limits of 'sexuality'. One is that 'sexuality' is best thought of as 'a field of meanings, discourses and practices that are interlaced with social institutions and movements' (Seideman, 1994: 169); a 'sexual regime' (Berlant and Warner, 1998: 548, footnote 2). Queer theory is also important because it draws attention to the ways in which this regime is hierarchical and normative, producing 'heterosexuality' as the basic idiom of the personal, and the social. It is a regime that produces 'heterosexuality' like the air we breathe, a diffuse all-pervasive presence (a sense of rightness), but, at the same time, out of mind, unnoticed, unrecognisable, often unconscious, and immanent to practice and to institutions.

The attribution of absence to the pervasive presence of heterosexuality plays a central role in linking certain qualities and values to that subject position. One characteristic attributed to heterosexuality as the unmarked is that of 'a state of nature' which gives rise to a multitude of positive connotations. Another is the link between heterosexuality and the ideal. A third is the assumption that heterosexuality is the very pinnacle of moral accomplishment (free from bias, the universal, not the partial). This is a heteronormative regime. The heteronormative sexual regime is not a single or uniform phenomenon. It is both ever-present and disparate shaping potentially connected settings; the home, family, school, workplace, police station, courtroom, street, neighbourhood, village, town, city, religious community, ethnic group, nation, 'international community', and so on. The list is not exhaustive. LGBT hate crime politics at its best needs to expose the workings of heteronormative regimes, expose their investment in violence, challenge their operations, and promote change.

To reduce 'LGBT' to an acronym for various sexualities is problematic in another way; it threatens to diminish the importance of gender. Let me illustrate the argument beginning with transgender experiences. Incidents of violence and harassment experienced by trans people are often accompanied by a barrage of insulting terms like 'poofta', 'pansy', and 'faggot' commonly associated with bias against lesbians and gay men. This is indicative of the way transgender experience is often reduced to and misunderstood as related to sexuality and treated as a form of 'homophobia' (Sharpe, 2002). Trans*gender* doesn't fit easily with categories that have long associations with 'sexuality'. Gender performance and gender identification is central to the trans experience in general and experiences of discriminatory violence in particular (see also Woods and Herman, this volume).

This example of the conflation of gender and sexuality also draws attention to the importance of actual and perceived gender practices in generating perceptions and experiences of sexual categories more generally. So when a woman's gender performance is read as masculine an assumption is commonly made that the woman is a lesbian. The significance of gender in the constitution of sexual distinctions has been a theme in gay scholarship on violence (Onken, 1998) and a matter highlighted in work on lesbian lives. Lesbian experiences of prejudice-related violence is often linked to a perpetrator's reading of the woman's gender performance; 'are you a boy or a girl' (Mason, 2002). More generally there is much work that notes the central importance of gender-related discrimination in lesbian experiences of bias-related violence (Majury, 1994; Mason, 1995, 2002; Robson, 1998). To reduce violence against lesbians to nothing more than a problem of discrimination related to sexuality misses the point that the discrimination is very much connected with violence by men against women.

But the relevance of gender in 'LGBT' hate crime is not limited to violence against transgender people and lesbians. It is also an important dimension of the violence experienced by gay men. Insulting terms are a common part of the repertoire of threats and intimidation aimed at men who are or are perceived to be 'gay' that discriminate against gender performances by men that are read as 'feminine'. My argument here is not to advocate the replacement of sexuality-related discrimination with gender discrimination but more to raise awareness of the importance of gender and to highlight the need to take account of the interconnections and differences between gender and sexuality.

LGBT as 'bad victims'

'L', 'G', 'B', 'T' people who have experienced violence often have an experience of being 'bad victims'. What do I mean by this? 'Bad victims' struggle to have the violence done to them recognised as violence. When you are taken to be a 'bad victim' perpetrators become victims and victims become perpetrators. The injuries done to you are taken as signs of your own wrongdoing. 'Bad victims' struggle to get the support of the State and State agencies such as the police. Attempts to get access to the safety and security that these agencies may provide is strictly limited and more likely to lead to punishment and further persecution. 'L', 'G', 'B', 'T' people have long been, and continue to be, categorised as 'bad victims'. Victims are perceived to be *bad* victims because the ongoing operation of prejudice makes otherwise ordinary lives and actions threatening, dangerous, disorderly, and so on. So, how does this come about?

Leslie J. Moran

1. Bad victims: Sexual orientation and gender prejudice as legitimate violence in criminal law

One way in which this state of affairs comes into being and is maintained is through the law itself. Law is a means of institutionalising discrimination and prejudice. It is also a mechanism for making some acts of prejudice-related violence legitimate. 76 countries currently have laws that institutionalise and legitimate same-sex and gender identity discrimination and violence. They all use criminal law to outlaw same-sex sexual acts between consenting adults (Itaborahy and Zhu, 2013). Most of these prohibitions only apply to sexual acts between men. The language used in many of these laws is worthy of attention. Terms such as 'sodomy' and 'buggery' and phrases such as 'carnal knowledge...against nature' and 'unnatural acts' are very common. They hark back to late medieval prohibitions first found in European legal systems (Moran, 1996). Exported as part of the civilising mission of colonisation, they continue to operate in ex-colonies around the world and have become naturalised being taken as evidence of local traditions (Human Rights Watch, 2008).

2. Bad victims: Sexual orientation and gender prejudice as legitimate violence in laws regulating family relations

Does the preoccupation with men in these laws mean that lesbians are unaffected by institutionalised prejudice and State violence legitimated through the law? The short answer is no. But women experience institutionalised prejudice and legitimate violence in different ways and in different legal settings. For example prejudice-related violence against women often happens in private and is regulated by way of private law, not criminal law. It is policed and enforced through civil law disputes about marital relations, family disputes, and divorce that operate through the civil justice process. Lesbians often experience the institutional violence of criminal law as victims of violence. Rape, sometimes called 'corrective rape', is a form of violence used by men to police lesbian sexuality. The phrase 'corrective rape' refers to the use of sexual violence to 'make' women perform and become heterosexual. While rape is in many jurisdictions a crime in which women are the only possible victim, traditions and practices of poor and inadequate policing, and infrequent and ineffective prosecutions resulting in low conviction rates, all point to systematic failures that turn the failure of law and thereby the crime into a quasi-legitimate form of prejudice-informed violence (Reid and Dirsuweit, 2002; Anguita, 2012).[2] Domestic murder and so-called 'honour crimes' are other forms of sexual violence that while formally prohibited, because of the problems of enforcement, have a quasi-legitimate quality (Manderson and Bennett, 2003).

3. Bad victims: decriminalisation as necessary but not sufficient

First, decriminalisation of same-sex acts between consenting male adults may be a necessary precondition indicating changing attitudes to LGBT people. It may be an important step opening up the possibility of LGBT people to be recognised as 'good victims'. But it is not sufficient in and of itself. As already noted, criminalisation of consensual same-sex acts is in many cases of marginal significance for lesbians, and decriminalisation may have little impact upon the gender discrimination that is central to their experience in discriminatory violence. Second, the libertarian model of decriminalisation, confining reforms to sexual acts that take place in private between consenting adults, may leave a wide range of other laws that institutionalise prejudice and legitimate state violence in place.

Third, decriminalisation does not necessarily make new criminal offences or new legal prohibitions that legitimate discrimination and link that discrimination to State violence impossible. So for example in Britain the right wing Tory government under Margaret Thatcher institutionalised new forms of sexual orientation discrimination in the now notorious section 28 of the Local Government Act of 1988. The reform outlawed the 'promotion of homosexuality' through local government and in schools (Smith, 1990). In 2013 the Russian legislature passed a law criminalising 'propaganda of non-traditional sexual relations among minors', which is a more recent example of a State institutionalising sexual orientation discrimination and legitimating prejudice-related violence (Martin, 2013).

Sexual and gender citizenship: Putting violence on the political agenda

In this section I want to examine LGBT initiatives that put discrimination-related violence on the agenda. I put this under the banner of 'citizenship' as it still remains the case that in liberal democratic models of society a key benefit of citizenship is the provision of safety and security by the State (Bell and Binnie, 2000; Phelan, 2001).

The factors that maintain LGBT people as 'bad victims' all work against LGBT people attaining the basic attributes of citizenship: safety and security. At the same time the experiences of exclusion and denial have been, and continue to be an important factor motivating activism that seeks to bring both State and individual violence associated with sexual and gender discrimination to an end. For example GALOP, a London-based LGBT community organisation that currently works to bring hate crime to an end and to improve criminal justice responses to hate crime, had its origins in monitoring police violence and discrimination against gay men and lesbians (GALOP, undated).

While decriminalisation is not a necessary first step before community activism around violence can grow, it is often a factor in the widening of LGBT community agendas to incorporate violence. Jenness and Grattet note that the addition of anti-violence work to the lesbian and gay movement agenda in the US was one of the community activist drivers behind the whole development of a hate crime social movement (2001: 23–24; see also Jenness and Broad, 1997). In this section I want to map out some of the issues that activism addresses. I also want to point out some of its problems.

One of the first and most important objectives is to gather data about the nature and extent of discriminatory violence. LGBT hate crime is at best under reported to the police. In many instances it is unreported. At worst when reported it is unrecognised and unrecorded. It remains the case that in many countries LGBT hate crime and LGBT victims of violence are 'hidden'; missing from the records. Absence of data is often mistaken as evidence that violence doesn't happen. For example in some European Union countries there is no (or very limited) official data on hate crimes, including hate crime relating to sexual orientation and gender identity: Bulgaria, Cyprus, Estonia, Greece, Hungary, Ireland, Italy, Latvia, Luxembourg, Malta, Portugal, Romania, Slovenia and Spain. It is a long list. The list of countries that were found to have 'comprehensive data' is much smaller: Finland, Netherlands, Sweden and the UK (European Union Agency for Fundamental Rights, 2012: 8). Gaps in official data is not a problem unique to countries in the European Union. It is a common characteristic across the globe.

Community activism involving the use of community victim survey is an important tool to overcome the effects of official silence. Community surveys gather together and report violence that is otherwise missing from those official records. It is a mechanism for giving a voice to those otherwise hidden from the history of everyday violence.

What do these surveys report? They tend to paint a depressing picture of lives blighted by everyday discriminatory violence. The vast majority of those responding to these surveys report they have experienced discriminatory violence. For many it is an experience of repeated violence. Harassment and 'low level' violence is the most common experience. Another key finding of community victim surveys is that the majority of incidents have never been reported to the police. The reasons for not reporting tend to fall into two categories. Many relate to experiences, perceptions and expectations of institutional discrimination in the police; bad past experiences with police; continuing threat of criminalisation of the victim; homophobic attitudes of the police; police indifference; the problem of 'coming out' to the police; and concern about how a report would be dealt with. Another set of reasons for not reporting is more associated with the type of violence experienced: it is too trivial, no loss was suffered, the police can't do anything about it, the police are not interested.

On the back of community activism 'victim surveys' of LGBT experiences are one of the initiatives undertaken by state agencies seeking to take hate crime against LGBT seriously. Two good examples of this type of initiative are *Out of the Blue* produced by the Police in New South Wales, Australia (1995) and a survey of *Women's experiences of homophobia and transphobia* commissioned by London's Metropolitan Police (Paterson et al., 2008). While this type of initiative may reflect police suspicion of community victim surveys, they also add to the legitimacy of these initiatives and help to overcome institutional silences about violence. They may also be a valuable resource in community calls for further police reform.

An initiative by the European Union Agency for Fundamental Rights (FRA) that includes LGBT hate crime brings many of these features together and gives them an extra twist. FRA is an agency set up by the EU to give advice and support on fundamental rights. The FRA fact sheet 'LGBT persons' experiences of discrimination and hate crime in the EU and Croatia' (2013a) offers some familiar 'key findings'. Some relate to the experiences of violence:

> A quarter (26 per cent) of all EU LGBT survey respondents had been attacked or threatened with violence in the previous five years.

And:

> About three in 10 of all transgender respondents said they were victims of violence or threats of violence more than three times in the past year.

A related finding is:

> A majority of respondents who had experienced violence (59 per cent) in the past year said that the last attack or threat of violence happened partly or completely because they were perceived to be LGBT.

Others record ongoing suspicion and fear of reporting incidents to the police:

> Fewer than one in five (17 per cent) reported to the police the most recent incident of hate-motivated violence that had happened to them.

Perceptions and expectations that the police would not take reports of the violence seriously and little expectation that anything would change are important reasons given for not reporting the violence. Fear of being 'outed' and negative consequences flowing from that is another important factor (2013b: 2).

The FRA initiative has a twist. It is a supra-national project generating data about all the countries of the EU. There is potential for comparisons and benchmarking between LGBT experiences in different nation states. But this is also problematic, if only because differences between nations and between LGBT experiences in different locations may be enormous, making comparisons difficult. At the same time a supra-national project such as this one may be welcome. It may provide a resource for, and considerable support to, LGBT communities and activists in locations in which community activism may be struggling to develop. It may also provide supra- and multi-national support and leverage to LGBT communities to assist in projects to encourage national change.[3]

LGBT victim surveys are not without problems. For example, there is no standard set of questions so it is difficult to compare experiences. Some surveys ask about experiences over a short period of time, one year, while others ask for information about experiences over a respondent's lifetime. Levels of violence experienced over a lifetime are likely to be greater than experienced in the last 12 months. The questions asked and answers given may provide only crude portraits of the violence experienced. They tend to tell a story of random acts of violence in public places – stranger danger – whereas there is a growing body of research suggesting much homophobic and transphobic violence takes place in and near the home, in the victim's neighbourhood, at work, or in places of learning (Mason, 2005; Moran, 2007b). Moreover, the lack of a victim survey, or on-going low levels of reporting to the police, may be used as a justification by policing and criminal justice agencies to dismiss the new data and taken as a licence to carry on as before. An alternative effect of community victim surveys may be that the police fail to examine their own, albeit limited data. This is ironic as no matter how small it is, this police data is a rich source of community data about experiences of violence that can be put to valuable use by the police to better understand victims' experiences and needs and to develop police responses to understand those experiences and to meet those needs (Moran, 2007b).

If recording otherwise 'hidden' discriminatory violence is an important first step, it is not the end of the matter. The experience of victims once they contact the police is crucial. Prejudice will undermine investigations and potentially undercut confidence in the police and criminal justice agencies more generally. The quality and effectiveness of the experience of the police investigation is also of vital importance. Failure to recognise the relationship between violence and discrimination will leave key aspects of the violence out of the picture. Failure to ask the right questions can have similar effects. The response of State prosecutors is also fundamental. Little progress will be made if the improvements within the police leave in place homophobic and transphobic responses by prosecutors. Experiences in the courtroom, and finally the activities of judges, all have a role to play. All may play a role in perpetuating official prejudice against LGBT people and commit acts of institutional discriminatory violence on the basis of sexual orientation and gender discrimination. Joined up thinking and action is essential if progress is to be made towards taking violence against LGBT people seriously.

I want to finish on a note of caution that has two dimensions. Both relate to the ultimate goal of 'hate crime' reform. The first focuses on the LGBT investments that are being made in criminalisation and punishment. A key characteristic of hate crime law reform is enhancement of the punishment given to those found guilty of hate crime. Additional punishment is said to be justified on the basis of the particular damage that is done to the individual, the immediate community that the status category refers to and the wider community. As Lamble (2011) has noted, this connects LGBT politics to what has been described as the 'punitive turn' and policies of mass incarceration. As she suggests, imprisonment tends to impact disproportionately on people who are marginal and subject to discrimination in a society. So the poor, members of racial and ethnic minorities, young people tend to be over represented in prison populations. Promoting enhanced punishment for violence against LGBT people may lead to LGBT investments in institutional practices that are profoundly discriminatory.

Also, LGBT advocates need to heed the warnings raised in other hate crime contexts. For example writing about the impact of reforms in England and Wales introducing enhanced sentences for racially aggravated acts of violence, Burney and Rose noted the potential of prosecutions to entrench social divisions rather than to heal them (2002, see Chapter 7). This does not necessarily lead to a conclusion that hate crime initiatives need to be abandoned but it does call for serious consideration to be given to the particular preoccupation with punishment. Should more priority be given to mediation and to initiatives to reconcile divided communities as a response to violence? In the final instance, what most victims want is for the everyday violence to stop so they can carry on their lives. Does criminalisation provide the 'best' option?

Last, but by no means least, turning to the State in general, and the police in particular, for safety and security may be problematic in other ways. David Garland's work (1996) warns that the criminal justice policy landscape is not necessarily consistent. It may be full of contradictions. More specifically initiatives to strengthen the power of the State, to get tough on crime, may well coincide with policies and practices that acknowledge the limits of the State to deliver safety and security. Hate crime is a classic example of this. On the one hand hate crime law reform introduces new 'get tough' criminal justice responses, for example by calls for more policing and by way of sentence enhancement reforms.

Yet these changes are taking place at the same time as governments are cutting funds for policing. As a result, the police are less able to respond. This impacts upon how policing LGBT hate crime is audited and evaluated. So for example changes are made to the criteria used to measure successful LGBT hate crime policing. Success is not about increasing prosecutions or successful determinations of guilt, but in making sure that the police respond to LGBT phone calls within x minutes or return calls about violent incidents within y hours.

The rise of multi-agency approaches to safety and security is another development that may well have benefits, but at the same time acknowledges the limits of the police. Strategies that raise the profile and importance of crime prevention and individual responsibility for safety are other responses that acknowledge a limited role for the State. LGBT people are encouraged to learn how better to negotiate the streets to minimise the dangers of homophobic and transphobic prejudice or to better protect their homes and commercial venues (Moran et al., 2004; Stanko and Curry, 1997). They are encouraged to insure against robbery or damage to property.

Conclusions

LGBT campaigning and activism, law and institutional reform, has at its end point two fundamental goals. One is to bring the violence to an end. The other is to ensure safety and security in the face of violence. They are fundamental goals of liberal democracies that are applicable to all citizens. They may be easy to state, but history and contemporary experiences suggest they are difficult to achieve. Social divisions that continue to structure societies work at the everyday level to produce insiders and outsiders. Sexuality and gender are two of those divisions. LGBT hate crime campaigning and activism seeks to expose the damaging effects of those divisions. The general goal is to eradicate their operation. The specific target is their operation within the criminal justice system and its delivery of safety and security to citizens. In this chapter I have outlined some of the key challenges this political project engages. In drawing attention to the potential for change, and some of the problems, the aim has been to raise awareness, promote critical engagement, and thereby promote the more effective realisation of the ultimate goal of respect and recognition for all citizens.

Notes

1 Other 'second tier' status categories include 'disability'.
2 The legality of rape in marriage is a form of legitimate violence against women. For a historical introduction see Weintraub, 1995.
3 There is also a critical literature on this type of initiative. For example see Binnie and Klesse, forthcoming; Stychin, 1998, 2003.

References

Anguita, L.A. (2012). 'Tackling corrective rape in South Africa: the engagement between the LGBT CSOs and the NHRIs (CGE and SAHRC) and its role'. *The International Journal of Human Rights*, 16(3): pp. 489–516.
Bell, J. and Binnie, J. (2000). The *Sexual citizen: Queer politics and beyond*. Cambridge: Polity Press.
Berlant, L. and Warner, M. (1998). 'Sex in Public'. *Critical Inquiry*, 24(2): pp. 547–566.
Binnie, J. and Klesse, C. (forthcoming). *Sexual Politics Beyond Borders: Transnational Activist Networks and LGBTQ Politics in Europe*. Manchester: Manchester University Press.
Burney, E. and Rose, G. (2002). *Racially Aggravated Offences: how is the law working?* Home Office Research Study 244, London, Home Office.
Crenshaw, K. (1995). 'Mapping the margins: intersectionality, identity politics and violence'. In: K. Crenshaw et al. (eds), *Critical Race Theory*, New York, The New Press, pp. 357–383.
DeLuzio Chasin, C.J. (2011). 'Theoretical issues in the study of asexuality'. *Archives of Sexual Behaviour*, 40(4): pp. 713–723.
Duggan, L. (2003). *The twilight of equality? Neoliberalism, cultural politics and the attack on democracy.* Boston: Beacon Press.
Emens, E.F. (2013). 'Compulsory Sexuality'. *Columbia Public Law Research Paper* No 13-331. Retrieved at http://papers.ssrn.com/sol3/papers.cfm?abstract_id=2218783
European Union Agency for Fundamental Rights (2012). *Making hate crime visible in the European Union: acknowledging victims' rights*. Luxembourg: European Union Agency for Fundamental Rights.
European Union Agency for Fundamental Rights (2013a). *LGBT persons' experiences of discrimination and hate crime in the EU and Croatia*. Retrieved at http://fra.europa.eu/en/publication/2013/lgbt-persons-experiences-and-hate-crime-eu-and-croatia
European Union Agency for Fundamental Rights (2013b). *European Union Lesbian Gay Bisexual Transgender survey; Results at a glance*. Vienna: European Union Agency for Fundamental Rights. Retrieved at http://fra.europa.eu/en/publication/2013/eu-lgbt-survey-european-union-lesbian-gay-bisexual-and-transgender-survey-results
Foucault, M. (1981). *The history of sexuality. Volume 1: An introduction.* London: Penguin.
GALOP (undated). 'History'. Retrieved at www.galop.org.uk/history/
Garland, D. (1996). 'The limits of the sovereign state: Strategies of crime control in contemporary society'. *British Journal of Criminology*, 36(4): pp. 445–471.
Human Rights Watch (2008). *This alien legacy: the origins of 'sodomy' laws in British Colonialism.* New York: Human Rights Watch.
Itaborahy, L.P. and Zhu, J. (2013). *State sponsored homophobia: Criminalisation, protection and recognition of same-sex love*, International lesbian, gay bisexual trans and intersex Association. Retrieved at http://old.ilga.org/Statehomophobia/ILGA_State_Sponsored_Homophobia_2013.pdf

Jenness, V. and Broad, K. (1997). *Hate Crimes: New Social Movements and the Politics of Violence*. Hawthorne, NY: Aldine de Gruyter.

Jenness, V. and Grattet, R. (2001). *Making hate a crime: From social movement to law enforcement*. New York: Russell Sage Foundation.

Lamble, S. (2008). 'Retelling racialized violence, remaking white innocence: the politics of interlocking oppressions in transgender day of remembrance'. *Sexuality Research and Social Policy: Journal of NSRC*, 5(1): pp. 24–42.

Lamble, S. (2011). 'Transforming carceral logics: 10 reasons to dismantle the prison industrial complex using a queer/trans analysis'. In: N. Smith and E.A. Stanley (eds), *Captive Genders: Trans Embodiment and the Prison Industrial Complex*. Oakland, U.S.: AK Press, pp. 235–266.

Lamble, S. (2014). 'Queer Investments in Punishment: Sexual Citizenship, Social Movements and the Expanding Carceral State'. In: J. Haritaworn, A. Kuntsman and S. Posocco (eds.), *Queer Necropolitics. Social Justice*. Oxford, UK: Routledge, pp. 151–171.

Law Commission (2013). *Hate Crime: the case for extending existing offences. Consultation paper 213*. London: Law Commission.

Majury, D. (1994). 'Refashioning the unfashionable: claiming lesbian identities in the legal context'. *Canadian Journal of Women and the Law*, 7(2): pp. 286–306.

Manderson, L. and Bennett, L.R. (2003). *Criminalizing marital rape in Indonesia: Violence against women in Asian societies*. New York: Routledge.

Martin, S. (2013). 'Interview, "It's not about whether you belong or don't belong"'. *Irish Times*, 12th September 2013.

Mason, G. (1995). '(Out)Laws: Acts of proscription in the sexual order'. In M. Thornton (ed.) *Public and Private: Feminist Legal Debate*, pp. 66-88. Melbourne: Oxford University Press.

Mason, G. (1997). 'Boundaries of Sexuality: Lesbian Experience and Feminist Discourse on Violence Against Women'. *Australian Gay and Lesbian Law Journal*, 7: pp. 41–56.

Mason, G. (2002). *The Spectacle of Violence*. London: Routledge.

Mason, G. (2005). 'Hate Crime and the Image of the Stranger'. *British Journal of Criminology*, 45(8): pp. 837–859.

Moran, L.J. (1996). *The Homosexual(ity) of Law*. London: Routledge.

Moran, L.J. (2007a). '"Invisible minorities": Challenging community and neighbourhood models of policing'. *Criminology and Criminal Justice*, 7(4): pp. 417–441.

Moran, L.J. (2007b). 'Homophobic violence in London: challenging assumptions about strangers, dangers and safety in the city'. In: A. Philippopoulos-Mihalopoulos (ed.), *Law and the City*. London: Routledge-Cavendish, pp. 77–96.

Moran, L.J. and Sharpe, A. (2004). 'Violence, Identity and Policing: The Case of Violence against Transgender People'. *Criminal Justice*, 4(4): pp. 395–417.

Moran, L.J., Skeggs, B., Tyrer, P. and Corteen, K. (2004). *Sexuality and the politics of violence and safety*. London: Routledge.

New South Wales (1995). *Out of the Blue: A police survey of violence and harassment against gay men and lesbians*. Sydney: New South Wales Police Service.

Onken, S.J. (1998). 'Conceptualizing Violence Against Gay, Lesbian, Bisexual and Transgendered People'. In: L.M. Sloan and N.S. Gustavsson (eds), *Violence and Social Injustice Against Lesbian, Gay and Bisexual People*, pp 5–24. Binghampton: The Haworth Press.

Paterson, S., Kielinger, V. and Fletcher, J. (2008). *Women's experiences of homophobia and transphobia*. London: Metropolitan Police Authority.

Phelan, S. (2001). *Sexual strangers: Gays, lesbians and the dilemmas of citizenship*. Philadelphia: Temple University Press.

Pillay, N. (2011). 'Homophobic hate crimes on the rise, UN human rights chief warns'. [Video]. Retrieved at www.un.org/apps/news/story.asp?newsid=38406&cr=pillay#.UibesVRwbs0

Reid, G. and Dirsuweit, T. (2002). 'Understanding systemic violence: homophobic attacks in Johannesburg and its surrounds'. *Urban Forum*, 13: pp. 99–126.

Robson, R. (1998). *Sappho goes to law school*. New York: Columbia University Press.

Seideman, S. (1994). 'Queer-ing Sociology, Sociologizing Queer Theory: An Introduction'. *Sociological Theory*, 12(2): pp. 166–177.

Sharpe, A. (2002). *Transgender Jurisprudence: Dysphoric Bodies of Law*. London: Cavendish.

Smith, A.M. (1990). 'A symptomology of an authoritarian discourse'. *New Formations*, 10 (Summer): pp. 41–65.

Stanko, E.A. and Curry, P. (1997). 'Homophobic violence and the self "at risk": interrogating the boundaries'. *Social and Legal Studies*, 6(4): pp. 513–532.
Stychin, C. (1998). *Nation by Rights*. Philadelphia: Temple University Press.
Stychin, C. (2003). *Governing Sexuality: The changing politics of citizenship and law reform*. Oxford: Hart Publishing.
Tatchell, P. (2002). 'Some people are more equal than others'. In: P. Iganski, *The Hate Crime Debate: Should Hate be Punished as a Crime?* London: Institute for Jewish Policy Research, pp. 54–70.
Tomsen, S. (2009). *Violence, prejudice and sexuality*, London: Routledge.
Weintraub, S.L. (1995). 'The marital rape exception: evolution to extinction'. *Cleveland State Law Review*, 43: 351–380.

22
Anti-transgender hate crime

Jordan Blair Woods and Jody L. Herman

This chapter is dedicated to the topic of crimes motivated by bias against a victim's actual or perceived gender identity or expression. Although any person can potentially experience crime motivated by bias against their gender identity or expression, transgender and gender non-conforming people are especially at risk of experiencing this type of bias-motivated violence. Hate crime is part of a wider pattern of discrimination and marginalisation that many transgender and gender non-conforming people experience in vital spheres of daily life, including housing, employment, public accommodations, and educational settings (Currah and Minter, 2005).

This chapter has three aims. First, the chapter will discuss some definitional issues involving this category of hate crime. Second, it will summarise existing statistics and empirical research on hate crime motivated by anti-transgender bias. Third, and finally, the chapter will discuss arguments for and against hate crime laws that include gender identity or expression.

In short, this chapter will show that the limited available data suggest that transgender and gender non-conforming people are frequent targets of verbal, physical, and sexual violence motivated by bias against their gender identity or expression. Because of methodological shortcomings, existing statistics likely underrepresent the extent of the problem. Some national governments and local jurisdictions in Western countries have enacted hate crime laws that include gender identity or expression as protected characteristics. Most hate crime laws in Western countries, however, currently exclude these characteristics. Members of transgender communities, transgender advocacy and service organisations, as well as transgender community advocates, disagree over whether hate crime laws are justified or beneficial to transgender and gender non-conforming people.

Conceptualising sex, gender, and sexual orientation

Before summarising hate crime data and hate crime legislation that include gender identity or expression, it is necessary to define some key terms as they will be used in this chapter. 'Sex' generally refers to a person's status as male or female as determined by their physical and biological attributes (Mackenzie, 1994). 'Gender' is the roles, meanings, behaviours, attitudes, and other qualities that are assigned to people based on their presumed sex

(Namaste, 1996). Gender has several components, including 'gender identity' and 'gender expression'. Gender identity 'encompasses our own personal awareness, i.e., our core internal knowledge of who we are as masculine, feminine, or other' (Sheridan, 2009: 35). Gender expression describes how a person presents their gender 'to the world through external symbols and behaviours such as clothing, accessories, hairstyle, body language, and tone of voice' (Meyer, 2010: 34). Gender expression is often a reflection of a person's gender identity. Concepts of sex, gender, gender identity, and gender expression are distinguishable from 'sexual orientation'. 'Sexual orientation' involves a person's emotional and intimate attractions to others – it does not reflect a person's awareness or expression of 'maleness' or 'femaleness'.

Although there is no universal definition of 'transgender' (Stotzer, 2009), the term has been defined broadly to refer to 'individuals whose gender identity or expression does not conform to the social expectations for their assigned sex at birth' (Currah et al., 2006: xiv). Transgender individuals may or may not have had hormonal or surgical interventions to express and to present the gender with which they identify (Factor and Rothblum, 2007).

Scholars have argued that there is a pervasive conflation of sex, gender, and sexual orientation concepts in Western societies (Valdes, 1995). In this regard, Currah and Minter (2005) have identified several definitional and conceptual challenges that legislatures have struggled with when creating transgender-inclusive laws. Three of these challenges are relevant to how legislatures have delineated (or failed to delineate) concepts of sex, gender, and sexual orientation when enacting transgender-inclusive hate crime legislation.

The first challenge involves whether legislatures should include 'gender identity' or 'gender expression' as separate categories in hate crime laws, or encompass those concepts in 'sex', 'gender', or 'sexual orientation' categories. Although legislatures have taken various approaches, one major disadvantage of not explicitly recognising gender identity or expression in the statutory language of hate crime laws – either by creating separate categories or by explicitly listing gender identity or expression in the definition of other terms, such as 'gender' – is that it creates uncertainty over whether hate crime laws offer protection on the basis of gender identity or expression. This omission decreases the likelihood that judges and law enforcement officers will view anti-transgender violence as falling under the purview of hate crime laws if they interpret laws strictly based on their statutory language.

The second challenge involves avoiding the 'status versus conduct trap' (Currah and Minter, 2005: 46). Some hate crime laws include 'gender identity', but not 'gender expression'. This omission runs the risk of excluding specific forms of gender expression from protection under hate crime laws. Consider a person who is violently targeted on a public street because they are cross-dressing (dressed in clothing that is traditionally worn by members with the opposite gender). If a hate crime law includes gender identity only, then it is uncertain whether the crime would fall under the protective scope of that law if the person's gender identity aligns with the person's sex assigned at birth.

Third, it is also challenging to determine which groups are protected by hate crime laws that include gender identity or expression. For instance, do these laws only protect victims who self-identify as transgender, or do they protect anyone who is targeted because of gender identity or expression regardless of their self-identified gender? There may also be questions of whether these laws apply to all transgender and gender non-conforming people, or only to particular groups (e.g., do the laws exclude cross-dressers?). These points raise important questions about inclusion and exclusion under the law, and more specifically, whether hate crime laws afford protection to the wide diversity of gender non-conforming identities and conduct.

Although this summary does not resolve these challenges, it illustrates that the ways in which legislatures operationalise gender identity concepts in hate crime legislation influence which people and conduct fall under the purview of these laws.

Data on anti-transgender hate crime

Three key themes emerge from the available data on hate crimes against transgender people. First, the existing data is sparse. Most of the data are subsumed in broader studies on hate crimes against lesbian, gay, bisexual, transgender, and queer (LGBTQ) people. Consequently, it is difficult to differentiate data that applies to anti-transgender hate crime from data that apply to sexual orientation only. Second, the existing data sources have a number of methodological shortcomings that prevent the data from capturing the full extent of anti-transgender hate crime. Third, in spite of these limitations, the existing data indicate that transgender and gender non-conforming people are frequent targets of hate-motivated violence, including sexual violence, physical violence, and verbal harassment. As noted above, this hate-motivated violence is part of a wider pattern of discrimination and marginalisation that transgender and gender non-conforming people regularly face.

Official hate crime statistics and victimisation surveys

The bulk of official hate crime statistics from law enforcement departments and other government agencies excludes gender identity/expression-based hate crime. Many countries do not collect this data because they do not have hate crime laws, or because their hate crime laws exclude gender identity or expression (Perry, 2001). For instance, 19 of the 56 participating states in the Office for Democratic Institutions and Human Rights' report on hate crime in Europe collected data on crimes motivated by sexual orientation bias,[1] but only nine of those states collected data involving crimes motivated by anti-transgender bias (ODIHR, 2012).[2] Moreover, many countries with hate crime laws that include gender identity or expression do not gather, or only recently have started to gather, data on gender identity/expression-based hate crime. For instance, in 2012 the United States Federal Bureau of Investigation added bias-motivation codes for gender identity in its annual Hate Crime Incident Report, which is the main official source for hate crime statistics in the United States (FBI, 2012).

Methodological shortcomings also limit what official statistics can and cannot tell about gender identity/expression-based hate crime. Official hate crime statistics only include specific types of hate-motivated offences (Rubenstein, 2004). Moreover, even when police departments collect comprehensive hate crime data, individual law enforcement officers may not recognise or categorise specific crimes as being motivated by bias against the victim's gender identity or expression (Perry, 2001). Local police jurisdictions also can be lax in gathering, collecting, or submitting hate crime data on gender identity/expression-based hate crime in countries with nationwide or regional schemes that serve to distribute this data to the public.

The most serious shortcoming of official hate crime statistics is underreporting. There are a variety of reasons why transgender and gender non-conforming people may not report hate crimes to law enforcement. First, they may fear that law enforcement officers and departments will mishandle or ignore their reports. Second, they may fear that law enforcement officers will only further victimise them for being transgender or gender non-conforming. A recent study on transgender people's experiences of hate crime in the European Union reported that the vast majority of respondents from all participating EU countries were not confident that law enforcement would treat them appropriately in accordance with their preferred gender (Turner et al., 2009). Moreover, the most recent report from the National Coalition of Anti-Violence Programs (NCAVP) – which tracks violence against lesbian, gay, bisexual, and transgender people in the United States – reported that transgender hate crime victims were 1.67 times as likely to experience police violence than non-transgender hate crime victims; transgender people of colour were 2.38 times as likely to experience police violence than participants who were not transgender people of colour (NCAVP, 2011).

Third, hate crime victims targeted because of their gender identities or expression may fear that reporting will cause the perpetrators to retaliate against them. Fourth, hate crime victims may not report the crimes to law enforcement to avoid drawing attention to their gender identities, especially if they have not revealed that they are transgender or gender non-conforming to others. Fifth, undocumented transgender and gender non-conforming people may fear that reporting hate crime will result in their deportation.

Victimisation surveys can potentially overcome the shortcoming of underreporting in official hate crime data by capturing hate crimes that were never reported to, or discovered by, law enforcement. Victimisation surveys, which typically are not conducted by law enforcement agencies, ask members of the population directly about their experiences of criminal victimisation. Many major victimisation surveys, however, do not include or only very recently have started to include questions about hate crimes motivated by bias against the victim's gender identity or expression. For instance, the Crime Survey for England and Wales (previously called the British Crime Survey) did not include gender identity as a hate crime motivation until 2011 (Smith et al., 2012). Hate crime data subsequent to this inclusion have not yet been released. The U.S. Census Bureau, which sponsors the National Crime Victimization Survey (NCVS), notes that it has collected data on hate crimes motivated by 'gender or gender identity bias' since 2010 (Sandholtz et al., 2013). The NCVS questionnaire, however, only asks whether respondents believe that they have been targeted because of their 'gender', and the most recent edition of the NCVS survey manual defines 'gender' explicitly as 'male or female'. This makes it difficult to separate anti-transgender hate crime from crimes motivated by bias against a person's gender more broadly. Therefore, popular victimisation surveys do not provide much insight into the extent of hate crime motivated by anti-transgender bias.

Data from advocacy and social service organisations

Due to the general exclusion of hate crimes motivated by bias against a victim's gender identity or expression from official hate crime statistics and major victimisation surveys, advocacy and social service organisations have taken a leading role in gathering and reporting this information. The most extensive organisation-based data comes from the United States. These surveys, however, also have methodological shortcomings, especially with respect to the representativeness of the survey samples. In 1997, Gender Public Advocacy Coalition (GenderPAC) in the United States conducted the first national survey on transgender violence. Of the 403 respondents, 78 per cent reported having been verbally harassed and 48 per cent reported having been victims of assault, including assault with a weapon, sexual assault or rape (Wilchins et al., 1997).

More recent reports from social service and advocacy organisations support the high prevalence of gender identity/expression-based hate crime. In 2011, the National Gay and Lesbian Task Force (NGLTF) and the National Center for Transgender Equality released a report on the 'National Transgender Discrimination Survey' (NTDS), which investigated 6,450 transgender and gender non-conforming people's experiences of discrimination across the United States (Grant et al., 2011). Although the NTDS did not include a general question about whether respondents had ever experienced bias-motivated violence, 26 per cent reported having been physically assaulted in various contexts (e.g., education settings, work, police interactions, homeless shelters, and public accommodations). Moreover, 10 per cent of respondents reported having been sexually assaulted for being transgender or gender non-conforming. In the most recent NCAVP survey, transgender people were 1.58 times as likely to experience injuries as non-transgender people because of hate-motivated violence, and 1.76 times as likely to require medical attention due to hate-motivated violence compared to the overall sample (NCAVP, 2011). Transgender people of colour were 28 per cent more likely to experience physical violence compared to survey participants who were not transgender people of colour.

A number of organisations outside of the United States have also released reports on gender identity/expression-based hate crime. In 2009, ILGA-Europe and Press for Change released the first study on transgender people's experiences of hate crime in the European Union (Turner et al., 2009). Of the 2,669 respondents, the most common forms of reported abuse were: comments (44 per cent), verbal abuse (27 per cent), threatening behaviour (15 per cent), physical abuse (7 per cent), and sexual abuse (2 per cent). In 2006, Press for Change – a legal support organisation for transgender people in the UK – released the largest UK survey of anti-transgender violence (Whittle et al., 2007). The study, which was based on an online survey taken by 873 trans self-identified respondents, reported that 73 per cent had experienced comments, threatening behaviour, physical abuse, verbal abuse, or sexual abuse while in public spaces.

Some organisations have also created projects to track individual cases of anti-transgender violence. The Trans Murder Monitoring (TMM) project is one example of a global-scale effort. Created in April 2009, the TMM project systematically monitors, collects, and analyses reports of homicides of transgender people worldwide. Transgender Europe's (2013) latest report revealed a total of 1,123 killings in 57 countries between January 1, 2008 and December 31, 2012. In major world regions, the highest number of reports came from countries with strong transgender movements, or transgender advocacy and social service organisations, including: Brazil (452), Mexico (106), and Colombia (65) [South and Central America]; United States (69) [North America]; Turkey (30) [Europe]; and Philippines (28) [Asia]. This finding is likely a reflection of better data collection in countries with stronger transgender movements, or transgender advocacy and social service organisations.

Empirical studies

Most of the empirical studies that investigate anti-transgender hate crime were also conducted in the United States. One common shortcoming in these studies is that assessments of hateful motivations are often based on victims' perceptions of the crimes, as opposed to perpetrators' self-reported motivations (Stotzer, 2009).

Stotzer's (2009) review of violence against transgender and gender non-conforming people in the United States is the most comprehensive review of this data to date. As Stotzer's review notes, several studies report that transgender people are common targets of sexual assault and rape (Clements-Nolle et al., 2006; Garofalo et al., 2006; Kenagy, 2005). Fewer studies have examined perpetrators' motivations of sexual violence against transgender and gender non-conforming people, but those that have reported that victims commonly perceive anti-transgender bias to motivate the incidents. In Xavier et al.'s (2007) study on transgender people in the U.S. state of Virginia, 27 per cent of the 350 transgender participants reported having been forced to engage in unwanted sexual activity after the age of 13, and 57 per cent of those participants reported that at least one of the incidents was motivated by bias against their transgender status, gender identity, or gender expression. Moreover, 13 per cent of the 248 participants in Xavier et al.'s (2005) needs assessment of transgender people of colour reported having been victims of sexual assault or rape, and many of them perceived those incidents to be motivated by anti-transgender bias.

The existing empirical research also indicates that transgender and gender non-conforming people are common targets of physical violence (Xavier et al., 2007), and that transgender sex workers are especially at higher risk of being subjected to physical violence (Cohan et al., 2006; Nemoto et al., 2004; Valera et al., 2000; Weinberg et al., 1999). Empirical research also supports the notion that many transgender and gender non-conforming people perceive acts of physical violence against them as motivated by bias against their gender identity or expression. In Xavier et al.'s (2007) study, 40 per cent of participants reported that they had been victims of physical assault, and over half of those victims were physically assaulted on multiple occasions. Over two-thirds (69 per cent) of participants reported that they perceived bias related to their transgender status, gender identity, or gender expression as the primary motivation for at least one of the incidents of physical assault. Reback et al.'s (2001) survey of 244 transgender people in Los Angeles County found that 47 per cent of the victims were physically abused or beaten because of their gender identity.

Empirical studies also report that transgender people are common victims of verbal harassment and abuse. In Clements-Nolle et al.'s (2006) study, 83 per cent of the 515 trans participants reported experiencing 'verbal gender discrimination'. Eighty per cent of participants in Reback et al.'s (2001) study reported that they were victims of verbal abuse because of bias against their gender identity. Strangers were the most common perpetrators of the verbal abuse (71 per cent), followed by police officers (37 per cent).

Research on anti-transgender hate crimes is growing as countries are becoming more aware of, and recognising, these crimes. In spite of methodological limitations, the combined data from all available sources supports the conclusion that hate crime motivated by anti-transgender bias is a pervasive problem. More research, however, is needed to explore the extent of this problem and the nuances of how it affects different segments of transgender communities.

The debate over hate crime laws that include gender identity or expression

Most hate crime laws in Western countries exclude gender identity or expression. Some countries and local jurisdictions, however, have enacted hate crime laws to combat violence motivated by anti-transgender bias. These laws can take three forms: (1) a separate criminal offence for gender identity/expression-based hate crime (e.g., United States [The Matthew Shepard and James Byrd, Jr., Hate Crimes Prevention Act of 2009, 18 U.S.C. Section 249]), (2) a broad penalty-enhancement provision for already existing crimes that grants judges the authority to consider hateful motivations when determining criminal sentences (e.g., Germany [Section 46 of the German Criminal Code]), and (3) a penalty-enhancement provision for already existing offences that explicitly applies to hateful motivations based on victims' gender identity or expression (e.g., Greece [Greece Penal Code, Article 66]; Scotland [The Offences (Aggravation by Prejudice) (Scotland) Act of 2009]; United Kingdom [Criminal Justice Act of 2003, Section 146]).

Regardless of their form, hate crime laws that include gender identity or expression implicate wider philosophical and political discussions about recognition – and more specifically, the consequences of not recognising violence against transgender and gender non-conforming people. Juang (2006: 714) argues that non-recognition of anti-transgender violence: (1) 'promotes hate crimes by allowing perpetrators to regard victims as targets who "deserve" to be hated'; (2) 'renders invisible the frequency of [hate] crimes'; (3) 'leads to a dismissive attitude by the criminal justice system, the media, and the public toward the consequences of hatred for its victims and to victims being blamed for "bringing it on themselves"'; and (4) '[makes it possible] to resign oneself to the "inevitability" of being hated'. These consequences of non-recognition inspire fundamental questions about how societies should recognise and address violence against transgender and gender non-conforming people. As explained below, transgender community members and advocates disagree over using the criminal law to recognise and address this violence.

Arguments for transgender-inclusive hate crime laws

Proponents of hate crime laws that include gender identity or expression have grounded arguments in theories of retribution, deterrence, and denunciation. Retribution justifies punishment based on the desert or moral blameworthiness of criminal offenders (Woods, 2008). From a retributivist perspective, some proponents of transgender-inclusive hate crime laws have stressed that hate crimes against transgender and gender non-conforming people are particularly violent (Green, 2000). Hate crime laws serve to match the severity of the crimes with the severity of the punishment.

Other proponents have invoked principles of deterrence to argue that hate crime laws are necessary to prevent violence against transgender and gender non-conforming people (Anti-Defamation League, 2013). This position assumes that attaching criminal penalties to gender identity/expression-based hate crimes will dissuade potential hate crime offenders and law-abiding members of society from committing them. It is important to note, however, that some transgender community members, advocates and scholars doubt that hate crime laws have any deterrent effect (Spade, 2009).

Some proponents have also relied on principles of denunciation, which justify punishment as a means to communicate collective disapproval of crime (Woods, 2008). From this perspective, some proponents argue that gender identity/expression-based hate crimes send powerful and threatening messages that instil fear in transgender communities; they contend that hate crime laws send a contrary message that the government neither tolerates nor condones violence motivated by gender identity or expression (Human Rights Campaign, 2013).

Arguments against transgender-inclusive hate crime laws

Hate crime laws have not received uniform support in transgender communities, especially in radical circles that are critical of criminal justice systems and the administration of punishment (Strout, 2012). Spade (2009: 296) observes that '[many trans] advocates point out that hate crime legislation has no payoff for trans people: it has never been shown to prevent violence or have any deterrent value. Instead, it increases the resources of a system that we know targets and endangers trans people, especially poor people and people of color.' One statistic supporting this view is that no state hate crime law in the United States resulted in a successful conviction for a bias-motivated murder of a transgender person until 2009, even though Minnesota enacted the first trans-inclusive state hate crime law in 1988 and about a dozen states had enacted these laws by 2009 (Spellman, 2009; Transgender Law & Policy Institute, 2009).

Moreover, Spade and Willse (2000: 41) have connected efforts to enact trans-inclusive hate crime laws to the activism priorities of mainstream 'gay' agendas, which they argue have three shortcomings: '[1] the failure to adequately address anti-racist, feminist, and socialist concerns; [2] the inability to challenge the structural basis of social inequalities; [3] the reification of gay identity to the exclusion of equal protection for all gender and sexual variance.' In their view, 'a movement built on this uncomplicated version of homophobia and the narrow conception of who needs protection does not at all serve a broad spectrum of gender and sexual outlaws' (2000: 50). Similarly, Kohn (2002: 260) has argued that 'hate crime legislation, beyond merely replicating the discrimination found in society, actually reinforces such discrimination by actively adopting legal structures premised on the concept of social hierarchy'.

Some transgender social service and advocacy organisations have also publicly opposed laws that increase the punishment for crimes motivated by gender identity or expression. For instance, in 2011, the U.S. state of Massachusetts enacted a transgender anti-discrimination bill that included a hate-crime punishment provision. Black and Pink, a radical 'open family' of queer prisoners and their allies, publicly opposed the bill, explaining: 'We do not believe that expanding Massachusetts' Hate Crimes statutes will bring greater safety to our communities, but rather gives greater strength to the criminal justice system that causes great harm to our communities' (Black and Pink, 2011). In 2009, several LGBTQ advocacy groups – Sylvia Rivera Law Project, Audre Lorde Project, FIERCE, Queers for Economic Justice, and Peter Cicchino Youth Project – opposed a similar transgender anti-discrimination bill in the U.S. state of New York. Some of their reasons for opposing the bill were:

- [Transgender] people, people of color, and other marginalized groups are disproportionately incarcerated to an overwhelming degree. . . . If we are incarcerating those who commit violence against marginalized individuals/communities we then place them behind walls where they can continue to target these same people.
- Hate crime laws are an easy way for the government to act like it is on our communities' side while continuing to discriminate against us.
- Hate crime laws focus on punishing the 'perpetrator' and ha[ve] no emphasis on providing support for the survivor or families and friends of those killed during an act of interpersonal violence.
- Hate crimes don't occur because there aren't enough laws against them, and hate crimes won't stop when those laws are in place. Hate crimes occur because, time and time again, our society demonstrates that certain people are worth less than others; that certain people are wrong, perverse, are immoral in their very being.

(QEJ, 2009)

The Sylvia Rivera Law Project – a legal aid organisation based in New York City that services transgender, intersex, and gender non-conforming people – maintains its public opposition to hate crime laws (SRLP, 2013).

Although a comprehensive evaluation of these critical perspectives is beyond the scope of this chapter, these criticisms – heard from the voices of people who gender identity/expression-inclusive hate crime laws intend to protect – raise important questions about whether the criminal punishment of violence motivated by bias against a victim's gender identity or expression fosters (or undercuts) the greater goals of transgender social movements and advocacy efforts. These perspectives also underscore the drawbacks of thinking about hate crime laws in a vacuum, without considering how they connect to the broader treatment of transgender and other gender non-conforming people – as well as other minority populations – in the criminal justice system.

Notes

1 These 19 states were Andorra, Belgium, Canada, Croatia, Cyprus, Denmark, Finland, France, Germany, Iceland, Ireland, Liechtenstein, Lithuania, Netherlands, Norway, Serbia, Sweden, the United Kingdom and the United States.
2 These nine states were Belgium, Canada, Finland, Germany, Norway, Portugal, Serbia, Sweden and the United Kingdom.

References

Anti-Defamation League (2013). ADL deeply concerned about alleged transgender hate crime in Silver Spring, MD. Mar. 14, 2013. Available at http://regions.adl.org/dc/adl-deeply-concerned-about-1.html (last retrieved May 23, 2013).
Black and Pink (2011). Non-support for Massachusetts' transgender equal rights bill. Available at www.blackandpink.org/revolt/non-support-for-massachusetts-transgender-equal-rights-bill/ (last retrieved May 23, 2013).
Clements-Nolle, K., Marx, R. and Katz, M. (2006). Attempted suicide among transgender persons: The influence of gender-based discrimination and victimization. *Journal of Homosexuality*, 51: 53–69.
Cohan, D., Lutnick, A., Davidson, P., Cloniger, C., Herylyn, A., Breyer, J., Cobaugh, C., Wilson, D. and Klausner, J. (2006). Sex Worker Health: San Francisco Style. *Sexually Transmitted Infections*, 82: 418–422.
Currah, P., Juang, R. M. and Minter, S. P. (eds). (2006). *Transgender rights*. Minneapolis: Minnesota University Press.
Currah, P. and Minter, S. (2005). Unprincipled exclusions: The struggle to achieve judicial and legislative equality for transgender people. In E. Bernstein and L. Schaffner (eds) (pp. 35–48). *Regulating sex: The politics of intimacy and identity*. London: Routledge.
Factor, R. J. and Rothblum, E. D. (2007). A study of transgender adults and their non-transgender siblings on demographic characteristics, social support, and experiences of violence. *Journal of LGBT Health*, 3: 11–30.
Federal Bureau of Investigation (FBI) (2012). *Hate crimes accounting: Annual report released*. Available at www.fbi.gov/news/stories/2012/december/annual-hate-crimes-report-released/annual-hate-crimes-report-released (last visited May 23, 2013).
Garofalo, R., Deleon, J., Osmer, E., Doll, M. and Harper, G. W. (2006). Overlooked, misunderstood and at-risk: Exploring the lives and HIV risk of ethnic minority male-to-female transgender youth. *Journal of Adolescent Health*, 38: 230–236.
Grant, J. M., Mottet, L. A., Tanis, J., Harrison, J., Herman, J. L. and Keisling, M. (2011). *Injustice at Every Turn: A Report of the National Transgender Discrimination Survey*. Washington: National Center for Transgender Equality and National Gay and Lesbian Task Force.
Green, J. (2000). Introduction to transgender issues. In *Transgender Equality: A Handbook for Activists and Policymakers*. Washington, DC: National Center for Lesbian Rights. Available at www.thetaskforce.org/downloads/reports/reports/TransgenderEquality.pdf (last visited May 23, 2013).
Human Rights Campaign (2013). Issue: Hate crimes. Available at www.hrc.org/issues/hate-crimes (last visited May 23, 2013).
Juang, R. (2006). Transgendering the politics of recognition. In S. Stryker and S. Whittle (eds), *The transgender studies reader*, pp. 706–719. New York: Routledge.
Kenagy, G. P. (2005). Transgender health findings from two needs assessment studies in Philadelphia. In W. Bockting and E. Avery (eds), *Transgender health and HIV prevention: Needs assessment studies from transgender communities across the United States*, pp. 49–56. Binghamton, NY: Haworth Medical Press.
Kohn, S. (2002). Greasing the wheel: How the criminal justice system hurts gay, lesbian, bisexual and transgendered people and why hate crime laws won't save them. *New York University Review of Law and Social Change*, 27: 257–280.

Mackenzie, G. O. (1994). *Transgender nation*. Bowling Green, OH: Bowling Green State University Popular Press.

Meyer, E. J. (2010). *Gender and sexual diversity in schools: An introduction*. New York: Springer.

Namaste, K. (1996). Genderbashing: Sexuality, gender, and the regulation of public spaces. *Environmental and Planning D: Society and Space, 14*: 221–240.

National Coalition of Anti-Violence Programs (NCAVP). (2011). *Hate violence against lesbian, gay, bisexual, transgender, queer, and HIV-affected communities in the United States in 2011*. New York: NCAVP. Available at www.avp.org/storage/documents/Reports/2012_NCAVP_2011_HV_Report.pdf (last retrieved on May 23, 2013).

Nemoto, T., Operario, D., Keatley, J. and Villegas, D. (2004). Social context of HIV risk behaviours among male-to-female transgenders of colour. *AIDS Care, 16*: 724–735.

Office for Democratic Institutions and Human Rights (ODIHR). (2012). *Hate crimes in the OSCE region: Incidents and responses. Annual report for 2011*. Warsaw, Poland: ODIHR/OSCE.

Perry, B. (2001). *In the name of hate: Understanding hate crimes*. New York: Routledge.

Queers for Economic Justice (QEJ) (2009). QEJ & allies announce non-support of gender non-discrimination act. Available at http://q4ej.org/qej-and-allies-announce-non-support-of-gender-non-discrimination-act (last retrieved May 23, 2013).

Reback, C. J., Simon, P. A., Bernis, C. C. and Gatson, B. (2001). *The Los Angeles transgender health study: Community report*. Los Angeles, CA: Authors. Available at http://friendscommunitycenter.org/documents/LA_Transgender_Health_Study.pdf (last visited May 23, 2013).

Rubenstein, W. (2004). The real story of U.S. hate crime statistics: An empirical analysis. *Tulane Law Review, 78*: 1213–1246.

Sandholtz, N., Langton, L. and Planty, M. (2013). *Hate crime victimization, 2003–2011*. Special report NCJ 241291: U.S. Department of Justice, Office of Justice Programs, Bureau of Justice Statistics. Available at www.bjs.gov/content/pub/pdf/hcv0311.pdf (last retrieved on May 23, 2013).

Sheridan, V. (2009). *The complete guide to transgender in the workplace*. Santa Barbara, CA: ABC-CLIO, LLC.

Smith, K. (ed.), Lader, D., Hoare, J. and Lau, I. (2012). *Hate crime, cyber security and the experience of crime among children: Findings from the 2010/11 British Crime Survey: Supplementary Volume 3 to Crime in England and Wales 2010/11*. London: Home Office.

Spade, D. (2009). Keynote address: Trans law reform strategies, co-optation, and the potential for transformative change. *Women's Rights Law Reporter, 30*: 288–314.

Spade, J. and Willse, C. (2000). Confronting the limits of gay hate crimes activism: A radical critique. *Chicano-Latino Law Review, 21*: 38–52.

Spellman, J. (2009). Transgender murder, hate crime conviction a first. CNN.com, Apr. 23, 2009. Available at www.cnn.com/2009/CRIME/04/22/transgender.slaying.trial/ (last visited May 23, 2013).

SRLP (Sylvia Rivera Law Project) (2013). SRLP on hate crime laws. Available at http://srlp.org/our-strategy/policy-advocacy/hate-crimes/ (last visited May 23, 2013).

Stotzer, R. (2009). Violence against transgender people: A review of United States data. *Aggression and Violent Behavior, 14*: 170–179.

Strout, J. (2012). The Massachusetts transgender equal rights bill: Formal equality in a transphobic system. *Harvard Journal of Law and Gender, 35*: 515–521.

Transgender Europe (TGEU) (2013). Constant rise in murder rates: Transgender Europe's Trans Murder Monitoring project reveals more than 1,100 reported murders of trans people in the last five years. Transgender Europe: Press Release: March 12, 2013. Available at www.transrespect-transphobia.org/uploads/downloads/2013/TMM-english/TvT-TMM2013-Update-PR_EN.pdf (last visited May 23, 2013).

Transgender Law & Policy Institute (2009). Hate Crime Laws (last edited Oct. 28, 2009). Available at www.transgenderlaw.org/hatecrimelaws/index.htm (last visited May 23, 2013).

Turner, L., Whittle, S. and Combs, R. (2009). *Transphobic hate crime in the European Union*. IGLA-Europe and Press for Change. Available at www.ucu.org.uk/media/pdf/r/6/transphobic_hate_crime_in_eu.pdf (last retrieved May 23, 2013).

Valdes, F. (1995). Queers, sissies, dykes, and tomboys: Deconstructing the conflation of 'sex,' 'gender,' and 'sexual orientation' in Euro-American law and society. *California Law Review, 83*: 1–377.

Valera, R. J., Sawyer, R. G. and Schiraldi, G. R. (2000). Violence and Post Traumatic Stress Disorder in a Sample of Inner City Street Prostitutes. *American Journal of Health Studies, 16*: 149–155.

Weinberg, M. S., Shaver, F. M. and Williams, C. J. (1999). Gendered Sex Work in the San Francisco Tenderloin. *Archives of Sexual Behavior, 28*: 503–521.

Whittle, S., Turner, L. and Al-Alami, M. (2007). Engendered penalties: Transgender and transsexual people's experiences of inequality and discrimination. London: Equalities Review. Available at www.pfc.org.uk/pdf/EngenderedPenalties.pdf (last retrieved May 23, 2013).

Wilchins, R. A., Lombardi, L., Priesing, D. and Malouf, D. (1997). *First national survey of transgender violence*. New York: Gender Public Advocacy Coalition.

Woods, J. B. (2008). Taking the 'hate' out of hate crimes: Applying unfair advantage theory to justify the enhanced punishment of opportunistic bias crimes. *UCLA Law Review, 56*: 489–541.

Xavier, J., Honnold, J. A. and Bradford, J. (2007). *The health, health-related needs, and lifecourse experiences of transgender Virginians*. Richmond: Division of Disease Prevention through the Centers of Disease Control and Prevention, Virginia Department of Health.

Xavier, J. M., Bobbin, M., Singer, B. and Budd, E. (2005). A Needs Assessment of Transgendered People of Color Living in Washington D.C. *International Journal of Transgenderism, 8*: 31–47.

23
A personal reflection on good and evil on the Internet

Sol Littman

One would hardly expect the 2,000-year-old *Dead Sea Scrolls* to become the subject of a contemporary battle on the Internet, yet, the young scholar, Raphael Golb, resorted to numerous blogs under diverse aliases to defend his father's theory of the Scrolls' origins.

> He started a blog; then another and another, each under a different name. The aliases begot other aliases known on the Internet known as sock puppets: 20, 40, 60, 80. The sock puppets debated with other posters, each time linking to other sock puppets to support their arguments, creating the impression of an army of engaged scholars espousing his [father's] ideas.[1]

Unfortunately, instead of sticking to the kind of high-minded academic discourse that would enhance the reputation of the Internet, Golb's puppets indulged in accusations of plagiarism and misrepresentation on the scholars who disagreed with his father.[2] But tracing his I.P. address identified Golb's 82 aliases and, as a result, he faced 51 charges of identity theft, aggravated harassment, criminal impersonation, forgery and unauthorized use of computers in a N.Y.U. library.

No knowledgeable person doubts that the Internet's invention has been a mixed blessing, that it has lent itself to tremendous good and unanticipated evil. Among the evils is the use of the Internet to trade in child pornography, seduce children, preach hate, engage in fraudulent sales, plant false rumours, and anonymously bully and slander classmates.

Yet, looking back on the history of information technology we have seen each advance greeted as a gift to the masses and a threat to the established order. Gutenberg's printing press was both welcomed and feared. On the one hand the Bible could be readily reproduced so that common men – at least those who were literate – could read the holy book for themselves and not be dependent on the hand-written manuscripts stored in monastery libraries. At the same time, many churchmen feared that having ready access to the scriptures without their guidance might lead to multiple interpretations of God's word. And as they predicted, Luther quoted scripture to attack the established church.

Similarly, the introduction of cheap pulp paper to replace costly sheets of linen paper was seen as revolutionary. Linen was suitable for the thoughtful essays of Addison and Steele but they had limited circulation and concerned themselves chiefly with the issues that occupied the aristocracy. Pulp paper lent itself to mass circulation of newspapers for a ha'penny. Now the weaver in the factory and the miner in the pits could afford to read the news and make his own judgments. The truth could be told and democracy strengthened.

However, the promise of newspapers was tainted by the "yellow journalism" practised by Randolph Hearst's daily newspaper chain with its scare headlines in huge print, faked interviews, false experts and a lavish use of graphic pictures. Supermarket tabloids such as the *National Enquirer* and the *Globe* did little to strengthen democracy by devoting themselves to sensational crime stories, the sex exploits of movie stars, and tales of aliens from outer space mating with humans.

Hopes were renewed by the invention of radio. Here was an instrument that sat in the listener's home. In radio's Golden Age, blue and red networks brought great dramas and the world's greatest composers into the living room. Arturo Toscanini led the NBC symphony orchestra in weekly concerts. Arthur R. Murrow and his colleagues reported from bomb-torn London, and learned men participated in panel discussions.

Surely, this was an instrument to inform and elevate its audience. But before long high-mindedness gave way to low entertainment, and "Top Ten" pop tunes replaced Mozart and Beethoven. Single-minded talk radio substituted for reasoned exchange of opinion; soap operas replaced the works of Puccini and Wagner.

Then came television. Radio sets, which had dominated living rooms, were shuffled into kitchens and bedrooms to make room for the center of attention. By the early 1950s television served as a combination of Broadway theater, movie house, museum, news purveyor, political forum, art gallery, and vaudeville show. For the first time, large audiences could watch live ballet and attend opera performances. But here again gold standards were tarnished; television programs were expensive to produce, broadcasting 24 hours a day required major capital and television artistry bowed to commerce; repetitive advertisements for purgatives and sex arousers crowded the airways. TV producers had to keep in mind a sponsor's whims and wishes. High-minded newscasts of the Murrow and Cronkite era gave way to rancorous talk shows.

But no technical advance in communications raised hopes as high as the Internet. Here was an instrument that didn't require a large capital investment; it didn't have to pass through the hands of editors and publishers; there were virtually no laws governing its operation. It was free of defined subject matter; you could call down the wrath of God on the government or post intimate information on the state of your digestion.

Many of the Internet's idealistic young prophets saw the Internet as the ultimate instrument for the sharing of opinion and information. The Internet, they claimed, would serve as a worldwide Agora, the ancient Greek forum in which all opinions would be heard and consensus reached by open argument.

Needless to say, this utopian dream had absolutely no chance of being realized. Within months of its launch, the Internet became an instrument of derision, assumptions parading as facts and claims impossible to validate.

Obviously, not everything about the Internet turned out to be bad. It had its many positive uses. It made communication between friends and family members quick and easy. It brought forth the Arab Spring by mustering crowds for demonstrations in Tahrir Square. It allowed political parties to solicit campaign funds from party members; it facilitated the petitioning of members of Congress. Blogs gave new perspectives on numerous issues; Facebook allowed us to describe ourselves, as we would prefer to be seen. Twitter's chief virtue was its 16-word limit but it trained a verbose nation in brevity. Texting produced a new language and a new series of abbreviations (u no wat I meen).

Yet, every virtue had its accompanying illness. On-line dating led to many successful marriages, but at the same time it gave sexual predators access to naïve teenagers. Its anonymity, coupled with its freedom and diversity, encouraged the expression of venomous racial and religious hate messages that went unchallenged and unpunished.

Ironically, this tool that initially promised democracy, became the favorite instrument for fascist-minded hate mongers, enabling them to reach vast audiences. Sometime in the early 1960s, George Lincoln Rockwell, commander of the American Nazi Party, decided to hold a rally in Michigan where he had a dozen active followers.[3] When no Michigan municipality would issue him a parade licence, he decided to hold the rally in the suburban backyard of one of his party members.

In the week prior to the rally, two or three young men were observed hurriedly sticking leaflets advertising the meeting under the windshield wipers of automobiles parked in downtown parking lots. Another young man in full Nazi regalia stood near the entrance of one of Detroit's high schools handing out printed invitations to George Lincoln Rockwell's Nazi-fest. The police soon chased him away.

In the eyes of Rockwell's followers the strenuous pamphleteering in parking lots and school entrances was well worth the effort; six veteran followers formed a guard of honor, Nazi flags blew in the breeze and a half dozen newcomers expressed interest in joining the movement.

Today, a single neo-Nazi lurking in his basement with a cheap computer can reach thousands of potential converts in a matter of minutes. He can send them the latest denunciation of the Jews, the most recent warning against race mixing, the most vitriolic description of undocumented Mexican immigrants, and the latest anti-government conspiracy theories. The question can be asked: Why is this permitted? A further question asks: How can it be prevented?

In reality hate utterances on the Internet can easily be blocked. Every Internet message is forwarded by a provider who has only to "pull the plug" to silence the sender. And on occasion it has been done in response to complaints with a minimum of fuss and bother. True, the sender can then seek out another provider but he is liable to meet the same fate wherever he goes.

Then why doesn't it happen this way? After all, the giant providers are private companies and like newspapers they are under no obligation to print every "letter-to-the-editor" or every op-ed article submitted. They have the ultimate right of "editorship." They can, if they wish, pick and choose. But the providers are reluctant to play the editorial role; they would rather take refuge in the notion that they are simply "carriers" who only deliver the package regardless of its content. They are deterred by the sheer volume of transmissions on their networks and the possibility of frivolous lawsuits launched by rejected senders.

There are ready answers to both these problems. In the same way that the default computer-user can eliminate spam by bopping specific words, phrases or company names, providers can be alerted to questionable material on their network. Also, given the violent nature of much of the hate material posted on the Internet the courts are unlikely to rule in their favor.

Let me make use of a recent event reported in the *New York Times* – the bizarre case of New York City police officer Gilberto Valle currently charged with conspiracy to kidnap and accessing a government data base without authorization.[4] Mr. Valle's wife, Kathleen Mangan-Valle, recounted how she had delved into her husband's chat history on a laptop one day, only to discover that he had been talking about killing various women, including her:

> I was going to be tied up by my feet and my throat slit, and they would have fun watching the blood gush out of me . . .

Subsequent e-mails had Mr. Valle saying things like "I have longed to butcher and cook female meat." The *Times* report suggests that "there's a huge amount of online activity devoted to cultivating horrific impulses towards women" that lurks in the darkest corners of the Internet that needs to be cleared out.

In the United States any talk of regulation runs smack into the issue of censorship and the guarantee of freedom of speech provided by the First Amendment. But the First Amendment applies chiefly to restriction or censorship by the government or a government agency, not private parties. A book or newspaper publisher is free to reject a manuscript for whatever reason, whether for its political viewpoint, lack of artistic merit, or the likelihood that it won't sell well. While the Valle case may be extreme, I know of no one who would argue that Valle's First Amendment rights would be trammelled if Yahoo, AOL, Gmail or some other provider had chosen to "pull the plug" on his insane utterings.

Not all restrictions are evil. Traffic laws limit our God-given freedom of movement. Speed limits, traffic lights, stop signs serve to keep traffic moving and prevent us from going the wrong way up a one-way street. Surely if we can abide traffic laws that protect our lives we can abide some limits on our freedom of expression in order to prevent senseless attacks on our reputations and the security of our gender, race, national origin and sexual preference.

I am well aware that millions of computer operators will protest any restriction on their digital activities, but millions also swore that no government was going to compel them to buckle up their seat belts or don helmets when they mounted their motorcycles. Thousands more refused to vaccinate their children against measles and whooping cough. Yet, as time went on, most people realized that vaccines, helmets and seatbelts saved lives – theirs and others.

Some may argue that the Internet is too ubiquitous, too diverse to be controlled. They claim – not without justice – that if an American provider pulls on an acknowledged bigot, the bigot will simply sign up with a provider in a foreign country. That is certainly true but doesn't necessarily deal the notion of regulation of the Internet a fatal blow. Instead, it points to the necessity of common international standards for all Internet operators. Some may argue that it is impossible to achieve that high degree of cooperation between nations in this day and age. Not necessarily. Piracy on the high seas was once considered a desirable activity among competing nations but in the end they realized they had more to lose than to gain and anti-piracy laws won the respect of all civilized nations.

Similarly, competing airlines faced great dangers in the skies as each set its own schedules and set its own safety standards. National airlines, frequently an object of pride for a country that had little else to offer, saw regulation as an attack on their sovereignty, yet eventually they all saw the light and organized the International Air Transport Association (IATA) headquartered in Montreal, Canada. Today, the IATA has 240 members who carry 84 percent of all air traffic.

If we can manage to set personnel standards and coordinate the highly complicated routes and schedules of airlines that fly in and over national boundaries, surely we can find a way to keep hate material, reputation assassination and sexual predation in check on the Internet. Given the importance and rapid efflorescence of the Internet, isn't it time that we reined our enthusiasm for this new medium and take a second look to determine what is worth promoting and what is best discarded?

Notes

1   *New York Times*, February 17, 2013, page 25.
2   Norman Golb, University of Chicago.
3   A disgruntled follower assassinated Rockwell in 1967.
4   *New York Times*, March 4, 2013.

24
Hate on the Internet

Sarah Rohlfing

Literature on hate crime is somewhat characterised by academic debate concerning the identification of the causal factors leading to hate-motivated behaviour (Jacobs and Potter, 1998; Sullivan, 1999; Hall, this volume). Extensive research into hate in general, for example, stereotyping and discrimination (Baron and Byrne, 1994; Brown, 1995), persuasion (Petty and Cacioppo, 1986; Chaiken, 1987), and prejudice (Allport, 1954), has already been carried out. The theories used to account for these elements in playing a role in negative attitudes and hate-motivated behaviour include classic psychological and social-psychological theories, such as social identity theory (Tajfel and Turner, 1986), the social identity model of deindividuation effects (Reicher et al., 1995), and deindividuation (Zimbardo, 1969; Diener, 1980). However, whilst these deliver some explanation into factors contributing towards why people may commit acts of hatred (Hall, 2005, 2013), current psychological research into underlying processes of hate crimes is still somewhat limited. Therefore, remarkably little is known about the underlying social and social psychological processes that give rise to hate-motivated offending behaviour (Bowling, 1999; Hall, 2010) and, specifically, the causal risk factors that potentially contribute towards both negative prejudiced attitudes and subsequent actions (Sibbitt, 1997; Green et al., 2003). In fact, hate crime has only recently been adopted as a psychological topic in social psychology textbooks (see Hogg and Vaughan, 2010).

Adding to these gaps in knowledge, and the general lack of adequate theoretical models with which to account for hate-motivated offending behaviour, are increasing political and wider social concerns about the role of the Internet in shaping hate-based attitudes and inciting criminal behaviour towards certain identifiable groups, such as those based on race, faith, sexual orientation, transgender and disability (OSCE, 2010; Home Office, 2009; ACPO, 2013; PCAA, 2011). Prior to the Internet, and particularly prior to Web 2.0, members of (organised) hate groups relied on various other, more traditional, means of communication to get their message across using propaganda (for example, leaflet dropping and/or the distribution of propaganda filled music via CDs or the radio, as well as the distribution of other print materials, and the like), to recruit new members to their cause and to threaten members of their 'target' groups. Naturally, these means required more physical effort from hate group members (for example, financial, physical presence, printing and distributing/delivering the materials), but these means were also more limited in terms of the size of the audience reached.

Sarah Rohlfing

This chapter consists of six sections, which examine and synthesise existing research and issues relating to online hatred. The sections are structured as follows:

The first section discusses the Internet as an additional medium or tool for hate groups to spread and incite hatred, and considers the challenges the Internet delivers for those whose responsibility it is to combat online hatred. The second section includes some of the relevant academic evidence in relation to online hatred. In particular, it refers to psychological and criminological examinations of the content of hate websites. It further discusses existing research on/with online hate group members. The findings derived from these studies are explained through their practical applications, including recruiting new members to the cause, the way audiences are targeted, who is targeted, the commission of acts of hatred, and some of the psychological underpinnings to these methods.

The third section of this chapter will examine some of the current research limitations, including the challenges that the complexity of online hatred delivers, the 'end-product-approach' taken by many researchers, and the lack of knowledge regarding the impact of online hatred on its victims. The fourth section discusses legislative challenges of online hatred. The main focus of this section refers to the lack of cross-jurisdiction agreement of hate crime legislation. It further examines the legal disagreements about what constitutes an online hate crime in relation to social networking and the responsibilities of Internet Service Providers (ISPs) to detect and remove hateful web-content.

The fifth section examines the consequences of online hatred to its victims by drawing on recent suicide cases attributed to online bullying. It then compares some of the potential similarities between the impacts of online bullying and online hatred to its victims. Finally, some concluding thoughts about the future of research into online hatred and related policy making are discussed.

The Internet

Since the introduction of the Internet, hate crimes can now be committed in the virtual world, especially using social media, including for example, Twitter, Facebook, and YouTube. Social networking sites, and the Internet more generally, have the potential for reaching many more members than other more traditional methods (Douglas, 2007), require much less effort, and are also more cost-effective (Whine, 1997; Perry, 2000). Indeed, as Douglas (2007) points out, connecting with others who share the same ideology can now simply be done by the clicking of a button. Therefore, the accessibility, immediacy and popularity of the Internet raises concerns over its potential for exploitation by those wishing to incite hatred against particular groups (Deshotels and Forsyth, 2007; Home Office, 2009).

Furthermore, according to Bargh and McKenna (2004) the Internet allows easy access to information and can connect people who would have previously been isolated from one another. They further argue that activities carried out on the Internet are largely anonymous, which reduces self-disclosure and contributes towards the formation of virtual relationships. The Internet further enables individuals with common beliefs to find and communicate with one another and build virtual communities all over the world. However, these virtual relationships also allow the reinforcement of socially unacceptable behaviours, including spreading messages of hatred (McDonald et al., 2009). For example, research on paedophilia (Durkin and Bryant, 1999) and self-injury (Adler and Adler, 2008) has demonstrated that existing online communities can reinforce and validate shared 'negative' beliefs among Internet users.

In addition, the position of the UK Home Office (2009: 11) under the previous Labour government supported academic findings and shared the concern that the Internet can be exploited for inciting online hatred. In particular, their position was that:

> Those inciting hatred can get their abhorrent messages out more quickly and to a wider range of people than ever before. The Internet is also a vehicle by which material that promotes or encourages violent extremism or terrorism may be spread. Some of this material may incite hatred or violence against particular groups and may constitute a criminal offence.

According to the statement above, the former government relied on the *assumption* that online hate materials may incite violence. However, this assumption has not yet been tested empirically. In addition to the lack of empirical evidence for this assumption, Amichai-Hamburger (2005), and Bargh and McKenna (2004) proposed that little is known about how the Internet influences peoples' behaviour in general. Gerstenfeld et al. (2003) argued more specifically that the impact of hate group websites remains unclear.

In addition to government, the media has also raised concerns about the Internet's direct responsibility for deviant behaviours (Bennett, 2008; Wolf, 2009). Yet, research has largely neglected the extent to which the Internet affects the prevalence of deviant behaviours (McDonald et al., 2009). Another problem is the lack of restrictions on what can and cannot be posted online. One issue within this domain relates to the freedom of speech. Opposing views argue that harmful speech is directly linked to harmful action and the aim of victimising minorities (USHMM, 2009). In the US, hate speech is constitutionally 'protected' by the First Amendment, which in the past had led people to use servers based in the US to advocate their extreme positions. It is therefore vital to investigate and clarify the link between hate messages on the Internet and active hate offending in order to fully understand and effectively respond to the problems it may present.

Academic contributions towards understanding online hate

Research from various disciplines into hatred has begun to focus on the virtual world, with a primary focus on content analyses of racist and white supremacist websites (Green et al., 1999; McDonald, 1999; Burris et al., 2000; Lee and Leets, 2002; Gerstenfeld et al., 2003; Bostdorff, 2004; Douglas et al., 2005; Hara and Estrada, 2005; Zhou et al., 2005), ethnographic studies with white supremacist forums (Glaser et al., 2002), and interview studies with white supremacists (Green et al., 1999). From these studies, three main aims of hate websites have been identified (Douglas, 2007), namely linking people and groups with similar views together (Blazak, 2001; Lee and Leets, 2002; Levin, 2002; Gerstenfeld et al., 2003; Anti-Defamation League, 2005), 'educating' non-white supremacists (Blazak, 2001; Douglas, 2007), and recruitment of new members to the cause (Lee and Leets, 2002; Turpin-Petrosino, 2002; Gerstenfeld et al., 2003; Douglas et al., 2005).

As part of this, the content of those websites rarely involves direct adverts for violence or hate (Gerstenfeld et al., 2003), but instead involves persuasive narratives and arguments presented on the hate group's websites (Lee and Leets, 2002). Examples include arguments against inter-racial mixing, superiority of Whites (for example, as supposedly chosen by God as the superior race), reinforcement of positive images of happy White people with their happy White babies (Lee and Leets, 2002), or social scientific justifications for White superiority (Douglas et al., 2005). Other findings suggest that hate websites target, and are appealing to, youngsters in particular (Blazak, 2001; Douglas, 2007; Perry, 2000). In support of this latter claim, Kellstedt (2003) argued that mass media influences children more than adults, because children's attitudes are often not yet as strongly developed as those of adults. According to Blazak (2001), hate groups encourage hate crimes in the non-virtual world by creating contexts in which actions seem justified. Some researchers have therefore suggested that this virtual influence could also lead to hate-related actions in the non-virtual world (Burch, 2001; Chau and Xu, 2007; Douglas, 2007).

There is some circumstantial evidence supporting the view that the virtual influence implied above can, indeed, lead to acts of hatred in the non-virtual world, suggesting that the Internet may actually 'act as a vehicle' to facilitate such acts. These include bombing attempts aimed at Jewish, Black and homosexual people which were planned by affiliated members of branches of the former World Church of the Creator (Breckheimer, 2001), and a fire bomb that gutted the headquarters of the Charlie Hedbo newspaper after publishing images of the prophet Muhammad in 2011. Yet, as noted previously, this evidence is circumstantial and therefore does not provide a clear basis for assuming that there is a clear and simple link between virtual exposure to hatred and non-virtual acts of hatred. Neither is there any academic research to back-up this circumstantial evidence. Instead, there is opposing evidence suggesting the relationship between one's attitude and subsequent behaviour remains inconsistent (Ajzen and Fischbein, 1977; Kraus, 1995; Crano and Prislin, 2006).

Furthermore, there is also some evidence suggesting that the relationship between a person participating in hostile or hate speech in the virtual world would not necessarily do so in the offline world (Douglas and McGarty, 2001, 2002). This has generally been attributed to the concept that people in the virtual world can act and remain anonymous in comparison to the non-virtual world. This process of people behaving differently when they are anonymous as opposed to when they are identifiable, has been attributed to the concept of deindividuation (Festinger et al., 1952; Zimbardo, 1969). This concept relies on the assumption that those who perceive themselves as non-identifiable (anonymous), whether in virtual or non-virtual contexts (the Internet or a physical crowd), lose themselves in the mass, and as a result lose their behavioural control, including adherence to social norms, usually practised in identifiable (non-anonymous) contexts. This anonymous (deindividuated) state is argued as leading to anti-normative behaviour because individuals feel they cannot be held accountable for their actions when being anonymous (Festinger et al., 1952; Zimbardo, 1969; Diener, 1980).

Whilst the concept of deindividuation has been challenged by several researchers on the basis of its lack of empirical support (Reicher et al., 1995) and conceptual limitations (Reicher and Potter, 1985; Reicher, 1987), the idea that anonymity leads to anti-normative behaviour is still common. For example, the social identity model of deindividuation effects (SIDE) (Reicher et al., 1995) suggests anonymity does not automatically lead to negative (anti-normative) behaviour. It also challenges the principle that, in contexts of anonymity, such as a large number of others, individuals simply lose their behavioural control in this mass. Instead, SIDE proposes that the individual shifts from their individual or personal identity towards a social or group identity. In particular, the theory suggests that in a non-identifiable (anonymous) context, such as a crowd or the Internet, an individual immerses themselves into the social group they identify with, and consequently adhere to the (positive and/or negative) standards of this group (Reicher et al., 1995). It further proposes that individuals can have several social identities because individuals may identify as belonging to more than one group. This proposition explains individuals' different behaviours in different contexts at different times (Reicher et al., 1995). Nevertheless, the jury is still out on the causal role anonymity plays in anti-social behaviour – and, by extension in online hate crimes.

The consequences of anonymity in virtual communication and subsequent virtual behaviour have also been investigated by computer-mediated-communication (CMC) researchers (for example, Joinson, 1998). CMC proposes that communication demonstrated in the virtual world is distinctive to the virtual world and therefore communication in the virtual world differs from that in the real world (Douglas, 2007; Spears and Lea, 1994). Whilst there is no evidence supporting that anonymity inevitably leads to negative virtual behaviour, there is some evidence suggesting that virtual communication can be hostile and disinhibited (Douglas and McGarty, 2001). Amichai-Hamburger (2013) argues also that anonymity in combination with an absence of social cues usual to virtual communication can often lead to disinhibition. He further argues that individuals are more likely to join virtual groups that could hold negative stigmas than join non-virtual groups, because they can a) hide their identity from a virtual group and b) avoid and escape non-virtual exposure to social stigmatisation for their group-membership (DeKoster and Houtman, 2008).

In a study with members of 'Stormfront', DeKoster and Houtman (2008) found that those members who experienced non-virtual stigmatisation used the community of the forum for refuge, whereas those who experienced no non-virtual stigmatisation did not display this sense of community. Furthermore, Corb (2011; see also this volume) interviewed 100 members of online White supremacist groups online and found that a) 65 per cent of respondents admitted to having been approached and/or influenced towards White supremacy on the Internet, and b) participants perceived the virtual world as having 'no boundaries' and 'everything goes', meaning that they could say whatever they wanted, because 'no one knows who you are . . .'.

A different, but related form of anonymous negative virtual communication is the recently emerging concept of 'trolling'. Trolls, who are often associated with online bullying, seem to experience pleasure and satisfaction out of the reactions, supporting or condoning, they receive for their often offensive and sometimes hateful virtual posts and comments. Whilst the consequences of trolling and bullying can be devastating to the recipients, such as committing suicide (discussed later), at this stage, trolls often receive no penalty for their online behaviour.

With the notion of various different underlying processes pointed out above, which have been attributed to hatred generally and online hatred specifically, and those who have yet to be investigated and determined, it becomes clear that the concept of hate crimes, whether being committed virtually or in the 'real' world, are a complex matter. Whilst psychology generally tries to categorise people in order to understand and explain related phenomena (such as introversion or extroversion, mental disorders, risk factors to delinquency, and so on), some phenomena (including autism, re-offending and hate crimes) might simply be too complex to put them into categories and assume that by displaying some identified variables, the outcome will always be the same. In the context of online hatred or hatred in general, even if research were able to identify variables that might predict future acts of hatred, would this justify intervention before the committing of the actual act? Of course not. Otherwise this concept would have been applied to other phenomena already.[1]

Research limitations

The complexity of hate crime related processes, pointed out above, is reflected by research generally focusing on one particular factor/process in attempts to explain the underlying processes involved in people committing hate crimes, irrespectively of being committed in the virtual or non-virtual world. This is of course understandable, bearing in mind that findings naturally need to be explained, and whilst a combination of variables are most likely to be in place during the expression of hatred, attempting to explain them in combination or even in percentage attribution might seem an impossible task, leaving these explanations open for criticism and further debate. Nevertheless, whilst delivering a good insight into the particular factor/process being investigated, the result is that the outcomes of research necessarily mask the complexity of the situation.

A further limitation in much existing research relates to the often applied 'end-product-approach' (focusing exclusively on those who are *already engaging* in online hate), which analyses hate website content, or studying white supremacists. Whilst this approach has provided a good basis for explaining why, in loose terms, 'haters' use the Internet for their purposes, questions, such as, how 'non-haters'[2] or 'peripheral haters' would be affected by the content of hate websites and hate materials; and more broadly whether the Internet can shape people's hatred towards others, remain unanswered. Some research (Rauch and Schanz, 2013; Rohlfing et al.; Rohlfing and Sonnenberg, both forthcoming) has therefore started to focus on people who are not yet, or are not at all, members of online hate groups in an attempt to shed light on some of the processes relevant for exposure to hate materials and hate speech, as well as online participation in hate speech interactions, instead of focusing on the 'end product hater'.

Additionally, the argument made by Douglas (2007) that the consequences of hate messages and hate materials are unknown still resonates to date. In addition to this gap in knowledge, other areas of interest and importance have emerged within the field of online hatred. One of these areas concerns the impact online hate crimes may have on their victims. Whilst this has now been recognised and subsequent research into the victim-impact of hate crimes in general is currently being carried out (Chakraborti and Garland, in process), the current knowledge of this impact is limited (but see Iganski, and Perry, both this volume). Furthermore, to the author's knowledge, no research to date has directly and explicitly investigated the impact of online victimisation on hate crime victims.

In a related field, Dooley et al. (2009) have argued that victims of cyber bullying perceive the severity of online bullying the same, or even worse, than face-to-face bullying. A similar investigation into the levels of depression of victims of cyber bullying and traditional bullying also revealed that those who were bullied online showed higher levels of depression (Wang et al., 2010). One may speculate that the impact of victimisation in online hate behaviour could also be viewed in a similar manner. This claim is based on two assumptions. First, perpetrators can commit their crimes anonymously (Greene, 2006; Anderson and Sturm, 2007; Chibbaro, 2007; Ybarra et al., 2007), which in turn might lead to an increase in victims' levels of fear as 'it could be anyone out in the street', as opposed to knowing 'the face' of the perpetrator. It might also be easier to judge if the perpetrator might commit future crimes if they are known to the victims, rather than being anonymous. Second, the abusive material is potentially available to millions of other Internet users (Wang et al., 2010), which could increase the public visibility of the victimisation and potential for incitement. It is however important to note here that the crimes referred to in this context are non-physical, but that any of these crimes can (and probably will) have negative impacts on their victims.

Legislative challenges

An advantage of the Internet for those wishing to incite hatred is presented by the 'loop holes' in the criminal justice systems across the globe. In other words, an offence such as posting racial slurs on the Internet may count as incitement to racial hatred and therefore be criminal in one country, but may not be classed as a criminal offence in another country (Douglas, 2007). Despite many countries around the world acknowledging that online hatred is a growing problem, and them investing large amounts of money to combat it (OSCE, 2010; No Hate Speech Movement, 2013), there remains a clear lack of consensus amongst countries' online hate legislation. Most of this can be explained by arguments relating to the right to freedom of expression and, in the United States, the First Amendment. Whilst the argument to protect one's right to freedom of expression is clearly important, the lack of consensus highlighted above can lead to difficulties in policing, regulation, and therefore in effectively tackling the problems that online hatred seems to present.

In the United Kingdom, the milestone case *R v Sheppard and Whittle* (2009 and 2010) has put the wheels in motion to address, at least in part, the issue relating to the lack of consensus in relation to inciting online hatred. In particular, the case established that offenders should be tried in the same jurisdiction in which they committed the offence (where the button to upload the hateful content was pressed), regardless of where the Internet servers are hosted. The importance of the decision of this case rests with the location of the host-server the accused parties used to upload their hateful materials (California, US), where the upload of these materials was not classed an offence. The parties were subsequently convicted of inciting racial hatred and their appeal dismissed on three points. First, almost everything in the case related to the UK (where the material was created, edited, uploaded and controlled). Second, the content of the material was aimed primarily at the British public with the intent of stirring up racial hatred. Third, the only foreign element was the location of the website server, which was only one stage in the transmission of the material.

However, the agreement about what constitutes criminal in relation to inciting online hatred and who should be included into hate crime legislation is not always clear-cut. For example, the media and the Crown Prosecution Service in the United Kingdom have recently experienced much controversy about celebrities and others making racial comments via social media (Voula Papachristou, 2012; the involvement of a 17-year-old over tweets to British Olympian Tom Daley, 2012 – see Hawkins, this volume) and in person (Luis Suarez, 2012; John Terry, 2012 – again, see Hawkins, this volume). Despite not all of the incidents stated above resulting in criminal convictions, they encouraged widespread debates on the limits to the right of free expression.

A further challenge towards effectively tackling the 'online hate problem' relates to lack of enforcement some ISPs' practice towards the removal and surveillance of hateful web-content. Instead, these rely on web-users agreeing to their terms and conditions, which often state that by agreeing to the website's terms and conditions, the user would agree not to do a number of things, including not uploading, posting or publishing offensive and/or abusive content. As a result, offensive, abusive and hateful web-content has to be reported before the service providers might remove it. One may therefore argue that there should be procedures in place to make the detection and removal of such content easier, and for this to be the responsibility of the service providers. One of these procedures could include the requirement that users who sign up for the service provide verifiable personal information. This could lead to two advantages. First, the provision of this information might decrease the level of perceived anonymity (discussed later), which in turn might influence and limit what information people chose to upload. Second, the information can be readily passed on to the authorities in instances where the user posts or uploads content that potentially constitutes a criminal offence.

Whilst it is not the view of the author of this chapter to suggest that the use of the Internet, or indeed access to hate websites, should be restricted in order to combat online hatred, some authors (such as Burch, 2001) have argued that censorship is one way of addressing some of the identified aims (discussed later) attributed to hate websites. A different view to this argument suggests that restrictions related to the use of the Internet would not only drive people wishing to incite hatred away from using public websites, and therefore not tackle the problem, but instead displace it elsewhere. This in turn would inhibit any effective monitoring of 'what goes on' (Douglas, 2007) and further limit the information available to develop prevention strategies and further research.

Consequences of online hate

The sad reality of the consequences online bullying can have on its victims is found in 43 acknowledged cases of teen suicides between 2003 and 2013. However, LeBlanc (2012) has argued that cyber bullying alone has not led to suicide, but instead other factors such as face-to-face bullying and mental disorders, such as depression, are also contributing factors. This does not really come as a surprise, considering that research has already found that victims of online bullying reported higher levels of depression (Wang et al., 2010). Nevertheless, the study found that cyber and face-to-face bullying had occurred in 78 per cent of those who committed suicide, suggesting that bullying in either form can have extreme consequences for victims. The most recent cases of children committing suicide as a direct consequence of cyber bullying include 13-year-old Hannah Smith in England (August 2013) and 15-year-old Rehtaeh Parsons in Canada (April 2013). Rehtaeh's death lead the Canadian government to introduce the Cyber-safety Act (Nova Scotia Bill 61, 2013), which aims to address and prevent cyber bullying. Other recent cases include that of 13-year-old Erin Gallagher, 15-year-old Ciara Pugley and 15-year-old Amanda Todd whose suicides are all believed to be directly linked to online bullying (O'Cionnaith, 2012). The evidence surrounding a link between cyber bullying and suicide is therefore not clear, but in any case cannot and should not be ignored.

In terms of online hatred and cyber bullying, there are some clear overlaps, including, for example, perpetrators' levels of anonymity and the availability of the posted information to potentially millions of Internet users. The main difference between online bullying and online hatred relates to part of the definition that online bullying has to be a repetitive act (Olweus, 1993; Smith et al., 2008), whereas offences relating to the incitement of hatred do not. One issue with this definition is that whilst it might be sufficient for the non-virtual world, in the virtual world, it seems not sufficient because it implies that posting offensive materials online once does not count as cyber bullying despite it being seen and potentially re-posted or taken further by many other Internet users. In particular, if several individual people post offensive material about an individual online, does that mean that the individual acts are not going to be classed as cyber bullying despite the individual being repeatedly exposed to the offensive materials?

Furthermore, even in the event of there 'only' being one offensive post, tweet, comment, or photo, the victim's perception of repetitive victimisation as a consequence of many others potentially seeing the information is simply ignored by this definition. Nevertheless, based on the similarities between incitement of hatred online and cyber bullying, one may argue that the consequences for their victims could also be similar. There remains, however, a lack of research to support this claim and, as pointed out above, even research into victims of hatred generally remains somewhat limited to date. Future research therefore has a long way to go in order to investigate and explain some of the questions pointed out so far.

Conclusions

Whilst the Internet and its easy accessibility are valuable for information seeking, social networking, as well as numerous other positive features for its many users, the Internet is also being exploited by hate groups, using these features to their advantage for recruiting members and for spreading the hateful messages to a potentially large audience. The Internet can link those who share ideologies together all over the world, which was not possible before its development. Instead, in the context of hatred and negative prejudice, individuals who had extreme views might not have been able to easily get support or agreement from other individuals or groups sharing their views, and therefore may have remained on the same level of prejudice. One may argue that through the ability to share and support similar ideologies on the Internet, individuals are now able to gain approval and support from others, and therefore strengthen their existing beliefs. The results of this process may escalate individuals' levels of prejudice. However, as discussed above, the underlying processes involved in acts of hatred and online hatred are complex and cannot be determined by identifying some individual contributing factors. In other words, even if the Internet contributes towards an escalation of one's level of prejudice, this does not automatically imply that one will then go on and commit acts of hatred.

The complexities of hate, and particularly online hate, have been demonstrated throughout this chapter. For example, whilst academia has identified and applied some relevant theories and processes relating to hate and online hate, the complexities of the phenomena leave some gaps in the existing body of knowledge. These gaps include, but are not limited to, the question of whether the Internet as a medium can lead and/or influence individuals or groups to commit acts of hatred, and the question about what the impact might be for victims of online hatred. Whilst there are undoubtedly many more unanswered questions in relation to online hatred, it is important to point out at this stage that to date academia has contributed a great deal towards explaining and understanding hatred in general (as evidenced in the chapters of this book), and that it will continue to do so, despite the continuing challenge of the pace of Internet development.

Besides the complexities online hatred delivers to researchers, online hatred also delivers challenges to policy makers and Internet Service Providers. In particular, the lack of agreement about what constitutes 'online hate crimes' across different countries inhibits effective policymaking and subsequent responses to them through law enforcement. In addition, this lack of agreement results in a lack of effective enforcement to monitor and remove hateful web content by the responsible Internet Service Providers. If definitions and policies were clearer, perhaps reinforcement of surveillance and removal of hateful web content by the service providers, as well as service providers assisting law enforcement agencies in any resulting investigations and prosecutions, would be possible and more effective.

Whilst the task to examine online hatred might seem daunting to some, particularly considering the complexities and challenges highlighted in this chapter, unravelling these complexities and clarifying and making sense of hatred, and particular online hatred, is undoubtedly necessary in order to effectively deal with the consequences and challenges that online hatred can pose for everyone involved, including victims, law enforcement and policy makers.

Notes

1 Please note, that it is not the intention to imply that the other phenomena named above, and especially mental disorders and risk factors into delinquency, are not complex. In fact, over-lap of symptoms between mental disorders and uncertain predictions of future acts of criminal behaviour in people who display risk factors of delinquency seems anything but simple.

2 In the context of this chapter, the term 'non-hater' is to be understood as someone who has no affiliations or relationship to any hate-group and is not pre-disposed towards expressing hateful views.

References

Adler, P. A. and Adler, P. (2008). The cyber world's self-injurers as loners: Deviant communities, relationships, and selves. *Symbolic Interaction, 31(1)*, 33–56. doi: 10.1525/si.2008.31.1.33

Ajzen, I. and Fischbein, M. (1977). Attitude-behavior relations: A theoretical analysis and review of empirical research. *Psychological Bulletin, 84(5)*, 888–918. doi: 10.1037/0033-2909.84.5.888

Allport, G. W. (1954). *The Nature of Prejudice*. Massachusetts: Addison-Wesley Publishing Co.

Amichai-Hamburger, Y. (2005). *The social net: Understanding human behaviour in cyberspace*. Oxford University Press.

Amichai-Hamburger, Y. (2013). *The Social Net: Understanding Our Online Behavior* (2nd edn.). New York: Oxford University Press.

Anderson, T. and Sturm, B. (2007). Cyberbullying from playground to computer. *Young Adult Library Services, Winter, 5(2)*, 24–27.

Anti-Defamation League (2005). *Attitudes Toward Jews in Twelve European Countries* (May 2005). Retrieved from www.adl.org: www.adl.org/israel/Eur_Poll_Israel_May_2005.pdf

Association of Chief Police Officers (2013). *ACPO Hate Crime Manual*. ACPO: London.

Bargh, J. A. and McKenna, K. Y. A. (2004). The internet and social life. *Annual Review of Psychology, 55(1)*, 573–590. doi: 10.1146/annurev.psych.55.090902.141922

Baron, R. A. and Byrne, D. (1994). *Social Psychology: Understanding Human Interaction*. (7th Edn.). Massachusetts: Allyn and Bacon.

Bennett, J. (2008, December 29). *Why she cuts*. Newsweek. Retrieved March 26, 2011 from www.newsweek.com/id/177135

Blazak, R. (2001). White Boys to Terrorist Men: Target Recruitment of Nazi Skinheads. *American Behavioral Scientist, 44(6)*, 982–1000. doi: 10.1177/00027640121956629

Bostdorff, D. (2004). The Internet rhetoric of the Ku Klux Klan: A case study in website community building run amok. *Communication Studies, 55(2)*, 340–361. doi: 10.1080/10510970409388623

Bowling, B. (1999). *Violent Racism: Victimisation, policing and social context*. New York: Oxford University Press.

Breckheimer, P. (2001). A Haven for Hate: The Foreign and Domestic Implications of Protecting Internet Hate Speech under the First Amendment. *Southern California Law Review, 75*, 1493–1528.

Brown, R. (1995). *Prejudice: Its social psychology*. Oxford: Blackwell.

Burch, E. (2001). Comment: Censoring Hate Speech in Cyberspace: A new Debate in New America. *North Carolina Journal of Law & Technology, 3(1)*, 175–192.

Burris, V., Smith, E. and Strahm, A. (2000). White supremacist network on the Internet. *Sociological Focus, 33(2)*, 215–234. doi: 10.1080/00380237.2000.10571166

Chaiken, S. (1987). The heuristic model of persuasion. In M. P. Zanna, J. M. Olson and C. P. Herman (eds), *Social Influence: The Ontario Symposium* (5th edn., pp. 3–39). Hillsdale, NJ: Erlbaum.

Chau, M. and Xu, J. (2007). Mining communities and their relationships in blogs: A study of online hate groups. *International Journal of Human-Computer Studies, 65*, 57–70. doi: 10.1016/j.ijhcs.2006.08.009

Chibbaro, J. S. (2007). School counsellors and the cyberbully: Interventions and mp- locations. *Professional School Counselling, 11(1)*, 65–68. doi: 10.5330/PSC.n.2010-11.65

Corb, A. (2011). *Into the minds of mayhem: White supremacy, recruitment, and the Internet*. Cambridge: Google Ideas.

Crano, W. D. and Prislin, R. (2006). Attitudes & Persuasion. *Annual Review of Psychology, 57*, 345–374. doi: 10.1146/annurev.psych.57.102904.190034

DeKoster, W. and Houtman, D. (2008). 'Stormfront is like a second home to me'. *Information, Communication & Society, 11(8)*, 1155–1176. doi: 10.1080/13691180802266665

Deshotels, T. H. and Forsyth, C. J. (2007). Postmodern masculinities and the eunuch. *Deviant Behaviour, 28*, 201–218. doi: 10.1080/01639620701232961

Diener, E. (1980). Deindividuation: the absence of self-awareness and self-regulation in group members. In P. Paulus (ed.), *The psychology of group influence* (pp. 1160–1171). Hillsdale, NJ: Erlbaum.

Dooley, J. J., Pyzalski, J. and Cross, D. (2009). Cyberbullying versus face to-face bullying: A theoretical and conceptual review. *Zeitschrift fur Psychologie [Journal of Psychology]*, 217(4), 182–188. Retrieved from http://0web.ebscohost.com.library.brookdalecc.edu/ehost/pdfviewer/pdfviewer?vid=12&hid=11&sid=95c1e0a1-76e8-4022-94ea-bee6242be665%40sessionmgr13

Douglas, K. (2007). Psychology, discrimination and hate groups online. In A. Joinson, K. McKenna, T. Postmes and U. D. Reips (eds), *The Oxford Handbook of Internet Psychology* (pp. 155–163). New York: Oxford University Press.

Douglas, K. M. and McGarty, C. (2001). Indentifiability and self-presentation: Computer-mediated communication and intergroup interaction. *British Journal of Social Psychology*, 40(3), 399–416. doi: 10.1348/014466601164894

Douglas, K. M. and McGarty, C. (2002). Internet identifiability and beyond: A model of the effects of identifiability on communicative behavior. *Group Dynamics*, 6(1), 17–26. doi: 10.1037/1089-2699.6.1.17

Douglas, K. M., McGarty, C., Bliuc, A. M. and Lala, G. (2005). Understanding Cyberhate: Social Competition and Social Creativity in Online White Supremacist Groups. *Social Science Computer Review*, 23(1), 68–76. doi: 10.1177/0894439304271538

Durkin, K. F. and Bryant, C. D. (1999). Propagandizing pederasty: a thematic analysis of on-line exculpatory accounts of unrepentant paedophiles. *Deviant Behaviour*, 20, 103–127. doi: 10.1080/016396299266524

Festinger, L., Pepitone, A. and Newcomb, T. (1952). Some consequences of de-individuation in a group. *The Journal of Abnormal Social Psychology*, 47(2), 382–389. doi: 10.1037/0057906

Gerstenfeld, P. B., Grant, D. R. and Chiang, C. P. (2003). Hate Online: A Content Analysis of Extremist Internet Sites. *Analyses of Social Issues and Public Policy*, 3(1), 29–44. doi: 10.1111/j.1530-2415.2003.00013.x

Glaser, J., Dixit, J. and Green, D. P. (2002). Studying Hate Crime with the Internet: What makes Racists Advocate Racial Violence? *Journal of Social Issues*, 58(1), 177–193. doi: 10.1111/1540-4560.00255

Green, D. P., Abelson, R. P. and Garnett, M. (1999). The distinctive political views of hate-crime perpetrators and white supremacists. In D. A. Prentice, D. T. Miller (eds), *Cultural Divides*, (pp. 429–464). New York: Russell Sage Foundation.

Green, D. P., McFalls, L. H. and Smith, J. K. (2003). Hate Crime: An Emergent Research Agenda. In Perry, B. (ed.). *Hate and Bias Crime: A Reader* (pp. 27–48). New York, Routledge.

Greene, M. B. (2006). Bullying in School: A Plea for Measure of Human Rights. *Journal of Social Issues*, 62(1), 9–125. doi: 10.1177/1461444809341260

Hall, N. (2013). *Hate Crime* (2nd edn.). London: Routledge.

Hall, N. (2010). Law Enforcement and Hate Crime: Theoretical Perspectives on the Complexities of Policing Hatred. In N. Chakraborti (ed.). *Hate Crime: Concepts, Policy, Future Directions* (pp. 169–193). Cullompton: Willan Publishing.

Hall, N. (2005). *Hate Crime*. Cullompton: Willan Publishing.

Hara, N. and Estrada, Z. (2005). Analyzing the mobilization of grassroots activities via the Internet: A case study. *Journal of Information Science*, 31(6), 503–514. doi: 10.1177/0165551505057013

Hogg, M. and Vaughan, G. (2010). *Social Psychology* (6th edn.). Harlow: Pearson Education Limited.

Home Office (2009). *The Cross-Government Action Plan*. London: Home Office.

Jacobs, J. B. and Potter, K. (1998). *Hate Crimes: Criminal law and identity politics*. New York: Oxford University Press.

Joinson, A. (1998). Causes and implications of disinhibition on the Internet. In J. Gackenbach (ed.). *The Psychology of the Internet* (pp. 43–60). New York: Academic Press.

Kellstedt, P. M. (2003). *The Mass Media and the Dynamics of American Racial Attitudes*. New York: Cambridge University Press.

Kraus, S. J. (1995). Attitudes and the Prediction of Behavior: A Meta-Analysis of the Empirical Literature. *Personality and Social Psychology Bulletin*, 21(1), 58–75. doi: 10.1177/0146167295211007

LeBlanc, J. C. (2012, October). *Cyber bullying Only Rarely the Sole Factor Identified in Teen Suicides*. Paper presented at the American Academy of Pediatrics National and Exhibition, New Orleans.

Lee, E. and Leets, L. (2002). Persuasive Storytelling by Hate Groups Online: Examining Its Effects on Adolescents. *American Behavioral Scientist*, 45(6), 927–957. doi: 10.1177/0002764202045006003

Levin, B. (2002). Cyberhate: A legal and historical analysis of extremists' use of computer networks in America. *American Behavioral Scientist*, 45(6), 958–988. doi: 10.1177/0002764202045006004

McDonald, H. S., Horstmann, N., Strom, K. J. and Pope, M. W. (2009). The Impact of the Internet on Deviant Behaviour and Deviant Communities. Institute for Homeland Security Solutions.

Retrieved March 26, 2011, from www.ihssnc.org/portals/0/IRW%20Literature%20Reviews%20 Deviance%20and%20the%20Internet.pdf
McDonald, M. (1999). CyberHate: Extending persuasive techniques of low credibility sources to the World Wide Web. In D. W. Schumann and E. Thorson (eds.), *Advertising and the World Wide Web* (pp. 149–157). Mahwah, NJ: Lawrence Erlbaum Associates.
No Hate Speech Movement (2013). *Combating Hate Speech Online*. Campaign Launch 22 March. Retrieved April 2, 2013, from www.nohatespeechmovement.org/
O'Cionnaith, F. (2012, October 29). Third suicide in weeks linked to cyberbullying. *Irish Examiner*. Retrieved from www.irishexaminer.com/ireland/third-suicide-in-weeks-linked-to-cyberbullying-212271.html
Olweus, D. (1993). *Bullying at school: What we know and what we can do*. Cambridge, MA: Blackwell.
Organisation for Security and Co-operation in Europe (2010). *Incitement vs. Freedom of Expression: Challenges of combating hate crimes motivated by hate on the Internet*. Report of the OSCE-ODIHR Expert Meeting in Warsaw. Retrieved May 20, 2011, from www.osce.org/odihr/68750
Parliamentary Committee Against Antisemitism Foundation (PCAA), (2011). *Ministerial Internet Hate conference – Spring 2011*. Retrieved 26 March 2011 from www.antisemitism.org.uk/events/event-listings
Perry, B. (2000). "Button-down terror": The metamorphosis of the hate movement. *Sociological Focus*, *33(2)*, 113–131. doi: 10.1080/00380237.2000.10571161
Petty, R. E. and Cacioppo, J. T. (1986). The elaboration likelihood model of persuasion. In L. Berkowitz (ed.). *Advances in experimental social psychology* (Volume 19, pp. 123–205). New York: Academic Press.
Rauch, S. M. and Schanz, K. (2013). Advancing racism with Facebook: Frequency and purpose of Facebook use and the acceptance of prejudiced and egalitarian messages. *Computers in Human Behavior*, 29(3), 610–615. doi: 10.1016/j.chb.2012.11.011
Reicher, S. D. (1987). Crowd behaviour as social action. In J. C. Turner, M. A. Hogg, P. J. Oakes, S. D. Reicher and M. S. Wetherell (eds). *Rediscovering the Social Group: A self-categorisation theory* (pp. 171–202). Oxford: Blackwell.
Reicher, S. D. and Potter, J. (1985). Psychological theory as intergroup perspective: A comparative analysis of 'scientific' and 'lay' accounts of crowd events. *Human Relations*, *38(2)*, 167–189. doi: 10.1177/001872678503800206
Reicher, S. D., Spears, R. and Postmes, T. (1995). A social identity model of deindividuation phenomena. *European Review of Social Psychology*, *6(1)*, 161–197. doi: 10.1080/14792779443000049
Sibbitt, R. (1997). *The Perpetrators of Racial Harassment and Racial Violence*. Home Office Research Study No. 176. Retrieved March 26, 2011, from the Great Britain Home Office Website: www.homeoffice.gov.uk/rds/pdfs/hors176.pdf
Smith, P. K., Mahdavi, J., Carvalho, M., Fisher, S., Russell, S. and Tippett, N. (2008). Cyberbullying: Its nature and impact in secondary school pupils. *Journal of Child Psychology & Psychiatry*, *49(4)*, 376–385. doi: 10.1111/j.1469-7610.2007.01846.x
Spears, R. and Lea, M. (1994). Panacea or panopticon? The hidden power in computer-mediated-communication. *Communication Research*, 21(4), 427–459. doi: 10.1177/009365094021004001
Sullivan, A. (1999, September 26). What's so bad about hate? The illogic and illiberalism behind hate crime laws. *The New York Times Magazine*. Retrieved March 26, 2011, from www.nytimes.com/1999/09/26/magazine/what-s-so-bad-about-hate.html
Tajfel, H. and Turner, J. C. (1986). The social identity theory of intergroup behavior. In S. Worchel and W. G. Austin (eds). *Psychology of intergroup relations* (pp. 7–24). Chicago, IL: Nelson-Hall.
Turpin-Petrosino, C. (2002). Hateful Sirens . . . Who Hears Their Song? An Examination of Student Attitudes Toward Hate Groups and Affiliation Potential. *Journal of Social Issues*, *58(2)*, 281–301. doi: 10.1111/1540-4560.00261
United States Holocaust Memorial Museum (2009). *Hate Speech and Group Targeted Violence*. USHMM: Washington DC.
Wang, J., Iannotti, R. J., Luk, J. W. and Nansel, T. R. (2010). Co-occurrence of Victimization from Five Subtypes of Bullying: Physical, Verbal, Social Exclusion, Spreading Rumors, and Cyber. *Journal of Pediatric Psychology*, *35(10)*, 1103–1112. doi: 10.1093/jpepsy/jsq048
Whine, M. (1997). The far right on the Internet. In B. D. Loader (ed.). *The governance of cyberspace: Politics, technology, and global restructuring* (pp. 209–227). London: Routledge.

Wolf, C. (2009, June 17). *The hate mongers' new tool: The Internet*. Retrieved March 26, 2011 from www.cbsnews.com/stories/2009/06/17/opinion/main5092743.XHTML

Ybarra, M., Mitchell, K. J., Finkelhor, D. and Wolak, J. (2007). Internet Prevention Messages: Targeting the Right Online Behaviors. *Archives of Pediatric Adolescence Medicine*, *161(4)*, 138–145. doi: 10.1001/archpedi.161.2.138D

Zhou, Y., Reid, E., Qin, J. H., Chen, H. and Lai, G. (2005). US domestic extremist groups on the web: Link and content analysis. *IEEE Intelligent Systems*, *20(5)*, 44–51. doi: 10.1109/MIS.2005.96

Zimbardo, P. G. (1969). The human choice: individuation, reason, and order versus deindividuation, impulse and chaos. In W. J. Arnold and D. Levine (eds), *Nebraska Symposium on Motivation* vol. 17 (pp. 237–307). Lincoln, NE: University of Nebraska Press.

25

Online hate and cyber-bigotry

A glance at our radicalized online world

Abbee Corb[1]

Not a day goes by that we are not exposed, in one way or another, to acts of hate, extremism and terrorism. Each day, the news media delivers stories of horrific acts of hate, bias and acts of terrorism. Hate and its respective crimes have been vilified in our everyday vernacular. Those perpetrated by the extremist groups and their "lone wolf"[2] soldiers have increased over the past decade. The rise in worldwide hate crimes, coupled with the changes in social and political environments, and the flourishing of various global groups, have been propagated and advanced through the use of technology by means of the Internet. These changes have lead to an increase in contentious websites, questionable material and, to say the least, dubious uses of available technology.

Extremist groups were amongst the first to make use of the Internet and realize the potential of the medium. From its inception the Internet has presented an unrestrained setting for extremist activity. The advent of the mainstream Internet from its Arpanet predecessor, Internet Relay Chat (a primitive synchronous conferencing system), USENET newsgroups, dial-up Bulletin Board System (BBS) services and the like, were the first places populated by extremists. In fact, in 1995, the first white supremacist hate-related website, *Stormfront*, went online, evolving from a dial-up BBS. *Stormfront*, a creation of American Klansman Don Black, was a more than ambitious effort to reach out and "educate the leaders of tomorrow" (Black, 1995). *Stormfront*, until recently had a mission statement defining its intention and its primary objective. It read "*Stormfront* is a resource for those courageous men and women fighting to preserve their White Western culture, ideals and freedom of speech and association – a forum for planning strategies and forming political and social groups to ensure victory" (Black, 1995). Since then, the canon has been readily accessible to anyone with access to the Internet. Youth and impressionable folks have always been the targets that have been catered to in this new-fangled venue.

Global extremist groups have a far-reaching impact. Despite their geographic location, the purveyors of hate rhetoric have been utilizing the latest technology and available tools, in all forms, to reach out, network, recruit, and further their influence and global impression. For example, in September 2013, Al Shabab used Twitter to "live-tweet" their deadly attack on the Westgate Mall in Nairobi.[3] Although the Twitter account used by the group was eliminated multiple times, their message was conveyed and re-tweeted by individuals and news media alike.

Radicals and extremists, it could be said, are using their Internet voice in a similar way that the Nazi Regime exploited the radio with the dissemination of hate tools and propaganda. They are furthering their message, gaining support and followers, educating and informing the diaspora of their various causes and goals. The Internet knows no borders, yet problems that arise as a result of the Internet and its various facets are indeed ones of international concern. It provides a forum where aged rhetoric can be presented in new-fangled ways. It is a place where political and social agendas can be shared and reacted to in real-time.

The placement of websites with providers located in countries with minimal or non-existent hate crime laws, coupled with foreign-based bulletin boards, and social networking sites, have aided in the ideological furtherance, recruitment and radicalization efforts of those active in the various extremist movements. In many instances the Internet has facilitated and enabled groups to dodge laws and evade those who enforce the laws. The Internet transcends borders and as such has given many governments the ability to ignore the problems and claim it is out of their jurisdiction. This leaves no checks and balances on multi-national corporations, particularly those registered in the U.S. where hate speech is protected by the First Amendment which allows for freedom of speech.

Music and games formulated to attract young people have been accessible online since the mid 1990s. For example, *Resistance Records* and other old school hate rock distribution companies made use of new technology when it became accessible. As such, their audience base grew. Dr. William Pierce and the *National Alliance* grasped the technology in its infancy, making use of IRC[4] to secure and recruit rock bands and to distribute the rights of their music. Pierce, the now deceased former leader of the *National Alliance* affirmed that "You are not merely consumers of a product . . . and we are not merely distributors of a product. Together we are fighting a war to awaken the survival instincts in a dying people. . . . Ours is not just a culture worth preserving. It is the only one worth preserving" (Pierce, 1995). Indeed, in a 2002 interview with *Wired* Magazine, Pierce stressed that *National Alliance* has "been a multimedia organization, interested in using communication, using every medium that we can to reach the public effectively." Pierce was featured in a clip distributed with the game talking about the "upcoming white revolution" (Scheres, 2002).

Of course, music purveyors, the likes of iTunes, sell the music to anyone with an account. However, in 2009, iTunes added a clause to its end-user agreement, stating:

> You may not use or otherwise export or re-export the Licensed Application except as authorized by United States law and the laws of the jurisdiction in which the Licensed Application was obtained. In particular, but without limitation, the Licensed Application may not be exported or re-exported (a) into any U.S.-embargoed countries or (b) to anyone on the U.S. Treasury Department's Specially Designated Nationals List or the U.S. Department of Commerce Denied Persons List or Entity List. By using the Licensed Application, you represent and warrant that you are not located in any such country or on any such list. You also agree that you will not use these products for any purposes prohibited by United States law, including, without limitation, the development, design, manufacture, or production of nuclear, missile, or chemical or biological weapons.[5]

In essence, although some of the songs present on iTunes and elsewhere contain hateful rhetoric, members of listed terrorist groups cannot purchase the music.

Some music groups, such as "Rahowa", an acronym for Racial Holy War, have songs that are vehemently anti-Semitic and contain racist jargon. The songs are used to influence their listeners and, at times, disseminate racist propaganda, and radicalize the youth. J. Cotter, in

Sounds of Hate: White Power Rock and Roll, aptly states that the propagation, persistence and viability of the white supremacist culture can be attributed to the messages conveyed in the lyrics of the music. This music validates the use of violence (Cotter, 1995). Extremist groups are able to radicalize young people through the use of music, videos and games, and the effects of music are far-reaching. Music has thus become a political device, source of income and a propaganda tool. Al Qaeda's supporters as well as other Islamic extremist groups have similarly made use of music on their websites as tools of recruitment and radicalization.

Currently extremists exploit social media and user-created content sites for the circulation of their wares. User-created content areas give rise to much trepidation. The exposure to graphic portrayals of violence in a context that provides ideological justifications for violence is a particularly lethal combination. In many cases the images play with your emotions showing terrible and horrific images (Corb, 2011). In some instances, the Internet and its many venues has become the cornerstone of communication for a number of groups who might not have a soapbox in the "real world". On November 22, 2012, the group Tehkreek-e-Taliban Pakistan (TTP) posted on their Umar Media Facebook page, "Dear brothers and sisters, 'the pen is mightier than the sword'. Now you have a chance to use this mighty weapon" (Shackle, 2013).

Technological changes, advancements, and the availability of new fangled means of communication have only extended the impact of extremist groups, terrorists and gangs who make use of it. Young people are, by and large, impressionable and therefore at risk of being swayed by non-conventional thoughts and rhetoric. In many instances, these young people are disenchanted by society. They find themselves disoriented, uncertain and occasionally lacking self-esteem. For these individuals, the misanthropy presented by websites of extremist groups and other entities may seem appealing and may attribute to their membership and recruitment.

Online hate rhetoric, cyber-hate and hate-bullying can easily impact and influence young people, as well as aid in the manipulations of their thoughts and views. Extremist group recruitment tactics operate for the most part on a proletarian level. Much recruitment and ideological dissemination takes place on user-created content sites, specifically Facebook, VKontakte,[6] Twitter and other social networking venues. Prevalent access to the Internet has similarly led to a dramatic increase in distasteful and questionable websites. Such Internet content "is offensive. It is crude, it is fascist and it mirrors the most infamous of Nazi Newspapers" (Littman, 1996).

Recruitment tactics can vary from group to group. One consistency, however, is the use of the Internet as a tool. For example, one group leader (Goudreau, personal correspondence, March 16, 2011) stated that the "Age of membership is 18 preferably but the youth are the future so high-school aged recruits are important for our youth corps and youth movement. Recruitment is via word of mouth and Internet networking sites and such". Similarly, Billy Roper, Chairman of *White Revolution* and *Nationalist Party of America* stated that his group makes use of many recruitment methods including: "literature distributions, rallies, protests and marches, demonstrations, music CDs, social media on the Internet, as well as our own websites, and most importantly, in terms of white power jujitsu, using the controlled media for our own purposes, to bring people to our websites and forums where we can speak to them without the Jewish media filter" (Roper, personal correspondence, March 17, 2011).

The Internet as a venue for conscription is easy and anonymous. Online recruitment and membership documents are easy to find and can be completed with great ease. The Net acts as a convenient virtual meeting place. It is a backdrop where like-minded and conflicted individuals can meet, form virtual relationships, and discuss and share their opinions and ideals:

> The Internet is great for communication. You can send email or chat with somebody anywhere in the world on the Internet for free. You can post messages on bulletin boards where potentially millions of people can read your information. The information can be posted anonymously or with a pseudonym. You can debate with anti-racists or just post racialist ideology and information. There are no limits to free speech on the Internet, anything goes. The glory of the Internet is its openness. There are few intermediaries if any, no editors, no borders and above all, no censors. Internet users can talk to anyone, anywhere, anytime about anything. They can be as private as they want, as straight-laced or as unbuttoned.[7]

Freedom of speech is also an inextricable part of the fabric of the Internet:

> There are places on the Internet where you can find information on books, literature, etc.... that you can download and print. If you have a computer ... be sure to blast into cyberspace, perhaps the greatest opportunity that has ever presented itself to the white resistance. The rules of the game are rapidly changing. We must be the first to master this new dimension.
>
> (McAleer, 1995)

Where previously these groups had a physical audience of a few dozen at their meetings, they now have access to millions of people worldwide, 24 hours a day, 365 days a year. Where it once took hours and days to transmit a message and coordinate a meeting, it now takes minutes, with the stroke of a key and the click of a button. Wyatt Kaldenberg, member of the defunct *White Aryan Resistance* and best remembered as the neo-Nazi skinhead who broke American talk show host Geraldo Rivera's nose on live television, stated:

> The Internet is more important than a march for the white man. One guy posting only one hour a day can get replies from many. 100 men marching in the street don't get that kind of response. Also, the streets are a legal bitch. People can get hurt or killed. With the Internet you can post using a false name, and no one will ever find out who you are. The most visible aspect of the neo-Nazi utilization of cyberspace has been the dispersal of propaganda.
>
> (Kaldenberg, 1995)

The Internet similarly empowers extremist entities. Technology has given rise to a relatively new medium where racist and extremist activity can take place and the Internet has become their virtual battleground. As Braun (1995) notes, "You can outlaw the swastika, ban the party etc. But you can never kill the idea. The Internet lets us spread the National Socialist idea". In addition, anyone can broadcast his or her message.

This phenomenon and thought process is not precluded to domestic white racist groups. In fact, a spokesman for terrorist group, Ahle Sunnat wal Jamaat (ASWJ) stated, "We use Facebook, Twitter and our own website for sharing daily news [...] Many people make propaganda against us and say we are a terrorist party. But when people see our comments on the Internet, they say that our agenda is right" (Chao, 2013). As well, many young Muslims can become radicalized online very quickly and with few warning signs, becoming potential terrorists before federal agencies can identify them (Smithson, 2012).

As well, the Canadian self-proclaimed leader of the *White Nationalist Front* regularly uploads motivational messages and recruitment videos to his followers on YouTube and Twitter and other sites.

Where once the fringe groups, terrorist and extremist entities had to depend upon conventional means and methods to disseminate their messages in the 'real' world, such as the physical distribution of flyers and schoolyard recruitment, they now for the most-part utilize the means of the Internet to communicate with a superior in numbers audience base in a more cost effective, personal, at times anonymous and private way than ever before.

Jamaat-ud-Dawa (JuD) is a major religious organization in Pakistan. JuD is listed by the United States, the United Nations and the European Union as a terrorist entity due to its alleged role in the 2008 Mumbai attacks. Abdul Rehman, of JuD's IT and social media wing, stated that though the group has had an online presence for at least a decade, its focus on social media is new: "Our Facebook and Twitter has the political aim of taking up our narratives," "There is a lot of propaganda against us. Twitter allows us to give our own official statements. The main purpose is to preach our message" (Shackle, 2013).

Organizations who were previously limited by time, finances, geographic boundaries and audience, now have the ability to network with new people. Minor splinter groups, which are technically savvy, have the ability to manipulate the reader into perceiving that they are broad-based groups with many followers.

In the late 1990s, Harold Covington, also known as Winston Smith, then leader of the NSWPP (*National Socialist White People's Party*) stated that "all of a sudden we've broken out of the bubble and people are LISTENING to us. They can use search engines to find us, which a lot of people couldn't do when we were restricted to cut and paste newsletters". The Internet, he declared, "Has made it possible for people who think as we do to FIND us and get connected. We are in essence bypassing the system news media."[8]

Groups can be easily found through a myriad of online search portals. Cross-pollination of ideas and interconnectivity of groups also adds to a potential increase in their audience. They can intermingle, align, and cross-pollinate their ideas with others in minutes, not previously possible before the Internet. The operative words here are *networking* and *opportunity*. The Internet represents an opportunity to network. With networking comes plotting, and with plotting comes conspiring and the potential to commit crimes, thus an entirely new set of circumstances is presented before us.

Extremist factions have historically leveraged new technologies to target the pre-radicalized and the radicalized. The advent of technology has aided the groups. White supremacists, terrorists, gangs, cults and extremist groups have all realized the complexities and potential of new and emerging technology, and as such have harnessed its power. As dissimilar as these groups are, similarities exist in that there are complex and somewhat anarchic consistencies in their recruitment techniques and propaganda distribution methods. Characteristically they all utilize the Internet for fundraising, recruitment, radicalization, training, instruction, propaganda, psychological warfare and the gathering of intelligence and counter intelligence. Bomb making instructions, warfare how-to's and the like are aplenty in the online world. A recipe for how to make pressure cooker bombs, which investigators say were used in the Boston Marathon attack, was most notoriously published in the al-Qaeda magazine "Inspire". The article was aptly titled "Make a bomb in the kitchen of your Mom" (Spencer, 2013).

A majority of the extremist activity and philosophical views have made the transition to the Internet: refined racist writings; offensive cartoon representations; the advocating of genocide; Holocaust denial and revisionism, and violent video game adaptations are but a few of elements found on the pages of the radical and extreme right. Each component of the online world and its related technologies plays a role in advancing the groups' agenda; be it propaganda distribution or recruitment. The Internet is a consistent driver and enabler for the process of radicalization across all genres. On the freewheeling net, everyone from white supremacists to Islamists and environmental radicals are connecting – then producing, sharing and consuming content that reinforces or encourages extremist views. Even some of the most mainstream social networking sites – like YouTube, Facebook, and Twitter – are host to extremist groups spouting their own narratives (Cunningham, 2013).

The Internet provides the impressionable mind of the potential recruit with direct and easy access to unfiltered fundamental and extremist ideology. For example, the Tsarnaev brothers of the 2013 Boston Marathon bombing, reportedly used an instruction manual from the English-language, Al-Qaeda-published "Inspire" magazine to build the crude, homemade bombs they used in the Boston Marathon attack. The founder originally published the magazine "as a PDF from the basement of his parents' home in North Carolina" writes (Foreign Policy) J.M. Berger, an author and analyst of extremist movements in the US and abroad (Cunningham, 2013). Kevin Goudreau, Chairman of the *White Nationalist Front* of Canada stated (personal correspondence, March 17, 2011), "the Internet has aided the movement and helped it grow exponentially . . . due to the anonymous nature of the Internet to mask ones' identity because of fear (sic.) . . . Because of social communism and getting to know like minded people of which is the norm rather than the fringe when in private."

Shrouded under a veil of impartiality and potential anonymity, the Internet permits the aspiring member to view the world and global conflicts through an extremist lens thus reinforcing the rhetoric, objectives and political arguments. The Internet has the capacity to serve as an enabler, thus, providing broad access to an array of information on targets and their various vulnerabilities. The Internet has in some ways become the single most important apparatus of the twenty-first century for the dissemination of misinformation. It is a tool used to provide coaching to youth who might not have otherwise had direct contact with recruiters.

The Internet plays an essential role in creating the social bonds that are necessary for radicalization and recruitment, as well as providing a setting for perpetuating radicalization among groups of recruits. If youth have begun to explore these areas and have formed bonds with other like-minded individuals (whether they are peers in similar situations or recruiters, online or offline), their radicalization may then progress inside these groups. Researchers have indicated that the Internet "can intensify a sense of identity" through the phenomenon of "group polarization," in which members of a specific radicalizing group perpetuate their own radicalization through continued discussion, perhaps with the facilitation of a terrorist recruiter (Madden, 2008).

August Kreiss of *Aryan Nations* and *Posse Comitatus* fame indicated (personal correspondence, March 11, 2011) that his group uses:

> Whatever methods are available to us. Prior to the Internet as we have it today was bulletin board services using dos programs. The fax machine, literature dropped at ones doors, canvassing areas that are experiencing racial tensions, leafleting, telephone hotlines and my favorite – mass distribution of "Who brought the slaves to Amerika" in Black communities waking them to the fact of it is the Jews that are their true enemy and the enemy of all the races and sub-races in the world.

Kreiss further went on to say, "We use any media that is available including Jewbook, *Myspace, MSN, Twitter, Google* and all the rest run by evil Jewry! We seek out potential candidates online until we are able to meet and greet in person" (Kreiss, personal correspondence, March 2011).

Tom Metzger, the prominent White supremacist and founder of *White Aryan Resistance* and *The Insurgent*, noted (personal correspondence, March 20, 2011) that although his group does not have a membership per se, it depends upon the Internet for the conveyance of the material he feels would be important to indoctrinate the lone wolf activist. He employs the use of websites, Internet based radio, and YouTube to transmit his message. Chairman of the *White Revolution*, Billy Roper (personal correspondence, March 17, 2011) indicated that his group had a great deal of success using Facebook, Myspace, and Twitter to recruit new members. Further, he indicated that networking with others who are already racially conscious, around the world, helped with recruitment.

In October of 2012, Tehkreek-e-Taliban Pakistan (TTP) used the Umar Media Facebook page to broadcast "online job opportunities", including "video-editing, translations, sharing, uploading, downloading and collection of required data". Offering an email address on which to contact the Taliban, the two adverts urged readers to spread the word in case the Facebook account was deleted. This showed foresight: Facebook soon closed the page. But social media are notoriously hard to police and it recently reopened, quickly gaining over 2,000 "likes" (Shackle, 2013).

The use of Facebook by TTP to recruit shows how militant and extremist organizations are increasingly aware of the importance of the Internet. Legitimate religious organizations and institutions make regular use of online tools. Networks of religious institutions, madrassas and other schools for example use forums and video platforms to share study materials and resource materials. Banned religious and extremist groups – which often carry out social work besides their more unsavory activities – exploit the Internet in the same way. But increasingly, many also see Twitter and Facebook as a chance to change their image and recruit members (Shackle, 2013).

Law enforcement personnel cannot always respond to hate speech in the virtual and global sphere. At times, response (or lack of response) by law enforcement proves to be unacceptable to the non-governmental organizations. As well, many federal governments lack coordinated strategies to combat online radicalization. Jurisdictional issues with respect to the placement of websites on servers in varying nations proved to be an issue as well. Many times websites belonging to the lunatic fringe are carefully placed on servers in countries where freedom of speech is protected by laws, similar to the First Amendment Rights in the United States. Freedom of Speech is both a privilege and a right. It becomes particularly problematic when it is abused, for instance when that speech has the propensity to incite violent actions against an identifiable group. However, many of the sites call themselves victims and blanket themselves in the rights accorded to them by the First Amendment and similar laws elsewhere. It should be noted, however, that the use of Facebook, Twitter and the like, open the groups to global scrutiny.

Extremist groups are international and prey upon the vulnerabilities of young people seeking a place to belong. They have kept abreast of the technological revolution and have leveraged it to their advantage. They have harnessed the power of the Internet and use it as a weapon of potential mass destruction for purposes of radicalization and recruitment. Seemingly, memberships fluctuate during times of economic and political change or unrest. Messages and rhetoric have been furthered through the use of technology. The Internet has become the best friend to the lunatic fringe, giving it an intercontinental voice that cannot be overlooked. The Internet has thus become a staple in providing those in their formative years with amusement, connectivity, and interaction. Groups have grasped and recognized this. They have adapted their strategies to adhere to what is trendy and sexy today. Radical entities make use of the power of the Internet to unite and incite. They reach out to impressionable people using popularized social networking venues in a venture to indoctrinate them with their deep-seated underlying, and at times fervidly racist and odious messages.

Notes

1 In 2011 Dr. Corb was commissioned to conduct a study for Google Ideas on white supremacy, the Internet and radicalization. Some of the contents of that study have been modified and adapted for this chapter.
2 Lone Wolves, being individuals who plan, surveil, and carry out their attack against a target in secrecy so as not to be infiltrated or exposed by others.
3 HSM Press Office twitter.com/hsm_pr
4 Internet Relay Chat – a form of synchronous conferencing.
5 ITunes Store, Legal, Terms and Conditions www.apple.com/legal/internet-services/itunes/us/terms.html (last accessed August 29, 2013).
6 VKontakte or vk.com is a Russian-based social networking site much like US-based Facebook. According to alexa.com, the web informatics company, it is the second largest social networking site, second to Facebook. 67 per cent of its users are European. The site name essentially translates to in touch in English. VK boasts to have 100 million active users (http://vk.com/about).
7 Beyond the Fringe, The Voice of CyberFree America, Vol. 17, No. 8 p.1.
8 Winston Smith, Beyond the Fringe, The Voice of Cyberfree America, Volume 17, Number 8. p.1.

Bibliography

A Skinhead's Story: An Interview with a Former Racist *Intelligence Report*, 2001 The Southern Poverty Law Center.
Anti-Defamation League. Racist Groups Using Computer Gaming to Promote Violence Against Blacks, Latinos and Jews. www.adl.org/videogames/default.asp
Albrecht, G., Backes, O. and Kühnel W. (eds) (2001), *Violent Crime between Myth and Reality* (pp. 195–235). Frankfurt.
Alexander, J.D., *Offline and Online Radicalization and Recruitment of Extremists and Terrorists*, September 2010. Western Illinois University.
Australian Human Rights Commission, Examples of Racist Material on the Internet. *Race Discrimination Unit, HREOC, October 2002*. www.heroic.gov.au/racial_discrimination/cyberracism/examples.html
Baacke, D. and Heitmeyer, W. (1985) *New Contradictions: Young People in the 80's*. Weinheim.
Baier, D. (2005) Deviant Behavior in Adolescence. *Magazine for Socialization Research and Education Sociology*, 4, 381–398.
Barefoot, Abigail. Former white supremacist speaks on solidarity, recovery. *Iowa State daily.com* Thursday, April 1, 2010. Updated Monday June 14, 2010.
Bartsch, Matthew and Stark, Holger. Islamism and the Like Button: Can Radicalization Via Facebook Be Stopped? *Spiegel Online*. March 15, 2011.
Beck, E. M. (2000) Guess who's coming to town: white supremacy, ethnic competition, and social change. *Sociological Focus*, 33: 152–174.
Beelmann, A. and K. J. Jonas (2009) *Diskriminierung und Toleranz: psychologische Grundlagen und Anwendungsperspektiven*. Wiesbaden: VS Verlag für Sozialwissenschaften.
Berkowitz, L. (1993) *Aggression: its causes, consequences, and control*. New York: McGraw-Hill.
Bernstein, R. (2004) *Racial innocence: white supremacy and the performance of American childhood*, Yale University Press: xviii, 377 p.
Black, D. (1995) Stormfront Mission Statement, retrieved from www.stormfront.org.
Blazak, R. (2001) White boys to terrorist men, *American Behavioral Scientist*, 44(6): 982–1000.

Blythe, Will (2000) The guru of white hate, *Rolling Stone*, New York, June 8. Iss 842, pp. 98–106.

Borstel, D. and Wagner, B. (2006) Opportunities and limits of the measures against Right wing extremist violence: Prevention and intervention. In W. Heitmeyer and M. Schröttle (eds), *Violence: description – analysis – prevention*. Bonn.

Borum, Randy (2004) Psychology of Terrorism. University of South Florida. http://worlddefensereview.com/docs/PsychologyofTerrorism0707.pdf

Braun, K. (August 5, 1995) Personal communication.

Brown, Staci (2000) Virtual Hate: The Internet has Rekindled the Zeal and Magnified the Power of Hate Groups. What can we do to fight back? *Sojourners*; Sep/Oct 2000.

Callahan, B. (1993) *Right young people: entry and exit: six biographical studies*. Bielefeld.

Callahan, B. and Becker, R. (2007) Right youth cliques: between unobtrusiveness and provocation: an empirical study. Schwalbach/TS: Weekly News Publisher.

Chao, Rebecca (2013, September 24). The Western Voices of al-Shabaab's Twitter Account. Techpresident, Retrieved September 24, 2013 from http://techpresident.com/news/wegov/24366/western-voices-al-shabaab-twitter

Chau, Michael and Xu, Jennifer (2006) A Framework for Locating and Analyzing Hate Group Blogs. In *Proceedings of the Pacific-Asia Conference on Information Systems*. Kuala Lumpur, Malaysia, July 6–9, 2006.

Chen, Hsinchun, with Chung, Wingyan, Larson, Cathy, Reid, Edna, et al. (2003) *Advanced Methodologies for Collecting and Analyzing Information from the "Dark Web" and Terrorism Research Resources*. Artificial Intelligence Lab: The Terrorism Knowledge Portal. The University of Arizona August 14. http://al.ellar.Arizona.edu/

Cooper, Abraham with Rick Eaton and Mark Weitzman (2010) Digital Terrorism and Hate: The First Decade and Beyond. *Genocide Prevention Now* Issue 2, Spring 2010.

Corb, Abbee (1998) The Extremists on the Internet. Toronto (rev. 2009).

Corb, Abbee (2008) *An examination and remedy to the systemic failures in Canadian* hate crime prosecution (position paper) Hate Crime Extremism Investigative Team: Toronto.

Corb, Abbee (2011) *Into the Minds of Mayhem: White Supremacy, Recruitment and the Internet*. Google Ideas, New York.

Corte, Ugo and Edwards, Bob (2008) White Power Music and the mobilization of racist social movements. *Music and Arts in Action*. Vol. 1. Issue. 1. June 2008. http://musicandartsinaction.net/index.php/mala/article/view/whitepowermusic

Cotter, John M. (1999) Sounds of Hate: White Power Rock and Roll and Neo-Nazi Skinhead Subculture. *Terrorism and Political Violence*, Vol. 11, No. 2 (Summer), pp. 111–40.

Cunningham, Erin (2013, April 25) Boston bombing revives debate over online extremism. GlobalPost. Retrieved April 25, 2013, from www.globalpost.com/dispatch/news/regions/americas/united-states/130424/boston-bombing-online-extremism-tamerlan-dzokhar-tsarnaev

Daniels, J. (2009) *Cyber racism: white supremacy online and the new attack on civil rights*. Lanham, MD: Rowman & Littlefield Publishers.

Dees, Morris (1993) *Hate on Trial: The Case Against America's Most Dangerous Neo-Nazi*. New York: Villard Books.

European Commission's Expert Group on Violent Radicalization (2008) Radicalization Processes Leading to Acts of Terrorism. Submitted to the European Commission on 15 May 2008. *Official Journal of the European Union*, L 111/9 of 25.04.2006.

Ezekiel, R. S. (1995) *The racist mind: portraits of American Neo-Nazis and Klansmen*. New York, Viking.

Falk, A. and Zweimüller, J. (2005) Unemployment and right wing extremist crime, www.iza.org/en/webcontent/publications/press/index_html?start_year=2005

Ferber, A. L. (1998) *White man falling: race, gender, and White supremacy*. Lanham, MD: Rowman & Littlefield.

Ferber, A. L. (2004) *Home-grown hate: gender and organized racism*. New York; London: Routledge.

Fink, Naureen Chowdhury and Hearne, Ellie, B. (2008) Beyond Terrorism: Deradicalization and Disengagement from Violent Extremism. International Peace Institute. October 2008. http://ipacademy.org/publication/meeting-notes/detail/24-beyond-terrorism-deradicalization-and-disengagement-from-violent-extremism.htm

Fishlock, Diana and Kemeny, Matthew (Tuesday, August 3, 2010) Rebel activity is on the rise nationally, expert says. *The Patriot News* www.penlive.com/midstate/index.ssf/2010/08/rebel_activity_is_on_the_rise.html

Flynn, Kevin (1989) *The Silent Brotherhood: Inside America's Racist Underground*. New York: Free Press.
Fuchs, M. (2003) Right wing extremism among young people *Kölner Zeitschrift für Soziologie und Sozialpsychologie*, 55: 654–678.
Gamper, M. and Willems, H. (2006) Right wing extremist violence – backgrounds, perpetrators and victims. In W. Heitmeyer and M. Schröttle (eds), *Violence: Description – Analysis – prevention*. Bonn.
Garcia, Gabriela (2010) iTunes Sells White Power Music. December 13. http://change.org
Graham, K. M. (2010) *Beyond redistribution: White supremacy and racial justice*. Lanham, MD: Lexington Books.
Green, D. (1998) From Lynching to Gay Bashing – the elusive connection between economic conditions and hate crime. *Journal of Personality and Social Psychology* 75(1), 82–92.
Grumke, T. and Wagner, B. (2002) Manual Right wing Radicalism: People, Organizations, Networks of the neo-Nazism to the middle of the company. (trans)
Hamm, M. S. (1993) *American skinheads: the criminology and control of hate crime*. Westport, CT: Praeger.
Hate on the Internet: A Response Guide for Educators and Families. Defining the Problem: The Internet as a Tool for Hate. (pp. 13–24) www.partnersagainsthate.org/publications/hol_defining_problem.pdf
Heitmeyer, W. (1987) *Right-extremist orientations among young people: empirical findings and Declaration of patterns of a study on the political socialization*. Weinheim.
Heitmeyer, W. (2002). Right-extremist violence. In W. Heitmeyer and J. Hagan (eds), *International Handbook of violence research* (pp. 501–546). Wiesbaden.
Hodges, E. and Isaacs, J. (2002) Learning of aggression in families and peer group. In W. Heitmeyer and J. Hagan (eds), *International Handbook of violence research* (pp. 619–639). Wiesbaden.
Hoffman, Bruce (2006) *Inside Terrorism*. New York: Columbia University Press.
Hofstadter, R. (1964) The pseudo-conservative revolt. In D. Bell (ed.), *The Radical Right* (pp. 75–95). Garden City: Doubleday.
Hopf, W. (1994) Right wing extremism among young people – not a deprivation issue? *Magazine for Socialization Research and Development Sociology*, 14, 194–211.
Husfeldt, V. (2006) Extreme negative attitudes towards immigrants: an analysis of factors in five countries. *Prospects*, 36(3), 355–374.
Ibanga, Imaeyen (June 12, 2009) Hate Groups Effectively Use Web as a Recruiting Tool. *ABC News*. http://abcnews.go.com/Technology/story?id=7822417 (last viewed September 10, 2013).
Jacobs, James and Kimberly Potter (2001) *Hate crimes: criminal law & identity politics. Studies in crime and public policy*. New York; Oxford: Oxford University Press: viii, 212 pp.
Jenkins, William D. (1990) *Steel Valley Klan: Ku Klux Klan in Ohio's Mahoning Valley*. Kent, OH: Kent State University Press.
Kaldenberg, W. (November 3, 1995) Personal communication. Stormfront mailing list.
Kaplan, J. and Bjørgo, T (1998) *Nation and race: the developing Euro-American racist subculture*. Boston, MA: Northeastern University Press.
Kennedy, Stetson (1990) *The Klan Unmasked*. Boca Raton, FL: Florida Atlantic University Press.
Kentucky Justice & Public Safety Cabinet (2007) *Hate Crime and Hate Incidents in the Commonwealth 2007* Prepared by the Kentucky Statistical Analysis Center http://justice.ky.gov/NR/rdonlyres/A0887299-05DC-4AAF-A20A-8FB7EFAC3A3E/0/2007HateCrimeReport_FINAL.pdf (last viewed July 17, 2013).
Keteyian, Armen (2010) The Violent World of White Supremacist Gangs: Armen Keteyian's Exclusive Investigation into a Heavily Armed, Violent Gang. *CBS Evening News* (Television Broadcast). Omaha, Nebraska. August 4.
King, Angela V. (2009) Web Based, Gendered Recruitment of Women by Organized White Supremacist Groups. Unpublished Master's Thesis, University of Central Florida, Orlando, Florida.
Lantigua, John (Saturday, July 26, 2008) Local organizer, other supremacists say Obama's run boosts their cause. *The Palm Beach Post*.
Lay, Shawn (ed.) (1992) *The Invisible Empire in the West: Toward a New Appraisal of the Ku Klux Klan of the 1920s*. Urbana, IL: University of Illinois Press.
Lethbridge, David (1994) *Aryan Nations: Christian Identity and Fascist Terror*. November 1994 Revised July 1995. The Bethune Institute for Anti-Fascist Studies.
Littman, Sol. (August 3, 1996) On hate mongering by white supremacists on the Internet, *The Beacon Herald*, Stratford.

Lopez, Clare M., Peer, Roland and Brim, Christine (2011) Religious Bias Crimes Against Muslim, Christian & Jewish Victims: American Trends From 2000–2009. Center for Security Policy: The Occasional Paper Series. March 9, 2011. www.centerforsecuritypolicy.org/g3.xml

Lutholtz, M. William (1991) *Grand Dragon: D.C. Stephenson and the Ku Klux Klan in Indiana*. West Lafayette, IN: Purdue University Press.

Maass, David (2010) White out: American Third Position, a White-nationalist political group, spreads to San Diego County. *San Diego City Beat*. Wednesday, September 8.

Madden, Christina L. (February 5, 2008) Typing TERROR in a Crowded Chat. *Policy Innovations*. www.policyinnovations.org/ideas/briefings/data/00002

McAleer, T. (Spring 1995) Plug into the Freedom of the Internet, *Resistance Magazine*, 13.

Michael, George (2003) *Confronting right wing extremism and terrorism in the USA*. New York: Routledge.

Minkenberg, Michael (2000) The Renewal of the Radical Right: Between Modernity and Anti-modernity. *Government and Opposition* Volume 35, Issue 2, pages 170–188, April.

Minkenberg, Michael (1998) *The New Radical Right in Comparison: United States, France, Germany*. Opladen: Westdeutscher Verlag.

Monks, Tara (2010) Maine Freedom of Speech: A White supremacist group is recruiting in Bucksport. *New York in Jury News* May 11.

Moore, Jack B. (1993) *Skinheads Shaved for Battle: A Cultural History of American Skinheads*. Bowling Green, OH: Bowling Green University Press.

Moore, Leonard J. (1993) *Citizen Klansmen: the Ku Klux Klan in Indiana, 1921–1928*. Chapel Hill, NC: University of North Carolina Press.

Mudde, C. (2000) *The Ideology of the Extreme Right*. Manchester: Manchester University Press.

Nelson, Joe (February 10, 2006) Spreading Web of Intolerance Racist Skinhead Project: Hate Grows in I.E. On the Internet *Daily Bulletin Ontario* California.

Newton, Michael (1991) *The Ku Klux Klan: an Encyclopedia*. New York: Garland.

Neumann, J. and Frindte, W. (2002) Violent Crimes against Foreigners *Journal of Conflict and Violence Research*, 4(2), 95–111.

Now white supremacists go door-to-door to try and recruit more members. Daily Mail Reporter *Mail Online* 16th March 2011.

Ohlemacher, T. (1998) *Xenophobia and Right wing Extremism: media coverage, population opinion and their interaction with xenophobic acts of violence, 1991–1997*. Hannover.

Olzak, S. (1992) *The Dynamics of Ethnic Competition and Conflict*. Stanford, CA: Stanford University Press.

Olzak, S. (2006) *The Global Dynamics of Racial and Ethnic Mobilization*. Stanford, CA: Stanford University Press.

Parker, Robert Nash and Tuthill, Louis (2006) *Youth Violence Prevention Among White Youth. Preventing youth violence in a multicultural society* (pp. 199–218). Washington, DC: American Psychological Association, xi, pp. 310.

Pierce, W. (1995) National Alliance Mission Statement retrieved from www.resistance.com

Pistole, John, Assistant Director Federal Bureau of Investigation Testimony Before the Senate Judiciary Committee, Subcommittee on Terrorism, Technology, and Homeland Security on Terrorist Recruitment in Prisons and the Recent Arrests Related to Guantanamo Detainees. Washington, DC. October 14, 2003.

Raftery, Miriam (May 9, 2009) SPLC Provides Tools to Curb Recruitment of Teens by Racist Hate Groups; Hate Crimes on the Rise. *East County Magazine* (last viewed August 12, 2013). www.eastcountymagazine.org./node/1102

Ray, L. and Smith, D. (2004) Racist Offending, Policing and Community Conflict *Sociology*; 38: 681–699.

Ray, Beverly and Marsh II, George E. (2001) Recruitment by Extremist Groups on the Internet. *First Monday*. Vol 6, Number 2–5 February 2001. http://firstmonday.org/htbin/cgiwrap/bin/ojs/index.php/fm/article/view/834/743

Reid, Edna and Chen, Hsinchun (2007) Internet-Savvy U.S. And Middle Eastern Extremist Groups *Mobilization: An International Quarterly Review* 12(2): 177–192.

Reinares, F. (2008) Radicalization processes leading to acts of terrorism. European Commission of Expert group on violent Radicalization.

Ridgeway, James (1990) *Blood in the Face: The Ku Klux Klan, Aryan Nations, Nazi Skinheads and the Rise of a New White Culture*. New York: Thunder Mountain Press.

Rose, D. D. (1992) *The Emergence of David Duke and the politics of race.* Chapel Hill: University of North Carolina Press.

Scheres, Julia (2002) Games Elevate Hate to Next Level. *Wired Magazine* February. www.wired.com/culture/lifestyle/news/2002/02/50523

Schafer, John R. and Navarro, J. (2003) *The Seven-Stage Hate Model: The Psychopathology of Hate Groups* FBI Law Enforcement Bulletin. March 2003. Vol.72. Number 3 www2.fbi.gov/publications/leb/2003/mar2003/mar03leb.htm

Searchlight (Organization) (2001) *White noise: Rechts-Rock, Skinhead-Musik, Blood & Honour: Einblicke in die internationale Neonazi-Musik-Szene.* Hamburg, Unrast.

Shackle, Samira (2013, August 15) The Twitter jihadis: how terror groups have turned to social media. *New Statesman,* Retrieved August 17, 2013, from www.newstatesman.com/2013/08/twitter-jihadis

Smithson, S. (2012) Report: Internet Radicalizes US Muslims quickly. *Washington Times.* February 27 (last viewed November 11, 2013).

Spencer, Richard (2013, April 16) Boston Marathon bombs: al-Qaeda's Inspire magazine taught pressure cooker bomb-making techniques. *The Telegraph.* Retrieved April 17, 2013, from www.telegraph.co.uk/news/worldnews/al-qaeda/9998886/Boston-Marathon-Bombs-al-Qaedas-Inspire-magazine-taught-pressure-cooker-bomb-making-techniques.html

Stanton, Bill (1991) *Klanwatch: Bringing the Ku Klux Klan to Justice.* New York: Weidenfeld.

Terrorism Research Center (2008) Internet Intelligence Report. *Target France.* January 10, 2008. ED. 4 Vol.2 www.totalintel.com

Tiven, Lorraine and Training, Peter (2003) Hate on the Internet: A Response Guide for Educators and Families. Partners Against Hate Anti-Defamation League, Washington, DC. December 2003. www.partnersagainsthate.org

Transnational Terrorism, Security & the Rule of Law (2008) Concepts of Terrorism: Analysis of the rise, decline, trends and risk. December 2008. A project financed by the European Commission under the Sixth Framework Programme. www.transnationalterrorism.eu

U.S. Department of Homeland Security (2009) Rightwing Extremism: Current Economic and Political Climate Fueling Resurgence in Radicalization and Recruitment. *Prepared by the Extremism and Radicalization Branch, Homeland Environment Threat Analysis Division. Coordinated with the FBI.* 7 April 2009. www.fas.org/rip/eprint/rightwing.PDF

Valdez, Al (2002) White Supremacist Gangs: From the Aryan Nations to the Posse Comitatus, white racist groups are still recruiting and spreading an often violent message. *Police: The Law Enforcement Magazine.* (October 1, 2002) www.policeman.com/Channel/Gangs/Articles/2002/10/In-the-Hood.aspx.

Van Duyn, Donald, Deputy Assistant Director, and Counterterrorism Division Federal Bureau of Investigation. Testimony on Prison Radicalization: The Environment, the Threat, and the Response. Senate Committee on Homeland Security and Governmental Affairs and Related Agencies. Washington, DC. September 19, 2006.

Weatherby, Georgie Ann and Scoggins, Brian (2005/06) A Content Analysis of Persuasion Techniques Used on White Supremacist Websites. *Journal of Hate Studies* Vol. 4: 9, pp. 9–31.

Wendel, Bradley W. (2002) "Certain Fundamental Truths": A Dialectic on Negative and Positive Liberty in Hate-Speech Cases. *Law and Contemporary Problems. Duke University School of Law.* Cited: 65 *Law & Contemp.Probs. 33 (Spring 2002).*

Woolf, Linda M. and Hulsizer, Michael R. (2004) Hate Groups for Dummies: How to Build a Successful Hate Group. *Humanity and Society,* Vol. 28, Number 1, February 2004.

Zeskind, L. (2009) *Blood and politics: the history of the white nationalist movement from the margins to the mainstream.* New York, Farrar Straus Giroux.

26
Hate crime in sport

Nick Hawkins

Sport by its very nature produces an environment which can be a force for good and which actively promotes equality and diversity amongst participants, officials and spectators. However, and conversely, the nature of sport sets people against each other and this can (and has) cause an environment in which incidents of hate crime can occur. This chapter therefore examines all aspects of hate crime in sport, in the UK and worldwide, and considers ways of tackling hate crime by looking at the role of sports authorities and police and prosecutors. Throughout the chapter, examples are given covering a range of sports.

Most sports have experienced hate crime, both on the pitch and in the stadium, varying from isolated individual acts to widespread racial (and other forms of) abuse of large sections of crowds. It is arguably the case that team sports suffer most, and in particular football, possibly due to the stronger and longer association of supporters with teams rather than individual sportsmen and women. It is also clear that hate crime is far more prevalent in male sport – with football providing a real contrast.

Hate crime in sport is a worldwide phenomenon and has been reported in every continent. The prevalence of multi-nation tournaments also provides the opportunity for perpetrators of hate crime to offend away from their home countries.

In considering the legal and regulatory framework that deals with hate crime it is necessary to look at the social and political context at any given time in any given country. For example it is hardly surprising that no attention was given to hate crime in sport in the USA before the civil rights movement, or in South Africa in the apartheid years.

Nonetheless sport has often led the way in highlighting and tackling hate crime, and thereby placing the issue into the public domain. Apartheid can only be described as institutional and legal racism and the international sporting community responded to it by excluding South Africa from many sports, thereby contributing to the isolation of the government.

History

The first black professional footballer in England was Arthur Wharton who played professionally in the nineteenth century. Although there is no record of any crime being committed against him, he was treated differently from other players and certainly not treated with the respect that his achievements deserved. It took until 1978 before Viv Anderson became the first black player to play for England in a full international match, and he was continually subjected to racial abuse in club and international matches. Racial abuse was prevalent in English football throughout the 1970s, 1980s and 1990s and the first specific legislation to tackle racial abuse in football in the UK was not introduced until 1991.

Two other examples show that racism in sport has been present since the rapid expansion of organised sports in the late nineteenth century. In the USA African-Americans were excluded from professional baseball in the 1890s leading to the formation of the Negro Leagues. Even when minorities are not excluded from mainstream sport they may choose to form their own competitions to avoid abuse, with the Jewish Football Leagues in England being but one example.

The Berlin Olympics in 1936 were scarred by racism, with Jewish athletes excluded from the German team, and the great Jessie Owens being snubbed by officials despite his success on the track.

Hate crime against visible minorities, or indeed against other nationalities, is easier to spot and deal with. Participants from minorities become easy targets but equally are obvious people to protect from abuse. Hate crime against less visible groups, such as the lesbian, gay, bisexual and transgender (LGBT) community, has been present as long as hate crime based on race or colour, yet has had a different effect on participants, with many choosing to hide or deny their sexuality. To date there has been no openly gay Premier League footballer in England, although in other sports international players have been able to be more open with an England cricketer and a Welsh Rugby Union player making public declarations about their sexuality.

Given the worldwide and historic nature of hate crime generally, it is no surprise that the prevalence of hate crime in a variety of forms has continued well into the twenty-first century. Fortunately, the 24-hour nature of the modern media means that offences are now widely publicised and authorities, whether political, sports or law enforcement have had to act to tackle the issue.

Regulation or legislation?

Participants in sport will almost invariably be subject to a number of concurrent jurisdictions. Spectators will always be subject to the criminal law of the country in which the sport is taking place, and they may also be in a contractual relationship with the owners or tenants of the venue. In this section, English football is used as an example to illustrate the practicalities of this, but the principles described below will apply to almost any sport.

It is not disputed that criminal law continues to apply on the field of play, nor that there are concurrent jurisdictions. Sportsmen have appeared in court and been convicted of assaults on other players, whilst others for not dissimilar incidents have been dealt with by the sport's disciplinary body. The same principles apply to hate crime.

Although resulting in an acquittal in a criminal trial the recent case of John Terry provides a clear example of concurrent jurisdiction. Following an allegation that he called another player a "black c**t" he was charged with using threatening, abusive or insulting words or behaviour or disorderly behaviour within the hearing or sight of a person likely to be caused harassment, alarm or distress, and the offence was racially aggravated in accordance with section 28 of the Crime and Disorder Act 1998, contrary to Section 5 of the Public Order Act 1986 and section 31(1)(c) and (5) of the Crime and Disorder Act 1998. After a trial lasting a week in July 2012 he was acquitted by the Senior District Judge who gave a detailed ruling. Terry did not deny using the words but denied the criminal offence.[1]

Nick Hawkins

On 27th September Mr Terry was found guilty by a Football Association Independent Regulatory Commission of breaching the FA rules on abusive behaviour and discrimination, which state that:

> E.3 (1): A participant shall at all times act in the best interests of the game and shall not act in any manner which is improper or brings the game into disrepute or use any one, or a combination of, violent conduct, serious foul play, threatening, abusive, indecent or insulting words or behaviour.

> E.4: A participant shall not carry out any act of discrimination by reason of ethnic origin, colour, race, nationality, faith, gender, sexual orientation or disability.

Full written reasons were given, and no appeal against either the finding or sentence was made.[2]

This case highlights the concurrent jurisdiction between the criminal law and the game's disciplinary framework. Had the game been one regulated by either UEFA or FIFA, then a third body would have had jurisdiction to deal with the matter.

In most cases it is desirable and consistent with principles of natural justice for a player to only face one hearing resulting out of a particular incident, but it is not illegal for both a criminal and a disciplinary hearing to take place. In England, the Association of Chief Police Officers, the Crown Prosecution Service, and the Football Association have committed to developing a protocol setting out principles as to who should investigate and have primary jurisdiction following an allegation of an on-field incident that could be a criminal offence. This ongoing work recognises that each case must be considered on its own individual facts, and that there can be no hard and fast rules when there is concurrent jurisdiction.

With regard to spectators, the position is different. If a spectator is alleged to have committed a criminal offence, for example racially abusing a player, then the only route for investigation and prosecution is through the criminal justice system of the country in which the incident occurs. A second "sanction" may be a ban imposed by the Club which hosted the game in which the incident occurred or with which the spectator is associated, and this is becoming much more common in professional football in Europe.

Criminal or inappropriate behaviour by a single spectator is unlikely to result in action being taken against clubs, but incidents involving large numbers of fans may result in charges being brought against a club or international association. UEFA's Disciplinary Regulations 2012 contain the following provision:

Article 14 Disciplinary measures against member associations and clubs

1. The following disciplinary measures may be imposed on member associations and clubs in accordance with Article 53 of the *UEFA Statutes*:
   a) warning,
   b) reprimand,
   c) fine,
   d) annulment of the result of a match,
   e) order that a match be replayed,
   f) deduction of points,
   g) declaration of a match forfeit,

h) playing of a match behind closed doors,
i) full or partial stadium closure,
j) playing of a match in a third country,
k) withholding of revenues from a UEFA competition,
l) prohibition on registering new players in UEFA competitions,
m) restriction on the number of players that a club may register for participation in UEFA competitions,
n) disqualification from competitions in progress and/or exclusion from future competitions,
o) withdrawal of a title or award,
p) withdrawal of a licence.

2 A fine shall be no less than €100 and no more than €1,000,000.[3]

This rule was used on a number of occasions in the 2012/13 season, including notably following repeated racist abuse of black England players in an Under-21 match against Serbia. UEFA's finding contained the following section:

> The UEFA Control and Disciplinary Body has ordered the Serbian Under-21 national team to play their next UEFA competition home match behind closed doors, following a number of incidents that occurred during and after the 2013 UEFA European Under-21 Championship play-off second-leg match against England at the Mladost Stadium in Krusevac on 16 October. The Football Association of Serbia (FSS) has also been fined €80,000.
>
> The sanction against the FSS has been imposed for the improper conduct of its supporters, specifically racist behaviour, during and at the end of the match, as well as for the improper conduct of the Serbia players at the end of the game.[4]

UK experience

The UK has considerable legislation that covers hate crimes, all of which applies equally to sport. In summary, there are specific offences which cover hate crime and there are racially aggravated versions of existing crimes which carry a greater maximum penalty (e.g. racially aggravated assault). There are general provisions which require courts to treat "hate crime" as an aggravating feature when sentencing offences that do not have specific hate crime provisions, Criminal Justice Act 2003 Section 145, Increase in Sentences for racial or religious aggravation and Section 146, Increase in Sentences for aggravation related to disability or sexual orientation.

Football in England

There are two principal statutes dealing with football-related offending. The Football Spectators Act 1989 creates a framework that allows for the imposition of Football Banning Orders, following conviction or complaint. Over the last decade the average number of bans in force has been around 3,000 of which 10 per cent would be on complaint. Schedule 1 of the Act lists offences that qualify for a Ban, and these included racially aggravated Public Order Act Offences and all offences under the Football (Offences) Act 1991.

Nick Hawkins

This second statute contains a specific provision dealing with chanting.

Section 3 Indecent or Racialist Chanting:
1. It is an offence to take part in the chanting of an indecent or racialist nature at a football match.
2. For this purpose:
   a) "chanting" means the repeated uttering of any words or sounds in concert with one or more others;
   b) "of a racialist nature" means consisting of or including matter which is threatening, abusive or insulting to a person by reason of his colour, race, nationality (including citizenship) or ethnic or national origins.

This legislation has been used with care by prosecutors in order to get the balance right between allowing humour and prosecuting grossly offensive chanting. In general this approach has been supported by fans who see no place in football for racism or other hate crime. Two examples show how the legislation has worked.

In October 2002 Port Vale played Oldham. Oldham had been the scene of race riots in May 2001. Around 100 Port Vale fans chanted "you're just a town full of Pakis". One of these fans was prosecuted and acquitted by a District Judge, but the case was appealed to the High Court that ruled that the use of the word "Paki" in football match chants is racially offensive. The case, brought under the Football Offences Act 1991, established that even without accompanying swearing or insults, chants on football terraces incorporating the word were racist and illegal.

In January 2009 a number of Spurs fans were convicted of "indecent" chanting following a game against Portsmouth FC in September 2008. They were identified from video footage and admitted chanting: 'Sol, Sol, wherever you may be, Not long now until lunacy, We won't give a f*** if you are hanging from a tree, You are a Judas c**t with HIV'. They received Football Banning Orders. This case has been described as significant by the Professional Footballers Association, and by KickItOut (a charitable organisation formed to combat racism in football and supported by the Football Association).

In both of these cases it was suggested that the chants were just "banter" and therefore were part and parcel of football culture and should be accepted. This is not a view accepted by police, prosecutors, or the game's authorities.

It is clear that tackling racism and other hate crime on the terraces cannot be achieved by one authority acting alone. In England, the accepted model for dealing with all offending in and around football is a multi-agency approach involving police, prosecutors, the Football Associations and Leagues, players and government departments. The media also plays a part as do clubs and the voluntary sector. Whilst it is hard to define exactly where the line is between a hate crime and banter, it is usually clear when the line has been crossed to such an extent that only a prosecution provides an appropriate resolution of the case.

Similar problems exist with homophobic chanting, and although prosecutions are rare, the leading gay rights organisation in the UK, Stonewall, has contributed to the debate and has lines of communications with police and prosecutors.

One of the problems in dealing with some "hate crime" and in particular chanting is that some words are used as a term of abuse by one group of fans and as a badge of honour by others. The best known example is the use of the word "yid" by Spurs fans to describe themselves, when chanting "yid" by other fans could be an offence. Education, as well as legislation and regulation, is a way of combating such chanting and a good example of this is provided by the production of a short film, "The Y Word" produced by two well-known Jewish fans and promoted by KickItOut.[5]

To combat the problem of English fans committing offences overseas and avoiding a meaningful sanction that has an impact in the UK the Football Spectators Act 1989 Section 14B allows the prosecution authorities to apply for a Football Banning Order on complaint (i.e. not following a conviction). Section 14C allows the Court to take into account the following:

> 4   The magistrates' court may take into account the following matters (among others), so far as they consider it appropriate to do so, in determining whether to make an order under section 14B above—
>   a) any decision of a court or tribunal outside the United Kingdom,
>   b) deportation or exclusion from a country outside the United Kingdom,
>   c) removal or exclusion from premises used for playing football matches, whether in the United Kingdom or elsewhere,
>   d) conduct recorded on video or by any other means.

This is typically used to deal with fans convicted or arrested for violence and disorder, but can and has been used to tackle hate crime. Before the football World Cup in Germany in 2006 significant efforts were made by both English and German authorities to deter hate crime, particularly in light of German history.

One English fan departed Leeds-Bradford airport on 9th June. Posters were clearly displayed in the airport advising supporters not to display provocative insignia. Similar messages had been given in the national and local media. He was arrested on 10th June in Frankfurt under S.86a of German Criminal Code (displaying of a banned symbol). He was photographed with a swastika on his back, a 'SS' motif on his back, a swastika on his chest and a 'J' motif on his arm. He was clearly drunk and passers-by indicated disgust in gesticulations and shaking of heads. After arrest he was on 100 euros surety and left Germany voluntarily. On arrival back in England he was placed before Leeds Magistrates' Court on 12th June. He admitted his behaviour and did not contest an application for a Football Banning Order, receiving one of 25 months.

This is believed to be the first example of hate crime being committed in one country during a sports tournament and being dealt with in the country of origin.

Football in Scotland

Sectarianism has long been seen as a plague on Scottish football, with "Old Firm" derby matches between Glasgow Rangers and Celtic being marked by sectarian chanting. In 2011 the Celtic manager was sent a parcel bomb. In response to this, and as part of a wider approach to tackling sectarianism, the Offensive Behaviour at Football and Threatening Communications (Scotland) Act 2012 was passed by the Scottish Parliament on 14th December 2011, and was brought into force on 1st March 2012. The Act criminalises behaviour that is threatening, hateful or otherwise offensive at a regulated football match including offensive singing or chanting. It also criminalises the communication of threats of serious violence and threats intended to incite religious hatred, whether sent through the post or posted on the Internet. The Act will only criminalise behaviour likely to lead to public disorder which expresses or incites hatred, is threatening or is otherwise offensive to a reasonable person.

The Act introduces two new offences, Offensive Behaviour at a regulated football match and Threatening Communications. Initial signs are that the legislation has had an effect with a marked reduction in incidents and arrests in the season 2012/13.

Even prior to the legislation the police and prosecutors in Scotland had been taking a robust approach to sectarianism, using the legal process to good effect. The leading case involved the singing of "the famine song" which was adopted by Rangers fans. In November 2008, a Rangers fan was found guilty of a breach of the peace (aggravated by religious and racial prejudice) for singing the song during a game in Kilmarnock. At his appeal in June 2009, three Scottish judges ruled that the song is racist because it targets people of Irish origin.[6]

Significantly, the Rangers fans' organisation, the Rangers Supporters' Trust, rejected claims that the song was racist, describing it as a "wind-up" albeit a "distasteful" one which is designed to mock not the famine itself, but Celtic fans' perceived affiliations with the Republic of Ireland. This echoes with the "banter" argument put forward by some English fans.

Cricket

In common with many governing bodies, the England and Wales Cricket Board (ECB) has made a statement of intent to combat hate crime and inequality, through its "One Game" campaign. The statement reads:

> The ECB is fully committed to the principles of equality of opportunity and aims to ensure that no individual receives less favourable treatment on the grounds of age, gender, disability, race, ethnic origin, nationality, colour, parental or marital status, pregnancy, religious belief, class or social background, sexual preference or political belief. This includes players, employees, participants, volunteers and spectators.[7]

The ECB launched a "Clean Bowl Racism" to coincide with the 1999 Cricket World Cup. This has since been supplemented by the "Let's Hit Racism For Six" campaign. This is also supported by the Professional Cricketers' Association.

England hosted the World T20 tournament in 2009, and the ECB set up a Security Directorate headed by a former Chief Constable. This adopted a similar approach to the football multi-agency approach involving the cricket authorities, ground safety officers, private security firms, the police and prosecutors. Clear reference was made to the unacceptability of behaviour that would amount to "hate crime" in both ground safety notices and official programmes. In a tournament involving 12 teams and 27 games, no serious incident was reported and no prosecution took place for an offence of hate crime. A similar approach was planned for the 2013 International Cricket Council Champions Trophy in England and Wales.

Rugby

Both codes of Rugby in the UK (Union and League) have largely avoided problems with hate crime, and any suggestions of racism are dealt with promptly. The Rugby Football League (the governing body) has launched a new game-wide 'Tackle IT!' Equality and Diversity programme which aims to increase awareness of issues such as racism, homophobia and other forms of discrimination and prejudice within Rugby League.[8] The Rugby Football Union has a "Code of Rugby" which includes "Reject cheating, racism, violence and drugs".

International experience

Space precludes a thorough examination of hate crime in sport across the world. It is trite to say that the problem is an international one and not limited to any individual country, nor is it limited to football, although that attracts the most publicity. In many countries the "banter" excuse for hate crime is replaced by an argument that the acts or words complained of are patriotic or nationalist, but it is difficult to see how targeting opposing players because of the colour of their skin can be described as anything other than "hate crime". Any quick Internet search will find numerous examples of hate crime in football across the world, and any citing of recent cases would be out of date almost as soon as it was written. The game's governing bodies have strict policies and rules and an examination of the websites of FIFA, UEFA and other regional governing bodies shows a reasonable consistency of approach.

In order to consider an international approach to hate crime, two specific sports are considered below, in each case looking at the regulations and at specific incidents.

International Rugby Board (IRB)

IRB regulation 20 covers misconduct, and section (c) lists the following as possibly constituting misconduct: "acts or statements that are, or conduct that is, discriminatory by reason of religion, race, sex, sexual orientation, disability, colour or national or ethnic origin". In the World Cup in New Zealand in October 2011 the Samoan player Fuimaono Sapolu tweeted that Welsh referee Nigel Owens was "racist" and "biased" after a match against Samoa. He was suspended from rugby for six months, although the punishment was suspended for two years. It is of note that he then received a three-week ban from the [English] RFU for another incident of "twitter" abuse. This then caused a reconsideration of his earlier suspension, which was not activated but which was increased to nine months suspended for three years.[9]

International Cricket Council (ICC)

The ICC has published an Anti-Racism Policy for International Cricket. Section 6 states that:

> The ICC and all of its Members should:
>
> a) not at any time offend, insult, humiliate, intimidate, threaten, disparage, vilify or unlawfully discriminate between persons based on their race, religion, culture, colour, descent, and/or national or ethnic origin ('**Inappropriate Racist Conduct**').[10]

This policy applies to players, officials and spectators and makes it clear that spectators could be ejected from grounds for a breach. The policy operates in parallel with the ICC Code of Conduct for players, which covers other kinds of non-racist offensive language, which must include homophobic comments.

The best known international case of racism involves the Australian mixed-race cricketer Andrew Symonds. During the winter of 2007/08 Australia toured India, and then India went to Australia. Symonds was racially abused by Indian fans throughout the tour, resulting in prosecutions in Mumbai. Whilst in Australia an Indian player was accused of racially abusing Symonds, but was only found guilty of using offensive [non-racial] language.

However, this problem is not confined to one winter. The previous winter both South African and Sri Lankan players were subjected to racist abuse in Australia, and in November 2012 a former Australian international cricketer had to defend himself against allegations of racism having used the word "kaffir" whilst telling a joke.

Olympics 2012

The London Olympics and Paralympics have been widely praised for the community atmosphere generated by Olympians, spectators, and in particular the volunteer "gamesmakers" who represented the diverse ethnic mix of the UK's population. Nevertheless there were isolated problems despite massive efforts by a number of authorities to educate and deter hate crime.

Two Olympians, a Swiss footballer and a Greek female athlete, were both excluded from their national teams for posting racist messages on the social media site, Twitter. This was not limited to athletes, with anti-Japanese messages being posted by American fans after the USA defeated the Japanese women's football team.

Perhaps the most serious offence involved a Lithuanian basketball fan that gave a Nazi salute during an Olympic basketball match. He was convicted of a racially aggravated offence at the Games and fined £2,500. Undercover police were at the basketball arena after complaints about the behaviour of Lithuanian fans in their previous match against Argentina, and he was seen to make a Nazi salute, whilst other fans made monkey noises towards the opposing team from Nigeria. The District Judge made clear the seriousness of his offence saying, "This type of conduct tarnishes the whole ethos of the Games." She said that his Nazi salute had been an insult to all those who had lost their lives in the Holocaust and his behaviour was "despicable".

Social media – a new phenomena?

The two most commonly used social media platforms (at the time of writing) are Facebook and Twitter. Each allows users to post messages without any editorial control, and which can be forwarded to an unlimited number of recipients. This phenomena is worldwide, and the problems created by this new form of mass media can be considered by reference to a small number of cases in the UK in 2011 and 2012.

Like many jurisdictions legislation exists in the UK that allows for prosecutions for criminal misuse of social media. Both section 1 of the Malicious Communications Act 1988 and section 127 of the Communications Act 2003 refer to communications that are grossly offensive, indecent, obscene, menacing or false.

Four cases are worthy of mention:

- On 17th March 2012 the footballer Fabrice Muamba suffered cardiac arrest in a game while playing for Bolton and almost died. A university student posted a number of messages on Twitter, the first of which began "LOL. F*** Muamba. He's dead!!!" He was jailed for 56 days and this sentence was upheld on appeal.
- In late 2011 the Newcastle footballer, Sammy Ameobi, was subjected to racist abuse on Twitter. Two teenagers were arrested and eventually admitted their guilt. Due to their age they were not prosecuted, but they had been subjected to a ban by Newcastle Football Club.
- In August 2012 former Portsmouth footballer, Tal Ben Haim was sent a threatening message by a disgruntled fan, which contained reference to him being Jewish. After admitting the offence the perpetrator was given a community punishment.

- The case that attracted the most publicity was the Twitter abuse of the British 18-year-old diver Tom Daley during the Olympics. Having come fourth in an event in the first week of the Olympics he received abusive messages from a 17-year-old from Dorset, and from a semi-professional footballer from South Wales. Neither was prosecuted, the first because of his age and the second because of his remorse, even though the message contained homophobic references, and the fact that the posting was only intended for a small number of friends. The views of the victim were sought and taken into account. Tom Daley's attitude was typical of many victims of hate crime when he made it clear that he just wanted the abuse to stop and the perpetrator to realise that what he was doing was wrong.

The decision to prosecute is not an easy one, requiring a prosecutor to balance the right to free speech on the one hand, and the requirement to protect victims on the other hand. Following an increase in the number of incidents, some of which involved sports personalities, the former Director of Public Prosecutions for England and Wales, Keir Starmer QC, issued guidelines to prosecutors and launched a public consultation, following roundtable discussions with a number of interest groups including sports administrators.[11]

Sports bodies have also had to deal with the misuse of social media by sportsmen and women. Where this misuse amounts to hate crime there is little doubt that it will fall foul of any anti-racism or anti-discrimination regulations issued by the relevant sport's governing body. Many sports bodies have issued guidance to their sportsmen and women, most notably the British Olympic Association before the London Games, and the Football Association before the start of the 2012/13 season.

Conclusion

Sport touches the lives of millions of people around the world. It is therefore no surprise that hate crime finds its way into sport. Whilst this is regrettable the one positive to come out of this is that the profile of sport makes it possible to highlight the evil of hate crime and to publicise successful efforts to combat and eradicate hate crime in sport.

Notes

1 http://news.bbc.co.uk/1/shared/bsp/hi/pdfs/13_07_12_r_v_john_terry.pdf
2 http://www.thefa.com/News/governance/2012/oct/john-terry-written-reasons-051012
3 http://www.uefa.com/MultimediaFiles/Download/Tech/uefaorg/General/01/81/94/48/1819448_DOWNLOAD.pdf
4 http://www.uefa.com/uefa/footballfirst/matchorganisation/disciplinary/news/newsid=1906957.html
5 http://www.kickitout.org/1307.php
6 http://www.scotcourts.gov.uk/opinions/2009HCJAC59.html
7 http://www.ecb.co.uk/ecb/one-game/statement-of-intent/
8 http://www.therfl.co.uk/the-rfl/equitydiversity/tackle-it
9 http://www.irb.com/mm/Document/Tournament/Mediazone/02/06/09/54/120109SupplementalJODecisionEliotaFuimaono-Sapolu.pdf
10 http://static.icc-cricket.com/ugc/documents/DOC_3B0C8F126B78199EF98077C462FD229D_1348137775374_513.pdf
11 http://www.cps.gov.uk/consultations/social_media_consultation.html

4
Combating hate and hate crime

27
Policing and hate crime

Paul Giannasi

The challenges of preventing, prosecuting and otherwise dealing with the effects of hate crimes are some of the toughest challenges facing modern police leaders. To do it effectively requires leaders, who often have confined geographical boundaries, to be cognisant of events in other continents. Crimes on our streets today can have their root-causes in conflicts from other millennia (see Hall in relation to historical events as 'triggers' for hate crime, this volume) and responses today will affect the trust felt by affected communities decades from now. This may sound like a grand statement but I believe it to be true.

Many of the world's most horrific incidences of civil disorder involve violence that we would consider to be hate crimes. By way of an example, the 62 people murdered in South Africa in May 2008 died in violence that many observers, including the International Organisation for Migration, believed targeted migrants in what became known as 'Xenophobic Murders'[1] The huge majority of terrorist attacks would fit into the hate crime framework and, whilst most States separate out the policy and legislation areas, the links are obvious, and monitoring the hostility that fuels both is key to any State's efforts to prevent the more extreme violence.

As well as the causal link to serious violence, hate crime can be seen in the 'ripples' of many major world events. The impact of the Gaza conflict in December of 2008 was felt in many diverse communities throughout the world. In the UK, for example, in the following two weeks the police recorded the amount of anti-Semitic crime that they would have expected to see in six months. Some sectarian conflicts that can play out as intra-religious hate crime have their origins in theological disputes dating back centuries. The mishandling of the Stephen Lawrence murder enquiry, in 1993, provides the clearest evidence of the impact of failures on the reputation of the agencies for many years to come.

The long-term impact of police action in response to hate crime is clearly demonstrated in the experiences in recent decades within the UK. My son is a young detective in a large city in England. He, and other young officers, are regularly challenged by people in the community about their ability to deliver fair and equitable service to minority ethnic communities. Individuals will often quote as evidence the police failings identified in the Stephen Lawrence Inquiry and particularly the finding that the police were 'Institutionally Racist', a term that has 'stuck' to the police in the eyes of many in the community. My son was just seven when Stephen was murdered but community confidence in his ability to deliver fair and equitable service is still challenged by the mishandling of the racist hate crime two decades earlier, by officers and leaders who have largely left the service.

The mishandling of the Stephen Lawrence murder is undoubtedly one of the most damaging incidents to police reputation in the span of my career since the mid 1980s. However, it is not the only instance of a potential hate crime having an impact on the police's relationship with the community. The mishandling of an enquiry into the murder of a transgender victim, Maxwell – known as 'Michelle' Confait – in 1972 lead to the re-writing of the rules of investigation in England and Wales in The Police and Criminal Evidence Act, 1984. More recently, the failure of the Police and local authorities to protect Fiona Pilkington and her disabled daughter Frankie, from protracted abuse was deemed, by their Coroner's Inquests, to have contributed to her decision to take their lives in 2007.

As damaging as the mishandling of hate crime investigations can be, positive, fair and compassionate handling can have the opposite effect. It may take many positive examples to overcome the harm caused by just one mishandled enquiry, however it is possible to build more positive relationships with affected communities.

In 2007, Gee Walker, the mother of Anthony Walker – who was brutally murdered in a racist attack in Liverpool in 2005 – was interviewed by the UK Government's Independent Advisory Group. In stark comparison to Doreen and Neville Lawrence's experience, who reasonably feel that the criminal justice system added to the burden of the tragedy they suffered, Gee Walker felt that the criminal justice system had helped her to begin to deal with that same tragedy of losing a child to horrific racist violence. She made note of the support that she had received from the police and Crown Prosecution Service and was particularly praising of the sentencing judge, Mr Justice Leveson, who explained to the court how the sentences for the murderers had been enhanced using the powers in section 145 of the Criminal Justice Act, 2003. She said it was the clearest indication to her, affected communities, and offenders, that the State did not tolerate racist violence.

Another example of the impact of hate and hostility is demonstrated below with examples of how positive police action to threats to a broad community can have a massive impact on community relationships and public disorder.

In this chapter, I will outline some of the significant operational challenges that the police face in their efforts to prevent hate crime, bring offenders to justice, and build positive relationships with the affected communities. I will use examples from the UK to demonstrate these challenges including:

- The under-reporting of hate crime.
- The relationship between hostility and public disorder.
- The challenges of policing hate crime on the Internet.
- Hate crime targeting disabled victims.

The under-reporting of hate crime

It is impossible for the police and partners to begin to understand simmering hostilities in our communities if authorities do not know about them. We know that many 'ordinary' crimes do not get reported to the police but also that hate crimes are massively under-reported and under-recorded. Accurate recording requires two key elements, firstly that the victim or some other person notifies authorities, but also that authorities recognise that the crime has an element of hostility.

In Chapter 9, I discussed how, in the UK, successive Governments have recognised the importance of reducing the under-recording of hate crime. For many political leaders this situation is counter-intuitive and some would want to play down the significance of the problem, either to protect their reputation, because they do not value the rights of those citizens who are most susceptible to hate crime, or to provide reassurance to affected communities. I would argue that transparency of data, strong leadership and effective responses to hate crime are essential to reducing the risk of major violence. The police have a key role in encouraging reporting, as do the many civil society groups, such as Human Rights First, who do excellent work to expose the extent of hate crimes in States where authorities cannot or will not report hate crime. They are able to expose the real experiences of affected communities and hold the States to account in international fora and the media.

In some States, such as the UK and USA, the extent of under-recording of hate crime is clear because, as well as reporting hate crime data, these States also assess the actual experiences of citizens through extensive, and statistically validated surveys. I discussed the British Crime Survey in Chapter 9, but it shows that in 2011/12 there were around 260,000 actual hate crimes although the police only recorded 43,000. The US Bureau of Justice Statistics examined the USA Victimization Survey and found that there were an average of 259,700 violent or property-related hate crimes. In 2011 the Federal Bureau of Investigation recorded 7,254 offences.

Whilst data from these two States cannot be directly compared because of recording practices and legislative disparities, it is compelling evidence to me as to why under-recording should be one of the greatest operational challenges for police and States. I believe that the 'closing of the gap' of these two sets of data is the clearest indication of State progress and over time the examination of their relationship will, for example, give States the confidence that falls in recorded crime are the result of less hostility in society, rather than victim apathy or police indifference.

One of the key approaches to improving reporting in the UK has been the promoting of third-party reporting schemes. These cover a broad range of activities and recognise that many victims cannot or will not report directly to the police, because of a lack of trust, inaccessibility or some other factor. Third-Party Reporting provides a range of different routes to enable reporting to authorities. These groups range from formal, national support groups to local, informal 'self-help' groups. They assist a victim to report or, where they cannot be encouraged to pass their details onto the police, details of the crime can be passed on anonymously. On the rare occasion in which the victim insists on anonymity, the police will record these crimes to inform their understanding of hostility and prevent future criminality. It is possible to convict offenders without a victim, for instance where an assault is covered by CCTV, although the chances of detection without victim cooperation are significantly reduced.

There are many different accounts of where this concept first originated but the first traces I can find in the UK were within the lesbian, gay, bisexual and transgender (LGBT) community in Manchester in the early 1990s. Manchester has a thriving LGBT social scene but in the 1990s many victims did not trust the police to deal with hate crime sensitively and attacks on them were massively under-reported. The police worked with community groups and set up outreach centres in nightclub venues, which were often staffed by LGB police colleagues. This outreach work and the willingness to record crimes anonymously were significant factors in improving the relationship between the police and a community often affected by hate crime.

The value of this policing approach was further evidenced in the aftermath of the nail-bomb attacks in London in April 1999. The 'white-supremacist', David Copeland, set off a series of explosive devices, attacking the Asian, Black and LGB communities, killing three people and injuring many more. These crimes are discussed further by Smith in this volume.

In response to the attack on the Admiral Duncan Pub in Soho, and in order to encourage witnesses to come forward, the Metropolitan Police placed a mobile police station in the area. It was made to be common knowledge that the police station was staffed by LGB police officers, many of whom had travelled from other parts of the country to assist the enquiry.

The impact of this move was significant and encouraged victims and witnesses to come forward, but it also had the effect of bringing forward victims of many other crimes who had been given the confidence to report, without fear of any adverse reaction from officers. This initiative provided clear evidence to police managers that victims can be encouraged to come forward if the police are proactive and deliver services tailored to meet the needs of the victim. This is the key challenge in delivering third-party reporting schemes.

These initiatives, and the bravery of a number of police colleagues who were prepared to 'break-ground' and become open about their sexual orientation, provided a significant advance in police relationships with the gay community in the UK. Perhaps a sign indicating the value of these initiatives was demonstrated in 2006, when Staffordshire Police was assessed to be the 'UK Employer of the Year' by the LGB community group, Stonewall.

In 2008, the Association of Chief Police Officers' (ACPO) Hate Crime Group carried out a review of existing third-party reporting schemes. It found that many, whilst well intended, failed to deliver tangible results. Others suffered from short-term delivery that could potentially water-down the value of all such schemes. It found that third party and assisted reporting remains relevant, whilst hate crime is still under-reported, in order to overcome some of the limitations and to ensure consistency throughout the UK. It agreed that the ACPO Hate Crime Group takes on the 'ownership' of the scheme that had had the greatest success, True Vision. It would develop and host the scheme and provide systems and materials to encourage reporting.

True Vision (www.report-it.org.uk) aims to provide information to victims and professionals, share materials for local delivery and allow for the online reporting of hate crime into local police control centres. The latter has proved to be a popular option to victims with over 3,000 reports being made to the police in 2012. The site has around 10,000 visits per month by visitors who view an average of seven pages. Whilst this includes many professionals, it is proving a popular service.

One of the other factors identified by the ACPO review was that information schemes are more likely to be effective to people who would know how to access services should they wish to do so. The more isolated sections of our communities are at least as likely to be victimised as others but are less likely to demand services. The ACPO guidance suggests that, before embarking on targeted activity in their community, they should have knowledge of who is susceptible to hate crime and who is less likely to seek services. They then need to consider the best way to target materials to those groups in a sensitive way.

One positive example of such targeted police activity was that Greater Manchester Police wanted to encourage reporting from their resident Jewish community who were experiencing hostility. They consulted with the community and found that one of the factors causing non-reporting was that religious observance stopped victims using a phone or vehicle during Shabbat. In order to overcome this inaccessibility, the police regularly placed a mobile police station near to the Synagogue. The result was an increase in reporting and improved relationships with the community.

The relationship between hostility and public disorder

It is perhaps logical that threatened communities will feel that their presence is threatened by serious or sustained attack. Both the individual and community attacks can lead to fear and tension. If that fear is not averted, there is a risk of escalation, retribution and ultimately public disorder. These fears can affect the majority as well as minority groups. In May 2013, following the horrific murder of Drummer Lee Rigby in Woolwich, London, which was widely believed to be fuelled by Islamist extremism, police in the UK recorded a significant rise in hate crimes targeting Muslims.

Whether this was fuelled by pre-existing hostility or newly created fear of attack is yet to be examined but the increased community tension was clear to see. It is perhaps logical that the more visible, marginalised and isolated communities will feel greater levels of fear.

Perhaps one of the clearest examples of escalating tensions was in the north of England in April, 2001, however it would be wrong to suggest that hate crime was the sole trigger of the disorder that broke out in many northern towns. In his official review of the disorder, Professor Ted Cantell describes many community factors such as integration, poverty and joblessness as being contributing factors to the incidents, but the trigger that led to the first conflict was an escalation of tension between the majority white and minority Asian communities. It is clear that reported and actual hate crime were trigger events that began this disorder which continued to spread, and over several weeks resulted in over £10.3 million of property damage, over 400 injured police officers and many years of effort needed to rebuild relationships.

On 21st April 2001, a 76-year-old man, Walter Chamberlain, was assaulted in the Chadderton area of Oldham in Greater Manchester, by a number of youths from Asian heritage. During the attack he received facial injuries that resulted in extreme bruising. Mr Chamberlain and his family insisted that his assault was not a racist attack but an attempted robbery, however the newspaper headlines suggested that it was. The national tabloids included headlines such as:

> *'Beaten for being white: OAP, 76, attacked in Asian no-go area'*
> *'Whites beware'*
> *'Beaten to a pulp . . . for being white:*
> WAR VETERAN, 75 ATTACKED IN ASIAN 'NO-GO AREA'

It is clear now that the media coverage caused anger and tension in sections of the majority white community. On Saturday 28th April 2001, Stoke City travelled to Oldham to play a scheduled football match. Whilst Stoke City, at that time, had a problem of violence within its supporter group, the fixture was not one that had traditionally been marred by confrontation. Football intelligence officers from Staffordshire Police had expected a small number of 'risk' supporters to travel to the match, but expected them to travel in small groups and not to seek violent confrontation with opposing fans. On this basis the policing operation was relatively low-key.

On the day a much larger group of 'risk' supporters arrived at the local rail station much earlier than they would normally travel. They met another group of men in Manchester who were outsiders, not normally associated with the club. At this point the police reassessed the operation and diverted reserves to Oldham. The group, estimated at 400–500 strong, arrived in Oldham and walked to the Chadderton area where they were involved in a prolonged incident of disorder. They damaged shops, homes and cars and attacked Asian residents. Rumours spread that they had beaten a pregnant Asian woman.

The coordinated attack on Chadderton was considered to be a backlash to the media coverage of the attack on Walter Chamberlain. Some on the periphery told police that they were there to 'send a message' to the Asian community and it was clear that they were particularly angered by the 'No-Go Area for Whites' claims. Given the history of racist groups and individuals trying to stir up tensions, police managers, including myself, believed that this creation of tension in target communities was a deliberate attempt to create the confrontation and disorder that we saw.

Once the original attack was over, the group moved off to watch the match and huge numbers of Asian men came out onto the street and demonstrated their anger at the disorder. The police mobilised resources and sought to maintain order, but there was some violent confrontations with police and tensions built. By the time the football supporters left the match large groups of local people were on the streets, but police lines had been bolstered and were largely able to keep groups apart.

The tensions that were present beforehand, and the anger at the attack on the area by the white group, spilled over into civil disorder which spread into several towns and cities over several weeks. The cost of the disorder, in terms of finance and fractured community relationships, lead to a re-examination of police practices, a greater commitment to community engagement and the development of more effective Community Intelligence with systems developed by Deputy Assistant Commissioner John Grieve after the 1999 Inquiry.

The comparison of societal damage in 2001 is stark when compared to the English Defence League (EDL) demonstrations of 2010–12. It is clear that, whilst the EDL is not an illegal organisation and would claim to be only opposed to Islamist 'extremist' activity, most of the community, including the Muslim community, would see the group as, at least, containing racist and anti-Muslim elements. It is easy to see similarities between the trigger incidents in 2001 and the tactics of some EDL supporters, who seek to demonstrate at sensitive areas, often on the back of media coverage of wrongdoings of individuals from the Muslim community.

Many of the protests have resulted in violence and police believe that one of the tactics deployed by some of the protesters is to try to inflame tension and provoke a violent reaction from the Muslim community. Their events usually attract a counter-protest from 'anti-Fascist' groups. As the series of protests developed, police began to coordinate activity through intelligence gathering, particularly from the Internet and social media. The police joined other agencies and community groups to give advice to affected areas and to ensure lessons were learned from earlier incidents.

One of the series of protests took place in Stoke-on-Trent on 23rd January 2010. The event became violent and many of the demonstrators attacked police officers who were defending sensitive locations such as mosques and businesses owned by Asian proprietors. In the run-up to the Stoke-on-Trent event, police carried out extensive community engagement, aimed at reassuring the community and preventing a backlash reaction. A senior police officer was appointed to act as the principal point of liaison. The engagement activity included events in schools, mosques and businesses and brought together a multi-faith group to show leadership and reassure fearful communities.

The police recruited, trained and included within their operation a series of volunteer Community Mediators. This engagement was intensified on the day of the event and continued until intelligence assessments suggested that tensions had diminished.

During the protest, a large number of demonstrators attempted to break free from the group. The police made a series of arrests, but also suffered injuries to a number of officers. In addition to the uniformed presence, the police also allocated a team of detectives to gather evidence from video recordings, forensic science and witnesses. They made a series of retrospective arrests in the weeks following the event for crimes that were recorded as hate crimes. This resulted in a total of 21 convictions for a range of offences including 'Racially and Religiously Aggravated' violence and public order offences. Offenders all appeared in court and received sentences of up to 16 months imprisonment.

The police and community representatives believe that the collaborative approach adopted had prevented a violent backlash from a very fearful community and had enhanced the levels of trust in the police and other agencies from affected communities.

The challenges of policing hate crime on the Internet

'The internet is the cause of, and solution to, most of our problems'.

The Internet has perhaps provided the first occasion in peacetime history where States have not been able to control or legislate against materials and information that has influence within their borders, and they have no real ability to influence its content. Whereas a generation ago, the vast majority of information we consume would have originated from organisations complying with local legislation and governance, this is now not the case, with significantly more information generated by organisations outside the reach of our governments. Many States pride themselves on having a free media to underpin their democratic ideals, but the decision not to regulate is a conscious and deliberate choice.

There is no single State or even multi-state body that can unilaterally control the Internet and the myriad of people who use it. The USA is undoubtedly the most influential State, given the prevalence of its territories as a base for operations, but it would still be incapable of effectively controlling activity due to its interactive nature, prevalence of anonymous posting and the opportunity for individuals to set up outside their territories. The USA legislature is also restrained by the limitations of the First Amendment to their Constitution, which bars Congress from passing laws that restrict, amongst other things, free speech.

There are several challenges to finding solutions to the problem of reducing the harm caused by hate material on the Internet. Some of the more pressing or difficult include:

I. The global nature of the Internet

As Littman's reflective piece (this volume) suggests, the Internet is truly unique in the history of communications for many reasons, not least of all its global nature. The fact that it is without a single base, a single commanding authority or a single technology is its strength, but presents a huge challenge for those tasked with preventing and detecting criminality that is planned, incited or even executed over the Internet.

II. Disparity in legislative approaches

There seems to be little appetite or capability of harmonizing legislation across different States, although there are some European commitments to legislate against the more serious incitement offences.

III. The huge void between the prevalence of hate and criminal justice capacity

There is a stark reality that in countries like the UK, where legislatures have sought to control behaviour through legislation such as the incitement of hatred offences, the prevalence of harmful material exponentially outweighs the capacity of criminal justice agencies to respond.

Academics have long since given up trying to measure the extent of hate material on the Internet and the police have resisted any temptation to trawl for offences, relying solely on responding to complaints made by the public. The reality of the situation is that one story in a newspaper or one video on the Internet can lead to several hundred instances of material being posted which is above the threshold set by the courts in UK Public Order Act offences.

Where States do have provisions for courts to order the removal of material, the financial and resource implications, together with the inevitable time delay, means that this model, which is favoured by many in the Internet industry, is both laborious and ineffective, and the harm intended by the material is often caused before the material could be removed.

IV. The valuable role of free speech in democracy, particularly in oppressive regimes

One very real concern for many States is the need to protect free speech, particularly in international regimes where journalism, democracy and basic freedoms are under threat. Some international non-governmental organisations have expressed concern that Internet controls, intended to reduce the harm caused by hate material, could also be used to oppress free-speech.

V. The speed of development and the fragmented nature of the industry

It is hard to imagine that the larger, more influential social media organisations that are so influential today did not exist 10 years ago. The rapid and fragmented growth of small groups means that we cannot expect the same social and historical insight that you would expect from established national and multinational groups who have developed over decades. Another challenge is that there isn't a single voice for these groups and most see themselves as being in aggressive competition, urgently seeking to provide their services as the bedrock for the emerging industry services and thereby capturing its advertising capabilities.

Another distinct characteristic of the Internet industry is that the social media service users are seen by most in their business model as commodities rather than customers. It is important to realise that the model of 'free use', that has proved so popular with consumers, means that the companies see the advertisers as the customers and seek to appease the public only insofar as necessary to retain their patronage. This means that they do not place such a high importance on traditional 'customer service', and many complainants have been left exasperated by the perceived lack of response from the companies.

In those countries such as the UK, where the Police have prosecuted Internet hate crimes, there are some important principles for courts to rule on. Two of the most important are the jurisdiction of any offence and whether the Internet is a 'public space' or a place of private communication as many legislatures have offences that can only occur in public spaces.

In the UK these two questions seem to have been addressed by the courts' interpretation of the legislation. In relation to jurisdiction, the UK Supreme Court has clarified this in the case of Sheppard and Whittle, who were convicted in July 2008 at Leeds Crown Court of several counts of publishing racially inflammatory material. Whilst on bail, they fled the UK

Policing and hate crime

to the USA where they claimed asylum, but were returned nearly one year later. On 10th July 2009 they were sentenced to terms of imprisonment.

Their material, which contained antisemitic text, Holocaust denial, and other racist content, was posted on a website, which was hosted in California. The Court held that as the material in question was uploaded in the UK and was available to the public at large, the offence occurred in the UK, and was therefore subject to British jurisdiction and was not extra-jurisdictional, as the defendants had argued. The convictions were upheld by the Court of Appeal and the Supreme Court.

In order to address some of the challenges listed above the UK Director of Public Prosecutions and the Association of Chief Police Officers have issued guidance on the investigation and prosecution of Internet hate offences in order to ensure consistency, manage demand and provide a balance between the rights to free speech and protection from harm.

Hate crime targeting disabled victims

The targeted abuse of disabled people is a relatively recent inclusion in hate crime policy, however it is certainly not a new phenomenon. As Quarmby (2011) argued, it is a burden that has been faced by many disabled people throughout history.

In England and Wales, hate crime against disabled people was recognised in the Criminal Justice Act, 2003, where section 146 included an instruction to courts to enhance the sentence of offenders shown to have demonstrated hostility on the grounds of the victim's disability or perceived disability. However, whilst this power came into force in 2005 it was not until 2007 that the attention of the criminal justice agencies was drawn to the problem.

As I discussed in Chapter 9, when the review of hate crime policy was being undertaken by criminal justice partners in England and Wales in 2007, there was a series of high profile crimes in which disabled people were targeted in degrading, abusive, torturous and even fatal violence. Some of the most high-profile crimes were prominent in the news as agencies considered which strands of hate crime should be included in the shared definition in the UK. One of the most alarming such crimes was the murder of Steven Hoskins. Steven was 38 when he was murdered in 2006, in St Austell, Cornwall. He had a learning disability and lived alone in a bedsit. He 'befriended' a group, including five individuals who would go onto abuse, torture and eventually murder him. The group included two men in their 20s and three teenagers, although only one of these was involved in the fatal incident.

Over a period of time, Steven's friendship was abused and he was subjected to prolonged humiliation and violence. He was tied up in his home, made to wear a dog's collar and lead before being dragged around his home. He had multiple injuries from cigarette burns and other violence. Steven was forced to confess to being a 'paedophile' and was found guilty in a 'kangaroo court'. As a punishment, Steven was sentenced 'to death'. He was forced to take around 70 paracetamol tablets before being taken to a nearby viaduct, where he was forced to climb over the railings. Shockingly, as Steven held onto the viaduct the youngest of those present, a 16-year-old girl, stamped on his fingers causing him to fall 35 metres to his death. Five offenders were convicted in relation to Steven's death; the 16-year-old girl and her 29-year-old boyfriend were convicted of murder, a 21-year-old man was convicted of manslaughter and two teenage boys were convicted of assault and false imprisonment. The hearing took place before disability was included in the national agreed hate crime definition and it does not appear that any of the criminal justice agencies considered it to be a disability hate crime.

Sadly, Steven's murder was not the only horrific disability hate crime to come to attention in 2007, others, such as the killings of Kevin Davies and Brent Martin, as well as the humiliation of Christine Lakinski as she lay dying in the street, all served to demonstrate the hostility that disabled people can suffer in society. However they did identify similarities in the behaviour of the offenders, whilst there may not be a 'common cause' amongst the perpetrators of these crimes, in the same way as there is with 'white supremacists', there was some stark similarities in their offending. Offenders were more likely to target victims repeatedly, offend in an escalating severity and operate in groups, abusing, humiliating and even torturing their victims. These deaths shocked police and prosecutors in the UK and disability was included in the national definitions, with police beginning to gather national data from 2008.

Another series of hate crimes came to the public attention in October 2007 when Fiona Pilkington drove with her 18-year-old daughter Francecca (Frankie) Hardwick to a lay-by near to their home in Leicestershire, which they shared with Frankie's brother Anthony, who was then 16. The bodies of the mother and daughter were later discovered in the burnt-out shell of the vehicle.

An inquest into their deaths was held in 2009, and the jury found that Fiona Pilkington killed herself and Frankie 'due to the stress and anxiety regarding her daughter's future, and ongoing antisocial behaviour'. The jury said the police's response had contributed to Fiona Pilkington's decision to 'unlawfully kill her daughter and commit suicide'. They said that 'Calls were not linked or prioritised' and they also highlighted the lack of action by local Borough and County Councils.

The Inquest was told that Frankie had a learning disability and that Fiona was her carer, and that Anthony also suffered from dyslexia. The family had suffered torment over a period of around 10 years before their deaths. Their abuse was varied in its nature and severity, taking place in many different locations and targeting all family members. Incidents ranged from rowdiness around their home through to occasions where Anthony was forced into a shed at knife-point and detained there until he was able to break free. There were other occasions where property around the family home was set on fire.

It does not appear from the evidence heard in the inquest or the subsequent investigation of the Independent Police Complaints Commission (IPCC) that the issue of the children's disability was a consideration when responding to incidents. At the time of their tragic deaths Leicestershire Police, in common with many police forces, did not include disability as one of its strands of hate crime recording. Sadly, Fiona and Frankie died a month before ACPO's Cabinet agreed to the common definition of hate crime that included disability.

The inquest and the IPCC investigation found fundamental flaws in the response of the police and local authorities. There were systemic and individual failings in the agencies' responses but perhaps most damaging was that the incidents tended to be responded in isolation, with different officials responding to the circumstances they faced at that time, rather than recognising the escalating harm caused by the holistic situation faced by the family.

Fiona had sought the support of agencies repeatedly but her family gave evidence that she died with a sense of desperation, fearing that there was no other escape from the torment that she and Frankie were suffering. It is worth taking time here to consider the situation Fiona faced – ask yourself, how could we envisage a life so tormented and frustrating that we would choose to take our own life and that of our child, in such horrific circumstances, in an attempt to escape the fear and suffering within our everyday life?

The exposure of police failings by the Coroner, by the IPCC, and later by the Equality and Human Rights Commission's Inquiry again showed that hate crime can have significant impact on public confidence in the police and their ability to deliver fair, equitable and effective service. The examination of the police response to Fiona Pilkington and her family's needs damaged police relationships, particularly with disabled people.

Police and prosecution leaders acknowledge that there was a need to urgently address the challenges of effectively responding to disability hate crime. In a speech in October 2008, the Director of Public Prosecutions (DPP), Sir Ken Macdonald QC (Now Lord Macdonald of River Glaven) said:

> I am on record as saying that it is my sense that disability hate crime is very widespread. I have said that it is my view that at the lower end of the spectrum there is a vast amount not being picked up. I have also expressed the view that the more serious disability hate crimes are not always being prosecuted as they should be . . . This is a scar on the conscience of criminal justice. And all bodies and all institutions involved in the delivery of justice, including my own, share the responsibility.

The DPP's sentiment was shared by Police leaders, with both services issuing detailed guidance to professionals in how to build the confidence in disabled people and to provide their basic rights to equitable security from the State. The gap between the 65,000 crimes recognised by the British Crime Survey and the 2,000 recorded by the police demonstrates the scale of that challenge.

Conclusion

This chapter has outlined some of the significant operational challenges that the police face in their efforts to prevent hate crime, bring offenders to justice, and build positive relationships with affected communities. Although there are undoubtedly many challenges in this complex area of policing, I have used the examples of the under-reporting of hate crime, the relationship between hostility and public disorder, the challenges of policing hate crime on the Internet, and hate crime targeting disabled victims to illustrate the scope and depth of these challenges. Although considerable progress has been made in the policing of hate crime in the UK in recent years, it is clear that these complexities ensure that this progress must continue.

Note

1 In 2008 South Africa did not have any criminal hate crime legislation and relied on civil litigation to counter hate speech.

Bibliography

College of Policing (2014). *Hate Crime Strategy and Tactical Advice*. London: College of Policing.
Director of Public Prosecutions for England and Wales (2013). Guidelines on prosecuting cases involving communications sent via social media (Accessed at www.cps.gov.uk/legal/a_to_c/communications_sent_via_social_media/index.html) London: DPP.
EHRC (2012). Out in the Open: tackling disability-related harassment – a manifesto for change. www.equalityhumanrights.com/uploaded_files/disabilityfi/out_in_the_open_dhi_manifesto.pdf. London: EHRC.
EHRC (2011). Hidden in Plain Sight: Inquiry into Disability Related Harassment. Retrieved from EHRC website: www.equalityhumanrights.com/uploaded_files/disabilityfi/ehrc_hidden_in_plain_sight_3.pdf . London: EHRC.
England and Wales Court of Appeal (Criminal Division) Decisions, *Sheppard & Whittle, R v* (2010) EWCA Crim 65 (29 January 2010). www.bailii.org/ew/cases/EWCA/Crim/2010/65.html
Federal Bureau of Investigation (USA), Hate Crime Statistics for 2011 (Accessed October 2013 at www.fbi.gov/about-us/cjis/ucr/hate-crime/2011/narratives/incidents-and-offenses).

Home Office (2001). *Building Cohesive Communities: a report of the Ministerial Group on Public Order and Community Cohesion*, London, Home Offfice.
International Organisation for Migration (2009). Towards Tolerance, Law and Dignity: Addressing Violence against Foreign Nationals in South Africa.
Langton, L., Planty, M. and Sandholtz, N. (2013). *Hate Crime Victimization, 2003–2011*, Bureau of Justice Statistics, Washington DC.
OSCE (2012). *Hate Crimes in the OSCE Region – Incidents and Responses. Annual Report for 2011.* Warsaw: OSCE.
Quarmby, K. (2011). *Scapegoat: Why We Are Failing Disabled People.* London: Portobello.
Smith, K., Lader, K., Hoare, J. and Lau, I. (2012). Hate Crime, Cyber Security and the Experience of Crime Among Children: Findings from the 2010/11 British Crime Survey. Retrieved from: www.homeoffice.gov.uk/publications/science-research-statistics/research-statistics/crime-research/hosb0612/hosb0612?view=Binary. London: Home Office.

28
Intelligence and hate crime

John G.D. Grieve

This chapter provides an update on some thinking about the role of intelligence-led policing in dealing with hate crime. It presents some further argument about earlier versions that appeared directly in Hall et al. (2009), but also indirectly in Grieve (2004/2009, 2009). There, an argument is developed that what are needed in general are community friendly police intelligence systems. There are tensions, practical and logical, between this aspiration and the proximate social and cultural, professional and political context, and distal wider and international environment in which any intelligence developments are taking place. This chapter expressly addresses the application of intelligence, with all the current context of concerns that have arisen, to the policing of hate crime.

The immediate context is increasing media, political, public concern over police intelligence following allegations about surveillance tactics, some of which are immediately relevant to hate crime (see for example Evans and Lewis, 2013) in a wider environment of allegations of international surveillance by the USA, UK and other countries, particularly relating to digital, cyber and 'cloud' intelligence gathering in counter terrorism (Guardian Newspaper 17.6.2013: 1–5 and many others). There is a wider environment pertaining to the post 'Wiki leaks' world (Guardian Newspaper 31.7.2013 and many others) and the National Security Agency (NSA) (USA)/Government Communications Headquarters (GCHQ) documents leaked by Edward Snowden, but also to the debate engendered in the UK by the Butler Report (2004) about the public use of intelligence in the build up to the Iraq War (Butler, 2004), and in the subsequent discussion of confidence in intelligence in the consent for intervention debates about Syrian use of banned weapons. Much of the broader current debate about intelligence that splashes over into debates about police intelligence in particular seems to have its origins in public perceptions of intelligence from the Iraq experiences. This emphasis on what appears to be *being done* may be contrasted with concerns that *not enough is being done* about the intelligence and investigative opportunities for 'trolling' that is hate based largely, but not exclusively, on gender abuse and threats on the Internet (Guardian Newspaper 30.07.2013: 30 and many others). Intelligence in all its guises is a hot topic. However intelligence is a tool in the policing response to hate crime and could usefully restore public confidence in many disparate communities in general, and with hate crime in particular.

John G.D. Grieve

There are many dimensions to these distal and proximate debates about the use of intelligence and its dissemination, some of which are discussed below using hate crime as a vehicle. The aim however is to promote intelligence in the investigation of these crimes. The chapter also concerns itself with other related aspects of investigation, such as information, analysis, knowledge flows, learning, adaptation and complexity. Similarly, this chapter looks back to where we have come from since the 1999 Stephen Lawrence Inquiry (SLI) in the UK, focusing on intelligence-led policing of hate crime, with some international comparison, and it endeavours to look ahead to where we might go next. In that way my hope is that this will further the debate, not just about hate crime and intelligence, but further the ambition that everyone benefits from a 'community friendly', intelligence-led policing strategy (Hall et al., 2009; Grieve, 2004/2009).

This chapter also seeks to challenge the dominant narrative that all is negative and the result of police (leadership) failure by exploring the issues and changes in attitudes and legislation. It is a partner to Grieve (2014, forthcoming in Pycroft and Bartollas, 2014) 'The Stephen Lawrence Inquiry: Complexity and Policing', which explores the value of complexity theory (not covered in detail here) in hate crime investigation, cultural and organisational change programmes, and complex adaptive systems of which intelligence-led policing against hate crime is an example. The word 'adaptive' is important here as systems of adaptation are seen to have real potential for changes, and organisational fear of change, not least in the intelligence arenas (see Murray, 2011 and Serena, 2011, for military examples).

Intelligence, investigation, legislation, hate crime and ethics

Intelligence, in the sense of 'information designed for action' (a definition derived from Sims, 1993), is only one aspect of the police investigative strategy and tactics. The investigative strategy, depending on the nature of the hate crime, and the resources available, may include (under the broad headings of) evidential opportunities, the search for witnesses, the gathering of evidence and documents, forensic retrieval, digital evidence of electronic footprints from CCTV to mobile phone information, social networks, lifestyle and the families of victims and perpetrators (specifically explored at more length later), communications (internal to policing and external in the search for assistance from the public) to name but a fraction of what may be needed in the search for the truth. Intelligence may play a part in any of those areas of activity.

It is possible that a hate crime intelligence system that managed to include all the concepts listed in the Table 28.1, together with a communication strategy that persuaded communities that it was in their interests to support it, would not only be a powerful driver for success against hate crime but would also be a public relations success for intelligence agencies more generally (Giannasi makes this case in the comparison of this in similar events of hate crime in the previous chapter of this volume).

Intelligence-led policing has a long history, which is explored elsewhere (Grieve, 2004/2009). Here though, the emphasis is on the ethical and political concerns. Early 'cause célèbre' (from 1834) included the widespread public distaste in the reaction to a plain clothes police officer (Sergeant William Popay of the (London) Metropolitan Police) who observed, over the course of a year, the preparations for public demonstrations against the government (Shpayer-Makov, 2011: 31). Nearly 180 years later this same distaste manifested itself again (Evans and Lewis, 2013) as they sought to expose the operating practice of undercover police officers in the UK.

Table 28.1 Summary: Comparative table of usages of the word 'intelligence'

Simms 1993 as interpreted by SID Project (see Grieve 2009 in Hall et al. 2009)	Butler 2004	Keegan 2003	National Intelligence Model (NIM) 2000 & Ratcliffe 2004/2009	Omand 2010 p.119	Other concepts and writers
Collection plan Information Designed for	Collect Acquire Analysis Key judgements. Role of dissent.	Acquire Analysis	Direct Collect Process Collate	Requirement Access Elucidation	Requirement Questions Hofstadter 1980 wider usages of the word 'intelligence'. Assessment, Grant 1981. Fricker, 2002
Action	Disseminate	Delivery Accept Implement	Formal Review Disseminate NIM emphasis on outcomes, products	Dissemination Action	
Impact					Leverage Kerr 2008a and 2008b.

Over the years the police have taken very different views of the role of intelligence. In 1881 Howard Vincent, himself part of a reform of policing following scandals, wrote:

> Police work is impossible without information, and every good officer will do his (sic) best to obtain reliable intelligence, taking care at the same time not to be lead away on false issues. Information must not be treasured up, until opportunity offers for action by the officer who obtains it, but should be promptly communicated to a superior, and those who are in a position to act upon it. Not only is this the proper course of action to take, in the public interest, but it will be certainly recognised, both by authorities and comrades, promoting esteem and confidence, which will bring their own reward.
>
> *(Vincent, 1881: 202)*

It is instructive that the last decade and a half has the development of hate crime legislation and hence police investigation and Crown Prosecution Service (CPS) prosecutions mirroring the national development of UK-wide intelligence-led policing. Dixon and Court in this volume demonstrate how, if shared, that same intelligence can assist in the rehabilitation of offenders. We have also seen a growth in intelligence assessments of the strategic, tactical, operational, practical, legal, ethical and political. This juxtaposition of the diverse elements in a timeline of these interwoven strands, as they relate to hate crimes, are important to help understand the way ahead. The immediate relevance of intelligence to hate crimes was apparent in the Stephen Lawrence[1] Public Inquiry (published in 1999) and in particular in the summary of arguments provided by Michael Mansfield QC in 1998:

> Where the offence occurs in the hours of darkness over a short space of time and the perpetrators disappear on foot into the locality, it then behoves investigating officers to act with speed and intelligence. Time is of the essence. With every passing hour . . .
> *(Stephen Lawrence Inquiry Transcript, Michael Mansfield QC closing speech Page 11063 lines 20–25)*

> In summary, there plainly has to be a compendious and effective local intelligence gathering operation in existence that can be accessed quickly by officers at any time, day or night, especially when those officers may not be familiar with the locality. The information itself should be categorised in such a way that it can be called up by reference to name, or description, or address, or offence, or modus operandi, or vehicle or associates. Computerisation must clearly have made this possible for the future.
> *(Stephen Lawrence Inquiry Transcript Michael Mansfield QC closing speech Page 11055 lines 2–12)*

This hugely useful statement about the significance of hate crime intelligence by a critic of ineffective policing and famous defence lawyer (which I have quoted before) unfortunately never made its way into the recommendations of the public inquiry. Another practical impact was the arrival of the UK National Intelligence Model in 2000, the year after the Stephen Lawrence Inquiry reported (see Flood and Gaspar (2004) in Ratcliffe (2004/2009) for a detailed account and chronology), which had a separate genesis to hate crimes.

The legislative background for intelligence-led policing is contained in the Police Act 1997, the Crime and Disorder Act 1998 (which both predated the Stephen Lawrence Public Inquiry), the Regulation of Investigatory Powers Act 2000 and subsequent guidance from the Surveillance Commissioners set up under that act, and the Human Rights Act 1998. The latter introduced an ethical context with the foundation concepts contained in the acronym PLAN BI (Proportional, Legal, Accountable, Necessary, and acting on the Best Information available at the time) (see Neyroud and Beckley (2001); Grieve et al. (2007: 107 et seq.)).

There are many dimensions to these debates about the use of intelligence and its dissemination. Ethically, there is the balance between secrecy in ensuring the security of the State and the safety of its citizens on the one hand, and the freedoms and rights of individuals on the other. In arriving at that balance, the concept of public consent has to be considered in any democracy. This presents vital, even fundamental concerns for policing.

The same sort of concerns arise for policing in the openness required by the media in their 'public scrutiny' role of responsible reporting and in informing the debate that gives rise to public consent or otherwise. The classic question follows on from this – who will watch the watchers? Be they the police or the media or those tasked with oversight of intelligence matters; elected, judicial or otherwise (see Lanchester, 2013 for an informative, but not exhaustive account of these issues and Neyroud and Beckley (2001) for a more general account).

Exploring some of these concepts may be useful. They may be grouped into two broad categories, those that were used as a guide before 1997 and those that emerged after and are still developing.

- **Legal and accountable** (in the sense that there was a written record, personalised to individuals, including justification for any decision making).

Intelligence and hate crime

- **Necessary** (in the sense that there was no other ways of gathering intelligence, or other methods had been tried and failed); instead of proportionate, the concept before 1997 which was concerned with the identification of serious crime or its prevention. Intrusion and proportionality (particularly around the notions of proportionate and balance – the tensions between different rights under separate sections of the Human Rights Act 1998), which emerged as more and more, sophisticated concepts in the decade and a half after 1997 (see Neyroud and Beckley (2001)).

In some senses the period 1997–2004 can be argued to be a watershed and even to be part of a wider paradigm shift in policing in the UK (see Hall et al., 2009). In the middle of that period the Stephen Lawrence Inquiry Report (SLI) was published in February 1999. It was followed almost immediately by the Home Secretary's Action Plan (1999), which responded to the recommendations in the report.

The sheer amount of legislative and policy change that followed, including the review of 'knowledge flows' in public inquiries, indicates some of the complexity of the issues disclosed and the learning and degree of change that was required to address the exposed concerns (see also Grieve in Pycroft and Bartollas (2014) about complexity theory and adaptation). The SLI recommendations and action plan did not specifically identify intelligence, though they had much to say about reporting, recording, retaining information and its subsequent investigation by police. This is directly pertinent to the intelligence-led policing of hate crime. There were at least 11 of the SLI recommendations that related to hate crime.

In 2002, Lord Laming headed a Public Inquiry into the tragic murder of an 8-year-old girl, Victoria Climbie who died in London in February, 2000. It exposed the missed opportunities to prevent her death and also identified issues about communication, information flow and the use of knowledge. It exposed the need for accurate and timely information shared to ensure understanding both within and between agencies (Laming, 2003: paragraph 1.43).

Later, Sir Michael Bichard's Public Inquiry Report (2004) examined the circumstances of the murders of Holly Wells and Jessica Chapman in Soham, and the ensuing police investigation. It identified six intelligence failures. These related to accessing and inputting on databases; failure to use databases properly and effectively; failure to share information, as well as confusion and lack of awareness of data legislation. The UK government identified IMPACT (Intelligence Management, Prioritisation, Analysis, Coordination and Tasking) as a programme of reform to implement Bichard's recommendations. The significance of this is identified by Harfield and Harfield (2008: 31) who show that the failures identified by Bichard mirror those of the Stephen Lawrence Inquiry.

Intelligence and family liaison

Nearly a quarter of the recommendations of the Stephen Lawrence Inquiry (1999) related to police relationships with victims' families, between those families and communities, and hence between the police and the communities. Considerable time was spent at the inquiry exploring family liaison issues (1999: Chapter 26 and at many other points). The development of family liaison as a specialist skill in policing, during and post the public inquiry, came from a rich mix of stakeholders. The thinking was ethical and victim oriented with inchoate boundaries. The improved service that followed, and the benefits it gave to the police and the families of future victims was an important gift from the Lawrence family and the SLI.

There had always been the concern that the family liaison officers would be viewed as spying on the family. Not least, and this is extremely sensitive, because in some historical

Table 28.2 Timeline Intelligence and Hate Crime Developments

Intelligence Developments	Hate Crime Developments	Notes and references
	1986 – Public Order Act contained Hate Crime Legislation although this term was not used, and identified a criminal offence of stirring up hatred on grounds of race, religion and sexual orientation	
1992–2000 Developments in London and Kent in Intelligence Policing systems		Harfield C and Harfield K (2008). Intelligence
	1993 – Stephen Lawrence murdered 22.04.93	SLI Report (1999) Hall et al. (2009)
	1993–1998 unsuccessful investigations, prosecutions and reviews into SL murder	SLI Report (1999) Hall et al. (2009)
1997 – HMIC publish 'Policing with Intelligence' 1997 – Police Act		
	1998 – Crime and Disorder Act introduces Hate Crime Legislation in aggravated offences which can lead to higher maximum sentences where involving hostility based on race or, later, religion	
1998 – Human Rights Act 1998 – Data Protection Act		
	1998–1999 Stephen Lawrence Public Inquiry set established	SLI Report (1999) Hall et al. (2009)
	1998 – Race and Violent Crime Task Force (RAVCTF) set up in August	Hall et al. (2009)
1998 – Intelligence Cell Analytic System (ICAS) intelligence system for tackling hate crime created Autumn 1998		
	1999 – SLI Report published in February	SLI Report (1999) Hall et al. (2009)
	Overwhelming political, media and public criticism of police investigations into hate crime in general and the Stephen Lawrence murder in particular. February 1998 et seq	
	1999 – Home Secretary's Action Plan published in March	SLI Report (1999) Hall et al. (2009)

Table 28.2 Continued

Intelligence Developments	Hate Crime Developments	Notes and references
2000 – Freedom of Information Act		
2000 – Regulation of Investigatory Powers Act becomes law 02.10.2000		Harfield C and Harfield K (2008). Intelligence
2000 – National Intelligence Model introduced		
2002 – Lord Laming's Inquiry into the murder of Victoria Climbie looks at information flow and knowledge use between agencies and within systems		Harfield C and Harfield K (2008). Intelligence
	2003 – Sections 145 and 146 of the Criminal Justice Act introduces enhanced sentencing for the 4 (later 5, with the addition of transgender) hate crime	
2004 – Bichard Public Inquiry Report into the murders of Holly Wells and Jessica Chapman identifies 6 intelligence failures		Bichard M. (2004). Bichard Inquiry Report. Harfield C and Harfield K (2008: 31). They identify similarities with failures in SLI.
	2007 – Hate Crime investigation and reporting clarified into five categories by police and CPS, as: race, religion, sexual orientation, disability, transgender identity	Law Commission 2013 Hate Crime: The case for extending existing offences. Consultation Paper 213.
	2012 – Gary Dobson and David Norris convicted of murder of Stephen Lawrence	
2012–2013 Wikileaks and NSA/GCHQ surveillance allegations	2013 – Allegations involving intelligence operations and Lawrence family. Internal inquiries supervised by IPCC. 2 Barristers appointed to review all documents	Guardian (2013) Evans and Lewis (2013)

murders, family members became suspects, and on some occasions they have even been convicted of killing other family members, or arranging for contract killers to carry out crimes for them. This of course has to be balanced against the likelihood of this being the case in the precise and unique circumstances of any such investigation.

Family liaison officers are taught to explain to the families they work with that they are first and foremost investigators. Although they have information and contacts who can help with, for example, bereavement counselling and other emotional and social needs, their primary tasks are to bring the offender to justice, by gathering evidence for a prosecution. Part of this process is to gather information from the family, which may or may not be considered useable as intelligence. 'Show me how someone lived and I will show you how they died' (or how and why a crime has been committed) is a mantra amongst investigators. This may be as simple as why they were on a particular train or in a shop; or it may be more compendious considerations about their lifestyle. Some of this may be sensitive and emerge as intelligence, although it may not always be possible for it to be translated into evidence in the criminal justice system. There is always the likelihood that it may have to be disclosed to the defence if there is any trial.

By contrast, there is much intelligence readily available as open source material. Some of this comes from academics (see for example Hall, 2013; Bowling, 1999; Juett et al. 2008 for a parallel example from drugs policing). Most often this will be strategic in nature, an area that is developed later in this chapter when considering the role of an Independent Advisory Group as an intelligence tool.

Intelligence and the politics of hate crime

The issue raised in the previous section, however remote the possibility of family involvement in the crime may be, is one of extreme sensitivity in hate crime. This extreme aspect of an investigation requires very careful handling and if it is not done sensitively and defensibly, it can arouse fury in families, their supporters, communities and politicians. Which brings the discussion to a tension in the requirements of politicians to use all lawful means to stop hate crime, their distaste for some aspects of intelligence gathering as part of an investigation, and the requirement for investigators to be impartial, firm, open minded, and healthily sceptical (see Laming, 2003, aided in this respect by John Fox, for a discussion of these investigative requirements in a different arena of police investigation).

One of the ways of addressing these challenges has been to set up a cross-government Hate Crime Programme (see Giannasi, Chapter 7 this volume), which is 'owned' by a number of senior politicians and has also attracted cross-party support. One aspect of this cross-government political dimension is the Independent Advisory Group, which functions as an intelligence generating body using the dimensions explored in Table 28.1 earlier. The group was set up with the tasks (amongst other roles) to assess and analyse information from a variety of sources, to provide advice, and bring the victim perspective to inform Government activity. It is discussed next.

The cross-government Hate Crime Independent Advisory Group and strategic intelligence

The origins of the group are instructive. One of the responses to the SLI Report and the Home Secretary's Action Plan was the creation of an Advisory Group to advise the Home Secretary. When this was disbanded by his successors a review was conducted by Professor Gus John (who had originally sat on the Burnage Public Inquiry – see Macdonald et al.,

1998). This review led first to the Race for Justice Advisory Group which then morphed into the broader-based Hate Crime Independent Advisory Group (IAG) with a 'wider than race' agenda.

This advisory group recruits its independent members and chair from a broad background of perspectives including academia, support groups and victims/advocacy groups. It meets and reports to Ministers and officials across government departments and is hosted by the Ministry of Justice and hence Justice Secretary, but also addresses the Attorney General as the chief Government law officer, the Home Office (to the Home Secretary), the Department of Community and Local Government, and the Minister responsible for Equality. The IAG also acts as the formal hate crime IAG to the Association of Chief Police Officers (ACPO) and advises the other parts of the criminal justice system.

More recently the group, the action plan and programmes it supports have been of considerable interest to the Foreign and Commonwealth Office as it seeks to use influence to support hate crime initiatives within Europe, and through work with the Organisation for Security and Cooperation in Europe (OSCE), Eastern Europe and the United States. What is significant, besides this global reach, for a domestic hate and intelligence perspective is that it took over some aspects of the domestic strategic monitoring tasks that had been initiated by ICAS and then taken up and later abandoned by the Home Secretary's Group. A recent intelligence related task was to explore the continuing impact of the Stephen Lawrence Inquiry recommendations.

Looking to the future

The emergence of the Internet as a vehicle to deliver and promote hatred presents some huge challenges to our future protection from hate. Hall (2013: 202) has a useful introduction to these 'Generation Y' issues – hatred in the twenty-first century using the Internet. In many ways these public communications provide opportunities to more effectively gather information and to develop intelligence from it, in ways never envisaged until recently. However, its ubiquitous and unstructured nature presents huge new challenges. Our 'stakeholders' list is now global, the jurisdiction of offending is often difficult to ascertain, and the legislative disparity creates challenges when criminality is organised globally or within 'virtual' crime organisations. Intelligence may be more readily available but the task of identifying the 13-year-old considering self-harm because of cyber-bullying or the self-radicalised 'Lone Wolf' planning to carry out attacks, requires a new perspective and application of the intelligence models discussed in this chapter (see also Rohlfing, and Corb, this volume).

Conclusions

There is no better mentor, for those considering the application of intelligence to challenging modern problems, than Patrick Beesly who chronicled the role of academics in the Battle of the Atlantic in World War Two. The author of this chapter has no hesitation in turning to him again for help.

> It is easy for all of us now, more than 40 years on to sift slowly through the relevant records, neatly arranged in chronological order, and ask ourselves, with the additional benefit of hindsight, why clues were missed, why appreciations were faulty, why incorrect decisions were taken. Those who have never experienced it should not forget the

> 'the fog of war' factor, the atmosphere of urgency, the pressures, the strain, day after day, week after week, year after year, the try to solve the problems and complete the jigsaw puzzle – or rather puzzles because in a world war, no single problem can be considered in isolation: there are dozens of them each calling for swift and most of them immediate action. The more senior the individual concerned the more likely it is that he (sic) will have to switch his attention at any time during the day – or night from one end of the world to the other, from the land to the sea or to the air, from the tactical situation to the long-term implications, from the possible reactions of the enemy to the behaviour of allies. Nothing is simple, nothing is certain, but everything is important.
>
> *(Beesly, 1990: 317/318. Intelligence and decision-making)*

It is dangerous and illogical to press models of World War Two too far when considering the policing of hate crimes. Amongst other issues the sheer scale of the suffering of millions is an inappropriate comparison to other crimes, unless we are considering genocide, however there are lessons to be learnt not least about the requirement of the police to be vigilant in early stages of the build up of hatred and incitement against 'out groups' (see for example Community Security Trust (CST)-funded Smith, 2008, for an excellent example of learning from the Holocaust for contemporary police officers worldwide).

There are outstanding tasks in respect of hate and intelligence that are worthwhile even in the context and environment that appears to be challenging and denigrating intelligence-led approaches of all kinds. It seems possible that the intellectual skills and intelligence tools that appear to be available for counter-terrorism could be applied to dealing with hate crimes. This would be more than a public relations exercise.

It has been argued in this chapter that in some senses the period between 1997 and 2000 was a watershed, and even a paradigm shift in intelligence-led policing in general as well as hate crime in particular. The decade and a half since 1997, coupled with the development of legislation for hate crime, parallels the development of intelligence-led policing more widely. Studying the interactions between the two can be instructive.

Note

1 Stephen Lawrence was murdered by a gang of racists in 1993, two of whom were convicted 19 years after the crime. A public Inquiry reported in 1999 on the context and environment in which a failed police investigation had occurred and concluded that institutional racism (that is 'unwitting, ignorant, thoughtless and stereotypical' conduct by police) had played a role in the failure. Intelligence which should have played a role in investigative success was an element in that finding. There were 70 recommendations by the public inquiry. (See TSO 1999 and Hall et al., 2009).

References

UK Legislation referred to in this chapter
Crime and Disorder Act 1998.
Human Rights Act 1998.
Police Act 1997.
Regulation of Investigatory Powers Act 2000.
Other useful references (not all referred to in the text)
ACPO (1975). Association of Chief Police Officers. *Report of the Sub Committee on Criminal Intelligence* (Baumber Report) London. ACPO.
ACPO (1978). *Steering Committee on Criminal Information Systems Working Party* (Pearce Report). London. ACPO.

ACPO (1986). *Report of the Working Party on Operational Intelligence* (Ratcliffe Report). London. ACPO.
ACPO (2000). *National Hate Crime Guide*. launched 11 September 2000. Updated by the College of Policing, ACPO, Ministry of Justice 2014. London. ACPO.
Ascoli D. (1979). *The Queen's Peace*. London. Hamish Hamilton.
Audit Commission (1994). *Tackling Crime Effectively*. London.
Audit Commission (1996). *Tackling Crime Effectively Part 2*. London. Audit Commission.
Baggini, J. and Stangroom, J. (eds). (2002). *New British Philosophy. The Interviews*. London. Routledge.
Beesly, P. (1990). *Convoy PQ17: A Study of Intelligence & Decision making*. Pages 292–322 in M. Handel. *Intelligence and Military Operations*. London. Cass.
Beesly, P. (2000). 2nd Edition. *Very Special Intelligence. A Story of the Admiralty's Operational Intelligence Centre 1939–1945*. London. Greenhill Books.
Bhatti, A. (2008). 'The mobiles are out and the hoods are up' Chapter 13 page 174 in Harfield, C., MacVean, A., Grieve, J. and Phillips, D. *The Handbook of Intelligent Policing, Consilience, Crime Control, and Community Safety*. Oxford. Oxford University Press.
Bichard, M. (2004). *Bichard Inquiry Report*. London. TSO.
Billingsley, R. and Bean, P. (2001). *Crime and informers* in Billingsley, R., Nemitz, T. and Bean, P. *Informers, policing, policy, practice*. Willan Publishing. UK.
Billingsley, R., Nemitz, T. and Bean, P. Edited. (2001). *Informers, policing, policy, practice*. Willan Publishing. UK.
Bowers, A. (2008). *Knowledge Management and the National Intelligence Model*. Chapter 20 in Harfield, C., MacVean, A., Grieve, J. and Phillips, D. *The Handbook of Intelligent Policing, Consilience, Crime Control, and Community Safety*. Oxford. Oxford University Press.
Bowling, B. (1999). *Violent Racism Victimisation, Policing and Social Context*. Oxford. Clarendon Press.
Bungay, S. (2000). *The Most Dangerous Enemy*. London.
Butler, Lord (2004). *Espionage and the Iraq war*. HC 898. London. The Stationery Office. Reprinted by Tim Coates London.
Critchley, T.A. (1967). *A History of Police in England and Wales*. London. Constable.
Davis, J. (2008). *Why Bad Things Happen to Good Analysts*. Chapter 10 in George, R. and Bruce, J. *Analyzing Intelligence. Origins, Obstacles and Innovations*. Washington. Georgetown University Press.
ESRC (2001). Alan Travis. *Partners in Crime. Policemen (sic) and Academics*. The Edge. *Journal of Economic and Social Research Council and Policy Forum for Executive Action*. Issue 8 November 2001.
ESRC (2002). Violence Research Project. Director Prof Betsy Stanko. Taking Stock. What do we know about interpersonal Violence, Economic and Social Research Council. Swindon. UK.
Evans, R.M. (2008). *Cultural Paradigms & Change: a Model of Analysis*. Chapter 8 page 105 in Harfield, C., MacVean, A., Grieve, J. and Phillips, D. *The Handbook of Intelligent Policing, Consilience, Crime Control, and Community Safety*. Oxford. Oxford University Press.
Evans, R. and Lewis, P. (2013). *Undercover: The True Story of Britain's Secret Police*, London. Faber and Faber.
Fleming, R. and Miller, H. (1994). *Scotland Yard*. London. Michael Joseph.
Flood, B. (2004) in Ratcliffe J. (ed.) (2004/2009). *Strategic Thinking in Criminal Intelligence*. 2nd Edition. Federation Press and Willan UK and personal communication September 9th, 2004.
Flood, B. and Gaspar, R. (2004/2009). *Strategic aspects of the UK National Intelligence Model*. Chapter 4 pages 47 to 65 in Ratcliffe, J. (ed.) (2004/2009) *Strategic Thinking in Criminal Intelligence*. 2nd Edition. Federation Press and Willan, UK.
Fricker, M. (2002). *Power Knowledge and Injustice* Chapter 5 in Baggini, J. and Stangroom, J. Edt. *New British Philosophy. The Interviews*. London. Routledge.
George, R. and Bruce, J. (2008). Edts. *Analyzing Intelligence. Origins, Obstacles and Innovations*. Washington. Georgetown University Press.
Grant, I. (1981). Units 26 and 27 *U202 Inquiry*. Open University. UK.
Grieve, J. (1998). *Intelligence as education for all*. In O'Connor, L., O'Connor, D. and Best, R. (1998) *Drugs, Partnerships for Policy, Prevention and Education*. London. Cassell.
Grieve, J. (2004/2009). *Developments in UK Criminal Intelligence*. Chapter 3. p 25 in Ratcliffe J. (2004/2009). 2nd Edition. *Strategic Thinking & Criminal Intelligence*. NSW Australia. Federation Press.
Grieve, J. (2008). *Lawfully Audacious – a Reflective Journey*. Chapter 1. p 13 in Harfield, C., MacVean, A., Grieve, J. and Phillips, D. *The Handbook of Intelligent Policing, Consilience, Crime Control, and Community Safety*. Oxford. Oxford University Press.
Grieve J. (2009). 'The Stephen Lawrence Inquiry: from intelligence failure to intelligence legacy'. Chapter 6. In Hall, N., Grieve, J. and Savage, S. *Policing and Legacy of Lawrence*. Devon. Willan.

Grieve, J. (2014). *The Stephen Lawrence Inquiry: Complexity and Policing* in Pyecroft, A. and Bartollas, C. Edited (2014). *Applying Complexity Theory: Whole Systems Approaches in Criminal Justice and Social Work*. Bristol, UK. Policy Press.
Grieve, J., Harfield, C. and MacVean, A. (2007). *Policing*. London. Sage.
Guardian Newspaper 17 June 2013: 1–5 Snowden Revelations about Intelligence.
Guardian Newspaper 31 June 2013 Hate on the Internet.
Guardian Newspaper 30 June 2013 Wikileaks.
Hall, N. (2005/13) (2nd Edition). *Hate Crime*. Devon. Willan.
Hall, N., Grieve, J. and Savage, S. (2009). *Policing and Legacy of Lawrence*. Devon. Willan.
Handel M. (1990). *Intelligence and Military Operations*. London. Cass
Harfield, C. and Harfield, K. (2005). *Covert Investigation*. Oxford. Oxford University Press.
Harfield, C. and Harfield, K. (2008). *Intelligence: Investigation, Community and Partnership*. Oxford. Oxford University Press.
Harfield, C., MacVean, A., Grieve, J. and Phillips, D. (2008). *The Handbook of Intelligent Policing, Consilience, Crime Control, and Community Safety*. Oxford. Oxford University Press.
HMIC (1997). Her Majesty's Inspectorate of Constabulary. *Policing With Intelligence, Criminal Intelligence – A Thematic Inspection of Good Practice*. London. Home Office.
Hofstadter, D. (1980). *Godel, Escher, Bach: An Eternal Golden Braid*. London. Penguin.
Howe, S. (1997). *Cross Border Intelligence*. Police Review. 5 December 1997.
Jackson, R. (2008). Conversations in Critical Studies on Terrorism. Counter-terrorism and Communities: an interview with Robert Lambert. *Critical Studies in Terrorism*. Vol.1, No.2, August 2008: 1–16. London. Routledge.
John, T. and Maguire, M. (2007). *Criminal Intelligence and the National Intelligence Model* in T. Newburn et al. *Handbook of Criminal Investigation*. Devon. Willan.
Juett, L., Smith, R. and Grieve J. (2008). *Open Source Intelligence – A Case Study: GLADA 'London – the Highs and Lows' 2003 and 2007*. Chapter 12 page 161 in Harfield, C., MacVean, A., Grieve, J. and Phillips, D. (Eds). *The Handbook of Intelligent Policing, Consilience, Crime Control, and Community Safety*. Oxford. Oxford University Press.
Keegan, J. (2003). *Intelligence in War*. Hutchinson. London.
Kerr, R.J. (2008a). *The Perfect Enemy. Reflections of an Intelligence Officer on the Cold War and Today's Challenges*. Chapter 3 page 37 in Harfield, C., MacVean, A., Grieve, J. and Phillips, D. *The Handbook of Intelligent Policing, Consilience, Crime Control, and Community Safety*. Oxford. Oxford University Press.
Kerr, R.J. (2008b). *The Track Record. CIA Analysis 1950–2000* in George, R. and Bruce, J. Edts. *Analyzing Intelligence. Origins, Obstacles and Innovations*. Washington. Georgetown University Press.
Laming, Lord (2003). *Victoria Climbie Inquiry*. Command 5730. London. TSO.
Lanchester, J. (2013). *When did we give our consent to a secret state?* London Guardian Newspaper 4 October 2013. pp 1, 36, 37.
Lowenthal, M. (2008). *Intelligence in Transition: Analysis after September 11 and Iraq*. Chapter 14 in George, R. and Bruce, J. Edts. *Analyzing Intelligence. Origins, Obstacles and Innovations*. Washington. Georgetown University Press.
Macdonald, I., Bhavnani, R., Khan, L. and John, G. (1998). *Murder in the Playground. The Burnage Report. Report of the Macdonald Inquiry into Racism and Racial Violence in Manchester Schools*. London. Longsight Press.
Metropolitan Police (1998). *Informant Working Group Report. Informing the Community: Developing Informant Risk Assessment to Reflect Community Concerns*. London. MPS.
Metropolitan Police (2000). *Breaking the Power of Fear and Hate*. London MPS and ACPO Manual.
Metropolitan Police (2000). *Managing and Preventing Critical Incidents*. London MPS.
Metropolitan Police (2000). *The Investigation of Racist, Domestic Violence and Homophobic Incidents, Minimum standards*. London MPS.
Metropolitan Police (2000). *Third Party Reporting*. London MPS.
Metropolitan Police and Home Office (2002). *Targeted Policing Initiative Joint Project. Understanding and responding to hate crime – Fact Sheets (1) Domestic Violence (2) Racial Violence (3) Homophobic violence*. London MPS.
Murray, W. (2011). *Military Adaptation in War. Fear of Change*. Cambridge University Press.
NCIS (1998). *International Conference for Criminal Intelligence Analysts. Meeting the Challenge from Serious Criminality*. NCIS.

NCIS (2000). *The National Intelligence Model*. National Criminal Intelligence Service. London.
Newburn, T., Williamson, T. and Wright, A. (eds) (2007). *Handbook of Criminal Investigation*. Devon. Willan.
Neyroud, P. and Beckley, A. (2001) *Policing, Ethics and Human Rights*. Cullompton. Willan.
Observer Newspaper 31 January 1999. '*Lets Nick Some Racists*'. London.
Omand, D. (2010). *Securing the State*. London. Hurst and Co.
O'Hara, P. (2005). *Why Law Enforcement Organisations Fail. Mapping the Organisational Fault Lines*. North Carolina. USA. Carolina Academic Press.
Pyecroft, A. and Bartollas, C. Edited (2014). *Applying Complexity Theory: Whole Systems Approaches in Criminal Justice and Social Work*. Bristol, UK. Policy Press.
Ratcliffe, J. (ed.) (2004/2009). *Strategic Thinking in Criminal Intelligence*. 2nd Edition. Federation Press and Willan. UK.
Rawlings, P. (2002). *Policing: a short history*. Cullompton. Willan.
Rowe, M. (2007). *Policing Beyond Macpherson. Issues in Policing, Race & Society*. Devon. Willan.
Savage, S. (2007). *Police Reform. Forces for change*. Oxford. Oxford University Press.
Serena, C. (2011). *A Revolution in Military Adaptation. The US Army in the Iraq War*. USA. Georgetown University Press.
Sheptycki, J. (2004). Organisational Pathologies in Police Intelligence Systems. Some Contributions to the Lexicon of Intelligence-led Policing. *European Journal of Criminology* Vol.1 No. 3 July 2004. London. Sage.
Shpayer-Makov, H. (2011). *The Ascent of the Detective*. Oxford University Press.
Sims, J. (1993). '*What is Intelligence?*' (paper 1) in Shulsky, A. and Sims, J. '*What is Intelligence?*' Working Group on Intelligence Reform. Washington. Consortium for the Study of Intelligence. Georgetown University.
Sissens, J. (2008). *An Evaluation of the Role of the Intelligence Analyst within the National Intelligence Model*. Chapter 9. Page 121 in Harfield, C., MacVean, A., Grieve, J. and Phillips, D. *The Handbook of Intelligent Policing, Consilience, Crime Control, and Community Safety*. Oxford. Oxford University Press.
Smith, D. (2008). *The Holocaust. A Guide for Police Personnel*. London. The Holocaust Centre funded by CST.
Smith, M. (1996). *New Cloak, Old Dagger: How Britain's Spies Came In from the Cold*. London. Gollancz.
Stenko, B. (2008). *Strategic Intelligence: Methodologies for Understanding What Police Services Already 'know' to Reduce Harm*. Chapter 17 page 227 in Harfield, C., MacVean, A., Grieve, J. and Phillips, D. *The Handbook of Intelligent Policing, Consilience, Crime Control, and Community Safety*. Oxford. Oxford University Press.
Stephen Lawrence Inquiry. Home Secretary's Action Plan. March 1999.
TSO (1999). *The Stephen Lawrence Inquiry*. Command 4262. London. TSO.
Vincent, C.E.H. (1881). *Police Code. Manual of the Criminal Law*. London. Cassell, Petter, Galpin and Co.
Wright, A. (2002). *Policing: An Introduction to Concepts and Practice*. Cullompton. Willan.

29
Forensic science and hate crime

Paul Smith

This chapter provides an overview of forensic science with reflections on its use in hate crime cases. It assumes little or no knowledge of forensic science by the reader and its purpose is to provide an overview of the key aspects in the application of science to hate crime. The context within which forensic science operates is discussed, and the contemporary issues and constraints affecting its use in practice are presented along with the fundamentals of forensic science. This is placed in context through the use of a case study. To facilitate this the London nail bombings are used as they exemplify the use of forensic science processes in a large complex investigation, which utilised a multi-disciplinary and multi-agency response along with the proactive use of intelligence resources, used to inform the strategic deployment of forensic science to the investigation.

Forensic science and hate crime

The absorption of forensic science in social culture has been comprehensively documented throughout the many textbooks and commentaries on the subject (Jackson and Jackson, 2008; Houck and Siegel, 2010; Fraser and Williams, 2009; James and Nordby, 2009). Since the 1980s, there has been juxtaposition between the advances and application of scientific methods to criminal justice issues and the profound media response, in many cases 'romanticising' the relationship, which has been accelerated by the popularity of programmes such as CSI (Harvey and Derksen, 2009). This relationship and the so-called 'CSI effect' is a common juncture for most forensic science texts to start from. However, irrespective of the abounded criticisms associated with venturing too close to the usual clichés, the impact of forensic science on popular culture has been so palpable that the banality of the reference needs to be tolerated. For this reason the social impact of forensic science has to be re-emphasised as it has become intrinsic to its perceived practical application, operational usefulness, and its deemed operational 'success' (Schweitzer and Saks, 2007). In this chapter it is being linked with another genre of study that propagates an equal amount of social fascination for very different reasons – hate crime.

As with most investigations, forensic science techniques are a 'tool in the box' for investigators, and for that reason form tangible links with other commentaries relating to the police response to hate crime and discussed in more detail elsewhere in this volume (see, for example, Giannasi, and Grieve). Furthermore, 'hate' is often classified as a motivating factor for many crimes where forensic science has been utilised (Macpherson, 1999; Foster et al., 2005). However, there is an apparent dearth of academic discussion explicitly linking the two genres in any meaningful way, and there is scope to study the relationship further beyond the remit of this chapter.

From a forensic science perspective, forensic science research and academic commentary is embroiled in techniques and scientific principles commonly deployable to a range of crime types and their extended application, both in a positive and negative sense (Robertson, 2012; Ludwig et al., 2012). But there is little on its specific application to hate crime, even though, as highlighted elsewhere in this text, many of the techniques have relevance depending on the incident context. From the hate crime perspective, there are far more tangible areas of inquest to focus academic critique, and, for forensic science, it is the development of new scientific functionality that is the focus, not necessarily the genre of crime. However, there are many aspects of forensic science research and practice that transposes validly to hate crime and warrants a more associated discussion and further inquiry, particularly with regard to the use of forensic science intelligence, for example, and its use as an intelligence tool in volume crimes (Rossy et al., 2013).

Evidently, both are equally pervasive in the social psyche. However, it is important to note that the key issues associated with hate crime warrants a change of focus from interest propagated through television and fictional media to interest and response generated through news media and reports of crimes deemed prominent to the social interest. This is particularly relevant to cases that have eked into public consciousness through perceived procedural or 'institutional' failures (Macpherson, 1999; Taylor, 1990; Scarman, 1981). This relationship, popularity and often the associated infamy of offenders and the perceived 'wrongdoers', irrespective of the media techniques and long-standing associations, make these two genres colossal in regards to the interest and, consequently, the material they generate. The causal impetus and subsequent demands for change can be commensurate with the outraged social sensitivities that such media and official reports evoke (Neal, 2003).

A fitting example of this is the Stephen Lawrence case. It provided a glut of opinion and media rhetoric that fuelled debate and action across the criminal justice spectrum and, in many respects, the subsequent Macpherson report propagated changes that resulted in a 'profound cultural shift for the police' (Hall et al., 2009). The media response and the public opinion that followed has been fervently tempered by the diligent, laudable and passionate efforts of the parents, family and a few good women and men who ensured the case was seldom far from the public conscience for the right reasons. Of note and of relevance is the cold case review and the new evidence it introduced (Wilson and Gallop, 2013; BBC News, 2012).

A microscopic blood spot which had dried into Gary Dobson's jacket, and fibres from Stephen's clothing found on both David Norris' and Gary Dobson's clothing were presented, discussed at length, and subsequently augmented the prosecution case to assist in their conviction at the re-trial (BBC News, 2011). The forensic science evidence was comprehensively reported and generated a great deal of media attention, and without further scrutiny of the underlying issues identified during cross examination, appears to further strengthen the portfolio of forensic science.

However, it was the months of painstaking work by the scientists that resulted in the confident presentation of the evidence. The months of work included research looking at how microscopic bloodstains absorbed in to the types of fibres found in Gary Dobson's coat accounting for as many eventualities that were conceivably possible. It is this level of endeavour and understanding of the variables affecting the hierarchy of propositions that goes unseen and unreported, but is often essential to support the facts presented at court (Wilson and Gallop, 2013). This level of intricate research and analysis was required to establish the differing probabilities of the evidence given the propositions, indicating whether the blood spot was left as a result of the offence in 1993, and not the result of any cross contamination at a later date (BBC News, 2012). This is central to the scientists' endeavours, however the complexity of the research and analysis along with associated variables is a prime indication that perceived 'success' of forensic science is not as prosaic as it is often portrayed and perceived through the media.

It is the author's intention to ground the epistemological approach in the realistic interpretation of operational functions, and emphasise the greater awareness of how the intricacies of forensic science are entwined with investigative and procedural context. This chapter provides a limited overview of the basic tenets of forensic science and its application to hate crime, focusing on the London nail bomber. However, the reader is also encouraged to appreciate the context of its operational deployment and the influence of prevailing and emerging change drivers affecting its application to hate crime (and all crime) and the constraints abound in modern policing (House of Commons Science and Technology Committee, 2013). The use of the case study serves as a review of the types of evidence recovered based on the nature of the crime and it will make comment on the nature of the analysis and interpretation. However, before looking at the case study the next section discusses the basic elements and observations in regard to the deployment of forensic science.

The fundamentals of forensic science and contemporary issues

The now ubiquitous reference to the exchange principle, posited by Locard (1920), has often been identified as the underpinning logic pertaining to the application of forensic science. The notion is introduced to students studying forensic science, and the simplicity of the "every contact leaves a trace" mantra is easy to understand and explain. It does loosely define the underpinning logic of forensic science, however it can be much more complicated than it first appears, and the phrase does not fully encapsulate the broader approaches suggested by Locard, particularly the holistic use of forensic science in case work (Roux et al., 2012). Fundamentally the primary objective is identifying interactions (and the exchanging matter) that offer the opportunity to recover relevant traces that can be matched to a source supporting a particular hypothesis. Broeders (2007) offers more balanced reflection on the administration of the principle in practice. He reiterates that it is not as prosaic as it first appears and is besieged by many variables that affect the transfer and persistence of evidence. Furthermore, with the enhanced sensitivities of many techniques direct contact is not always necessary, particularly in regards to Deoxyribonucleic Acid (DNA). However, this is a very general view that does not fully account for the disparities and differences that abound in the investigation and, as a corollary, with forensic science and the techniques used.

These differing variables affecting application notwithstanding, the context of the interaction needs to be considered. For example, there may be little benefit recovering finger marks from a door at the scene of a domestic incident, particularly if both parties have access to the address, however if it is a burglary then finding the finger marks of the intruder is intrinsic to placing him or her at the scene, after all they should not be there (Houck and Siegel, 2010). This is a simple example, but it is often a persistent problem. Many see forensic science evidence as irrefutable but often the evidence can be innocently explained and it is understanding the nature of the evidence and appropriately interpreting it that is at the centre of prudently using forensic science and formulating a robust strategy (Fraser, 2007).

The various textbooks build on this premise and discuss specific scientific applications and their suitability to analyse trace evidence, biological evidence, marks and impressions and others (Jackson and Jackson, 2008; Houck and Siegel, 2010; Fraser and Williams, 2009; James and Nordby, 2009). However, it is very difficult in a concise chapter to encompass all potential evidence; just about anything that sheds and persists can potentially leave a detectable trace. Evidence and the traces it bares can be analysed for the physical and chemical properties, which can then be compiled and recorded to help establish a probability value of it matching the known source. However, the complexities proliferate through the search, recovery, and analysis and through establishing the discriminatory value, which can require considerable skill and knowledge to interpret. This is applicable throughout the continuum of its analysis; through scene preservation, during the examination of the crime scene, in the laboratory and, arguably most importantly, presenting the evidence to the court.

There are many variables present at crime scenes, and new developments and techniques, or the novel use of established techniques, are applied when required often with some success, for example, the use of cat DNA to assist in a murder inquiry (The Independent, 2013). In this regard many applications proliferate through demand from investigative requirement. There is now a resurgence of new forensic science relevant research, which seems to have lulled since the sad demise (or enforced closure) of the Forensic Science Service (House of Commons Science and Technology Committee, 2013). However, fingerprints and DNA evidence are most prominent in operational practice (Roux et al., 2012). To borrow an adage from technology acceptance the pervasiveness of these techniques can be attributable to them being 'useful' and 'usable' (Venkatesh et al., 2003). *Useful* as they can be speculatively searched against a database, and *usable* as, in modern times it is relatively easy to recover the evidence from the scene and, through enhanced technological capability, the scientist has become very efficient at analysing the evidence and presenting the probability of it matching the known record (Butler, 2011), however it is granted that the 'individualisation' mantra is not without its problems and critics (Saks and Koehler, 2008).

In its most basic sense this requires the evidence to be found and recovered at the scene. The 'crime scene' does not necessarily pertain to a geophysical location, it may also refer to artefacts recovered in relation to the incident, and so it varies from large expansive landscapes, to the smallest object recovered in relation to the investigation. This may be footwear, an article of clothing, a firearm, anything that can be examined to glean relevant evidence relating to the interaction and the context of the crime. Miller (2009) posits it can be referred to as the macroscopic and microscopic crime scene. Therefore control of the 'macroscopic scene' is essential to preserve and interpret the microscopic evidence recovered from within. For example, during the London nail bombings in 1999, control of a large area was required to ensure minimum disruption to the smaller evidence, bomb fragments, and so on. Each fragment was essential to interpreting events, and the location and nature of the injuries to the victims (Vermette, 2012; Persaud et al., 2003; Leibovici et al., 1996).

As in all disciplines relating to criminal justice, there are factors in forensic science that will confound, constrain and adversely impact on the validity and admissibility of the evidence. These factors are found throughout the processing continuum from the search, recovery and analysis of forensic science evidence. Based on the media portrayal and the increased reliability on science and technology, it is easy for the lay observer to assume forensic science is infallible and wholly reliable. In the author's experience, forensic scientists on the whole are highly professional and have methods in place to robustly test and assure competency. However, there are exceptions and well-documented failures (Cole, 2012).

It is naïve to assume that we have infallible systems and practitioners. There are laudable endeavours to maintain and ensure the highest levels of practice, and to bring international coherence and parity in service provision where possible (House of Commons Science Select Committee, 2013; Rankin et al., 2012; Silverman, 2011; Jamieson, 2011). Since the closure of the Forensic Science Service, many eminent scientists (forensic and otherwise) have voiced displeasure and castigated the systems and differing paradigms of evolving service provision in the United Kingdom (Wilson and Gallop, 2013; Jamieson, 2011). This is particularly divided on the issues of insourcing of forensic provision to the police, along with the competing private markets and procurement strategies (ibid.).

Police laboratories and operating forensic science laboratories are required to aim to achieve ISO 17025 standard status since the European Union (EU) mandate was published in 2009 (Rennison, 2011). Competency testing and the move towards increased accountability notwithstanding, there will always be the human elements of working practice in any working environment. The causes are not always down to personal incompetency of course, it will relate to the social and operational conditions that affect the administration of practice and deployment of the resource (House of Commons Science Select Committee, 2013). There are everyday pressures that ensue along with budgetary constraints and so forth, all with the potential to compound and limit the analysis of forensic science evidence.

The broader point of discussion is the real world frailties affecting the deployment and application of science and the author makes no apology for entrenching this chapter in the real world constraints affecting the use of forensic science. There are a plethora of textbooks covering the scientific techniques and applications, and it is relatively easy to regurgitate the textbook formulae on the application of scientific methodologies, but is fundamentally pointless as there are many excellent texts which already achieve that aim, many of which are referenced here. It accomplishes nothing in regard to portraying the intricacies of forensic practice and their use and application to hate crime. This chapter takes a real world stance acknowledging that forensic science embodies a resource to be used intelligently and prudently based on the context of the investigation. The context here is hate crime and as with its application to other crime types is a powerful tool when used appropriately and in the right conditions, but awareness of the broader implications needs to be forestalled.

Arguably 'success' in regards to using forensic science in any operational scenario is dependent on cohesion of the varying facets of the investigation. The evidence submitted for analysis needs to be appropriately recovered, preserved, and accompanied by a robustly delivered submission strategy that meets the overarching requirements. Furthermore, the scientist needs to undertake analyses that meet the investigative objectives. It can be assumed that the application of forensic science involves the unified deployment of disparate resources. Baber et al. (2005) posit that crime scene investigations, and by extension forensic science, can be viewed as distributed cognition where the varying narratives build through each stage from the commission of the offence, interpretations of the first responder, to the agents involved in differing stages of the investigation and the application of their skills to determine what has probative value and what does not. Each stage builds its own narrative based on the interrelationship between agents operating across the continuum of the investigation.

Smith et al. (2008) further comment on the formation of ad hoc teams throughout this continuum, and subsequently the successful deployment is reliant on not just maintaining personal competency and appropriate laboratory processes, but the augmentation and amalgamation of routes of connectivity, intermittent interpretation and dissemination of the appropriate evidence and data. In essence, where there is disparity in objectives, there needs to be a clearly defined pathway of communications that meets the unified goal of solving the crime. This can be achieved by propagating a systems level approach to promote holistic understanding of the entire process. No more is this requirement better illustrated than in the nail bomb case study.

Though constrained, this section has sought to present the prevalent issues and some fundamentals in regard to the operational use of forensic science. The next stage is extrapolating these observations to hate crime through a case study. The focus is on articulating the crime type, and the factors to consider when deciding on the appropriate strategies.

Forensic science case study – the London nail bombings

Over three successive weekends in April 1999 bombs exploded in Brixton, Brick Lane, and the Admiral Duncan public house in Old Compton Street, Soho. Three people were killed and many more were injured (Guardian, 2000). The areas where the bombs exploded were either areas with a high concentration of ethnic minorities, or the central area of congregation for London's gay community. Soon after the demographics of the areas targeted were established it became apparent that the motivation was based on extremist views in regards to race and minority communities.

David Copeland was convicted of the offences and was sentenced to six life sentences in July 2000. He was described as 'a Neo-Nazi extremist' (ibid.) and subsequently his motivations for carrying out the bombings were seemingly based on a political viewpoint manifest through 'hatred' for the communities he targeted. However, the causal influences, as in many other crimes, were not only attributed to his political motivations; he was presented by the defence as a paranoid schizophrenic. There is perhaps a discussion to be had on the legal rhetoric and bargaining here, however as explained throughout this book, and in other publications (Hall et al., 2009), the causal impetus is complex and heterogeneous and should not be seen in isolation. Similarly, understanding the diversity in motivational factors and maintaining an open mind in the investigative approach is imperative to the outcome of the case. This is re-emphasised later.

The premise taken here is the use of forensic science is embroiled within a broader framework of reciprocating data that informs the actions taken by investigators, and the interpretative functions of the evidence are crucial to maximise the evidence potential. There were many factors that assisted in the ultimate arrest and conviction of David Copeland and, as with all investigations, it is the multidisciplinary deployment of the techniques to the investigative endeavours that are required to establish the broader picture and ensure as many facts relating to the case can be established. The case study touches on many issues of relevance including the use of CCTV, utilising the publishing of 'commodified violence' online where David Copeland manufactured the bombs after accessing the Internet (Slater, 2005).

There are established techniques and 'recipes' available which do 'commodify' the illicit manufacture of substances and devices and David Copeland's actions are a good example of this, as highlighted by Slater (2005). This is but a fraction of the criminal risks propagated by the Internet and related media, and its influences on crime in all manners are well documented, and well beyond the scope of this chapter (but see Rohlfing, and Corb, this volume). However, it is important here in terms of defining the interactions across the continuum of the offence and it is important in the broader remit of intelligence building and corroborating actions. All aspects of the evidence parameters and the associated interactions whether they are virtual or physical are important and support the other aspects of the investigation. For example, the interrogation of digital media (Casey, 2011) provides information, in this case the nature of the explosive device, and therefore informs the forensic scientist and, when used holistically, the information builds a reliable hierarchy of propositions to better inform the hypothesis and offer greater reliability in the final interpretations.

In cases like the nail bomber the proactive use, or the efficient use, of accumulated intelligence is key to help intercept and disrupt those who intend to cause harm. Further, intelligence is important to maximise the prudent use of forensic science for investigative purposes, reciprocally, there is a requirement for forensic science to be used more effectively in intelligence (Rossy et al., 2013). At this juncture it is important to briefly discuss the broader use of intelligence in the London bombings. David Copeland was described as a 'lone wolf', operating alone and therefore difficult to intercept through the use of intelligence. However, 'soon after Copeland's arrest it had emerged that neither Special Branch nor MI5 held a file on him, despite his active involvement in the British National Party and the more extreme National Socialist Movement' (Searchlight, 2010: 10). This, at the time, raised questions for the intelligence community, as events like the bombings frequently do; however, the point here is that all evidence and intelligence needs to be coordinated and used effectively, this is sometimes easier said than done. However, in the last twenty years information technology capabilities have improved, and the international intelligence community continue to review their methods commensurate with the occurrence of various incidents (9/11 Commission Report, 2002).

As discussed previously, the examination of the interaction points develop through accumulated knowledge and through the primary scene, in this case the bomb site, and as the intelligence builds and more information is forthcoming further points of interaction are established and the list of secondary scenes develop. For example, during the initial points of the investigation detectives gather information through a range of sources, CCTV, eye witnesses, etc.; subsequently the profile builds and the associated parameters widen. The scene(s) are preserved and/or commandeered and the influx of information needs to be coordinated and resulting actions undertaken accordingly.

It is known now that the explosive device was taped to the inside of a sports bag, and there are many facts that were established as the inquiry progressed. The forensic strategy will be established and may involve defining the exact type of sports bag used and disseminating images to investigating officers helping to establish the retailers and utilise any intelligence available from that perspective. However, the validity of any data is reliant on robust methods to process the scene and gather reliable evidence, therefore it is useful to provide a review of the underpinning processes used to prudently manage the scene and the evidence recovered therein.

The initial actions undertaken during an incident of this nature need to establish its full geophysical extent and to execute control as soon as possible (Vermette, 2012). In this context the priority is preserving life and reducing injury to those in and around the incident; also, surrounding areas may be placed in a state of alert. Within these parameters and where possible the integrity of the scene needs to be maintained which follows once the area is safe and secure and the injured have been dealt with. There needs to be control of entry and egress preserving the evidential context, this is particularly relevant to the explosives scene where the pieces of evidence are widespread but will still offer important contextual and probative value (ibid.).

Often it is the ethical and safe approach to managing the scene and the forensic science evidence found within that is overlooked. There is sometimes a preponderance in the literature

Forensic science and hate crime

with the analyses and techniques used which sometimes overlooks the scene process required to manage evidence with due process, preventing further harm, and to address with empathy to the needs of the victims and their families. At this juncture there is a requirement to address the functional aspects of the forensic examination juxtaposed to fulfilling the obligation to provide information to the relatives. There is also a juxtaposition between reciprocal flows of information. As news and media reports increase the accumulation of phone calls from relatives increases and a list of 'missing' individuals if required can be used to begin compiling the necessary comparative data to formulate the identification of any victims. The known demographic of the area evidently makes an initial corroboration of the nature of the target and subsequently the motives of the offender, which can guide and focus early enquiries. However, there is always a need to use caution on speculating too widely and being too narrowly focused on specific information at the expense of other hypotheses. There is a need to respond to new information and test it objectively to reduce the fixation on one probable hypothesis; the process needs to be iterative. The investigator needs to focus holistically and be open-minded to determining the appropriate response.

The physical identification of the victim can be straightforward, however it can be significantly compounded by decomposition, disfigurement through impact, or a general lack of leads to provide a link to help establish identity. Also the nature of the incident, for example, the disorganisation caused by the explosion (Vermette, 2012; Mohanty, 2012) that followed the nail bombings can significantly complicate endeavours and requires a well-rehearsed multi-agency response that is well coordinated. This ensuing chaos and disorganisation and the difficulties in assuming control does make the process of gathering forensic science evidence complicated, but it is mentioned here to emphasise that the application of forensic science is not an isolated process. Subsequently, as the nature of victim identification is often assumed through physical and/or biological markers such as fingerprints, DNA, odontology, through scars/tattoos, the presence of prostheses, and so on, the nature of the injuries determines which identification techniques are viable and available in any given situation. It is the skills of the investigation teams and crime scene personnel to ratify and identify the applicable method assessing the situation and utilising a multidisciplinary approach to formulate the identification calling in the relevant experts and systems to assist as and when required. As stated earlier, it is also reliant on having comparable data, which may be gathered through intelligence, or speculatively searched depending on the background of the victim.

It is useful to note the difference in requirements of the evidence to serve the alternating purposes of the enquiry. The same principles, and where relevant scientific methodologies, are utilised to identify suspects and victims but there are differing legal provisions required in order to govern the process and to ensure that the evidence recovered is admissible to the court. This is most relevant when approaching the methods and procedures used to locate, identify, detain and to treat the suspect when in custody. It is beyond the scope of this chapter, however the legislative provisions govern all aspects of the process and investigators and scientists follow the legislation and appropriate protocol to maximise best evidence throughout the process.

In the context of the nail bombings, identifying David Copeland was facilitated through multidisciplinary means utilising intelligence and emerging data to propagate a call by detectives to the home address. On arrival he admitted the offences to the detectives and this was corroborated by the Neo-Nazi materials found at the premises (Guardian, 2000). However, it is important not to rely heavily on the confession at the early stage, and continue to maximise the evidence potential before the opportunity is lost. Based on establishing interactions, as the CCTV information from the three bombings was surveyed his interaction with the surroundings could be established and the resulting scenes examined to recover any trace that corroborates the developing hypothesis. The appropriate recovery of the evidence should show its context within the scene, for example, every shard recovered from the device, the location should be recorded and photographed, measured and plans drawn to show its location to aid interpretation (Vermette, 2012). Subsequently, the fragments can potentially be matched to origin and/or linked to the place where the device was manufactured.

There is a great deal of potential in maximising the recovery and efficient use of the more conventional forensic science evidence. However, as discussed earlier, it is important to establish its location, the nature of the explosion and to learn the lessons from other similar terrorist explosive attacks (Harrison et al., 2007). The forensic principles of explosive investigation are linked to the type and amount of explosive, and the environment where the explosion takes place. The rapid expansion of the explosive causes the surrounding casing, for example, the 'container', nails, ball bearings, etc. to fragment and cause significant damage to surrounding objects and personnel (Mohanty, 2012).

As highlighted by Hart et al. (2002), injuries caused by explosions are rare outside of war situations, however the observations are important not only in regards to the investigation, but also in terms of learning from experience and responding to the incident. Persaud et al. (2003) comment on the nature of the otological injuries recorded making an inference with the location in relation to the blast origin. This is important as it highlights the need for unity in response bringing together the required range of disciplines that compiles information that informs future investigations. Leibovici et al. (1996) concur, they provide the results of a study based on the injuries sustained between open air and confined space explosions, the benefit of these studies adds to the forensic knowledge and informs hypothesis. In many circumstances the use of any of the forensic sciences is grounded in our understanding of the known scientific record and the exploitation of that record to add a discriminatory value that informs hypothesis.

Conclusion

The depth of discussion within a book chapter is limited. However, there is scope to develop more detailed studies on the application of forensic science to a range of hate crime case studies. For example, there is a wealth of detail linked to the Stephen Lawrence enquiry and the Fiona Pilkington case, both with significant underpinning forensic science evidence that assisted in each enquiry for very different reasons. There is also more to discuss regarding the application of forensic intelligence to persistent perpetrators of hate crime and a more in-depth discussion on analyses of traces and linking the outcomes through the utilisation of techniques established and developed within other aspects of forensic science.

The intention of this chapter was to introduce some of the key aspects associated with forensic science and present them for consideration to the readers of hate crime. Hopefully a few long established myths will be dispelled and the representation of forensic science in fiction will remain where it belongs – as good entertainment and nothing more. The full complexity of delivering forensic science to hate crimes, and all other investigations for that matter, is entrenched in the realisation that though the science is long established, the ability to interpret based on scene context is a skill and an art that is developed through extensive experience. Furthermore, there is an opportunity to extrapolate further towards the bespoke dissemination of forensic science methods to the benefit of assisting hate crime investigations.

References

9/11 Commission Report (2002). Available at www.9-11commission.gov/report/911Report.pdf

Baber, C., Smith, P.A., Cross, J., Hunter, J.E. and McMaster, R. (2005). Crime scene investigation as distributed cognition. *Pragmatics & Cognition* 14(2) pp. 357–385.

Barnett, K.G. and Cole, M.D. (eds) (2010). *Crime scene to court: the essentials of forensic science* (3rd edn.). Cambridge: The Royal Society of Chemistry.

Broeders, A.P.A. (2007). Principles of Forensic Identification Science. In T. Newburn, T. Williamson and A. Wright (eds), *Handbook of Criminal Investigation* (pp. 303–337). Cullompton: Willan Publishing.

Butler, J.M. (2011). *Advanced Topics in DNA Typing: Methodology*. London: Academic Press.

Casey, E. (2011). *Digital Evidence and Computer Crime: Forensic Science, Computers, and the Internet*. London: Academic Press.

Cole, S.A. (2012). Forensic Science and Wrongful Convictions: From exposer to contributor to corrector. *New England Law Review*, 46(4).

Foster, J., Newburn, T. and Souhami, A. (2005). *Assessing the Impact of the Stephen Lawrence Inquiry. Home Office Research Study 294*. London: Crown Copyright.

Fraser, J. (2007). The Application of Forensic Science to Criminal Investigation. In T. Newburn, T. Williamson and A. Wright (eds), *Handbook of Criminal Investigation* (pp. 303–337). Cullompton: Willan Publishing.

Fraser, J. and Williams, R. (2009). *Handbook of Forensic Science*. Cullompton: Willan Publishing.

Hall, N., Grieve, J. and Savage, S. (2009). *Policing and the legacy of Lawrence*. Cullompton: Willan.

Harrison, S.E., Kirkman, E. and Mahony, P. (2007). Lessons Learnt from Explosive Attacks. *Journal of the Army Medical Corps*, 153(4) pp. 278–282.

Hart, A.J., Mannion, S., Earnshaw, P. and Ward, P. (2002). The London Nail Bombings: The St. Thomas' Hospital Experience. *Injury*, 34(11) pp. 830–833.

Harvey, E. and Derksen, L. (2009). Science Fiction or Social Fact? An exploratory analysis of popular press reports on the CSI effect. In M. Byers and V.M. Johnson (eds) *The CSI Effect* (pp. 3–28). Plymouth: Rowman & Littlefield.

Houck, M. and Siegel, J. (2010). *Fundamentals of forensic science* (2nd edn.) London: Academic Press.

House of Commons Science and Technology Committee. (2013). *Forensic Science: Second Report of Sessions 2013–14*. London: Crown Copyright.

Jackson, A.R.W. and Jackson, J.M. (2008). *Forensic science* (2nd edn.). Harlow: Pearson Education Ltd.

James, S. and Nordby, J. (2009). *Forensic science: an introduction to scientific and investigative techniques*. Boca Raton: CRC Press.

Jamieson, A. (2011). Forensics: Stronger scientific scrutiny needed in Britain. *Nature*, 464, 1266.

Leibovici, D., Gofrit, O.N., Stein, M., Shapira, C., Noga, Y., Heruti, R.J. and Shemer, J. (1996). Blast Injuries: Bus versus open-air bombings – A comparative study of injuries in survivors of open air versus confined space explosions. *Journal of Trauma-injury, Infection and Critical Care*, 41 (6) pp. 1030–1035.

Locard, E. (1920). *L'enquête criminelle et les méthodes scientifiques*. Paris: Flammarion.

Ludwig, A., Fraser, J. and Williams, R. (2012). Crime Examiners and Volume Crime Investigations: An empirical study of perception and practice. *Forensic Science Policy & Management: An International Journal*. 3(2) 53–61.

Macpherson, W. (1999). *The Stephen Lawrence Inquiry*. London: Crown Copyright.

Miller, M. (2009). Crime Scene Investigation. In S.H. James and J.J. Nordby (eds) *Forensic science: an introduction to scientific and investigative techniques* (pp. 167–188). Boca Raton: CRC Press.

Mohanty, B. (2012). Physics of Explosion Hazards. In A. Beveridge (ed.). *Forensic Investigation of Explosives* (Second Edition, pp. 79–118). London: Taylor and Francis.

Nail bomber convicted of murder (2000). Retrieved from the Guardian website: www.theguardian.com/uk/2000/jun/30/uksecurity

Neal, S. (2003). The Scarman Report, the Macpherson Report and the Media: how newspapers respond to race-centred social policy interventions. *Journal of Social Policy*, 32(1) pp. 55–74.

Persaud, R., Hajioff, D., Wareing, M. and Chevretton, E. (2003). Otological Trauma Resulting from the Soho Nail Bomb in London, April 1999. *Clinical Otolaryngology & Allied Science*, 28(3) pp. 203–206.

Pet cat's DNA helps convict owner who killed his friend after an argument (2013). Retrieved from The Independent website: www.independent.co.uk/news/uk/crime/pet-cats-dna-helps-convict-owner-who-killed-his-friend-after-an-argument-8761995.html

Rankin, B.W.J., Taylor, G. and Thompson, T.J.U. (2012). Should Higher Education respond to recent changes in the forensic science marketplace? *New Directions*, Issue 8, 27–32.

Rennison, A. (2011). *Codes of Practice and Conduct for forensic science providers and practitioners in the Criminal Justice System*. London: Crown Copyright.

Robertson, J. (2012). Forensic Science, an enabler or dis-enabler for criminal investigation? *Australian Journal of Forensic Science*. 44(1) pp. 83–91.

Rossy, Q., Ioset, S., Dessimoz, D. and Ribaux, O. (2013). Integrating forensic information in a crime intelligence database. *Forensic Science International*; Jul 10, 2013, 230 1–3, pp. 137–146.

Roux, C., Crispino, F. and Ribaux, O. (2012). From Forensics to Forensic Science. *Current Issues in Criminal Justice*. 24(1) pp. 7–24.

Saks, M.J. and Koehler, J.J. (2008). The Individualization Fallacy in Forensic Science Evidence. Available at: works.bepress.com/michael_saks/1

Scarman, Lord J. (1981). *The Brixton Disorders, 10–12th April*, London: Crown Copyright.

Schweitzer, N.J. and Saks, M.J. (2007). The CSI Effect: Popular fiction about forensic science affects the public's expectations about real forensic science. *Jurimetrics*, 47 pp. 357–364.

Searchlight (2010). Lone Wolves: Myth or Reality. Available at: www.lonewolfproject.org.uk/resources/LW-complete-final.pdf

Silverman, B. (2011). *Research and Development in Forensic Science: A Review*. London: Crown Copyright.

Slater, S. (2005). The Commodification of Violence on the Internet. *The Internet Journal of Criminology*, available at: www.internetjournalofcriminology.com/Slater%20-%20THE%20COMMODIFICATION%20OF%20VIOLENCE%20ON%20THE%20INTERNET.pdf?pagewanted=all

Smith, P.A., Baber, C., Hunter, J. and Butler, M. (2008). Measuring Team Skills in Crime Scene Examination: Exploring Ad-hoc Teams. *Ergonomics*, 51(10) pp. 1463–1488.

Stephen Lawrence murder: Dobson and Norris found guilty. (2012). Retrieved from the BBC News website: www.bbc.co.uk/news/uk-16283806

Stephen Lawrence trial: 'Blood on Gary Dobson's jacket'. (2011). Retrieved from the BBC News website: www.bbc.co.uk/news/uk-15965801

Taylor, P.M. (1990). *The Hillsborough Stadium Disaster*. London: Crown Copyright.

User Acceptance of Information Technology: Toward a Unified View. *MIS Quarterly*, 27(3) pp. 425–478.

Venkatesh, V., Morris, M.G., Davis, G.M. and Davis, F.D. (2003). User Acceptance of Information Technology: Toward a unified view. MIS Quarterly 27:3, pp. 425–478.

Vermette, J.-Y. (2012). General Protocols at the Scene of an Explosion. In A. Beveridge (ed.) *Forensic Investigation of Explosives* (Second Edition, pp. 79–118). London: Taylor and Francis.

Wilson, T.J. and Gallop, A.M.C. (2013). Criminal Justice, Science and the Marketplace: The Closure of the Forensic Science Service in Perspective. *The Journal of Criminal Law*: February 2013, Vol. 77, No. 1, pp. 56–77.

30

"You're a victim, don't become a perpetrator"

A study of the 'moral career' of racist hate crime victims

Corinne Funnell

This chapter presents findings from an ethnographic study funded by the Economic and Social Research Council which took place across two phases, first in the spring of 2009 and, second, between May 2010 and June 2011. The aim of the research was to explore victims' perceptions and experiences of racist hate crime in light of the victim-centred definition of 'hate crime' adopted by the criminal justice system in England and Wales. Accepted on the recommendation of the Macpherson report (1999), which investigated the racist murder of Stephen Lawrence in 1993, the Association of Chief Police Officers (ACPO) defined (at that time) a hate incident as:

> Any incident, which may or may not constitute a criminal offence, which is perceived by the victim or any other person, as being motivated by prejudice or hate.
>
> *(ACPO, 2005: paragraph 2.2.1)*

Whereas 'hate incidents may not constitute a criminal offence' 'all hate crimes are hate incidents' (ACPO, 2005: paragraph 2.2.2). Indeed:

> The perception of the victim or any other person is the defining factor in determining a hate incident. The apparent lack of motivation as the cause of an incident is not relevant as it is the perception of the victim or any other person that counts. The prejudice or hate perceived can be based on any identifying factor including disability, age, faith, sexual orientation, gender identity and race.
>
> *(ACPO, 2005: paragraph 2.2.6)*

The wider research project sought to provide a detailed account of the processes of racist hate crime victimization and to provide empirical research that critically assesses the idea that it is indeed a process (Bowling, 1999). This is important because whilst Chakraborti (2009: 123) states that Bowling's conceptualization of racism as a process captures the 'low-level or everyday experiences' of hate crime and the ways in which they cumulatively cause harm to the victim, their family and community, there is nothing, certainly within the last decade, which elucidates the situated meanings and experiences of the process of victimization. Moreover,

Bowling's (1993, 1994, 1999 and 2003) conceptualization of racist victimization as a 'process' rather than an event has shaped the development of hate crime scholarship in both North America (for example Perry, 2001, 2003a, 2003b) and the UK (Chakraborti and Garland, 2009; Hall, 2005; Iganski, 2008).

There has, in fact, been little in the way on how victims come into being (Rock, 2002) generally, or victimological research specifically into the nature and impact of racist hate crime victimization, especially that which accesses and gives voice to victims' experiences (Boeckmann and Turpin-Petrosino, 2002: 222), or which demonstrates the potential of social scientific enquiry through, for example, use of the ethnographic method (Vera and Feagin, 2004). Consider, for example, that Herek et al.'s (2002: 337) findings suggest that labelling 'an incident a hate crime may have a disempowering effect on the victim' and yet, implicit in the current definition is a requirement for the victim not only to identify themselves as such but also to claim victim status from a police service characterised by ongoing poor relations for some minority communities.

On balance what is absent from the research literature is an investigation of racist hate crime from a victim-informed perspective at 'ground level' (Chakraborti and Garland, 2009: 126) that explores how victims perceive hate crimes and what meanings they give to those experiences. What is required is an analysis of victimization as 'an emergent process of signification like many others, possibly involving the intervention and collaboration of others whose impact and meaning change from stage to stage, punctuated by benchmarks and transitions, and lacking any fixed end state' (Rock, 2002: 17).

The research took place at an agency located in England that was run by victims of racist incidents for such victims and which provided a casework-based service. The organization had institutionalized the subjective (ACPO) "Stephen Lawrence definition"; that is to say, unless the victim misled the caseworker, they were guided in their work by it and proactively applied the perception-based definition in determining whether or not to open a case and in the management of cases. Amongst themselves and in discussions with potential/clients and others, the caseworkers were concerned to find out if the claimant or a third party perceived themselves to be a victim of a hate crime. This was frequently referred to as meaning "we are client led", and caseworkers emphasized this in their dealings with clients and other parties such as police officers. Besides participant observational fieldwork, which involved accompanying the caseworkers in the course of their duties, nine ethnographic interviews were conducted with caseworkers and 16 unstructured interviews took place with victims.

The experience of victimization is analysed here with reference to a principal aspect of the caseworkers' role, which was to "empower" clients. The focus is victims' perceptions of acts of provocation by the perpetrator and 'under-protection' by the police service and the potential for "retaliation" by the victim. Running through the analysis is a consideration of the operation in practice of the victim-centred Stephen Lawrence definition of hate crime in terms of how those who perceived that they were victims maintained or lost victims status vis-à-vis recording agencies such as the police service, but also how victims could be constituted as perpetrators. The chapter thus highlights 'the interpretive definitional processes implicated in assignment of victim status' (Holstein and Miller, 1990: 104).

"Empowerment"

The "empowerment" of victims was the defining feature of the caseworkers' role. Chahal (2008: 26) explains that Reese (1991: 268) sees the aim of empowerment 'as social justice'. Indeed, casework practice mirrored the (online) *Oxford Dictionaries* (2012) definition of 'empower', which is 'to make (someone) stronger and more confident, especially in controlling their life and claiming their rights' and echoes Cogan's (2003: 473) discussion of the rationale behind empowering victims. Caseworkers thus focused on strategies both to enable victims to regain control of their lives, such as by encouraging them to report incidents or by doing so on their behalf, and by responding to the harms caused by victimization, and also through seeking to ensure that they were procedure- and rights-aware in respect of a range of services and systems. The process of "empowerment" was thus multi-faceted and, importantly, was predicated on the understanding that supporting victims entailed enabling them to respond to actual and potential victimization.

The "empowerment" function also had a pastoral element and this had two principal organizing foci. The first was to ensure equality of service provision by police officers. Whilst this concern permeates the analysis that follows, it will not feature as an analytically distinct issue apart from to observe that the caseworkers' tasks included "pushing the police" and "monitoring the police investigation", both with regard to recording crimes and incidents and in respect of the ongoing management of cases. The second aspect of the "empowerment" function in relation to the pastoral care of victims was directed toward ensuring that perceived failures of the criminal justice and other systems did not combine with wider processes of racism and discrimination, to result in some clients not only losing their claim to victim status, but acquiring the status of perpetrator.

During "a case opening" it was usual practice for caseworkers to advise their clients not to "retaliate" or not to "take things into your own hands" or to remind them "you're a victim, don't become a perpetrator". Rather, clients were encouraged to call the caseworker to "offload" and were reminded to do so throughout the life of a case. Michelle, for example, wanted to retaliate because the police had not brought the offenders to justice and, in consequence, they continued to victimize her and her family by, for example, petrol bombing the family's cars and constantly sending racially abusive and threatening messages by text, Facebook and post. Michelle said:

> I can understand why people take the law into their own hands sometimes. I really can. I really can understand.
>
> *(Field note 18/5/11)*

Salma, her caseworker, advised:

> Don't let her provoke you into anything, because look you know, you've just moved to your new house and hopefully things will sort between you and [your husband]. So just don't let her have the last laugh . . . do you know, just give her the satisfaction of what she wanted, of basically seeing your family destroyed.
>
> *(Field note 18/5/11)*

This advice was typical of that routinely given to clients but, another important motif is apparent, and that is the way in which acts of provocation interacted with other minor and major acts of racism to contribute to the experience of victimization. Often committed without leaving any evidence, the only sign that stealthy committed acts of provocation had occurred was the response of the victim in the form of a retaliatory act. Indeed, hate crimes presented as complex competing narratives and when cases involved acts of "provocation" and "retaliation", the caseworker's focus was on maintaining their client's victim status, hence the advice not to "retaliate" from the outset. Whilst caseworkers understood how retaliatory acts were embedded in the processes of perpetrator victimization and police responses, when clients ignored the advice not to retaliate, caseworkers as well as the police arguably saw clients as not constituting 'ideal victims' (Christie, 1986). As such, there was little in the way of repair work that could be done to restore victim status, hence the major focus on advising and supporting victims not to 'retaliate'.

'Retaliation' was discernible in three distinct contexts, which often interrelated. First, in response to direct acts of 'provocation' by the perpetrator and which, like other modes of victimization, were considered to be part of the tactics employed by perpetrators to target victims. Second, retaliatory acts arose as a consequence of victims' loss of confidence and trust in the police to protect them (and their family) and bring the offender to justice; they took the law into their own hands. Third, akin to the 'slow burn' defence identified in cases of domestic violence, the process of victimization – in terms of repeat victimization – exacted a toll on some victims and they engaged in retaliatory conduct. These three different contexts are apparent in the following excerpt from an interview with a caseworker, which shows how such acts are embedded in the process of victimization:

> Jyoti: I mean what we say is "I know it's a very difficult" . . . you've got to put yourself in those shoes. If you're subject to constant racial harassment or taunts or an assault you know day in day out from neighbours or on the street or whatever it may be and you're just trying to get on with your daily life and you're like "Please leave me alone and let me *live* my life. I'm not bothering you so don't bother me". That's the general feeling we get from most clients. It's like "I just want to live my life, leave me alone. I'm not bothering you". . . . Live a normal life is what you know we call it without you know that, that's all they want. . . . But . . . they're subject to constant harassment, racial harassment. What happens is, if you can imagine like, . . . you know *anger* builds up inside and you just think *why* are you doing this to me, *why* are you doing it? And a lot of clients *do* say "I've *had* enough" you know. "I've had . . . I've put up with this *long* enough, I *don't* need to". You know I think . . . some of them will say you know "Sometimes I think I'm just gonna turn around and shout abuse back at them". That's one of the things they want to do. It may not be racist but just tell them what they think. Or sometimes people say "If they do come to my house again or if they come onto my property and shout at my kids or shout at my family [pauses], if they are on my property then I'll just defend and do whatever it needs to get them off". You know or "If they hit me I'll hit them back". Because if there're threats made . . . to say "I'm going to hit you" or "I'm going to beat your son up" or "We're going to *kill* him" for example, then . . . I mean parents or . . . dads for example as well *won't* take that very lightly because they're there to protect their families and they'll be like "Don't say that because I'll actually . . . Don't make threats" and then some of them you know *want* to retaliate and say "I'm going to hit back and lash out".

> Corinne: So why don't they get the police involved then instead of . . .

> Jyoti: Um . . . this is the thing now. Some cases there aren't [pauses] police involved yet and it depends what stage we get. But most times if there are police involved and things haven't sort of worked out . . . Say for example when you've got a case it also is very dependent when you've reported things to the police, upon evidence. [Pauses and then laughs] Which is one of the things which is . . . I *know* it's needed but sometimes it's very difficult because when you've got neighbourly disputes going on for example . . .

A study of the 'moral career' of racist hate crime victims

Space precludes the opportunity to discuss all three different contexts for retaliatory action and so the main focus will be on 'provocation' and 'under protection'. Whilst these are presented here as analytically distinct, in practice, not least because of the ongoing nature of victimization, the contexts overlapped and interlocked.

Provocation

Jason's experience illustrates how and why "provocation" by perpetrators and "retaliation" by victims frequently permeated and shaped the experience of victimization and jeopardized clients' claims to victim status. In response to receiving racially imbued death threats and his experience of frequent acts of provocation such as name calling by his neighbour, Jason retaliated verbally:

> Jason: I said to him "If there is one thing I'm sticking up for you bastard and it's the colour of my skin" and then he *used* that against me as a counterclaim when he went to [give] his statement.
>
> Corinne: So did he take it to be that you were threatening him?
>
> Jason: Absolutely. He tried to turn it to say that I was threatening him but even though he had done all the threatening . . .

Jason articulated the nature of the dilemma faced by victims:

> . . . where's the fine line between you going out there and counterattacking and sticking up for yourself or *taking* all the verbal abuse and walking back in your door?

Jason was able to maintain his victim status by playing an audio-recording on his mobile telephone of the exchange to police officers and so proved that the incident unfolded in the way that he claimed and that he was thus not the aggressor. As Jason's case illustrates, hate crimes are competing narratives, which can include acts of "provocation", (potential) retaliatory acts and "counter allegations". It is the retaliatory act, however, that can set the context for the "counter allegation" and put the victim at risk of being cast as the perpetrator because those perceived to be involved in criminal activities do not make 'ideal victims' (Christie, 1986: 25). As noted, there was little in the way of repair work that victim and caseworker could do once this occurred, rather the criminal justice process had to be allowed to take its course. In Jason's case, however, there was an 'ideal victim' and an 'ideal perpetrator' (Christie, 1986: 25) not only because of the evidence that Jason was able to produce but because the perpetrator was known to the police and had a history of similar offending.

One caseworker (Salma) encountered a perpetrator and her boyfriend in two unrelated cases and recognised acts of provocation in both. In the first case:

> They provoked someone so much . . . they called my other client's son the n word [pauses] . . . because he's white and his son's dual heritage . . . Oh God! And then they . . . they grabbed the little boy OK and the dad must have just gone crazy. He grabbed a Samurai sword and he [pauses] . . . hit one of the guys there.

The nature of the provocation was different in the second case, however, where the victims (Michelle and her family) were related to the perpetrators and the incendiary acts were the 'constant name calling' because: 'they want a reaction . . . Why would they otherwise do it? If they know that people won't give them a reaction they wouldn't do it . . .' (Salma). Indeed, the issue of social and physical proximity in terms of how it facilitated ongoing victimization and the likelihood of a retaliatory response was evident in many cases, and was reflected in Michelle's account:

> Michelle: . . . I've just had enough. I feel like going and knocking on her door and just beating the hell out of her. I really do. Because, that's my worry now, because they know where we live.
>
> Corinne: So you don't feel like it's threatening or intimidating? It's more. . .
>
> Michelle: No, not at the moment. She's just trying to get a reaction from me, and she knows if she keeps pushing she will get . . .
>
> Corinne: She's trying to provoke you?
>
> Michelle: . . . she will get one and I know straightaway, as soon as I knock on . . . she's only got to see me in her street and she'll just call the police on me anyway, I know she will. She's just pushing me now.
>
> Corinne: So you think that she's trying to provoke you?
>
> Michelle: Because she's got away with it all. Yeah. She's got away with it. She has got away with everything. Because look at that other case, when she lived in her previous property, that was because she was calling her old neighbour's stepson, I don't like the word, n-i-g-g-e-r, because he ended up retaliating, he ended up in Elban Crown Court. He got banned from Roseville and everything.

When victims did react to perpetrators' acts of provocation, caseworkers described this as the client 'letting them get to them'. Referring to Michelle's case, the caseworker said:

> And that's one of the reasons why the police hasn't been able to press any charges [pauses] . . . and like you know by speaking to [the perpetrators] on the phone and sending text messages that kind of made their case weaker.
>
> *(Salma)*

"Physical" retaliation on the part of the victim in this context was explained by caseworkers as arising usually after the victim had initially ignored (racist) verbal provocation and was subsequently physically provoked by the perpetrator. A caseworker explained the situational dynamics in this way:

> . . . [the victim doesn't] respond to what's being said to them so then [the perpetrator tries] to make it physical because obviously the verbal doesn't seem to be having an effect. Despite it having an effect we always say "Do not respond". So then they think "I'm not going to respond" . . . "Don't respond, report it. Report it, report it, report it." We always encourage reporting. . . . because they're not getting anything out of the

person so they think let's have a fight you know . . . and I can show my power to you that way . . . which is strange.

(*Jyoti*)

Mr Seck's case illustrates physical retaliation arising in this way with regard to his children, including his young teenage son Jawara. According to his caseworker, youths would congregate outside the family home and chant abuse and death threats and would also follow Jawara and his younger sister when they left the home. Besides using 'racial verbal abuse' they would jostle him and say:

"Do you want to fight? I want a fight. Come on let's fight" and trying to provoke him into fighting. He said "I don't want to . . . I don't want to fight".

(*Jyoti*)

On one occasion, however, Jawara punched one of the perpetrators in the face and in consequence lost his victim status when he was constructed as perpetrator by police officers.

Provocation was a prominent feature of many cases and the following descriptions by victims explain how the act is enmeshed in the process of victimization:

. . . we are only dirty gypsies and spitting at us every time she's passing. She *do* not care who is out there. She don't care who you are or what you are, she'll pass and she'll grin and smile . . . [waiting] for somebody to attack her. She want to be attacked. She *really* want you to attack her so she can go to the police . . . *All* the time. But she's not getting that from me. Cos the more she's doing that to me the more I'm walking away cos I know well what she's playing at. . . . She's doing that *every single* day.

(*Dawn*)

Yeah he tries and gets [my boyfriend] to fight in the past, and I'm really lucky my boyfriend's actually more calm than me. He is super calm, he takes from him and then [the neighbour-perpetrator] realised the only way to get to him is to be really rude to me and say these things to myself 'cos obviously well [if] you can't get to him you can get to him via me 'cos if I'm upset he's gonna want to say something.

(*Cora*)

Retaliatory acts in response to provocation by the perpetrator were often framed as a form of defence of self or significant others. Indeed, expressly stated culturally imbued notions of male gender identity and role associated with family arose in this context (see for example Jyoti's comments above). A typical example occurred in Sara's case when, following a minor road incident involving her family's car and that of another [white] family in their car, Sara was punched and her husband pushed the assailant back. Sara's husband was charged with assault whereas no charges were brought against the man who assaulted her; she was told that there were no witnesses to the incident, which of course does not explain either outcome. Here Sara explains her husband's acts to defend her in response to acts of provocation:

It is like this, he thumped me, he bruised my eyes he did. He have no right to touch me and for us you know, I was going to say Muslim people – don't touch their wife. Don't

> go near their wife and their kids. My husband doesn't even like when people say. . . he's used to it now, because sometimes you go, "Why don't you f off". We don't have this f off and this b word, it's unrespectable. [The police] didn't do nothing [in response to the assault] and they got my husband in the police station, they arrested him, they had DNA, . . . they treated him like a criminal. I said, I'm not going to report nothing. But I can control myself. You know, I shout and I scream. It's my husband I'm aware of, because the minute he will break that . . . but he's holding himself, you know, he's straining himself, but that's because I'm there. So many times he pick me up and say, "Get out of my way!". But I did save his life so many times. But I don't want to live my life saving my husband's life.

Sara's experience not only captures the dilemmas faced by victims, it highlights many of the recurrent themes documented in the wider research project including: the mundane nature of interactions that can trigger racist incidents; the presence of children as witnesses if not primary and secondary victims (children were present in both cars); the requirement by police officers for evidence; reasons for not reporting; culturally-based understandings of and responses to victimization; the victim-offender dyad; and relations between people from black and minority ethnic communities and the police service. Furthermore, Sara's account reflects victims' everyday experience of a differential response from police officers towards them and the perpetrator where, when faced with competing accounts, the officer believed – or at least acted upon – the alleged perpetrator's account. The issue brings to mind a case reported by Bowling (1999: 49) in 1978 against Sikh brothers:

> For the black community it seemed that the victims of an attack were the ones arrested and the 'offence' of self-defence was the one punished.

The provocation-retaliation aspect of Sara's case also raises another important common experience of the majority of clients and this concerns the belief that not only did the police not listen to them, they did listen to the perpetrator. Sara's caseworker reflected upon this in a discussion about her case:

> And there is fear there of you becoming a perpetrator and that's where [her husband] was left where they were actually victims and had been victims for a long time . . . And . . . that really is very, very sad. Because . . . even the fact that the police will listen . . . to the other party more than this party.
>
> *(Jyoti)*

The experience of being treated as a criminal and the sense of injustice that arose from the disparity in the police response towards victim and perpetrator, all speak to inequality in service provision. Indeed, many participants suggested that the police operated on racist assumptions about people from black and minority ethnic (BME) groups and a few felt that perpetrators relied on the fact that this occurred in order to carry out acts of victimization. At this juncture, and before considering 'under-protection' which was the second context in which retaliatory acts arose, it is important to consider victims' perceptions of the police.

For many victims and caseworkers, racism aside, the failure of police officers to discharge their responsibilities or to do so other than in a perfunctory fashion arose from a range of reasons, many of which have been documented in the literature. Two victims summed up the views and experiences of many:

They're crap they are. Sorry. I'm being honest. They don't . . . maybe they're not funded enough, maybe they haven't got time, maybe they want concrete proof, but they've got to listen to us people, because we go through it every single day. They've got to listen and take action, proper action, even if it's just . . . I don't know, caution those other people who was saying that.

(Sara)

Like to me every time the police come and just take *one* look at me they don't think like . . . they don't say who's to blame. They just put the blame straight on me [pauses] without doing what they are supposed to do and do their job properly.

(Dawn)

The victims' accounts sit, however, with aspects of 'institutional racism' identified by Grieve and French (2000: 14):

Institutional racism is about stereotyping; it is about being unwitting; it is about ignorance; it is about failing to recognise a racist/hate crime; it is about not listening or understanding and not being interested in listening or understanding; it is about white pretence and black people being seen as a problem.

I often heard caseworkers, sometimes with clients, saying in respect of the police:

If you're white you're alright. If you're brown keep down. If you're black go back.

Interestingly, this saying mirrors the lyrics of a 1956 song entitled *Black, brown and white blues* sung by Big Bill Broonzy that was rereleased in 2000. Explaining the meaning behind the expression Mandeep said:

. . . the thing that has [pauses] . . . been said by the mostly Caribbean people and they know how they been victimized [pauses] . . . how they're picked on . . . stop and searches *even* though the policy came up we shouldn't be stopping more BME people for stop and search. *But* even *recent* statistics show that there are more BME people stopped and searched for no *reason* whatsoever and hence, when they come to [the agency] then we challenge on what grounds have this person been stopped *so* many times in a certain period and at times there is no answer and then the appropriate inspector said "Yes I will speak to the . . . team". And it's just not fair . . . And I think that's why history has been repeated . . . started off with the [pauses] [local riots] . . . [and in another region] as well. . . . when people see justice not [pauses] there and they're not being treated in the way they *should* be treated . . . Hence they confront.

This of course, chimes with commentators such as Bridges (2012) and Benyon (2012) writing on the 'urban disorder' of August 2011.

'Under-protection'

Retaliatory acts on the part of some victims were strongly related to their experience of policing, in terms of 'under-protection' as well as 'over-policing'. Before considering retaliatory responses in this context, however, it is important to consider the related question of evidence. A subject worthy of discussion in its own right, space does not permit the matter significant attention. As noted above, evidence was of central concern to victims and caseworkers because their reports of victimization were frequently rejected or relinquished on the basis that their perceptions could not be substantiated. Although of course, evidence is explicitly stated not to be required by the ACPO guidance in respect of reporting and recording hate crimes (2005: paragraph 5.4.2), because victim perception is the 'defining factor' (*ibid.*: paragraph 2.2.6). In response to such challenges, however, victims engaged in a range of evidence-gathering practices, which not infrequently generated physical if not legal dangers. The latter would include, for example, charges of false imprisonment for taxi drivers and shop keepers as a result of attempting to detain perpetrators whilst waiting for the police to arrive or issues in relation to data or child protection for photographing or filming minors whilst they committed racist acts. At the very least, an absence of probative evidence could result in a decision by police officers that they would take "no further action" and, in these circumstances, not only would the victim remain exposed to further victimization, they might feel compelled to "retaliate".

Mirroring the psychological consequences of victimization to be found in the hate crime literature (see for example Craig-Henderson, 2009: 23–24 and Dunn, 2009), but generating new insights, participants described how "frustration", "anger" and "hurt" could variously coincide to result in acts of "retaliation" in the absence of the protection and support of the police and housing services. This situation was explained by caseworkers in the following ways:

> It is frustration . . . most of the people just want to move away from it and when they can't . . . it's been taking longer and longer and longer because they cannot move away from there, the harassment is ongoing, there is problem with gathering evidence, the police are being called over and over again and in the end they say what's what the point in calling the police because they're not going to do anything, the council are not doing anything. Well I might as well take it on and I'll do it . . . I'll do it myself and there are a few cases where they *want* to do it but then we try to talk them out of it, to say "Look why do you want to be criminalised? You are not a criminal. Don't put yourself in that position because that guy – whoever is doing that to you – has probably already got records on him anyway so he doesn't care if he gets one more. But why do you want to have this stain . . . on your life" and we try to talk them out of it.
>
> *(Mandeep)*

> And so [if] there is racial verbal abuse being shouted over the garden fence or at someone as they come in and out of their house or day in day out for example. But, if no one's seen it [pauses] . . . [or] you know you don't know who it is . . . there is no action the police can take.
>
> *(Jyoti)*

Capturing both the process of 'slow burn' and the impact of lack of service provision Jason explained the impact of constant harassment by his neighbour:

> Jason: . . . what I fear is what *I* would do to *him*, not what he would do to me and that's it. I've said this to the police, I've said to Mandeep, I've said this to [the housing provider] [pauses] I said I would fear what *I* would do to *him* because *all* that history before [pauses] will mount up and mount up . . .

Corinne: Do you feel angry?

Jason: I feel *very* angry. I feel angry at [the housing provider].

Bilbar, discussing the impact of victimization, explains here how under-protection could lead to acts of retaliation and also highlights the 'slow burn' effect of hate crime victimization:

Bilbar: Overall you lose confidence in system. And [pauses] *frustration* is there. This is *very* dangerous. One thing is depression. One thing is the frustration. Frustration builds up. You are keyed up for that. You *know* your hands are tied. He insults you and then you *can't* . . . So what happen when it come to situation where you had an opportunity? You very likely seize the opportunity.

Corinne: To retaliate?

Bilbar: [Makes gesture confirming that he is referring to retaliation] That's dangerous. [Pauses] Does it make sense?

Corinne: Mmm. Yes.

Bilbar: So, it's not only one kind of emotional phase you go through this builds up different level, different stages. And somewhere, one level [taps table once], one stage [taps table once] . . . [pauses] trigger takes over you. So . . . it's answer to your question some days I'll get depressed. Had enough. One . . . that moment of time you do . . . next moment you get opportunity . . . to retaliate . . . and you do it . . . you seize it so . . . it wasn't only . . . I get depressed. There is something else. *Anger* and . . . the frustration was building up as well which kicks you [snaps fingers] . . . tip over.

The caseworkers' advice not to retaliate was not heeded in several cases including a "Chinese take-away case" where constant harassment made the clients "so fed up with the teenagers, you cannot imagine". Whilst securing the premises one evening the shopkeeper went back inside momentarily and "the perpetrator" locked the shop owner inside his shop and, much to his annoyance he could only be released with the help of the police:

So next time when they saw this group of teenagers they decided to take them into their own hands and lock them into . . . the shop. They were trying to sort them out but how you could do that? . . . These teenagers straightway reported to the police to say "Oh they assaulted me".

(Qiaohui)

The caseworker immediately followed this with an important point and one that was a feature of all these cases:

So in that case . . . you think you fed up with the police, police hasn't done anything but in this way you turn yourself into perpetrator.

Thus a lack of confidence or belief that the police would take action carried the risk of verbal and/or physical acts of "retaliation" where the victim took "the law into their own hands". Poor perceptions and experiences of the police service thus impacted greatly on reporting behaviour but also shaped the 'moral career' (Goffman, 1963) of the victim. That is to say, the process of labelling could involve the reconstruction of victims' histories and identities from that of victim to one that was stigmatized and deviant. The process of victimization thus included within the interactional dynamics that were the hate crime encounters, retaliatory acts that denied victims 'ideal victim' status because they were constituted as perpetrators by the services that they perceived had failed them. Dev's experience is typical of those encountered. He feared that he might take action himself when he believed that the police had failed to respond effectively and reflected that if the agency had not "forced" the police to act then he would have had to:

Dev: . . . end up . . . risking myself.

Corinne: What, to take action yourself you mean?

Dev: Yes, exactly. I mean my wife and kids . . . I mean I'm working for them; not [to] enjoy myself. So if something happened to my wife and kids, I'm not going to wait for the police.

Corinne: Wait for the police?

Dev: Simple as that. . . . I don't want to put myself in a risk, this is why I ask the police "Please, please".

Dev went on to describe how the anguish of victimization and lack of police response caused him to risk putting himself "in danger as well" by physically retaliating should another incident arise. These feelings were of course experienced alongside those arising from acts of victimization. Whilst caseworkers could "understand" their clients' feelings in such situations, the strong and consistent message was that they were not to risk becoming perpetrators and not to "go down to their level".

Conclusion

As the foregoing analysis demonstrates claims of hate crime victimization often presented as complex and competing narratives which influenced both the construction of the victim and perpetrator by the agencies involved and the form and content of the hate crimes and incidents. Yet the person who sought to claim hate crime victim status often seemed to be on the back foot. Frequently victims claimed to have reported incidents or crimes to the police and/or housing provider but without consequence; and they would often produce evidence of their endeavours. Not infrequently, some rightly claimed that the alleged perpetrator had also made allegations to the same authorities, often after a victim had retaliated, but that these had been followed up, thereby creating a situation where the victim had to rebut the "counter allegation". Thus, once an alleged perpetrator made an allegation, victims engaged in a process whereby they had to challenge the perpetrator's construction of them. Moreover whilst hurdles such as a requirement for evidence operated in practice to deny victim status to those who self-identified themselves as victims, arguably those with idealized attributes had the strongest claim to this label. In turn, those who engaged in retaliatory conduct – whether because they felt provoked by the perpetrator or compelled to take the law into their own hands or experienced 'slow burn' – lost their claim and, in consequence, faced the possibility of ongoing and sometimes escalating victimization and, in some instances, criminalization. In all these cases the dominant issue was the failure of the victim's perception to trump police discretion in the reporting and recording of racist incidents. Such instances represent an exercise of power by officers – a reassertion of police officer discretion denied by the current definition. Therefore, whilst the victim-orientated definition defines who *is* a victim, it is everyday 'interactional practice' (Holstein and Miller, 1990) which determines who *can* be a victim.

References

Association of Chief Police Officers (ACPO). 2005. *Hate crime: delivering a quality service – good practice and tactical guidance*. London: Home Office Police Standards Unit.

Benyon, J. 2012. England's urban disorder: the 2011 riots. *Political Insight* 3(1), pp. 12–17.

Boeckmann, R. and Turpin-Petrosino, C. 2002. Understanding the harm of hate crime. *Journal of Social Issues* 58(2), pp. 207–225.

Bowling, B. 1993. Racial harassment and the process of victimization: conceptual and methodological implications for the local crime survey. *British Journal of Criminology* 33(2), pp. 231–250.

Bowling, B. 1994. Racial harassment in East London. In: Hamm, M. ed. *Hate crime: international perspectives on causes and control*. Cincinnati: Anderson Publishing Company, pp. 1–36.

Bowling, B. 1999. *Violent racism: victimization, policing and social context*. Oxford: Clarendon Press.

Bowling, B. 2003. Racial harassment and the process of victimization: conceptual and methodological implications for the local crime survey. In: Perry, B. ed. *Hate and bias crime: a reader*. London: Routledge, pp. 61–76.

Bridges, L. 2012. Four days in August: the UK riots. *Race and Class* 54(1), pp. 1–12.

Chahal, K. 2008. Empowerment, racist incidents and casework practice. *Housing, Care and Support* 11(2), pp. 22–29.

Chakraborti, N. 2009. A glass half full? Assessing progress in the policing of hate crime. *Policing* 3(2), pp. 121–128.

Chakraborti, N. and Garland, J. 2009. *Hate crime: impact, causes and responses*. London: Sage.

Christie, N. 1986. The ideal victim. In: Fattah, E. ed. *From crime policy to victim policy: reorienting the justice system*. Basingstoke: Macmillan, pp. 17–30.

Cogan, J. 2003. The prevention of anti-lesbian/gay hate crimes through social change and empowerment. In: Perry, B. ed. *Hate and bias crime: a reader*. New York: Routledge, pp. 465–477.

Craig-Henderson, K. 2009. The psychological harms of hate: implications and interventions. In: Iganski, P. ed. *Hate crimes. The consequences of hate crime*. Westport: Praeger, pp. 15–30.

Dunn, P. 2009. Crime and prejudice: needs and support of hate crime victims. In: Iganski, P. ed. *Hate crimes. The consequences of hate crime*. Westport: Praeger, pp. 123–141.

Goffman, E. 1963. *Stigma: notes on the management of spoiled identity*. Middlesex: Penguin Books.

Great Britain 1999. *The Stephen Lawrence Inquiry. Report of an Inquiry by Sir William Macpherson of Cluny*. London: The Stationery Office (Cm 4262-1).

Grieve, J. and French, J. 2000. Does Institutional Racism Exist In the Metropolitan Police Service? [Online] pp. 7–19. In: Green, D. ed. *Institutional racism and the police: fact or fiction*. London: Institute for the Study of Civil Society. Available at: www.civitas.org.uk/pdf/cs06.pdf [Accessed 9 April 2013].

Hall, N. 2005. *Hate crime*. Cullompton: Willan.

Herek, G., Cogan, J. and Gillis, J. 2002. Victim experiences in hate crimes based on sexual orientation. *Journal of Social Issues* 58(2), pp. 319–339.

Holstein, J. and Miller, G. 1990. Rethinking victimization: an interactional approach to victimology. *Symbolic Interaction* 13, pp. 103–122.

Iganski, P. 2008. *'Hate crime' and the city*. Bristol: The Policy Press.

Oxford Dictionaries. 2012. [Online]. Available at: http://oxforddictionaries.com/definition/english/empower [Accessed: 25 June 2012].

Reese, S. 1991. *Achieving Power.* Sydney: Allen and Unwin.
Perry, B. 2001. *In the name of hate: understanding hate crimes.* London: Routledge.
Perry, B. 2003a. *Hate and bias crime: a reader.* London: Routledge.
Perry, B. 2003b. Where do we go from here? Researching hate crime. *Internet Journal of Criminology* [Online]. Available at: www.internetjournalofcriminology.com. [Accessed: 5 January 2009].
Rock, P. 2002. On becoming a victim. In: Hoyle, C. and Young, R. eds. *New visions of crime victims.* Oxford: Hart, pp. 2–22.
Vera, H. and Feagin, J. 2004. The study of racist events. In: Bulmer, M. and Solomos, J. eds. *Researching race and racism.* London: Routledge, pp. 66–77.

31
Working with perpetrators

Liz Dixon and David Court

The family campaign and subsequent public inquiry (Macpherson, 1999) into the murder of Stephen Lawrence raised awareness and concern about the prevalence and nature of racist attacks in the UK, as well as the impact of these offences on victims and wider communities. The publication of the inquiry report heralded revolutionary changes in the prosecution of race hate crime as the police service and other criminal and community justice agencies began to address the phenomenon of racist crime.

The focus on this form of criminal activity has had the effect of extending the criminal gaze to other strands of hate crime and to the appreciation that there are moving targets when thinking about potential victims. This chapter seeks to reflect on this ongoing work with convicted perpetrators of hate crime. The authors draw on practitioner experience in London specifically. They reflect on the emerging landscape to establish how far the lessons learned with race hate perpetrators can apply to other forms of hate. However, we initially refer to some of the academic literature that has developed apace since 'Lawrence'.

In 1997, the Home Office commissioned Rae Sibbitt to conduct research into perpetrators of racist hate crime. She visited community and criminal justice organisations and reported that it was very difficult to find a stereotypical racist perpetrator. She observed that there were perpetrator communities rather than individuals and that different age groups participate differently in the production of racist incidents and crime. Sibbitt concludes that 'the elders' socialise their prejudices into the younger offenders who act out these prejudices when offending. Aaron Beck's (2000) work on in-group and out-group dynamics provided evidence that we are biased in favour of our own 'group' and that this also has a significant impact on perpetrators' prejudice. Reflection from practice experience of work with reactive offenders shows how this bias is formed and entrenched in defence against the perceived threat of outsiders and interlopers that helps distance 'the other'.

Ray et al. (2004) carried out research into racist offending following disturbances in the north of England in cities including Oldham, Rochdale, and Bolton, during the summers of 2000 and 2001, as further discussed by Giannasi, in Chapter 27 of this volume. Offenders were prepared to admit to violence, but did not acknowledge the racism; rather they appeared to feel slighted. The research highlighted perpetrator shame and envy when faced with different Black and minority ethnic communities, whom the perpetrators *perceive to* have more social capital, better economic prospects and that their social capital seems stronger (Ray et al., 2004). This shame fuelled their antisocial, racist behaviour. Beck (1999) elaborates on the themes of hurt becoming hate and gives an account rooted in cognitive therapy that practitioners have found helpful in explaining why some perpetrators act on their prejudices when offending. This does not necessarily fit with the London picture, but it highlights the importance of attending to the local demographics, to offenders' socialisation, their cultural experiences and the community myths, prejudices and perceived grievances.

Roger Hewitt's research in Greenwich focused again on community experiences and perpetrator profiles. In his book 'White Backlash' (2005) he looks at how those communities experienced demographic, economic and political upheavals in the previous decades. He suggests that the implementation of 'clumsy anti-racist government policies' in that context was hugely damaging. White people he met and spoke with were horrified by the racist attacks but felt that the majority white communities were being labelled as racist because of the minority 'far-right' presence in the borough, and the ripple effect of constant media attention.

Hewitt produced a powerful training video for the Greenwich local authority (2005). With his publication called 'Routes of Racism' he captured these reactions and the perpetrator mindset. He found that there are 'community profiles' which produce race offending. He said certain factors can act as pre-conditions to race unrest, namely entrenched local racism; local social and economic deprivation; passive engagement in leisure activities; few affordable youth facilities; high levels of adult criminality linked with wider criminal networks; and, a violent youth subculture.

When working with more entrenched racist offending, our practitioner experience resonated with Hewitt's research and contemporary research commissioned by the National Probation Service at the time. This highlighted common offender profiles or dynamic risk factors, which include:

- a minimisation and denial of racial element of the offending;
- blaming the victim and counter accusations;
- an absence of victim empathy;
- distorted sense of provocation;
- a sense of entitlement and alienation;
- distorted ideas about the victims and racial differences;
- a poor sense of their own racial/cultural identity.

Challenging offending

There are inherent difficulties in assessing motivation where the crime is attitudinal as denial and minimisation are the norm. The courts' enhanced sentencing powers for crimes of hate can serve as a disincentive to admit to such offending at the outset. Moreover in our experience denial can be conscious and unconscious; there is often a lack of insight which, along with shame and stigma (Ray et al., 2004), can act as a barrier to intervention. Those challenging the behaviours need to be acutely sensitive to their own attitudes around prejudice, race, religion, disability and sexuality. These can impact and be modelled within their own interaction with perpetrators and can influence or even derail the intervention, and lead to collusion, so training to manage these dynamics is essential (Dixon, 2002).

The term 'Hate Crime' is used to describe offences 'where the perpetrator's prejudices against any identifiable group of people is a factor in determining who is victimised' (UK

Criminal Justice definition). In practice, it is more usual to interview offenders who have been convicted for offences where the hostility is more an aggravating and additional factor within the offence, rather than the sole reason for the crime.

Some perpetrators are well known for causing a nuisance generally and present as persistent 'generalist' offenders. Underlying prejudices (frequently sub-conscious) serve to aggravate the incidents, assaults and criminal behaviours. The harassment involved can be 'fleeting', 'impulsive' and 'circumstantial', which will require a specific response from the agency involved, even if that does not amount to a crime report. However, the behaviour needs to be marked and victims protected. The damage inflicted is often the same regardless of the motivation. That said, staff need to be able to differentiate between perpetrators whose behaviour is less entrenched and more 'peer related' and circumstantial, as opposed to those who pose a future risk and where the offending is more targeted. Racial and other forms of hate tend to occur as an aggravating rather than motivating factor (Court, 2003 and Burney and Rose, 2002) and are treated as such by the courts and subsequent interventions.

Working with perpetrators not only impacts upon re-conviction but also improves knowledge of why and when hate crime occurs. It can also provide information that can be used to develop successful interventions if shared within partnerships. For instance, focusing on perpetrator socialisation processes is revealing that many of the tensions and prejudices are arising from limited, positive inter-ethnic interaction and an attendant susceptibility to negative media reporting of immigration issues. They can also respond to localised community myths and jealousies, rather than any attachment to organised hate crime groups.

We have found McDevitt's typology, used in the USA Juvenile Justice Department to be particularly useful (McDevitt et al., 2002). This resonates with our own experiences and identifies four groups of offender. The McDevitt et al. typology (2002) distinguishes between different motivations used within interventions.

- **The 'thrill seekers':** Those who are 'attracted' to the offending because of the thrill or 'buzz' it provides. They are influenced by a wider peer group and will 'tag along', often getting drawn into violence without any regard for the victim. Such offenders are often known to the Youth Offending Team and the Local Authority's Housing Department for a variety of offences and anti-social activities. We may consider their activities territorial rather than specifically motivated by hate, even though the victim's experience will be the same. This will resonate with housing workers, where children and adolescents act out prejudice that they pick up from adults. The solution lies in directing the youth into purposeful activities and challenging the prejudice and stereotypes. As practitioners, we challenge their offending and raise awareness of the impact of their prejudices. It may be that mediation and restorative justice, in some instances, can be developed to assist with these cases. However, these interventions do require and depend upon good accurate assessment and knowledge of resources. The object of the intervention is to get them to refrain from offending and to develop strategies so that they can manage their prejudices and be less anti-social.
- **The 'reactive/defensive offenders':** Usually older, frequently with few previous criminal convictions, members of this group will have a sense of grievance and believe that they are acting to protect against a perceived threat to their way of life. They will have a sense of due entitlement and look on any service provision to Black people or newcomers (asylum seekers/refugees/immigrants) as preferential treatment. Offences frequently occur when alcohol acts as a dis-inhibitor. Victims can be minority ethnic neighbours, shop staff, local authority workers and police officers. The developed

programme, called the Diversity Awareness and Prejudice Pack (DAPP) toolkit, along with alcohol interventions can be invaluable for this group. Also staff find that focusing on their own experiences and issues around their own racial identity can help prepare the way for raised awareness about perpetrator prejudices and the impact of this on their behaviour.

- **The 'retaliatory offender':** This is the offender who reacts to the racial aggression or prejudices and negative stereotyping he or she receives and 'hits' back. His or her offending may be hate related and needs addressing but is motivated by a desire to 'get even' and 'retaliate'. A focus on developing a more robust personal identity is often an effective intervention. Offences can be against authority figures, such as the police, or people from new arrival communities, especially if the offender is from a more established minority ethnic community.

- **The 'mission offenders':** The offending of this group is premeditated and targeted. Often inspired by a 'higher order', they may have mental health problems; David Copeland, the 'London nail bomber' (discussed elsewhere in this volume by Giannasi and Smith) may be considered such an offender. We would also include 'politically motivated offenders', i.e. those attached to or sympathetic to extremist parties or organisations (British National Party or National Front activists). Staff have developed good alliances with multi-agency partners and community groups to both carry out risk management and, in some cases, risk reduction when working with Mission Offenders.

Practitioners have found that this typology is helpful in making assessment about reoffending risks and interventions that can resonate with their experience (Court, 2003). With mission offenders, the primary aim has to be to ensure victim protection as the offending is premeditated and targeted. Work with 'thrill seekers' is often geared at diverting them into pro-social attitudes and working on their capacity to resist negative peer pressure, as this can also drive the offending. The American psychologist, Gordon Allport (1954), talked about the escalation of prejudice that takes place when nothing is done to challenge prejudice and this, in turn, leads to racial violence.

The Greenwich Hate Crimes Project

The Greenwich Hate Crimes Project was one of four projects funded by the Government to drive effective practice with race hate crime after the examination of the Stephen Lawrence murder. The project was a multi-agency initiative, which initially focused on addressing race hate crime offending, but later evolved to include religious, homophobic and disability hate-related offending. The multi-agency approach enabled intelligence sharing and ensured that the victim experience was addressed safely and sensitively. This multi-agency approach assisted in raising awareness and aspirations around prosecutions and prevention. It developed professionals' skills in effective community engagement, knowledge about the nature of prejudice and strategies to help offenders at a very basic level manage their prejudice and in some cases transform it.

At the beginning of the project in 2005, it was unclear as to whether it would be possible to work with individuals who had been convicted of racially motivated or aggravated offences. Some earlier work revealed that the successful implementation of the structured interventions in Greenwich was possible, as 76 per cent of offenders completed the required level deemed appropriate to their level of risk. This allowed the interventions to be used on a wider scale with hate crime offenders. DAPP interventions were monitored in a database, which covers both Greenwich and Lewisham. There was also a pilot in a young offenders unit where the interventions were monitored for some qualitative evaluation.

The joint expertise and commitment drove innovation and best practice. The Greenwich project provided a blueprint for future offender work, attracting national awards at its inception in recognition of the innovative and effective work.

Multi-agency work

The recommendations from the Stephen Lawrence Inquiry strenuously advised agencies to invest in multi-agency work that proved to be critical to successful work with perpetrators. We have found that close liaison with the arresting police officer, the Community Safety Unit, and often housing and other criminal justice agencies where relevant, intelligence is essential in presenting a clear picture of what happened and what was intended. Staff need to be equipped with relevant material given the widespread minimisation and reduction in charges.

In the first instance this pertains to assessments – it is imperative that we find out who knows about the offender. The multiagency forums developed in Greenwich facilitated the sharing of community and criminal intelligence. Housing departments often knew the perpetrators – they had often been involved in neighbourhood disputes and were subject to antisocial behaviour disorders.

We learnt about the staged civic sanctions to mark anti-social behaviour and to support victims (Lemos and Crane, 2000). The forum members could see when to impose Acceptable Behaviour Contracts (ABCs) and Anti-Social Behaviour Orders (ASBOs), as well as when to instigate civil legal proceedings. They became aware of the importance of contact with the police and intelligence sources. Probation staff can minimise the offending behaviour and we learned that staff could not rely on self-disclosure from the perpetrator. Hearing all accounts of a crime is important so that you do not inadvertently 'collude'. Moreover, Court assessments should be viewed as the start of a process, rather than the 'final' assessment.

Multi-agency working also proved useful in helping London staff to develop their interviewing and intervention skills – we learned how to navigate these dialogues where counter-accusations were the norm. London staff were not prepared for the fact that the perpetrators would blame the victims and have a counter-narrative to the victim account. Housing workers dealt with this scenario on a regular basis with perpetrators and victims of harassment and developed interview schedules to assist them in dealing with the antagonism that they met when they challenged tenants' prejudices.

Shared databases serve the whole community as informed and planned interventions reduce re-offending and protect other tenants and the public at large.

Programmes and mentoring. We are aware that all the agencies have an interest in work with perpetrators. Social workers, mentors or youth offending staff can implement intervention plans. There may be some housing support workers who could get involved in these projects. The challenges involved are similar to those that probation practitioners face in which offender counter-accusation and denial are common, despite the clear evidence on Crown Prosecution papers and witness statements of the ferocity of attacks and the presence of harassment.

When working with more serious offenders, where the offending is entrenched, one needs to draw on multi-agency assessment and referrals to other specialist processes such as the Community Safety Units or Multi-Agency Public Protection Panels. Identification of appropriate interventions can be very diverse with appropriate choices including eviction warnings, ASBOs or a threat to withdraw tenancy.

Seconded officer

The project paid for a seconded probation officer to work with offenders aged 18 and over who have been convicted of hate crime offences. In order to use the probation officer's time most effectively their priorities were to focus on direct work with convicted offenders, assessing offenders prior to sentence and working on their prejudiced beliefs, as well as managing their social behaviours after sentence.

The project went from a planning stage straight to the implementation. The project did not stay 'in the laboratory' as the project staff learnt by error and modification. There was a commitment toward reduction of reoffending and rehabilitation and the combined focus and concern raised aspirations and developed professional expertise.

Observations from direct work with perpetrators

The Programme developed guidance for court report writers with a view to helping them accurately assess the depth of an offender's prejudice and animosity towards the target victim or the target group, and the likelihood of harm to the general public, specific individuals or communities. When this has been completed, resources can then be focused where they are most required. The key question has to be 'what is the most effective and proportional response to this offence and offender?'. The guidance and accompanying 'client questionnaire' exercise proved invaluable for report writers and we drew on the guidance developed for work with perpetrators of domestic violence.

With regard to direct face-to-face work it was clear that we were not able to draw on offenders' altruism or remorse both of which were largely absent at the time of conviction. It was better to concentrate on developing engagement in order to facilitate exploration of prejudice, chipping away at the cement rather than the brick. Labelling offenders as racist was experienced as an insult and was often counterproductive. We instinctively used some of the desistance themes in listening to narratives and promoting new scripts and narratives.

It is important that professionals are aware of all of the known facts and it is advisable to think about and plan questions using structured materials such as those found in the DAPP. It is also advisable to rehearse strategies and get used to the sound of your voice when talking about race. This can diffuse the tension that often accompanies racial allegations and get perpetrators to reflect on the irrationality of their views.

We have found that using a motivational approach helps with the work and to focus on *the uncontested elements of the incidents involved*. This is also a good way of developing rapport for later interventions. We have found that open-ended questions help illicit information.

Staff need to be polite and be aware that there are often a range of emotions associated to the incidents that will affect the dynamics of any intervention or interview. Staff need to avoid labelling and we advise avoidance of calling people racist – it is better to focus on the behaviour and what happened and to highlight the harm caused and to focus on ways to prevent it.

The seconded officer and other specialist staff found common themes that applied, irrespective of the racial background of the offender. These include low empathy and high personal need, poor parenting and damaged relationships. Offenders often present with high levels of impulsiveness and aggressiveness. Alcohol abuse or dependency was another common theme. Staff are advised to be aware of these factors but not to allow them to become a distraction or means of avoiding the work. Staff are also able to 'signpost' perpetrators to support agencies and remain focused on challenging their offending.

In London we found that inviting perpetrators to reflect on their socialisation experiences via the 'autobiography exercises' and the 'relationship webs' helped them develop some insight into where their attitudes and even prejudices had come from. We have alluded to the unconscious racial element of some of the behaviour – perpetrators have often internalised negative images of black and Asian people and are drawing of these phenotypes – this impacts on a dehumanisation of the victim.

Perpetrators overwhelmingly commit their crimes at times of agitation and personal distress. They are also prone to externalise blame, both for the offence and also for their own personal and social problems, thus those who harass neighbours do not believe that their racial views impact as directly as they do.

Interventions are geared at raising victim awareness, victim concern and eventually victim empathy. One example of this is an offender who was required to discuss a particularly aggressive attack, where the victim was kicked to the floor. He eventually reflected that had the victim been white he would not have been so badly assaulted and in this way started to see the link between his prejudices and behaviours. The link to other forms of targeted offending is obvious. Only very specific and informed intervention is likely to uncover and tackle this form of offending. The causation may be multi-faceted and this needs to be addressed before embarking on any programme of intervention.

Modules 4 and 5 of the intervention programme start to focus on victims' experiences and staff are trying to assess and nurture offender empathy. The toolkit draws on Finkelhor's theory of offending (and Matza's techniques of neutralization – see Hall, this volume) to look at the process and purpose of offenders' actions. This helps break down the denial and minimisation of offending, and highlight how prejudice contributes to the 'dehumanisation process'. In our experience both staff and perpetrators value these exercises. These latter modules are particularly relevant for medium and high-risk perpetrators serving prison sentences. If successful, then perpetrators acknowledge that they unconsciously dehumanise the 'other' and the perpetrators may go further in seeing the prejudicial attitude acting as an accelerant. Dixon and Court testify to the increased ferocity of the attacks in addition to the ripple effect on the community (Dixon and Court, 2003).

Training

The importance of training for all staff cannot be overestimated as this gives knowledge and builds competence and confidence. In our experience staff require guidance in developing the risk assessment skills required with this work. This is emotive work, as it requires that practitioners engage with individuals' core identities. To be successful, the practitioner must show a genuine but not collusive interest in how the offender has developed their perceptions and their interpretation of their environment, both human and economic. The practitioner must, therefore, be skilled and confident in motivational interviewing, person-centred methods, and the application of the principle of responsivity.

Staff use the structure of the DAPP to assist the offender to identify how they have constructed their personal and social and racial identities. Staff have to be alert to the influence of political ideologies. The training is critical to help staff to avoid colluding with the denial and to make sure they do not overreact to situations.

London Probation Trust (LPT) carried out an evaluation of this work in HMPYOI Feltham and one of the findings was that staff who had not attended training were less likely to use the DAPP exercise to engage in dialogues on prejudice and racial identities and focused on the less challenging parts of the toolkit. The LPT training reflects the multidisciplinary nature of work and has been developed with a partnership with staff from the Greenwich racial attacks monitoring unit. Listening to victims' experience has helped develop expertise both in terms of training and programme development.

In drawing upon victims' testimonies to understand the process of offending, policy makers and those running interventions have also learned more about the role that language plays in escalating behaviours and developing the intent to offend.

Those involved with perpetrators work hard to learn about distorted victim perceptions and to assist offenders to develop identities that are more pro-social. They highlight the importance of gathering both criminal and community intelligence, prior to working with those charged with hate crime offences, and the need to have 'relevant materials' at their disposal prior to engaging with the work. This is similar to the way that we would work with sex offenders or perpetrators of Intimate Partner Violence.

Iganski's 2007 and 2008 examination of local, situational analyses with their focus on context are also helpful to practitioners, demonstrating why they need to work with local communities to gather community intelligence, and to learn about target groups and available solutions.

So it is that professionals involved in the monitoring of hate crime in a community have learned to familiarise themselves with community demographics, community cohesion, the target groups and victims. The professional therefore needs to be proactive, to prepare for the intervention and concomitant interviews, given community and situational specific dynamics. It is essential that practitioners assemble available community intelligence and read all the prosecution papers, the most important of which are the witness statements. In this way, they are victim focused, will avoid collusion, support victims and address ongoing issues of risk, to maximise opportunities to reduce and manage those risks.

The need to have flexible intervention is imperative given changing presentations of offending, moving targets and the greater confidence in our capacity to promote change at all stages. Practitioners from criminal and community justice agencies and schools highlight the importance of visual interventions and these include the use of film, video and photography to help with education and looking for different perspectives.

One of the more powerful exercises in DAPP is called the 'community project', relying on the practitioners to design a project, which will involve the offender in their 'diversity journey'. A senior probation officer in Liverpool used to send offenders down to the docks to walk the slave trade trail and get them to report back to her on that experience. In Greenwich, offenders go to the Racial Attack Monitoring Unit to meet staff working with victims and are confronted with an emotive photo collage illustrating the cost of racial hatred. The Heartstone project gets pupils and offenders to consider different perceptions and elements of their communities in an effort to promote pride and develop concern. It also helps develop empathy, awareness, challenges ignorance and denial and facilitates changing the view of events and communities.

Conclusion

London Probation Trust now uses Restorative Justice (RJ) approaches (see Walters, this volume) and this has provided an opportunity to assist the victims of hate crime and to get offenders to better appreciate the harm caused. Many of the victims of racial aggravated offending have elected to engage in RJ and have told LPT facilitators that they want to let the harmer know about the impact of the offence and they welcome the opportunity to have some say in making reparation. One female victim of a racially aggravated road rage attack said she wanted the offender to work on his self-development and to find ways to manage his prejudices so that other victims do not suffer. The perpetrator is now engaging in the DAPP and has agreed that the victim can see the work that he has done. He is also writing a letter to her to express his remorse.

The authors have commented on how work with perpetrators of racial hate crime has informed other forms of, namely, homophobic and disability related hate crime. A more recent challenge is to work with individuals charged under the terrorist legislation and those who present as 'of concern'. Some Probation Trusts, including Yorkshire and London, who are supervising significant number of TACT (those charged under the terrorist acts) offenders have developed toolkits.

The London toolkit has evolved from the original DAPP and is made up of exercises and articles designed to promote focused dialogue and identity exercises aimed at assisting the offender to see how their religious identity became dominant and distorted. A relatively recent initiative has been the development of structured scripts to assist the staff in managing the very challenging dynamics with politically and religiously motivated offenders.

Staff in the National Offender Management Service have worked to develop programmes and drawn on a variety of sources, to develop the knowledge-base of hate and gang-crime identity literature. They have also designed a useful risk assessment tool, the 'Extremist Risk Guidance', which assess the perpetrators under four domains – beliefs, motivation, capacity and attitudes. We use these assessment tools to help us identify politically motivated hate crime offenders and to implement risk management and public protection measures accordingly.

We conclude by reiterating again the importance of working together with other criminal justice and community agencies, faith based and victims groups to find ways to reach people, whose attitudes and behaviours create harm to victims. Ultimately, the aim is to reduce the risk of re-offending and start to repair the damage caused by hate crime.

Bibliography

Allport, G. (1954) *The nature of prejudice*. Cambridge, MA: Addison-Wesley.
Beck, A. (1999) *Prisoners of Hate: The Cognitive Basis of Anger, Hostility and Violence*. New York: Harper Collins Publishers.
Bowling, B. (1998) *Violent Racism: Victimisation, Policing and Social Context*. Oxford: Clarendon Press.
Burney, E. and Rose, G. (2002) *Racist Offences – How is the Law Working? The Implementation of the Legislation on Racially Aggravated Offences in the Crime and Disorder Act 1998* (Home Office Research Study 244). London: Home Office.
Court, D. (2003) 'Direct work with racially motivated offenders', *Probation Journal* 1 (50) pp. 52–58.
Dixon. L. (2002) 'Tackling Racist Offending: A Generalised or Targeted Approach?' *Probation Journal* 49 (3).
Dixon, L. and Court, D. (2003) Good Practice with Racially motivated offenders, *Probation Journal* 50 (2) pp. 149–153.
Dixon, L. and Ray, L (2007) Current issues and developments in race hate crime. *Probation Journal* 54 (2) June 2007.
Heartstone project. www.users.globalnet.co.uk/~eastwich/project2.htm
Hewitt, R. (1996) *Routes of Racism*. Stoke-on-Trent: Trentham Books.
Hewitt, R. (2005) *White Backlash and the politics of multiculturalism* Cambridge: Cambridge University Press.

Iganski, P. (2007) *Evaluation of the London-Wide Race Hate Crime Forum as a Model of good practice between statutory criminal justice agencies and the voluntary sector non governmental organizations.* London: London Probation Service.
Iganski, P. (2008) *Hate Crime and the City.* Bristol. The Policy Press.
Lemos, G. (2005) *The search for tolerance: Challenging and changing racist attitudes and behaviour among young people.* Joseph Rowntree Foundation.
Lemos, G. and Crane, P. (2000) *Racial Harassment on the Ground.* Joseph Rowntree Foundation.
Macpherson, W. (1999) *The Stephen Lawrence Inquiry – report* CM 4262-1. London: HMSO.
McDevitt, J., Levin, J. and Bennett, S. (2002) Hate Crime Offenders and extended typology. *Journal of Social Issues* 58 (2) pp. 303–318.
Ray, L., Smith, D and Wastell, L (2004) Shame, rage and racist violence. *British Journal of Criminology* 44 pp. 350–368.
Sibbitt, R. (1997) *The Perpetrators of Racial Harassment and Racial Violence.* Home Office Research Study 176. London: Home Office.
Victim Support UK. (2006) *Crime and Prejudice Research into Hate Crime in England and Wales.* Available at www.victimsupport.org.uk

though
32
Helping offenders to 'think again'
A practitioner's perspective on developing an intervention for hate offenders

Eila Davis

In 2004 I was funded by the Home Office to adapt an existing individual intervention, the (Priestley) One to One programme (2001) (hereafter called OTO), for use with what were then termed 'racially motivated offenders'. From what I knew about relevant research, I felt strongly that the motivational and empowering style of OTO could benefit this type of offender and reduce the risk of creating more victims. The political context was, of course, the aftermath of the Stephen Lawrence Inquiry (Macpherson, 1999) and the advent of legislation against racially aggravated offences. Closer to home, the introduction of evidence-based practice with offenders was in full swing, stirring up mixed views throughout the Probation Service. Some practitioners welcomed a more structured and prescriptive form of rehabilitation, whereas others were doubtful and wary, fearing that scope for professional creativity and judgement was being curtailed.

Despite the respect that its author, Philip Priestley, commands, the OTO programme, with its national, accredited status and defined method, was seen by some as a symbol and tool of a new restrictive and counterproductive era of probation practice. That it was originally developed for general offenders, yet was now being adapted to suit hate crime perpetrators, was viewed by vocal detractors as motivated by politics and expedience, rather than logic and theoretical coherence. It was within this somewhat highly charged arena that I began to consider how best to adapt OTO to suit hate crime perpetrators. My first step was to explore how theory, in relation to hate crime, could most effectively translate into practice.

Considerable professional contact with a diversity of general and 'specialist' offenders had created a strong impression that the thinking of Carl Rogers (1980), which inspired the concept of motivational interviewing, is fundamental to meaningful engagement and rehabilitation. Motivational interviewing adheres to four principles: 'express empathy', 'develop discrepancy' (by creating cognitive dissonance), 'support self-efficacy', and finally 'roll with resistance', which entails avoiding direct disagreement and confrontation in dialogue with the client (Miller and Rollnick, 2002). I was interested in the potential for developing a hate crime intervention that had these four edicts at its heart.

I was conscious that a Rogerian thread – 'physician heal thyself' – ran perceptibly through the OTO programme, with its emphasis upon enabling the participant to think and behave in a more purposeful and positive way. To gauge the potential utility of this approach with hate crime perpetrators, I turned to research that sheds light on their characteristics, which related at that time mainly to 'racially motivated offending'. A consistent theme that emerged, which will be discussed in more depth below, was the extent to which perpetrators – often beneath an outward display of mendacity and bravado – feel adrift from the society of which they are part and lack a sense of place and purpose.

Of course, such factors can be traced in the disposition of many 'general offenders' too, which leant credence to adapting OTO, originally developed for general offenders, to suit this type of perpetrator. In that many members of the non-offending public have entrenched prejudicial attitudes (Cunneen et al., 1997; Sibbitt, 1997; Tomsen, 2009; Hall, 2005; Levin, 2007) there must, it seems, be other things that determine the 'likelihood' to commit a hate crime. Conversely, the regularity with which individuals from minority communities experience hate crime suggests that there are many potential perpetrators and that such offending is not especially specialist.

Further studies have added to our body of knowledge and contributed to the emergence of the Think Again intervention, which I developed in 2010/11. West Yorkshire Probation Trust Research Unit is currently evaluating its effectiveness. In the short term, high levels of compliance and engagement have been achieved; with anecdotal feedback from participants suggesting it has had a positive impact on their thinking and behaviour.

Think Again is faithful to the ethos of the adapted OTO programme but is delivered as part of standard reporting and is more modest in length. As with OTO, it steadfastly avoids straying into a style that might be experienced as educative and paternalistic, a risk inherent to interventions that provide arguably irrelevant factual information intended to 'myth-bust' earlier views.

Instead, within Think Again, the participant is empowered to consider the reliability of *any* information that we, as human beings, absorb as fact. This would include, by association but not direct reference, the beliefs that have narrated their offending. In this way, the 'development of discrepancy' (one of the four Motivational Interviewing principles) occurs in the form of an *internal* dialogue, born of a seed the practitioner has planted. This ongoing conversation with self is inevitably more powerful and enduring than dialogue with a practitioner trying – however skilfully – to dislodge beliefs in which the perpetrator is invested.

Research undertaken by Ray et al. (2002) would seem to underpin the benefits of this subtle but logical technique. It suggests that the probable personal history of the offender is one in which they have grown used to blame, lack of respect and condemnation (contributing to and shaping a sense of personal 'shame'). The researchers caution that further treatment of this kind could increase the negative emotions that have led the perpetrator to offend, with obvious consequences. This is an important pointer for practice, in that any approach *experienced* by the perpetrator as blaming or condemnatory, even when we do not intend it to be, is likely to be ineffective.

The above study (Ray et al., 2002) indicated that perpetrators of racist offences typified the client group with whom the Probation Service engages. Most had general offending histories. They lived in run down areas in which there was an almost exclusively White population and widespread racist attitudes. Many used violence quite a lot (in various contexts) as a perceived means of resolving difficult situations.

The interviewees saw themselves as lacking in identity, overlooked and having no strong community tie compared with their victims. The researchers became aware of an important distinction between the interviewees' cognitive denial of racist beliefs (which happened frequently) and the underlying feelings about self that may drive the offence. They refer to the work of Scheff and Retzinger (1991) who explore the concept of *shame* as an emotional state that leads to powerlessness and a feeling of abandonment. The state of shame potentially translates into irrational, harmful behaviours towards other individuals seen as contributing to the unhappy situation one is in.

Beck (2000) describes the way in which we can all tend to see ourselves as part of a particular group (the 'in' group) and distinguish between that group and another to which we don't feel we belong (the 'out' group). A hate crime perpetrator may have a heightened sense of themselves as being part of the 'in' group, members of which find common ground in hostility towards the dehumanized 'out' group. Hate crime can emerge from this context, because perpetrators are not held back from offending by thoughts of how the victim will be affected.

Extending Beck's argument, we might then think that a fundamental part of addressing hate crime would be trying to get the perpetrator to understand how it feels to be the victim of this type of offence. Of course this plays a part in our interventions with many types of offender and does to some extent feature in 'Think Again'. A meta analysis by Jolliffe and Farrington (2003) casts doubt, however, on how much increasing victim empathy helps to reduce offending, not just with hate crime perpetrators but in general. On this basis it does not form a cornerstone of the approach. Instead, what we can learn from Beck is that increasing the perpetrator's awareness of other types of group to which they could, or may already, belong and contribute, dilutes their association with the former 'in' group and hence their dehumanization of the 'out' group as perceived.

Insufficient research has as yet taken place into the motivations of perpetrators who target other protected characteristics, such as sexual orientation, disability or transgender. Writing about homophobic attitudes (but not specifically about homophobic hate crime) Herek et al. (1999) outline three types:

1 'Experiential' – that is interpreting social realities on the basis of earlier contact with gay people.
2 'Defensive' – which entails imposing one's own discontent and disorientation onto someone seen as 'other'; to bolster self esteem and distract from inner troubles.
3 'Symbolic' – in which prejudice finds expression through aligning oneself with social constructs hostile to the 'out' group, thereby gaining a gratifying sense of solidarity with others, who also seek to exclude.

Such suggested dispositions seem very similar to some of the characteristics of racially motivated offenders and would indicate that a holistic and motivational approach, as advanced in Think Again, may have a beneficial impact.

In respect of disability hate crime, Quarmby (2008) suggests that it is based on contempt. Her report considers whether the perceived limitations of the victim serve to 'dehumanize' them in the perpetrator's mind. Conceivably, the victim's obvious adversity may be an irritating and upsetting reminder to the perpetrator of their own vulnerabilities, which is then projected onto the victim through gestures of contempt. Quarmby (2008) highlights that, especially with more serious hate crimes, disabled people often know the perpetrator. The study cautions us not to see the disabled victim's perceived vulnerability as being the cause of the offence, highlighting that many offences go beyond taking advantage of the victim's limitations and are overtly cruel and tormenting. It suggests that to associate causation with a victim's vulnerability risks 'normalising' the targeting of disabled people.

Whittle et al. (2007) note that a catalyst for harassment of trans individuals is the point of transition towards a changed gender. That is to say their trans status becomes more obvious as they start presenting in the gender they are acquiring. As yet, there is limited information about the pathology of offenders who target trans people.

Even though there is not much information about the typology of 'other' types of hate crime perpetrator, because research on racially motivated offending indicates attitude to self could be more relevant than their view of the specific group/s against which they have offended, it is reasonable to suggest that hate crime perpetrators – whomever they target – may have similar characteristics and risk factors, that lead them to offend. As such Think Again has potential utility with any type of hate crime perpetrator.

Turning to external risk factors, how might the perpetrator's allegiance to a particular group, such as a far-right group, influence our practice and assessment of risk? Practitioners may understandably assess that active participation in the activities of such a party is directly relevant to the risk of re-offending, hence a legitimate area to challenge in supervision, or weave into the delivery of Think Again. It is interesting to consider how fruitful or otherwise this may be.

In terms of what draws individuals into such parties, Billig and Cochrane (1990) suggest that membership increases during harsh socio-economic times when simple understandings of how to resolve financial hardship, for instance reducing immigration, are seen as attractive solutions. Exploring this possibility, Green et al. (2001) and Brimicombe et al. (2001) did not find a clear relationship between economic deprivation and increased hate crime. Iganski (2008), however, identified that amongst indigenous White communities, socio-economic deprivation *when combined* with the arrival of unfamiliar newcomers, creates a volatile mix that increases racist and religious hate crime.

Whilst membership of an extreme, if legal, political party does not inevitably lead to hate crime, the reinforcement of racist attitudes may increase the risk of susceptible individuals expressing their views through offending (Billig and Cochrane, 1990; Perry, 2003; Hewitt, 2005). On the face of it, this might suggest that in order to rehabilitate the perpetrator, their allegiance to the political party must be addressed. Such a stance, however, risks both entrenching the service user and sweeping aside the possibility that the trigger for the actual offending may – at least in part – be environmental not ideological.

Cognitive behavioural theory invites us to consider the significance of the immediate, often frenetic physical environment upon actions, particularly when someone has limited capacity to manage their responses in the heat of the moment (a feature of many types of offending behaviour). Within this framework, the ethos within Think Again would point the practitioner towards improving the individual's self-management, rather than directly questioning the wisdom of, or moral justification for, their association with the party. If they do participate in the party's legal, if provocative, activities, such as protest marches, and there is no requirement preventing them from doing so, the aim would be for them to resist the impact of that incendiary external environment so that taking part does not ignite into the commission of hate crime. Of course, their self-management may then extend into electing for themselves not to participate in potentially high-risk behaviour.

At the same time, within Think Again, the practitioner collaborates with the perpetrator to mediate their underlying sense of alienation, a likely factor behind their allegiance to the party in question. This dual stance adheres directly to the edicts of rolling with resistance (by not presuming to directly question their identification with the party); and supporting self-efficacy, in that they are being encouraged to make more considered choices but in the short term better manage their reactions, even when the pull of the immediate environment is strong. Encouraging them towards a greater sense of their own place and potential will simultaneously loosen the grip that allegiance to the party has on their emotions and intellect.

Concurring with this approach, Bragg (2006), the folk singer and political activist, notes what he describes as deliberate exploitation of the fears of White working class communities by far-right parties. Drawing on impressions gained from the part of outer London in which he grew up, Bragg highlights that patriotism has been distorted to lend respectability to what are in reality inflammatory racist beliefs. He suggests that people affected by socio-economic uncertainty and a changing demographic are drawn to such organizations, in order to experience a sense of participation and connection.

Bragg's considered observation would suggest that a valid focus for our energies, in contact with the perpetrator, is enabling them to develop alternative, viable paths to achieving a sense of belonging and shared purpose. In this way, they may eventually question *for themselves* their allegiance to the party in question and opt to take another route, without any overt challenge from the practitioner.

Resonating with Bragg's observations, Osler and Starkey (2000) found that young people who invest in racist attitudes often feel adrift from wider society and do not see themselves as having a stake or foothold in it. Osler and Starkey's analysis suggests that if perpetrators can recognize their potential to contribute to situations in a positive way it will benefit their view of self, with favourable implications for a reduced risk of re-offending. 'Think Again' includes, therefore, content intended to increase the participant's sense of being a member of a society in which they can play a useful part.

In a study conducted in four London boroughs, Sibbitt (1997) concluded that racially motivated perpetrators were of all ages, both male and female, and often acted in groups. Perpetrators' racist views were actually typical of some of the opinions held within their communities. Behaving in a racist way seemed to distract the perpetrator and their 'audience' from deep-seated problems that they did not know how to deal with, such as a limited sense of their own identity, unease about the future, or health problems. Thinking about what this means for rehabilitation, it would suggest that developing problem-solving abilities, which enhance the perpetrator's potential to manage everyday situations more effectively, reduces the impulse to offend. Such an approach is supported by a literature review on racially motivated offenders commissioned by the Home Office (Hollins and Palmer, 2001). The review concluded that many 'risk factors' amenable to change, such as limited emotional control and ineffective problem solving, are similar to those of general offenders.

Internal risk factors associated with racially motivated offending (i.e. White perpetrator) were defined in 2001 by a sub group of the Home Office Accreditation Panel, comprising practitioners and academics with specialist knowledge of the topic. The identified factors gave me a helpful starting point in understanding how to work with this type of offender. They are reproduced below:

- *Poor and problematic moral reasoning* – the process of dehumanization as part of the justification for offending. This is addressed in Think Again via moral dilemmas and more subtly through input on citizenship.
- *Cognitive deficits* – limited ability to distinguish between fact and myth, offenders showing rigid thinking. This is responded to via a simple exercise at an early stage of Think Again and cast back throughout, to *indirectly* reinforce the point.
- *Distorted victim perspective* – perpetrators may have limited victim empathy, the more so perhaps when wanting to avoid the stigma of having committed a hate crime. They may struggle to empathise with the victim, whom they have consigned in their mind to the 'out' group. Because overt consideration of the victim perspective could create resistance, this is developed subtly and indirectly at various stages in the intervention, as well as featuring explicitly in the offence analysis and via the 'Who am I?' exercise. This exercise provides a few facts about a fictional character, which might create a particular

impression. That impression is then gently displaced by the additional information provided. The exercise is delivered as a collaborative learning journey for both participant and practitioner. It is a nuanced way of developing discrepancy in the participant's mind; directly addressing the risky human tendency to fill with assumption gaps left by incomplete information, without labouring its particular relevance to their offending history.

- *Predisposition to violence as a means of conflict resolution* – many hate crimes feature violence, which may be the habitual way that the perpetrator responds to tense or frustrating situations, in order to 'resolve' them. Hence Think Again creates opportunities to practise the skills of assertion, negotiation and self-management.
- *Conflict of an individual's cultural identity* – the perpetrator may have a limited sense of their own ethnic heritage and the reality of what that means in contemporary society, which can generate resentment when faced with overt expressions of cultural identity within minority ethnic groups (such as symbols, dress or festivals). This is addressed through specific exercises intended to generate a more positive and coherent sense of their own background and identity.
- *A perception of territorial invasion* – a sense of other cultures present within society in some way undermining their own. In response to this identified risk factor, Think Again encourages the participant to recognize their personal strengths and potential so that their possessive loyalty to a particular geographical area, as a means of shoring up their own identity, starts to reduce.
- *A distorted worldview* – the sub group considered that some hate crime perpetrators can be prone to accept myths and distortions as fact, which they then act on. Instead of 'correcting' or 'educating' them, the practitioner conducts a series of exercises that enable the participant to make more considered judgements, across the board, as to the reliability of what they see and hear.
- *Individuals draw on the social support in perpetrator communities* – within 'perpetrator communities' beliefs are reinforced by the idea of a hierarchy of social/ethnic groups and a sense of belonging to an 'in' group. This risk factor is particularly focused upon towards the end of the intervention once a positive working relationship has been established.
- *The erosion of traditional characteristics associated with gender identity* – This is addressed implicitly by encouraging the participant towards a more positive sense of their individual strengths and potential.

With consideration, the material can be adapted and drawn from to suit work with perpetrators from minority groups, or to address inter-ethnic offending. When the material is used in this way some important factors need to be borne in mind. Where the perpetrator is a member of a minority community, their offending does not reflect the same historic societal status that may (unconsciously or otherwise) inform that of perpetrators from the majority community. Indeed, their offending may to some extent be an expression of frustration at the discrimination that they have experienced in all sorts of situations.

Practitioners are encouraged to realize that the impact of hate crime upon a member of the majority community, whilst harmful, is inevitably different to when you are part of a minority and may have had to weather such experiences throughout your life. Of course, that is not to say that the perpetrator's actions should be ignored or condoned, or that elements of prejudice have not influenced their offending. Their offending can potentially be reduced by way of the same broad approach. They too may well have limited problem-solving skills and could benefit from Think Again's emphasis upon empowerment and upon recognizing their strengths and potential. An approach that helps them to plan better and improve their emotional control could also be useful to them. The practitioner needs, however, to work sensitively with the context from which the offending originated. The participant may gain from a focus on self-management and on thinking about cause and effect, in view of the particular pressures to which they are subject, as a member of a minority community.

More generally, in terms of suitability for Think Again, all participants would be expected to show some motivation to address their offending through taking part in the intervention. This does not mean that they have to recognize or 'admit' that their actions in committing the offence/s were discriminatory.

As has been established, a defining characteristic of many perpetrators appears to be the inversion or deflection of self-doubt by investing in a shared ideology, which then provides a framework for offending. This description brings to mind the possible typology of some individuals drawn into serious gang- and group-related offending. Exploring the potential common ground between these two offender typologies, my attention was drawn to the likely relevance of strain theory to both hate crime and gang-related offending. Strain theory maintains that structural (socio-economic) pressures and/or personal strain created, by striving to maintain a foothold against the odds, can create a context in which crime occurs; either as an expression of that strain or a means to an end (Agnew, 2002).

Signalling theory likewise points to a theoretical resonance between hate crime perpetration and offending by members of criminal gangs and groups. Symbols of hate, like tattoos and graffiti, have obvious parallels with the tags and insignia used by gang members to show solidarity with each other as members of the 'in' group, whilst simultaneously signalling hostility and threat to the 'out' group.

Another common feature of both gang-related offending and hate crime perpetration is 'neutralization' via the conscious and explicit 'appeal to higher loyalties', such as allegiance to a group and its associated ideology, to justify and rationalize offending (Sykes and Matza, 1954). As established codes of conduct and moral boundaries are suspended, the risk of serious offending, made possible by appealing to higher loyalties, can increase.

The ideas outlined above provide a glimpse into the benefits of thinking about hate crime perpetration in the wider context of broader explanations for offending, in order to increase our understanding of how best to intervene with this type of offender. In summary, research would suggest that:

- The attitudes and beliefs of the perpetrator can't in themselves explain why a hate crime has been committed, in that many members of the public hold similar views but do not offend. An approach that focuses primarily on attitudes and beliefs would seem, therefore, to be the wrong road to go down in our work with hate crime perpetrators. Interventions that depend on this type of material but that are nonetheless delivered in a motivational and encouraging way may have some impact on the risk of re-offending. It is possible, however, that their positive outcomes owe more to the therapeutic style with which they are delivered than their actual content.
- Offenders who commit hate crime commonly lack a strong, positive sense of their own potential, place and purpose, which may be an underlying driver for their offending and a valid focus therefore in their rehabilitation.
- Increasing victim empathy may not be key to reduced re-offending.
- Hate crime perpetrators have much in common with general offenders and often have general offending histories.
- An approach *experienced* as in any way critical or blaming could intensify the negative feelings about self that have contributed to offending, with obvious consequences.

For these reasons it can be suggested that an intervention that is rounded, problem solving in content, and motivational in style, is likely to be more effective than one that attends directly to discriminatory attitudes and their origins.

Above all the tone to be struck is one of collaboration, with both parties engaged as a partnership in the quest to reduce the risk of further offending. Achieving this outcome does not mean the participant has to 'admit' to being, for example, homophobic or racist. In fact this is unnecessary and potentially counterproductive. The aim of Think Again, informed by evidence, is that the participants position themselves in life to make more clear headed and empathic choices, which will maximize the potential for them to avoid behaving in this way again.

References

Agnew, R. (2002) Foundation for a general strain theory of crime and delinquency. *Criminology* 30, 47.

Beck, A. (2000) *Prisoners of Hate: The Cognitive Basis of Anger Hostility and Violence*. London, Harper Collins.

Billig, M. and Cochrane, R. (1990) Values of political extremists and potential extremists: a discriminant analysis. *European Journal of Social Psychology* 9 (2), 205–222.

Bragg, B. (2006) *The Progressive Patriot*. Bantam Press.

Brimicombe, A.J., Ralphs, M.P., Sampson, A. and Tsui, H.Y. (2001) An Analysis of the Role of Neighbourhood Ethnic Composition in the Geographical Distribution of Racially Motivated Incidents. *British Journal of Criminology* 41, 293–308.

Cunneen, C., Fraser, D. and Tomsen, S. (eds) (1997) *Faces of Hate: Hate Crime in Australia*. Sydney, Hawkins Press.

Densley, J. (2013) *How Gangs Work*. Palgrave Macmillan.

Green, D., McFalls, L. and Smith, J. (2001) Hate Crime an Emergent Research Agenda. In Perry, B. (ed.). *Hate and Bias Crime: A Reader*. New York, Routledge.

Hall, N. (2005) *Hate Crime*. Abingdon, Routledge.

Herek, G.M., Gillis, J.R. and Cogan, J.C. (1999) Psychological sequelae of hate crime victimization amongst lesbian gay and bisexual adults: Prevalence, psychological correlates, and methodological issues. *Journal of Interpersonal Violence* 12, 195–215.

Hewitt, R. (2005) *White Backlash and the Politics of Multiculturalism*. Cambridge, Cambridge University Press.

Hollins, C. and Palmer, E. (2001) *Literature review on work by the Probation Service with racially motivated offenders*. London, National Probation Service (unpublished).

Iganski, P. (2008) *Hate Crime and the City*. Bristol, The Policy Press.

Jolliffe, D. and Farrington, D.P. (2003) Empathy and offending: a systematic review and meta analysis. *Aggression and Violent Behaviour* 9 (5), 441–476.

Levin, J. (2007) *The Violence of Hate* (2nd edition). London, Pearson.

Macpherson, Sir W. (1999) *The Stephen Lawrence Inquiry: Report of an Inquiry by Sir William Macpherson of Cluny*. London, The Stationery Office.

Miller, R. and Rollnick, S. (2002) *Motivational Interviewing: Preparing People for Change* (2nd edition). New York, Guilford Press.

Osler, A. and Starkey, H. (2000) Citizenship, Human Rights and Cultural Diversity. In Osler A. (ed.) *Citizenship and Democracy in Schools: Diversity Identity and Equality*. Stoke-on-Trent, Trentham.

Perry, B. (ed.) (2003) *Hate and Bias Crime: A Reader*. Abingdon, Routledge.

Priestley, P. (2001) *The One to One Cognitive Behavioural Offending Behaviour Programme*. London, National Probation Directorate.

Quarmby, K. (2008) *Getting Away with Murder*. London, Scope.

Ray, L., Smith, D. and Wastell, L. (2002) Shame Rage and Racist Violence. *The British Journal of Criminology* 44, 350–368.

Rogers, C. (1980) *A Way of Being*. Boston, Houghton Mifflin.

Scheff, T.J. and Retzinger, S.M. (1991) *Emotion and Violence: Shame and Rage in Destructive Conflicts*. Lexington, MA, Lexington Books.

Sibbitt, R. (1997) *The Perpetrators of Racist Violence and Harassment*. London, Home Office.
Sykes, G.M. and Matza, D. (1954) Techniques of Neutralization: A Theory of Delinquency. *American Sociological Review* 22 (6), 664–670.
Tomsen, S. (2009) *Violence Prejudice and Sexuality*. Abingdon, Routledge.
Whittle, S., Turner, L. and Al-Alami, M. (2007) *Engendered Penalties: Transgender and Transsexual People's Experience of Inequality and Discrimination*. A Research Project and Report Commissioned by the Equalities Review.

33
Repairing the harms of hate crime
A restorative justice approach

Mark Walters

Much has been written in this handbook about the causes and consequences of hate crime. As with most other forms of harmful and/or wrongful behaviour, the state's main response is to criminalise and punish offenders. There are sound reasons why legislatures should pursue such an approach to tackling hate-motivated offences. Legislation promotes an important symbolic message to society by denouncing the immorality of various forms of bigotry. Simultaneously, the law provides a message of support to minority groups that the state will protect them from targeted victimisation (Iganski, 1999). Within most jurisdictions, hate crime statutes have the effect of enhancing the punishments of hate offenders. These laws have been cogently grounded in retributive theories of punishment with the argument being that the increased seriousness of hate motivation must be met with a more severe penalty (Lawrence, 1999). However, critics have noted that penalty enhancements do little to actively repair the emotional, social and cultural damage caused by hate-motivated incidents (Shenk, 2001; Moran et al., 2004).

In recent years, governments have begun to pursue new approaches to justice that focus on restoring the harms caused by crime. The use of restorative justice for example, has been utilised by a growing number of jurisdictions searching for more effective measures of crime control (see Johnstone and Van Ness, 2007; Sullivan and Tifft, 2008). Yet despite the rapid expansion of restorative justice within many criminal justice systems, there remains a resistance towards its use for hate crime.[1] This is mainly due to the concern that restorative encounters will expose victims to further victimisation (Walters and Hoyle, 2010). There is also the risk that a restorative approach to hate crime will be perceived as a "soft option", thereby working in direct contrast to the harsher penalties which legislation provides.

This chapter does not deny there are important benefits to be gained from criminalising hate (see Walters, 2013). It does, however, question whether the Government's focus on enhancing the punishment of offenders is the most effective method of challenging the causes and consequences of hate crime. In particular, it is asserted that retributive responses to hate crime often fail to provide any meaningful or long-term resolution within cases involving ongoing and persistent targeted abuse. The main problem is that retributive justice is focused on finding individual responsibility for discrete criminal acts. Such an approach fails to consider the fact that isolated hate offences frequently form one part of a "process" of victimisation

(Bowling, 1998). Furthermore, research has also suggested that many incidents occur within broader inter-personal conflicts between local community members (Netto and Abazie, 2012; Walters and Hoyle, 2012). These are disputes that often involve multiple actors and a multitude of causal factors, including amongst other issues: noise pollution, alcohol and drug abuse, and mental health problems.

Such complex and ongoing conflicts are rarely resolved using traditional policing measures and/or retributive penalties, mainly because these measures overlook the situational contexts within which much hate abuse occurs. The failure of conventional justice measures to resolve most hate crimes means that victims continue to feel unsupported by the state and, in turn, remain subject to repeat victimisation (Smith et al., 2012).

This chapter examines whether restorative justice can help to repair the harms caused by hate crime. It begins by briefly summarising several commonly used restorative practices that have been examined empirically in the context of hate crime offending. The chapter then explores the key process variables within restorative practice that have been identified as aiding the recovery of hate victims. These include: "story-telling" (i.e. the vocalisation of harms); support provided by restorative facilitators; and assurances of desistance as provided by offenders. The final part of the chapter examines the potential limitations of restorative justice, including the secondary harms that "community" participants may expose hate victims to. It is here that the chapter outlines the measures that restorative practitioners must undertake in order to guard against the risks posed to victims of hate crime by restorative justice.

Introducing restorative justice for hate crime

There has been a proliferation of restorative-based practices within criminal justice systems throughout the world over the past 20 years (Johnstone and Van Ness, 2007). Such has been their popularity that legislatures have sought to introduce restorative interventions into the legal frameworks for criminal justice within countries such as Australia, Canada, the United States, the United Kingdom and New Zealand – to name just a few (McCold, 2008). Yet while the use of restorative justice has expanded rapidly, there remains no agreed definition of what it is (Gavrielides, 2007). This has not, of course, prevented theorists from expounding upon the values and principles central to restorative theory (see Johnstone and Van Ness, 2007). Perhaps the most commonly referenced definition found within the extant literature is that which is provided by Tony Marshall who states that:

> Restorative justice is a process whereby parties with a stake in a specific offence collectively resolve how to deal with the aftermath of the offence and its implications for the future.
>
> *(1999: 5)*

This process-led definition emphasises collective resolution through inclusive dialogue. However, it can be criticised for not explaining how "resolution" is best achieved or what values are central to realising such a goal. Others have therefore argued that restorative justice must be focused on achieving an outcome, such as material or emotional reparation (Walgrave, 2007). For instance, Howard Zehr argues that crime is a "wound in human relationships" which requires convalescence (Zehr, 1990: 181). As such, perpetrators of crime have "obligations to restore and repair" the damage that they cause. Like Marshall, Zehr argues that this is best achieved by bringing together the "stakeholders" in the offence – typically the victim, offender and other affected community members. Fundamental to this process is that the participants explore together the harms caused, before collectively determining how these harms should be repaired (Zehr and Mika, 1998).

Restorative practices

While there remains a degree of disparity amongst restorativists as to the definition of restorative justice, most, if not all, agree that it is a theory and/or practice of justice, which has at its heart the values of "encounter", "repair" and "transformation" (Johnstone and Van Ness, 2007). A number of practices have been introduced over the past 20 years that aim to embrace all, or at least some, of these values. Two of the most commonly used restorative practices are victim-offender mediation (VOM) and community mediation. Both VOM and community mediation programmes have been used as an alternative to retributive penalties or as an addition to them post sentence. Mediators can employ both direct and indirect (shuttle) meetings between (complainant) victims and (accused perpetrators) offenders, allowing each participant to discuss the causes and consequences of an offence/incident (supporting the value of "encounter").

Similar to mediation schemes are the newer Family Group Conferences (FGC) (first emerging within the youth justice system in New Zealand in 1989, see Maxwell and Morris, 1993). Though models vary to some extent, FGCs typically involve a face-to-face meeting between the victim, offender and their family members in a safe environment. FGCs are often used as part of the sentence that is handed down to (especially young) offenders (see Maxwell and Morris, 1993). Some conferences will also engage state agency workers such as police officers, social workers and/or housing officers.

The primary aims of all of these restorative practices are to encourage those who have harmed to take responsibility for their actions and to repay the damage they have caused directly to the victim (i.e. the concept of "repair") (Raye and Roberts, 2007). Facilitators of meetings typically start by asking the (accused) perpetrator to explain his or her actions. Victims are then provided with the space to articulate their experiences of victimisation. The process usually ends with an agreement between the stakeholders, outlining the undertakings agreed by the parties – including any reparations. These agreements provide a mechanism for change and as such signify a renewed relationship has been formed between stakeholders (thereby supporting "transformations").[2]

As restorative practices have proliferated, so too have empirical studies into its effectiveness as a justice process. Although a review of the growing body of research is outside the scope of this chapter, it is worth noting here that the vast majority of studies have found that a higher percentage of victims are satisfied with restorative interventions (particularly FGC) when compared to conventional justice processes (see *inter alia* Sherman and Strang, 2007). Participants are also more likely to perceive restorative justice to be procedurally fair, with facilitators being seen as more impartial than conventional justice practitioners (Shapland et al., 2007). Moreover, facilitators are more likely to provide adequate information about the victim's case in good time (Strang, 2002).

Research has also indicated that victims are provided with a greater opportunity to express how the incident has affected them when compared with other forms of criminal justice (Shapland et al., 2007). Of particular significance to this chapter is that a growing number of studies have suggested that restorative justice helps to alleviate the emotional traumas caused by crime, including reducing feelings of fear, anger and insecurity (see e.g. Strang, 2002).

Restorative justice for hate crime?

While numerous studies have examined the impact that restorative justice has on victims and offenders of crime in general, very few have explored its potential in cases involving hate-motivated offences. Several academics have, however, begun to highlight various case studies where restorative justice has been used for hate crime (see Umbreit et al., 2002; Gavrielides, 2007, 2012; Coates et al., 2013). These qualitative studies have suggested that identity and/or cultural barriers between participants (those causal to the commission of hate incidents) can be broken down via the dialogic processes typical of restorative interventions.

For instance, Robert Coates et al. provide several US-based case studies that illustrate the benefits of using a restorative approach to resolving different types of hate crime. In one case study in Oregon, the offender had made death threats to an Islamic cultural centre after the terrorist attacks of September 11th. In response, a mediation meeting was set up between the offender and the victim and his family. At the first meeting the offender showed some signs of contrition but at the end of the meeting both parties felt that more needed to be done to bridge the emotional gap that remained between them. The offender was angry that one of the participants had accused him of being an unfit parent, while the victim had been unhappy that the offender had made no eye contact with him. A second meeting was therefore arranged during which the offender opened up to the group, telling them of his experience of losing his child and being angry at the world. The offender apologised for his actions and as part of his reparation was asked to attend lectures on Islam, which he did. He also agreed to attend counselling for his anger issues and later became involved in helping at a juvenile detention centre. The pursuit of a dialogical process between the stakeholders of this offence clearly had the effect of humanising both parties. Ultimately, it was the bridging of empathic divides which allowed both sides to move on with their lives in a more positive and peaceful way (Coates et al., 2013).

Research by Mark Walters and Carolyn Hoyle has also highlighted the potential of restorative justice to repair the harms of hate. In their study of a Hate Crimes Project, run by a community mediation centre in south London, they found that the majority of victims who participated in the mediation process found it to be a positive experience (Walters and Hoyle, 2012). In total, 23 victims of hate-motivated incidents/crimes[3] were interviewed about their experiences of the mediation process, in addition the authors also observed 15 mediation meetings. Walters and Hoyle reported that 17 of the 23 interviewees who were interviewed stated that the mediation process directly contributed to an improvement in their emotional wellbeing. Fifteen interviewees went on to state that their feelings of anxiety were reduced directly after mediation while 14 also stated that their levels of anger towards the accused perpetrator decreased, and 13 reported that they were now less fearful of the offender. The authors also reported that in 11 of the 19 separate cases researched,[4] incidents ceased directly after mediation, while a further six cases were resolved after the mediator went on to engage other local agencies within the process, including: housing officers, police officers and social services (see further discussion on multi-agency partnerships in restorative justice in Walters, 2014a: Chapter 6).

The qualitative research into restorative justice for hate crime has also provided useful information on the process variables that are key to aiding the emotional recovery of victims and preventing the recurrence of victimisation. The most important of which include: having an opportunity to take part in the process; explaining to the other party how the incident had affected their life; witnessing the other party's comprehension of how the incident/conflict had affected them; receiving support from the mediator and, perhaps most importantly, obtaining assurances that their victimisation would stop (see Walters, 2012). It is to these key variables that we now turn.

"Story-telling"

The victimisation of those perceived as "different" is often marked by a process of marginalisation through which victims are exposed to a sense of heightened vulnerability (Chakraborti and Garland, 2012). The reorientation of victims of hate crime from a position of disempowerment to that of empowerment and self-worth must therefore begin by bringing victims centre stage in the justice process. The most powerful way of achieving this is to offer victims a voice. As restorative justice focuses on harm reparation, the victim is encouraged to focus his or her voice on expressing the harms that he or she has experienced (Zehr, 1990). Kay Pranis describes this process as "storytelling", she notes that:

> Having others listen to your story is a function of power in our culture. The more power you have, the more people will listen respectfully to your story. Consequently, listening to someone's story is a way of empowering them, of validating their intrinsic worth as a human being.
>
> *(2001: 7)*

Victims who share their experiences of prejudice are frequently rescued from the margins of society where they feel isolated and ignored. It is by stepping onto the restorative stage that they are able to find a place of greater personal security. The significance of hate crime victims forming their own narrative is exemplified by the value that is attached to talking about cultural or ethnic identity. A restorative practitioner (previously interviewed by the author) illustrates the importance of this process:

> They [the victim of anti-Semitic harassment and his father] went to great lengths telling me about their own family history and who of their own family members they'd lost during periods of time [referring to the Holocaust], and showing me memorabilia in the house, paintings and things which had been done by relatives who were no longer with us, very personal stuff. And probably half an hour or more spoke about those sorts of issues . . . Their identity was very, very important to them. And they went to lengths to tell me how proud they were to be Jewish. And they certainly want to maintain and hang on to that identity and those roots.[5]

It became patently clear to this practitioner that the victims' healing process needed to begin with them talking, not just about their experience of hate abuse, but vis-à-vis who they were and why their identity meant so much to them.

Practitioner support

The support that is offered by restorative practitioners is also an immense source of comfort to victims of hate crime. The very fact that facilitators are prepared to sit down and listen to the experiences of victims will often come as a great relief to them. This is especially the case where traditional methods of crime control have left victims feeling "let down" by the state; especially where police officers and anti-social behaviour units offer little by way of a resolution for the victim (see e.g. Pilkington case, "Police errors in 'bullying' deaths revealed at inquest" *The Guardian*, 18th September 2009). Hence, a key ingredient in the recovery of hate victims is, quite simply, that they are no longer being ignored by local agencies that are focused only on punishing offenders. However, it is not just that restorative practitioners are more inclined to listen than their retributive counterparts. They are also better placed to provide the type of listening that counts. This is because, unlike police officers and criminal prosecutors, restorative facilitators are concerned with *engaging* victims in a process that seeks to put them at the centre of the justice process. Pivotally, facilitators encourage victims to have a say about how *their* case should be resolved.

Promises of desistance

It has already been mentioned that a high proportion of hate victims are subjected to repeat victimisation (Smith et al., 2012). Of fundamental importance to any restorative process, therefore, is that it brings an end to the victim's ordeal. Restorative justice aims to reform the behaviours of offenders via a non-stigmatising process that encourages individuals to take responsibility for their actions. Much will depend on the emotional connections that are made between the participants during restorative encounters and the reparative work that the defendant agrees to undertake. It is outside the scope of this chapter to analyse, in detail, the potential for restorative justice to reform hate offenders (see Walters, 2014b). I note simply that a short-lived justice process will be of limited effect in rehabilitating hate offenders; especially where the prejudices that motivated the perpetrator may have been learned over many years.[6]

Still, for the purposes of this chapter it is worth highlighting that a goal of restorative justice should be to obtain an assurance from the offender that he will not repeat his or her harmful behaviours. As already noted earlier, Walters and Hoyle (2012) found that the community mediator observed in south London incorporated such assurances into the vast majority of signed agreements. This aspect of mediation was positively received by most victims who felt that it helped them to move on from their experiences of hate victimisation. We need only consider the fact that a high proportion of hate incidents are repeated over long periods of time to appreciate how essential these promises of desistance are to victims.[7]

The dangers of ineffective facilitation and the perils of "community" participation

The tentative findings from the author's previous studies and the various case studies provided by others (Gavrielides, 2007, 2012; Coates et al., 2013) offer promising data on the potential of restorative justice to repair the harms caused by hate. However, this is by no means to say that restorative justice will be a panacea for hate crime. There are various risks posed by bringing stakeholders of such incidents together via dialogical processes. A major concern raised by some critics of restorative justice is that the involvement of community participants from different cultural backgrounds holds the potential for some stakeholders to dominate the process (Cunneen, 2003). Adam Crawford (2002) notes that the aims and objectives of restorative justice can be undermined where the "community" in question is fragmented, hierarchical and unequal. Such a concern is particularly significant in cases of hate crime where victims are likely to belong to already stigmatised and marginalised identity groups (Perry, 2001). This has led some theorists to question whether the more informal processes found within restorative practices will provide opportunities for offenders to reassert their sense of superiority over those perceived as vulnerable (Stubbs, 2007).

The inclusion of the offender and his or her community supporters within restorative dialogue is further confounded by diverging cultural norms between the stakeholders (Smith, 2006). Participants may hold conflicting religious beliefs and possess disparate social and moral values (Smith, 2006; Crawford, 2002). The resulting "social distance" between stakeholders of hate crime can consequently mean that the participants of restorative justice will struggle to form empathic connections with each other. This means that individuals are less likely to empathise with each other's experiences and, in turn, the stereotypes, which divide victims and offenders, are less likely to be broken down (see Harris et al., 2004). If offenders fail to appreciate the consequences of their hate-motivated actions they will be less likely to offer contrition or provide genuine forms of reparation. Instead, victims' "stories" may only serve to provoke the offender and his or her supporters, resulting in further hostile responses towards the victim. In such circumstances, restorative justice risks becoming another mechanism through which victims of hate crime are further subjugated for being "different".

Protecting against re-victimisation

The perils of inclusive participation within restorative justice must remain at the forefront of practitioners' minds if restorative practices are to be successfully applied to hate crimes. Indeed, if there is a significant risk of exposing victims to further harm we must seriously contemplate whether it is worth using such an approach in the first place. We must therefore ask: can restorative justice ensure that it does not expose the vast majority of victims of hate-motivated crime to further harm? There is no cast iron guarantee that every victim will be protected from re-victimisation. Nevertheless, I can say that during my time observing restorative justice meetings and interviewing victims and practitioners involved in hate crime cases it was very rare for a victim to feel disadvantaged at any point during the process (see Walters, 2014a).

By far the most effective way of preventing domination or re-victimisation within meetings is to ensure that all participants are thoroughly prepared before the process (Coates et al., 2013: 168). This involves facilitators meeting with each of the participants before any direct dialogue takes place. Many facilitators will hold what is sometimes referred to as "mini conferences" where each of the stakeholders are asked to explain what has happened, how it has affected them and their reasons for their behaviour. It is during such meetings that practitioners can explore with the offender how deeply prejudices are felt, whether a demonstration of hostility during the commission of an offence is tangential to the main cause of crime and, finally, whether the offender is likely to repeat hostilities during direct communication. It will also be important for facilitators to ensure that all participants are engaged *voluntarily* and that the offender is prepared to take responsibility for his actions (even if the offender denies that he or she was motivated by prejudice) (see Walters, 2014a: Chapter 8).

Only once the facilitator has determined that both victim and offender understand the aims and objectives of restorative justice, and that they are willing to participate in direct communication, should a direct meeting be arranged. At this stage the facilitator must then outline ground rules for direct communication. This should entail facilitators explaining that all discussions are to be based around the principles of respect and equality. Facilitators may also wish to state that there should be no "finger pointing" and that abusive language will not be tolerated during dialogue. The goal is to provide each participant with an opportunity to talk and for others to listen. If these components of restorative justice are strictly adhered to, re-victimisation and domination during meetings rarely materialise.

Including appropriate supporters

I have already mentioned earlier that communities can be fragmented and hierarchical entities, within which cultures of prejudice are frequently cultivated (Sibbitt, 1997). A source of the offender's own bigotries may therefore be his own community; especially those closest to him or her, including family members and friends. Restorative practitioners who invite community members (supporters) into the dialogic process risk providing social support to the offender's prejudiced actions, rather than the social disapproval that restorative dialogue seeks to convey (Braithwaite, 1989). In these cases, facilitators must determine whether inclusion of the offender's supporters will aggravate the restorative process, if, for example, their input has the effect of neutralising the offender's wrongdoing. Such a situation will ultimately limit the sincerity of any reparation that is agreed between the parties and therefore will do little to alleviate the distress caused by hate crime.

Those who seek to neutralise the immorality of hate may be circumvented during the preparation stage of restorative justice. This is achieved where practitioners seek out alternative supporters who condemn rather than support the offender's prejudiced views. Supporters may include, for example, teachers, sports coaches, friends or other well-meaning relatives.[8] The inclusion of participants for whom the offender respects and/or cares for but who denounce the offender's actions, paves the way for behavioural transformation.

But what if these positive supporters do not exist, or are unavailable at the time of the meeting? In such circumstances the facilitator may have no other option but to allow the offender to involve his chosen "community of care". In fact, refusal to include these individuals runs the risk of undermining the offender's willingness to participate. There are other significant reasons why the offender's closest community supporters should be included in the restorative process. Most noteworthy is that restorative practices that fail to include the offender's closest kinship risk paying lip service to the "community" which is of greatest influence over him or her. In other words, if offenders are to be truly reintegrated back into a community where they are less likely to reoffend, facilitators may need to include those who are a source of the offenders' bigotry in the hope that both his or her prejudices, and those of his or her "community", are effectively challenged and modified.

The inclusion of potentially unconstructive community supporters within restorative dialogue must be counterbalanced during the preparation stage of restorative justice. This process works in exactly the same way as described above for offenders. If it becomes clear that the supporter will remain antagonistic, the facilitator may need to utilise indirect mediation. This will entail mediation meetings being conducted separately with the facilitator. The mediator then conveys information back and forth to the participants, while additionally seeking to resolve the conflict between the parties. In the end, one can only hope that both the victim's and offender's narratives will help to break down identity barriers. Within the many cases where this becomes possible, individuals can be humanised and damaged relationships can be transformed.

Conclusion

If restorative justice is to be used for hate crime it must be administered by practitioners who rigorously administer the key values of "encounter", "repair" and "transformation". The promise of restorative justice for hate crime lies mainly in its harm-repairing capabilities. Indeed, there are few other *criminal justice* practices that address effectively the complex dynamics of hate. Essentially, the dialogical processes central to restorative justice provide a platform upon which victims of hate crime can find a voice. It is this voice that helps individuals from stigmatised groups to move from positions of isolation and despair to that of empowerment and recovery. Moreover, the promises of desistance, which frequently make up part of restorative agreements, allow victims to return to their community without the constant fear of repeat victimisation. These are benefits that must not be seen as "soft options" but as directly addressing the causes and consequences of hate crime.

Yet while restorative practices can clearly *help* to repair harm and reform the behaviours of some offenders (at least in relation to the participating victim), practices must not be viewed as a panacea for hate crime. In particular, restorative justice (at least in its current forms) is not furnished with the means to challenge the broader socio-cultural inequalities causal to most hate-motivated crimes (Perry, 2001). In this sense, restorative practices must operate within the boundaries of society's hierarchical structures. These are structures that will continue to actively oppress those labelled as "different".

The unequal society we live in inevitably gives rise to power differentials between participants of restorative justice. This means that restorative facilitators must remain alive to the risk of domination and re-victimisation during dialogue. Nevertheless, these risks must not prevent us from striving to tackle more effectively the causes and consequences of hate crime. This chapter has suggested that the harms of hate crime can be partly alleviated through restorative dialogue, while the pitfalls of direct communication can be avoided where practitioners spend sufficient time preparing participants and outlining the rules of engagement. As such, there is much to be encouraged by from the use of restorative justice for hate crime. Looking ahead, common standards of practice must be introduced in order to ensure practices are consistently administered by fully trained practitioners. Fundamental to the use of restorative justice for hate crime will be the thorough preparation of *all* participants by facilitators who adhere strictly to the restorative values articulated throughout this chapter. Only then will the success stories highlighted here be replicated elsewhere.

Notes

1 During the author's doctoral study into restorative justice for hate crime a pilot project was launched by Brighton and Hove Police Service into the use of a police-led restorative cautioning scheme for hate crimes/incidents. Over an 18-month period (and after many communications from senior officers to encourage police constables to use the new disposal) there remained no cases referred to the scheme.
2 More recently, restorative justice has been adopted by police services that use restorative cautions or restorative disposals to deal with "low-level" offences (Hoyle, 2007; O'Mahony and Doak, 2013). These are often used as an alternative to traditional cautioning.
3 Hate incidents were defined as "Any incident, which may or may not constitute a criminal offence, which is perceived by the victim or any other person, as being motivated by prejudice or hate" (ACPO, 2005).
4 23 interviewees were interviewed regarding 19 separate cases of hate crime victimisation.
5 This case study is explored in greater detail in Walters (2014a).
6 Not to mention the personal and socio-economic problems which often underlie much of the perpetrator's offending behaviour (see Gadd, 2009).
7 As we saw above, in most cases hate incidents stopped after mediation.
8 In cases where there are more than one offender, facilitators should consider holding separate meetings.

Bibliography

Association of Chief Police Officers (ACPO) (2005), *Hate Crime: Delivering a Quality Service: Good Practice and Tactical Guidance*, London: Home Office.

Bowling, B. (1998), *Violent racism: victimization, policing, and social context*, Oxford: Oxford University Press.
Braithwaite, J. (1989), *Crime, Shame, and Reintegration*, Cambridge: Cambridge University Press.
Chakraborti, N. and Garland, J. (2012), "Reconceptualizing hate crime victimization through the lens of vulnerability and 'difference'", *Theoretical Criminology*, 16: 499–514.
Coates, R., Umbreit, M. and Vos, B. (2013), "Responding to hate crimes through restorative dialogue", in G. Johnstone (ed.), *A Restorative Justice Reader*, London: Routledge.
Crawford, A. (2002), "The state, community and Restorative Justice: heresy, nostalgia and butterfly collecting", in L. Walgrave (ed.), *Restorative Justice and the Law*, Cullompton: Willan.
Cunneen, C. (2003), "Critical Thinking about Restorative Justice", in E. McLaughlin, R. Fergusson, G. Hughes, and L. Westmarland (eds.) *Restorative Justice Critical Issues*, London: Sage.
Gadd, D. (2009), "Aggravating Racism and Elusive Motivation", *British Journal of Criminology*, 49(6): 755–771.
Gavrielides, T. (2007), *Restorative justice theory and practice: addressing the discrepancy*, New York: Criminal Justice Press.
Gavrielides, T. (2012), "Contextualising Restorative Justice for Hate Crime", *Journal of Interpersonal Violence*, 27(8): 3624–3643.
Harris, N., Walgrave, L. and Braithwaite, B. (2004), "Emotional dynamics in Restorative Justice", *Theoretical Criminology*, 8(2): 191–210.
Hoyle, C. (2007), "Policing and Restorative Justice", in G. Johnstone and D. Van Ness (eds), *Handbook of Restorative Justice*, Cullompton: Willan Publishing.
Iganski, P. (1999), "Why Make Hate a Crime?", *Critical Social Policy*, 19(3): 386–95.
Iganski, P. (2008), *Hate Crime and the City*, Bristol: The Policy Press.
Johnstone, G. and Van Ness, D. (2007), "The meaning of restorative justice", in G. Johnstone and D. Van Ness (eds), *Handbook of Restorative Justice*, Cullompton: Willan Publishing.
Lawrence, F. M. (1999), *Punishing hate: bias crimes under American law*, London: Harvard University Press
Marshall, T. F. (1999), *Restorative Justice: An Overview*. Home Office, London: Research Development and Statistics Directorate.
Maxwell, G. and Morris, A. (1993), *Family, Victims and Culture: Youth Justice in New Zealand*, Wellington: Institute of Criminology, Victoria University of Wellington and Social Policy Agency.
McCold, P. (2008), "The recent history of restorative justice: mediation, circles, and conferencing", in D. Sullivan and L. Tifft (eds), *Handbook of Restorative Justice: Global Perspective*, Abingdon: Routledge.
Moran, L., Skeggs, B. with Tyrer, P. and Corteen, K. (2004), *Sexuality and the Politics of Violence and Safety*, London: Routledge Taylor & Francis Group.
Netto, G. and Abazie, H. (2012), "Racial harassment in social housing: the case for moving beyond action against individual perpetrators", *Urban Studies*, 50(4): 1–17.
O'Mahony, D. and Doak, J. (2013), "Restorative Justice and Police-Led Cautioning", in G. Johnstone (ed.), *A Restorative Justice Reader*, Abingdon: Routledge.
Perry, B. (2001), *In the Name of Hate: Understanding Hate Crimes*, New York: Routledge.
Pranis, K. (2001), "Building Justice on a Foundation of Democracy, Caring and Mutual Responsibility", accessed at: www.doc.state.mn.us/rj/pdf/rjbuildingjustice.pdf
Raye, B. and Roberts, A. (2007), "Restorative processes", in G. Johnstone and D. Van Ness (eds), *Handbook of Restorative Justice*, Cullompton: Willan Publishing.
Shapland, J., Atkinson, A., Atkinson, H., Chapman, B., Dignan, J., Howes, M., Johnstone, J., Robinson G. and Sorsby, A. (2007), *Restorative justice: the views of victims and offenders: The third report from the evaluation of three schemes*, London: Ministry of Justice Research.
Shenk, A. H. (2001), "Victim-offender mediation: the road to repairing hate crime injustice", *Ohio State Journal on Dispute Resolution*, 17: 185–217.
Sherman, L. and Strang, H. (2007), *Restorative Justice: The Evidence*, London: The Smith Institute.
Sibbitt, R. (1997), *The perpetrators of racial harassment and racial violence*, Home Office Research Study 176, London: Home Office.
Smith, K. (2006), "Dissolving the Divide: Cross-Racial Communication in the Restorative Justice Process", *Dalhousie Journal of Legal Studies*, 15: 168–203.
Smith, K. (ed.), Lader, D., Hoare, J. and Lau, I. (2012), *Hate crime, cyber security and the experience of crime among children: Findings from the 2010/11 British Crime Survey: Supplementary Volume 3 to Crime in England and Wales 2010/11*, London: Home Office.

Strang, H. (2002), *Repair or Revenge: Victims and Restorative Justice*, Oxford: Oxford University Press.
Stubbs, J. (2007), "Beyond apology? Domestic violence and critical questions for restorative justice", *Criminology and Criminal Justice*, 7: 169–187.
Sullivan, D. and Tifft, L. (eds) (2008), *Handbook of Restorative Justice: A Global Perspective*, Abingdon: Routledge.
Umbreit, M., Coates, R. and Vos, B. (2002), *Community Peacemaking Project: Responding to Hate Crimes, Hate Incidents, Intolerance, and Violence Through Restorative Justice Dialogue*, Minnesota: Center for Restorative Justice.
Walgrave, L. (2007), "Integrating criminal justice and restorative justice", in G. Johnstone and D. Van Ness (eds), *Handbook of Restorative Justice*, Cullompton: Willan Publishing.
Walters, M. A. (2012), "Hate crime in the UK: promoting the values of dignity and respect for young victims through restorative justice", in T. Gavrielides (ed.), *Rights and restoration within youth justice*, Whitby, Ontario: de Sitter Publications.
Walters, M. A. (2013), "Conceptualizing 'Hostility' for Hate Crime Law: Minding 'the Minutiae' when Interpreting Section 28(1)(a) of the Crime and Disorder Act 1998", *Oxford Journal of Legal Studies*, doi: 10.1093/ojls/gqt021.
Walters, M. A. (2014a), *Hate Crime and Restorative Justice: Exploring Causes, Repairing Harms*, Oxford: Oxford University Press.
Walters, M. A. (2014b), "Restorative approaches to working with hate crime offenders", in N. Chakraborti and J. Garland, *Hate crime*. Bristol: The Policy Press.
Walters, M. A. and Hoyle, C. (2010), "Healing harms and engendering tolerance: The promise of restorative justice for hate crime", in N. Chakraborti (ed.), *Hate Crime: Concepts, policy, future directions*, Cullompton: Willan Publishing.
Walters, M. A. and Hoyle, C. (2012), "Exploring the Everyday World of Hate Victimisation through Community Mediation", *International Review of Victimology*, 18 (1): 7–24.
Zehr, H. (1990), *Changing lenses: a new focus for crime and justice*, Scottdale: Herald Press.
Zehr, H. and Mika, H. (1998), "Fundamental Concepts of Restorative Justice", *Contemporary Justice Review*, 1: 47–55.

34
Challenging sectarianism

Graham Spencer

> We are drawn towards a thing because we believe it is good. We end by being chained to it because it has become necessary.
>
> *Simone Weil*

It is the British painter Graham Sutherland who is associated with the expression 'the precarious tension of opposites' and it is an expression which, regardless of how he intended it, has particular relevance for understanding identity, since that too emerges through the precarious tension which Sutherland referred to, a tension where that what we think we are is enmeshed with what we think we are not and where one helps shape and define the other. Since opposites are invariably bound by a relationship of differences it is apparent that we need what we are not in order to make sense of what we are. Where, as part of this entanglement, we move within worlds that encourage us to connect (or regard) on the one hand and disconnect (or disregard) on the other.

The precarious tension is intensified in a conflict situation when, as relations deteriorate, a reluctance to dialogue corresponds with a preference for monologue. In the event of this decline in relations, talking (or shouting) takes over from listening and results in others being reduced to objects of displeasure and ridicule. It is in the context of this depersonalisation that hate and suspicion begin to flourish and where identity takes on increasing importance against the 'they' that 'we' want to exclude and isolate. Such a reaction also highlights how 'our' identity so often rests on a denial of that fact, or at least an overlooking of it, and how 'our' homogenisation of 'them' also creates a homogenisation of 'us', locking both into stereotypes of opposition.

The precarious tension of opposites is a useful conceptual starting point for thinking about sectarianism and how claims about identity invariably emphasise insecurity and security simultaneously. If sectarianism is a rigid adherence by individuals to particular groups and organisations, then the question arises as to how this rigidity operates and what it depends on. In that context the separation between 'us' and 'them' relies strongly on the idea that 'we' must collectively act to prevent 'they' from doing what 'we' do not like and to do this 'we' need to advocate fear which increases the desire for security and so conformity. This security is designed to address the fear, but also exaggerate feelings of insecurity. The others from who 'we' need protection are seen to be responsible for the insecurity 'we' feel, but this insecurity is also needed by 'us' to reaffirm the security we seek and so return us to who 'we' think 'we' are. The threat of losing identity is therefore essential for preserving identity since it serves as a reminder of who 'we' want to be and not be.

The construction of society, as Mary Douglas points out, is a product of narratives that emphasise 'external boundaries, margins and internal structure'. These narratives, Douglas argues, reinforce those boundaries, margins and internal structures in order to 'contain power to reward conformity and repulse attack' (Douglas, 2002: 141). Narratives are thus integral to building common perceptions of identity, but also integral for excluding those who do not share that identity, or who are opposed to it. The idealised or preferred notion of society is one which necessarily uses the external threats to its boundaries as a means for maintaining those boundaries and the ideological structures that they give form to. However, those boundaries are also porous and it is the possibility of permeation and transformation that makes internal forces a threat to identity, since internal forces are responsible for maintaining the boundaries and keeping others out. The internal lines of society are drawn from matters of morality where contestations about right and wrong are negotiated in relation to the boundaries within which they take place. In acute form, where the moral becomes subject to disputed meanings, tensions rise and this creates the ground for sectarianism. A dynamic of polarisations can emerge, as Douglas observed, that then stress narratives of purity and danger.

Perceptions of other social groups and communities being a threat to the identity of 'our' social groups and communities offers a means to re-assert order and structure, but in the process tends to reduce those others to less than human. They become little more than dirt and in being seen as such allow traditional boundaries to be restated as cleaner and better. As Douglas puts it when drawing on the relationship between dirt and cleanliness: 'In chasing dirt, in papering, decorating, tidying we are not governed by anxiety to escape disease, but are positively, re-ordering our environment, making it conform to an idea' and we do this in order to create a 'unity of experience' (ibid: 2). This 'tidying' or 'reordering' not only reflects a need for mimetic desire and behaviour (Girard, 2007) but also indicates the importance of guarding against dangerous beliefs and enemies that threaten to contaminate or erode. In the process this action also invariably involves exaggerated claims about perceived dangers so as to induce vigilance and resistance against polluting outside influences. As Douglas explains it, 'ideas about separating, purifying, demarcating and punishing transgressions have as their main function to impose system on an inherently untidy experience' and it 'is only by exaggerating the difference . . . that a semblance of order is created' (ibid: 4). Moreover, 'order implies restriction' whilst 'disorder by implication is unlimited', so signifying danger and threat (ibid: 95).

Transition in society is the most dangerous state for identity preservation since it 'is neither one state nor the next, it is "undefinable"' (ibid: 97). This interregnum is the period of uncertainty and instability which can lead to defensive actions that rather than easing the uncertainty, contribute to it. The past cannot be gone back to and the future is prevented by fears over where it might lead. In Gaston Bachelard's nuanced study *The Poetics of Space*, the tension of opposites is seen as a 'dialectic of division' creating an interpretive context of '*yes* and *no*, which decides everything' and in extreme cases leads to 'a basis of images that govern all thoughts of positive and negative' (Bachelard, 1994: 211). Drawing heavily on myths which emphasise difference, Bachelard notes how when articulated and presented as straightforward polarisations, differences can become locked into a 'simple geometrical opposition' which 'becomes tinged with agressivity' and in this environment those who symbolise and promote the oppositions become 'incapable of remaining calm' (ibid: 212). Here, Bachelard contends, the 'dialectics of *here* and *there* has been promoted to the ranks of absolutism' locking each community into a mirror reflection of the other in terms of imitative moves and gestures where the object of desire matters more when it is of interest to the other. In a conflictive situation, what one side wants becomes an object of attachment for the other side too and not because it is needed, but because the other side wants it. At this point scapegoating mechanisms are used to re-impose a sense of stability and equilibrium. Although the scapegoat is rarely the cause of a perceived problem, he/they offer the aggrieved community a common point of focus and so act to restore some sense of (temporary) balance as the scapegoat is isolated or removed. Interesting here too is how the scapegoat inculcates a desire for rejection and hatred rather than compassion and how that hatred binds the community into an image of coherence, shared interest and common purpose more than compassion, which lacks clarity and hinders equilibrium (Girard, 1986).

In such a climate tensions can manifest through what Bauman calls 'derivative fear', which he defines as 'the sentiment of being susceptible to danger; a feeling of insecurity and vulnerability' that itself 'even in the absence of a genuine threat' acquires a 'self-fulfilling prophecy' (Bauman, 2006: 3). Confirmation of one's fears requires some justification of the other's dangerous intent, thereby legitimising fear and the resultant actions that follow. However, what lurks within this imagination is a form of panic, where we become as much frightened of our own inability to confront and overcome the fear as we are of those we see as responsible for it and this can lead to a collapse in trust and confidence (Tester, 2013: 71). At such a moment those who are fearful become aware of their own fragility and it is the realisation of that fact that gives rise to panic and fear (ibid: 12). Our fear arises not just because we meet uncertainty, but because we have lost contact with the order that gives us security. The transition from fear to panic is a matter of shift from dream to nightmare. If our dreams are an attempt to bring order to our concerns and worries then the nightmare is the realisation that we cannot. That we are out of control and subject to forces beyond our own. As Tester puts this difference, 'Fear is the *possibility* that fragility might be revealed. Panic is the *certainty* fragility *has been* revealed. Fear suggests an existential condition of anticipation, whereas panic suggests a condition of crisis' (ibid: 12). Fear also exists as a response to death or annihilation, where the greater the fear the greater the call for the reassertion of security, order and identity. At a communal level fear stands as evidence (because others feel and believe it) of potential or perceived loss (and so death) and in a context of contested communal identities and political priorities this can easily lead to an escalation of hatred and violence.

In their study of sectarianism, Liechty and Clegg (2001) argue that destructive relationships invariably arise as a result of 'hardening the boundaries between groups' (other factors include ignoring, humiliating and dehumanising, seeking to dominate, and attacking or intimidating others (Liechty and Clegg, 2001: 103)) and what gives this hardening substance are actions, attitudes, beliefs and structures that are a fusion of political and religious outlooks. In that the demarcations of boundaries are a reflection of 'physical and symbolic markers of difference' (Diener and Hagen, 2012) it is apparent that such boundaries also function to reassert historical narratives that emphasise superiority, whilst those outside those boundaries necessarily lack such qualities and so exist in a state of inferiority. These boundaries, in their more volatile state, stress 'aggressive assertions of difference' (ibid: 17) of the kind discernible in dysfunctional family relationships, where oppositions arise as dynamics of defence and find meaning through what Ugazio calls 'family semantic polarities' (Ugazio, 2013).

Bound by a conflictive environment, antagonistic communities compete for a sense of belonging and insist that the other is an obstruction to that belonging set on its demise. Here we find some consistency with the kind of reaction that arises in the family environment, where the influence of parental demands provides a set of references which children seeking independence and individuality (those denied this space and raised in coercive environments appear to become 'enforced types', subject to depression and phobias) rebel against in order to bolster self-definition and identity formation. The family environment, like the social environment, enables and encourages individuals to see themselves as successes in relation to perceived failures, or failures in relation to perceived successes. Early experiences of identity in family life create a sense of belonging and good/bad differences that have emotional resonance that similarly exist in organisational settings where polarisations are used to form and sustain dominant meanings and relations (ibid: 66).

In its more extreme expression, rigid self-definition and identification hinders the possibility of 'closeness' with others and carves the world into what Ugazio calls 'permitted' and 'forbidden' stories (ibid: 93). But emotional distancing from others brings with it heightened anxieties that can create phobic reactions, raising the 'fear of being involved in a relationship because it creates the terror of falling into the grip of the other and no longer being able to escape from the entanglement created by the bond' (ibid: 95). This results in the inability to navigate safely or with self-assuredness through the emotions of fear/anxiety about the 'bad self', and mortification/annihilation scenarios that arise in the struggle to maintain what is seen as the 'good self'. And if both points of identification dominate, the worldview becomes subject to constant anger, loathing and distancing. Worse, the 'search for certainty' that shapes this self-image brings with it 'decisional paralysis', where the individual is unable to respond reflexively and effectively to change and the ever-present threat of oblivion or dissolution (ibid: 135). While fear and anxiety relate to concerns about keeping the 'bad self' at bay, mortification and annihilation relate to the inability to keep the 'good self' present and both are common attributes of obsessive organisations as well as individuals (ibid).

The role of the individual in the group, and so wider society, is important because love-hate prejudices, as Allport highlights, emerge from individual values, making social and communal judgements a matter of personal belonging (Allport, 1979: 36). It is from the personal that man acquires the propensity to 'form generalizations, concepts, categories, whose content represents an oversimplification of his world of experience' (ibid) and it is those features of his existence that incline him to associate with some and not others. Those he does associate with we might think of as the 'in-group' and those he prefers to disassociate with we might think of as the 'out-group'. With the in-group the tendency is to find meaning by thinking in terms of 'we', whilst the out-group exists as 'they' (ibid: 31).

Importantly, though, as Allport points out 'we' is often an '*achieved* status', in contrast to 'they' who retain an '*ascribed* status' (ibid: 33) and though both involve simplification in construction, the in-group uses positive stereotypes for this purpose while the out-group is contrived through negative stereotypes (the stereotype does not only exaggerate belief in relation to a particular categorisation, but, importantly, functions 'to justify our conduct in relation to that category' (ibid: 191)). Inside the in-group 'each individual tends to see in his in-group the precise pattern of security that he himself acquires' (ibid: 36) and so the in-group creates a feeling of intimacy and security that the out-group is denied. And it is through this depersonalisation that the in-group is able to maintain a perceived sense of superiority. This superiority ensures not only that one is drawn to the in-group, but that one is actively discouraged from engaging with the out-group unless such interaction confirms the sense of in-group superiority. In an intense form the in-group reflects a personal desire to aggressively assert control and superiority to the point of defining in-group values as little more than expressions of hatred of the out-group (ibid: 37). This is often reciprocated by the out-group, so locking both into a clash of loyalties that function through a lens of 'identical scope' (ibid: 44), effectively homogenising identities of each group in a reciprocal process of mutual hatreds.

In conflict situations polarised narratives, which give definition to identity, can be exaggerated to hysterical levels, evoking emotional reactions on a simplistic basis of pleasure or displeasure, and bringing immediate responses to scenarios which 'entertain no complications and perceive no shadings' (Young-Bruehl, 1996: 220). In such a climate 'institutionalised obsessionality' prevails and is encouraged (ibid: 341). Rituals are used to confirm the superiority/inferiority of status between in-groups and out-groups and prejudice is used to regulate relations and perceptions, while self-image is protected through the vigilance of paranoia (ibid: 343). Resorting to the absolutism of polarised positions, prejudice looks to 'obsessional ceremonials' which adhere to precise expression, serve to re-assert differences and warn against the contamination of outsiders (ibid: 347). The demonstration of paranoia, for Young-Bruehl, can be found in 'the means by which obsessionals displace out onto the world the battle they feel in themselves between their bad desires and their moral strictures, their wishes and their warning lights, their fantasies and their "Thou shalt not's"' (ibid: 349).

The fear and judgement that sustains such prejudice, to the extent that it takes on harmful and humiliating expression, requires the absence of empathy. Indeed, from this perspective, empathy is the 'danger within' in that it risks moving one towards, rather than away from, the other. As Nussbaum puts it on this issue 'In fear, a person's attention contracts, focusing intently on her own safety . . . In empathy the mind moves outward, occupying many different positions outside the self' (Nussbaum, 2012: 146).

In relation, we might argue that empathy is the counterforce to fear because it moves us towards what we are afraid of (which in this case is the other) and in so doing risks exposing the fallacy of that fear, exposing it as groundless and illusory. Perhaps one of the most challenging responses we can offer to those we are suspicious or fearful of is compromise (challenging because when we enter into an exchange that risks compromise we also risk finding out that our view of the other was misplaced or wrong), since compromise is an act of co-operation (Margalit, 2010: 37).

Even in a situation where one might enter into an exchange and come out more successful than before, there is still the recognition, as Margalit reminds us, that the legitimacy and force of the other's 'claim is recognised and acknowledged in human terms' (ibid: 41). And it is in the process of exchange, rather than the outcome, that compromise begins to have effect by enabling each to become alert to the human qualities of the other. During such an interaction the depersonalisation of the other that previously endured starts to collapse and with it 'they' are seen more in terms of their own concerns rather than only through the concerns of 'us'. In this way, the act of exchange, of co-operation, brings with it a 'transformative role in humanizing the enemy' (ibid: 42), moving the protagonists from a desire to degrade, humiliate or destroy to the recognition that identity fears and concerns are conjoined and need each other to survive.

However, compromise also brings problems since it flows in the opposite direction to the sectarian impulse which requires 'keeping your principled position uncompromised' and views co-operation as a diminution of security and identity (ibid: 148). It is this fear over perceived dilution that encourages resistance to compromise since the legitimacy of a particular cause may not only be undermined, but exposed as not worth belonging to (ibid: 151).

Compromise undermines the sectarian tendency because, while sectarianism emphasises the disadvantage of dialogue and the advantage of monologue, compromise does the opposite. In his excellent analysis of compromise, Margalit observes that sectarianism emerges most effectively when exaggerated claims are not made subject to critical self-evaluation and scrutiny. This requires manipulating the conditions that exist to 'inflate a minor disagreement over beliefs, or practices, until it becomes impossible for the sectarians and those not of their party to live together'. In this environment the sectarian 'behaves like a social amoeba: even when there is only one cell, it manages to split itself. In an adverse environment the sectarian-like amoeba tends to become a cyst, isolating itself totally from the outside world in order to stay alive' (ibid: 153). Isolating himself from those who exist outside of his own imagined community the sectarian maintains a heightened vigilance against 'mixing categories' and fears about such impurities keep boundaries in sharp relief. It is because of this that those within such a boundary tend to re-define themselves against the constant threat of any possible 'reaching out' or receptiveness to the concerns and anxieties of those outside (ibid: 157).

The physical manifestation of sectarian division can be seen in the existence of walls that split communities in conflict spaces and that stand not just as a reflection of imagination, but attempts to determine movement and behaviour. Walls (ironically also called 'peace walls' or 'peace lines'), as we can see in Northern Ireland and Israel, are an indication of enforced distance. These walls communicate that those who inhabit the space either side are unable or unwilling to contemplate living amongst those on the other side. These are people, the wall suggests, that not only don't want to live with their neighbours but who can't even imagine talking to them. The wall is a symbol of the inability to compromise, but more than that it signifies absence of any curiosity about the other. Instead it assumes a certainty about the other which reinforces the pointlessness of dialogue. The wall implies that the minds of those who live alongside it are made up (or have been made up for them) about others and that mixing with those others would risk a serious contamination to the 'clarity' of that which separates one side from the other.

Although the wall offers security it does not resolve the state of insecurity that led to its imposition. That problem remains and so the wall does not remove the basis of fear. It merely reminds those who live against it that fear is as certain and indisputable as the wall is. In its representation as a marker of conflict the wall defines not only geographical boundaries but imaginary ones too. It shapes the perceptions of those who live under its influence (Di Cintio, 2013: 213) and as such it becomes a focus for identity, 'a congregation point' (ibid: 216) and a place of concentrated tension.

It is also 'a "solution" that entrenches the problem' and which acts to 'prevent people from either community from ever seeing each other beyond ossified boundaries' (ibid). Such walls 'stand not just as architecture but archaeology. Fossilized artefacts of enduring division' (ibid: 256). The wall is a monument to the failure to dialogue and so a failure to act humanely. It stands to maintain division and although for those who live alongside it the wall may be an instant and understandable reminder of its ability to keep 'us' safe from 'them', it also ensures the continuation of this fear and the failure to overcome it. The wall therefore stands to keep fear in place and its unchanging nature is a prompt to the dangers of ignoring that fear.

The wall's presence in conflict zones and the barbed wire that invariably tops it symbolises a form of alienation, which becomes justified because 'the political costs do not exceed the advantages'. The costs in question arise from economic as well as political calculations where 'Productivity depends on the efficient management of flux, and the ordering of space must ensure the greatest possible control over circulation' whilst trying to allow for some freedom of movement (Razac, 2002: 112–113). The wall's limitation of space and its territorial delineations are a metaphor for the territorialisation of thought and the delineations of imagining others. Its inanimate presence is a prompt to the illusions of security found in the static as well as the inevitable insecurity that it seeks to contain. And historical continuity is reinforced by the wall's solidness. It is a symbol that the boundaries of identity are also solid and not malleable; that they are unchanged and unchanging. It does not suggest that anything has shifted and so offers some comfort that the past is protected and preserved. It keeps out those who are undesired and keeps in those who are desired. Another irony of this situation, as Razac observes in his fine analysis of barbed wire and segregated space, is that a 'wall or enclosure can be counterproductive to security because it attracts attention' and, as in the case of Northern Ireland and Israel, routinely becomes a focus for frustration and hostility; as proof of the inability of one community to live with the other.

The Northern Ireland example is a poignant one to examine how the tension between opposites has traditionally been used to bind identity and meaning. Within the unionist/loyalist/Protestant community there has been a tendency to try and preserve status and political standing through stressing the need to maintain Northern Ireland's status as part of the UK. Within the nationalist/republican/Catholic community (note how three categorisations on each side reflect a counterbalancing dynamic) there has been a tendency to argue that Northern Ireland's status should be subsumed into a single Ireland and so its UK status should be ended. This makes for a convenient narrative of polarisation, with fears deriving from mirror reflections of each other. A desire to hold on to something is different from a desire for be released from it in that while the former finds comfort in a static analysis, the latter finds comfort in a dynamic analysis. Such fears also operate as extensions of each other, so while for the former the future brings constant fear, for the latter the present is the constant fear and while one community is anxious about change happening, the other is anxious about change not happening. Here, the fear and anxiety of one community remains counterbalanced by the fear and anxiety of the other. This is surely the precarious tension of opposites in action since the image of the dynamic only takes on meaning in relation to the static and vice versa.

Reactions to symbols of identity can be seen in protests and demonstrations in Northern Ireland which began late 2012 and continued through the summer of 2013 (still unresolved at the time of writing) over restrictions on the British flag being flown and marches taking place and where, for those resisting this change such symbolism remains a matter of identity preservation. Here, there exists a counterbalancing force that argues a 'post-conflict' society requires moving away from narratives and symbols that are representative of the past and so domination and inequality. So, while one community seeks to preserve the past the other seeks to change it. Both communities (at least those who seem concerned the most) have one thing in common – the past – and both struggle to (re)construct it to complement identity interests. Moreover, as the issue becomes more important for one side so it takes on more importance for the other and this is because each side wants to be seen to have achieved, and be associated with a successful resolution of the problem. Unfortunately, this resolution is all too often associated with perceived humiliation which locks each side into increasing hostility and this is because as the issue becomes more important the stakes are raised in terms of success and failure. Ideally, the neutral observer would see this predicament as a failure on both sides, but the concept of neutrality has little value here.

One way of perhaps seeking some compromise on this issue would be to encourage both sides to think about what future they want instead of what past they want and to use 'all' rather than 'us' or 'them' to provide the context for engagement. Most parents wish their children 'better' lives – so what would a better life look like for all children and subsequent generations? To try to unlock the resistance of each side there is a need to think of a future which looks outside of the immediate 'us' and 'them' fixations of now, moving both sides into a frame of thinking which is inclusive rather than exclusive and imagining a future with a decent society, where humiliation is minimised and, where possible, eradicated (Margalit, 1996). This would require a context where differences become 'blended' and refocused on another point of mutual interest (the future), rather locked into intransigence by immediate and short-term focus on win or lose scenarios. Moving the contentions over current developments into a process and so a longitudinal context also starts to remove the pressures and threats of now and de-escalate the antagonisms.

Struggles between the desire to resist and release again conveniently provide us with polarised narratives. Communities have the potential to bind but also blind (Haidt, 2012) and are similarly subject to oscillations between these extremes. In a conflict situation fears become mutually re-enforcing and indeed reliant on each other. This makes it easier for one to blame the other and for that other to reciprocate such blame. The success of the peace process in Northern Ireland came not just from shifting the focus away from the divided communities to the British and Irish governments, but also because of a new trajectory created by the possibility of change. The importance of process in this transition is self-evidently central, but so was dialogue and using a range of avenues for communication that went around, over and through the conventional walls of division. The context for difference was shifted onto a terrain of mutual interest and it was on that terrain that compromise was forged. This new arena, in building communication and dialogue, created expectations of change and although this brought new fears it also brought about a common point of understanding. It was this common point of understanding that enabled the parties to get over fears to find agreement (even if it was an agreement to disagree (Powell, 2009: 108)).

This success was built on the momentum of process and in recent times it is process that has begun to stall, with the political representative of both communities in Northern Ireland now finding it harder to sell the image of progress. And once process starts to grind to a halt compromise becomes harder simply because defensive positions become less flexible. Once the static begins to gain hold then it is not surprising that communities tend to resort to traditional positions and re-assert the more uncompromising parts of identity. The problem of thinking not flexibly (which encourages pragmatism and compromise) but rigidly (which discourages pragmatism and compromise) can also be glimpsed in the difference of two key documents produced by the Northern Ireland Assembly on sharing and cohesion. The first *A Shared Future: Improving Relations in Northern Ireland* was published in March 2005 and the second *Programme For Cohesion, Sharing and Integration* was published in July 2010. *A Shared Future* was designed to emphasise reconciliation and in so doing implied a dynamic of convergence in addressing conflict issues. The tone was located firmly in a future-based context of movement and process. The document *Programme For Cohesion* provided a different focus, however, effectively retracting from the movement and pragmatism suggested in *A Shared Future*.

In an evaluation of the changed orientation from the 2005 document to the 2010 document the Institute for British Irish Studies based at University College Dublin concluded in its report '*From "A Shared Future" to "Cohesion, Sharing and Integration": An Analysis of Northern Ireland's Policy Framework Documents*' (October 2010) that while *A Shared Future* provided 'a vision of constant cultural change and dynamism' the *Programme for Cohesion* document framed cultures and identities 'as given and stable entities'. The suggestion is that envisaging change as movement outside boundaries had shifted to managing change inside boundaries. Though it would be unfair to claim this is a regressive strategy, one can see the potential problem this would be likely to create for inclusive thinking about the future.

The absence of the dynamic means the dominance of the static and when dealing with issues of conflict this risks locking the different parties, groups and communities into looking backwards rather than forwards. In that situation there is a considerable likelihood that they will resort to re-asserting principles rather than pragmatism and so conventional narratives about identity are likely to re-emerge. The static in this regard has dangers in that it provides fertile ground for the sectarian to operate and is unlikely to be of benefit to the moderate voice which is less likely to advocate clear lines and more likely to advocate ambiguous ones (necessary to include rather than exclude). The sectarian does not thrive in the world of ambiguity where fears are less pronounced and lines are blurred. As a peace process stalls there is an increased chance that the opposing sides will seek to blame each other for that stalling so augmenting problems and providing the more extreme voice with greater potency as the dangers of failure give credence to the 'we-told-you-so' commentary. And in such a climate fears increase, barriers to progress are erected and the narratives of polarisation are re-energised, all of which benefit the sectarian more than the libertarian.

Boundaries, walls and fears indicate the more fixed aspects of identity and the desire to preserve and protect what one is. Essential for this are rigid depictions of the 'other' who has little to offer 'us'. Though it would be ridiculous to claim that the sectarian mind inhabits all in conflict societies, it is nevertheless apparent that a sectarian minority can create fears and tensions which can hold that society back and in turn incite further violence and hatred. In this instance, it is movement, or process, that the sectarian fears most, at one level viewing this as contributing to the dissolution of identity, and, at another, presenting the 'other' as a distorted construct, who is revealed as such through engagement and dialogue. A new future-oriented context which moves beyond 'us' and 'them' and which facilitates expectations of compromise, precisely because identity is conceived in terms of a wider social context rather than a communal one, has the ability to dissolve the sectarian tendency. But it must continue to move and be ongoing and it must be inclusive. Constant process requires constant adaptation and at a social level emphasises a common point of reference for social and political change. Without it identity starts to become a static rather than developing experience, not only inhibiting constructive change, but also returning communities to the siege mentality and defensiveness from which the sectarian benefits most.

References

Allport, G.W. *The Nature of Prejudice* (New York: Basic Books, 1979).
Bachelard, G. *The Poetics of Space* (Boston, MA: Beacon Press, 1994 ed).
Bauman, Z. *Liquid Fear* (Cambridge: Polity Press, 2006).
Di Cintio, M. *Walls* (London: Union Books, 2013).
Diener, A. C. and Hagen, J. *Borders* (Oxford: Oxford University Press, 2012).
Douglas, M. *Purity and Danger* (London: Routledge, 2002 ed).
Girard, R. *The Scapegoat* (Baltimore: The Johns Hopkins University Press, 1986).
Girard, R. *Evolution and Conversion* (London: Continuum, 2007).
Haidt, J. *The Righteous Mind* (London: Penguin, 2012).
Liechty, J. and Clegg, C. *Moving Beyond Sectarianism* (Blackrock/Dublin: The Columba Press, 2001).
Margalit, A. *The Decent Society* (Cambridge, MA: Harvard University Press, 1996).
Margalit, A. *On Compromise* (Princeton: Princeton University Press, 2010).
Nussbaum, M. C. *The New Religious Intolerance* (Cambridge, MA: Harvard University Press, 2012).
Powell, J. *Great Hatred, Little Room* (London: The Bodley Head, 2009).
Razac, O. *Barbed Wire: A History* (London: Profile Books, 2002).
Tester, K. *Panic* (London: Routledge, 2013).
Ugazio, V. *Semantic Polarities and Psychopathologies in the Family* (London: Routledge, 2013).
Weil, S. *Gravity and Grace* (London: Routledge, 2002 edition).
Young-Bruehl, E. *The Anatomy of Prejudices* (Cambridge, MA: Harvard University Press, 1996).

35
Deradicalization

Daniel Köhler

'Deradicalization' as a concept denotes a process of individual or collective cognitive change from criminal, radical or extremist identities to a non-criminal or moderate psychological state. 'Deradicalization' has to be strongly differentiated from 'Disengagement', which denotes the mere behavioural role change (from offending to non-offending) while leaving the ideological or psychological aspect aside (cf. Bjørgo and Horgan, 2009; Dechesne, 2011; Horgan, 2009b; Horgan and Braddock, 2010; Noricks, 2009). Thus, individuals can be disengaged (i.e. not engaging criminal behaviour) while still being committed to a radical ideology. On the other hand, it may also happen that individuals remain part of a radical group and commit crimes without adhering to the cause. 'Deradicalization' and 'Disengagement' belong to the arsenal of interventional anti-terrorism and counter-extremism tools (in addition to repression and prevention tools). Still, the term remains, for the most part, inadequately defined or conceptualized (Horgan and Braddock, 2010), although it has a strong counterpart in criminological desistance research. Differentiating between primary and secondary desistance (Farrall and Maruna, 2004; Gadd, 2006; Maruna, 2001, 2004; Maruna et al., 2006), Maruna et al. describe "the movement from the behaviour of non-offending to the assumption of the role or identity of a 'changed person'" (Maruna et al., 2006: 274), which "involve[s] identifiable and measurable changes at the level of personal identity or the 'me' of the individual" (ibid.: 274; cf. Giordano et al., 2002; Lemert, 1951; Maruna, 2001; Shover, 1996).

Deradicalization research was predated by desistance research, which started in the late 1930s and gained speed in the early 1970s and 1980s (cf. Farrall and Maruna, 2004: 358). Deradicalization research quickly followed, with the first study in the field published in 1988 (Aho, 1988). Yet despite some recent increased interest in deradicalization, the field remains largely the realm of three researchers (Omar Ashour, John Horgan, Tore Bjørgo) and thus academically narrow (Ashour, 2007, 2008a, 2008b, 2009; Bjørgo, 2006, 2011; Bjørgo and Horgan, 2009; Horgan, 2006, 2008a, 2008b, 2009a, 2009b; Horgan and Braddock, 2010; Noricks, 2009), especially in comparison to the closely related field of radicalization research.

Individual motivations and influences to exit and deradicalize

Research on motivation and processes of individual deradicalization is still in its infancy compared to the amount of work done in the field of radicalization research, and has thus been rightly considered under-researched (cf. Dechesne, 2011; Horgan and Braddock, 2010). Nonetheless, some studies have been able to establish a basic understanding of the underlying motives and factors involved. The differentiation between certain categories of elements influencing the personal motivation to exit radical groups has proven useful, such as changes within the group, of individual preferences, or within external circumstances (Reinares, 2011), as well as the concept of 'push' and 'pull' factors (Aho, 1988; Bjørgo and Horgan, 2009).

In general, exiting a radical group or desisting from criminal offense involves an *individual decision* (cf. Bjørgo and Horgan, 2009; Fink and Haerne, 2008; Gadd, 2006; Laub and Sampson, 2001; Noricks, 2009), sometimes incorporating the *desire for change* and the *will to lead a 'normal' life* (Bjørgo and Horgan, 2009; Fink and Haerne, 2008; Horgan, 2006, 2009a, 2009b). A *personal traumatic experience*, which might create a 'cognitive opening', has been found to be an essential criteria/aspect by many researchers (e.g. Bjørgo and Horgan, 2009; Fink and Haerne, 2008; Garfinkel, 2007; Laub and Sampson, 2001; Noricks, 2009). Other important elements for deradicalization have been found to include (Bjørgo, 2009: 36–40): negative social sanctions, the loss of faith in the ideology and politics of the group or movement, the perception that 'things are going too far', the disillusionment with the inner workings and activities of the group, lost confidence, status and position within the group, and/or exhaustion ('push factors'). Age, career prospects and personal future, family and responsibilities are among the 'pull' factors to end a radical or criminal career (cf. Bjørgo, 2009; Bushway et al., 2001; Kazemian, 2007; Laub and Sampson, 2001; Warr, 1998).

In summary, external (e.g. events, changes in environment) and internal (e.g. burnout, ideological doubt) factors usually play together and influence such decisions, and may precede each other. However, the motivational and process-related aspects of deradicalization are still very much under-researched and the insights remain insufficient (cf. Dechesne, 2011; Farrall and Maruna, 2004; Horgan and Braddock, 2010; Kazemian, 2007; Laub and Sampson, 2001; Noricks, 2009).

As the deradicalization process is neither one-directional nor irreversible, several factors have found to be strong inhibitors of starting the process in the first place or stopping and reversing it at a later stage. Bjørgo (2009: 40–42), for instance, has highlighted the positive characteristics of the group, negative sanctions from the group, the loss of protection from former enemies, possible negative sanctions from the criminal justice system, the lack of an alternative 'place to go', and the fear that career prospects might be ruined as major factors. In general, insufficient support from the society (or a 'significant other') towards the individual wanting to leave radical groups significantly increases the risk of re-radicalization, higher reoffending rates, and sometimes an accelerated radicalization process (cf. e.g. Maruna et al., 2006).

Practical aspects of deradicalization work

Practical deradicalization work depends to a large degree on an efficient exchange between research and practitioners, although this happens rarely. Methods and cornerstones of deradicalization work developed from 'the bottom up', during practical drop-out assistance, should ideally meet indicated factors of the deradicalization process found by academic studies. The combination of research, analysis and practical work not only provides the basis for evaluation of existing practical methods and programs but also the necessary framework for future development and adaptation of deradicalization techniques, since radical movements and radicalization processes are hardly a monolithic phenomenon and themselves adapt to societal circumstances. This is why several widely and academically accepted cornerstones of deradicalization work (or the promotion of secondary desistance) need to be included as the most basic knowledge for practitioners and academics alike as an initial point for further discussion. Most of the factors stem from desistance research but apply to deradicalization of extremists as well.

One of the first and most important characteristics of deradicalization is that the term describes a comparatively long and complex *process* (cf. Bjørgo, 2009; Bushway et al., 2001; Ebaugh, 1988: 181; Farrall and Maruna, 2004; Gadd, 2006; Horgan, 2008a, 2009a, 2009b; Kazemian, 2007; Laub and Sampson, 2001; Maruna, 2004; Maruna et al., 2006; Noricks, 2009; Warr, 1998), which means that deradicalization is neither a singular moment, nor a linear evolution – it can be *disturbed*, *reversed* (cf. Laub and Sampson, 2001: 12), *reaffirmed*, *slowed down* or *re-initiated* through events and other external factors (cf. Farrall, 2002: 212; Gadd, 2006: 180; Maruna, 2001: 26). This means that deradicalization programs have to be *long-term oriented* and *lasting*.

While in criminology the time span of absence from criminal behaviour for an individual to be counted as 'desisting' ranges between six and 24 months (Laub and Sampson, 2001: 9), ideological deradicalization might take significantly longer. The average duration of individual cases at EXIT-Germany, for example, is between three and four years. This finding directly determines the essential need and role of the 'significant other' – a third party involved as assistant during the deradicalization process (cf. Demant et al., 2008; Gadd, 2006; Garfinkel, 2007; Maruna et al., 2006) – in which the concerned individual is an *active and equal participant*, rather than a 'patient' or 'client' (cf. Laub and Sampson, 2001: 50; Maruna et al., 2006: 278). Without external help, unassisted deradicalization might lead to re-radicalization into similar or different stigmatized and radical groups, sometimes even exceeding the previous radicalism (cf. Braithwaite, 1989; Gadd, 2006: 196; Maruna et al., 2006: 273).

Successful deradicalization is often associated with an *effective de-labelling process* for the society to be able to accept the former extremist and offender as a 'normal' part (Maruna et al., 2006), involving *recognized external experts without a previous positive or negative relationship* to the individual seeking help, which confers credibility to the individual role and belief change (cf. Ebaugh, 1988: 184; Maruna et al., 2006: 275; Meisenhelder, 1977: 329). Former peers, family and friends are, of course, not generally trustworthy players in society's re-labelling of the individual as a 'reformed' extremist, due to their obvious positive interest in this process. Similarly, government agencies (e.g. police and intelligence service) might also not be the right partners for this process. Due to their interest in gaining intelligence and informants, as well as their legally defined role to focus on behaviour rather than ideology, these agencies, although highly valuable and essential in *disengagement* work, should not take the lead in *deradicalization*. Sometimes the involvement of government agencies as the main assistant to deradicalization might even add to the stress, danger and complexity faced by the individual and turn out to be a disadvantage in the long run.

This guarantee by the 'significant other' might include rituals – e.g. a publicly visible exit – especially if the group to be left is perceived as highly institutionalized with a high degree of collective identity (cf. Ebaugh, 1988: 201; Meisenhelder, 1977). These strong and effective but also potentially dangerous rituals might be included in the process not only to burn any possible bridges leading back into the group but also to 'prove' to the society the 'seriousness' of the individual's intentions. The judgment between the costs and benefits of a 'silent' vs. a 'public' exit is typically influenced by factors, such as the individual's former status and the intensity of the public labelling as an extremist.

The exit process – which might 'mirror' the entry process to a certain degree in terms of motives and dynamics (Garfinkel, 2007) – often requires basic practical elements to be dealt with for the concerned individual. A *geographical relocation* for example (cf. Garfinkel, 2007; Laub and Sampson, 2001) might be essential for a 'decent and secure accommodation' (Gadd, 2006: 180) as well as for the 'knifing off' of individual offenders from their immediate environment (Caspi and Moffitt, 1995; Laub and Sampson, 2001: 49), which has been found to have a minimising effect on reoffending in criminology (e.g. Osborn, 1980) and is a standard procedure in deradicalization work.

Employment, education and personal relationships are also among the factors widely proven to be essential for successful desistance and deradicalization (cf. Bjørgo and Horgan, 2009; Fink and Haerne, 2008; Gadd, 2006; Garfinkel, 2007; Laub and Sampson, 2001). Others include the need for personal reassessment and re-evaluation of one's past (Gadd, 2006: 180) – including most importantly the ideology – the change of explanatory self-narratives to positive and change-oriented frameworks (Maruna, 2004) and the perception of 'earned redemption' (cf. Bazemore, 1998; Gadd, 2006; Maruna et al., 2006) by the concerned individual. A major challenge of successful deradicalization, however, is the complex practical and psychological effect of role residuals (Ebaugh, 1988: 182) – elements of the former ideology or role still influential in the individual's life. The former national identity or perception of 'freedom' as examples of two ideologically-formed political values might actively continue to affect a person's ability to reintegrate and deradicalize (see Leiser, 2012; Wouters, 2012).

On a more abstract level, comparisons of numerous Deradicalization and Disengagement Programs (DDPs) worldwide resulted in the recognition of three main pillars essential to be addressed in order to maximize the chance of success: the affective, pragmatic and ideological levels of the individual have to be methodologically included in the program to equally strong degrees (see Rabasa et al., 2010: 41 et seq.). While the dismantling of ideological frameworks is absolutely essential by definition for any deradicalization program, the pragmatic level consists of practical life circumstances (e.g. employment, education, drug treatment). The affective level, in contrast, includes emotional networks and environments countering the former radical one, which typically need comprehensive strengthening.

The strategic value of Deradicalization and Disengagement Programs (DDP)

Beyond their value as individual support to leave radical groups, leave behind a life of crime and violence and reintegrate into society, DDPs have a more substantial function within a society's anti-terrorism and counter-extremism strategy. Their strategic value (cf. Dechesne, 2011) lies in the targeted destruction of groups' hierarchies and denying them ideological stability. Every exit forces the group to internally explain the event to the active members. The normal reaction will be to dismiss the former member as corrupt, untrustworthy and psychologically unstable, as working for the enemy, being a traitor and the like. Even if this solves internal tensions and the immediate threat of subsequent exits, these explanations conflict with the fact that former members were an accepted part of the group, which means that neither the ideology nor the group itself was capable of detecting the deficiencies of that particular individual and/or turning them into a loyal member.

Every exit reveals the possible failures of ideology and group coherence to the group and demands not insignificant efforts and resources to counter the deteriorating effect. In short, exits of group members keep radical groups in a constant state of explanatory drift and dynamics, preventing the ideological and collective stabilization necessary to reach a critical mass and reproduce. This mechanism applies only to smaller groups, of course. In Germany, numerous cases of whole groups collapsing as the consequence of a drop out are known. Large international terrorist networks however will hardly be affected in the described way.

Nevertheless, DDPs do yield additional values. Through the insights and personal experiences of the former radicals, targeted prevention and the creation of effective counter-narratives become possible. This works due to the close-up knowledge of how, where and who certain radical groups recruit as members, what is considered attractive and which topics, styles and opportunities are necessary to reach the potential recruit. One of the most successful counter-narrative examples known was created by EXIT-Germany in late 2011 during the largest European right-wing rock festival in Germany. The NGO distributed 300 free T-shirts to concert participants, designed with the latest style and motives of the movement. After one wash, the T-shirt changed its imprint to the slogan: 'If your T-Shirt can do it, so can you. We will help you to free yourself from right-wing extremism. EXIT-Germany.' Possible only due to the combined knowledge of experienced case managers (when and how to distribute?), former extremists (what motive, style, what message after washing?) and marketing experts (which printing technique?), the initiative resulted in the triplication of individual drop out attempts and sparked an international debate about deradicalization as well as the threat of right-wing extremism.[1] In this way, EXIT-Germany is one of the few DDPs that directly involves former extremists in their research and prevention work (for instance, through workshops with former extremists at schools), as well as counsellors. Thus, DDPs provide significant and unique knowledge of radical groups, radicalization processes and related aspects of extremism and terrorism, which have proven to be highly valuable for research, prevention and the design of effective policies.

Examples of other Deradicalization and Disengagement Programs

A comprehensive analysis of every major modern DDP is beyond the scope of this chapter (several high quality, in-depth studies are available, such as Horgan and Braddock, 2010; Noricks, 2009; Rabasa et al., 2010). Instead, a short overview of the most important programs will be given to further contextualize the previous theoretical findings and provide a starting point for further consideration. In general, a distinction can be made between state and non-state programs, and between programs mainly designed either for disengagement (reintegration or demobilization) or for deradicalization. While western state-run programs are mostly designed as classical reintegration programs leaving aside ideology, Middle Eastern state-led programs heavily rely on a theological component (especially programs in Yemen and Saudi Arabia). Researchers, however, have criticized that the ideological component in most programs has been insufficiently developed (cf. e.g. Dechesne, 2011), claiming even that 'not targeting the ideological orientation of radicalized individuals but their action orientation' (Noricks, 2009: 314) would be more feasible.

Demobilization and reintegration programs using, in part, similar techniques and aims to those of modern DDPs, can be dated back to the 1970s. The demobilization of the Palestine Liberation Organization's (PLO) Black September included significant incentives for marriage and starting a family (cf. Dechesne, 2011: 287). Italy tried an analogue program to facilitate the dissolution of the Red Brigades (ibid.), as did Northern Ireland as part of the 'Good Friday Agreement' from 1998 (cf. Horgan and Braddock, 2010: 269) and Colombia with the 'Disengagement and Reincorporation' program for former FARC members since

1997 (ibid.: 271). Large scale state-funded deradicalization programs in Indonesia, Yemen ('Religious Dialogue Committee' since 2002) as well as Saudi Arabia's counselling program (since 2003) have received widespread international attention as they included theological (i.e. ideological) debate and challenge for incarcerated Islamist terrorists (cf. Horgan and Braddock, 2010; Noricks, 2009; Rabasa et al., 2010). These programs have become role models for similar attempts in Egypt, Jordan, Algeria, Tajikistan, Malaysia, Singapore, Yemen, Iraq and Thailand (ibid.). Other state-run programs have been started in Denmark, the UK and the Netherlands (cf. Noricks, 2009; Rabasa et al., 2010). However, these programs were not the first structured attempts to dismantle a radical ideology (in contrast to the earlier programs by the PLO, Northern Ireland and Colombia, which focused on reintegration and practical aspects of it). In 1997, the first EXIT program for right-wing extremists willing to leave their radical environment was established in Norway under the lead of Tore Bjørgo (cf. Bjørgo and Horgan, 2009: 136). The three-year project was not designed, however, as an institutionalized program but rather as a case-based mobile counselling team. In 1998, inspired by the Norwegian project, EXIT-Sweden was founded (ibid: 138) by a former neo-Nazi leader. In the year 2000, the former high-ranking criminal police officer Bernd Wagner and former neo-Nazi leader Ingo Hasselbach founded EXIT-Germany as the first German DDP, after previous uncoordinated deradicalization cases had been carried out in the country since 1988 by criminal police agencies under the auspices of Wagner.

Evaluation problems and standards of deradicalization work

Two major problems of DDPs are the effective and credible evaluation of the effort and resources applied in regard to the effects yielded, as well as the establishment of practical standards that the programs can be held accountable to. The first problem directly stems from the essential differentiation between deradicalization and disengagement. While disengagement can be monitored and evaluated fairly easily (through the simple absence of criminal behaviour and the measurement of reoffending or recidivism rates), deradicalization (i.e. a cognitive transformation) is of course impossible to determine with absolute accuracy. This has led both to the proposal to focus on disengagement (Noricks, 2009: 314) and to heavy criticism of Middle Eastern state-run deradicalization programs, which however have reported astonishing rates of success (cf. Horgan and Braddock, 2010; Noricks, 2009).

The first steps towards evaluation must therefore be *transparency* (through publically accessible and high quality self-evaluation) and *externality* (evaluation conducted by independent experts in the field). Evaluation should be *quantitative*, measuring, for instance, participant numbers and statistics, reintegration factors (such as the rate of employment, reoffending, completion or abort rates of related procedures), efficiency of internal structures and financial costs; as well as *qualitative*, through in-depth studies of methods, efficacy, effectiveness and internal organization through participatory observation, interview studies and case studies. While the qualitative element should evaluate if the methods applied by the program are capable of changing individual ideological frameworks and behaviour, the quantitative element is supposed to evaluate these methods' efficacy on a large scale. Important is the evaluation along a certain timeline. It is thus not sufficient to present simple numbers of program participants and their biographical backgrounds as well as their reoffending rates shortly after program completion.

These steps however, can only be the start of a sophisticated evaluation mechanism, which is still the subject of heavy debate. Several different approaches, like the 'Multi Attribute Utility Technology (MAUT)' (Horgan and Braddock, 2010) or multidimensional, vertical, and horizontal evaluations (Romaniuk and Fink, 2012), are still being discussed (a topic which surpasses the scope of this chapter). Nevertheless reviewing the literature on deradicalization and desistance, effective DDPs should employ minimal standards to ensure efficacy, such as: no offering of financial incentives, being institutionally independent from governmental agencies sustainable and long lasting, ideological reassessment as the basis of practical work, provision of security, comprehensiveness and individuality.

EXIT-Germany as a case study of deradicalization

EXIT-Germany,[2] founded in the year 2000, is part of an NGO network named the 'Centre for Democratic Culture' in Berlin, which has been operating since 1997. Both were founded by the former criminal police officer Bernd Wagner (EXIT in cooperation with the former neo-Nazi Ingo Hasselbach). Since then, the Centre has established numerous specialized NGOs under its umbrella, working broadly in the field of counter-extremism and anti-terrorism, education, counselling, deradicalization and research. Thus, the Centre can be described as a comprehensive civil society-based competence network on extremism and terrorism. The Centre is also the only organization in the world working on right-wing extremism as well as Islamist extremism (e.g. 'Arbeitsstelle Islamismus und Ultranationalismus ASTIU'; Family Counselling Program 'Hayat') under the same structure (albeit with separated units), which allows for the continuous exchange of methods, experiences and developments.

Another cornerstone of the Centre is its own internationally-oriented research division, the Institute for the Study of Radical Movements (ISRM),[3] with the main task of providing high quality research based on the empirical data mined from the Centres' DDPs, of cooperating with external academics for evaluation and research and of making all findings publically available and transparent. EXIT-Germany includes family counselling, a prison program, a working group of former extremists, comprehensive prevention (e.g. workshops in schools), capacity building (e.g. for police officers, teachers, prison staff), community coaching (e.g. for institutions and governments in the field of anti-terrorism and counter-extremism strategies) and of course individual case management.

The cornerstone of EXIT-Germany's work is the highlighted role of ideology as the main driving force behind behaviour. Consequently EXIT-Germany tries to embed personal reassessment of a person's past and former ideology into every aspect of the deradicalization process. In contrast to EXIT-Sweden, EXIT-Germany is not state-funded but nevertheless undergoes continuous evaluation through quantitative and qualitative external and internal procedures. The most recent quantitative evaluation was carried out by the German government in early 2012 (Bundesregierung, 2012) and compared the program to the only other nationwide DDP in Germany run by the Federal Intelligence Service. With 443 completed cases since 2000 (until March 2012) and a recidivism rate of roughly 2 percent (ibid.: 3–4), the program highly outranked the state-run program (with 100 cases between 2001 and 2012 and a recidivism rate of roughly 8 percent) both in case based success measures as well as cost effectiveness. However, it is worth noting that the state program offers less transparency, due to its location within the Intelligence Service, and is mainly designed as disengagement assistance.

EXIT-Germany mainly attracts mid- to high-level drop outs, cadres highly radicalized with mostly over 10 years in the organized neo-Nazi movement, as well as many semi-terrorist individuals. Qualitative evaluations with in-depth interview studies have also been conducted regularly, the latest in 2012 in cooperation with Cambridge University (cf. e.g. Rommelspacher,

2006; Wouters, 2012). Integrating a multi-dimensional framework (macro-, meso-, micro-social) into long-term individual case management on the basis of ideological reassessment, the program was found to be one of the most successful DDPs in the world and named a 'role model project in the field of social integration' by the European Commission/European Social Funds in 2012.

Conclusion

Concluding this overview, deradicalization as a field of research and as a practical counter-terrorism and anti-extremism tool is still in its infancy but one of the most promising future areas for academics and policy makers in that regard. Nevertheless a strong need for more comprehensive and substantial research in individual deradicalization processes, as well as comparative interdisciplinary works is among the factors impeding the development of deradicalization programs. In addition policy makers still need to recognize the strategic value of deradicalization tools for domestic security and to combat other forms of asymmetric threats (e.g. foreign fighters) and a tendency to 'reinvent the wheel', i.e. starting national programs from the bottom up vs. learning from other successful experiences, also are points for future action. What nevertheless is clear from the existing research and practical experience is that DDPs are a valuable contribution to a comprehensive democratic culture, to the security and safety of every citizen, and an essential tool to combat terrorist and extremist threats.

Notes

1 See: www.youtube.com/watch?v=CSIbsHKEP-8 (accessed: February 2013) or: www.spiegel.de/international/germany/tee-d-off-right-wing-extremists-tricked-by-trojan-shirts-a-779446.html (accessed: February 2013).
2 www.exit-deutschland.de
3 www.istramo.com

References

Aho, J. A. (1988). Out of hate: A sociology of defection from neo-Nazism. *Current Research on Peace and Violence, 11*(4), 159–168.
Ashour, O. (2007). Lions Tamed? An Inquiry into the causes of De-Radicalization of the Egyptian Islamic Group. *Middle East Journal, 61*(4), 596–597.
Ashour, O. (2008a). De-Radicalization of Jihad? The Impact of Egyptian Islamist Revisionists on Al-Qaeda. *Perspectives on Terrorism II/5, 11*(14).
Ashour, O. (2008b). Islamist De-Radicalization in Algeria: Successes and Failures. *The Middle East Institute Policy Brief* (21).
Ashour, O. (2009). *The Deradicalization of Jihadists: Transforming Armed Islamist Movements*. New York and London: Routledge.
Bazemore, G. (1998). Restorative Justice and Earned Redemption: Communities, Victims, and Offender Reintegration. *American Behavioral Scientist, 41*(6), 768–813.
Bjørgo, T. (2006). Reducing Recruitment and Promoting Disengagement from Extremist Groups: The Case of Racist Sub-Cultures. In C. Benard (ed.), *A Future for the Young: Options for Helping Middle Eastern Youth Escape the Trap of Radicalization*. Santa Monica: RAND Corporation.
Bjørgo, T. (2009). Processes of disengagement from violent groups of the extreme right. In T. Bjørgo and J. Horgan (eds.), *Leaving Terrorism Behind. Individual and collective disengagement* (pp. 30–48). New York: Routledge.
Bjørgo, T. (2011). Dreams and disillusionment: engagement in and disengagement from militant extremist groups. *Crime, Law and Social Change*, 1–9.

Bjørgo, T. and Horgan, J. (2009). *Leaving Terrorism Behind: Individual and Collective Disengagement.* London and New York: Routledge.

Braithwaite, J. (1989). *Crime, shame, and reintegration.* Cambridge and New York: Cambridge University Press.

Bundesregierung (2012). *Antwort der Bundesregierung auf die Kleine Anfrage der Abgeordneten Ulla Jelpke, Heidrun Dittrich, Dr. Lukrezia Jochimsen, weiterer Abgeordneter und der Fraktion DIE LINKE. – Drucksache 17/8937 –.*

Bushway, S. D., Piquero, A. R., Broidy, L. M., Cauffman, E. and Mazerolle, P. (2001). An Empirical Framework for Studying Desistance as a Process. *Criminology, 39*(2), 491–516.

Caspi, A. and Moffitt, T. E. (1995). The continuity of maladaptive behavior: From description to understanding in the study of antisocial behavior. In D. Cicchetti and D. J. Cohen (eds.), *Risk, disorder, and adaptation.* (Vol. 2, pp. 472–511). Oxford: John Wiley and Sons.

Dechesne, M. (2011). Deradicalization: not soft, but strategic. *Crime, Law and Social Change, 55*(4), 287–292.

Demant, F., Slootman, M., Buijs, F. J. and Tillie, J. (2008). *Decline and Disengagement – An Analysis of Processes of Deradicalisation.* Amsterdam: Institute for Migration and Ethnic Studies (IMES).

Ebaugh, H. R. F. (1988). *Becoming an Ex. The Process of Role Exit.* Chicago: University of Chicago Press.

Farrall, S. (2002). *Rethinking what works with offenders: probation, social context and desistance from crime.* Cullompton: Willan.

Farrall, S. and Maruna, S. (2004). Desistance-Focused Criminal Justice Policy Research: Introduction to a Special Issue on Desistance from Crime and Public Policy. *The Howard Journal, 43*(4), 358–367.

Fink, C. N. and Haerne, E. B. (2008). *Beyond Terrorism: Deradicalization and Disengagement from Violent Extremism.* International Peace Institute.

Gadd, D. (2006). The role of recognition in the desistance process: A case analysis of a former far-right activist. *Theoretical Criminology, 10*(2), 179–202.

Garfinkel, R. (2007). *Personal Transformations. Moving from Violence to Peace.* United States Institute of Peace.

Giordano, P., Cernkovich, S. and Rudolph, J. (2002). Gender, Crime, and Desistance: Toward a Theory of Cognitive Transformation. *American Journal of Sociology, 107*(4), 990–1064.

Horgan, J. (2006). Psychological Factors Related to Disengaging from Terrorism: Some Preliminary Assumptions and Assertions. In C. Benard (ed.), *A Future for the Young: Options for Helping Middle Eastern Youth Escape the Trap of Radicalization.* Santa Monica: RAND Corporation.

Horgan, J. (2008a). Deradicalization or Disengagement? A Process in Need of Clarity and a Counterterrorism Initiative in Need of Evaluation. *Perspectives on Terrorism, 2*(4).

Horgan, J. (2008b). From Profiles to Pathways and Roots to Routes: Perspectives from Psychology on Radicalization into Terrorism. *Annals of the American Academy of Political and Social Science, 618,* 80–94.

Horgan, J. (2009a). Individual disengagement: a psychological analysis. In T. Bjørgo and J. Horgan (eds.), *Leaving terrorism behind: individual and collective disengagement.* (pp. 17–29). London and New York: Routledge.

Horgan, J. (2009b). *Walking away from terrorism: accounts of disengagement from radical and extremist movements.* London and New York: Routledge.

Horgan, J. and Braddock, K. (2010). Rehabilitating the Terrorists?: Challenges in Assessing the Effectiveness of De-radicalization Programs. *Terrorism and Political Violence, 22*(2), 267–291.

Kazemian, L. (2007). Desistance From Crime: Theoretical, Empirical, Methodological, and Policy Considerations. *Journal of Contemporary Criminal Justice, 23*(1), 5–27.

Laub, J. H. and Sampson, R. J. (2001). Understanding Desistance from Crime. *Crime and Justice, 28*(2001), 1–69.

Leiser, A. (2012). Freedom and Identity. Their Role in the Perceived Experiences of Former Right-Wing Extremists. *ISRM Working Paper Series, 02/12.*

Lemert, E. M. (1951). *Social pathology; a systematic approach to the theory of sociopathic behavior* (1st ed.). New York: McGraw-Hill.

Maruna, S. (2001). *Making good: how ex-convicts reform and rebuild their lives* (1st ed.). Washington, D.C.: American Psychological Association.

Maruna, S. (2004). Desistance from Crime and Explanatory Style: A New Direction in the Psychology of Reform. *Journal of Contemporary Criminal Justice, 20*(2), 184–200.

Maruna, S., Lebel, T. P., Mitchell, N. and Naples, M. (2006). Pygmalion in the reintegration process: Desistance from crime through the looking glass. *Psychology, Crime and Law*, *10*(3), 271–281.

Meisenhelder, T. (1977). An Exploratory Study of Exiting from Criminal Careers. *Criminology*, *15*(3), 319–334.

Noricks, D. M. E. (2009). Disengagement and Deradicalization: Processes and Programs. In P. K. Davis and K. Cragin (eds), *Social Science for Counterterrorism. Putting the Pieces Together*. Santa Monica: RAND Corporation.

Osborn, S. G. (1980). Moving Home, Leaving London and Delinquent Trends. *British Journal of Criminology*, *20*(1), 54–61.

Rabasa, A., Pettyjohn, S. L., Ghez, J. J. and Boucek, C. (2010). *Deradicalizing Islamist Extremists*. Santa Monica: RAND Corporation.

Reinares, F. (2011). Exit From Terrorism: A Qualitative Empirical Study on Disengagement and Deradicalization Among Members of ETA. *Terrorism and Political Violence*, *23*(5), 780–803.

Romaniuk, P. and Fink, C. N. (2012). *From Input To Impact. Evaluating Terrorism Prevention Programs*. Center on Global Counterterrorism Cooperation.

Rommelspacher, B. (2006). *"Der Hass hat uns geeint": junge Rechtsextreme und ihr Ausstieg aus der Szene*. Frankfurt/Main and New York: Campus.

Shover, N. (1996). *Great pretenders: pursuits and careers of persistent thieves*. Boulder, CO: Westview Press.

Warr, M. (1998). Life-Course Transitions and Desistance from Crime. *Criminology*, *36*(2), 183–216.

Wouters, M. (2012). Moving Forwards? Breaking With Right-Wing Extremism in Present Day Berlin. *ISRM Working Paper Series*, *03/12*.

Index

abortion clinics 27
Acceptable Behaviour Contracts (ABCs) 385
accountability, police intelligence 346
Addressing Hate Crime in Ontario 167
advocacy organisation, LGBT 281–2, 285
African Americans 154–5, 319
age and online recruitment tactics 308
Ahle Sunnat wal Jamaat 309
Al-Qaeda 308, 310, 311
Al-Shabab 306
alcohol 216, 383, 384, 386
Alleanza Nazionale 140
allegiance to group 74, 394, 397
alternative subcultures 5–6, 15, 226–36
Ameobi, Sammy (footballer) 326
animosity against ethnic groups 255
animus 155, 156–7; test 62
anomie 70–1, 73
anonymity: online perpetrator 296–7, 298, 311; victim (in reporting) 333
anti-discrimination measures: Australia/NZ 178, 179, 180; US, transgender 285
anti-Semitism (anti-Jewish prejudice) 4, 129–37; Canada 134–5, 135, 165; community impact 47; ideology 89; Internet 291, 311; Iran and 88; sport 322–3, 326; story-telling by victims of 404; *see also* Holocaust; 'yid' chant
Anti-Social Behaviour Orders (ASBOs) 385
Anti-Terrorism, Crime and Security Act (2001) 112
Apartheid South Africa 318
appeal to higher loyalties 74, 397
Aryan Nations 311
ASBOs (Anti-Social Behaviour Orders) 385
asexuality 267
Asian victims: in Australia 176, 181; UK shopkeepers 6, 249–65
Asian youths and the Oldham riots 335–6
Association of Chief Police Officers (ACPO) 15, 107, 320, 339, 367; anti-Semitism and 131; definition of hate crime 367; review of third-party reporting schemes 334

Australia 5, 174–89; cricket against India 325; cricket against South Africa 326; disability 194, 197; LGBT 272
Australian Communication and Media Authority (ACMA) 178
Australian Institute of Health and Welfare (AIHW) 195
Australian Nationalist Movement (ANM) 176, 180
autobiography exercises 387
Autonome Nationalisten 145

bad victims, LGBT as 269–71, 271
baseball 319
Battle of the Atlantic (WWII), intelligence 351
behavioural injuries 43–4
belonging 75
Ben Haim, Tal (footballer) 326
benefits claimants (UK) 88
Berlin Olympics 319
Bichard inquiry 347, 349
Birmingham, Asian shopkeepers 250–1
bisexual people *see* Lesbian, Gay, Bisexual and Transgender or queer
black LGBT people 30; *see also* African Americans
Blocco Studentesco 146
Boston Marathon attack 310, 311
Bragg, Billy (folk singer) 394–5
British (concepts of being) 253, 254, 255
British Crime Survey *see* Crime Survey of England and Wales
British National Party (BNP) 141, 147, 213
bullying, online (cyber-bullying) 294, 298, 300
Byrd, James (and Matthew Shepard) 49, 155, 157, 176, 194, 283

California 61, 156, 158
Canada 4, 163–73; anti-Semitism 134–5, 135, 165; targeted violence 53–4; White Nationalist Front 310, 311
Canadian Human Rights Act 164, 165
Canadian Human Rights Commission 164, 165

430

Index

Canadian Human Rights Tribunal 165
CasaPound 145, 146–7
Catholic–Protestant conflict in UK *see* sectarianism
causation theory 69–80, 394–5; disability hate crime 212, 394
Celtic football club 323, 324
Chadderton and Oldham riots 335–6
Chamberlain, Walter 335, 336
change: implications for 55–7; positive, catalyst for 49, 55
chanting (singing) at football 113, 322–3, 323, 324
'chavs' 231
children and young people: helping offenders 395; N. Ireland 124; online hate 307, 308, 312
Christian identity 89; *see also* sectarianism
civil responses in Australia/NZ 177–9
Civil Rights Act (1968) 153, 154, 155
Civil Rights Movement (US) 154–5
civil society organisations (CSOs) 3, 96, 100
Civil War (US) 154
Civitas 144
Climbie, Victoria 347
cognitive behavioural theory 394
cognitive deficits 395
cohesion (community) 54
Cohesion, Sharing and Integration (CSI) document 125
collateral damage (communities) 52–4
Committee on the Elimination of Racial Discrimination 96
Communications Act (2003) 326
community/communities: alternative subcultures and 228–9; Canada 169; impact on 3, 47–58; including (in restorative justice) appropriate supporters from 407; involvement in restorative justice, perils 405–6; LGBT and 271–2; perpetrator, individual drawing on support in 396, 407; targeted 50–2, 56, 159
community project (in Diversity Awareness and Prejudice Pack) 388
Community Security Trust (CST) 131–3
compromise in sectarianism 415–16, 417, 418
concepts *see* theories and concepts
condemnation of the condemners 74
Confait, Maxwell ('Michelle') 322
Conference on Security and Cooperation in Europe (CSCE) 95
confidence (victim), improving (UK) 115
conflict: of individual's cultural identity 396; resolution, predisposition to violence 396
conscription and recruitment online 307, 308–9, 310, 311, 312
constitutionality of hate crime laws (US) 157
contextual and psychological factors: interplay of 73–4

Copeland, David 25–6, 107, 176; and London nail bombings 8, 107, 334, 356, 358, 361–4, 384
Covington, Harold (aka Winston Smith) 310
cricket: England and Wales 324; international 325–6
Crime and Disorder Act (1998) 24, 25, 60, 62, 112, 319, 346
crime scene 359
'crime scripts' 207, 210, 211, 215, 216
Crime Survey of England and Wales (formerly British Crime Survey) 14, 34–46, 111, 131, 198; gender identity and 281; policing and 333, 341
Criminal Code: Australia/NZ 175, 178, 180; Canadian 163, 164, 165, 166, 167, 168, 169, 196
Criminal Justice Act (2003) 24, 25, 113, 196, 208, 216, 321, 332, 339, 349
Criminal Justice Inspectorate for Northern Ireland (CJINI) 123
Criminal Justice System (UK): disability hate crime 208, 210, 211, 215, 216; monitored hate crime definition 35; prevalence of hate and the capacity of 338
criminological perspectives 3; disability hate crime 213–14
Cronulla riots 178
Cross-Government Hate Crime Programme 108
Crown Prosecution Service (CPS) 26, 27, 31, 107, 108, 110, 113; data 111; disability hate crime 208, 216–20
culture (and cultural groups) 48, 83–4; Australia/NZ 175–7; conflict of an individual's cultural identity 396
cyber-bullying (online bullying) 294, 298, 300
Czech Republic, Gypsies/Travellers/Roma 243

Daley, Tom 327
Danish Association (Den Danske Forening) 144
data (and its collection incl. surveys) and statistics: anti-Semitism 129, 130; Asian shopkeeper hate crime 250–1; Europe 97, 99, 99–100, 100; LGBT hate crime 271–2, 273, 280–3; UK 110–11, 114–15, 250–1; US 155, 157–9
Davies, Kevin, killing 339
Dead Sea Scrolls 289
decriminalisation of same-sex acts 270–1
defensive/reactive hate crimes 84, 383–4, 393; disability hate crime and 213; UK 213; US 159
definitions (of hate crime) 13–23; alternative subculture hate crime 232; Canada 166–7; disability hate crime 194–6; legal 47–8; monitored hate crime 109–10; online bullying 300

431

Index

deindividuation (online) 293, 296
democracy: free speech and 338; Internet and 290
demonstration test 63
denial: in Australia/NZ 177; of injury 74, 215; of responsibility 74, 215; of the victim 74, 215
Denmark, far-right 144
denunciation grounds 65; transgender hate crime 284
Deoxyribonucleic Acid (DNA) evidence 358, 359, 363
deradicalisation 420–9
derivative fear 413
desistances (from crime) 401, 405, 408, 420, 422
'difference' (in characteristics/attributes) 16, 17, 19, 20, 73, 75, 76, 250, 413; doing 15, 77, 228, 256, 261; protecting forms of 63–5, 181–3; story-telling and 404; *see also* othering
differential association 73
Director of Public Prosecutions 339, 341
dirty (notion of), Gypsies/Travellers/Roma 240
disabled people 5, 193–225, 339–41, 393; causation of hate crime 212, 394; Crime Survey of England and Wales 36; differences from other hate crimes 196–8; murders 209, 210, 339–40; N. Ireland 122, 123; policing of hate crime 200, 339–41; prevalence of hate crime 198–9; reporting of hate crimes 28, 197, 198, 198–9, 199–202; terminology 194–6; UK 88, 193, 194, 195, 196, 197, 198, 199, 200, 201, 207–25
discrimination 81; Australia/NZ 178–9, 182, 183; discriminatory (group) selection test 62, 156, 181, 182; Gypsies/Travellers/Roma 237, 241–2, 243, 244, 245; LGBT 266–74; *see also* anti-discrimination measures
disengagement 420, 422, 423–5, 425
distorted perspectives/views: of victim 388, 395–6; worldview 296
distrust (affected communities) 51–2
Diversity Awareness and Prejudice Pack (DAPP) 211, 384, 384–5, 387, 388, 389
Dobson, Gary 349, 357–8
documentation *see* recording and documentation
doing difference 15, 77, 228, 256, 261
domestic abuse/violence 64, 88, 108; disabled people 197, 211
domestic murder 270
dominance/domination 75, 76; men over women 252; physical 261; preventing 406; subculture hate crime and 231–2
drift 73
Dutch Party for Freedom 139
Dutch People's Union 142

Eastern Europe, Gypsies/Travellers/Roma 239, 241–2, 243, 245

economics 85–6
education, Canada 170
emotional injuries 40–3, 44
empathy (and its lack) 387, 395, 415; for Gypsies/Travellers/Roma 240
empirical studies of transgender hate crime 282–3
empowerment 368–71
England *see* United Kingdom
English Defence League 145, 147–8, 336
Equality Act (2010) 113–14
Equality and Human Rights Commission 112, 340; disability hate crime and 208, 211, 213, 220, 221
ethnic minorities *see* culture; racism
Europe (and European Union) 3, 13–14, 95–104; anti-Semitism 131–4; disability in 194, 196; extremism/far right 4, 132–4, 138–52; Gypsies/Travellers/Roma in 6, 237–48; obstacles to tackling hate crime 99–102; transgender in 280–1, 282
European Commission Against Racism and Intolerance (ECRI) 96, 99
European Court of Human Rights (ECHR) 96
European Union Agency for Fundamental Rights *see* Fundamental Rights Agency
European Union Minorities and Discrimination Survey (EU-MIDIS) 97, 100, 242, 243
European Union Monitoring Centre on Racism and Xenophobia (predecessor to Fundamental Rights Agency) 96–7
exiting from radical groups 421, 423–7; EXIT-Germany 422, 424, 425, 426–7; EXIT-Sweden 425, 426; process 423
experiences and impacts/consequences (victims): community 3, 47–58; personal *see* personal injuries; sharing (in restorative justice) 404
experiential prejudice and motivation 393
extremism and radicalism (incl. far right) 4; anti-Semitism and 130, 132, 133, 134, 135; definitions/labels 138; economics and 85, 86; Europe 4, 132–4, 138–42; Germany 142, 145, 424; Gypsies/Travellers/Roma and 242, 243; online 7, 318–27; search for respectability 143–4; *see also* terrorism

face-to-face work 386, 402
Facebook 147, 290, 294, 308, 309, 310, 311, 326, 369
facilitators, restorative *see* practitioners
Facing Facts programme 100
faith *see* religion
family: liaison, and intelligence 347–8; relations, sexual orientation and gender prejudice as legitimate violence in laws regulating 270; in restorative practices 402
far-right extremism *see* extremism

Index

fascism 140, 141, 146, 149; Mussolini's 146; *see also* neo-Nazism and neo-fascism
fear 77, 415; derivative 413
federal government and law: Australia 175; US 153–6
females *see* women
football: chanting (singing) 113, 322–3, 323, 324; England 113, 319, 326, 335–6; Scotland 323–4
Football (Offences) Act (1991) 113, 321
Football Spectators Act (1989) 321, 323
forensic science 8, 356–66; case study 361–4; fundamentals and contemporary issues 358–61
France: anti-Semitism 133–4, 135; extremism 141, 143–4, 144–5; Gypsies/Travellers/Roma 242; Muslim headscarves 87
freedom of speech 113, 148, 196, 292, 295, 306, 307, 309, 312, 327, 338–9
friends, disability hate crime by ('mate crime') 197, 209–10, 214, 218, 219
Front National (FN) 141, 143–4
Fundamental Rights Agency (EU Agency for Fundamental Rights) 96, 97, 98, 99, 100; anti-Semitism and 129, 130, 134; disability and 194, 199; LGBT and 267, 272–3, 274; predecessor to (=EUMC) 96

Gallagher, Erin, suicide 300
games, online 307
gang membership 252–3
gay people *see* Lesbian, Gay, Bisexual and Transgender or queer
gender issues 6; expression 279, 280, 281, 282, 283, 283–6; identity *see* identity; self-identity; perpetrators and 6; theories and concepts 267–9, 278–80
Gender Public Advocacy Coalition (GenderPAC) 281
genocide of WWII (the Holocaust) 404; denial 83, 141, 165, 166, 176, 310, 339; Gypsies/Travellers/Roma in 239, 244
geography 84–5; geographical relocation of individual 423; *see also* international perspectives
Germany: exiting from radical groups (EXIT-Germany) 422, 424, 425, 426–7; far right 142, 145, 424; Nazi era *see* Nazi Germany
Glasgow Rangers v. Celtic football clubs 323, 324
global perspectives 3–5, 93–189
Golb, Raphael 289
Golden Dawn 142
goths 226, 227, 229, 230, 232
Goudreau, Kevin 311
government *see* policy; state
Greater Manchester Police: alternative subcultures and 15, 226, 232, 233, 234, 239; anti-Semitism and 132

GRECE (Groupement de Recherche et d'Etudes pour la Civilisation Européenne) 144–5
Greece, far right 142
Greenwich 382, 385, 388; Hate Crimes Project 384–5
Griffin, Nick 141
group(s) 381; allegiance to 74, 394, 397; alternative subcultures 227–34; bonding 74; group animus model 156; selection (discriminator selection) test 62, 156, 181, 182; *see also* in groups; out groups
Groupement de Recherche et d'Etudes pour la Civilisation Européenne (GRECE) 144–5
Gypsies 6, 237–48

Hague-based International Association of Prosecutors 101
happiness, disability and hate crime and erosion of 209–10
harassment: alternative subcultures 226–8; disabled persons 208, 209, 210, 213, 215, 219; LGBT 269, 272
Hardwick, Francecca, 176, 208, 340
harms, repairing 400–10
hate crime (general aspects): conventional boundaries 14–16; definitions *see* definitions; extending boundaries and rethinking 16–19, 24–32; hidden truths 19–20; impacts *see* experiences and impacts; international perspectives 3–5; perpetrators *see* perpetrators; repairing harms 400–10; theories and concepts *see* theories and concepts; typology of motivations 159, 197, 212, 260, 383–4, 394; understanding *see* understanding; victims *see* victims
Hate Crime Community Working Group (Canada) 167
Hate Crime Independent Advisory Group 350–1
Hate Crime Laws – A Practical Guide (ODIHR) 101
Hate Crime Statistics Act (1990) 155
Hate Crimes Sentencing Enhancement Act (1995) 155
hate incidents *see* incidents
hegemonic masculinity 251–2, 252
heterosexuality 261, 268–9; normative 251, 268–9
Hidden in Plain Sight report 112
higher loyalties, appeal to 74, 397
Himmler, Heinrich 239
history (of hate crime) 82–3, 164; Gypsies/Travellers/Roma 237–40; in sport 318–19
holistic approach 77, 86; to prosecution 101
Home Office: disability hate crime and 198; Internet concerns 295; interventions and 391, 395
homosexuals: outlawing promotion of 271; sport and homophobia 322, 327; *see also* Lesbian, Gay, Bisexual and Transgender or queer

433

Index

'honour crimes' 270
Hoskins, Steven 339
hostility 60; disability 207, 211, 214, 216; public disorder and 335–7; racial or religious, proving 62–3; UK and recognition or evidence of 110
household crime 35, 36, 37, 43
Human Rights Act (Canada 1977) 164, 165
Human Rights Act (NZ 1993) 175, 178, 182
Human Rights Act (UK 1998) 346, 347, 348
humiliation concerning masculine identity 256
Hungary: anti-Semitism 134, 135; extremism 134, 135, 142–3; Gypsies/Travellers/Roma 241, 243

Iannone, Gianluca 146
identification of nail bombing victims 363
identity 20; alternative subcultures 228–9, 230; choosing 230; Christian 89; cultural (individual's), conflict of an 396; gender 6, 30, 36, 37, 183, 249–65, 278–88, 396; politics 26–8; social group 412; symbols of *see* symbolism; *see also* self-identity
ideology 88–9
ILGA-Europe 282
impact *see* experiences and impacts
in groups 74, 75, 227, 256, 260, 381, 393, 396, 414, 415
incapacity benefit (UK) 88
incidents (of hate): monitored 109; N. Ireland 122; responding to 106–7
inclusion and inclusivity: alternative subcultures 229, 231, 233, 234; effects of hate crime on national commitments to 49; limits 54
Independent Police Complaints Commission (IPCC) 340
India–Australia cricket 325
indigenous people: Australia/NZ 175–6, 183; US (Native Americans) 49
information-sharing (between agencies): UK 107
information technology 289–90; *see also* media
Inspire (Al-Qaeda's) 310, 311
Institut Civitas 144
Institute for Conflict Research 123
institutional response in Australia/NZ 175–7, 182
Intelligence Cell Analytic System (ICAS) 348, 351
intelligence-led policing 7, 343–55
intentional selection of victims (US) 156–7
International Association of Prosecutors (Hague-based) 101
International Day against Homophobia and Transphobia 266
international governmental organisations (IGOs), European 96, 98, 99, 100, 102

international perspectives 3–5, 93–189; deradicalisation 424–5; online recruitment 312–13; sport 325–6; *see also* geography
Internet (online) 6–7, 289–317; academic contributions towards understanding of hate crime on 295–7; consequences of hate 300; extremist activity 7, 318–27; personal reflections of good and evil on 289–92; policing (incl. legislation on hate) 298–300, 337–9; UK 115
Internet Service Providers 299, 301
intersectionality (concept/theory of) 2, 25–31, 207–8, 251–3; identity politics and 26–8; LGBT and 268
intersex 267
interventions 329–429; with offenders *see* rehabilitation; police *see* police
Intifada: in France 134; Second Palestinian 132, 133
investigations (police) 344–7
IRA (Irish Republican Army) 119, 120
Iran and Israel 88
Irish Republican Army (IRA) 119, 120
Islamic people (Muslims) 25; community impact 57; English Defence League and 147; France, and anti-Semitism 133; France, and wearing of headscarves 87; historical triggers for hate of 83; Internet and Islamophobia 148; Internet and radicalisation of 308, 309, 311; 9/11 attacks and Islamophobia 25, 55, 83, 87; restorative justice for hate crime against 403; women 29, 51–2, 53, 55, 57; *see also* Al-Qaeda; Al-Shabab; Tehkreek-e-Taliban Pakistan
Israel: anti-Semitism and 132; Iran and 88; 'peace wall' 416; *see also* Palestinian Intifada
Italy: far right 140, 145, 146–7; Gypsies/Travellers/Roma 241, 242, 243
iTunes 307

Jamaat-ud-Dawa 309
Jews, prejudice against *see* anti-Semitism; 'yid' chant
Jobbik 134, 142–3
John, Professor Gus 107, 350–1
Johnson, Steve 177
Jones, Alan (Australian shock-jock) 178
justice: punitive *see* punishment; restorative 8–9, 388, 400–10

Kaldenberg, Wyatt 309
killing *see* murder
King (Jr.), Martin Luther 155
'kith and kin' racism 253
'known' to disabled victims, persons 198, 200; *see also* friends
Kreiss, August 311–12
Ku Klux Klan (KKK) 86, 89, 154

Index

Lakinski, Christine, murder 212, 214, 340
Laming inquiry 347, 349
Lancaster, Sophie (and Sophie Lancaster Foundation) 26, 226–7, 229, 232, 233
law *see* legislation; police
Law Enforcement Officers Programme (LEOP) of the ODIHR 101
Lawrence, Stephen 8, 35, 105, 114, 115, 331–2, 352, 364, 368, 384; Macpherson Inquiry and Report 15, 25, 105, 106–7, 108, 114, 252, 331, 344, 346, 347, 351, 357, 367, 381, 385, 391
Le Pen, Marine 141, 143–4
League for Human Rights of B'nai Brith (Canada) 134–5
learned behaviour and disability hate crime 213
legislation/law and regulations (adverse): Gypsies/Travellers/Roma in UK 241; LGBT/transgender 270–1, 283–6
legislation/law and regulations (beneficial) 3, 59–68; Australia/NZ 175–9, 180, 181; Canada 163–4, 165; definitions of hate crime 47–8; enforcement *see* police; Internet 298–300, 337, 338; LGBT hate crime 279; models 60–1; sport and 319–21; thresholds 61–2; UK 24, 26, 60, 62–3, 112–14, 319–20, 323, 323–4, 344–7; US 153–7; *see also* prosecution; punishment; sentencing
Leicester Hate Crime Project 19
lesbian(s) 30; rape 270
Lesbian, Gay, Bisexual and Transgender or queer (LGBTQ) 6, 20, 212–13, 266–77; advocacy organisations 281–2, 285; as bad victims 269–71, 271; data on hate crime 271–2, 273, 280–3; law 270–1, 283–6; murders 155, 176, 183, 270, 282; N. Ireland 122, 123; policy 27, 29, 30; theories and concepts 267–9, 278–80; UK 267, 333–4; *see also* homosexuals; sexuality and sexual orientation; transgender people
Local Government Act (1988) 271
London: interventions 385, 387–9; nail bombings 8, 107, 334, 356, 358, 361–4, 384; Olympics (2012) 326, 327; Paralympics (2012) 207, 326

Macdonald, Sir Ken (now Lord M of River Glaven) 342
Macpherson (Stephen Lawrence) Inquiry and Report 15, 25, 105, 106–7, 108, 114, 331, 344, 346, 347, 351, 352, 357, 367, 381, 385, 391
Making Hate a Crime 266
Making hate crime visible in the European Union: acknowledging victims' rights 100
male identities *see* masculine identities
Malicious Communications Act (1988) 326
Manchester, LGBT 333–4; *see also* Greater Manchester Police

Martin, Brent, killing 209, 212, 339
masculine identities (and male gender role) 249–65; disability and 213; ethnic minorities and 6, 249–65
Massachusetts transgender anti-discrimination bill 285
'mate crime' 197, 209–10, 214, 218, 219
Matthew Shepard and James Byrd, Jr. Hate Crimes Prevention Act (2009) 155–6, 157, 194
media: Australia/NZ 177, 178; Internet concerns 295; religion and 87; social *see* social media; *see also* information technology
mediation, victim–offender (VOM) 402, 403, 407
mentoring 385
Mertonian strain theory 71
message crimes 50–2
Metropolitan Police Service 344; London nail bombing and 334; Stephen Lawrence murder and 25, 106
Metzeger, Tom 312
mission crimes and offenders 83, 384; US 159
mobilisation (community) 54–5
monitored hate crime, definition 109–10
monitored hate incident 109
'moral career' of racist hate crime victims 367–80
moral reasoning, poor and problematic 395
motivations 393, 421; in interventional work 386, 391, 392, 393, 397; tests 61; typology of 159, 197, 212, 260, 383–4, 394; UK 109
Muamba, Fabrice (footballer) 326
multidisciplinary/multi-agency approaches 385; disability hate crime 196, 209–10, 217; forensic science 361, 363; LGBT hate crime 274; working with perpetrators 384, 385
murder/killing 335, 347, 348, 349; alternative subcultures 226, 227, 229, 233; Australia/NZ 176, 177, 183; Canada 166; disabled people 209, 210, 339–40; domestic 270; Jews 129, 133; LGBT/transgender 155, 176, 183, 270, 282; racially-motivated 49, 105, 106, 107, 154, 331, 332, 367, 381, 384; sectarian 120; South Africa 331; *see also* genocide; physical injuries; violence
music, online 307–8
Muslims *see* Islamic people
Mussolini 140, 146

nail bombings, London 8, 107, 334, 356, 358, 361–4, 384
National Alliance (Italy - Alleanza Nazionale) 140
National Alliance (USA) 307
National Center for Transgender Equality 281
National Coalition of Anti-Violence Programs (NCAVP) 281, 282

435

Index

National Crime Victimization Survey (NCVS) 158; transgender 281
National Front (France - Front National) 141, 143–4
National Gay and Lesbian Task Force (NGLTF) 281
National Intelligence Model (UK) 344, 346, 349
National Offender Management Service 389
National Socialist 309, 310
National Socialist White People's Party 310
National Transgender Discrimination Survey (NTDS) 282
Nationalist Party of America 308
Native Americans 49
Nazi Germany (1930s/40s) 85, 239, 307; Berlin Olympics 319; *see also* Holocaust; neo-Nazism
Nazi salute, Lithuanian Olympian in London 326
necessity of police intelligence 347
neo-Nazism (Nazi ideology) and neo-fascism 25–6, 83, 132, 134; deradicalisation 425, 426; Europe 141, 142, 143, 145, 147, 148; forensic science 361, 363; Olympics (2012) 326; online 291, 309; UK 147; US 291; *see also* Nazi salute
Netherlands, far-right parties (Dutch...) 139, 142, 148
networking, opportunity online 310
neutralisation 71, 74, 397, 407
New South Wales (NSW) 174, 176, 177, 178, 180, 181, 182; LGBT hate crime 272
New Zealand 5, 174–89
9/11 attacks 25, 55, 83, 87, 362, 403
non-governmental organisations (NGOs) 45; anti-Semitism and 130, 131, 134, 135; deradicalisation and 426; in Europe 99, 101, 130
non-party far-right organisations 144–5
normality (ordinariness) of hate crime 18, 19, 78, 83
normative heterosexuality 251, 268–9
Northern Ireland, sectarianism 4, 9, 117–25, 417, 418
Northern Ireland Association for the Care and Resettlement of Offenders (NIACRO) 124
Northern Ireland Life and Times (NILT) Survey 125
Northern Ireland Social Attitudes (NISA) Survey 125
NPD (Nationaldemokratische Partei Deutschlands) 142

offenders *see* perpetrators
Office for Democratic Institutions and Human Rights (ODIHR) 14, 15, 61, 95, 98–101, 105; disability and 194, 198, 199

Oldham riots 335–6
Olympics: Berlin 319; London 326, 327
One to One (OTO) programme 391, 392
online hate *see* Internet
on-roaders 252
opposites, precarious tension of (in sectarianism) 411, 417
oppressive regimes and free speech 338
ordinariness (normality) of hate crime 18, 19, 78, 83
Organization for Security and Co-Operation in Europe (OSCE) 13, 95, 98–9, 99–100, 101, 105; anti-Semitism and 129, 130, 134; disability and 194, 198, 199, 200; gypsies/travellers/Roma and 243, 244
othering 15, 30; Gypsies/Travellers/Roma and 237, 245; racism and 253; *see also* difference
out groups 75, 381, 393, 395, 397, 414–15; alternative subcultures 227–8

paedophiles 27, 219, 229, 294
Pakistani Taliban (Tehkreek-e-Taliban Pakistan) 308, 312
Palestinian Intifada, Second 132, 133
Paralympics, London 207, 326
paramilitary groups (N. Ireland) 118, 119, 120
Parsons, Rehtaeh, suicide 300
Pathological Religion 87
peace process: N. Ireland 119, 120, 124, 125, 418; stall in 419
'peace walls/lines' 416
penalty enhancement 8, 60–1, 400; Australia/NZ 180; gender identity/expression and 283; UK 62–3; US 157
perception-based recording 106
perpetrators (incl. offenders) 381–410; disability hate crime 5, 200–1, 210–16; preventing victims becoming 367–80; provocation by 369, 370, 371–5; rehabilitation *see* rehabilitation; understanding 210–15, 220; US statistics 159; working with 8–9
personal injuries (experience/impact/consequences) 2, 34–46, 367–80; denial of 74, 215; physical injuries *see* physical injuries; psychological consequences 40–3, 376
physical dominance 261
physical identification of nail bombing victims 363
physical injuries 38–40; London nail bombings 361, 362, 363, 364; *see also* murder; violence
Pilkington, Fiona 18, 208, 209, 212, 332, 340, 364
plea-bargaining and racism 107
pogroms against Gypsies/Travellers/Roma 239; *see also* genocide

Index

police (and policing/law enforcement) 7–8, 331–42; Australia/NZ 176, 177, 178, 179–81, 182; Canada 163–4, 166, 167–8, 169, 170; disability hate crime 200, 339–41; forensic science *see* forensic science; intelligence and 7, 343–55; Internet 298–300, 337–9; LGBT hate crime 270, 272–4; ODIHR Law Enforcement Officers Programme (LEOP) training 101; online hate 312; UK 106–9, 331–53; US 159; *see also* Association of Chief Police Officers
Police Act (1997) 346, 348
Police Service of Northern Ireland (PSNI) 123
policy and politics 24–32, 87–8; intelligence 350; silo approach to policy *see* silo and victim group approach
political European far-right parties 139–43
populism 141, 145, 149
Porrajmos 239
positive change, catalyst for 49, 55
Posse Comitatus 311
power 75, 76, 89; *see also* empowerment
practitioners/facilitators, restorative: ineffective facilitation by, dangers 405–6; support from 401, 404–5
precarious tension of opposites (in sectarianism) 411, 417
prejudice 60, 81–2; alternative subcultures 226–8; experiences *see* experiences and impacts; gender 270
Press for Change 282
Preventing and Responding to Hate Crime (ODIHR) 101
Priestley, Philip (of OTO Programme) 391
probation staff/officers 385, 387–8, 392; seconded 386
prosecution: Australia/NZ 179; Europe 101; N. Ireland 123; sport 320, 322, 324, 326, 327; UK 110, 111, 112, 113, 114, 340; US 153, 155, 155–6, 157, 159; *see also* Crown Prosecution Service
protection: forms/classes to protect 63–5, 181–3; insufficient 375–8
Protestant–Catholic conflict in UK *see* sectarianism
provocation 369, 370, 371–5; retaliation to *see* retaliation
psychology 81–2; context and 73–4; victimisation and psychological consequences 40–3, 376
public disorder and hostility 335–7
Public Order Act (1986) 112, 219, 319, 321, 338, 348
Public Prosecution Service 123
Pugley, Ciara, suicide 300
punishment (punitive justice) 65–6, 400; increased/enhanced 25; LGBT crime 273–4, 284, 285
punks 230, 232

queer theory 268; *see also* Lesbian, Gay, Bisexual and Transgender or queer

Race for Justice (2003 Professor Gus John's report) 107, 350–1
Race for Justice (2006 Task Force report) 107–8
Race for Justice work programme 108
Racial Attack Monitoring Unit (Greenwich) 388
racial separatism 89
racism (against racial/ethnic minorities): Australia/NZ 176, 178, 179, 180, 182, 183, 249–65; Canada 166; Crime Survey of England and Wales 36, 37; Europe 96, 97, 99; interventions 384, 386, 387–9, 392, 393, 394, 395; masculine identity and 6, 249–65; 'moral career' of victims 367–80; murders 49, 105, 106, 107, 154, 331, 332, 367, 381, 384; N. Ireland 122, 123; proving racial hostility 62–3; social factors 72; sport 318–27; targeted crime and violence 249–65; UK 106–9, 112, 113, 147, 249–65; US (incl. African Americans) 153–5; *see also* culture; White Supremacists
radicalisation 421, 422; online 311, 312; *see also* deradicalisation
radicalism *see* extremism and radicalism
radio 290
Rangers football club 323, 324
rape, lesbian victims 270
rational choice theory 78
reactive hate crimes *see* defensive/reactive hate crimes
rebellion 72
recognition (of hate groups - and its politics) 26; Gypsies/Travellers/Roma 244–5
Reconstruction Era in US (1865–1877) 154
recording and documentation: Canada 170; disability hate crime 198, 199; improving 107; LGBT hate crime 271, 272, 273; perception-based 106; under-recording in UK 114
recruitment online 307, 308–9, 310, 311, 312
regulation(s) *see* legislation and regulations
Regulation of Investigatory Powers Act (2000) 346, 348
rehabilitation of/interventions with offenders 381–410; Canada 170; deradicalisation 420–9; disability hate crime 211
relationship webs 387
religion/faith/theology 86–7; ideology in 89; proving religious hostility 62–3; UK 36, 37, 112; *see also* sectarianism *and specific religious groups*
repairing harms of hate crime 400–10
reporting of hate crimes by victims (and under-reporting/reluctance to report) 97, 98, 102, 332–5; anti-Semitism 129; Canada 167, 169; disability 28, 197, 198, 198–9, 199–202; police and 333; Roma 242; transgender 280; UK 107, 332–5; US 158, 159, 333

437

Index

research: on gendered masculine identities in targeted violence against ethnic minorities 250–1; on Internet hate crime, limitations 297–8; on personal injuries of hate crime 34–5
resentment towards ethnic minorities 253, 254, 255, 256, 258
responsibility of denial 74, 215
restorative justice 8–9, 388, 400–10; introducing 401–4; practices 402; practitioners in *see* practitioners
retaliation (and retaliatory hate crime) 53, 369–76, 377, 378, 384; US 159
re-victimisation 406
Rigby, Lee, murder 335
right-wing extremism 4
Roma 6, 237–48
Romania, Gypsies/Travellers/Roma 242
Roper, Billy 308, 312
routine activities theory 78, 216
Royal Ulster Constabulary 119
rugby: international 325; UK 324–5

same-sex sexual acts, decriminalisation of 270–1; *see also* Lesbian, Gay, Bisexual and Transgender or queer
scene of crime 359
Scotland: disabled victims 201; football 323–4
Scotland, Baroness 108–9
Second World War *see* Holocaust; Nazi Germany; World War II
seconded officer 386
sectarianism 117–25, 411–19; N. Ireland 4, 9, 117–25, 417, 418; Scottish football 323–4
security (and insecurity) and sectarianism 411–12, 413, 414, 416, 417; N. Ireland 120–2
segregation, N. Ireland 120–2
self-control 77, 253–6; gendered masculinity and 260–1
self-destructive activities 52
self-identity 228; gendered 250, 253, 260, 279, 282
sentencing: aggravation element 61, 182, 183; Australia/NZ 182, 183; UK legislation 113; US legislation 155
Serbia: Gypsies/Travellers/Roma 241–2; under-21 football match against England 321
sex workers 17, 27, 64; transgender 283
sexuality and sexual orientation: Australia/NZ 182–3, 183; theories and concepts 267–9, 278–80; UK 36, 37, 112; *see also* gender; Lesbian, Gay, Bisexual and Transgender or queer
shame 256, 381–2, 392–3
shared values and views: of community, impact on 52–4; of perpetrators 74

Shepard, Matthew (and James Byrd) 49, 155, 157, 176, 194, 283
Sheppard and Whittle case 299, 338–9
Sibbitt, Rae, race crime and commissioning by Home Office 381
signalling theory 397
significant others 373, 421, 422
silo and victim group approach 2, 24, 28, 268; challenging 24–32
situational crime prevention 78
Smith, Hannah, suicide 300
Smith, Winston (aka Harold Covington) 310
social factors: disability hate crime 213; racism 72
social group identity 412
social justice, punitive justice in name of 65–6
social media (incl. Internet) 294, 308, 310, 312, 338; English Defence League on 147; sport and 326–7
social psychology 82
social services, transgender hate crime data 281–2, 285
social support in perpetrator communities, individuals drawing on 396, 407
sociological perspectives 3
Soham murders 347
Sophie Lancaster Foundation 226, 232, 233
South Africa: Apartheid 318; cricket against Australia 326; murder 331
specialist staff *see* staff
spectators at sport 319, 320–1, 321, 323, 325, 326; chanting/singing (football) 113, 322–3, 323, 324
speech: freedom of 113, 148, 196, 292, 295, 306, 307, 309, 312, 327, 338–9; hate *see* vilification; *see also* chanting
sport 7, 318–27
Spurs (Tottenham Hotspurs) 322, 322–3
staff (specialist) 385, 386; training 387–8; *see also* multidisciplinary/multi-agency approaches; practitioners; probation staff
state (government) agency discrimination: Gypsies/Travellers/Roma 241–2; LGBT 270
state (government) law: Australia/NZ 175, 180; US 156; *see also* policy
statistics *see* data
status versus conduct trap with gender 279
stereotypes 81
Stoke City FC travelling to Oldham 335–6
Stoke-on Trent protests 336
Stop the Islamisation of America (SIOA) 148
Stop the Islamisation of Nations (SION) 148
Stormfront (website) 297, 306
story-telling 401, 404
strain 71–3, 77; gendered 253–6
strand-based approach 24–8; breaking away from 31

Index

Strike Force Macnamir 177
Strong Religion 87
structural theories (of causation) 75–6, 77
subcultures 73; alternative 5–6, 15, 226–36; as choice 229–31
subordination and alternative subcultures 231–2
substantive offence 61; Australia/NZ 180
suicide 52; online hate and 300
support (of victims): including appropriate supporters 407; from restorative facilitators/practitioners 401, 404–5; understanding of impact for 44–5
Supreme Court: UK 338, 339; US 154, 157, 159
Sweden, exiting from radical groups (EXIT-Sweden) 425, 426
Sylvia Rivera Law Project 285
symbolism 393; law in Australia/NZ 183–4; in sectarianism (incl. N. Ireland) 120–2, 417
Symonds, Andrew 325
Systems for Investigation and Detection (SID) project 345

Taliban, Pakistani (Tehkreek-e-Taliban Pakistan) 308, 312
targeted crime and violence 48, 50, 64; in communities 50–2, 56, 159; ethnic minorities 249–65
Task Force *Race for Justice* (2006 report) 107–8
Tehkreek-e-Taliban Pakistan (TTP) 308, 312
television 290
territory 84, 261; invasion 242, 254, 396
terrorism 87, 331; 9/11 attacks 25, 55, 83, 87, 362, 403; Islamic 133, 309, 310; *see also* extremism
Terry, John (footballer) 319–20
theology *see* religion
theories and concepts (of hate crime) 2–3, 11–92, 70, 250–2; disability hate crime 211–15; LGBT hate crime 267–9, 278–80; racism 368–9; sectarianism 411; transgender hate crime 278–9; *see also* causation
Think Again intervention 392, 393, 394, 395, 396, 398
thrill-seeking 73, 74, 228, 383; disability hate crime 212; interventions 383; US 159
Todd, Amanda, suicide 300
tolerance, effects of hate crime on national commitments to 49
Tolerance and Non Discrimination Information System (TANDIS) 98, 99
Tottenham Hotspur (Spurs) 322, 322–3
Toulouse shootings at Jewish school 133
Training Against Hate Crimes for Law Enforcement (TAHCLE) programme 101
training of staff 387–8
Trans Murder Monitoring (TMM) project 282

transgender people (and transphobia) 6, 26, 278–92, 393; black 30; data 280–3; definition 279; N. Ireland 122, 123; trans woman 51–2, 53, 56; *see also* Lesbian, Gay, Bisexual and Transgender or queer
Travellers 6, 237–48
trolling 297
Troubles (N. Ireland) 4, 121, 124, 125; legacy 119–20
trust, loss in affected communities 51–2
TV 290
Twitter 290, 294, 306, 308, 309, 310, 311, 312, 326, 327
typology of motivations 159, 197, 212, 260, 383–4, 394

UEFA's Disciplinary Regulations (2012) 320–1
Umar Media Facebook page 308, 312
under-protection 375–8
under-reporting *see* reporting
understanding of hate crime 69–91; understanding online hate 295–7; understanding perpetrators 210–15, 220; understanding for supporting victims 44–5
undesirable groups 17, 26
Union of the Physically Impaired Against Segregation (UPIAS) 194
United Kingdom (UK) 3–4, 14, 105–16; alternative subcultures 5–6, 15, 226–36; anti-Semitism 131–3, 135; benefits claimants 88; 'difference' in 75; disability 88, 193, 194, 195, 196, 197, 198, 199, 200, 201, 207–25; extremism 141, 145, 147–8; football *see* football; Gypsies/Travellers/Roma 241, 243; Home Office *see* Home Office; internet 291–2, 299; legislation 24, 26, 26, 60, 62–3, 112–14, 319–20, 323, 323–4, 344–7; LGBT hate crime 267, 333–4; policing (incl. intelligence) 106–9, 331–53; policy development 106–9; racism 106–9, 112, 113, 147, 249–65; sport 321–4; *see also* Crime Survey of England and Wales; Northern Ireland; Scotland
United Nations and LGBT 266
United States (USA) 4, 153–62; disability hate crime 193–4, 195, 196, 197, 198, 199, 200; law 153–7; reporting/under-reporting; US 158, 159, 333; transgender hate crime 280, 281–2, 282–3, 284–5

Valle, Gilberto 291–2
van Tongeren (leader of ANM movement) 180
victim(s) 191–327, 367–80; bad, LGBT as 269–71, 271; confidence, improving (UK) 115; denial of the 74, 215; difference *see* difference; disabled, relationship to perpetrator 198, 200–1; distorted perspective

439

of 388, 395–6; intentional selection (US) 156–7; mediation between offender and (VOM) 402, 403, 407; nail bombing, physical identification 363; preventing becoming a perpetrator 367–80; protection *see* protection; of racist hate crime, moral career 367–80; reporting by *see* reporting; re-victimisation 406; understanding for supporting 44–5; *see also* silo and victim group approach *and specific victim groups*
victimisation 368–79; alternative subcultures 227, 228, 229, 231, 233; Gypsies/Travellers/Roma 241; process of 368–79; story-telling and 404; transgender 280–3; US, surveys 158–9
Victoria (Australia) 174, 176, 179, 180, 181, 183
vilification (hate speech) 62; Australia/NZ 174, 178–9, 180, 182; Gypsies/Travellers/Roma 237, 243; online 298, 312
violence: in conflict resolution, predisposition to 396; in Crime Survey of England and Wales 38–40; disability-related 207, 209, 210, 211, 212, 213, 215; domestic *see* domestic abuse/violence; female victims 270; Gypsies/Travellers/Roma 241, 242; LGBT-related, legitimacy in law 270; LGBT-related, on political agenda 271–4; sectarian (N. Ireland) 117, 118–19, 119, 120, 121, 122, 125; targeted *see* targeted crime and violence; transgender 279, 280, 281, 282–5; *see also* genocide; murder; physical injuries; pogroms
virtual world of the Internet 295–7, 300
vulnerability 17, 31, 51, 64–5, 404; alternative subcultures 228; disabled people 195, 201, 203, 210, 217, 393; masculine identity and 250–1; offender interventions 393

Wales *see* United Kingdom
Walker, Anthony 107, 332
walls in sectarianism 416–17
Warsaw Declaration (2005) 96
Weak Religion 87
Western Australia 62, 176, 180–1
Western Europe, Gypsies/Travellers/Roma 240, 242, 244, 245
Wharton, Arthur 318–19
What is a Hate Crime? (Canadian documentary) 167
White Aryan Resistance 312
White Nationalist Front (Canada) 310, 311
White Revolution 308, 312
White Supremacists 89, 154; Internet 295, 297, 298, 306, 308, 310, 311, 312
Wilders, Geert 139
women (females) 28; dominance of men over 252; Muslim 29, 51–2, 53, 55, 57; transgender 51–2, 53, 56; violence against 270; *see also* domestic abuse/violence; lesbians
Women's experiences of homophobia and transphobia 272
workplace and sectarianism in N. Ireland 121
World War II Battle of the Atlantic, intelligence 351; *see also* Holocaust; Nazi Germany
worldview, distorted 296
worldwide perspectives 3–5, 93–189

'yid' chant at Spurs 322–3
young men involved in violence against ethnic minorities 253; opinions 253–60; *see also* children and young people

Zundel, Ernst 165